MACROECONOMICS

PRINCIPLES AND APPLICATIONS

ROBERT E. HALL

STANFORD UNIVERSITY

MARC LIEBERMAN

VASSAR COLLEGE

SOUTH-WESTERN College Publishing

An International Thomson Publishing Company

Publishing Team Director: Jack C. Calhoun
Acquisitions Editor: John Alessi
Developmental Editor: Dennis Hanseman
Marketing Manager: Lisa Lysne
Project Manager: Justified Left
Production House: WordCrafters Editorial Services, Inc.
Composition: GGS Information Services
Cover and Internal Designer: Joseph M. Devine
Internal Photo Researcher: Feldman & Associates
Team Assistants: Kristen Meere, C. Renee Bowsky, Julie Behan

Library of Congress Cataloging-in-Publication Data

Hall, Robert Ernest, 1943–
Macroeconomics : principles and applications / Robert Hall, Marc Lieberman.
p. cm.
Includes index.
ISBN 0-538-84759-X
1. Macroeconomics. I. Lieberman, Marc. II. Title.
HB172.5.H346 1998
339—dc21 97-17926
CIP

2 3 4 5 6 7 8 9 VH 5 4 3 2 1 0 9 8
Printed in the United States of America

ITP® International Thomson Publishing
South-Western College Publishing is an ITP Company.
The ITP trademark is used under license.

PREFACE

TO THE INSTRUCTOR

This book is about economic *principles*—and how those principles are applied in the *real world*. It was conceived, written, and rewritten to help your students focus on those basic principles.

All of the existing books we have seen—and used—are *substitutes* for the instructor. They try to replicate what happens in class, as if there *were* no class. Moreover, many of them are encyclopedic—they cover every possible topic and subtopic *just in case* you might want to present them

Our approach is very different. We believe in *complementarity* between textbook and instructor, letting each specialize in the task for which it is best suited. A text has a comparative advantage as a study and reference tool, since the instructor cannot be pulled down off the shelf at a moment's notice. Therefore, a text's primary goal should be a well-organized, logical exposition of economic analysis with a minimum of distraction. As an instructor, you have the comparative advantage in bringing current events into the classroom, sparking controversy and discussion, and fleshing out the material in a highly personal way. A textbook—by its nature—cannot do any of these tasks well. This book is designed to support you—and to stay out of your way. Our philosophy is to treat fewer topics, and to treat them fully. We have tried hard not to write an encyclopedia of economics.

Macroconomics: Principles and Applications has a distinctive approach:

- **We stress the basic principles of economics.** Economic theory makes repeated use of some fundamental ideas that appear again and again in many contexts. To truly understand what economics is all about, students need to learn what these central ideas are, and they need to see them in action in different contexts. We've identified and stressed eight *basic principles of economics* in this text. These are:
    - Maximization Subject to Constraints
    - Opportunity Cost
    - Specialization and Exchange
    - Markets and Equilibrium
    - Short-Run versus Long-Run Outcomes
    - Marginal Decision Making
    - Policy Tradeoffs
    - The Importance of Real Values

A full statement of each principle appears in Chapter 1, and again later when it is first used. Then, whenever the principle is used again in future chapters, it is identified with a key symbol shown in the margin.

- **We avoid nonessential material.** When we believed a topic was not essential to an introductory understanding of economics, we left it out. We have also avoided interviews, news clippings, and boxed inserts with only distant connections to the core material. The features your students *will* find in our book are there to help them understand basic economic theory itself, or to help them explore sources of information on their own using the Internet.
- **We explain difficult concepts patiently.** Because we have avoided the encyclopedic approach, we can explain the topics we *do* cover thoroughly and patiently. We try to lead students, step-by-step, through each aspect of the theory, through each graph, and through each numerical example. Moreover, in the process of developing this book, we asked other experienced teachers to tell us which aspects of economic theory are hardest for their students to learn, and we've paid special attention to the trouble spots. Of course, full, patient explanations take up space, too. This is why our book is only *somewhat* shorter than other texts, even though our focus is more concentrated.
- **We use concrete examples.** Students learn best when they see how economics can explain the world around them. Whenever possible, we develop the

theory using real-world examples. When we employ hypothetical examples, because they illustrate the theory more cleanly, we try to make them realistic. In addition, each chapter ends with a thorough, extended application of new material.

Special Pedagogical Features

We've chosen features that reinforce the basic theory, rather than distract from it. Here is a list of the most important ones, and how we believe they help students focus on essentials.

- *Using the Theory* sections, which present extended applications, appear at the end of each chapter. While there are plenty of real-world examples and facts in the body of the chapter, helping to illustrate each step along the way, we also felt it important to have one extended application that unifies the material in the chapter. In the Using the Theory sections, students see how the tools they've learned can explain something about the world—something that would be difficult to explain without those tools.
- *Myth* sections are designed to dispel confusions about the economy that students *bring with them* to the class—ideas that they may have gotten from the media or from friends or family. Confronting these myths head-on helps to resolve dissonance between prior beliefs and current course content. We try to head off confusion before it occurs.
- *Dangerous Curves* explanations are designed to eliminate confusion that sometimes arises *as* students read the text—the kinds of mistakes we see year after year in their exams.
- *Internet references* point students to resources that contain truly up-to-the-minute information. We prefer Internet references, rather than the traditional approach of including news stories in the text, for two reasons. First, we want to minimize distractions; and second, what is current news at the time of writing is stale by the time of publication.

What's Different Here, and Why

In addition to the special features just described, you will find some important differences in topical approach and arrangement. These, too, are designed to make the theory stand out more cleanly, and to make learning easier. These are not pedagogical experiments, nor are they innovation for the sake of innovation. On the contrary, we are sensitive to the burden of adapting an existing syllabus to a new text. The pedagogical differences you will find in this text are the product of years of classroom experience.

A few of the differences may require minor adjustments in class lectures, and these are listed below. But we would be remiss if we merely listed them without also pointing out why we believe they are improvements. Please indulge us a bit as you read through this list.

- **Scarcity, Choice, and Economic Systems** (Chapter 2): This early chapter, while covering standard material like opportunity cost, also introduces some central concepts much earlier than other texts. Most importantly, the chapter introduces the concept of *comparative advantage,* and the basic principle of *specialization and exchange.* We have moved them to the front of our book because we believe they provide important building blocks for much that comes later.
- **Long-Run Macroeconomics** (Chapters 7 and 8): This text presents long-run growth before short-run fluctuations. But unlike many other texts, which treat growth in an entirely descriptive way, our treatment is analytical. Chapter 7 develops the long-run, classical model at a level appropriate for introductory students. Chapter 8 then *uses* the classical model to explain the causes—and costs—of economic growth in both rich and poor countries.

  We believe it is better to treat the long run before the short run, for two reasons. First, the long-run model makes full use of the tools of supply and demand, and thus provides for an easier transition from the preliminary chapters (1, 2, and 3) into macroeconomics. Second, we believe that students can truly understand economic fluctuations only if they understand *how* and *why* the long-run model breaks down over shorter time periods. This, of course, requires a full treatment of the long-run model first.
- **Booms and Recessions** (Chapter 9): This unique chapter provides a bridge from the long-run to the short-run macro model, and paves the way for the short-run focus on *spending* as the driving force behind the Keynesian model.
- **Aggregate Demand and Aggregate Supply** (Chapter 13): One of our pet peeves about other introductory texts is the too-early introduction of aggregate demand and aggregate supply curves, *before* teaching where these curves come from. Students then confuse the *AD* and *AS* curves with their microeconomic counterparts, requiring corrective action later. In this text, the *AD* and *AS* curves do not appear un-

til Chapter 13, where they are fully explained. Our treatment of *AS* is based on a very simple mark-up model that our students have found very accessible.

- **Exchange Rates and Open-Economy Macroeconomics** (Chapter 17): Many students find international macroeconomics the most interesting topic in the course, especially the material on exchange rates and what causes them to change. Accordingly, you will find unusually full coverage of exchange rate determination in this chapter. This treatment, while extensive, is kept simple and straightforward, relying exclusively on supply and demand. And it forms the foundation for the discussion of open-economy macroeconomics that ends the chapter.

Building a Syllabus

We have arranged the contents of each chapter, and the table of contents as a whole, according to the order of presentation that we recommend. But we've also built in some flexibility. For example, we've retained the traditional placement of international trade and finance toward the end of the book (Chapters 16 and 17). But if you wish to highlight international trade, you could assign Chapter 16 immediately following Chapter 3. In fact, once the core chapters (4 through 13) have been taught, the remaining chapters (14–17) can be presented in virtually any order.

Finally, we have included only those chapters that we thought were both essential and teachable in a one-semester course. But not everyone will agree about what is essential. While we—as authors—cringe at the thought of a chapter being omitted in the interest of time, we've allowed for that possibility. Nothing in Chapter 14 (monetary policy), Chapter 15 (fiscal policy and the deficit), Chapter 16 (international trade), or Chapter 17 (international finance) is required to understand the other chapters in the book. Skipping any of these should not cause continuity problems.

Teaching Aids for the Instructor

- The Instructor's Manual contains chapter summaries, lecture outlines, teaching tips and activities, ideas for interactive teaching, and solutions to all end-of-chapter problems and exercises.
- The Macroeconomics Test Bank contains over 2,500 multiple-choice questions. It is available in both printed and electronic forms.
- Full-color transparencies are available for most of the key graphs and illustrations in the text.
- Our Web site gives students access to a variety of perspectives on economic issues of the day. It contains a series of accessible position papers that explain competing viewpoints on key policy issues. The site also contains news updates linked to the text, teaching and learning resources, and a variety of other interesting features.
- Tutorial software allows students to create, modify, and use key graphs.
- A CNN video provides a variety of short video clips on various aspects of economics.
- Many of the text's figures and tables are available as Microsoft PowerPoint files.

A Request

Although we've worked hard on this book, we know we'll be able to improve it further in future editions. For that, our fellow users are indispensable. We invite your comments and suggestions wholeheartedly. We especially welcome your suggestions for additional "Myths" and "Dangerous Curves." You may send your comments to either of us care of South-Western College Publishing.

Bob Hall
Marc Lieberman

ACKNOWLEDGMENTS

This book is a case study of the principle of specialization and exchange. So many people contributed their valuable skills and expertise, especially the staff of South-Western College Publishing. First and foremost among them is our development editor, Dennis Hanseman. Not only does he hold a Ph.D. in economics, but he also possesses a rare ability to take the viewpoint of someone new to economics. His knack for spotting potential areas of confusion, his stubborn insistence on absolute clarity at every turn, and his innumerable contributions in planning and executing the project were immensely valuable. Jack Calhoun, formerly acquisitions editor at South-Western and now team director there, originally signed us as authors, so it is fair to say that this book would not exist without him. He was a relentless advocate for South-Western as a superior publishing company (a description that turned out to be entirely accurate), and a great problem solver once the project was under way. John Alessi, who took over midstream from Jack, jumped into the project with enthusiasm, energy, and skill. Lisa Lysne did a superior job of marketing and advertising this book and coming up with creative ways to explain what it was all about. Joe Devine created the design features for the text, and accomplished a near impossible task: designing a cover that both authors like a lot.

In addition to those at South-Western, we would like to thank Sue Ellen Brown, of Justified Left, and Ann Mohan at WordCrafters, who turned our manuscript into a beautiful book. Bruce Watson and Jennifer Stephan contributed many of the end-of-chapter questions. Geoffrey Jehle, of Vassar College, Heinz Kohler, of Amherst College, and Mike Pogodzinski, of San Jose State University, also made important contributions.

Finally we would like to thank our many reviewers, who carefully read the draft manuscript and provided, literally, more than a thousand suggestions for changes and improvements as we drafted and redrafted. While we had no intention of writing a book that would be "all things to all people," and could not incorporate every suggestion, our reviewers helped us make the book "more things for more people." Among those whose suggestions we found particularly valuable are the following:

David Aschauer, Bates College
Robert Averitt, Smith College
Neil Becker, University of Kansas
Alexandra Bernasek, Colorado State University
William Brown, Claremont-McKenna College
Cynthia Browning, Smith College
David Buffum, College of the Holy Cross
Paul Comolli, University of Kansas
Daniel Condon, University of Illinois, Chicago
James Peery Cover, University of Alabama
A. Edward Day, University of Central Florida
Bruce Dalgaard, St. Olaf College
John Duffy, University of Pittsburgh
Donald Dutkowsky, Syracuse University
Roger Nils Folsom, San Jose State University
Rodney Fort, Washington State University
David Gillette, Truman State University
Lisa Grobar, California State University, Long Beach
Philip Grossman, Virginia Polytechnic Institute
David Hakes, University of Northern Iowa
Daniel Hammond, Wake Forest University
John Heywood, University of Wisconsin, Milwaukee
Randall Holcombe, Florida State University
Frederick Inaba, Washington State University
Joyce Jacobsen, Wesleyan University
Helen Jensen, Iowa State University
Elizabeth Kelly, University of Wisconsin, Madison
Philip King, San Francisco State University
Catherine Krause, University of New Mexico
Ashley Lyman, University of Idaho
Michael Magura, University of Toledo
Robert Margo, Vanderbilt University
Howard Marvel, Ohio State University
Laurence McCulloch, Ohio State University
Janet Mitchell, Cornell University
W. Douglas Morgan, University of California, Santa Barbara
Randy Nelson, Colby College
Norman Obst, Michigan State University
Virginia Owen, Illinois State University
Steve Petty, Oklahoma State University
Morteza Rahmatian, California State University, Fullerton
Alan Richards, University of California, Santa Cruz
Jolyne Sanjak, SUNY, Albany
David Schaffer, Haverford College
Michael Smitka, Washington and Lee University
Rohini Somanathan, Emory University
Walter Wessels, North Carolina State University
Robert Whaples, Wake Forest University
Thomas White, Assumption College
David Wong, California State University, Fullerton

Personal Note from Marc Lieberman. I want to especially thank four people for helping me with this project in ways that are impossible to measure. Geoffrey Jehle, Professor of Economics at Vassar College, provided excellent advice on writing, organizing, and thinking about the material, as well as continual encouragement to keep going. Tami Yellin was both understanding and generous when I had to drop out of a collaborative film project to make time for this book. And my parents, Harold and Charlene Lieberman, showed remarkable patience and support when their son had to cancel family visits—several times—due to deadlines.

Personal Note from Bob Hall. Charlotte Pace, who keeps my office humming at Stanford, contributed in many ways, especially raising the art of copy checking and proofreading to new levels of excellence. My son Chris served as college culture consultant for the book. My wife, Susan Woodward—a financial economist—helped in so many ways, and happily tolerated the domestic dislocations that inevitably accompany a project like this one. She read and commented on many of the chapters and drafted material in her areas of interest. And she made Marc very happy by cooking dinner for him.

TO THE STUDENT

You may have already noticed that this note is substantially shorter than our note to instructors. And for good reason. The entire book has been written with you in mind. Here, we just want to give you some advice on using some special features of this book, and suggest some helpful supplements.

- **Getting started:** The first chapter tells you what economics *is,* and gives some tips on how to study it.
- **The Basic Principles:** As you will see, much of economic theory boils down to a small number of fundamental ideas, which appear again and again in many contexts. In this book, we've identified eight of them, and we call them the *basic principles of economics.* The entire list is presented in Chapter 1, and each principle is discussed, in more detail, in a later chapter when it is first used. Throughout the book, each time the principle appears again, it is identified with a key symbol, as shown at left. When you see one of these keys, it's a signal to stop and think about how the principle is being used.

- **Dangerous Curves:** Professors *do* talk about other things besides the mistakes their students make on exams. But when the subject comes up, it is surprising that our experiences are so similar. Year after year, no matter how hard we try, the same confusions pop up. We've tried to identify the most common ones in our "Dangerous Curves" feature, which you will find throughout the text. You may want to skip them as you read through the chapter the first time, and concentrate on them later—especially before exam time.

- **Myths:** From reading the newspaper, watching the news on TV, or even talking to your friends, you have probably developed a number of ideas about the economy and how it operates. Some of these ideas will be accurate but, unfortunately, others are dead wrong. We've identified some of the more common myths you may have encountered, and have tried to dispel them using the concepts you'll learn in this book. Again, these can be skipped as you read through the chapter the first time, but make sure you come back to them later.

- **Using the Theory:** Each chapter ends with an application that demonstrates how the tools you've learned can help you understand something new about the world, something that would be hard to understand *without* those tools. These applications should be read the first time you go through the chapter. They can be read again later as a useful review of how economic tools are used.

- **Mathematical Appendix:** For the most part, the only math you need to understand this book is what you learned in high school—and only a small part of that. The required math, as well as the basics of graphs, are reviewed in the mathematical appendix at the end of the book. If you are very rusty, you might want to read the appendix in its entirety, early on. Otherwise, just know that it's there, and refer to it when you need it.
- The Hall/Lieberman **Web site** contains a variety of helpful features that will enrich your study of economics. Check it out on a regular a basis at http://hall-lieb.swcollege.com

LEARNING AIDS

The following items are also available to help you learn economics:

- **The Study Guide:** Learning is different from memorizing. This textbook has been written to help you understand each concept. Nevertheless, to really master the material, there is nothing like repeated problem solving. Much as practicing helps a pianist, the Study Guide written to accompany this book will help you strengthen your knowledge of economics. (ISBN: 0-538-85473- 1)
- **MACROECONOMICS ALIVE!** is an exciting CD-ROM that contains animated lessons, economic tool-building exercises, and simulations that will help you learn economics interactively. (ISBN: 0-538-85471-5)

These learning aids can be ordered through your campus bookstore.

We are honored to help your instructor welcome you to the field of economics. We hope you find the experience of reading this book a fulfilling one—as fulfilling as the experience we had writing it.

Bob Hall
Marc Lieberman

ABOUT THE AUTHORS

Robert E. Hall is one of the world's most eminent economists. He is Senior Fellow at the Hoover Institution and Professor of Economics at Stanford University where he conducts research on inflation, unemployment, taxation, monetary policy, and the economics of high technology. He received his Ph.D. from MIT and has taught there as well as at the University of California, Berkeley. Hall is Director of the research program on Economic Fluctuations of the National Bureau of Economic Research, and Chairman of the Bureau's Committee on Business Cycle Dating, which maintains the semiofficial chronology of the U.S. business cycle. He has published numerous monographs and articles in scholarly journals, and is the co-author of the popular intermediate text, *Macroeconomics: Theory, Performance, and Policy.* Hall has advised the Treasury Department and the Federal Reserve Board on national economic policy, and has testified on numerous occasions before congressional committees.

Marc Lieberman is Associate Professor of Economics at Vassar College and a visiting lecturer at Princeton University, where he received his Ph.D. He has presented his extremely popular Principles of Economics course at Vassar, Harvard, the University of California-Santa Cruz, and the University of Hawaii. Lieberman is co-editor and contributor to *The Road to Capitalism: Economic Transformation in Eastern Europe and the Soviet Union.* In addition, he has consulted with the Bank of America and the Educational Testing Service. In his spare time, he is a professional screenwriter. He co-wrote the script for *Love Kills,* a movie that aired on the USA Cable Network and is now available in video stores around the world.

BRIEF CONTENTS

CONTENTS

PART I

PRELIMINARIES

PART II

MACROECONOMICS: BASIC CONCEPTS

PART III

LONG-RUN MACROECONOMICS

PART V

MONEY, PRICES, AND FLUCTUATIONS

PART VI

MACROECONOMIC POLICY

PART VII

THE INTERNATIONAL ECONOMY

C H A P T E R 1

WHAT IS ECONOMICS?

CHAPTER OUTLINE

Economics. The word conjures up all sorts of images: monolithic corporate headquarters, highly paid executives in business suits, complicated graphs and charts, manic stock traders on Wall Street, an economic summit meeting in a European capital, a somber television news anchor announcing bad news about higher unemployment. . . . You probably hear about economics several times each day. But what *is* economics? How does it fit into human knowledge? How does the world benefit from it?

First, economics is a social science. It studies those aspects of human behavior relating to working, producing goods, distributing them, and consuming them. Economics explains how prices are set in markets where buyers and sellers come together to trade.

Second, economics has practical value to people, businesses, and government. An economist designed the system used by the public broadcasting system to decide what shows to produce. Economists have developed theories that have reduced risk in financial markets, enabled more people to obtain insurance against fire and theft, and helped to protect consumers against defective products. Economic principles have influenced decisions about taxation, Social Security, unemployment insurance, inflation, business regulations, international trade, and many other government policies.

If you have never studied economics before—and if your ideas about it come mostly from the media—then you may have some misconceptions about what the field is all about. Let's dispel some of these misconceptions right now.

MYTHS

MYTHS ABOUT ECONOMICS

"ECONOMICS IS THE SAME AS *BUSINESS*."

The confusion between business and economics is easy to understand, because economics has much to say about business. Indeed, a mastery of economic principles will help anyone planning to start a business or go to work for an established firm. But since economics is a social science, it looks at business activities with the goal of understanding how they fit into the broader picture of our society, while the field of business takes an exclusively how-to approach.

"ECONOMICS IS ABOUT MAKING MONEY IN STOCKS, BONDS, AND REAL ESTATE."

A knowledge of economics will certainly help you understand what goes on in financial markets, and it is indispensable for anyone hoping to become a savvy investor. There is even a branch of economics—called *finance*—that focuses on markets such as those for stocks and bonds. But economics is not about the ins and outs of trading things for profit. Indeed, economics teaches us that it is very difficult to beat the market on a continuing basis and that most of those who claim they can do so are deluding themselves and their clients.

"SINCE THE ECONOMY ITSELF IS SO COMPLEX, ONLY SPECIALISTS WITH YEARS OF TRAINING CAN HOPE TO UNDERSTAND IT."

Our global, national, and even local economies are very complex, but this does not mean that the study of economics needs to be complex. In this text, you will see that some simple ideas can give you surprisingly powerful insights into the economy. Indeed, the art of economics—and the main activity of those who practice it—is to extract simple, understandable truths from an increasingly complex world.

"ECONOMICS IS BORING."

Economics deals with questions like these:

- Why, in recessions, are millions of Americans who want to work unable to find jobs?
- Why might a government purposely create an economic downturn, throwing millions out of work?
- Where will the jobs be when you graduate from college, and which professions will pay the highest salaries?
- Why do highly trained physicians earn $200,000 per year, while actors like Jim Carrey and Demi Moore earn more than 50 times that amount to star in movies?
- Why does the cost of many services, such as long-distance telephone calls, continue to fall, while the cost of others—for example, college education—keeps rising relentlessly?
- Why does the U.S. government take more care to prevent the public from buying cheap peanuts grown for export than it does to keep plutonium out of the hands of terrorists?

If you find these questions uninteresting, then you may as well close this book now. Economics will, indeed, bore you. But if you are like most people—curious, but often confused by what goes on in the world—you will find economics to be interesting and perhaps even fascinating.

ECONOMICS, SCARCITY, AND CHOICE

Economics is first and foremost a *social science,* so its primary purpose is to explain something about *society.* In this sense, it has much in common with psychology, sociology, and political science. But economics is very different from these other social sciences, both in terms of *what* economists study and *how* they study it. Economists ask fundamentally different questions, and they answer them using tools that other social scientists would find rather exotic. **Economics** can be defined as *the study of choice under conditions of scarcity.* This definition may appear strange to you. Where are the familiar words we ordinarily associate with economics, words such as "money," "stocks and bonds," "prices," and "budgets"? As you will soon see, economics deals with all of these things and more. It even reaches beyond what we ordinarily think of as the economy.

ECONOMICS The study of choice under conditions of scarcity.

SCARCITY AND THE INDIVIDUAL

Think for a moment about your own life—the activities of your day, the possessions you enjoy, the surroundings in which you live. Is there anything you don't have at this moment that you would *like* to have? Anything that you have, but that you would like *more* of? If your answer is "no," then congratulations—either you are well advanced on the path of Zen self-denial, or else you are a close relative of Ted Turner. The rest of us, however, would benefit from an increase in our material standard of living. This simple truth is at the very core of economics. It can be restated this way: We all face the problem of **scarcity.**

SCARCITY A situation in which the amount of something available is insufficient to satisfy everyone's desire for it.

Almost everything in your daily life is scarce. You would benefit from a larger room or apartment, so you have a scarcity of space. You have only two pairs of shoes and could use a third for hiking; you have a scarcity of shoes. You would love to take a trip to Chicago, but it is difficult for you to find the time or the money to go—trips to Chicago are scarce.

Because of scarcity, each of us is forced to make choices. We must allocate our scarce *time* to different activities: work, play, education, sleep, shopping, and more. We must allocate our scarce *spending power* among different goods and services: food, furniture, movies, long-distance phone calls, and many others.

Economists study the choices we make as individuals and how those choices shape our economy. For example, the goods that each of us decides to buy ultimately determine which goods business firms will produce. This, in turn, explains which firms and industries will hire new workers and which will lay them off.

Economists also study the more subtle and indirect effects of individual choice on our society. Will most Americans continue to live in houses, or—like Europeans—will most of us end up in apartments? Will we have an educated and well-informed citizenry? Will museums and libraries be forced to close down? Will traffic congestion in our cities continue to worsen, or is there relief in sight? These questions hinge, in large part, on the separate decisions of millions of people. To answer them requires an understanding of how people make choices under conditions of scarcity.

SCARCITY AND SOCIETY

Think for a moment about the goals of our society. We want a high standard of living for all citizens, clean air, safe streets, and good schools. What is holding us back from accomplishing all of these goals in a way that would satisfy everyone? You probably already know the answer: scarcity.

Society's problem is a scarcity of **resources**—the things we use to make goods and services. Economists classify resources into three categories:

RESOURCES The land, labor, and capital that are used to produce goods and services.

LABOR The time human beings spend producing goods and services.

CAPITAL Long-lasting tools used in producing goods and services.

HUMAN CAPITAL The skills and training of the labor.

LAND The physical space on which production occurs, together with the natural resources found beneath it.

1. **Labor** is the time human beings spend producing goods and services.
2. **Capital** consists of the long-lasting tools that people use to produce goods and services along with their labor. This includes *physical capital* such as buildings, machinery, and equipment, as well as **human capital**—the *skills and training of the labor force.*
3. **Land** is the physical space on which production takes place, and also the natural resources found under it or on it, such as oil, iron, coal, and lumber.

Anything produced in the economy comes, ultimately, from some combination of these resources. Think about the last lecture you attended at your college. You were consuming a service—a college lecture. What went into producing that service? Labor was being supplied by your instructor. Many types of capital were used as well. The physical capital included desks, chairs, a blackboard or transparency projector, and the classroom building itself. It also included the computer your instructor may have used to write out his or her lecture notes. In addition, there was human capital—your instructor's specialized knowledge and lecturing skills. Finally, there was land—the property on which your classroom building sits.

Besides the three resources, other things were used to produce your college lecture. Chalk, for example, is a tool used by your instructor, so you might think it should be considered capital, but it is not. Why not? Because it is not *long lasting.* Typically, economists consider a tool to be capital only if it lasts for a few years or longer. Chalk tends to be used up as the lecture is produced, so it is considered a *raw material* rather than capital.

But a little reflection should convince you that a piece of chalk is, itself, produced from some combination of the three resources (labor, capital, and land). In fact, all of the raw materials needed to produce the lecture—the energy used to heat or cool your building, the computer paper used for your instructor's lecture notes, and more—come, ultimately, from society's three resources. And the scarcity of resources, in turn, causes the scarcity of all goods and services produced from them.

Goods and services are not just important to us as individuals; we also use them to accomplish our social goals. Safe streets, for example, are an important social goal. To achieve this goal, we must have police protection, and this requires police vehicles, police stations, courthouses, and more. To produce these things, we use the labor of autoworkers, bricklayers, and electricians; natural resources such as sand, iron, and copper; and machinery like cement mixers, cranes, and electric drills. These very same resources, however, could instead be used to produce *other* desirable things, such as new homes, hospitals, automobile factories, or schools. As a result, every society must have some method of *allocating* its scarce resources—choosing which of our many competing desires will be fulfilled and which will not be.

Many of the big questions of our time center on the different ways in which resources can be allocated. The cataclysmic changes taking place in Eastern Europe and the former Soviet Union arose from a very simple fact: The method these countries used to allocate resources was not working. The never-ending debates between Democrats and Republicans in the United States and between Tories and Labourites in England, and similar debates throughout the world's democracies reflect subtle but important differences of opinion about how to allocate resources. Often, these are disputes about whether the private sector can handle the allocation of resources on its own or whether the government should be involved.

SCARCITY AND ECONOMICS

The scarcity of resources—and the choices it forces us to make—is the source of all of the problems you will study in economics. Households have limited incomes for satisfying their desires, so they must choose carefully how they allocate their spending among different goods and services. Business firms try to make profit, but they must pay for their inputs, so they must carefully choose *what* to produce, *how much* to produce, and *how* to produce it. Local, state, and federal governments must work with limited budgets, so they must carefully choose which goals to pursue. Nations often lack critical resources within their own borders, so they must trade with other nations to achieve their full economic potential. Economists study these decisions made by households, firms, governments, and nations to explain how our economic system operates, to forecast the future of our economy, and to suggest ways to make that future even better.

THE WORLD OF ECONOMICS

The field of economics is surprisingly broad. It extends its reach from the mundane—why does a pound of steak cost more than a pound of chicken?—to the personal and profound—how do couples decide how many children to have? With a field this broad, it is useful to have some way of classifying the different types of problems economists study and the different methods they use to analyze them.

MICROECONOMICS AND MACROECONOMICS

The field of economics is divided into two major parts: microeconomics and macroeconomics. **Microeconomics** comes from the Greek word *micros,* meaning "small." It takes a close up view of the economy, as if looking through a microscope. Microeconomics is concerned with the behavior of *individual* actors on the economic scene—households, business firms, and governments. It looks at the choices made by these actors and how they interact with each other in *specific* markets and industries. What will happen to the cost of movie tickets over the next five years? How many jobs will open up in the fast-food industry? How will the Japanese electronics industry be affected by a U.S. tax on imports? These are all microeconomic questions, because they analyze individual *parts* of the economy, rather than the whole.

MICROECONOMICS The study of the behavior of individual households, firms, and governments, the choices they make, and their interaction in specific markets and industries.

Macroeconomics—from the Greek word *macros,* meaning "large"—takes an *overall* view of the economy. Macroeconomics is not concerned about individual firms, individual households, or even individual industries; it concentrates on what is happening in the economy as a whole. Instead of focusing on the production of carrots or computers, macroeconomics lumps all goods and services together and looks at the economy's *total output.* Instead of focusing on the employment of unskilled workers or manufacturing workers, it considers *total employment* in the economy. Instead of asking why credit card loans carry higher interest rates than home mortgage loans, it asks what makes interest rates *in general* rise or fall. In all of these cases, macroeconomics focuses on the big picture and ignores the fine details.

MACROECONOMICS The study of the economy as a whole.

POSITIVE AND NORMATIVE ECONOMICS

The micro versus macro distinction is based on the level of detail we want to consider. Another useful distinction has to do with the *purpose* in analyzing a problem. **Positive economics** deals with what is—with *how* the economy works, plain and simple. If we lower income tax rates in the United States next year, will the budget deficit increase? If so, by how much? And what effect will this have on total employment? These are all positive economic questions. We may disagree about the answers, but we can all agree that there *are* correct answers to these questions if only we can discover them.

POSITIVE ECONOMICS The study of what *is,* of how the economy works.

NORMATIVE ECONOMICS The study of what *should be;* it is used to make value judgments, identify problems, and prescribe solutions.

Normative economics concerns itself with what should be. It is used to make judgments about the economy, identify problems, and prescribe solutions. While positive economics is concerned with just the facts, normative economics requires us to make value judgments. When an economist advises that we cut government spending—an action that will benefit some citizens and harm others—the economist is engaging in normative analysis.

Positive and normative economics are intimately related in practice. For one thing, we cannot properly argue about what we should or should not do unless we know certain facts about the world; every normative analysis therefore contains within it an underlying positive analysis. But while a positive analysis can, at least in principle, be conducted without value judgments, a normative analysis is always based, at least in part, on the values of the person conducting it.

WHY ECONOMISTS DISAGREE. The distinction between positive and normative economics can help us understand why economists so often disagree. Suppose you are watching a television interview in which two economists are asked whether the United States should eliminate all government-imposed barriers to trading with the rest of the world. The first economist says, "Yes, absolutely," while the other says, "No, definitely not." Why the sharp disagreement?

The difference of opinion may be *positive* in nature: The two economists may have sharply divergent views about what would actually happen if trade barriers were eliminated. Differences like this sometimes arise because economic knowledge is far from perfect.

More likely, however, the disagreement will be *normative*. Economists, like everyone else, have different values. In this case, both economists might agree that opening up international trade would benefit *most* Americans, but harm *some* of them. Yet they may still disagree about the wisdom of this policy move because they have different values. The first economist might put more emphasis on benefits to the overall economy, while the second might put more emphasis on preventing harm to the group that would be hurt. Here, the two economists have come to the same *positive conclusion*, but their *different values* lead them to different *normative conclusions*.

Unless these two economists are given ample time to express the basis for their opinions—which rarely happens in news articles and happens even more rarely on television—the public will hear only the disagreement. People may then conclude that economists cannot agree about how the economy works when the *real* disagreement is over which goals are most important for our society.

One of the most important things you will learn in introductory economics is the distinction between normative and positive disagreements. You will see that there is much more agreement on positive economic issues than on normative ones and that economists know more about the economy than the never-ending arguments over policy would suggest.

FIELDS OF ECONOMICS

Just as doctors specialize in different areas of the body—heart, lungs, or eyes—economists have found it valuable to specialize in different types of economic issues. The following list of *fields* is by no means exhaustive, but it will help you appreciate the scope of economics and the types of questions that arise.

Public Economics focuses on the role of government in the economy. What sorts of goods and services should be provided by government, and which should be left to the private sector? Could the U.S. tax system be redesigned to improve its fairness, on the one hand, and its efficiency, on the other? What is the economic relationship between individual states and the federal government, and how does it affect how each raises and spends money? What special problems arise when certain decisions are made collectively in the voting booth, instead of the marketplace?

Finance is concerned with the functioning of the stock, bond, currency, real estate, and commodities markets. Its ultimate goal is to understand what role these markets play in the overall economy and what sorts of policies will help or hinder their performance. Financial economists study how households decide which financial assets to buy and how firms choose between alternative methods of raising funds for expanding their businesses.

Monetary economics includes all aspects of our monetary system and its impact on the overall economy. How does the behavior of private banks affect the economy? What guidelines should central banks—like the U.S. Federal Reserve system—follow to help stabilize the economy? Why does the general level of prices sometimes rise rapidly and at other times hardly change at all? Why are there so many different interest rates in the economy? Is our financial system stable and resilient, able to withstand shocks? Or is it teetering on the brink of collapse, as best-selling paperbacks often suggest?

International economics embraces all aspects of the economic relations between nations. Why do nations trade with each other? What are the benefits from trade, and how are they distributed among a nation's population? What happens when governments interfere with trade? What determines the value of a nation's exchange rate in foreign currency markets? How does the exchange rate affect the national economy? Why do some nations have a trade deficit, and what can they do about it?

Labor economics studies all issues surrounding work and pay. How do individuals decide which career to pursue, how much education to obtain, and how many hours to work? How are wages determined, and what accounts for the vast differences in household incomes observed in most nations? How do government policies affect the type of work we do and the pay we receive for it?

Industrial organization examines how firms interact in markets. How do firms respond to the actions of their rivals? Is the public interest best served when an industry has many competing firms, a few firms, or only one? What happens when the government steps in and tries to change the rules of the game?

Law and economics considers the legal institutions that support economic activity. What is a contract, and what role do contracts play in the overall economy? When should the government intervene to protect consumers and other firms from a powerful and successful firm, such as Microsoft, and when is it better for the government to leave an industry alone? Are jury verdicts of hundreds of millions of dollars good or bad for the economy?

Comparative economic systems helps us classify and compare the economies of different nations. How should the successes and failures of an economic system be judged? Which types of economies perform best and why? Why have the former Soviet-bloc nations decided to abandon central planning in favor of market capitalism, and what can be done to ease the transition from one system to another?

Development economics focuses on growth in the less developed countries of the world, located mostly in Africa, the Middle East, South Asia, and Latin America. Some of these nations are rapidly lifting themselves out of poverty, while others continue to stagnate. What accounts for the low standard of living in these nations? What policies can help them catch up to the richer countries? What are the obstacles—political and economic—standing in the way of enacting these policies?

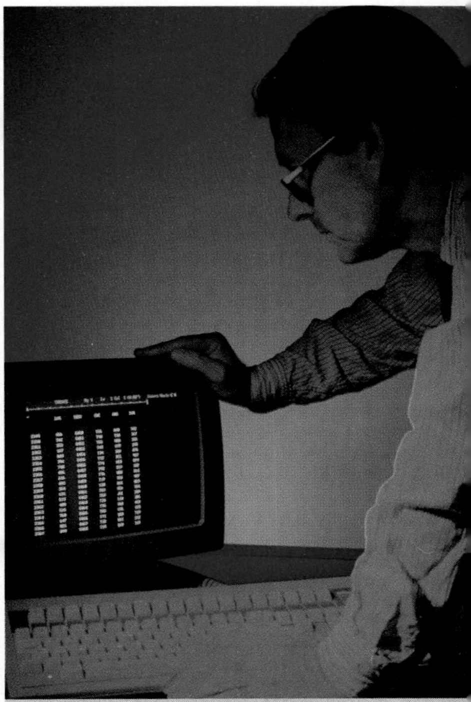

WWW

Name:
Resources for Economists on the Internet

Description:
Directory of economic resources on the Internet maintained by Bill Goffe, the University of Southern Mississippi

Resource:
Resources for Economists on the Internet provides links to economic sites of interest, including economic data sites, publications, and job listings.

Address:
http://econwpa.wustl.edu/EconFAQ/EconFAQ.html

WHY STUDY ECONOMICS?

Students take economics courses for all kinds of reasons. You may recognize some of your own goals among the following or realize that there are more reasons to study economics than you had previously thought.

To Understand the World Better

Much of what happens in the world can be better understood by applying the tools of economic analysis. The list ranges from the global and cataclysmic—wars, famines, epidemics, depressions, and crime waves—to the local and personal—the worsening traffic conditions in your city, the raise you did or didn't get last month, or the long line of people waiting to buy tickets for a popular concert. Economics has the power to help us understand these phenomena because they result, in large part, from the choices we make under conditions of scarcity.

Economics has its limitations, of course. But it is hard to find any aspect of life about which economics does not have *something* important to say. Economics cannot explain why so many Americans like to watch television, but it *can* explain how networks and cable stations decide which programs to offer. Economics cannot protect you from a robbery, but it *can* explain why some people choose to become thieves and why no society has chosen to eradicate crime completely. Economics will not help you solve the problems of your love life, resolve unconscious conflicts from your childhood, or help you overcome a fear of flying, but it *can* explain how many skilled therapists, ministers, and counselors there will be to help us solve these problems.

To Gain Self-Confidence

Understanding basic economic principles and expanding your grasp of cause and effect in world events can increase your confidence as you face a world full of opportunities and hardships. You may no longer feel that there are mysterious, inexplicable forces out there that are shaping your life, buffeting you like the bumpers in a pinball machine, determining whether or not you'll be able to find a job, what your salary will be, whether you'll be able to afford a home, and in what kind of neighborhood. After learning economics, you may be surprised to find that you no longer toss out the business page of your local newspaper because it appears to be written in a foreign language. You may no longer flip to another channel the instant the TV news announcer says, "And now for news about the economy. . . ." You may find yourself listening to economic forecasts and arguments with a critical ear, catching mistakes in logic, misleading statements, or out-and-out lies. When you master economics, you gain a sense of mastery over the world, and thus over your own life as well.

To Achieve Social Change

If you are interested in making the world a better place, economics is indispensable. There is no shortage of serious social problems worthy of our attention—unemployment, hunger, poverty, disease, child abuse, drug addiction, violent crime—and economic factors play a key role in all of them. Economics can help us understand the origins of these problems, explain why previous efforts to solve them have failed, and enable us to design new, more effective solutions.

To Help Prepare for Other Careers

Economics has long been the most popular college major for individuals intending to work in business, but in the last two decades it has also become popular among those planning careers in politics, international relations, law, medicine, engineering, psychology, and more. This is for good reason: Practitioners in each of these fields often find themselves confronting economic issues. For example, lawyers increasingly face judicial rulings based on the principles of economic efficiency. Doctors who understand basic economic principles can better price their services and understand the consequences of proposed changes in national health care policy. Industrial psychologists need to understand the economic implications of any workplace changes they advocate.

To Become an Economist

Only a tiny minority of this book's readers will decide to become economists themselves. This is welcome news to the authors, and after you have mastered the concept of supply and demand, you will understand why. But if you do decide to pursue a career as an economist—obtaining a master's degree or even a Ph.D.—you will find many possibilities for employment. Of 16,780 members of the American Economic Association who responded to a recent survey,[1] 65 percent were teachers at colleges or universities. The rest were engaged in a variety of activities in both the private sector (21 percent) and government (14 percent). Economists are hired by banks to assess the risk of investing abroad; by manufacturing companies, to help them determine new methods of producing, marketing, and pricing their products; by government agencies, to help design policies to fight crime, disease, poverty, and pollution; by international organizations, to help create aid programs for less developed countries; by the media, to help the public interpret global, national, and local events; and even by nonprofit organizations, to provide advice on controlling costs and raising funds more effectively.

THE METHOD OF ECONOMICS

One of the first things you will notice as you begin to study economics is the heavy reliance on *models*. Indeed, the discipline goes beyond any other social science in its insistence that every theory be represented by an explicit, carefully constructed model.

A **model** is *an abstract representation of reality*. Architects built cardboard models of buildings before construction begins. In high school chemistry, you may have seen a model of an atom—a plastic-and-wire contraption, with red, blue, and green balls representing protons, neutrons, and electrons. These are physical models: three-dimensional replicas that you can pick up and hold. Economic models, on the other hand, are built not with cardboard, plastic, or metal, but with words, diagrams, and mathematical statements.

MODEL An abstract, simplified representation of reality.

The Art of Building Economic Models

Look back at the definition of the word "model." The two key words are *abstract* and *representation*. A model is not supposed to be exactly like reality. Rather, it *represents* the real world by *abstracting*, or taking from it that which will help us understand it. There is much in the real world that a model must leave out.

When you build a model, how can you know which details to include and which to leave aside? There is no simple answer to this question. The right amount of detail depends on your purpose in building the model in the first place. There is, however, one guiding principle: *A model should be as simple as possible to accomplish its purpose.* This means that a model should contain all *necessary* details—but no *unnecessary* ones.

1 *American Economic Review*, December 1993, p. 635.

To help make this more concrete, think about a map. A map is a model—it leaves out many details of the real world, such as trees and houses and potholes; it represents the earth's three-dimensional surface by collapsing it into two dimensions; and it is small—much smaller than the area it represents. When you buy a map, how much detail are you looking for?

Let's say you are in San Francisco, and your purpose—the reason you need a map—is to find the best way to drive from Fisherman's Wharf to the downtown civic center. In this case, you would want a very detailed city map, with every street, park, and plaza in San Francisco clearly illustrated and labeled. A highway map—which ignores these details—wouldn't do at all.

But now suppose your purpose is different: to select the best driving route from San Francisco to Cincinnati. Now, you want a highway map. A street map covering the entire route would have *too much* detail. All of that extraneous information would only obscure what you really need to see.

Although economic models are more abstract than road maps, the same principle applies in building them: The level of detail that would be just right for one purpose will usually be too much or too little for another. When you feel yourself objecting to a model in this text because something has been left out, keep in mind the purpose for which the model is built. In introductory economics, the purpose is entirely educational. The models are designed to help you understand some simple, but powerful, principles that describe how the economy operates, and to enable you to come to important conclusions about the world. Keeping the models simple makes it easier to see the basic principles at work and remember them later.

Of course, economic models have other purposes besides education. They can help businesses make decisions about pricing and production, help households decide how and where to invest their savings, and help governments and international agencies formulate policies. Models built for these purposes will be much more detailed than their educational counterparts, and you will learn about them if you take more advanced courses in economics. But even complex models are built around a very simple framework—the same framework you will be learning in introductory economics.

ASSUMPTIONS AND CONCLUSIONS

Every economic model begins with *assumptions* about the way decision makers in the economy behave and then uses simple logic to arrive at conclusions about the world. There are two types of assumptions in a model: simplifying assumptions and critical assumptions.

SIMPLIFYING ASSUMPTION Any assumption that makes a model simpler without affecting any of its important conclusions

A **simplifying assumption** is—like it sounds—a way of making a model simpler, without affecting any of its important conclusions. The purpose of a simplifying assumption is to rid a model of extraneous detail, so its essential features can stand out more clearly. A road map, for example, makes the simplifying assumption, "There are no trees," because information about trees would not help us find our way. An economic model might include the assumption that there are only two goods that households can choose from or that there are only two nations in the world—not because these things are true, but because they make the models easier to follow and do not change any of the important insights we can get from them.

CRITICAL ASSUMPTION Any assumption that affects the conclusions of a model in an important way.

A **critical assumption**, by contrast, is an assumption that affects the conclusions of a model in important ways. When you use a road map, you make the critical assumption, "All of these roads are open." If that turns out not to be true, your conclusion—the best route to take in getting from one place to another—might be vastly different.

In an economic model, there are always one or more critical assumptions. You don't have to look very hard to find them, because economists like to make these assumptions explicit, right from the outset. This helps them scrutinize each other's ideas and ensures that the source of any disagreement can be quickly and accurately identified.

Two Fundamental Assumptions

The economy is complex. In the time it takes you to read this sentence, America's 250 million people will produce about $300,000 worth of goods and services, the U.S. government will collect about $55,000 in taxes and spend a bit more than that, and U.S. firms will exchange about $40,000 worth of goods and services with firms in more than a hundred different countries.

Economists make sense of all this activity—and more—by categorizing the decision makers in the economy into three broad groups: households, business firms, and governments. In *micro*economic models, the focus is on the behavior of *individual* households, firms, and government agencies and how they interact with each other. In *macro*economic models, we group these decision makers together into sectors—the household sector, the business sector, the government sector, and the foreign sector—and study how each sector interacts with the others. In all of these models, however, we find the same two underlying critical assumptions. They are so universal that we may fairly consider them part of the foundation of economic thought.

Fundamental Assumption #1. The first assumption has to do with the goal individual decision makers are trying to accomplish. It can be stated as follows:

> *Fundamental Assumption #1: Every economic decision maker tries to make the best out of any situation.*

Often, making the best out of a situation means *maximizing some quantity*. Business firms, for example, are usually assumed to maximize profit. Households maximize utility—their well-being or satisfaction. In some cases, however, we might want to recognize that firms or households are actually groups of individuals with different agendas. While a firm's owners might want the firm to maximize profits, the managers might want to consider their own power, prestige, and job security. These goals may conflict, and the behavior of the firm will depend on how the conflict is resolved.

While economists often have spirited disagreements about *what* is being maximized, there is virtually unanimous agreement that any economic model should begin with the assumption that *someone* is maximizing *something*. Even the behavior of groups—like the decision makers in a firm or officials of the federal government—is assumed to arise from the behavior of different maximizing individuals, each pursuing his or her own agenda.

Fundamental Assumption #1 seems to imply that we are all engaged in a relentless, conscious pursuit of narrow goals—an implication contradicted by much of human behavior. As you read this paragraph, are you consciously trying to maximize your own well-being? Perhaps. You may be fully aware that reading this will improve your grade in your economics course and that a better grade, in turn, will help you achieve other important goals. But most likely, you aren't thinking about any of this. In truth, we only rarely make decisions with conscious, hard calculations. Why, then, do economists assume that people make decisions in a formal way, when they are more likely to decide informally, without calculations?

This is an important question. Economists answer it this way: The ultimate purpose of building an economic model is to *understand behavior*—the behavior of households, firms, government, and the overall economy. As long as people behave *as if* they are maximizing something, then we can build a good model by *assuming that they are.* Whether they *actually, consciously* maximize anything is an interesting philosophical question, but its answer doesn't affect the usefulness of the model. Thus, the belief behind Fundamental Assumption #1 is that people, for the most part, behave *as if* they are maximizing something.

Milton Friedman, Nobel-prize winning economist, put it this way:

> *Consider the problem of predicting the shots made by an expert billiard player. It seems not at all unreasonable that excellent predictions would be yielded by the hypothesis that the billiard player made his shots* as if *he knew the complicated mathematical formulas that would give the optimum directions of travel, could estimate accurately by eye the angles, etc., describing the location of the balls, could make lightning calculations from the formulas, and could then make the balls travel in the direction indicated by the formulas. Our confidence in this hypothesis is not based on the belief that billiard players, even expert ones, can or do go through the process described; it derives rather from the belief that, unless in some way or other they were capable of reaching essentially the same result, they would not in fact be* expert *billiard players.*[2]

Friedman's last point is important: In many cases, we can have added confidence in Fundamental Assumption #1 because those who do not act as if they are following it will be replaced by those who do. A top-notch pool player *must* behave like an expert in the physics of movement, or else he will be beaten by someone who does. Thus, when all is said and done, all of the top-ranked pool players will behave as if they know physics. Similarly, any politician who deviates too much from vote-maximizing behavior will not be in office very long, and any business firm that doesn't maximize profits will tend to be replaced by one that *does.*

One last thought about Fundamental Assumption #1: It does not imply that people are selfish or that economists think they are. On the contrary, economists are very interested in cases where people take the interests of others into account. For example, much economic life takes place in the family, where people care a great deal about each other. Fundamental Assumption #1 would then be applied to the family as a whole. That is, we would assume that the family is trying to make the best out of any situation, rather than any one individual within it.

Economics also recognizes that people often care about their friends, their neighbors, and the broader society in which they live. Useful economic models have been built to explore charitable giving by individuals and corporations, volunteer activity, and ethical behavior such as honesty, fairness, and respect for fellow citizens.

FUNDAMENTAL ASSUMPTION #2. A second critical assumption underlying all economic models is a simple fact of life:

> *Fundamental Assumption #2: Every economic decision maker faces constraints.*

2 Milton Friedman, "The Methodology of Positive Economics," in his *Essays in Positive Economics* (Chicago: University of Chicago Press, 1935).

Society's overall scarcity of resources constrains each of us individually in much the same way as the overall scarcity of space in a crowded elevator limits the freedom of movement of each rider. Because of the scarcity of resources, households are constrained by limited incomes, business firms are constrained by requirements that they pay for all of the inputs they use, and government agencies are constrained by limited budgets.

Together, the two fundamental assumptions help define the approach economists take in answering questions about the world. To explain why there is poverty, illiteracy and crime, to explain the rise and fall of industries and the patterns of trade among nations, or to explain why some government polices succeed while others fail, economists always begin with the same three questions:

1. Who are the individual decision makers?
2. What are they maximizing?
3. What constraints do they face?

This approach is used so heavily by economists that it is one of the *basic principles of economics* you will learn in this book.

A Few Words on Macroeconomics

In microeconomics, it is easy to see the two fundamental assumptions at work, since the decision makers, what they maximize, and their constraints are spelled out right from the beginning. In macroeconomics, however, the actions of individual decision makers are often hidden in the background. Instead of worrying about individual households, firms, or government agencies, macroeconomists worry about the household, business, or government *sector*. Still, macroeconomists strive to clarify the role of the two fundamental assumptions in their models, to build the "microfoundations" of macroeconomics.

Choosing Among Theories

Economics is, above all, a practical science. It helps us to understand how choices are made in the face of scarcity, to understand the consequences of those choices, and to formulate policies that will make the economy work better. Economic theories—and the models used to represent them—help us achieve these goals. But often there will be more than one theory that attempts to explain how the economy, or some part of it, operates. How can we choose among alternative theories?

This is an important question and a major preoccupation of economists who are trying to advance the state of economic knowledge. And most economists agree: The best theory is the one that enables us to *predict* most accurately what will happen. One way to check a model's validity quickly—without waiting for the future to unfold—is to see how well it *helps us understand the behavior we see around us*. To do this, economists must look at past information on economic variables, such as the prices of different goods or the amount of output produced by a firm, an industry, or the entire nation. Generally, the best model is the one that is most consistent with the data.

"HOW MUCH MATH DO I NEED?"

Economists often express their ideas using mathematical concepts and a special vocabulary because each of these allows them to express themselves more precisely than with ordinary language. Whereas someone who has never taken economics might say, "When used textbooks are easy to buy, students won't buy new textbooks," a student of economics would say, "When the price of used textbooks falls, the demand curve for new textbooks shifts leftward."

Does the second statement sound strange to you? It should. First, it uses a special term—a *demand curve*—that you haven't yet learned. Second, it uses a mathematical concept—a *shifting curve*—with which you might not be familiar. But while the first statement might mean a number of different things, the second statement—as you will see in Chapter 3—can mean only *one* thing. By being precise, we can steer clear of unnecessary confusion. If you are worried about the special vocabulary of economics, you can relax. All of the new terms will be defined and carefully explained as you use them.

But what about the math? Here, too, you can relax. While professional economists often use sophisticated mathematics to solve problems, only a little math is needed to understand the *principles* they use to solve them. And virtually all of this math comes from high school algebra and geometry.

Still, you may not have used *any* of your high school math in a long time, and a little brushing up might be in order. This is why we have included a *mathematical appendix* at the end of the book. It covers some of the most basic concepts—such as the equation for a straight line, the concept of a slope, and the calculation of a percentage change—as well as a few special tools that you may not have encountered before. You may want to glance at this mathematical appendix now, just so you'll know what's there. Then, from time to time, you'll be reminded about specific parts of the appendix when you are most likely to need them.

THE BASIC PRINCIPLES OF ECONOMICS

As you learn economics, you will encounter a variety of different theories, ideas, and techniques—each suited to analyzing a particular problem. But a few of these ideas are so central that they are used again and again in solving economic problems in a variety of different contexts. And these ideas are not only useful in their own right; they also form the foundation on which the rest of economic theory is built. In this book, we will call them the *basic principles of economics:*

BASIC PRINCIPLES OF ECONOMICS A small set of basic ideas that are used repeatedly in analyzing economic problems. They form the foundation of economic theory.

> *The* **basic principles of economics** *are ideas that are used again and again to analyze economic problems. They form the foundation upon which economic theory is built.*

In this sense, the body of economic theory is like an upside-down pyramid, with a few basic principles at the narrow bottom and the many ideas that spring from them forming the wider top.

In this book, you will learn eight basic principles of economics. The "key" symbol will appear in the margin each time one of them is introduced for the first time. Then, each time the principle is *used* in the text—to analyze a problem or to help form a more specific theory—you will be alerted with the same symbol, in the margin.

For example, earlier in this chapter, you learned about the two *fundamental assumptions* that economists make to solve problems. Together, they form the first of the basic principles you will learn about. Let's now introduce this principle formally:

MAXIMIZATION SUBJECT TO CONSTRAINTS

> *The economic approach to understanding a problem is to identify the decision makers and then determine what they are maximizing and the constraints that they face.*

As you will see, the principle of *maximization subject to constraints* will be used again and again in this book.

What about the rest of the basic principles? Following is the complete list, which you are welcome to read through. But don't expect to understand them . . . yet. By the time you've finished reading this book, however, you will understand what these principles mean, how they are used, the connections between them, and why they are so basic to economics.

The Eight Basic Principles of Economics

- **Maximization Subject to Constraints:** *The economic approach to understanding a problem is to identify the decision makers and then determine what they are maximizing and the constraints that they face.*
- **Opportunity Cost:** *All economic decisions taken by individuals or society are costly. The correct way to measure the cost of a choice is its opportunity cost—that which is given up to make the choice.*
- **Specialization and Exchange:** *Specialization and exchange enable us to enjoy greater production and higher living standards than would otherwise be possible. As a result, all economies have been characterized by high degrees of specialization and exchange.*
- **Markets and Equilibrium:** *To understand how the economy behaves, economists organize the world into separate markets and then examine the equilibrium in each of those markets.*
- **Short-run versus Long-run Outcomes:** *Markets behave differently in the short run than in the long run. In solving a problem, we must always know which of these time horizons we are analyzing.*
- **Marginal Decision Making:** *To make the best of a situation, decision makers should consider the incremental or marginal effects of taking any action. This is why economists use marginal analysis to understand and predict economic decisions.*
- **Policy Tradeoffs:** *Government policy is constrained by the reactions of private decision makers. As a result, policy makers face tradeoffs: Making progress toward one goal often requires some sacrifice of another goal.*
- **The Importance of Real Values:** *Since our economic well-being depends, in part, on the goods and services we can buy, it is important to translate nominal values—which are measured in current dollars—to real values—which are measured in purchasing power.*

You may want to flip back to this list from time to time, especially when you see the "key" symbol in the margin and need to refresh your memory about the principle that it refers to.

HOW TO STUDY ECONOMICS

As you read this book or listen to your instructor, you may find yourself nodding along and thinking that everything makes perfect sense, perhaps even that economics is easy. Indeed, it *is* rather easy to follow economics, since it's based so heavily on simple logic. But *following* and *learning* are two different things. You will find—preferably *before* your first exam—that economics must be studied actively, not passively. If you are reading these words lying back on a comfortable couch, a phone in one hand and a remote control in the other, you are, sorry to say, going about it in the wrong way. Active studying means reading with a pencil in hand and a blank sheet of paper in front of you. It means closing the book periodically and *reproducing* what you have learned—reiterating the steps in each logical argument, retracing the cause-and-effect links in each model, and drawing the graph or graphs that represent the model. It means *thinking* about the basic principles of economics and how they relate to what you are learning. It is hard work, but the pay-off is a good understanding of economics and a better understanding of your own life and the world around you.

SUMMARY

Economics is the study of choice under conditions of scarcity. As individuals, and as a society, we have unlimited desires for goods and services. Unfortunately, the *resources*—land, labor, and capital—needed to produce those goods and services are scarce. Therefore, we must choose which desires to satisfy and how to satisfy them. Economics provides the tools that explain those choices.

The field of economics is divided into two major areas. *Microeconomics* studies the behavior of individual households, firms, and governments as they interact in specific markets and industries. *Macroeconomics,* by contrast, concerns itself with the behavior of entire economies. It considers total output, total employment, and the overall price level.

Economics makes heavy use of *models*—abstract representations of reality. These models are words, diagrams, and mathematical statements used to capture the essence of a problem. All models are simplifications, but a good model will have just enough detail *for the purpose at hand.*

Almost all economic models involve two fundamental assumptions. The first is that every decision maker tries to make the best out of any situation; the second is that every decision maker faces constraints. In every situation, then, it is important to determine: (1) who are the decision makers, (2) what are they maximizing, and (3) what constraints do they face?

KEY TERMS

economics	capital	macroeconomics	simplifying assumption
scarcity	human capital	positive economics	critical assumption
resources	land	normative economics	basic principles of economics
labor	microeconomics	model	

REVIEW QUESTIONS

1. What basic fact of life gives rise to the problems studied in economics? Discuss how this fact arises in households, business, and government. Which of the two fundamental assumptions of economics embodies this fact?

2. Explain whether the following would be classified as microeconomics or macroeconomics?
   a. Research into why the economy prospered in the 1980s.
   b. A theory of how consumers decide what to buy.
   c. An analysis of Microsoft's share of the computer software market.
   d. Research on the impact of interest rates on the level of investment in the economy.

3. Discuss whether the following statements are examples of positive economics or normative economics, or whether they contain elements of both:
   a. An increase in the federal government budget deficit causes interest rates to rise.
   b. The goal of any country's economic policy should be to increase the welfare of its poorest, most vulnerable, citizens.
   c. Excess regulation of small business is stifling the economy. Small business has been responsible for most of the growth in employment over the last 10 years, but regulations are putting a severe damper on the ability of small businesses to survive and prosper.
   d. The 1980s were a disastrous decade for the U.S. economy. Income inequality increased to its highest level since before World War II.

4. In which subfield of economics would each of the following questions most likely be studied?
   a. How will an increase in the minimum wage affect unemployment among unskilled workers?
   b. What determines the price of a bond?
   c. Does trading with other nations benefit the United States?
   d. Would lower tax rates on income be better for the U.S. economy?

5. What determines the level of detail that an economist builds into a model?

6. How would an economist respond to the following criticism?

"The problem with economics is that so much of it is unrealistic. Take, for example, the idea that consumers try to maximize their utility, or well-being. When I go into a store to buy something, I don't stand in the aisles with my calculator trying to compute exactly which purchase will make me the happiest."

CHALLENGE QUESTIONS

1. Dissect the following statements by coming up with a list of critical assumptions that could lie behind them. Discuss whether each assumption would be classified as normative or positive.
   a. The United States is not really a democratic society.
   b. Capitalism is a fair, equitable economic system.

2. At a dinner in 1945, the great English economist John Maynard Keynes made the following toast: "[To] economics and economists, who are the trustees, not of civilization, but of the possibility of civilization."

   In light of the overview of economics provided in this chapter, discuss what Keynes may have meant by this remark.

Visit Resources for Economists on the Internet (http://econwpa.wustl.edu/EconFAQ/EconFAQ.html) and look within the table of contents. Browse through the topics and visit a few of the sites listed. Are you surprised by the amount of economic information available? What type of information do you find here that you believe will be useful to this course?

C H A P T E R

2

SCARCITY, CHOICE, AND ECONOMIC SYSTEMS

CHAPTER OUTLINE

What does it cost you to go to the movies? If you answered seven or eight dollars, because that is the price of a movie ticket, then you are leaving a lot out. Most of us are used to thinking of cost as the money we must pay for something. A Big Mac costs $2.50, a new Toyota Corolla costs $15,000, and so on. Certainly, the money we pay for a good or service is a *part* of its cost, but it is not necessarily the entire cost or even the largest part of the cost. Economics takes a broader view of costs, recognizing monetary as well as nonmonetary components.

THE CONCEPT OF OPPORTUNITY COST

The total cost of any action—buying a car, producing a computer, or even reading a book—is what we must give up when we take that action. This cost is called the *opportunity cost* of the action, because any economic activity uses up scarce resources and therefore requires us to give up the *opportunity* to enjoy other things for which those resources could have been used.

The ***opportunity cost*** *of any choice is what we give up when we make that choice.*

Opportunity cost is the concept of cost that should be used in decision making.

Opportunity Cost for Individuals

OPPORTUNITY COST The value of the best alternative sacrificed when taking an action.

Virtually every action we take as individuals uses up scarce money or scarce time or both. Hence, every action we choose requires us to sacrifice other enjoyable goods, services, and activities for which we could have used our time and money. For example, it took a substantial amount of the authors' time to write this textbook. Suppose that the time devoted to writing the book could instead have been used by one of the authors to either (1) go to law school, (2) write a novel, or (3) start a profitable business.

Do all of these alternatives together make up the opportunity cost of writing this book? Not really. The time released from not writing the book would not be sufficient to pursue all of these activities. Only those alternatives that would actually have been chosen should be identified as the opportunity cost of writing the book. But which one would have been chosen? The one that is *next most* attractive to the decision maker. The opportunity cost of any choice, then, is the next most attractive alternative that must be sacrificed. The other, less valuable alternatives would not have been chosen and therefore play no role in making a decision.

To explore this notion of opportunity cost further, let's go back to an earlier question: What does it cost to see a movie? Suppose some friends ask Jessica to a movie located 10 minutes from campus. To see the movie, Jessica will use up scarce *funds* to buy the movie ticket and scarce *time* traveling to and from the movie and sitting through it. The *money* she uses for the movie ticket would otherwise have been spent on a long-distance phone call to a friend in Italy—her next best use of the money—and the *time* would otherwise have been devoted to studying for her economics exam—her next best use of time. For Jessica, then, the opportunity cost of the movie consists of two things: (1) a phone call to her friend *and* (2) a higher score on her economics exam. Seeing the movie will require Jessica to sacrifice *both* of these valuable alternatives, since the movie will cost Jessica both money and time.

Now consider Samantha, a highly paid consultant who lives in New York City, several miles from the theater, and who has a backlog of projects to work on. As in Jessica's case, seeing the movie will use scarce *funds* and scarce *time*. But for Samantha, the particulars will be different. First, the money costs are greater: There is not only the price of the movie ticket, but also the round-trip cab fare, which could bring the direct money cost to $20. However, this is only a small part of Samantha's opportunity cost. Let's suppose that the *time* it takes Samantha to find out when and where the movie is playing, hail a cab, travel to the movie theater, wait in line, sit through the previews, and travel back home is four hours—not unrealistic for seeing a movie in Manhattan. Samantha's next best alternative for using her time would be to work on her consulting projects, for which she would earn $150 per hour. In this case, we can measure the entire opportunity cost of the movie in monetary terms: first, the direct money costs of the movie and cab fare ($20), and second, the *forgone income* associated with seeing the movie ($150 × 4 hours = $600), for a total of $620!

At such a high price, you might wonder why Samantha would ever decide to see a movie. Indeed, the same reasoning applies to almost everything Samantha does besides work: It is very expensive for Samantha to talk to a friend on the phone, eat dinner, or even sleep—all of these activities require her to sacrifice the direct money costs plus another $150 per hour of foregone income. Should Samantha ever choose to pursue any of these activities? The answer for Samantha is the same as for Jessica or anyone else: yes—*if* the activity is more highly valued than what is given up. It is not hard to imagine that, after putting in a long day at work, leisure activities would be very important to Samantha—worth the money cost *and* the forgone income required to enjoy them.

With an understanding of the concept of opportunity cost and how it can differ among different individuals, you can understand some behavior that might otherwise appear strange. For example, why do high-income people rarely shop at discount stores like Kmart, preferring full-service stores where the same items carry much higher price tags? It's not that high-income people *like* to pay more for their purchases, but that discount stores are generally understaffed and crowded with customers, so shopping there takes more time. While discount stores offer a lower *money* price, they impose a higher *time cost*. For high-income people, these stores are actually more costly than stores with higher price tags. We can also understand why the most highly paid consultants, entrepreneurs, attorneys, and surgeons often lead such frenetic lives, doing several things at once and packing every spare minute with tasks. Since these people can earn several hundred dollars for an hour of work, every activity they undertake carries a correspondingly high opportunity cost. Brushing one's teeth can cost $10, and driving to work can cost hundreds! By combining activities—making phone calls while driving to work, thinking about and planning the day while in the shower, or reading the morning paper in the elevator—the opportunity cost of these routine activities can be minimized.

OPPORTUNITY COST AND SOCIETY

From an individual's point of view, it is useful to think of opportunity cost as arising from the scarcity of *time* or *money;* for society as a whole, it arises from the scarcity of society's *resources*. Since human wants are unlimited, while society's resources are not, no society can produce enough of everything to satisfy everyone's desires simultaneously. Therefore,

> *All production carries an opportunity cost: To produce and enjoy more of one thing, we must shift resources away from producing something else.*

Consider a goal on which we can all agree: better health for our citizens. What would be needed to achieve this goal? More medical checkups for more people and greater access to top-flight medicine when necessary. These, in turn, would require more and better trained doctors, more hospital buildings and laboratories, and more high-tech medical equipment such as CAT scanners and surgical lasers. In order for us to produce these goods and services, we would have to pull resources—land, labor, machinery, and raw materials—out of producing other goods and services that we also enjoy. The opportunity cost of improved health care, then, consists of these other goods and services we would have to do without.

THE PRINCIPLE OF OPPORTUNITY COST

Opportunity cost is one of the most important ideas you will encounter in economics. The concept sheds light on virtually every problem that economists consider, whether it be explaining the behavior of consumers or business firms or understanding important social problems like poverty or racial discrimination. In all of these cases, economists apply the *principle of opportunity cost.*

PRINCIPLE OF OPPORTUNITY COST All economic decisions taken by individuals or society are costly. The correct way to measure the cost of a choice is its opportunity cost—that which is given up to make the choice.

> ***The Principle of Opportunity Cost:*** *All economic decisions taken by individuals or society are costly. The correct way to measure the cost of a choice is its opportunity cost—that which is given up to make the choice.*

OPPORTUNITY COST

PRODUCTION POSSIBILITIES FRONTIERS

Let's build a simple model to help us see how the principle of opportunity cost can be applied to society's choices. We'll start with a *simplifying assumption*—that the production of all goods and services has been predetermined, except for those in *two* categories: health care and movies. This may seem like a strange juxtaposition: Why pit health care—which requires inputs such as doctors, laboratories, and medical equipment—against movies—which require inputs such as actors, writers, film, studios, and theaters? The answer is that all of these inputs are ultimately made from the same general categories of resources: land, raw materials, labor, and capital. To have more of one requires us to pull resources out of the other.

To be even more specific, let's measure health care by the *number of lives saved* and movies by the *number of major feature films produced.* This does, indeed, represent a viable choice for society: One way to have more and better health care would be to produce fewer movies each year, freeing up resources that could then be devoted to building more laboratories, training more doctors, and producing more diagnostic equipment.

Figure 1 illustrates society's alternatives in graphical form. The curve in the figure is society's **production possibility frontier** (PPF), *giving the different combinations of goods that can be produced with the resources and technology currently available.* In this case, the number of lives saved through medical intervention is measured along the vertical axis, and the number of feature films produced appears along the horizontal axis. The PPF tells us the *maximum quantity* of movies we can produce for each quantity of lives saved, or the maximum number of lives saved for each different quantity of films. Positions beyond the frontier are unattainable with the technology and resources at the economy's disposal; society's choices are limited to points *on* or *inside* the PPF.

PRODUCTION POSSIBILITIES FRONTIER (PPF) A curve showing all combinations of two goods that can be produced with the resources and technology currently available.

Point *A* represents one choice society could make: to use all available resources for health care and none for making movies. In this case, we would have zero movies, but we would save 1,000,000 lives each year with the health care system. Point *B* represents the opposite extreme: All available resources would go into film production and none into health care. We would then be able to enjoy 500 major Hollywood movies each year, but would have to forgo every opportunity to save lives.

If points *A* and *B* seem absurd to you, remember that they are, indeed, two *possible* choices for society, but choices no society would actually make. We want both psychological *and* physical health, so we want to be entertained as well as to be cured of illness. This requires us to choose a *mix* of health care and movies.

Suppose we desire such a mix, but the economy, for some reason, is currently operating at the undesirable point *A*—maximal health care, zero films. Then we need to shift some of society's resources from health care to entertainment. We could move from point *A* to point *C* and produce 100 movies each year, but, as a consequence, we'd have to cut back on health care and save 50,000 fewer lives. The opportunity cost of 100 films, then, would be 50,000 human lives.

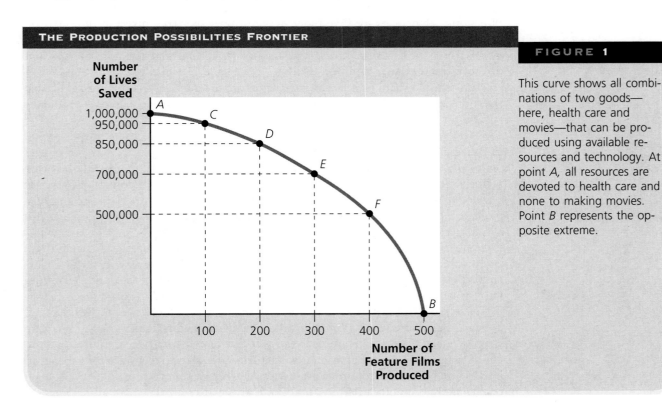

THE PRODUCTION POSSIBILITIES FRONTIER

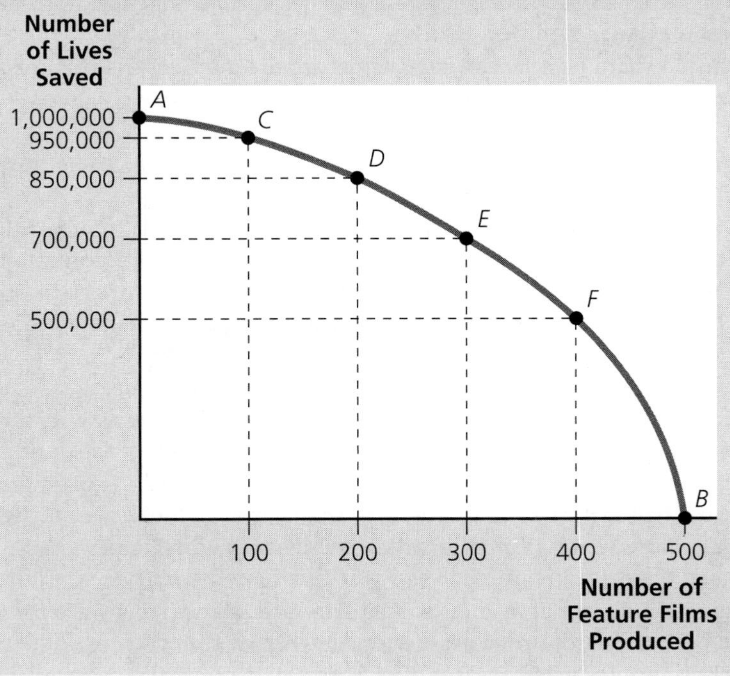

FIGURE 1

This curve shows all combinations of two goods—here, health care and movies—that can be produced using available resources and technology. At point *A,* all resources are devoted to health care and none to making movies. Point *B* represents the opposite extreme.

INCREASING OPPORTUNITY COST. The move from point *A* to point *C* in Figure 1 got us 100 more movies, but cost us 50,000 in lives saved. From point *C*, let us once again imagine shifting enough resources out of health care to produce an additional 100 movies. Notice that, this time, there is an even *greater* cost: 100,000 fewer lives saved. The opportunity cost of movies has risen. You can see that as we continue to increase movie production by increments of 100—moving from point *D* to point *E* to point *F*—the opportunity cost of movies keeps right on rising, until the last 100 films cost an additional 500,000 lives.

The behavior of opportunity cost described here—that the more films we produce, the greater the opportunity cost of producing still more of them—applies to a wide range of choices facing society. It can be generalized as the **law of increasing opportunity cost:**

LAW OF INCREASING OPPORTUNITY COST The more of something that is produced, the greater is the opportunity cost of producing one more unit.

> *The more of something we produce, the greater is the opportunity cost of producing still more.*

The law of increasing opportunity cost causes the PPF to have a *concave* shape, declining more steeply as we move rightward and downward. To understand why, remember—from high school math—that the slope of a line or curve is just the change along the vertical axis divided by the change along the horizontal axis. Along the PPF, as we move rightward, the slope corresponds to the change in the number of lives saved divided by the change in the number of films produced or, equivalently, the change in the number of lives saved *per additional film produced.* The absolute value of this slope is the opportunity cost of one more film. Since the opportunity cost increases as we move rightward and produce more films, the absolute value of the PPF's slope must rise—the PPF gets steeper and steeper—giving us the concave shape we see in the figure.

You may be wondering if the law of increasing opportunity cost applies in both directions. That is, as we save more lives, do we experience a rise in the opportunity cost of saving a life? A glance at Figure 2 should convince you that the answer is yes. There, you can see how equal increments in *lives saved* require the sacrifice of greater and greater numbers of films.

Why should there be a law of increasing opportunity cost? Why must it be that the more of something we produce, the greater the opportunity cost of producing still more?

Most resources—*by their very nature*—are better suited to some purposes than to others. At point *B*, where we are producing only films, we are making movies with many resources that are poorly suited to this purpose and that would be much better suited for work in health care. For example, at point *B*, potentially brilliant surgeons are employed as film directors, actors, camera operators, and so on; hospitals are being used as film studios; and laser equipment originally designed for eye surgery is instead being used to provide special effects.

As we move leftward along the PPF, shifting resources out of movies and into health care, we would first shift those resources *best suited to health care*—for example, a surgeon who could save many lives in the emergency ward, but is not doing too well as a film editor. This means that, moving from *B* to *C*, we are shifting resources that were not really contributing all that much to film production, but will contribute quite a bit to health care. This is why, at first, the PPF is very steep: We get a *large* increase in lives saved for only a *small* decrease in the number of films made. As we continue moving leftward, however, we are forced to shift into health care resources that are better and better suited to making films. As a result, the PPF becomes flatter. Finally, we arrive at point *A*, where all resources—

INCREASING OPPORTUNITY COST OF SAVING A LIFE

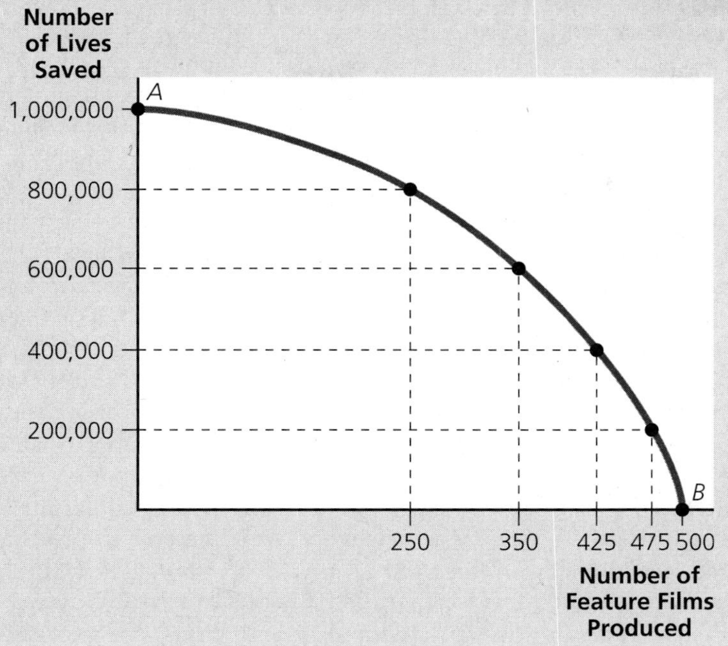

FIGURE 2

As more lives are saved, the cost of saving an additional life—measured in terms of movies sacrificed—rises. Equal increments in lives saved require the sacrifice of greater and greater numbers of films.

no matter how well suited for moviemaking—are working in the health care industry. Film studios would be used as hospital wards and spotlights used to illuminate operating rooms. Kevin Costner might be your ophthalmologist, Arnold Schwarzenegger might be working a suicide hot line, and Sharon Stone might be operating a CAT scanner.

The principle of increasing opportunity cost applies to all of society's production choices, not just that between health care and entertainment. If we look at society's choice between food production and oil production, we would find that some land is better suited to growing food and some land to drilling for oil. As we continue to shift resources out of food production and into oil production, the land we are shifting is less and less suited to producing oil, and the opportunity cost of producing additional oil will therefore increase. The same principle applies in choosing between civilian goods and military goods, between food and clothing, or between automobiles and public transportation: The more of something we produce, the greater is the opportunity cost of producing still more.

THE SEARCH FOR A FREE LUNCH

At the beginning of this chapter, it was argued that every decision to produce *more* of something requires us to pay an opportunity cost by producing less of something else. Economist Milton Friedman summarized this idea in his famous remark that "There is no such thing as a free lunch." The logic of this remark is seen every time we *move along* a PPF, sacrificing one thing in order to have more of another.

But what if an economy is not living up to its productive potential, but is instead operating *inside* its PPF? For example, in Figure 2, the economy might be producing 250 films and enough medical care to save 400,000 lives—a point *inside* its PPF. (Identify this point in Figure 2.) Shouldn't it be able to produce more of *both* goods by simply moving *to* its PPF, with no opportunity cost whatsoever? Here it looks like Milton Friedman was wrong—there *is* such a thing as a free lunch! But why would an economy ever be operating inside its PPF? There are two possibilities.

TECHNICAL INEFFICIENCY. One case where economies operate inside their PPFs arises when resources are being wasted. Be careful about the word "waste," however, because it means different things to different people. Suppose a plywood manufacturer does not use every scrap of lumber that comes into the factory; many wood chips end up on the floor and are swept into the trash. The plywood manufacturer is clearly using more lumber than is absolutely necessary to produce output. Does this mean that the company is wasting lumber?

You might be tempted to answer yes automatically. But what if the only way to eliminate this supposed waste is for the manufacturer to hire more inspectors to monitor the firm's operations more closely? This option would be *costly* to the manufacturer and *costly to society as well,* since the additional labor could instead be used to produce something else, say, better roads. Perhaps society would *benefit* more from the improved roads than it would benefit from using the additional wood chips. In situations like this, where using less of one input (such as lumber) requires using more of some other input (such as labor), it is not clear whether the manufacturer—or society as a whole—would be better off making the change.

But what if there is a way for the plywood manufacturer to produce the same output using less lumber *and no more of any other input.* For example, by rearranging its existing labor force, so that the best woodcutters are used to cut wood and the other workers do jobs such as sanding and gluing, the firm might be able to get more plywood out of each piece of lumber. Any manager who did not take advantage of an opportunity like this would be truly wasting resources. Eliminating this kind of waste would make the manufacturer better off—since production could increase without any increase in costs—and make *society* better off—since there could be more plywood without having to sacrifice anything. When all waste of this sort has been eliminated, production is **technically efficient**—the maximum possible output is being produced from a given collection of inputs.

TECHNICAL EFFICIENCY A situation in which the maximum possible output is being produced from a given collection of inputs.

Technical *in*efficiency is illustrated in Figure 3, where the PPF is drawn for the choice between plywood and paper—two goods that use lumber as a key input. Point *A* on the PPF shows us that, given plywood production of 400 units, the maximum production of paper would be 600 units. However, with technical inefficiency, the economy might be at a point like *B—inside* the PPF. The economy is not producing the maximum possible output from the resources—for example, lumber—at its disposal. Eliminating the technical inefficiency would allow us to move from point *B* inside the PPF to a point *on* the PPF. We could move from point *B* to point *C* and produce more plywood; from *B* to *A,* producing more paper; or from *B* to *E,* producing more of *both* goods. In any of these cases, we can have more of one thing without having to produce less of anything else, and so we can avoid paying any opportunity cost for the additional production.

Before you get the idea that finding free lunches like this is an easy task, be forewarned that cases of technical inefficiency are rare. When you study microeconomics, you will see that owners and managers of firms have powerful incentives to eliminate most instances of technical inefficiency.

RECESSIONS. Another situation where an economy operates inside its PPF is a *recession*—a slowdown in overall economic activity. During recessions, many resources are idle. There is widespread *unemployment*—people *want* to work, but are unable to find jobs. Factories shut down, so we are not using all of our available capital or land either. An end to the recession would move the economy from a

TECHNICAL INEFFICIENCY

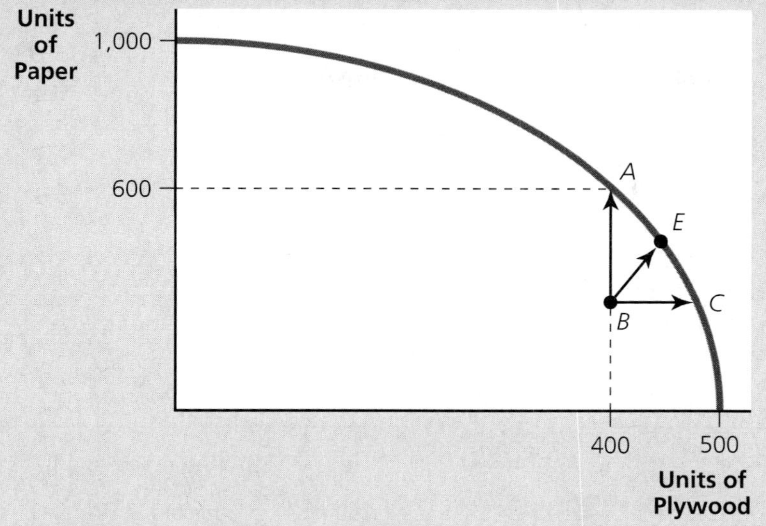

FIGURE 3

An economy employing a *technically inefficient* combination of resources operates inside the PPF, at a point such as *B*. Eliminating the inefficiency allows it to produce more paper with no less plywood (point *A*), more plywood with no less paper (point *C*), or more plywood and more paper (at a point such as *E*).

point *inside* its PPF to a point *on* its PPF—using idle resources to produce more goods and services without sacrificing anything.

This simple observation can help us understand, in part, why the United States and the Soviet Union had such different economic experiences during World War II. In the United States, the average standard of living improved considerably as we entered the war; in the Soviet Union, it deteriorated severely. Why?

Figure 4 shows why. Here, the PPFs illustrate the choice between military goods and civilian goods. When the United States entered the war in 1940, it was still suffering from the Great Depression—the most serious and long-lasting economic downturn in modern history, which began in 1929 and hit most of the developed world. For reasons you will learn when you study macroeconomics, entering the war ended the depression in the United States and moved our economy from a point like *A*, inside the PPF, to a point like *B*, *on* the frontier. Military production increased, but so did the production of civilian goods. Although there were shortages of some consumer goods, the overall result was a rise in the material well-being of the average U.S. citizen.

In the Soviet Union, things were very different. In the 1930s, the Soviet economy—which was internationally isolated—was able to escape entirely the effects of the depression infecting the rest of the world. Thus, it was already operating *on* or near its PPF, at a point like *C*. Entering the war—which meant an increase in military production—required a movement *along* its PPF, to a point like *D*. For the Soviet Union, the drop in civilian production—and the resulting drop in living standards—was the opportunity cost that had to be paid in order to fight the war.[1]

1 Another explanation for the different experiences of the United States and Soviet Union can also be illustrated with PPFs. Since the war was not fought on our turf, we had no significant destruction of physical capital within the 48 states. But large parts of the Soviet Union were decimated. Similarly, while the human loss for the United States was significant, the Soviet loss was about 20 times greater. In the Soviet Union, the huge decrease in labor, as well as in physical and human capital, shifted the PPF significantly *inward*—with fewer resources, there could be less production of civilian goods for a given amount of military goods. This, too, explains the decline in Soviet living standards.

FIGURE 4

UNEMPLOYMENT AND PRODUCTION

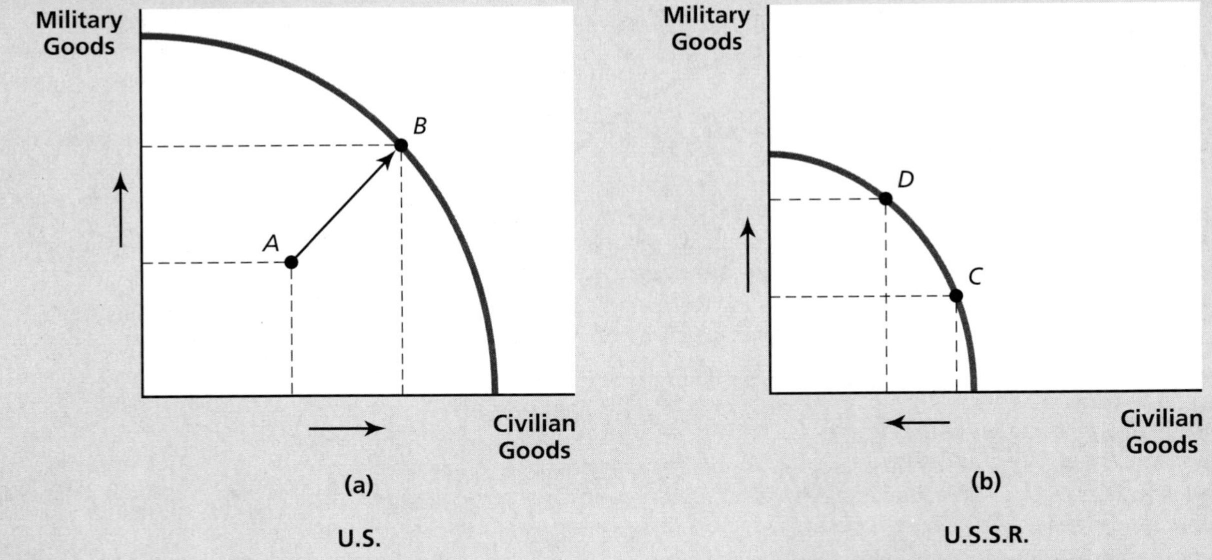

At the onset of World War II, the U.S. economy was experiencing unemployment, at point *A* in panel (a). War production eliminated the unemployment and the economy moved *onto* its PPF at point *B* with more military goods *and* more civilian goods. The Soviet Union, by contrast, began the war with no unemployed resources. It could increase military production only by moving *along* its PPF and sacrificing civilian goods, from point *C* to point *D*.

An economic downturn—such as the Great Depression of the 1930s—does seem to offer a clear-cut free lunch, but even here, appearances can be deceiving. When you study macroeconomics, you will see that there are a variety of government actions that can help to end recessions. But each of them comes with its own costs, such as a risk to the future health of the economy. Some would argue that *any* form of intervention gives the government added power and poses a threat to individual liberty. Of course, we may feel that it is worth paying these costs to end a recession, but that is a different matter. Once again, we see that a *truly free* lunch is not so easy to find.

ECONOMIC SYSTEMS

As you read these words—perhaps curled up on a couch or sitting upright on a chair in the library—you are experiencing a very private moment. It is just you and this book; the rest of the world might as well not exist. Or so it seems. . . .

Actually, even in this supposedly private moment, you are connected to the rest of the world in ways you may not have thought about. In order for you to be reading this book, we, the authors, had to write it. Someone (his name is Dennis Hanseman) had to edit it, to make sure that all necessary material was covered and that the sentences would read smoothly and easily. Someone else had to draw the diagrams. Others had to run the printing presses and the binding machines, and still others had to pack the book, ship it, unpack it, put it on a store shelf, and then sell it to you. And there is more: People had to manufacture paper and ink, the boxes used for shipping, the computers used to keep track of inventory, and so on.

It is no exaggeration to say that thousands of people were involved in putting this book in your hands.

And there is still more. The chair or couch upon which you are sitting, the light shining on the page, the heat or the air conditioning in the room, the clothes you are wearing—these are all things that you are using right now, things produced by *somebody else.*

Take a walk in your town or city, and you will see even more evidence of our economic interdependence: People are collecting garbage, helping schoolchildren cross the street, transporting furniture across town, constructing buildings, repairing roads, painting houses. Everyone is producing goods and services for *other people.*

Why is it that so much of what we consume is produced by somebody else? Why are we all so heavily dependent on each other for our survival and our material well-being? Why doesn't each of us—like Robinson Crusoe on his island—produce our own food, clothing, housing, and anything else we desire? And how did it come about that *you*—who did not produce any of these things yourself—are able to consume them?

These are all questions about our *economic system*—the way our economy is organized. Ordinarily, we take our economic system for granted, like the water that runs out of our tap. But now it is time to take a closer look at the plumbing: to learn how our economy works and how it serves so many millions of people, enabling them to survive and prosper.

SPECIALIZATION AND EXCHANGE

If we were forced to, most of us could, indeed, become economically self-sufficient. We could stake out a plot of land, grow our own food, make our own clothing, and build our own homes. But no society is characterized by such extreme self-sufficiency. On the contrary, every economic system known to history over the past 10,000 years has been characterized by two features: (1) **specialization,** in which each of us concentrates on a limited number of productive activities; and (2) **exchange,** in which most of what we desire is obtained by trading with others, rather than producing for ourselves. These two features are at the heart of a basic principle of economics:

SPECIALIZATION A method of production in which each person concentrates on a limited number of activities.

EXCHANGE The act of trading with others to obtain what we desire.

> ***The Principle of Specialization and Exchange:*** *Specialization and exchange enable us to enjoy greater production, and higher living standards, than would otherwise be possible. As a result, all economies have been characterized by high degrees of specialization and exchange.*

SPECIALIZATION AND EXCHANGE

PRINCIPLE OF SPECIALIZATION AND EXCHANGE Specialization and exchange enable us to enjoy greater production and higher living standards than would otherwise be possible. As a result, all economies are characterized by high degrees of specialization and exchange.

There are three reasons that specialization and exchange enable us to enjoy greater production. The first has to do with human capabilities: Each of us can learn only so much in a lifetime. By limiting ourselves to a narrow set of tasks—laying bricks, managing workers, writing music, or designing computer software—we are each able to hone our skills and become experts at one or two things, instead of remaining amateurs at a lot of things. It is easy to see that an economy of experts will produce more than an economy of amateurs. A second gain from specialization results from the time needed to switch from one activity to another. When people specialize, and spend more time doing one task, there is less unproductive "downtime" from switching activities.

Before considering the third gain from specialization, it is important to note that these first two gains—acquiring expertise and minimizing downtime—would occur even if all workers were identical, as the following, rather extreme example should help make clear:

Sherrie, Gerri, and Kerry are identical triplets who not only carry identical genes, but have had identical life experiences. The triplets decide to open up their own photocopy shop and quickly discover that there are three primary tasks to be accomplished each day: making photocopies, dealing with customers, and servicing the machines.

Suppose first that the triplets decide *not* to specialize. Each time a customer walks in, *one* of the triplets will take the order, walk over to the photocopy machine, make the copies, walk back to the counter, collect the money, make the change, and give a receipt. In addition, each time a machine runs out of paper or ink, the triplet who is using the machine must remedy the problem. You can see that there will be a great deal of time spent going back and forth between the counter, the copy machines, and the supply room. Moreover, none of the triplets will become an expert at servicing the machines, dealing with customers, or making photocopies. As a result of the downtime between tasks, and the lack of expertise, the triplets will not be able to make the maximum possible number of copies or handle the maximum possible number of customers each day.

Now, let's rearrange production to take advantage of specialization. We'll put Sherrie at the counter, Gerri at the photocopy machine, and Kerry at work keeping the machines in working order. Suddenly, all of that time spent going back and forth is now devoted to more productive tasks. Moreover, Sherrie becomes an expert at working the cash register, since she does this all day long. Gerri becomes an expert at making copies, figuring out the quickest ways to position originals, turn pages, and determine the proper settings. And Kerry learns how to quickly diagnose and even anticipate problems with the machines. Each task is now performed by an expert. You can see that specialization increases the number of copies and customers that the triplets can handle each day.

The gains from specialization were first explained by Adam Smith in his book, *An Inquiry into the Nature and Causes of the Wealth of Nations,* published in 1776. Smith explained how specialization within a pin factory dramatically increased the number of pins that could be produced there. In order to make a pin, he wrote,

One man draws out the wire, another straightens it, a third cuts it, a fourth points it, a fifth grinds it at the top for receiving the head; to make the head requires three distinct operations; to put it on is a [separate] business, to whiten the pins is another; it is even a trade by itself to put them into the paper; and the important business of making a pin is, in this manner, divided into about eighteen distinct operations, which, in some manufactories, are all performed by distinct hands.

Smith went on to observe that 10 men, each working separately, might make 200 pins in a day, but through specialization, they were able to make 48,000! What is true for a pin factory or a photocopy shop can be generalized to the entire economy: Even when workers are identically suited to various tasks, total production will increase when workers specialize.

TABLE 1

TIME REQUIREMENTS

	1 Quart of Berries	1 Fish
Maryanne	1 hour	1 hour
Gilligan	1½ hours	3 hours

Of course in the real world, workers are *not* identically suited to different kinds of work. Nor are all plots of land, all natural resources, or all types of capital equipment identically suited for different tasks. This observation brings us to the *third* gain from specialization.

FURTHER GAINS TO SPECIALIZATION: COMPARATIVE ADVANTAGE. Imagine a shipwreck in which there are only two survivors—let's call them Maryanne and Gilligan—who wash up on opposite shores of a deserted island. Initially unaware of each other, each is forced to become completely self-sufficient, using the 12 hours of daylight to perform two tasks necessary for survival: catching fish and picking berries.

On one side of the island, Maryanne finds that it takes her one hour to pick one quart of berries or to catch one fish, as shown in Table 1. She decides to devote five hours to berry picking and seven hours to fishing, and her total production—five quarts of berries and seven fish—is entered in the first row of Table 2.

On the other side of the island, Gilligan—who is less adept at both tasks—requires an hour and a half to pick a quart of berries and three hours to catch one fish, as listed in Table 1. Gilligan decides to spend three hours picking berries—yielding two quarts—and nine hours fishing—catching three fish, as listed in the second row of Table 2. The last row of Table 2 shows total production on the island, obtained simply by adding up the berries and fish produced by these two stranded castaways.

One day, Maryanne and Gilligan discover each other. After rejoicing at the prospect of human companionship, the two decide to work out a system of production that will work to their mutual benefit. Let's rule out any gains from specialization that might arise from minimizing downtime or from becoming an expert, as occurred in the photocopy shop example. Will it still pay for these two to specialize? The answer is yes, as you will see after a small detour.

Absolute Advantage: A Detour. When Gilligan and Maryanne sit down to figure out who should do what, they might fall victim to a common mistake: basing their decision on *absolute advantage*. An individual has an **absolute advantage** in the production of some good when he or she can produce it using *fewer resources* than another individual can. On the island, the only resource being used is labor time, so the reasoning might go as follows: Maryanne can pick one quart of berries more quickly than Gilligan (see Table 1), so she has an *absolute advantage* in berry picking. It seems logical, then, that Maryanne should be the one to pick the berries.

ABSOLUTE ADVANTAGE The ability to produce a good or service using fewer resources than other producers use.

But wait! Maryanne can also catch fish more quickly than Gilligan (see Table 1), so she has an absolute advantage in fishing as well. If absolute advantage is the criterion for assigning work, then Maryanne should do *both* tasks. This, however, would leave Gilligan doing nothing, which is certainly *not* in the pair's best inter-

SELF-SUFFICIENCY — **TABLE 2**

	Quarts of Berries	Number of Fish
Maryanne	5	7
Gilligan	2	3
Total Island	7	10

ests. What can we conclude from this example? That absolute advantage is an unreliable guide for allocating tasks to different workers.

Comparative Advantage. A better principle to guide the division of labor on the island is comparative advantage:

COMPARATIVE ADVANTAGE The ability to produce a good or service at a lower opportunity cost than other producers.

> *A person has a **comparative advantage** in producing some good if he or she can produce it with a smaller opportunity cost than some other person can.*

Notice the important difference between absolute advantage and comparative advantage: You have an *absolute* advantage in producing a good if you can produce it with fewer *resources* than someone else can; but you have a *comparative* advantage if you can produce it with a smaller *opportunity cost.* As you'll see, these are not necessarily the same thing.

Let's determine who has a comparative advantage in fishing. For Maryanne, catching one fish takes an hour, time which could instead be used to pick one quart of berries. Thus, for Maryanne, the opportunity cost of one fish is one quart of berries. For Gilligan, however, catching one fish takes three hours, time which he could instead use to pick two quarts of berries. The opportunity cost of one fish for Gilligan, then, is two quarts of berries. Comparing the two numbers, we see that Maryanne can catch fish with a lower opportunity cost in berries, so she has a *comparative advantage* in catching fish.

Now let's turn to berry picking. In the time it takes Maryanne to pick one quart of berries (one hour), she could alternatively catch one fish. Thus, for Maryanne, the opportunity cost of one quart of berries is one fish. For Gilligan, however, an extra quart of berries takes an hour and a half, which could be used instead to catch, on average, half a fish. Thus, for Gilligan, the opportunity cost of one quart of berries is half a fish. Hence, it is Gilligan, and not Maryanne, who has the lower opportunity cost for a quart of berries. Therefore, Gilligan—who has an *absolute* advantage in nothing—has a *comparative* advantage in berry picking.

Now let's see what happens if the two decide to specialize according to their respective comparative advantage. Maryanne would devote her 12 hours to fishing, catching 12 fish each day. Gilligan would pick berries all day, getting eight quarts. These results are summarized in Table 3. Comparing them with Table 2, you can see that when each of the two specializes according to his or her comparative advantage, total production on the island will be greater: The two will produce one quart more berries, and two more fish each day.

What is true for our shipwrecked island dwellers is also true for the entire economy:

SPECIALIZATION AND EXCHANGE

> *Total production of every good or service will be greatest when individuals specialize according to their comparative advantage. This is another factor behind the principle of specialization and exchange.*

Notice that comparative advantage identifies a gain from specialization that is conceptually distinct from the gains discussed earlier. In this example, neither Maryanne nor Gilligan becomes better at fishing or berry picking due to specializing, nor due to the downtime saved from doing one task instead of two. The gains from comparative advantage come about for an entirely different reason: because each individual is better suited to some tasks than others. More specifically, when someone has a comparative advantage in producing something, it means that they can produce it with a lower opportunity cost than someone else can. When *everyone* is producing according to the principle of comparative advantage, we ensure

SPECIALIZATION — **TABLE 3**

	Quarts of Berries	Number of Fish
Maryanne	0	12
Gilligan	8	0
Total Island	8	12

that the opportunity cost of everyone's production is as low as possible. In this way, society can produce more of everything with the same resources, as the principle of specialization and exchange tells us.

Now let's turn from our fictional island to the real world. Do we observe that production is, in fact, consistent with the principle of comparative advantage? Indeed, we do. A journalist may be able to paint her house more quickly than a housepainter, giving her an *absolute* advantage in painting her home. Will she do both activities herself? Except in unusual circumstances, no. The journalist no doubt has a *comparative* advantage in writing news articles. Indeed, most journalists—like most college professors, attorneys, architects, and other professionals—hire house painters, leaving themselves more time to practice the professions in which they enjoy a comparative advantage.

Even comic-book superheroes seem to behave consistently with comparative advantage. Superman could no doubt cook a meal, fix a car, chop wood, and do virtually *anything* faster than anyone else on the earth. Superman, we could say, had an absolute advantage in everything, but a clear comparative advantage in catching criminals and saving the known universe from destruction, which is exactly what he spent his time doing.

SPECIALIZATION IN PERSPECTIVE. The gains from specialization, whether they arise from developing expertise, from minimizing downtime, or from the principle of comparative advantage, can explain many features of our economy. For example, college students need to select a major and then, upon graduating, to decide on a career. Those who follow this path are rewarded with higher incomes than those who dally. This is an encouragement to specialize. Society is better off if you specialize, since you will help the economy produce more, and society rewards you for this contribution with a higher income.

Another phenomenon: Most of us end up working for business firms that employ dozens, or even hundreds or thousands, of other employees. Why do these business firms exist? Why isn't each of us a *self-employed* expert, exchanging our production with other self-employed experts? Part of the answer is that organizing production into business firms pushes the gains from specialization still further. Within a firm, some people can specialize in working with their hands, others in managing people, others in selling goods and services, and still others in keeping the books. Each firm is a kind of minisociety within which specialization occurs, resulting in greater production and a higher standard of living than we would achieve if we were all self-employed.

Specialization has enabled societies everywhere to achieve standards of living unimaginable to our ancestors. But it can have a downside as well, if it goes too far. In the old film *Modern Times,* Charlie Chaplin plays a poor soul standing at an assembly line, attaching part number 27 to part number 28 thousands of times a day. In the real world, specialization is rarely this extreme. Still, it has caused some jobs to be repetitive and boring. In some plants, workers are deliberately moved from one specialty to another to relieve boredom.

Nor is maximizing our material standard of living our only goal. Might we be better off *increasing* the variety of tasks we do each day, even if this meant some sacrifice in production and income? For example, in many societies, one sex specializes in work outside the home and the other specializes in running the home and taking care of the children. Might families be better off if children had more access to *both* parents, even if this meant a somewhat lower family income? This is an important question. While specialization produces material gains, there are *opportunity costs* to be paid in the loss of other things we care about. The right amount of specialization can be found only by balancing the gains against these costs.

RESOURCE ALLOCATION

It was only 10,000 years ago—a mere blink of an eye in human history—that the Neolithic revolution began, and human society switched from hunting and gathering to farming and simple manufacturing. At the same time, human wants grew beyond mere food and shelter into an appetite for the infinite variety of things that can be *made*. Ever since, all societies have been confronted with three problems, which together make up the problem of **resource allocation**. The three problems are:

RESOURCE ALLOCATION A method of determining which goods and services will be produced, how they will be produced, and who will get them.

1. *Which* goods and services should be produced with society's resources?
2. *How* should they be produced?
3. *Who* should get them?

The way a society chooses to answer these questions—i.e., the method it chooses to allocate its resources—will in part determine the character of its economic system.

Let's first consider the *which* question. Should we produce more health care or more movies, more goods for consumers or more capital goods for businesses? Where on the production possibilities frontier should the economy operate? As you will see, there are a number of methods societies can use to answer these questions.

The *how* question is a bit more complicated. Most goods and services can be produced in a variety of different ways, each method using more of some resources and less of others. For example, there are many ways to dig a ditch. We could use *no capital at all* and have hundreds of workers digging with their bare hands. We could use *a little bit of capital* by giving each worker a shovel and thereby use less labor, since each worker would now be more productive. Or we could use *even more capital*—a power trencher—and dig the ditch with just one or two workers. In every economic system, there must always be some mechanism that determines how goods and services will be produced from the infinite variety of ways available.

Finally, the *who* question. Here is where economics interacts most strongly with politics. There are so many ways to divide ourselves into groups: men and women, rich and poor, workers and owners; families and single people; young and old. . . the list is endless. How should the output of our economy be distributed among these different groups and among individuals within each group?

Determining *who* gets the output is always the most controversial aspect of allocating resources. Over the last half-century, our society has become more sensitized to the way goods and services are distributed, and we increasingly ask whether that distribution is fair. We have observed that men get a disproportionately larger share of output than women, whites get more than African-Americans and Hispanics, and middle-aged workers get more than the very old and the very young.

We have also focused on the distribution of particular goods and services. Should scarce donor organs be rationed to those who have been waiting the longest, so that everyone has the same chance of survival? Or should they be sold to the highest bidder, so that those willing and able to pay the most will get them? Should productions of Shakespeare's plays be subsidized by the government to permit more people—especially more poor people—to see them? Or should the people who enjoy these plays pay the full cost of their production?

THE THREE METHODS OF RESOURCE ALLOCATION. Throughout history, there have been three primary mechanisms for allocating resources. In a system of *tradition,* all three problems are solved in somewhat the same way that families solve similar problems. Historically, this method of resource allocation operates in small villages. The elders confer to determine what is produced, how it is produced, and who receives the output.

Tradition was the dominant mode of resource allocation for most of human history and remains strong in many tribal societies and small villages in parts of Africa, South America, Asia, and the Pacific. Adherence to tradition validates the powers of the elders. The village is small enough that the elders can assign tasks based on personal knowledge of abilities. Traditional principles of fairness govern the distribution of output.

Traditional village economies tend to be stable and predictable, but have one very serious drawback: They don't grow. With everyone locked into the traditional patterns of production, there is little room for innovation and technological change, or even a reorganization of work patterns for mutual advantage. Traditional economies are therefore likely to be stagnant economies.

In a **command system,** resources are allocated by explicit instructions from some higher authority. *Which* goods and services should be produced? The ones we're *ordered* to produce. *How* should they be produced? The way we're *told* to produce them. *Who* will get the goods and services? Those the authority *tells* us should get them.

COMMAND SYSTEM An economic system in which resources are allocated according to explicit instructions from a central authority.

In a command system, a government body *plans* how resources will be allocated. That is why command economies are also called centrally planned economies. Command economies can be vastly larger than village economies. Under a system of command, it is relatively easy to organize large productive units, such as steel plants or automobile factories.

Command economies are disappearing fast. Until a few years ago, examples would have included the former Soviet Union, Poland, Rumania, Bulgaria, Albania, and many others. Beginning in the late 1980s, all of these nations have, to significant degrees, abandoned central planning. The only examples left are Cuba, China, and North Korea, and even these economies—though still dominated by central planning—are moving away from it.

The third method of allocating resources—and the one with which you are no doubt most familiar—is the market, a system in which resources are allocated as a result of individual decision making. In a **market economy,** neither long-held traditions nor commands from above guide our economic behavior. Instead, we are largely free to make choices ourselves. *Which* goods and services will be produced? Whichever ones producers *choose* to produce. How shall they be produced? However producers *choose* to produce them. *Who* will get these goods and services? Producers will sell to anyone who *chooses* to buy them.

MARKET ECONOMY An economic system in which resources are allocated through individual decision making.

There are, of course, limitations on this freedom of action, some of them imposed by government to ensure an orderly, just, and productive society. We cannot kill, steal, or break contracts—even if that is our desire—without suffering serious consequences, and we must pay taxes to fund government services. But the most important limitations are the constraints imposed on each of us by the scarcity of resources.

This last point is crucial: In a market system, individuals are not simply free to do what they want—they are constrained by the resources they control. And in this respect, we do not all start in the same place in the economic race. Some of us—like the Rockefellers and the Kennedys—have inherited great wealth; some—Bill Gates, the novelist Joyce Carol Oates, and the model Isabella Rosellini—have inherited great intelligence, talent, or beauty; and some, such as the children of successful professionals, are born into a world of helpful personal and professional contacts. Others, unfortunately, will inherit none of these advantages. In a market system, those who control more resources will have more choices available to them than those who control fewer resources.

When each person acts according to his or her own desires, with no guidance from command or tradition, won't chaos ensue? How, in such a free-for-all, are resources actually *allocated*?

The answer is contained in a single word: *prices.*

PRICE The amount of money that must be paid to a seller to obtain a good or service.

THE IMPORTANCE OF PRICES. A price is *how much money a buyer must pay to a seller for a good or service.* Price is not the same as *cost,* which in economics means *opportunity cost—everything* that is sacrificed to buy the good. While the price of a good is a *part* of its cost to the buyer—since the money spent on the good could have been used to buy something else—it is not the only cost. For example, the price does not include the value of the *time* sacrificed to buy something. Buying a new jacket will require you to spend time traveling to and from the store, trying on different styles and sizes, and waiting in line at the cash register. In some cases—like Samantha's decision to go to a movie—the value of the time sacrificed is so great that the cost is much greater than the price.

Nevertheless, prices are important. In many cases, the price of a good is the most significant aspect of its cost, especially for large purchases such as a home or automobile. And while the opportunity cost of a good depends on individual characteristics (the value of your time, how far you live from the store, etc.), the price is an objective number that is faced by everyone in a market.

Prices confront individual decision makers with some of the costs of their choices. Consider the example of buying a new car, where the price makes up most of the cost. The price, together with your limited income, makes it easy to see that buying a new car will require you to buy less of other things. In this way, the opportunity cost to *society* of making another car is converted to an opportunity cost *for you.* If you value a new car more highly than the other things you must sacrifice for it, you will buy it. If not, you won't buy it.

Why is it so important that people face the opportunity costs of their actions? The following thought experiment can answer this question. Imagine that the government passed a new law: When anyone buys a new car, the government will reimburse that person for it immediately. The consequences would be easy to predict. First, on the day the law was passed, everyone would rush out to buy new cars. Why not, if cars are free? The entire stock of existing automobiles would be gone within days—maybe even hours. Many people who didn't value cars much at all, and who hardly ever used them, would find themselves owning several—one for each day of the week, or to match the different colors in their wardrobe. Others who weren't able to act in time—including some who desperately need a new car for their work or to run their households—would be unable to find one at all.

Over time, automobile companies would step up their production to meet the surge in demand for cars, and then we would face another problem: the government's yearly "automobile budget," which would be hundreds of billions of dollars. Ultimately, we would all bear the cost of the increased car production, since the government would have to raise taxes. But we would pay as *taxpayers,* not as car owners. And our hefty tax bill would be supporting some rather frivolous uses for cars. Chances are, we would all be worse off because of this new policy. By eliminating a price for automobiles, and severing the connection between the opportunity cost of producing a car and the individual's decision to get one, we would have created quite a mess for ourselves.

Understanding the Market System. The market is simultaneously the most simple and the most complex of the systems for allocating resources. From the point of view of individuals, the market is simple in that there are no traditions or commands to be memorized and obeyed. Instead, each of us responds to the prices we face as we *wish* to, unconcerned about the overall process of resource allocation. Most markets are *self-governing:* The goods that are traded, the way they are traded, and the price at which they trade are determined by the traders themselves; no direction from above is needed to keep markets working.

But from the economist's point of view, the system is quite complex, because resources are allocated indirectly, as a *by-product* of individual decision making, rather than through directly observed traditions or commands. It often takes some skillful economic detective work to determine just how individuals are behaving and how resources are being allocated as a consequence. To reinforce your understanding of economics, it helps to do some of this detective work yourself, sorting out the mysteries of resource allocation from the behavior that you observe in the real world. This book will provide plenty of examples, but you can find many more on your own.

Resource Allocation in the United States. The United States has always been considered one of the strongest examples of a market economy. Millions of distinct products are traded in these self-governing markets. Our grocery stores are always stocked with broccoli and tomato soup, the drugstore always has Kleenex and aspirin—the list of products that make their way from manufacturer to your shopping cart is endless.

But even in the United States, there are numerous cases of resource allocation *outside* the market. For example, families are important institutions in the United States, and many economic decisions are made within them. Families tend to operate like traditional villages, not like market economies—few families charge prices for the goods and services provided inside the home.

One can find examples of command in our economy as well. Various levels of government collect, in total, about a third of our incomes as taxes. We are *told* how much tax we must pay, and there are serious penalties for noncompliance, including imprisonment. This affects the distribution of output in important ways, since our right to the nation's production is determined by the income we have left *after* we pay these taxes. Government also produces certain services—such as mail delivery and law enforcement. In these cases, decisions about *which* specific goods to produce and *how* to produce them are made by government agencies and passed down the chain of government command to those actually providing the services.

There are also other ways, aside from strict commands, that the government limits our market freedoms. Regulations designed to protect the environment, maintain safe work places, and ensure the safety of our food supply are just a few examples of government-imposed constraints on our ability to do what we want with our endowments.

What are we to make, then, of resource allocation in the United States? There are cases where markets are constrained, but these are the exception rather than the rule. For each example we can find where resources are allocated by tradition or command, or where government restrictions seriously limit some market freedom, we can find hundreds of examples where individuals make choices according to their own desires. The things we buy, the jobs at which we work, the homes in which we live—in almost all cases, these come to us as market choices. The market, though not pure, is certainly the dominant method of resource allocation in the United States.

RESOURCE OWNERSHIP

So far, we've been concerned with how resources are allocated. Another important feature of an economic system is how resources are *owned.* Who makes available each parcel of land, each worker's labor, and each piece of capital equipment used in production? Who receives the payment when resources are purchased by producers?

Under *communal* ownership, resources are owned by everyone—or by no one, depending on your point of view. They are simply there for the taking, with no person or organization imposing any restrictions on their use or charging any fees. It is hard to find economies with significant communal ownership of resources. Karl Marx believed that, in time, all economies would evolve toward communal ownership, and he dubbed the resulting system **communism**, although none of the economies that invoked Marx's principles was able to achieve this goal. This is not surprising: Communal ownership on a broad scale can work only when individuals will not come into conflict over how resources are used. In other words, a prerequisite for the arrival of communism is the end of *scarcity*—an unlikely prospect in the foreseeable future.

COMMUNISM An economic system in which most resources are owned in common.

Nevertheless, there are examples of communal ownership on a smaller scale. Traditional villages maintain communal ownership of land and sometimes cattle. In some of the cooperative farms in Israel—called *kibbutzim*—land and capital are owned by everyone, and there may be a single television, a single kitchen, or a single dining room—all communally owned. Conflicts may result when individuals differ over how these resources should be used, but these conflicts are resolved by consensus, rather than by decree or by charging fees for their use.

In many countries, including the United States, families operate on the principle of communal ownership. The house, furniture, television, telephone, and food in the refrigerator are treated as if owned jointly. Once again, conflicts result, and systems for allocating the *use* of these facilities must be developed, often through habit or custom. We can also find examples of communal property in the broader economy. Sidewalks, streets, and most beaches—in theory, the state may own these, but in practice, all citizens are free to use them as they see fit.

Under **socialism**, the *state* owns all or most of the resources. The prime example here is the former Soviet Union, where the state owned all of the land and capital equipment in the country. In many ways, it also owned the labor of individual households, since it was virtually the only employer in the nation and unemployment was considered a crime.

SOCIALISM An economic system in which most resources are owned by the state.

Examples of state ownership of resources abound in nonsocialist economies as well. In the United States, national parks, state highway systems, military bases, public colleges and universities, and government buildings are all state-owned resources. Over a third of the land in the country is owned by the federal government. The military, even under our current volunteer system, is an example in which the state owns the labor of soldiers—albeit for a limited period of time.

When most resources are owned *privately*—as in the United States—we have **capitalism.** Take the book you are reading right now. If you turn to the title page, you will see the imprint of South-Western College Publishing Company. This is a *private* company, owned by another company—International Thomson Publishing—which, in turn, is owned by *private* individuals. These individuals, in the end, own the facilities of South-Western: the buildings, the land under them, the office furniture and computer equipment, and even the reputation of the company. When these facilities are made available to produce and sell a book, it is the private owners who will receive the income, mostly in the form of company profits. Similarly, the employees of South-Western are private individuals. They are *selling* a resource they own—their labor time—to South-Western, and receive income—wages and salaries—in return.

CAPITALISM An economic system in which most resources are owned privately.

But even the United States—which is one of the most capitalistic countries in the world—does not have pure capitalism. Many resources, as we've seen, are owned by the state, and some are owned communally. In addition, the government often imposes restrictions on the use of, and income earned from, privately owned resources. The income we earn from supplying our resources to firms is subject to income taxes, and the gains from selling our resources are subject to the capital gains tax. Recently, the federal government was embroiled in controversy when it declared that much swampland in Florida is an important natural resource, worthy of protection from economic development. As a result, this swampland—although owned by private individuals—cannot be used as these individuals see fit. Such environmental regulations—as well as zoning restrictions and licensing fees—are all examples in which government limits the rights of private owners.

TYPES OF ECONOMIC SYSTEMS

An **economic system** is composed of two features: a mechanism for *allocating* resources and a mode of resource *ownership*. If we ignore the rare cases where communal ownership or allocation by tradition are dominant, we are left with four basic types of economic systems, indicated by the four quadrants in Figure 5. In the upper left quadrant, we have *market capitalism* (often called the **market system**), in which resources are allocated primarily by the market and owned primarily by private individuals. Today, most of the economies of the world are market capitalist systems, including all of the countries of North America and Western Europe, and most of those in Asia, Latin America, and Africa.

ECONOMIC SYSTEM A system of resource allocation and resource ownership.

MARKET SYSTEM An economic system involving resource allocation by the market and private resource ownership.

In the lower right quadrant is *centrally planned socialism,* under which resources are mostly allocated by command and owned by the state. This *was* the system in the former Soviet Union and the nations of Eastern Europe until the late 1980s. Today, these countries' economic systems are going through cataclysmic change, moving from the lower right quadrant of the diagram to the upper left; that is, these nations are simultaneously changing both their systems of resource allocation and their systems of resource ownership.

Although market capitalism and centrally planned socialism have been the two paramount economic systems in modern history, there have been others. The upper right quadrant represents a system of *centrally planned capitalism,* in which resources are owned by private individuals, yet allocated by command. Countries such as Sweden and Japan—where the government is more heavily involved in allocating resources than in the United States—flirt with this type of system. Nations

FIGURE 5

TYPES OF ECONOMIC SYSTEMS

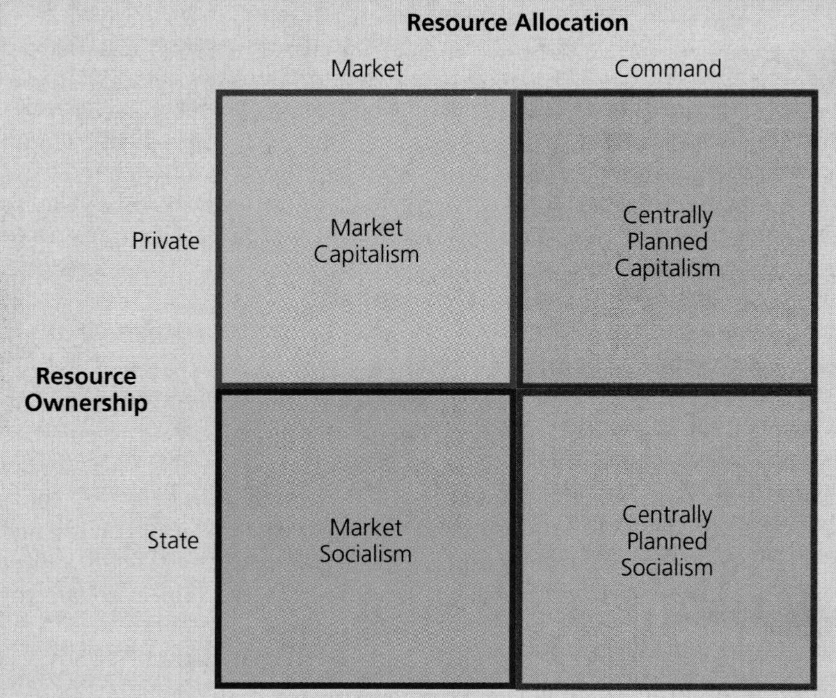

at war—like the United States during World War II—also move in this direction, as governments find it necessary to direct resources by command in order to ensure sufficient military production.

Finally, in the lower left quadrant is *market socialism,* in which resources are owned by the state, yet allocated by the market mechanism. The possibility of market socialism has fascinated many social scientists, who believed it promised the best of both worlds: the freedom and efficiency of the market mechanism and the fairness and equity of socialism. There are, however, serious problems—many would argue, unresolvable contradictions—in trying to mix the two. The chief examples of market socialism in modern history have been little more than short-lived experiments—in Hungary and Yugoslavia in the 1950s and 1960s—in which the results have been mixed at best.

ECONOMIC SYSTEMS AND THIS BOOK. In this book, you will learn how market capitalist economies operate. This means that the other three types of economic systems in Figure 5 will be consciously ignored. Ten years ago, these statements would have been accompanied by an apology: "True, much of the world is characterized by alternative economic systems, but there is only so much time in one course. . ." In the past decade, however, the world has changed dramatically: About 400 million people have come under the sway of the market as their nations have abandoned centrally planned socialism; another billion or so may soon be added if China changes course. The study of market capitalism is now, truly, the study of how modern economies operate. No more apologies are needed.

OPPORTUNITY COST AND THE INTERNET

USING THE THEORY

The Internet raises interesting and challenging issues of resource ownership and allocation. More than 40 million people around the world used the Internet by the end of 1996, and the number has been doubling every year. Huge quantities of resources have been diverted away from producing other goods and services to make the Internet available to more people for more hours. Among these resources are labor—to install the lines, operate the servers, and provide technical assistance to users—and capital—modems, computers, and fiber-optic cable. Use of the Net often strains against the capacity of service providers and against the capacity of the system as a whole. Each time usage increases, society must either divert resources to increasing capacity or allow worsened congestion on the Net. So far, society has chosen to increase capacity: The Internet infrastructure has been growing at near incredible speed, and, for the most part, serious congestion has been avoided.

Who pays for the Internet? In the United States, the payment comes from a variety of sources. Taxpayers bore part of the burden of creating the Internet—the government provided millions of dollars in subsidies to the initial network. Organizations that provide Internet service also pay part of the cost. Large universities, for example, often pay yearly fees of $100,000 or more to maintain their connection. Commercial Internet service providers—such as America Online, Compuserve, AT&T, and Sprint—must also pay these access fees. And all service providers—colleges and universities as well as commercial providers—must pay for their own equipment and user support.

But what was *your* cost the last time you used the Internet to send an e-mail to a friend or to search for information on the World Wide Web? If you used your college's computer system, you almost certainly faced a price (a direct money cost) of zero. Your college pays the yearly fee, and you can stay on-line as long as you want, without paying a penny. Thus, the only opportunity cost *you* faced was the value of your time spent on-line. If there was nothing pressing, rewarding, or particularly fun for you to do that afternoon or evening, the value you placed on your time was relatively low. As a result, you might have been on line for an hour or more while composing an e-mail, downloading a hundred-megabyte file of uncertain value, or watching an Internet video because there wasn't much else to do. These sorts of choices—by you and millions of other college students—affect the allocation of resources in our society: More resources are diverted toward the Internet and away from other uses. And ultimately, you and others will pay the cost. You may pay through a higher college tuition if fees to your college are raised, or through higher telephone charges when you make calls, but—unless your college changes its policy on Internet use—you will probably *not* be charged a fee for using the Internet.

Until recently, it was only at colleges, universities, or government organizations that Net users paid no direct price. Those who subscribed to commercial services paid a fixed monthly fee, with an additional charge for each hour of use over some preset number. For these commercial users, there *was* a price for spending another hour on the Net.

But all that changed in 1996. In February of that year, AT&T, in order to attract customers to its new Internet service, offered a special deal: a flat rate of $19.95 per month for *unlimited* time on line. Other commercial providers quickly matched the flat-rate policy. While users were still paying a price to *subscribe* to the commercial service, the price for *additional hours* on-line was suddenly eliminated. Usage shot up and the Internet became clogged: At peak times, users around the country faced slower response times and annoying delays in hooking up.

Then, on December 1, the situation worsened dramatically: America Online—the largest commercial provider, with more than seven million customers—finally joined the rest of the industry and offered its own $19.95 flat rate. This vastly increased the number of users who faced no price for additional hours. The effect was almost immediate. Within days, America Online found that its users were hooking up 30 percent more frequently and staying on-line 20 percent longer. Over the next two weeks, the company found itself in a vicious circle. Due to congestion, many of its customers faced hours of delays while trying to hook up. As a result, they were reluctant to let go once they connected. Since the only price they paid was a few cents per minute in local phone bills, customers would leave their computers hooked up while they went to lunch, walked the dog, or even went to sleep for the night. This, of course, made it more difficult for others to hook up, which made them hang on even longer when they were finally connected, and so on. When America Online responded by automatically disconnecting its users after a few minutes of inactivity, they responded in turn by downloading special programs to simulate active use and maintain their connections. One reporter described the situation this way: "It's as if a diner at a fixed-price buffet had someone hang on to his seat after lunch, so he could still have a place for dinner."[2]

What does all this imply about resource allocation? First, that resources may be *overallocated* toward the Internet: When people use the Net in ways that have low value, we must sacrifice other valuable goods and services in order to increase the Net's capacity. Second, that resources are allocated *among* Net users in a rather haphazard way. Instead of allocating time on-line to those who value it most and are willing to pay the most for it, it is allocated to those lucky enough to hook up at a particular moment, regardless of the value they place on the service. If some users remain logged on while walking their dog, others cannot hook up at all. These include surgeons waiting to receive crucial information about a pending operation, businesses trying to close important deals with their clients, and government officials tracking everything from data on the economy to the military activities of hostile countries.

Of course, *society* faces an opportunity cost for the additional use of the Internet, even when individuals do not incorporate that cost into their choices. Who bears this opportunity cost? Part of the cost is borne by the users who place a high value on the service, but cannot connect. Part is borne by consumers of *other* goods that will not be produced as resources are diverted toward increasing the Net's capacity. And—if flat rates remain in force—some will be paid by Internet users as a whole, as providers raise their flat rate to cover the increased cost of their operations.

Regardless of who pays, the recent experience with the Internet reinforces two important ideas discussed in this chapter: the principle of opportunity cost and the crucial role of prices in allocating resources. It is largely through *prices* that our society's opportunity cost becomes our *own* opportunity cost. When a price is reduced to zero—like the price of additional hours on the Net—much of our individual opportunity cost disappears, so we do not properly incorporate the costs to our society into our own decision making. The result is an allocation of resources that we are not very happy about.

---

2 Peter H. Lewis, "An 'All You Can Eat' Price Is Clogging Internet Access," *New York Times*, December 17, 1996, p. A1.

As the Internet becomes a more central part of our lives, it is likely that more of the resource allocation tools of the market economy will be used to solve congestion problems. Instead of flat monthly fees, service providers will charge for time, just as long-distance phone companies charge by the minute for phone calls. The personal cost of using the Internet will come closer to the social opportunity cost.

SUMMARY

One of the most fundamental concepts in economics is *opportunity cost.* The opportunity cost of any choice is what we give up when we make that choice. At the individual level, opportunity cost arises from the scarcity of time or money; for society as a whole, it arises from the scarcity of resources—land, labor, and capital. If we produce and enjoy more of one thing, we must shift resources away from producing something else. The *principle of opportunity cost* tells us that the correct measure of cost is opportunity cost—what we give up when we make a choice. The *law of increasing opportunity cost* tells us that the more of something we produce, the greater the opportunity cost of producing still more.

In a world of scarce resources, each society must determine its economic system—its way of organizing economic activity. All *economic systems* feature *specialization*—where each person and firm concentrates on a limited number of productive activities—and *exchange*—through which we obtain most of what we desire by trading with others. Specialization and exchange enable us to enjoy higher living standards than if we each consumed only what we produced ourselves.

Every economic system determines how resources are owned and how they are allocated. In a market system, resources are owned primarily by private individuals and allocated primarily through markets. Prices signal the relative scarcity of goods and resources and coordinate the actions of individual decision makers.

KEY TERMS

opportunity cost
principle of opportunity cost
production possibilities frontier (PPF)
law of increasing opportunity cost
technical efficiency
specialization
exchange
principle of specialization and exchange
absolute advantage
comparative advantage
resource allocation
command system
market economy
price
communism
socialism
capitalism
economic system
market system

REVIEW QUESTIONS

1. How might opportunity cost be used to explain the fact that people often stop at convenience stores to buy items that are available at lower prices in large grocery stores?
2. Warren Buffett is one of the world's wealthiest men, worth billions of dollars. For someone in his income bracket, the principal of opportunity cost simply doesn't apply. True or false? Explain.
3. What are some possible reasons a country might be operating inside its PPF?
4. Why is a PPF concave, i.e., bowed out from the origin?
5. What are three reasons specialization leads to a higher standard of living?
6. List the three questions any resource allocation mechanism must answer. Briefly describe the three primary kinds of economic systems that have evolved to answer them.
7. What is the chief allocative mechanism in a market economy? How does it help to determine answers to the three questions mentioned in question 6?
8. Why can't the United States be described as a *pure market system economy?*
9. True or false?: "Resource allocation and resource ownership are essentially the same thing. Once you know who owns the resources in an economy, you also know by what mechanism those resources will be allocated." Explain your answer.

PROBLEMS AND EXERCISES

1. You are considering what to do with an upcoming weekend. Here are your options, from least to most preferred: (1) Study for upcoming midterms; (2) fly to Colorado for a quick ski trip; (3) go into seclusion in your dorm room and try to improve your score on the computer game "Doom." What is the opportunity cost of a decision to play the computer game all weekend?

2. You and a friend have decided to work jointly on a course project. Frankly, your friend is a less than ideal partner. His skills as a researcher are such that he can review and outline only two articles a day. Moreover, his hunt-and-peck style limits him to only 10 pages of typing a day. On the other hand, in a day you can produce six outlines or type 20 pages. According to the principle of comparative advantage, who should specialize in which task? Why?

CHALLENGE QUESTIONS

1. Graph the PPF for an economy that faces constant, rather than increasing, opportunity costs in the production of two goods.

2. How would you show economic growth, i.e., an increase in the overall productive capacity of an economy, in terms of one or more PFF curves?

3. Consider an economy devastated by war. What would be likely to happen to its PPF for the production of any two goods?

4. Martin Feldstein, former economic advisor to President Reagan, has described the essence of a market economy as "self-interest checked by competition within a framework of law." Based on what you have learned about the market system in this chapter, discuss what you think that description means.

Go to the following Web site: http://www.csuchico.edu/econ/links/econlinks.html and try to "get a free lunch" by "clicking" on the waiter. Answer the following questions: Can you get a free lunch if a friend invites you out on his or her expense account? Why or why not?

C H A P T E R

3

SUPPLY AND DEMAND

Father Guido Sarducci, a character on "Saturday Night Live," once observed that a few years after we graduate from college, we remember only about five minutes worth of material. Then why not have a Five Minute University, where you'd learn only this crucial material and dispense with the rest? The economics course, Sarducci argued, would require just a few seconds, during which all students would learn the words "supply and demand."

With luck, you will remember more than five minutes' worth of knowledge from your time in college. What is interesting about Sarducci's observation, however, is that so many people do use the phrase "supply and demand" without understanding what it means. In a debate about health care, poverty, or the high price of housing, you might hear someone say, "Well, it's just a matter of supply and demand," as a way of dismissing the issue entirely. Others use the phrase with an exaggerated reverence, as if supply and demand were an inviolable physical law, like gravity, about which nothing can be done.

In fact, supply and demand is just an economic model—nothing more and nothing less—designed to explain *how prices are determined in a market system.* Why has this model taken on such an exalted role in the field of economics? Because prices, themselves, play such an exalted role in the economy, guiding the actions of individual buyers and sellers and determining how our resources are allocated. In a market system, once the price of a good has been determined, only those willing to pay that price will get it. Thus, prices determine which households will get which goods and services and which firms will get which resources. If you want to know why the laptop computer industry is expanding while the daily newspaper industry is shrinking or why homelessness is a more pervasive problem in the United States than hunger, you need to understand how prices are determined. Thus, supply and demand is doubly useful: It explains the workings of particular industries, and it also helps us understand the operation of the economy as a whole.

CHAPTER OUTLINE

MARKETS
The Size of the Market
Competition in Markets

DEMAND
Price and Quantity Demanded
The Demand Schedule and the Demand Curve
Changes in Demand

SUPPLY
Price and Quantity Supplied
The Supply Schedule and the Supply Curve Changes in Supply

PUTTING SUPPLY AND DEMAND TOGETHER

WHAT HAPPENS WHEN THINGS CHANGE?

A MYTH ABOUT SUPPLY AND DEMAND

THE PRINCIPLE OF MARKETS AND EQUILIBRIUM

GOVERNMENT INTERVENTION IN MARKETS
Price Ceilings
Price Floors
Supply and Demand and Normative Economics

USING THE THEORY: ANTICIPATING A PRICE CHANGE

In this chapter, you will learn how supply and demand work and how to use them. You will also learn about the strengths and limitations of the model. It will take more time than Guido Sarducci's economics course, but in the end you will know much more than just the words "supply and demand."

MARKETS

Listen to an economist for any length of time, and sooner or later you'll hear the word *market.* In ordinary language, a market is an actual location where buying and selling take place; such as a supermarket, an outdoor market, or a flea market. In economics, a market is defined not by its location, but by its participants:

MARKET A group of buyers and sellers with the potential to trade.

*A **market** is a group of buyers and sellers with the potential to trade.*

Economists think of the economy as a collection of individual markets. In each market, the collection of buyers and sellers will be different and will depend on what is being traded. There is a market for oranges, another for automobiles, another for real estate, and still others for corporate stocks, French francs, and anything else that is bought and sold.

THE SIZE OF THE MARKET

In some cases, the buyers and sellers in a market will be residents of the same town; in other cases, they will be spread around the country or even the world. The market for haircuts is a local market, since most of us will not travel long distances for a haircut, and few barbers or hairdressers will make long-distance house calls at rates we would pay. The market for oil, however, is a global market, since oil is relatively cheap to transport, and buyers and sellers anywhere in the world can easily communicate and trade with each other.

Often, we have some latitude in choosing the geographic breadth of a market, and the choice will depend on our purpose. To explain how and why real estate prices differ from one place to another, we can divide buyers and sellers into different localities and define one market for real estate in Poughkeepsie, another in Kalamazoo, and so on. But if the purpose is to explain the overall rise in real estate prices in the United States over the last 20 years, it is better to lump all buyers and sellers into a single, national market.

COMPETITION IN MARKETS

In some markets, either the buying or the selling side is dominated by a few large players. Did you eat cereal for breakfast this morning? Then chances are your cereal came from one of four large sellers—Kelloggs, Post, General Mills, or Quaker—since, together, they sell about 90 percent of all breakfast cereal in the United States. The market for windshield wiper motors is similarly dominated by a few large buyers—the carmakers.

When there are relatively few buyers or sellers in a market, each one will have some influence on the price of the product. Kelloggs knows that it can charge a higher price for its cereal if it is willing to sell fewer boxes and that—to increase sales—it can charge a lower price. Similarly, General Motors knows that it can influence the price it pays for wiper motors by negotiating with its suppliers or changing the quantity it buys.

IMPERFECTLY COMPETITIVE MARKET A market in which a single buyer or seller has the power to influence the price.

*When a buyer or seller has the power to influence the price of a product, we say that the market is **imperfectly competitive.***

The markets for automobiles, computer software, hospital care, and magazines are all imperfectly competitive.

In other markets, by contrast, there are so many buyers and sellers that each is just a tiny part of the whole. Wheat, for example, is grown on thousands of U.S. farms and purchased by thousands of millers. It is easily transported, so any farmer can sell to any miller. If a single farm doubles or triples its production of wheat, or a single flour mill dramatically increases its purchases of wheat, nothing will happen to the market price for wheat: The individual farmer and miller are just too small to have any impact. Therefore, they treat the price of wheat as something predetermined, outside of their control.

When there are so many buyers and sellers that each is too small to affect the price, the market is ***purely competitive*** *or, more simply,* ***competitive.*** *In a competitive market, each buyer and seller treats the market price as a given.*

PURELY COMPETITIVE MARKET A market in which no buyer or seller has the power to influence the price.

What has this got to do with supply and demand? Earlier, we suggested that supply and demand is useful for understanding how prices are determined in a *market system.* Now, we will narrow down the application of supply and demand still more:

Supply and demand explains how prices are determined in competitive markets.

This is an important restriction, and you might therefore be tempted to conclude that supply and demand aren't very useful in practice. After all, very few markets strictly satisfy the requirement of pure competition; most markets are—at least to some degree—imperfectly competitive. But even when competition is somewhat imperfect, supply and demand can often provide a good approximation to what is going on, and it has proven to be the most versatile and widely used model in the economist's tool kit. Neither personal computers nor orange juice is traded in purely competitive markets. But ask an economist to tell you why computer prices have come down over the last 15 years or why the price of orange juice rises after a freeze in Florida, and the answer will use supply and demand.

Supply and demand are like two blades of a scissors: The demand blade tells us how much of something people want to buy, and the supply blade tells us how much sellers want to sell. To analyze a market, we need both blades—and they must both be sharp. In this and the next section, we will be sharpening those blades, learning separately about supply and demand. Then, when we have a thorough understanding of each one, we'll put them together—and put them to use.

DEMAND

We often express our desires or needs with simple declarative sentences: "I need a two-bedroom apartment" or "I want to see the ballet twice each month." To an economist, these declarations are incomplete. Suppose the cheapest two-bedroom apartment in your neighborhood rents for $1,500, but you've just found a great deal on a one-bedroom for $500. Might you change your mind and decide you need only one bedroom? Suppose you move to a small town with no ballet company, and to see one requires a $200 round-trip ticket and half a day in travel time. Might you go less often?

Economics deals with *choices* rather than needs or wants. In deciding what to buy, and how much of each item, people make the best choices they can, given the constraints they face.

PRICE AND QUANTITY DEMANDED

QUANTITY DEMANDED The total amount of a good that all buyers in a market would choose to purchase at a given price.

> *The **quantity demanded** of any good is the total amount that buyers in a market would choose to purchase at a given price.*

There are a few things to keep in mind about quantity demanded. First, it can refer either to an individual buyer—"the quantity of running shoes demanded by Leticia"—or to *all* buyers in a market—"the quantity of running shoes demanded in the United States." The interpretation we use depends on the problem we are analyzing. In this chapter, we focus on quantity demanded in an entire market.

Second, quantity demanded tells us about *buyers' choices*—not about what will actually happen in a market. We don't worry—yet—about how much buyers will *actually* be able to buy in the market. That will be sorted out later, when we put demand and supply together.

Finally, quantity demanded refers to *buyers,* a rather general term. In markets for consumer goods and services—hamburgers, rental apartments, dry-cleaning services, bus rides, and so on—the buyers are *households.* But households are not the only buyers in the economy. Firms are buyers in markets for productive inputs, such as farm labor, security guards, raw iron, or tractor-trailers. And government agencies are buyers in markets for jet fighters, police officers, and public school teachers. This chapter deals primarily—but not exclusively—with consumer markets, in which households are the buyers.

What determines the amount of a good that households want to buy? The most important influences are:

- the price of the good
- household income and household wealth
- the prices of related goods
- population in the market
- expectations of future prices
- tastes

That's quite a list. But notice that, in the definition of quantity demanded, only one of these variables appears: the *price* of the good. Why this stress on price? The supply-and-demand model is designed to explain how prices are determined in markets. It seems natural, then, to begin our exploration of demand with the influence of prices.

THE LAW OF DEMAND. How does a change in price affect quantity demanded? You probably know the answer to this already: When something is more expensive, people will buy less of it. This common observation applies to walnuts, air travel, magazines, education, time on the Internet, and virtually everything else that people buy. For all of these goods and services, price and quantity are *inversely related*—that is, when price rises, quantity demanded falls; when price falls, quantity demanded rises. This inverse relationship is observed so regularly in markets, that economists call it the *law of demand:*

LAW OF DEMAND As the price of a good increases, the quantity demanded decreases.

> *The **law of demand** states that when the price of a good rises, and everything else remains the same, the quantity of the good demanded will fall.*

Read that definition again, and notice the very important words, "everything else remains the same." The law of demand tells us what would happen *if* all of the other influences on buyers' choices remained unchanged, and only one—the price of the good—changed.

This is an example of a common practice in economics. In the real world, many variables change *simultaneously*. But to understand the economy, we must understand the effect of each variable *separately*. Imagine that you were trying to discover which headache remedy works best for you. You wouldn't gain much information if you took an Advil, a Tylenol, and a Bayer aspirin all at the same time. Instead, you should make just *one* change at a time and observe its effects. To understand the economy, we go through the same process—conducting mental experiments in which only one thing changes at a time. The law of demand tells us what happens when we change just the price of the good and hold constant all other influences on buyers' choices, such as the prices of related goods, households incomes, and so on.

THE DEMAND SCHEDULE AND THE DEMAND CURVE

To make our discussion more concrete, let's look at a specific market: the market for maple syrup in Wichita. Table 1 shows the **demand schedule** for maple syrup in this market—*a list of different quantities demanded at different prices, with all other variables held constant.* Notice that these numbers obey the law of demand: As the price of maple syrup increases, the quantity demanded falls.

DEMAND SCHEDULE A list showing the quantities of a good that consumers would choose to purchase at different prices, with all other variables held constant

Figure 1 is a diagram that will appear again and again in your study of economics. In the figure, each price-and-quantity combination in Table 1 is represented by a point. For example, point *A* represents the price $4.00 and quantity 4,000, while point *B* represents the pair $2.00 and 6,000. When we connect all of these points with a line, we obtain the famous *demand curve,* labeled with a *D* in the figure.

*The **demand curve** shows the relationship between the price of a good and the quantity demanded, holding constant all other variables that affect demand. Each point on the curve shows the quantity that buyers would choose to buy at a specific price.*

DEMAND CURVE The graphical depiction of a demand schedule; a line showing the quantity of a good or service demanded at various prices, with all other variables held constant.

The demand curve in Figure 1—like virtually all demand curves we might observe—follows the law of demand: A rise in the price of the good causes a decrease in the quantity demanded. This is why the *demand curve slopes downward.*

The law of demand tells us that demand curves slope downward.

DEMAND SCHEDULE FOR MAPLE SYRUP IN WICHITA

TABLE 1

Price (per bottle)	Quantity Demanded (bottles per month)
$1.00	7,500
$2.00	6,000
$3.00	5,000
$4.00	4,000
$5.00	3,500

FIGURE 1

THE DEMAND CURVE

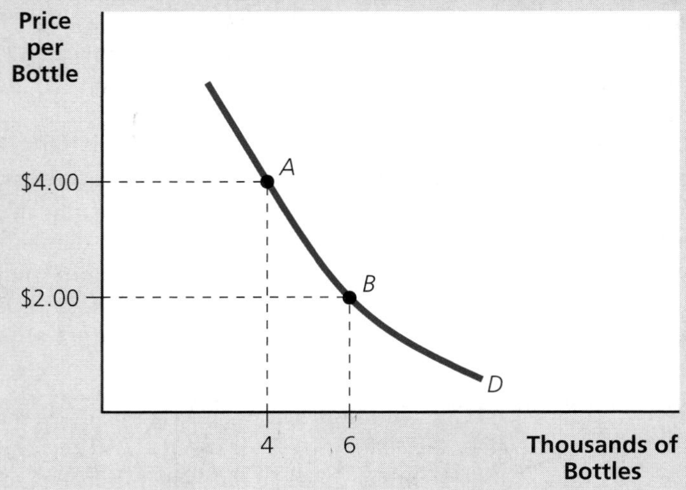

The downward-sloping demand curve, *D,* shows the quantity of a good that would be purchased at each price, holding constant all other variables affecting demand. At $4.00 per bottle, 4,000 bottles of maple syrup are demanded (point *A*). At $2.00 per bottle, 6,000 bottles are demanded (point *B*).

CHANGES IN DEMAND

Underlying any demand curve is some assumption about the other variables that affect buyers' choices. For example, the demand curve in Figure 1 might tell us the quantity demanded at each price, *assuming* that average household income in Wichita is $30,000, that the price of pancake mix is $2.00 per box, and so on. In the real world, of course, these variables can and do change. What happens then? The answer is, *The entire relationship between price and quantity demanded will change.* We call this a **change in demand,** because the word "demand" means the entire relationship between price and quantity demanded.

CHANGE IN DEMAND A shift of a demand curve in response to a change in some variable other than price.

A change in demand is a change in the entire relationship between price and quantity demanded. An increase in demand means that buyers would choose to buy more at any price; a decrease in demand means that they would choose to buy less at any price.

A change in demand would mean an entire new set of quantities demanded at each price and an entirely new demand curve. For example, an increase in demand might change the demand schedule as shown in Table 2, where the second column lists the original quantities demanded at each price and the third column lists the new, higher quantities demanded.

As you can see in the table, at each price the quantity demanded is greater than before. Figure 2 plots the new demand curve from the quantities in the third column of the table. The new demand curve lies to the *right* of the old curve. For example, at a price of $2.00, the old demand curve told us that the quantity demanded was 6,000 bottles (point *B*). After the increase in demand, buyers would want to buy 8,000 bottles at that price (point *F*).

CHANGE IN QUANTITY DEMANDED A movement along a demand curve in response to a change in price.

INCOME The amount that a person or firm earns over a particular period.

WEALTH The total value of everything a person or firm owns, at a point in time, minus the total value of everything owed.

Changes in demand are represented by a shift *in the demand curve. When demand increases, the demand curve shifts to the right; when demand decreases, the demand curve shifts to the left.*

INCREASE IN DEMAND FOR MAPLE SYRUP IN WICHITA

TABLE 2

Price (per bottle)	Original Quantity Demanded (bottles per month)	New Quantity Demanded after Increase in Demand (bottles per month)
$1.00	7,500	9,500
$2.00	6,000	8,000
$3.00	5,000	7,000
$4.00	4,000	6,000
$5.00	3,500	5,500

Now let's look at the different variables that can cause demand to change and shift the demand curve.

DANGEROUS CURVES

Language is important when speaking about demand. If you say, "People demand more maple syrup," you might mean that we are moving along the demand curve, like the move from point *A* to point *B* in Figure 2. Or you might mean that the entire demand curve has shifted, like the shift from D_1 to D_2 in the figure.

To avoid confusion (and mistakes on exams!), always use the special language that distinguishes between these two cases. When we *move along* the demand curve, we call it a **change in quantity demanded.** A change in quantity demanded is always caused by a change in the good's price. But when the entire demand curve shifts, we call it a *change in demand.* A change in demand is always caused by a change in something *other* than the good's price.

INCOME AND WEALTH. Your **income** is what you earn over a period of time—say, $3,000 per month or $36,000 per year. Your **wealth**—if you are fortunate enough to have some—is the total value of everything you own—cash, bank accounts, stocks, bonds, real estate, paintings, or any valuable property—minus everything you owe—home mortgage, credit card debt, student loans, and so on.

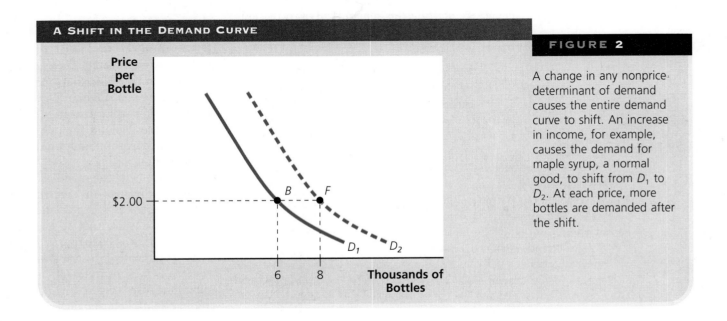

A SHIFT IN THE DEMAND CURVE

FIGURE 2

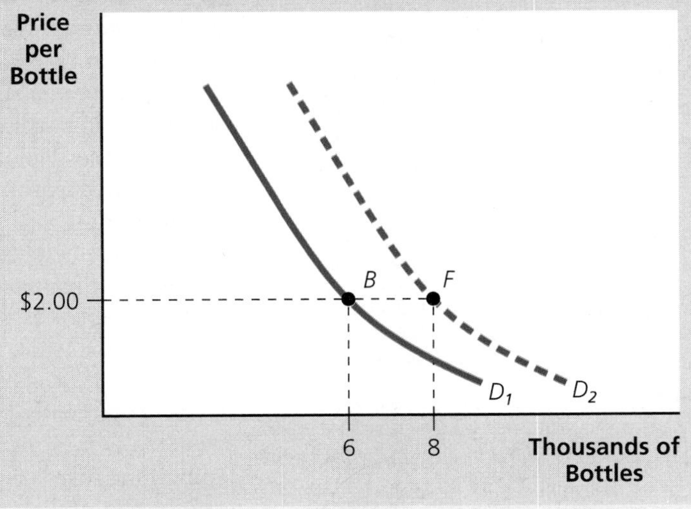

A change in any nonprice determinant of demand causes the entire demand curve to shift. An increase in income, for example, causes the demand for maple syrup, a normal good, to shift from D_1 to D_2. At each price, more bottles are demanded after the shift.

NORMAL GOOD A good that people demand more of as their income rises.

Greater amounts of income or wealth widen the range of purchases you can consider. For most goods, a rise in income or wealth will *increase* demand—buyers would want to buy more at any price. We call these **normal goods.** Housing, airline travel, and health club memberships are all examples of normal goods.

> *The demand for most goods (normal goods) is positively related to income or wealth. A rise in either income or wealth will increase demand and shift the demand curve to the right.*

INFERIOR GOOD A good that people demand less of as their income rises.

But the opposite could also occur: A rise in income or wealth could *decrease* demand. Such goods are called **inferior goods,** and there are many examples. Ground meat is a cheap source of protein, but not most people's idea of a fine dining experience. Higher income or wealth would enable consumers of ground meat to buy steaks, decreasing their demand for ground meat. For similar reasons, Greyhound bus tickets, low-rent housing units, and single-ply paper towels are probably inferior goods. For all of these goods, an increase in consumers' income or wealth would decrease demand, shifting the demand curve to the left.

SUBSTITUTE A good that can be used in place of some other good and that fulfills more or less the same purpose.

PRICES OF RELATED GOODS. A **substitute** is a good that can be used in place of another good and that fulfills more or less the same purpose. For example, many people use maple syrup to sweeten their pancakes, but they could use a number of other things instead: bananas, sugar, fruit, jam, or corn syrup. Each of these can be considered a substitute for maple syrup.

When the price of a substitute for a good rises, people will choose to buy *more* of the good itself. For example, when the price of jam rises, some of those using it will switch to maple syrup, which will then be relatively cheaper.

> *A rise in a substitute's price will cause an increase in demand for the good, shifting the demand curve to the right.*

COMPLEMENT A good that is used *together with* some other good.

Of course, if the price of a substitute falls, we have the opposite result: Demand decreases, shifting the demand curve to the left.

There are many examples in which a change in a substitute's price affects a market. A drop in the price of postage stamps would cause a decrease in the demand for electronic mail, a rise in private school tuition will cause an increase in the demand for public school education, and a fall in the rental price of videos would decrease the demand for movies at theaters. In each of these cases, we assume that the price of the substitute is the only price that is changing.

A **complement** is the opposite of a substitute: It is something used *together with* another good. Pancake mix is a complement to maple syrup,

DANGEROUS CURVES

It is easy to confuse *income* with *wealth,* because they are both measured in dollars and either can be used to buy goods and services. But they are not the same thing. Your income is measured *over a period of time.* (You earn $10.00 *per hour* or $400 *per week.*) Your wealth, by contrast, is measured *at a moment in time.* (On January 1, 1998, you have $5,436 in wealth.)

Since income and wealth are not the same thing, a household might have a high value for one and very little of the other. For example, when the French accountant Paul Gaugin moved to a South Seas island in 1891 to become a painter, he sold everything he owned and paid back all of his debts. The money he had left over was his wealth, which was relatively high. But during the next several years, he had virtually no income.

On the other hand, if you have a high-paying job, but you spend all of your income each year, you might not accumulate much in savings or other valuable assets. Your income would be high, but your wealth would be low.

since these two goods are used frequently in combination. If the price of pancake mix is higher, the cost of a pancake breakfast will be higher, and some consumers will switch to other breakfasts—bacon and eggs, for example—that don't include maple syrup. The demand for maple syrup will then decrease. In general,

a rise in the price of a complement decreases the demand for a good, shifting the demand curve to the left.

This is why we expect a higher price for automobiles to decrease the demand for gasoline and a lower price for movie-theater popcorn to increase the demand for movie tickets.

POPULATION. Over time, as the population increases in an area, the number of buyers will ordinarily increase as well. This is why an increase in population generally causes an increase in demand for a good. The growth of the U.S. population over the last 50 years has been an important reason (but not the only reason) for rightward shifts in the demand curves for food, rental apartments, telephones, and many other goods and services.

EXPECTATIONS. Expectations of future events can affect demand. For example, if buyers anticipate a rise in the price of maple syrup, they may purchase more *now,* to get it before the price goes up; the demand curve would shift to the right. If people expect a drop in price, they may postpone current purchases, hoping to take advantage of lower prices later. This would shift the demand curve leftward. Expectations are particularly important in the markets for financial assets such as stocks and bonds and in the market for real estate. For example, you would be more likely to buy a new home at any current price if you thought the price would rise over the next few years, rather than fall or remain the same.

TASTES. Suppose we know the number of buyers in Wichita, their expectations about the future price of maple syrup, the prices of all related goods, and the average level of income and wealth in Wichita. Do we have all the information we need to draw the demand curve for maple syrup in Wichita? Not really. Because we do not yet know how consumers in Wichita *feel* about maple syrup. How many of them eat breakfast? How many make pancakes or waffles for breakfast? How often? And how many of these consumers *like* the taste of maple syrup? Do they notice the difference between real and artificial maple syrup, which are two different goods in this analysis? And what about all of the other goods and services competing for consumers' dollars: How do the buyers feel about them?

The questions could go on and on, identifying various characteristics about the buyers that influence their attitudes toward maple syrup. The approach of economics is to lump all of these characteristics together and call them, simply, *tastes.* Economists do not try to explain where these tastes come from or what makes them change—that is left to other social scientists. Instead, economists concern themselves with the *consequences* of a change in taste, whatever the reason for its occurrence.

When tastes change *toward* a good (people favor it more), demand increases, and the demand curve shifts to the right. When tastes change *away* from a good, demand decreases, and the demand curve shifts to the left. In general, tastes tend to be rather stable, so economists most often look elsewhere when trying to explain a change in demand. But there are cases where changes in tastes are the most significant change. For example, intense antismoking advertising and laws restricting

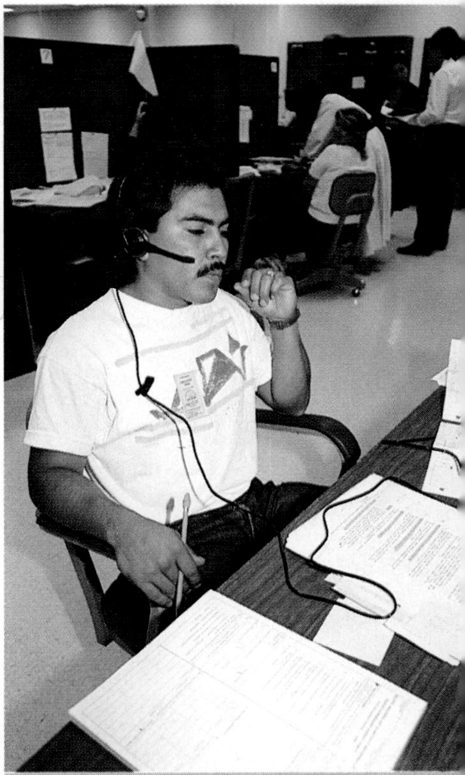

WWW

Name:
U.S. Department of Commerce, Bureau of the Census

Description:
Federal government collector and provider of economic and demographic data

Resources:
The Census Bureau, in addition to tracking the U.S. population, provides economic statistics, among other things, on businesses and markets, income, population, and prices. The Census Bureau also provides the latest *Statistical Abstract of the United States* for free to download.

Address:
http://www.census.gov/

TABLE 3

CAUSES OF A CHANGE IN DEMAND AND A SHIFT IN THE DEMAND CURVE

Demand decreases, and the demand curve shifts leftward, when:	Demand increases, and the demand curve shifts rightward, when:
income ↓ (normal good)	income ↑ (normal good)
wealth ↓ (normal good)	wealth ↑ (normal good)
price of substitute ↓	price of substitute ↑
price of complement ↑	price of complement ↓
expected future price ↓	expected future price ↑
tastes change away from the good	tastes change toward the good

smoking have changed tastes away from cigarettes over the past three decades. This has decreased the demand for cigarettes, shifting the demand curve to the left.

Table 3 summarizes the important variables that change demand and shift the demand curve.

SUPPLY

Now we switch our focus from the buying side to the selling side of the market. When we introduced demand, we discussed a common error: the tendency to regard our desire for something as a fixed amount, instead of viewing it as a variable that can change. We often make a similar mistake with supply. We might hear someone say, "There is only so much oil we can drill from the ground," or "There is no place left to build new office space in Manhattan." And yet, our known oil reserves have increased dramatically over the last quarter century, as oil companies have found it worth their while to look harder for oil. Similarly, the amount of office space in Manhattan continues to grow, as 12-story buildings are knocked down and replaced with 50-story ones. Supply, like demand, can change, and the amount of a good supplied in a market will depend on the *choices* made by those who produce it.

QUANTITY SUPPLIED The total amount of a good or service that all producers in a market would choose to produce and sell at a given price.

DANGEROUS CURVES

A troubling thought may have occurred to you. In the list of variables that shift the demand curve in Table 3, shouldn't we include the amount supplied by sellers? Or, to put the question another way, Doesn't demand depend on supply?

The answer is no. The demand curve tells us how much buyers *would choose* to buy at alternative prices. It provides answers to a series of hypothetical questions: "How much maple syrup *would* consumers choose to buy if the price were $3.00 per bottle? . . . if the price were $3.50 per bottle . . .," and so on. Sellers' decisions about how much to sell have no effect on the demand curve, since they do not affect the answers to these hypothetical questions.

"But wait," you object. "Surely, if sellers decide to sell more, people will buy more." True, but not because of a shift in the demand curve. As you'll see a bit later, if sellers want to sell more, consumers will buy more only because the *price* of the good decreases. This is represented by a movement *along* the demand curve, not a shift of the curve itself.

PRICE AND QUANTITY SUPPLIED

The **quantity supplied** of any good is the *total amount that sellers in a market would choose to produce and sell at a given price.*

There are a few things to keep in mind about quantity supplied. First, it can refer to an individual seller, like your local Kinko's copy shop, or to the combined choices of *all* sellers in a market—all photocopy shops in your area. In this chapter, we focus on quantity supplied in an entire market.

Second, quantity supplied, like quantity demanded, tells us about *choices*—not about what will actually happen in a market. When thinking about supply, we postpone wondering about how much sellers will *actually* be able to sell in the market. We just ask how much they would *choose* to sell at each price.

Finally, quantity supplied refers to *sellers* in general. Typically, the sellers are business firms that produce goods and services, as in the markets for coffee, haircuts, new cars, and airline travel. In these markets, each business firm will choose to produce and sell the quantity of output that gives it the highest possible profit. But in some markets, households are the sellers. For example, households sell their labor time to the business firms that employ them in the labor market. Households are also often sellers in markets for real estate, stocks and bonds, and used cars. This chapter, however, deals primarily with markets in which business firms are the sellers.

What determines the amount of a good that firms in a market want to sell? The most important influences are:

- the price of the good
- the prices of inputs used to produce the good
- the prices of alternative goods the firm could produce
- the technology used in production
- productive capacity in the industry
- expectations about the future of the good

We'll begin our analysis of supply by considering the impact of changes in a good's price.

The Law of Supply. How does a change in price affect quantity supplied? When a seller can get a higher price for a good, producing and selling it becomes more profitable. Producers will devote more resources toward its production and increase the quantity they would like to sell. For example, a rise in the price of vases will encourage ceramics manufacturers to shift resources out of the production of other things (coffee mugs, dishes, and so on) and toward the production of vases. It might also attract new ceramics producers into the market, who will add their production to that of the existing firms.

In general, price and quantity supplied are *positively related:* When the price of a good rises, the quantity supplied will rise as well. This relationship between price and quantity supplied is called the law of supply, the counterpart to the law of demand we discussed earlier.

> *The* ***law of supply*** *states that when the price of a good rises, and everything else remains the same, the quantity of the good supplied will rise.*

Law of supply As the price of a good increases, the quantity supplied increases.

Once again, notice the very important words, "everything else remains the same." Although many other variables influence the quantity of a good supplied, the law of supply tells us what would happen if all of them remained unchanged as the price of the good changed.

The Supply Schedule and the Supply Curve

Let's continue with our example of the market for maple syrup in Wichita. Who are the suppliers in this market? Since maple syrup is easy to transport, any producer on the continent can sell in Wichita. In practice, these producers are located mostly in the forests of Vermont, upstate New York, and Canada. In this case, the

TABLE 4 **SUPPLY SCHEDULE FOR MAPLE SYRUP IN WICHITA**

Price (per bottle)	Quantity Supplied (bottles per month)
$1.00	2,500
$2.00	4,000
$3.00	5,000
$4.00	6,000
$5.00	6,500

quantity supplied is the amount of maple syrup all of these producers together would offer for sale in Wichita at each price for maple syrup.

SUPPLY SCHEDULE A list showing the quantities of a good or service that firms would choose to produce and sell at different prices, with all other variables held constant.

Table 4 shows the **supply schedule** for maple syrup in Wichita—a *list of different quantities supplied at different prices, with all other variables held constant.* As you can see, the supply schedule obeys the law of supply: As the price of maple syrup rises, the quantity supplied rises with it.

Now look at Figure 3, which shows the curve whose importance in economics is matched only by the demand curve we drew earlier. In the figure, each point represents a price–quantity pair taken from Table 4. For example, point *C* in the figure corresponds to a price of $2.00 per bottle and a quantity of 4,000 bottles per month, while point *D* represents the price–quantity pair $4.00 and 6,000 bottles. Connecting all of these points with a solid line gives us the *supply curve* for maple syrup, labeled with an *S* in the figure.

SUPPLY CURVE A graphical depiction of a supply schedule; a line showing the quantity of a good or service supplied at various prices, with all other variables held constant.

*The **supply curve** shows the relationship between the price of a good and the quantity supplied, holding constant the values of all other variables that affect supply. Each point on the curve shows the quantity that sellers would choose to sell at a specific price.*

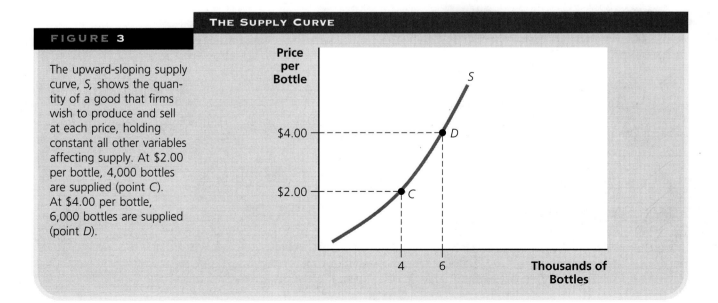

FIGURE 3 **THE SUPPLY CURVE**

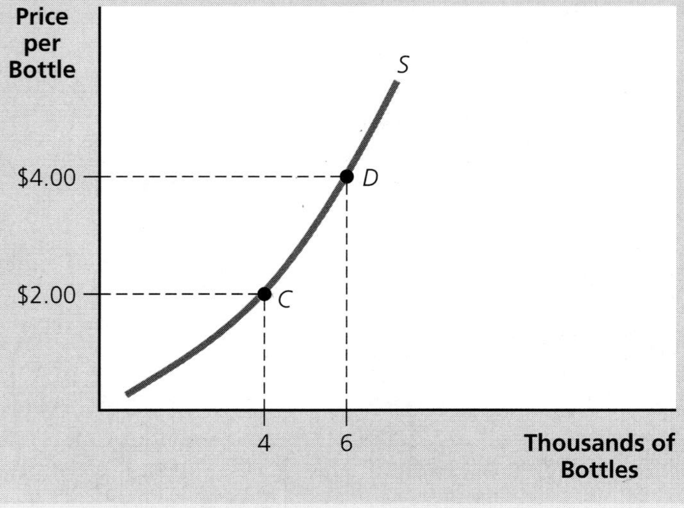

The upward-sloping supply curve, *S*, shows the quantity of a good that firms wish to produce and sell at each price, holding constant all other variables affecting supply. At $2.00 per bottle, 4,000 bottles are supplied (point *C*). At $4.00 per bottle, 6,000 bottles are supplied (point *D*).

Notice that the supply curve in Figure 3—like all supply curves—is *upward sloping*. This is the graphical representation of the law of supply: An increase in price causes an increase in quantity supplied.

The law of supply tells us that supply curves slope upward.

CHANGES IN SUPPLY

Both the supply schedule in Table 4 and the supply curve in Figure 3 hold constant all other variables that might affect supply: the prices of inputs, expected future prices, and so on. This allows us to concentrate on the relationship between price and quantity supplied. But if any of these variables we've been holding constant were to change, *the entire relationship between price and quantity supplied would change.* We call this a **change in supply,** because the word "supply" stands for the entire relationship between price and quantity supplied.

CHANGE IN SUPPLY A shift of a supply curve in response to some variable other than price.

A change in supply is a change in the entire relationship between price and quantity supplied. An increase in supply means that sellers would choose to sell more at any price; a decrease in supply means that they would choose to sell less at any price.

Table 5 illustrates how an increase in supply affects the supply schedule: The quantity supplied at each price increases. Figure 4 shows the old and new supply curves after an increase in supply. Notice that the new supply curve lies to the *right* of the old curve. For example, at a price of $4.00, the quantity supplied was 6,000 bottles on the old curve (point *D*) and 8,000 bottles on the new curve (point *J*). Changes in supply are represented by a *shift* in the supply curve. When supply increases, the supply curve shifts to the right; when supply decreases, the supply curve shifts to the left.

CHANGE IN QUANTITY SUPPLIED A movement along a supply curve in response to a change in price.

Now let's look a little more closely at the variables that can cause a change in supply and shift the supply curve.

DANGEROUS CURVES

To avoid confusion, always apply the same language convention for supply that we discussed earlier for demand. When we *move along* the supply curve, we call it a **change in quantity supplied.** A change in quantity supplied is always caused by a change in the good's price. When the entire supply curve shifts, we call it a *change in supply.* A change in supply is caused by a change in something *other* than the good's price.

TABLE 5

INCREASE IN SUPPLY OF MAPLE SYRUP IN WICHITA

Price (per bottle)	Quantity Supplied (bottles/month)	Quantity Supplied after Increase in Supply
$1.00	2,500	4,500
$2.00	4,000	6,000
$3.00	5,000	7,000
$4.00	6,000	8,000
$5.00	6,500	8,500

FIGURE 4

A SHIFT IN THE SUPPLY CURVE

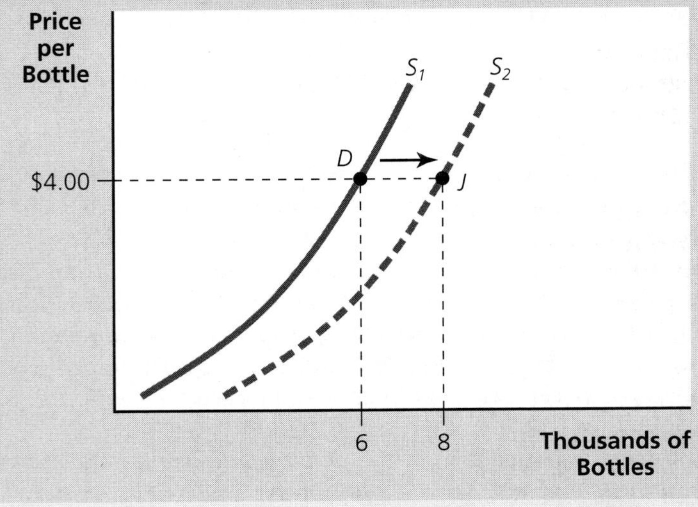

A change in any nonprice determinant of supply causes the entire supply curve to shift. A decrease in labor costs, for example, causes the supply of maple syrup to shift from S_1 to S_2. At each price, more bottles are supplied after the shift.

PRICES OF INPUTS. Producers of maple syrup use a variety of inputs: land, maple trees, water, labor, glass bottles, bottling machinery, transportation, and more. A higher price for any of these means a higher cost of producing and selling maple syrup, making it less profitable. As a result, we would expect producers to shift some resources out of maple syrup production, causing a decrease in supply.

In general,

a rise in the price of an input causes a decrease in supply, shifting the supply curve to the left.

We would expect a rise in the price of rubber to decrease the supply of tires and a decline in the price of paper to increase the supply of paperback books.

PRICES OF RELATED GOODS. Firms and other sellers can often choose among a variety of goods and services to produce and sell, all of which use roughly the same inputs. A maple syrup producer could cut down its maple trees and supply lumber instead or could dry its maple syrup and sell its output as maple *sugar*. These other goods that *could* be produced are called **alternate goods.**

ALTERNATE GOODS Other goods that a firm could produce using some of the same types of inputs as the good in question.

A rise in the price of an alternate good will decrease the supply of a good, shifting the supply curve leftward.

A rise in the price of maple *sugar* will make producing it more profitable, so producers will devote more of their output to maple sugar, *decreasing* the supply of maple syrup. Similarly, a higher price for oats will decrease the supply of wheat, and a lower price for hardcover books should increase the supply of paperbacks.

The same good supplied to a *different* market is an alternate good. For example, if we are considering the market for guitar lessons in Baraboo, Wisconsin, then "guitar lessons in Madison" is an alternate good, since guitar teachers could supply their services in either place. If the price of guitar lessons in Madison rises, holding everything else constant, *including the price of lessons in Baraboo,* we expect a decreased supply of guitar lessons in Baraboo.

TECHNOLOGY. Suppose there is a technological advance in producing maple syrup, say, a new, more efficient tap or a new bottling method. If this reduces the cost of producing maple syrup, producers will want to make and sell more of it at any price. In general, cost-saving technological advances will increase the supply of a good, shifting the supply curve to the right. Over the past two decades, cost-saving technological change has helped to increase supply in the markets for telephone calls, computers, and cable television service.

DANGEROUS CURVES

The list of variables that shift the supply curve in Table 6 does not include the amount that buyers want to buy. Is this a mistake? Doesn't demand affect supply?

The answer is no. The supply curve tells us how much sellers *would choose* to sell at alternative prices. It provides answers to a series of hypothetical questions, such as "How much maple syrup would firms choose to sell if the price were $4.00 per bottle? . . . if the price were $3.50 per bottle . . .," and so on. Buyers' decisions do not affect the answers to these questions, so they cannot shift the supply curve.

Of course, this does not mean that sellers don't respond to changes in demand. As you'll see a bit later, an increase in demand will ultimately cause an increase in the amount sellers will *actually* sell, but only by increasing the price of the good. This is represented by a movement *along* the supply curve, not a shift in the curve itself.

PRODUCTIVE CAPACITY. An increase in the number of firms in an industry or an increase in the size of each firm will increase supply, shifting the supply curve rightward. If half of the maple trees in Vermont perished, the total productive capacity of maple syrup suppliers would shrink, decreasing the supply of maple syrup. If more firms moved into the market and started their own maple syrup farms, supply would increase. Over the past several years, many new firms have begun producing laptop computers, leading to an increase in productive capacity and an increase in supply in this market.

EXPECTATIONS OF FUTURE PRICES. Imagine that you are the president of Sticky's Maple Syrup, Inc., and your research staff has just determined that the price of maple syrup will soon rise dramatically. What would you do? You should *postpone* producing—or at least selling—your output until later, when the price will be higher and profits will be greater. Applying this logic more generally,

A rise in the expected price of a good will decrease the supply, shifting the supply curve leftward.

A belief that the price of commercial lots in Trenton is about to rise will decrease the supply of such lots—fewer of them will be offered for sale at any given price.

Table 6 summarizes the different variables that change the supply of a good and shift the supply curve.

PUTTING SUPPLY AND DEMAND TOGETHER

What happens when buyers and sellers, each having the desire and the ability to trade, come together in a market? The two sides of the market have different agendas: Buyers would like to be charged the lowest possible price, while sellers would like to sell at the highest possible price. Is there chaos when they meet, with buyers and sellers endlessly chasing after each other or endlessly bargaining for advantage, so that trade never takes place? A casual look at the real world suggests not. In most markets, most of the time, there is order and stability in the encoun-

TABLE 6

CAUSES OF A CHANGE IN SUPPLY AND A SHIFT IN THE SUPPLY CURVE

Supply decreases, and the supply curve shifts leftward, when:	Supply increases, and the supply curve shifts rightward, when:
price of an input ↑	price of an input ↓
price of an alternate good ↑	price of an alternate good ↓
productive capacity in the industry ↓	productive capacity in the industry ↑
expectations of future price ↑	expectation of future price ↓
	there is a cost-saving technological advance

ters between buyers and sellers. In most cases, prices do not fluctuate wildly from moment to moment, but seem to hover around a stable value. This stability may be short lived—lasting only a day, an hour, or even a minute in some markets—but still, for this short time, the market seems to be at rest. Whenever we study a market, therefore, we look for this state of rest—a price and quantity at which the market will settle, at least for a while.

EQUILIBRIUM A state of rest; a situation that, once achieved, will not change unless some external factor, previously held constant, changes.

Economists use the word **equilibrium** when referring to a state of rest. More formally, an equilibrium is *a situation that, once achieved, will not change unless something we have been holding constant changes.* What will be the price of maple syrup in Wichita? And how much will people actually buy each month? We can rephrase these questions as follows: What is the *equilibrium price* of maple syrup in Wichita, and what is the *equilibrium quantity* of maple syrup exchanged? These are precisely the questions that the supply-and-demand model was designed to answer.

We can use Figure 5—which combines the supply and demand curves for maple syrup in Wichita—to find the equilibrium in this market, using the process of elimination. Let's first ask what would happen if the price of maple syrup in Wichita were $1.00 per bottle. At this price, we see that buyers would offer to buy 7,500 bottles each week, while sellers would offer to sell only 2,500 per week. We say

FIGURE 5

MARKET EQUILIBRIUM

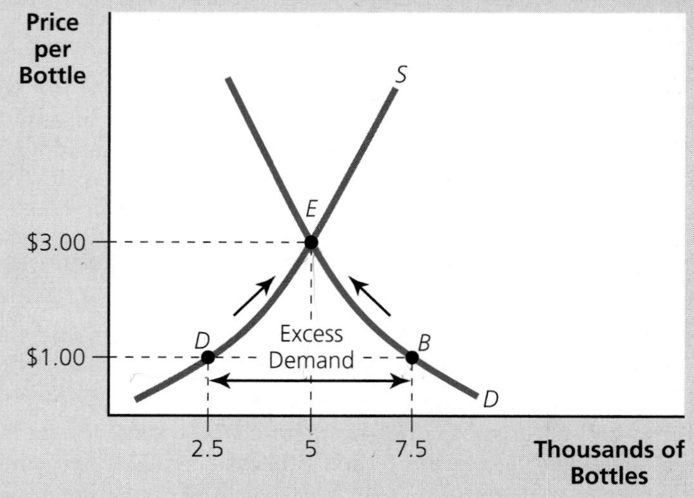

The intersection of the supply and demand curves at point *E* determines the market price of maple syrup ($3.00 per bottle) and the number of bottles exchanged (5,000). At a lower price, such as $1.00 per bottle, buyers would like to purchase more bottles (7,500) than producers are willing to supply (2,500). The resulting excess demand of 5,000 bottles causes the price to rise.

that there is an **excess demand** of 5,000 bottles. What will happen? Buyers will compete with each other to get more maple syrup than is available, offering to pay a higher price rather than do without. The price will then rise. You can see that \$1.00 per bottle is *not* the equilibrium price we seek, since—if the price *were* \$1.00—it would automatically tend to rise.

EXCESS DEMAND At a given price, the excess of quantity demanded over quantity supplied.

Before we consider other possible prices, let's look a bit closer at the changes we would see in this market as the price rose. First, there would be a decrease in quantity demanded—a movement along the demand curve leftward from point *B*. At the same time, we would see an increase in quantity supplied—a movement along the supply curve rightward from point *D*. As these movements continued, the excess demand for maple syrup would shrink and, finally—at a price of \$3.00—disappear entirely. At this price, there would be no reason for any further price change, since quantity supplied and quantity demanded would both equal 5,000 bottles per month. There would be no disappointed buyers to offer higher prices. In sum, if the price happens to be below \$3.00, it will rise to \$3.00 and then stay put.

Now let's see what would happen if, for some reason, the price of maple syrup were \$5.00 per bottle. Figure 6 shows us that, at this price, quantity supplied would be 6,500 bottles per month, while quantity demanded would be only 3,500 bottles—an **excess supply** of 3,000 bottles. Sellers would compete with each other to sell more maple syrup than buyers wanted to buy, and the price would fall, so \$5.00 cannot be the equilibrium price. The decrease in price would move us along both the supply curve (leftward) and the demand curve (rightward), decreasing the excess supply of maple syrup until it disappeared, once again, at a price of \$3.00 per bottle. Our conclusion: If the price happens to be above \$3.00, it will fall to \$3.00 and then stop changing.

EXCESS SUPPLY At a given price, the excess of quantity supplied over quantity demanded.

You can see that any price higher or lower than \$3.00 cannot be an equilibrium price, since if the price is higher, it will tend to drop, and if it is lower, it will tend to rise. You can also see—in Figure 6—that if the price is exactly \$3.00, there would be neither an excess supply nor an excess demand. Sellers would choose to sell 5,000 bottles per week, and this is exactly the quantity buyers would choose

EXCESS SUPPLY AND PRICE ADJUSTMENT

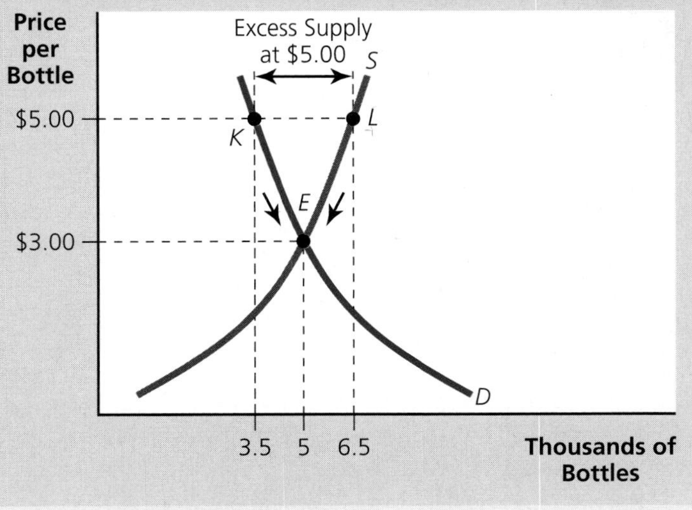

FIGURE 6

At any price above \$3.00 per bottle, the market for maple syrup will be out of equilibrium. The excess supply of 3,000 bottles at a price of \$5.00 causes the market price to fall. As the price falls, quantity supplied decreases and quantity demanded increases. At point *E*, the market is back in equilibrium.

to buy. There would be no reason for the price to change. Thus, $3.00 must be our sought-after equilibrium price and 5,000 our equilibrium quantity.

No doubt, you have noticed that $3.00 happens to be the price at which the supply and demand curves cross. This leads us to an easy, graphical technique for locating our equilibrium:

To find the equilibrium price and quantity in a market, draw the supply and demand curves. The equilibrium is the point where the two curves intersect.

The intersection of the supply and demand curves helps us to understand the concept of equilibrium even more clearly. At the intersection, the market is operating on *both* the demand and the supply curves. When the price is $3.00, buyers and sellers can *actually* buy and sell the quantities they would *choose* to buy and sell at $3.00. There are no dissatisfied buyers unable to find the goods they want to purchase, nor are there unhappy sellers, unable to find buyers for the products they have brought to the market. This is why $3.00 is the equilibrium price. In this state of rest, there is a balance between the quantity supplied and the quantity demanded.

But that point of rest will not necessarily be a lasting one. Remember that in order to draw the supply and demand curves in the first place, we had to assume particular values for all the other variables—besides price—affecting quantity demanded and quantity supplied. If any one of these variables were to change, then either the supply curve or the demand curve would shift, and our equilibrium would change as well. Economists are very interested in how and why the equilibrium changes in a market, so this is what we'll explore next.

WHAT HAPPENS WHEN THINGS CHANGE?

Point *E* in Figure 7 shows the equilibrium—a price of $3.00 and quantity of 5,000 bottles—in the market for maple syrup in Wichita. But now suppose that average

FIGURE 7

A SHIFT IN DEMAND AND A NEW EQUILIBRIUM

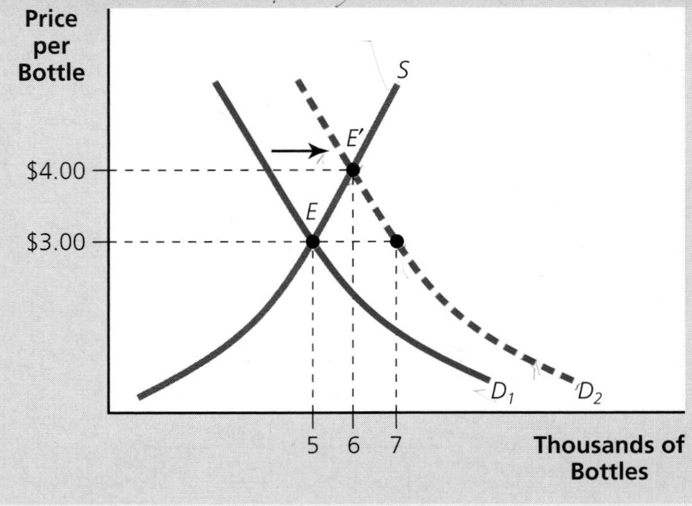

An increase in household incomes increases demand from D_1 to D_2. At the old price of $3.00 per bottle, there is now an excess demand. As a result, price rises until excess demand is eliminated at point *E*′. In the new equilibrium, quantity demanded again equals quantity supplied. The price is higher and more bottles are produced and sold.

household income in Wichita increases. We have already seen that the demand curve will shift rightward—from D_1 to D_2. At the original price of \$3.00 per bottle, there will be an excess demand of 2,000 bottles, forcing the price up. The rise in price will move us along the supply curve, from point E to point E'. Using our terminology, we would say that *an increase in demand* causes an increase in price, which, in turn, causes an *increase in quantity supplied.*

The end result is an increase in the equilibrium price—from \$3.00 to \$4.00—and a rise in the equilibrium quantity—from 5,000 to 6,000 bottles. In general,

Any change that shifts the demand curve rightward will increase both the equilibrium price and the equilibrium quantity.

Similarly,

Any change that shifts the demand curve leftward will cause the equilibrium price and quantity to decrease.

Figure 8 illustrates another type of change. Here, the wages of workers in the maple syrup industry have decreased, so the supply curve shifts rightward, from S_1 to S_2. Now, we have an excess supply of 2,000 bottles at the original price of \$3.00, so the price will decline. The fall in price moves us rightward along the demand curve, from point E to point E'. Here, an *increase in supply* causes the price to fall, which causes an *increase in quantity demanded.* Our new equilibrium occurs along S_2, at a lower price—\$2.00—and a higher quantity—6,000 bottles. To generalize,

Any change that shifts the supply curve rightward will decrease the equilibrium price and increase the equilibrium quantity.

A SHIFT IN SUPPLY AND A NEW EQUILIBRIUM

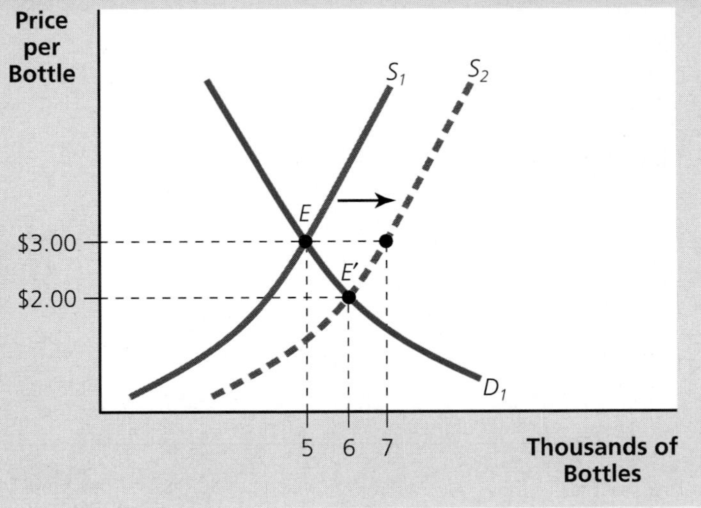

FIGURE 8

A decrease in wages causes supply to increase from S_1 to S_2. At the old equilibrium price of \$3.00, there is now an excess supply. As a result, the price falls until excess supply is eliminated at point E'. In the new equilibrium, quantity demanded again equals quantity supplied. The price is lower, and more bottles are produced and sold.

Similarly, any change in the opposite direction will shift the supply curve to the left, and give us the opposite results:

Any change that shifts the supply curve leftward will cause the equilibrium price to rise and the equilibrium quantity to fall.

So far, we've considered the consequences of a change in a single variable only. But what happens to the market equilibrium when two or more variables are allowed to change simultaneously? Figure 9 illustrates how we would analyze a situation like this. Here, we assume that there is a decrease in the price of pancake mix, a complement for maple syrup, and, simultaneously, a rise in the price of maple *sugar,* an alternate good. The drop in the price of the complementary good shifts the demand curve rightward, from D_1 to D_2, while the rise in the price of the alternate good shifts the supply curve leftward, from S_1 to S_2. The impact on the equilibrium price is unambiguous: It must increase, since each of these shifts pushes the equilibrium price higher. The effect on the equilibrium quantity, however, is ambiguous: it could go either way, depending on which of the shifts—supply or demand—is greater. In the figure, we've illustrated the case where equilibrium quantity increases, because the rightward shift in demand—making quantity increase—is greater than the leftward shift in supply—making quantity decrease. You may want to prove to yourself that we could just as easily have illustrated a *decrease* in equilibrium quantity, simply by making the supply shift a bit larger or the demand shift a bit smaller.

DANGEROUS CURVES

If you look back at Figure 2, you will see that when demand increases, the demand curve shifts rightward, but it also shifts upward. It is tempting to say, therefore, that "demand goes up." But this way of describing a shift causes problems when applied to the supply curve. Look at Figure 4, which illustrates an increase in supply. The supply curve shifts rightward, *but it also shifts downward.* If you say, "supply goes up," that might mean "vertically up," which would be a *leftward* shift of the supply curve—a decrease in supply.

To prevent this confusion, avoid using the terms "up" and "down" when referring to changes in supply and demand. Instead, use "right" and "left." An increase in supply or demand is always a *shift to the right;* a decrease in supply or demand is always a *shift to the left.*

FIGURE 9

A SIMULTANEOUS SHIFT OF SUPPLY AND DEMAND

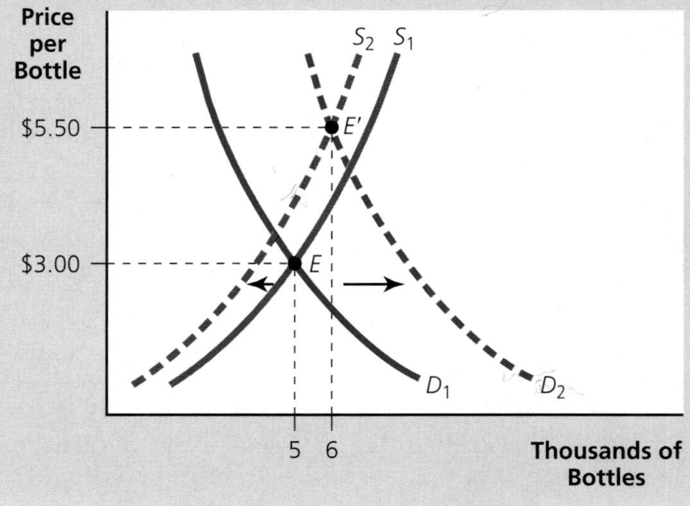

A decrease in the price of pancake mix causes demand to increase to D_2 while a rise in the price of maple sugar causes supply to decrease to S_2. Both price and quantity adjust until a new equilibrium is attained at point E' with a higher price and a higher quantity.

Effect of Supply and Demand Shifts on Equilibrium Price (*P*) and Quantity (*Q*)

TABLE 7

	Increase in Demand (rightward shift)	No Change in Demand	Decrease in Demand (leftward shift)
Increase in Supply (rightward shift)	P? $Q\uparrow$	$P\downarrow$ $Q\uparrow$	$P\downarrow$ Q?
No Change in Supply	$P\uparrow$ $Q\uparrow$	No change in P or Q	$P\downarrow$ $Q\downarrow$
Decrease in Supply (leftward shift)	$P\uparrow$ Q?	$P\uparrow$ $Q\downarrow$	P? $Q\downarrow$

Figure 9 illustrates only one of the possible combinations of shifts in supply and demand. But there are others. Table 7 summarizes what we *know* will happen to the equilibrium price (*P*) and quantity (*Q*), and what remains uncertain, in each case. For example, the figure showed us the effect of an increase in demand coupled with a decrease in supply, and in the table the result is found in the bottom, leftmost cell: The equilibrium price rises, while the equilibrium quantity might rise, fall, or remain the same.

This is a good time to put down the book, pick up a pencil and paper, and see whether you can *work* with supply and demand curves, rather than just follow along as you read. Try to draw a diagram that illustrates each of the possibilities in Table 7.

THE PRINCIPLE OF MARKETS AND EQUILIBRIUM

In this chapter, you've seen an example of how economists approach a problem. We began by asking how the prices of the things we buy are actually determined. To answer that question, we abstracted from the complex, real-world economy and viewed it as a number of distinct *markets*. We then chose to analyze one of those markets—the market for maple syrup—by looking for its *equilibrium* price and quantity. The supply-and-demand model is just one example of this approach, and there are many others, as you will see. This method of identifying a market and examining its equilibrium is one of the basic principles of economics:

Markets and Equilibrium

> ***The Principle of Markets and Equilibrium:*** *To understand how the economy behaves, economists organize the world into separate markets and then examine the equilibrium in each of those markets.*

Principle of Markets and Equilibrium To understand how the economy behaves, economists divide the world into separate markets and then examine the equilibrium in each of those markets.

You have already seen part of the reason that this approach is so valuable: It can explain how the price in a market is determined and what causes that price to change. But the approach takes us even further. It helps us predict important changes in the economy and prepare for them. And it helps us design government policies to accomplish our social goals and avoid policies that are likely to backfire. In the next section, we apply the principle of *markets and equilibrium* to some cases where government intervention is unlikely to accomplish our goals and even causes unintended harm. In later chapters, you will see some examples of effective government policies that can help market economies work even better.

MYTHS

A MYTH ABOUT SUPPLY AND DEMAND

"CHANGES IN SUPPLY OR DEMAND CAUSE SHORTAGES AND SURPLUSES."

Surpluses and shortages refer to situations where quantity supplied and quantity demanded in a market are not equal to each other. More specifically, a shortage occurs when quantity demanded is *greater* than quantity supplied. In this case, some buyers who have chosen to buy cannot find a willing seller. A surplus occurs when quantity demanded is *smaller* than quantity supplied, and some sellers cannot find willing buyers.

The media is full of statements attributing shortages and surpluses to changes in supply and demand. We have been told that the United States faces a shortage of oil because our use of it is growing too rapidly, that Seattle has a shortage of housing due to an increase in population, or that we face a coffee shortage due to a poor harvest in Colombia. Similarly, you might hear about a surplus of wheat because of good weather during the year, or a surplus of laptop computers because producers thought the price would be higher and manufactured too many of them.

Each of these statements can be translated into an assertion that a shift in a demand or supply curve has caused a shortage or surplus. In fact, however, shifts in supply and demand—by themselves—do *not* cause these problems. To see why, let's explore the "shortage" side of the myth in more detail.

In Figure 10(a), we see how an increase in demand for housing—say, due to an increase in population—causes the demand curve for housing to shift rightward. The equilibrium moves from E to E', and the equilibrium price of housing rises from P_1 to P_2. At E', the quantities of housing demanded and supplied are equal,

FIGURE 10 **CHANGES IN SUPPLY AND DEMAND DO NOT CAUSE SHORTAGES**

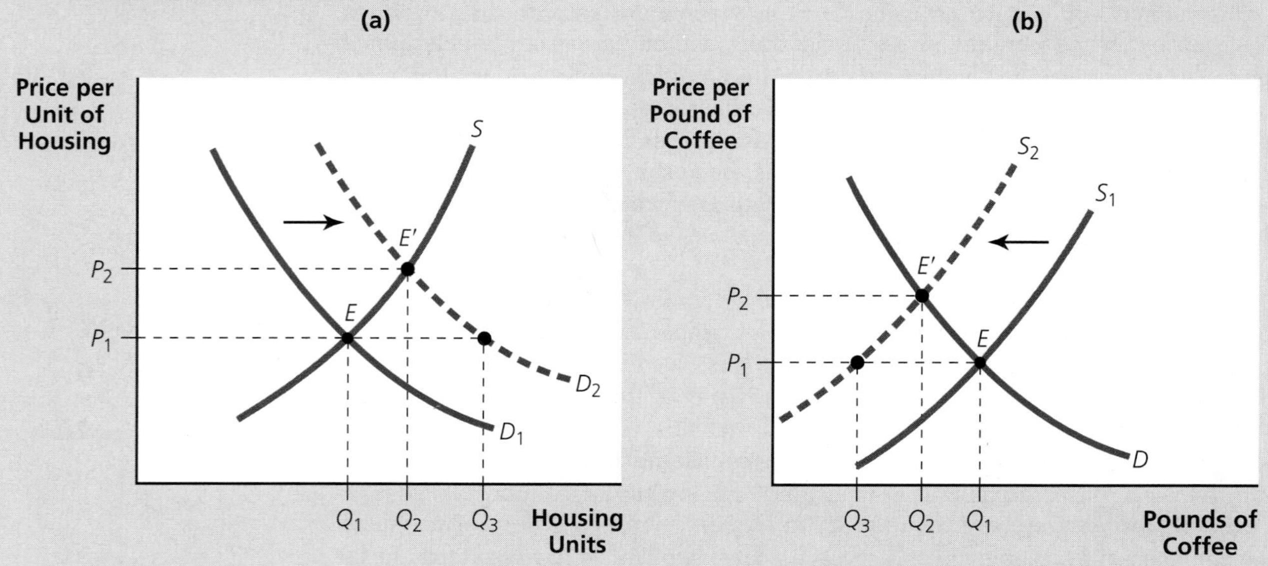

In (a), an increase in demand leads to excess demand at the original price, P_1. The price rises until a new equilibrium is established at point E'. In (b), a decrease in supply also leads to excess demand at the original price. Again, price rises until the excess demand is eliminated.

just as they were before demand increased. All buyers can find a willing seller. There is no shortage of housing.

Figure 10(b) illustrates a decrease in the supply of coffee due to a poor harvest. Once again, as long as the price is free to rise to its new equilibrium value, P_2, no shortage will result.

Why does this myth about the origin of shortages persist? Because in some cases, the market price is not permitted to adjust to its new, higher equilibrium level. Look again at Figure 10(a). If the price of housing were held at P_1 by law, the increase in demand would indeed result in a shortage, equal to the distance Q_1–Q_3. In Figure 10(b), if the price of coffee were fixed at P_1, a decrease in supply would cause a coffee shortage equal to the distance Q_1–Q_3.

But it is incorrect—or at least incomplete—to say that an increase in demand or a decrease in supply causes a shortage. Rather, there are *two* causes: (1) a change in demand or supply; *and* (2) something preventing the price from rising. Unless both of these conditions are present, there will be no shortage. Since economists view shifts in supply and demand curves as normal events in any market, they will usually attribute a shortage to what is *abnormal*—the failure of the price to rise.

The same logic applies to surpluses. As you can verify on your own (by drawing the relevant diagrams), an increase in supply or a decrease in demand is not enough—by itself—to create a surplus. In addition, something must *prevent* the price from falling to its new equilibrium. In the next section, we'll discuss some examples where a market price fails to move to its new equilibrium value because of government intervention.

GOVERNMENT INTERVENTION IN MARKETS

In our discussion so far, we've seen how competitive markets—through the mechanism of supply and demand—will settle at an equilibrium price and quantity. But society, or some groups within society, may be unhappy with this equilibrium. Most often, there is dissatisfaction with the equilibrium price: Apartment dwellers often complain that their rents are too high, while dairy farmers complain that the price of milk is too low.

Responding to this dissatisfaction, governments will sometimes intervene in markets, putting ceilings or floors on prices that prevent the market from attaining its equilibrium. Although these interventions often enjoy strong political support, they may have perverse effects. Economic analysis usually recommends alternative ways to accomplish the same goals at lower cost.

PRICE CEILINGS

Look at Figure 11, which shows the market for maple syrup in Wichita, with an equilibrium price of \$3.00 per bottle. If that price is viewed as too high, a government agency might be tempted to establish a **price ceiling** in this market: a regulation preventing the price from rising above the ceiling.

PRICE CEILING A government-imposed price that may not legally be exceeded.

Suppose the ceiling is \$2.00 per bottle, and it is strictly enforced. Then producers will no longer be able to charge \$3.00 for maple syrup, but will have to content themselves getting \$2.00 instead. In Figure 11, we will move down along the supply curve, from point *E* to point *R*, decreasing quantity supplied from 5,000 bottles to 4,000. At the same time, the fall in price will move us along the demand curve, from point *E* to point *V*, increasing quantity demanded from 5,000 to 6,000. These changes in quantities supplied and demanded together create an excess demand for maple syrup of 6,000 − 4,000 = 2,000 bottles each month. Ordinarily, the excess demand would force the price back up to $3.00, but now the price ceiling prevents this from occurring. What will happen?

There is a practical observation about markets that helps us arrive at an answer:

SHORT SIDE OF THE MARKET At a given price, the smaller of quantity demanded and quantity supplied.

*When quantity supplied and quantity demanded differ, the **short side of the market**—whichever of the two quantities is less—will prevail.*

This simple rule follows from the voluntary nature of exchange in a market system: No one is forced to buy or sell more than they want to. With an excess demand, sellers are the short side of the market. Since we cannot force them to sell any more than they want to—4,000 units—buyers will not be able to purchase all they want.

But this is not the end of the story. Because of the excess demand, all 4,000 bottles produced each month will quickly disappear from store shelves, and many buyers will be disappointed. The next time people hear that maple syrup has become available, everyone will try to get there first, and we can expect long lines at stores. When we include the *opportunity cost* of the time spent waiting in line, the ultimate effect of the price ceiling may be a *higher* cost of maple syrup for many consumers.

And there is still more. Suppose the price ceiling cannot be perfectly enforced. With so many unsatisfied potential buyers—many of whom would pay more than $2.00 per bottle if they could only find a willing seller—suppliers will be tempted to *violate* the price ceiling. And even if suppliers abide by the law, other individuals can try to buy maple syrup at $2.00 per bottle and sell it for a higher price. The result is a very active **black market**, where goods are sold illegally at prices higher than the legal ceiling.

BLACK MARKET An illegal market in which goods are sold at prices above the legal ceiling.

Ironically, the black-market price will exceed the original, freely determined equilibrium price of $4.00 per bottle. To see why, look at Figure 11. With a price ceiling of $2.00, sellers supply 4,000 bottles per month. Suppose all of this is bought

PRICE CEILINGS AND BLACK MARKETS

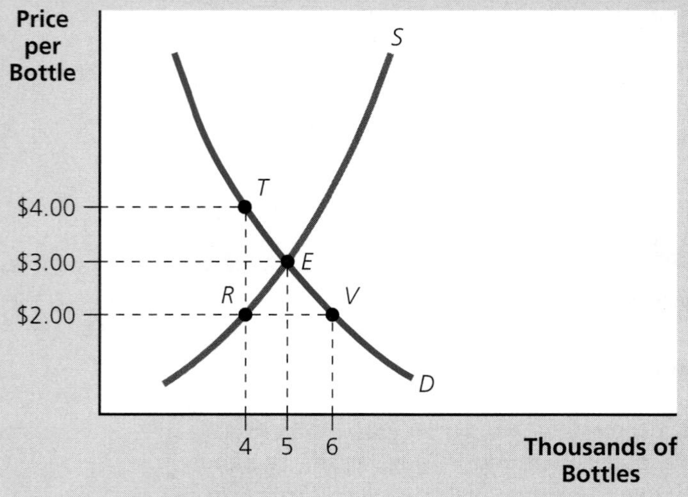

FIGURE 11

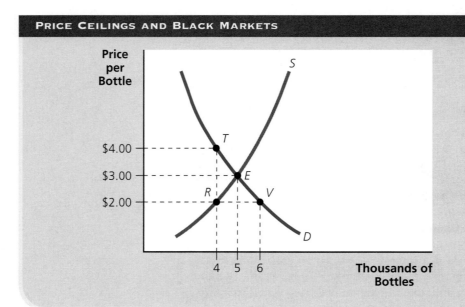

A government-imposed price ceiling of $2.00 per bottle reduces the legal quantity sold to 4,000 bottles, leaving an excess demand of 2,000 bottles. A black market may arise in which scalpers purchase the available 4,000 bottles and sell them (illegally) at the highest price consumers are willing to pay for that quantity—$4.00 per bottle, determined at point *T* on the demand curve.

by middlemen—maple syrup scalpers, if you will—who then sell it at the highest price they can get. What will this price be? We can use the demand curve to find out. At $4.00 per bottle (point *T*), the scalpers would just be able to sell all 4,000 bottles. They have no reason, therefore, to charge any less than this.

The unintended consequences of price ceilings—long lines, black markets, and, sometimes, higher prices—explains why they are generally a poor way to bring down prices. Experience with price ceilings has generally confirmed this judgment, so in practice they are rare. There are two exceptions, however.

First, governments impose a price ceiling of *zero* on certain trades that society finds unacceptable to treat as market transactions at all. For example, organs for transplant operations—such as hearts and livers—can be donated, but not sold.

The other exception is **rent controls**—city ordinances that specify a maximum monthly rent on many apartments and homes. If you live in a city with rent control, you will be familiar with its consequences. In any case, you may want to reread this section with the market for apartments in mind. How are shortages and long lines manifested? Do rent controls always decrease the cost of apartments to renters? And who are the middlemen who profit in this market?

RENT CONTROLS A government-imposed maximum on rents that may be charged for apartments or homes.

PRICE FLOORS

Sometimes, governments try to help sellers of a good by establishing a **price floor**—a minimum amount below which a price is not permitted to fall.

PRICE FLOOR A government-imposed minimum price below which a good or service may not be sold.

Suppose that the Maple Syrup Producers Association is able to convince the government to set a price floor of $5.00 per bottle. To see the effects on the market, look back at Figure 6. At $5.00 per bottle, producers would like to sell 6,500 bottles, while consumers want to purchase only 3,500. The excess supply of 6,500 − 3,500 = 3,000 would ordinarily push the market price down to its equilibrium value, $3.00, but the price floor prevents this. What will happen?

That depends on *how* the price floor is implemented. Suppose the government merely declares it illegal to sell maple syrup at any price below $5.00. If this law were obeyed, our short-side rule of markets tells us that buyers would prevail: They would purchase 3,500 of the 6,500 bottles produced, and producers would be unable to sell the remainder.

Producers would have an incentive to violate the price floor by selling some of their maple syrup for less than $5.00. A black market would develop for cheap maple syrup. Price floors are just as hard to enforce as price ceilings.

This is why governments usually maintain their price floors *indirectly*, with a rather aggressive—and foolproof—method. In our example, a special government agency might be established—let's call it the Maple Syrup Board—that would buy maple syrup from any seller at $5.00 per bottle. With this announcement, no supplier would ever sell at any price below $5.00, since selling to the government would always be preferred. With the price effectively stuck at $5.00, private buyers will buy 3,500 bottles per month—point *K* on the demand curve in Figure 6. But since quantity supplied is 6,500, the government will find itself buying 6,500 − 3,500 = 3,000 bottles each month. In other words, the government maintains the price floor by *buying up* the entire excess supply. This prevents the excess supply from doing what it would ordinarily do: drive the price down to its equilibrium value.

Governments in many countries have a long history of intervention in agricultural markets, including the use of price floors to prop up the incomes of farmers. In the United States, price floors for milk, cheese, eggs, and a variety of fruits and vegetables have been established. This policy has many critics—including most economists—who argue that the government spends too much money buying agricultural products it doesn't need and that the resulting higher prices distort the public's buying and eating habits—often to their nutritional detriment. Moreover, many of the farmers who benefit from price floors are wealthy individuals or large, powerful corporations, which do not need the assistance.

Maintaining a price floor, as described here, would cause a government to endlessly accumulate growing stocks of food. To prevent this, governments usually supplement price support programs with direct controls on supply. Our Maple Syrup Board would gain the power to limit the number of trees each producer could tap. As you can see, the desire to raise prices can get the government deeply involved in production decisions, rather than leaving them to the market.

SUPPLY AND DEMAND AND NORMATIVE ECONOMICS

Supply and demand offers us important lessons about the economy. The lessons are both positive—telling us *what* will happen when there is a change in a market—and normative—suggesting what sorts of policies we *should or should not* pursue.

Most economists believe that the mechanism of supply and demand is an effective way to allocate resources. "Let the market determine prices," they say, "and let each of us respond to those prices as we wish." When someone proposes to interfere with this mechanism, economists listen—but skeptically. The burden of proof, they believe, should lie with those who favor intervention. Why do economists feel this way?

Answering this question requires a more thorough understanding of the economy than we can provide after just three chapters of this book. Be assured, though, that when you finish your introductory study of economics, you will know why economists treat supply and demand with such respect. All of the basic principles you have learned so far—opportunity cost, specialization and exchange, and, of course, markets and equilibrium—and the other principles you *will be* learning—will help you understand economists' high regard for the market mechanism.

USING THE THEORY

ANTICIPATING A PRICE CHANGE

In the late 1980s, many East Coast colleges purchased expensive equipment that would enable them to switch rapidly from oil to natural gas as a source of heat. The idea was to protect the colleges from a sudden rise in oil prices, like the one they had suffered in the 1970s.

In the fall of 1990, Iraq invaded Kuwait, and oil prices skyrocketed. Finally, the colleges got a chance to put their new equipment to use, as they switched from burning oil to burning natural gas. But college administrators, expecting big savings on their energy bills, were in for a shock: They did not save much at all. When they received the bills from their local utilities, they found that the price of natural gas—like the price of oil—had risen sharply. Many of these administrators were angry at the utility companies and accused them of price gouging. Iraq's invasion of Kuwait, they reasoned, had not affected natural gas supplies at all, so there was no reason for its price to rise.

Were the college administrators right? Was this just an example of price gouging by the utility companies, taking advantage of an international crisis to increase their profits? A simple supply-and-demand analysis will give

THE MARKET FOR OIL

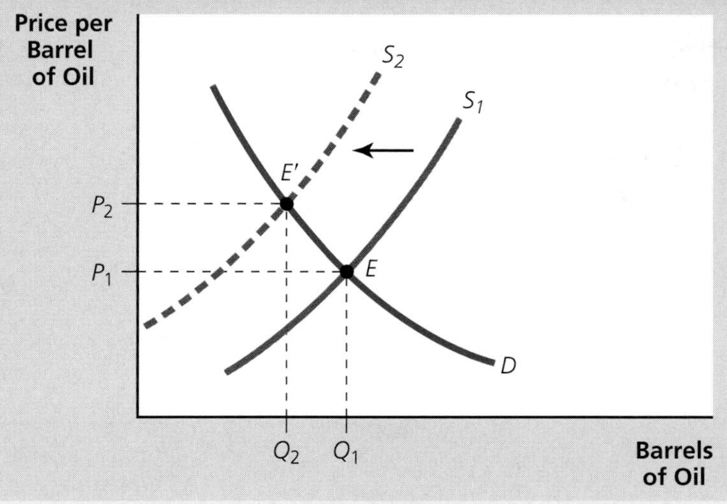

FIGURE 12

Before the Iraqi invasion of Kuwait, the oil market was in equilibrium at point E. The invasion and the resulting embargo on Iraqi oil decreased supply to S_2. Price increased to P_2 and the quantity exchanged fell to Q_2.

us the answer. More specifically, it will enable us to answer two questions: (1) Why did Iraq's invasion of Kuwait cause the price of oil to rise; and (2) Why did the price of natural gas rise as well?

Figure 12 shows supply and demand curves in the world market for oil. Before the invasion, the market was in equilibrium at E, with price P_1 and total output Q_1. Iraq's invasion and continued occupation of Kuwait—one of the largest oil producers in the world—led to a worldwide embargo of oil from Iraq and Kuwait. As far as the oil market was concerned, it was as if these nations' oil fields no longer existed—a significant decrease in the oil industry's productive capacity. If you look back at Table 6, you will see that a change in productive capacity is one of the causes of a shift in the supply curve. In this example, in which productive capacity decreases, the supply curve for oil shifts to the left. The new equilibrium at E' occurs at a lower quantity and a higher price. This change in the oil market was well understood by most people—including the college administrators—and no one was surprised when oil prices rose.

But what has all this got to do with natural-gas prices? Everything, as the next part of our analysis will show. Oil is a *substitute* for natural gas. A rise in the price of a substitute, we know, will increase the demand for a good. (Look back at Table 3 if you need a reminder.) In this case, the increase in the price of oil depicted in Figure 12 caused the demand curve *for natural gas*—depicted in Figure 13—to shift rightward. The price of natural gas rose, from P_3 to P_4.

The administrators were right that the invasion of Kuwait did not affect the supply of natural gas. What they missed, however, was the invasion's effect on the demand for natural gas. With a fuller understanding of supply and demand, they could have predicted—*before* investing in their expensive switching equipment—that any rise in oil prices would be accompanied by a rise in natural gas prices. Armed with this knowledge, they would have anticipated a much smaller saving in energy costs from switching to natural gas and might have decided that there was a better use for their scarce funds.

FIGURE 13

THE MARKET FOR NATURAL GAS

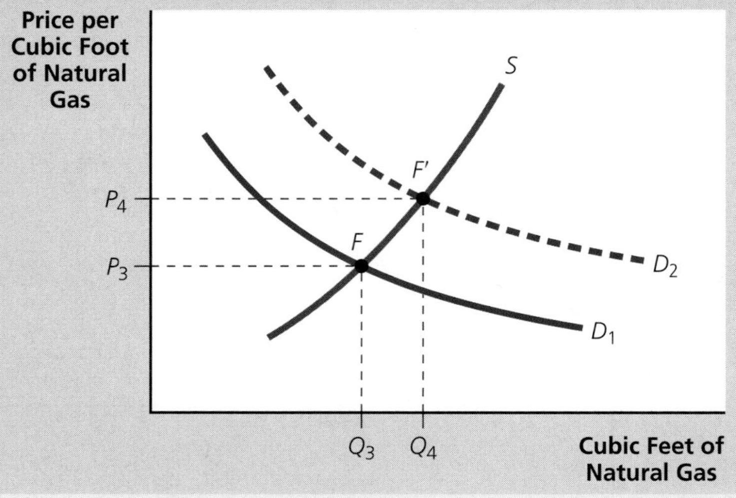

Oil is a substitute for natural gas. A rise in the price of oil increases the demand for natural gas. Here, demand increased from D_1 to D_2 and price rose from P_3 to P_4.

SUMMARY

In a market economy, prices are determined through the interaction of buyers and sellers in *markets.* A market with many buyers and sellers is *purely competitive;* if at least one buyer or seller has the power to influence the price of a product, the market is *imperfectly competitive.*

The model of *supply and demand* explains price determination in purely competitive markets. The *quantity demanded* of any good is the total amount buyers choose to purchase at a given price. The *law of demand* states that quantity demanded is inversely related to price; it tells us that the *demand curve* slopes downward. The demand curve is drawn for given levels of income, wealth, tastes, and prices of substitute and complementary goods. If any of those factors changes, the demand curve will shift.

The *quantity supplied* of a good is the total amount sellers choose to produce and sell at a given price. According to the *law of supply,* supply curves slope upward. The supply curve will shift if there is a change in the price of an input, the price of an alternate good, productive capacity, or expectations of future prices.

The *principle of markets and equilibrium* tells us that to understand how the economy operates, we should think of a system of markets and then examine the equilibrium in each of those markets. Equilibrium price and quantity in a market are found where the supply and demand curves intersect. If either of the curves shifts, price and quantity will change as the market moves to a new equilibrium.

KEY TERMS

market
imperfectly competitive market
purely competitive market
quantity demanded
law of demand
demand curve
change in demand
change in quantity demanded
income
wealth
normal good
inferior good
substitute
complement
quantity supplied
law of supply
supply schedule
supply curve
change in supply
change in quantity supplied
alternate goods
equilibrium
excess demand
excess supply
principle of markets and equilibrium
price ceiling
short side of the market
black market
rent controls
price floor
minimum wage

REVIEW QUESTIONS

1. How does economists' use of the word "market" differ from its use in everyday speech?

2. List and briefly explain the determinants of demand and the determinants of supply.

3. Discuss the distinction between substitutes and complements. Which of the following illustrate substitutes, which represent complements, and which are neither?
   a. Coke and Pepsi
   b. Computer hardware and computer software
   c. Beef and chicken
   d. Salt and sugar
   e. Ice cream and frozen yogurt

4. Rank each of the following markets according to how close it comes to pure competition:
   a. Wheat
   b. Personal computer hardware
   c. Gold
   d. Airline tickets from New York to Kalamazoo, Michigan

5. Are the following goods more likely to be normal or inferior?
   a. Lexus cars
   b. Second-hand clothes
   c. Imported beer
   d. Baby-sitting services
   e. Recapped tires
   f. Futons
   g. Home permanents
   h. Restaurant meals

6. Define what the term "equilibrium" means in economics.

7. Discuss why the price in a free market cannot stay above or below equilibrium for long, unless there is outside interference.

8. What does it mean to say that the "short side" of the market prevails?

9. State whether each of the following will cause a change in demand or a change in supply, and in which direction:
   a. Input prices increase.
   b. Income in an area declines.
   c. The price of an alternate good increases.
   d. Tastes shift away from a good.

PROBLEMS AND EXERCISES

1. Throughout the 1970s and 1980s, red meat fell out of favor with many consumers. On a supply-and-demand diagram, illustrate the effect of such a change on equilibrium price and quantity in the market for beef.

2. Discuss, and illustrate with a graph, how each of the following events will affect the market for coffee:
   a. A blight on coffee plants kills off much of the Brazilian crop
   b. The price of tea declines sharply
   c. An economic boom results in higher wages (be explicit about your assumptions here)
   d. Coffee is shown to cause cancer in laboratory rats
   e. Coffee prices are expected to rise rapidly in the near future

3. The following table gives the quantities of gasoline demanded and supplied in Los Angeles in a recent month.

Price per Gallon	*Qty. Demanded millions of gals.*	*Qty. Supplied millions of gals.*
$1.20	170	80
$1.30	156	105
$1.40	140	140
$1.50	123	175
$1.60	100	210
$1.70	95	238

   a. Graph the demand and supply curves
   b. Find the equilibrium price and quantity
   c. Illustrate on your graph how a rise in the price of cars would affect the gasoline market
   d. The California state government, alarmed by recent increases in gas prices, imposes a price ceiling of $1.20 per gallon. How will this affect the market? Specifically, calculate the resulting shortage or surplus.

4. How will each of the following affect the market for Levi's jeans in the United States?
   a. The price of denim cloth increases.
   b. An influx of immigrants arrives in the United States.
   c. A recession causes household incomes to decrease.
   Illustrate each answer with a supply-and-demand diagram.

5. Indicate which curve shifted which way to account for each of the following?
   a. The price of furniture rises as the quantity bought and sold falls.
   b. Apartment vacancy rates increase while average monthly rent on apartments declines.
   c. The price of personal computers continues to decline as sales skyrocket.

6. The market for rice has the following supply-and-demand schedule:

P (per ton)	Q_D (in tons)	Q_S (in tons)
10	100	0
20	80	30
30	60	40
40	50	50
50	40	60

   To support rice producers, the government imposes a price floor of $30 per ton. What quantity will be transacted in this market? Why?

CHALLENGE QUESTIONS

1. Let demand be given by the equation $Q_D = 500 - 50P$ and supply by the equation $Q_S = -25 + 25P$. What will be the equilibrium price and quantity?

2. A Wall Street analyst observes the following equilibrium price–quantity combinations in the market for soft drinks over a four-year period:

Year	*P*	*Q*
1	10	20
2	15	30
3	20	40
4	25	50

   She concludes that the market defies the law of demand. Is she correct? Why or why not?

3. Assume the labor market in the aircraft industry is in equilibrium. However, defense cutbacks result in decreased demand for airplanes and hence for aircraft workers. Will the result inevitably be unemployment in the industry? Why or why not?

4. Consider the following labor market scenario. You observe an influx of new workers into a region, but no decline in the wage, and worsening unemployment. What is the most likely explanation for this situation?

5. As discussed in this and the preceding chapter, prices act as an allocative mechanism, determining how available supply is distributed among all who want a particular good. In the case of a price ceiling, this price mechanism is frustrated. Consider the market for rental housing. If a ceiling is set below the market price:
   a. Will there be a shortage or a surplus of rental housing?
   b. Since price can no longer allocate housing, what other mechanisms might emerge? What factors might determine who gets a rent-controlled apartment and who does not? (You might find it helpful to read an article about rent control in cities such as Berkeley, California, or New York.)

WWW

First, draw a demand curve for a "normal" good. Next, visit the Census Bureau's most recent *Statistical Abstract of the United States* (http://www.census.gov/stat_abstract/) and find the "Statistics in Brief," addressing disposable personal income ("Part 2"). Determine what has happened to disposable personal income per person for the dates given. Draw what you predict would happen to your demand curve if everything else was held constant over that period of time. If your hypothetical good were an "inferior" good, would that change your answer? Explain.

CHAPTER

4

WHAT MACROECONOMICS TRIES TO EXPLAIN

From high orbit, astronauts see a stunning image: the earth—their own planet—suspended in the blackness as if by magic. Viewed from that great distance, the world's vast oceans look like mere puddles, its continents like mounds of dirt, and its mountain ranges like wrinkles on a bedspread. In contrast to our customary view from the earth's surface—of a car, a tree, a building—this is a view of the big picture.

What, you may be wondering, could this possibly have to do with economics? Actually, quite a bit: These two different ways of viewing the earth—from up close or from thousands of miles away—are analogous to two different ways of viewing the economy. When we look through the *micro*economic lens—from up close—we see the behavior of *individual decision makers* and *individual markets*. When we look through the *macro*economic lens—from a distance—these smaller features fade away, and we see only the broad outlines of the economy.

Which view is better? That depends on what we're trying to do. If we want to know why rents are so high in big cities, why computers are getting better and cheaper each year, or why the earnings of anesthesiologists are falling, we need the close-up view of microeconomics. But to answer questions about the *overall* economy—What determines the amount of unemployment? How fast will the average standard of living rise over the next decade? Why do interest rates fall in a recession? How fast will prices rise?—we need the more comprehensive view of *macro*economics.

Most people find the insights of macroeconomics interesting in their own right, but they can also be valuable in a more personal way: by helping you understand the forces that will shape your own future. Will there be a job for you when you graduate from college? How much will it pay? Will you be able to afford a house on your salary? A trip to Europe? Many years from now, will you be able to send your children to college, or live comfortably when you retire? Future macroeconomic developments will influence the answers to these questions.

CHAPTER OUTLINE

Moreover, an understanding of macroeconomics is crucial to the decisions you will make in the voting booth. Should you believe Candidate *A,* who says the way to increase our standard of living is to balance the government's budget by cutting government spending, or Candidate *B,* who maintains we'll be better off if we *increase* government spending on education, highways, and scientific research? What about the candidate who says we must keep Japanese cars out of the country to preserve American jobs, and the other who says that trade with other nations leads to more and better jobs for Americans? Should we believe those who say we are ruining the country by not *saving* enough, or those who say we aren't *spending* enough to keep Americans working? Macroeconomics helps us make up our minds on these important questions.

MACROECONOMIC CONCERNS

While there is some disagreement among economists about *how* to make the macroeconomy perform well, there is widespread agreement about the goals we are trying to achieve:

Economists—and society at large—agree on three important macroeconomic goals: rapid economic growth, full employment, and stable prices.

Why is there such universal agreement on these three goals? Because achieving them gives us the opportunity to make *all* of our citizens better off. Let's take a closer look at each of these goals and see why they are so important.

RAPID ECONOMIC GROWTH

If you were a typical American worker living at the beginning of this century, you would work about 60 hours every week, and your yearly salary—about $450—would buy a bit less than $8,000 would buy today. You could expect to die at the age of 47, and if you fell seriously ill before then, your doctor wouldn't be able to help much: There were no X-ray machines or blood tests, and little effective medicine for the few diseases that could be diagnosed. You would probably never hear the sounds produced by the best musicians of the day, or see the performances of the best actors, dancers, or singers. And the most exotic travel you'd enjoy would likely be a trip to a nearby state.

Today, the typical worker has it considerably better. He or she works about 35 hours per week, for an average yearly income of about $35,000, not to mention fringe benefits like health insurance, retirement benefits, and paid vacation. Thanks to advances in medicine, nutrition, and hygiene, the average man can expect to live to 73, and the average woman to 80. And more of the worker's free time today is really free: There are machines to do laundry and dishes, cars to get to and from work, telephones for quick communication, and—increasingly—personal computers to keep track of finances, appointments, and correspondence. Finally, during their lifetimes, most Americans will have traveled—for enjoyment—to many locations in the United States, and abroad.

What is responsible for these dramatic changes in economic well-being? *Rapid economic growth.* Because our output of goods and services has risen faster than the population, the average person can buy much more today—more food, cloth-

U.S. REAL GROSS DOMESTIC PRODUCT, 1921–1996

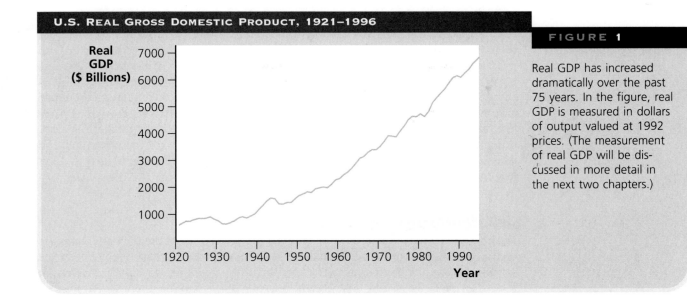

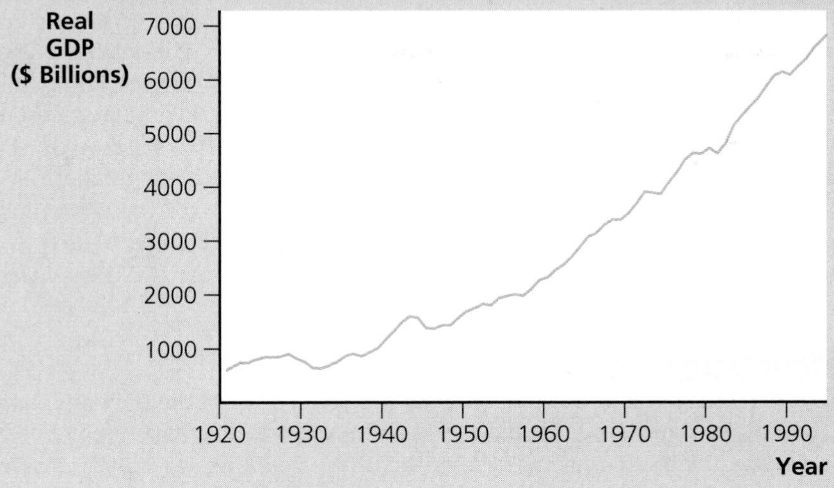

FIGURE 1

Real GDP has increased dramatically over the past 75 years. In the figure, real GDP is measured in dollars of output valued at 1992 prices. (The measurement of real GDP will be discussed in more detail in the next two chapters.)

ing, housing, medical care, entertainment, and travel—than at the turn of the century.

Economists monitor economic growth by keeping track of *real gross domestic product* (*real GDP*)—the total quantity of goods and services produced in the United States in a year. When real GDP rises faster than the population, output per person rises, and so does the average standard of living.

As you can see in Figure 1, real GDP has increased dramatically over the past 75 years. Part of the reason for the rise is an increase in population: More workers can produce more output. But real GDP has actually increased *faster* than the population: During the past 75 years, while the U.S. population has not quite tripled, the quantity of goods and services we produce each year has increased more than tenfold. Hence, the remarkable rise in the average American's living standard.

But when we look closer, we see something disturbing: Although output per person continues to grow, its *rate* of growth has decreased since the 1970s. From 1950 to 1973, output per person grew, on average, by 2.6 percent per year. But from 1973 to 1996, growth slowed to 1.5 percent annually. This may seem like a very slight difference, hardly worthy of the term "slowdown." But over long periods of time, such small differences in growth rates can cause huge differences in living standards. For example, suppose that from 1973 to 1996, output per person had grown at its previous pace of 2.6 percent per year instead of its actual rate of 1.5 percent. Then—over those 23 years—every man, woman, and child would have been able to consume an additional $16,000 in goods and services, valued at today's prices. (Think what you could do with an additional $16,000.) Economists and government officials are very concerned with the slowdown in growth.

Because growth increases the size of the economic pie, it makes it possible for every citizen to have a larger slice. This is why economists agree that growth is a good thing. But in practice, growth does *not* benefit everyone. Living standards will always rise more rapidly for some groups than for others, and some may even find their slice of the pie shrinking. For example, since the late 1980s, economic growth has improved the living standards of the highly skilled, while less skilled workers have actually become worse off. Partly, this is due to improvements in technology that have lowered the earnings of workers whose roles can be taken by computers and machines. But very few economists would advocate a halt to growth as a solution to the problems of unskilled workers. Some believe that, in the long run, everyone will indeed benefit from growth. Others see a role for the government in taxing successful people and providing benefits to those left behind by growth. But in either case, economic growth—by increasing the size of the overall pie—is seen as an important part of the solution.

HIGH EMPLOYMENT

Economic growth is one of our most important goals, but not the only one. Suppose our real GDP were growing at, say, a 3-percent annual rate, but 10 percent of the workforce was unable to find work. Although the economy would be growing at a healthy pace, we would not be achieving our full economic potential—our average standard of living would not be as high as it *could be.* There would be millions of people who wanted jobs, who *could* be producing output we could all use, but who would not be producing anything. This is one reason why consistently *high employment*—or consistently *low unemployment*—is an important macroeconomic goal.

But there is another reason, too. In addition to its impact on our average standard of living, unemployment also affects the distribution of economic well-being among our citizens. People who cannot find jobs and are unable to earn a wage or salary suffer. Their incomes—and their ability to buy goods and services—decrease.

FIGURE 2

U.S. UNEMPLOYMENT RATE, 1921–1996

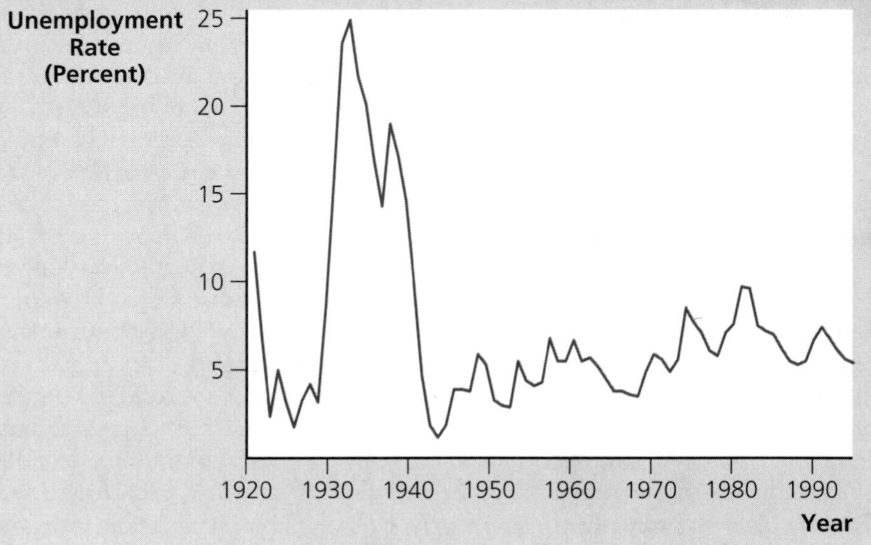

The unemployment rate fluctuates over time. During the Great Depression of the 1930s, it was extremely high, reaching 25 percent in 1933. In the early 1980s, the rate exceeded 11 percent.

And even though many of the jobless receive unemployment benefits and other assistance from the government, the unemployed typically have lower living standards than the employed.

One measure economists use to keep track of employment is the *unemployment rate*—the percentage of the workforce that would like to work, but cannot find jobs. Figure 2 shows the average unemployment rate during each of the past 75 years. Notice that the unemployment rate is never zero—there are always *some* people looking for work, even when the economy is doing well. But in some years, unemployment is unusually high. The worst example occurred during the Great Depression of the 1930s, when millions of workers lost their jobs and the unemployment rate reached 25 percent: One in four potential workers could not find a job. More recently, in the early 1980s, the unemployment rate rose above 11 percent.

The nation's commitment to high employment has twice been written into law. With the memory of the Great Depression still fresh, Congress passed the *Employment Act of 1946,* which required the federal government to "promote maximum employment, production and purchasing power." It did not, however, dictate a target rate of unemployment the government should aim for. A numerical target was added in 1978, when Congress passed the *Full Employment and Balanced Growth Act,* which called for an unemployment rate of 4 percent.

A glance at Figure 2 shows how seldom we have hit this target over the last few decades. Today, virtually all macroeconomists believe that the target is unrealistically low and that we should be shooting for a higher unemployment rate—somewhere between 5 and 6 percent. In future chapters, you will learn why economists believe in a higher target for unemployment and what we can and cannot do to achieve it.

EMPLOYMENT AND THE BUSINESS CYCLE. When firms produce more output, they hire more workers; when they produce less output, they tend to lay off workers. We would thus expect real GDP and employment to be closely related, and indeed they are. In recent years, each 1-percent drop in output has been associated with the loss of about half a million jobs. In order to achieve consistently high employment, then, we must have consistently high output. Unfortunately, output has *not* been very stable. If you look back at Figure 1, you will see that while real GDP has climbed upward over time, it has been a bumpy ride. The periodic fluctuations in GDP—the bumps in the figure—are called **business cycles.**

Figure 3 shows a close-up view of a hypothetical business cycle. When output rises, we are in the **expansion** phase, which continues until we reach a **peak.** Then, as output falls, we enter a **recession**—a period when output is abnormally low. When output hits bottom, we are in the **trough** of the recession.

Of course, real-world business cycles never look quite like the smooth, symmetrical cycle in Figure 3, but rather like the jagged, irregular cycles of Figure 1. Recessions can be severe or mild, and they can last several years or less than a single year. When a recession is particularly severe and long lasting, it is called a **depression.** In the 20th century, the United States experienced just one decline in output serious enough to be considered a depression—the worldwide *Great Depression* of the 1930s. From 1929 to 1933, the first four years of the Great Depression, U.S. output dropped by almost half.

But even during more normal times, the economy has gone through many recessions. Since 1959, we have suffered through two severe recessions (in 1974–75

BUSINESS CYCLES Fluctuations in real GDP around its long-term growth trend.

EXPANSION A period of increasing real GDP.

PEAK The point at which real GDP reaches its highest level during an expansion.

RECESSION A period during which real GDP declines to an abnormally low level.

TROUGH The point at which real GPD reaches its lowest level during a recession.

DEPRESSION An unusually severe recession.

FIGURE 3

THE BUSINESS CYCLE

Over time, real GDP fluctuates around an overall upward trend. Such fluctuations are called *business cycles.* When output rises more rapidly than usual, the economy experiences a *boom;* when output falls to an abnormally low level, we are in a *recession.*

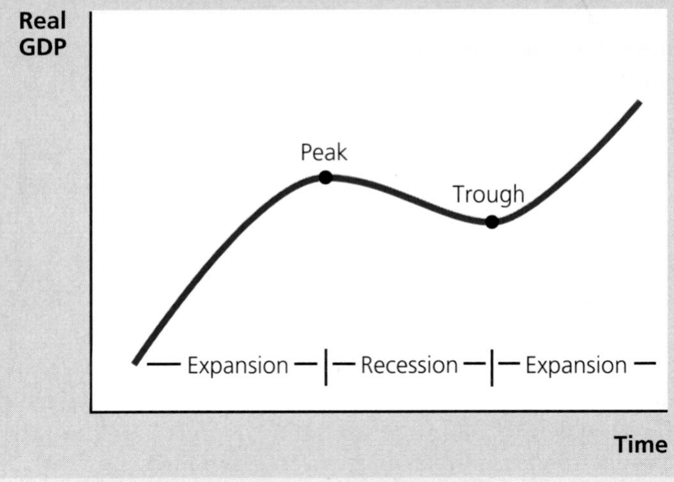

and 1981–82) and several less severe ones, such as the recession of 1990 to 1991. Later in this book, you will learn about some of the causes of recessions, why we cannot seem to eliminate them entirely, and what we *may* be able to do to make them milder in the future.

STABLE PRICES

Figure 4 shows the annual inflation rate—the percentage increase in the average level of prices—over the past 75 years.[1] With very few exceptions, the inflation rate has been positive—prices have risen in each of those years. But notice the wide variations in inflation: In 1979 and 1980, we had double-digit inflation—prices were rising by 10 percent or more per year. During that time, polls showed that people were more concerned about inflation than any other national problem—more than unemployment, crime, poverty, pollution, or anything else. In the 1990s, the inflation rate has averaged less than 3 percent per year, and we hardly seem to notice it at all. Pollsters no longer even include "rising prices" as a category when asking about the most important problems facing the country.[2]

Other countries have not been so lucky. In the 1980s, several Latin American nations experienced inflation rates of thousands of percent per year. In the early 1990s, some of the newly emerging nations of Central Europe and the former Soviet Union suffered annual inflation rates in the triple digits. An extreme case was the new nation of Serbia, where prices rose by 1,880 percent in the single month of August 1993. If prices had continued to rise at that rate all year, the annual inflation rate would have been 363,000,000,000,000,000 percent.

Why are stable prices—a low inflation rate—an important macroeconomic goal? Because inflation is *costly* to society. With annual inflation rates in the thousands

1 The figure is based on the Consumer Price Index, the most popular measure of the price level, as well as historical estimates of what this index *would* have been in the early part of the century. We'll discuss the Consumer Price Index and other measures of inflation in more detail in later chapters.

2 See, for example, issues of *The Gallup Poll Monthly* (Princeton, NJ: The Gallup Poll, various years) in the mid-1990s.

U.S. ANNUAL INFLATION RATE, 1922–1995

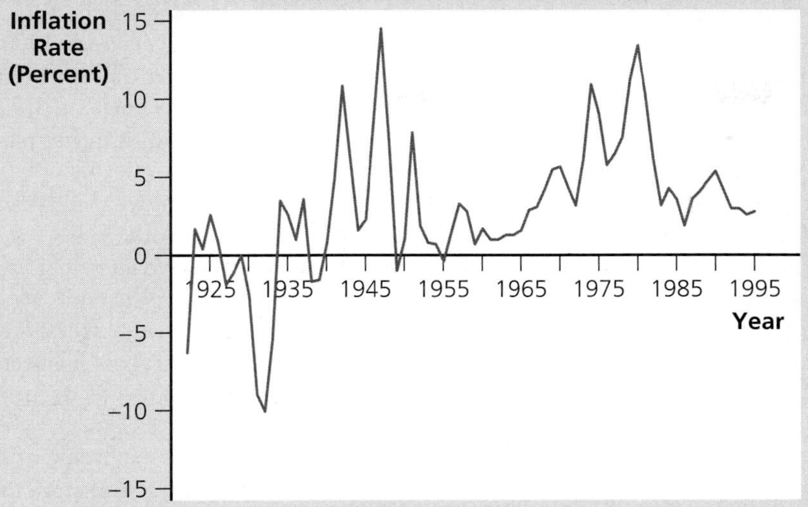

FIGURE 4

In most years, the inflation rate has been positive. The overall price level increased during those years.

of percent, the costs are easy to see: A nation's monetary system breaks down entirely, and people must waste valuable time and resources bartering with each other—for example, trading plumbing services for dentistry services. With so much time spent trying to find trading partners, there is little time left for producing goods and services. As a result, the average standard of living falls.

With more modest inflation—like the double-digit rates the United States experienced in the late 1970s—the costs to society are less obvious and less severe. But they are still significant. And when it comes time to bring down even a modest inflation rate, painful corrective actions by government are required. These actions often cause output to decline and unemployment to rise. For example, in order to bring the inflation rate down in the early 1980s (see Figure 4), government policy purposely caused the recessions of 1980 and 1981–82, reducing output (Figure 1) and increasing unemployment (Figure 2).

The previous paragraph raises a number of questions. How, precisely, does a modest inflation harm society? Why would a recession reduce inflation? And how does the government create a recession? If you're a bit confused, don't worry. You are just beginning your study of macroeconomics, and we have a lot of ground to cover.

THE MACROECONOMIC APPROACH

If you have already studied *micro*economics, you will notice much that is familiar in *macro*economics. The *basic principles of economics* play an important role in both branches of the field. But the macroeconomic approach is very different from the microeconomic approach in significant ways. Most importantly, in *micro*economics, we typically apply the basic principle of *markets and equilibrium* to *one market at a time*—the market for soybeans, for neurosurgeons, or for car washes. In *macro*economics, by contrast, we want to understand how the entire economy behaves. Thus, we apply the principle of markets and equilibrium to *all markets si-*

multaneously. This includes not only markets for goods and services, but also markets for labor and for financial assets like bonds and foreign currency.

How can we possibly hope to deal with all of these markets at the same time? One way would be to build a gigantic model that included every individual market in the economy. The model would have tens of thousands of supply and demand curves, which could be used to determine tens of thousands of prices and quantities. And with today's fast, powerful computers, we could, in principle, build this kind of model.

But it would not be easy. We would need to gather data on every market in the economy and understand how each market related to all of the others. As you might guess, this would be a formidable task, requiring thousands of workers just to gather the data alone. And in the end, the model would not prove very useful. We would not learn much about the economy from it: With so many individual trees, we could not see the forest. Moreover, the model's predictions would be highly suspect: With so much information and so many moving parts, high standards of accuracy are difficult to maintain. Even the government of the former Soviet Union, which directed production throughout the economy, was unable to keep track of all the markets under its control. In a market economy, where production decisions are made by individual firms, the task would be even harder.

AGGREGATION The process of combining different things into a single category.

What, then, is a macroeconomist to do? The answer is a word that you will become very familiar with in the chapters to come: **aggregation**—the process of combining different things into a single category and treating them as a whole. Let's take a closer look at how aggregation is used in macroeconomics.

AGGREGATION IN MACROECONOMICS

Aggregation is a basic tool of reasoning, one that you often use without being aware of it. If you say, "I applied for 15 jobs last month," you are aggregating 15 very different workplaces into the single category, jobs. Whenever you say "my friends, . . .," you are combining several very different people into a single category: people you consider friends.

Aggregation plays a key role in both micro- and macroeconomics. Microeconomists will speak of the market for automobiles, lumping Toyotas, Fords, BMWs, and other types of cars into a single category, or the market for physicians, lumping together general practitioners, dermatologists, ophthalmologists, and other types of doctors.

But in macroeconomics, we take aggregation to the extreme. Because we want to consider the entire economy at once, and yet keep our model as simple as possible, we must aggregate all markets into the broadest possible categories. For example, we lump together all the millions of different goods and services—computers, coffee tables, egg rolls, newspapers—into the single category, *output*. Similarly, we combine the thousands of different types of workers in the economy—doctors, construction workers, plumbers, college professors—into the category, *labor*. By aggregating in this way, we can create workable—and reasonably accurate—models that teach us a great deal about how the overall economy operates.

MACROECONOMIC CONTROVERSIES

Macroeconomics is full of disputes and disagreements. Indeed, modern macroeconomics—which began with the publication of *The General Theory of Employment, Interest, and Money,* by British economist John Maynard Keynes in

1936—originated in controversy. Keynes was taking on the conventional wisdom of his time—*classical economics*—which held that the macroeconomy worked very well on its own, and the best policy for the government to follow was *laissez faire*—"leave it alone." As he was working on *The General Theory*, Keynes wrote to his friend, the playwright George Bernard Shaw, "I believe myself to be writing a book on economic theory which will largely revolutionize—not, I suppose, at once but in the course of the next ten years—the way the world thinks about economic problems." Keynes's prediction was on the money: After the publication of his book, economists argued about its merits, but 10 years later, the majority of the profession was won over; they had become Keynesians. This new school of thought held that the economy does *not* do well on its own (one needed only to look at the Great Depression for evidence) and requires continual guidance from an activist and well-intentioned government.

DANGEROUS CURVES

In many English words, the prefix *macro* means "large" and *micro* means "small." As a result, you might think that in microeconomics, we study economic units in which small sums of money are involved, while in macroeconomics we study units involving greater sums. But this is not correct: The annual output of General Motors is considerably greater than the total annual output of countries such as Estonia or Guatemala, yet when we study the behavior of General Motors, we are practicing *micro*economics, and when we study the causes of unemployment in Estonia, we are practicing *macro*economics. Why? Microeconomics is concerned with the behavior and interaction of *individual* firms and markets, even if they are very large; macroeconomics is concerned with the behavior of *entire economies,* even if they are very small.

From the late 1940s until the early 1960s, events seemed to prove the Keynesians correct. Then, beginning in the 1960s, several distinguished economists began to challenge Keynesian ideas. Their counterrevolutionary views—which in many ways mirrored those of the classical economists—were strengthened by events in the 1970s, when the economy's behavior began to contradict the most important Keynesian ideas. While some of the early disagreements have been resolved, others have arisen to take their place.

Some of today's controversies are purely *positive* in nature. For example, one of the aggregates you will learn about is the *budget deficit*—the extent to which a government's spending exceeds its revenues. Many economists believe that the large budget deficits we have had in recent years—ranging from 3 to 5 percent of our real GDP—have prevented us from achieving one of our macroeconomic goals: rapid economic growth. But other economists believe just the opposite: that deficits of this size have very little, if any, impact on economic growth, and that shrinking the deficit would not make much difference. This is an example of an entirely *positive* disagreement: Both sides of the controversy place high value on rapid economic growth, but have different views of how the macroeconomy works.

Other controversies are entirely *normative* in nature. Two economists might agree that current deficits are hindering economic growth, but they might disagree strongly about the wisdom of deficit reduction because of differences in *values*. One economist places relatively more value on growth, the other on government programs in danger of being cut.

Sorting through the controversies is even more difficult because positive differences often have normative roots. It is no coincidence that economists with strong anti-interventionist leanings (a normative belief) generally conclude that government can't do much to change the course of the economy (a positive conclusion), while those who favor government intervention (normative) believe that it has helped keep the economy on track (positive).

Name:
United States Government Printing Office (GPO)
Description:
Federal Government printer and disseminator of governmental documents
Resources:
The GPO site enables users to search a variety of governmental databases, including materials from the U.S. Congress, the Council of Economic Advisers, and the Office of Management and Budget. Of particular note are databases containing key economics indicators, the *Economic Report of the President,* the *Congressional Record,* and the *Budget of the United States Government.*
Address:
http://www.gpo.gov/

As you study macroeconomics, you will learn how to sort through the maze of disagreements that often arise within the field. You will find that economists, like all other human beings, hold different values, and often hold them strongly. Not surprisingly, disagreements among economists are often emotionally charged. But there is also more agreement than meets the eye. Most macroeconomists agree on many basic principles, and we will stress these as we go. And even when there are strong disagreements, there is surprising agreement on the approach that should be taken to resolve them.

AS YOU STUDY MACROECONOMICS . . .

Macroeconomics is a fascinating and wide-ranging subject. You will find that each piece of the macroeconomic puzzle connects to all of the others in many different ways. Each time one of your questions is answered, 10 more will spring up in your mind, each demanding immediate attention. This presents a problem for a textbook writer, and for your instructor as well: What is the best order to present the principles of macroeconomics? We could follow the line of questions that occur to the curious reader, but this would be an organizational disaster. For example, learning about unemployment raises questions about international trade, but it also raises questions about government spending, government regulations, economic growth, wages, banking, and much, much more. And each of these topics raises questions about still others. Organizing the material in this way would make you feel like a ball in a pinball machine, bouncing from bumper to bumper. Still, the pinball approach—bouncing from topic to topic—is the one taken by the media when reporting on the economy. If you have ever tried to learn economics from a newspaper, you know how frustrating this approach can be.

In our study of macroeconomics, we will follow a different approach: presenting material as it is *needed* for what follows. In this way, what you learn in one chapter will form the foundation for the material in the next, and your understanding of macroeconomics will deepen as you go.

But be forewarned: This approach requires considerable patience on your part. Many of the questions that will pop into your head will have to be postponed until the proper foundations for answering them have been laid. It might help, though, to give you a *brief* indication of what is to come.

In the next two chapters, we will discuss three of the most important aggregates in macroeconomics: output, employment, and the price level. You will see why each of these is important to our economic well-being, how we keep track of them with government statistics, and how to interpret these statistics with a critical eye.

Then, in the remainder of the book, we study how the macroeconomy operates, starting with its behavior in the long run. Here, you will learn how the economy hangs together and why it performs *reasonably* well *most* of the time. You will also learn what makes an economy grow and which government policies are likely to help or hinder that growth.

Then, we turn our attention to the short run. You will learn why the economy behaves differently in the short run than in the long run, why we have business cycles, and how these cycles may be affected by government policies. Then we'll expand our analysis to include the banking system and the money supply, and the special challenges they pose for government policy makers. You'll learn why the macroeconomic policies that had been so successful in the 1950s and

1960s stopped working in the 1970s and 1980s, and what this implies for the 1990s and beyond.

Finally, we'll turn our attention to the global economy. You'll learn how trade with other nations constrains and expands our options at home and how economic events abroad influence our own economy. You will also learn why the United States has run persistent trade deficits with the rest of the world and what that means for our citizens.

This sounds like quite a lot of ground to cover, and indeed, it is. But it's not as daunting as it might sound. Remember that the study of macroeconomics—like the macroeconomy itself—is not a series of separate units, but an integrated whole. As you go from chapter to chapter, each principle you learn is a stepping-stone to the next one; little by little, your knowledge and understanding will accumulate and deepen. Most students are genuinely surprised at how well they understand the macroeconomy after a single introductory course. With a little work, you will be one of them.

SUMMARY

Macroeconomics is the study of the economy as a whole. It deals with issues such as economic growth, unemployment, inflation, and government policies that might influence the overall level of economic activity.

Economists generally agree about the importance of three main macroeconomic goals. The first of these is rapid economic growth. If output—real gross domestic product—grows faster than population, the average person can enjoy an improved standard of living.

High employment is another important goal. In the U.S. and other market economies, the main source of households' incomes is labor earnings. When unemployment is high, many people are without jobs and must cut back their purchases of goods and services.

The third macroeconomic goal is stable prices. This goal is important because inflation imposes costs on society. Keeping the rate of inflation low helps to reduce these costs.

In this text, we will study macroeconomics using models—simplified representations of reality. Because an economy like that of the United States is so large and complex, the models we use must be highly aggregated. For example, we will lump together millions of different goods to create an aggregate called "output" and combine all their prices into a single "price index."

For good or ill, macroeconomics is a field full of controversy. Some controversies are *positive;* they reflect disagreements about how the economy works. Others are *normative,* reflecting differences of opinion about what government policies are appropriate.

KEY TERMS

business cycles
expansion
peak
recession
trough
depression
aggregation

REVIEW QUESTIONS

1. Discuss the similarities and differences between macroeconomics and microeconomics.
2. What is the basic tool macroeconomists use to deal with the complexity and variety of economic markets and institutions? Give some examples of how they use this tool.
3. List the nation's macroeconomic goals and explain why each is important.
4. Consider an economy whose real GDP is growing at 4 percent per year. What else would you need to know in order to say whether the average standard of living is improving or deteriorating?

CHALLENGE QUESTION

Speculate about some factors that might help explain the post-1973 growth slowdown. What changes in the economy or in society as a whole may have contributed to this phenomenon ?

Economists often argue that the state of the macroeconomy is an important factor in determining the outcome of national elections. Some believe that the "misery index," the sum of the inflation rate and the unemployment rate, can be used to predict the fate of the incumbent. That is, if the misery index is high or increasing, the incumbent will face trouble; if the index is low or decreasing, however, the incumbent stands a good chance of reelection.

Visit the GPO (http://www.gpo.gov/) and find the database containing economic indicators (look for GPO Access — http://www.access.gpo.gov/su_docs/aces/aaces002. html). Select the economic indicators database and search for the term "employment." When the search results appear scroll down to the most recent listing of "Employment, Unemployment, and Wages." With this information, use the figures for "Civilian Labor Forces" and "Unemployment—Total" to calculate the unemployment rate for the latest month. That is, (Unemployment/Civilian Labor Force) × 100 = Unemployment Rate.

Go back to search for "consumer prices." When the search results appear scroll down to the most recent listing of "Consumer Prices—All Urban Consumers." With the information, calculate the percentage change in the Consumer Price Index over the past 12 months.

Combine your calculated unemployment rate and your inflation rate to find the current misery index. Calculate the index for 1994, 1992, and 1988. Does the condition of the macroeconomy seem to have been important in predicting the results of national elections in those years?

C H A P T E R

5

PRODUCTION, INCOME, AND EMPLOYMENT

On the first Friday of every month, at 8:00 A.M., dozens of journalists mill about in a room in the Department of Labor, waiting for the arrival of the press officer from the government's Bureau of Labor Statistics. When she enters the room, carrying a stack of papers, the buzz of conversation stops. The papers—which she passes out to the waiting journalists—contain the monthly report on the experience of the American workforce—a summary of everything the government knows about hiring and firing at businesses across the country; about the number of people working, the hours they worked, and the incomes they earned; and about the number of people *not* working and what they did instead. All of this information is broken down by industry, state, city, race, sex, and age. But one number looms large in the journalists' minds as they scan the report and compose their stories: the percentage of the labor force that could not find jobs, or the nation's *unemployment rate.*

Once every three months, a similar scene takes place at the Department of Commerce, as reporters wait for the release of the quarterly report on the nation's output of goods and services and the incomes we have earned from producing it. Once again, the report will include tremendous detail—a breakdown of output by industry and by the sector that purchased it (ordinary households, businesses, government agencies, and foreigners) and a breakdown of the income earned by wage earners, by property owners, and by those who run their own small businesses. And once again, the reporters' eyes will focus on a single number, a number that will dominate their stories and create headlines in newspapers across the country: the nation's *gross domestic product.*

The government knows the impact its reports on employment and production will have on the American political scene, and on financial markets in the U.S. and around the world, and so it takes great pains to ensure fair and equal access to the information. For example, the Bureau of Labor Statistics allows journalists to look

CHAPTER OUTLINE

PRODUCTION AND GROSS DOMESTIC PRODUCT
- GDP: A Definition
- The Expenditure Approach to GDP
- Other Approaches to GDP
- Measuring GDP: A Summary
- Real versus Nominal GDP
- The Importance of Real Values: A Basic Principle
- How GDP Is Used
- Problems with GDP

EMPLOYMENT AND UNEMPLOYMENT
- Types of Unemployment
- The Costs of Unemployment
- How Unemployment Is Measured
- Problems in Measuring Unemployment

USING THE THEORY: SOCIETY'S CHOICE OF GDP

at the employment report at 8:00 A.M. on the day of the release (the first Friday of every month). But all who see the report must stay inside a room—appropriately called the lockup room—and cannot contact the outside world until the official release time of 8:30 A.M. At precisely 8:29 A.M., the reporters are permitted to hook up their laptop modems, and then a countdown begins. Finally, at precisely 8:30 A.M.—not a second before—they are permitted to transmit their stories. At the same instant, the Bureau posts its report on an Internet Web site. (The URL is http://stats.bls.gov/blshome.html)

The reactions to the government's reports come almost immediately. Within seconds, wire-service headlines appear on computer screens across the country—"Unemployment Rate Up Two-Tenths of a Percent" or "Nation's Production Steady." Within minutes, financial traders, acting on these clues about the economy's future, make snap decisions to buy or sell, and prices move in the stock and bond markets. Further headlines will result—"Stock Market Plunges on Unemployment Data" or "Bonds Rally on Output Report." Within the hour, politicians and pundits will respond with sound bites, attacking or defending the administration's economic policies.

Why is so much attention given to the government's reports on production and employment, and—in particular—to those two numbers: gross domestic product and the unemployment rate? Because they describe aspects of the economy that dramatically affect each of us individually and our society as a whole. In this chapter, we will take our first look at production, income, and employment in the economy. The purpose here is not to explain what causes these variables to rise or fall—that will come a few chapters later, when we begin to study macroeconomic models. Here, we will focus on the reality behind the numbers: what the statistics tell us about the economy, how the government obtains them, and how they are sometimes misused.

PRODUCTION AND GROSS DOMESTIC PRODUCT

You have probably heard the phrase gross domestic product—or its more familiar abbreviation, GDP—more than once. It is one of those terms about the economy that are frequently used by the media and by politicians. In the first part of this chapter, we take a close look at GDP, starting with a careful definition.

GDP: A DEFINITION

The U.S. government has been measuring the nation's total production since the 1930s. You might think that this is an easy number to calculate, at least in theory: Simply add up the output of every firm in the country during the year. Unfortunately, measuring total production is not so straightforward, and there are many conceptual traps and pitfalls. This is why the definition of GDP is so precise—and so important:

GROSS DOMESTIC PRODUCT (GDP) The total value of all final goods and services produced for the marketplace during a given year, within the nation's borders.

The nation's ***gross domestic product (GDP)*** *is the total value of all final goods and services produced for the marketplace during a given year, within the nation's borders.*

Quite a mouthful. Is everything in this definition really necessary? Absolutely. To see why, let's break the definition down into pieces and look more closely at each one.

FIGURE 1

STAGES OF PRODUCTION

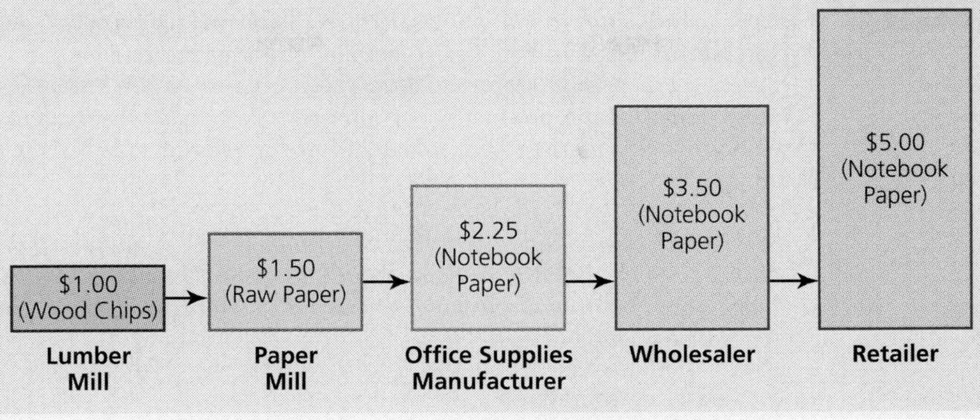

The total value . . .

How often do you hear that you can't add apples and oranges? But that is just what government statisticians must do when they measure our total output. In a typical day, American firms produce millions of *loaves* of bread, thousands of *pounds* of peanut butter, millions of *yards* of VCR tape, hundreds of *hours* of television programming, and so on. How can we combine all these different types of products—each measured in its own type of units—into a single measure? The approach of GDP is to add up the *dollar value* of every good or service—the number of dollars each product is *sold* for. As a result, our total product is measured in dollar units as well. For example, in 1996, the GDP of the United States was about $7,581,000,000,000—give or take a few billion dollars.

Using dollar values has two important advantages. First, it gives us a common unit of measurement for very different things, thus allowing us to add up "apples and oranges." Second, it ensures that more valuable goods (like a hundred computer chips) will count more in our GDP than less valuable ones (a hundred tortilla chips).

. . . of all final . . .

When measuring production, we do not count *every* good or service produced in the economy, but only those that are sold to their *final users.* An example will illustrate why.

Figure 1 shows a simplified version of the stages of production needed to produce a ream (500 sheets) of notebook paper: A lumber company cuts down trees and produces wood chips, which it sells to a paper mill for $1.00. The mill cooks, bleaches, and refines the wood chips, turning them into paper rolls, which it sells to an office supplies manufacturer for $1.50. This manufacturer cuts the paper, prints lines and margins on it, and sells its to a wholesaler for $2.25, which sells it to a retail store for $3.50, and then—finally—it is sold to a consumer—perhaps you—for $5.00.

Should we add the value of *all* of this production, and include $1.00 + $1.50 + $2.25 + $3.50 + $5.00 = $13.25 in GDP each time a ream of notebook paper is produced? No, this would clearly be a mistake, since all of this production ends

INTERMEDIATE GOODS Goods used up in producing final goods.

FINAL GOOD A good sold to its final user.

up creating a good worth only $5 in the end. In fact, the $5 you pay for this good already *includes* the value of all the other production in the process.

In our example, the goods sold by the lumber company, paper mill, notebook-paper manufacturer, and wholesaler are all **intermediate goods**—goods used up in the current period to produce something else. But the retailer (say, your local stationery store) sells a **final good**—a product sold to its *final user* (you). If we separately added in the production of intermediate goods when calculating GDP, we would be *overcounting* them, since they are already included in the value of the final good.

> *To avoid overcounting intermediate products when measuring GDP, we add up the value of final goods and services only. The value of all intermediate products is automatically included in the value of the final products they are used to create.*

. . . goods and services . . .

We all know a "good" when we see one: We can look at it, feel it, weigh it, and, in some cases, eat it, strum it, or swing a bat at it. Not so with a service: When you get a medical checkup, a haircut, or a car wash, the *effects* of the service may linger, but the service itself is used up the moment it is produced. Nonetheless, final services are as much a part of our total production as are final goods.

Services have become an increasingly important part of our total output in recent decades. The service sector has grown from 31 percent of total output in 1950 to 53 percent of total output in 1996.

. . . produced . . .

In order to contribute to GDP, something must be *produced.* This may sound obvious, but it is easy to forget. Every day, Americans buy billions of dollars worth of things that are *not* produced, or at least not produced this year, and so are not counted in this year's GDP. For example, people may buy land, or they may buy financial assets such as stocks or bonds. While these things cost money, they are not counted in GDP because they are not "goods and services produced." Land (and the natural resources on it or under it) is not produced at all. Stocks and bonds represent a claim to ownership or to receive future payments, but they are not themselves goods or services.

In addition, people and businesses buy billions of dollars in used goods during the year, such as secondhand cars, homes, used furniture, or an old photo of Elvis talking to an extraterrestrial. These goods were all produced, but not in the current period. We include only *currently produced* output when figuring this year's GDP.

DANGEROUS CURVES

You've learned that GDP excludes the value of many things that are bought and sold—such as land, financial assets, and used goods—because they are not *current production of goods and services.* But all of this buying and selling *can* contribute to GDP indirectly. How? If a dealer or broker is involved in the transaction, then the dealer or broker is producing a current service: bringing buyer and seller together. The value of this service is part of current GDP.

For example, suppose you bought a secondhand version of this book at your college bookstore for $25. Suppose, too, that before selling the book to you, the store had bought it from another student for $15. Then the purchase of the used textbook will contribute $10 to this year's GDP. Why? Because $10 is the value of the bookstore's services; it's the premium you pay to buy the book in the store, rather than going through the trouble to find the original seller yourself. The remainder of your purchase—$15—represents the value of the used book itself, and is *not* counted in GDP. The textbook was already counted when it was newly produced—in this or a previous year.

. . . for the marketplace . . .

GDP does not include *all* final goods and services produced in the economy. Rather, it includes only the ones produced for the marketplace—that is, with the intention of being *sold*. Because of this restriction, we exclude many important goods and services from our measure. For example, when you clean your own home, you have produced a final service—housecleaning—but it is *not* counted in GDP, because you are doing it for yourself, not for the marketplace. If you *hire* a housecleaner to clean your home, however, the final service is included in GDP; it has become a market transaction.

The same is true for many services produced in the economy. Taking care of your children, washing your car, mowing your lawn, walking your dog—none of these services are included in GDP if you do them for yourself, but all *are* included if you pay someone to do them for you.

. . . during a given year . . .

This part of the definition of GDP is important for several reasons. First, it tells us that GDP is an example of a **flow variable**—a measure of a *process* that takes place over a *period* of time:

FLOW VARIABLE A measure of a process that takes place over a period of time.

Gross domestic product is a flow variable: It measures a process—production—over a period of time.

The value of a flow depends on the length of the period over which we choose to measure it. For example, if you are asked, "What is your *income*?" (another flow variable), your answer will be different depending on whether the question refers to your hourly, weekly, monthly, or yearly income. The same is true of GDP: We can measure it per day, per month, or per year. (For example, on a typical day in 1996, the U.S. produced \$21 billion worth of final goods and services.) In practice, however, the basic period for reporting GDP is a year.

Not all macroeconomic variables are flow variables; some are **stock variables**—measures of things that *exist* at a *moment* in time. The U.S. population, the number of homes in the nation, the current value of your wealth—all these are stock variables, because they are values measured at a particular instant. In this case, we never need to add the phrase per week or per month, since there is no *period* attached to the variable. (For example, it makes no sense to ask "What is your wealth per month?" Instead, we would ask, "What is your wealth *right now*?"

STOCK VARIABLE A measure of an amount that exists at a moment in time.

GDP is measured and reported each *quarter*. But be careful: Quarterly GDP is almost always reported at an *annual rate*. For example, in the first quarter of 1996, we produced \$1,857 billion in final goods and services; but the GDP was reported at the *annual* rate of $4 \times \$1{,}857 = \$7{,}428$ billion. This is what we *would* have produced in 1996 if production had continued at the first quarter's rate for the entire year.

. . . within the nation's borders.

Finally, we come to the last part of the definition: GDP measures output produced *within U.S. borders*—whether or not it was produced by American citizens or residents. This means we include output produced by *foreign-owned* resources (including foreign workers) located in the United States and exclude output produced by Americans located in other countries. For example, when Paul McCartney, a resident of Britain, gives a concert tour in the United States, the value of his services are counted in U.S. GDP and not in British GDP. Similarly, the output pro-

TABLE 1

GDP IN 1996: THE EXPENDITURE APPROACH (BILLIONS OF DOLLARS)

Consumption Purchases		Private-Investment Purchases		Government Purchases		Net Exports	
Services	$2,973	Plant and Equipment	$791	Government Consumption	$1,177	Exports	$847
Nondurable Goods	$1,546	New-Home Construction	$313	Government Investment	$235	Imports	$957
Durable Goods	$634	Changes in Business Inventories	$22				
Consumption =	**$5,153**	**Private Investment =**	**$1,126**	**Government Purchases =**	**$1,412**	**Net Exports =**	**−$110**

$GDP = C + I^a + G + NX$
$= \$5,153 + \$1,126 + \$1,412 + (-\$110)$
$= \$7,581$

Source: Economic Report of the President, 1997 (average of 1996 second and third quarter annual rates).

duced by an American nurse working temporarily in an Ethiopian hospital is part of Ethiopian GDP and not U.S. GDP.

THE EXPENDITURE APPROACH TO GDP

The Commerce Department's Bureau of Economic Analysis (BEA)—the agency responsible for gathering, reporting, and analyzing movements in the nation's output—calculates GDP in several different ways. The most important of these is the *expenditure approach*. Because this method of measuring GDP tells us so much about the structure of our economy, we'll spend the next several pages on it.

In the expenditure approach, we divide output into four categories according to which group in the economy purchases it. The four categories are:

1. *consumption goods and services (C),* purchased by households;
2. *private investment goods and services (I^a),* purchased by businesses;[1]
3. *government goods and services (G),* purchased by government agencies; and
4. *net exports (NX),* purchased by foreigners.[2]

This is an exhaustive list: Every buyer of U.S. output belongs to one of these four sectors. Thus, when we add up the purchases of the four sectors, we must get GDP:

EXPENDITURE APPROACH Measuring GDP by adding the value of goods and services purchased by each type of final user.

In the ***expenditure approach*** *to measuring GDP, we add up the value of the goods and services purchased by each type of final user:*

$$GDP = C + I^a + G + NX.$$

As you can see in Table 1, applying the expenditure approach to GDP in 1996 gives us $GDP = C + I^a + G + NX = \$5,153 + \$1,126 + \$1,412 + (-\$110) = \$7,581$ billion.

1 The reason for the superscript "a" on Investment will be explained shortly.
2 The meaning and importance of the term *net* will become clear shortly.

Now let's take a closer look at each of the four components of GDP.

CONSUMPTION SPENDING. Consumption (C) is both the largest component of GDP—making up about three-quarters of total production in recent years—and the easiest to understand:

Consumption is the part of GDP purchased by households as final users.

CONSUMPTION The part of GDP purchased by households as final users.

Almost everything that households buy during the year—restaurant meals, gasoline, new clothes, doctors' visits, movies, rent, electricity, and more—is included as part of consumption spending when we calculate GDP.

But notice the word *almost*. Some of the things households buy during the year are *not* part of consumption, because they are not part of GDP at all. (Can you identify what they are? [*Hint*: See an earlier "Dangerous Curves" warning.])

There are also some quirky exceptions to the definition of consumption. For example, two things are included even though households do not actually buy them: (1) the total value of all food products that farm families consume for themselves (meat, dairy products, fruit, and vegetables) and (2) the total value of the shelter provided by homes that are owned by the families living in them. The government estimates (and adds to GDP) what farm families *would* pay if they had to buy all of their farm products in the marketplace like everyone else and the rent that homeowners *would* pay for their homes if they were renting from someone else. Another exception is that the construction of new homes—even when households buy them—is not counted as consumption, but rather as private investment.

PRIVATE INVESTMENT SPENDING. What do oil-drilling rigs, cash registers, office telephones, and the house you grew up in all have in common? They are all examples of *capital goods*—goods that will provide useful services in future years. When we sum the value of all of the capital goods in the country, we get our **capital stock.** As the name suggests, this is a *stock* variable—a value that exists at a moment in time.

CAPITAL STOCK The total value of all goods that will provide useful services in future years.

Understanding the concept of capital stock helps us understand and define the concept of investment. A rough definition of **private investment spending** is *capital formation*—the *increase in the nation's capital stock* during the year. Investment, like the other components of GDP, is a *flow* variable—a process (capital formation) that takes place over a period of time.

PRIVATE INVESTMENT SPENDING The sum of business plant and equipment purchases, new home construction, and inventory changes.

More specifically, private investment has three components: (1) business purchases of plant and equipment; (2) changes in business firms' inventory stocks (stocks of unsold goods); and (3) new home construction. Each of these components requires some explanation.

Business Purchases of Plant and Equipment. This category might seem confusing at first glance. Why aren't plant and equipment considered intermediate goods? After all, business firms buy these things in order to produce other things. Doesn't the value of their final goods include the value of their plant and equipment as well?

Actually, no, and if you go back to the definition of intermediate goods, you will see why. Intermediate goods are *used up* with the current year's production. But a firm's plant and equipment is intended to last for many years; only a small part of it is used up to make the current year's final goods. Thus, we regard the firm itself as the final user of any plant and equipment it buys during the year.

For example, suppose our paper mill—the firm that turns wood chips into raw paper—buys a new factory building that is expected to last for 50 years. Then only a small fraction of that factory building—one fiftieth—is used up in any one year's production of raw paper, and only a small part of the factory building's value will be reflected in the value of the firm's current output. But since the factory is produced during the year, we must include its value *somewhere* in our measure of total production. In calculating GDP, we therefore count the factory building as an investment good.

Plant and equipment purchases are always the largest component of private investment. In 1996, businesses purchased and installed $791 billion worth of plant and equipment, which was about two-thirds of total private investment spending that year. (See Table 1.)

New Home Construction. As you can see in Table 1, new home construction made up a significant part of total private investment in 1996. But it may strike you as odd that this category is part of investment spending at all, since most new homes are purchased by households and could reasonably be considered consumption spending instead. Why do the national income accounts treat new home construction as investment spending?

Largely because residential housing is an important part of the nation's *capital stock*. Just as an oil-drilling rig will continue to provide oil-drilling services for many decades, or goods in inventory can be sold in future years, so, too, will a home continue to provide shelter services into the future. If we want our measure of private investment spending to roughly correspond to the increase in the nation's capital stock, we must include this important category of capital formation in investment spending.

Changes in Inventories. Inventories are goods that have been produced, but not yet sold. They include goods on the shelves of stores, goods being shipped or making their way through the production process in factories, and raw materials waiting to be used. Why do we include the changes in firms' inventories as part of GDP? When goods are produced but not sold during the year, they end up in some firm's inventory stocks. If we did *not* count changes in inventories, we would be missing this important part of current production. Remember that GDP is designed to measure total production, not just the part of production that is sold during the year.

To understand this more clearly, suppose that in some year, the automobile industry produced $100 billion worth of automobiles, and that $80 billion was sold to consumers. Then the other $20 billion remained unsold and was added to the auto company's inventories. If we counted consumption spending alone ($80 billion), we would underestimate automobile production in GDP. To ensure a proper measure, we must include not only the $80 billion in cars sold (consumption spending), but also the $20 billion change in inventories (private investment spending). In the end, the contribution to GDP is $80 billion (consumption) + $20 billion (private investment) = $100 billion, which is, indeed, the total value of automobile production during the year.

What if inventory stocks *decline* during the year, so that the change in inventories is negative? Our rule still holds: We include the change in inventories in our measure of GDP—but in this case, we must add a *negative* number. For example, if the automobile industry produced $100 billion worth of cars, but consumers bought $120 billion, then $20 billion worth of cars must have come from inventory stocks—cars that were produced (and counted) in previous years, but that re-

Long-run growth in GDP is also important for another reason: to ensure that the economy generates enough additional jobs for a growing population. In order to prevent the unemployment rate from rising, real GDP must increase by about 2.5 percent each year—the upper horizontal line in the figure. You can see that real GDP growth has, on average, been sufficient for this purpose as well.

To sum up: We use GDP to guide the economy in two ways. In the short run, to alert us to recessions and give us a chance to stabilize the economy. In the long run, to tell us whether our economy is growing fast enough to raise output per capita and our standard of living, and fast enough to generate sufficient jobs for a growing population. You can see that GDP is an extremely useful measure. But it is not without its problems.

PROBLEMS WITH GDP

Our GDP statistics are plagued by some important inaccuracies. One problem is *quality changes.* Suppose a new ballpoint pen comes out that lasts four times as long as previous versions. What *should* happen to GDP? Ideally, each new pen should count the same as four old pens, since one new pen offers the same *writing services* as four old ones. But the analysts at the Bureau of Economic Analysis (BEA) would most likely treat this new pen the same as an old pen and record an increase in GDP only if the total number of pens increased. Why? Because the BEA has a limited budget. While it does include the impact of quality changes for many goods and services (such as automobiles and computers), the BEA simply does not have the resources to estimate quality changes for millions of different goods and services. These include many consumer goods (clearer televisions that need fewer repairs, razor blades that shave closer and last longer, telephones with clearer reception, and services such as call forwarding), medical services (increased surgery success rates and shorter recovery periods), and retail services (the added convenience of 24-hour supermarkets and faster checkout times due to optical scanners). As a result, GDP probably understates true growth from year to year.

A second problem arises from the *underground economy,* which contains hidden economic activity, either because it is illegal (drugs, prostitution, most gambling) or because those engaged in it are avoiding taxes. Since these activities cannot be measured accurately, the BEA does not *directly* include production in the underground economy when it computes GDP. Although the BEA does make indirect adjustments for underground economic activity, many economists believe that these adjustments are insufficient. As a result, GDP may understate total output. However, since the *relative* importance of the underground economy does not change rapidly, the BEA's estimates of *changes* in GDP from year to year should not be seriously affected.

Finally, except for food grown and consumed by farmers and for housing services, GDP does not include **nonmarket production**—goods and services that are produced, but not sold in the marketplace. All of the housecleaning, typing, sewing, lawnmowing, and childraising that people do themselves, without hiring anyone else, are excluded from GDP. Whenever a nonmarket transaction (say, typing your own final paper) becomes a market transaction (hiring a typist to do it for you), GDP will rise, even though total production (typing one paper) has remained the same. This can lead to a distortion of the change in GDP over long periods of time, since—over the last half-century—much production has, indeed, shifted away from the home and community to the market. Parenting, which was not counted in past years' GDP, has become day care, which *does* count, currently contributing more than $4 billion annually to GDP. Similarly, home-cooked food has been replaced

NONMARKET PRODUCTION Goods and services that are produced, but not sold in a market.

by takeout, talking to a friend has been replaced by therapy, and the neighbor who watches your house while you're away has been replaced by a store-bought alarm system or an increase in police protection. In all of these cases, real GDP increases, even though production has not.

What do these problems tell us about the value of GDP? That for certain purposes—especially interpreting *long-run* changes in GDP—we must exercise extreme caution. For example, suppose that, over the next 20 years, the growth rate of GDP slows down. Would this mean that something is going wrong with the economy? Would it suggest a need to change course? Not necessarily. It *could* be that the underground economy or unrecorded quality changes are becoming more important, or that certain activities—like parenting and cooking—are shifting back toward the home and away from the market. Any of these could cause the official GDP growth rate to *understate* the true growth in output.

When it comes to *short-term* changes in the economy, however, we can have much more confidence in using GDP. Look back at our discussion of problems with GDP. The distortions tend to remain roughly constant over the short run. If GDP suddenly drops, it is extremely unlikely that the underground economy has suddenly become more important, or that there has been a sudden shift from market to nonmarket activities, or that we are suddenly missing more quality changes than usual. Rather, we can be reasonably certain that output and economic activity are slowing down.

Short-term changes in real GDP are fairly accurate reflections of the state of the economy. A significant short-term drop in real GDP virtually always indicates a decrease in production, rather than a measurement problem.

This is why policy makers, business people, and the media pay such close attention to GDP as a guide to the economy from quarter to quarter.

EMPLOYMENT AND UNEMPLOYMENT

When you think of unemployment, you may have an image in your mind that goes something like this: As the economy slides into recession, an anxious employee is called into an office and handed a pink slip by a grim-faced manager. "Sorry," the manager says, "I wish there were some other way. . . ." Perhaps, in your mind, the worker spends the next few months checking the classified ads, pounding the pavement, and sending out resumes in a desperate search for work, but—if times are hard—without success. And perhaps, after months of trying, the laid-off worker gives up, spending days at the neighborhood bar, drinking away the shame and frustration, and sinking lower and lower into a vicious cycle of despair and inertia.

For some people, joblessness begins and ends very much like this—a human tragedy, and a needless one. On one side, we have people who want to work and produce something; on the other side is the rest of society, which could certainly use more goods and services. Yet somehow, the system isn't working, and the jobless cannot find work. The result is often hardship for the unemployed and their families, and a loss to society in general.

But this is just one face of unemployment, and there are others. Some instances of unemployment, for example, have little to do with macroeconomic conditions. And frequently, the amount of suffering that goes with a spell of unemployment is much less than in our grim story.

TYPES OF UNEMPLOYMENT

Economists have found it useful to classify unemployment into four different categories, each arising from a different cause and each having different consequences.

FRICTIONAL UNEMPLOYMENT. Frictional unemployment is short-term joblessness experienced by people who are between jobs or who are entering the labor market for the first time or after a long absence. For example, imagine that you have a job, but that you think you'd be happier at some other firm. Since you can't search for a new job while working full time, you may decide to quit your job and begin looking elsewhere. In an ideal frictionless world, every potential employer would immediately know that you were available, and you would immediately know which job you'd prefer most, so you would become reemployed the instant you quit; you would not be unemployed between jobs. Of course, in the real world, it takes time to find a job—time to prepare your resume, to decide where to send it, to wait for responses, and then to investigate job offers so you can make a wise choice. It also takes time for employers to consider your skills and qualifications and to decide whether you are right for their firms. During all that time, you will be unemployed: willing and able to work, but not working.

FRICTIONAL UNEMPLOYMENT Joblessness experienced by people who are between jobs or who are just entering or re-entering the labor market.

There are other examples of this type of unemployment. A parent—most often, a mother—reenters the labor force after several years spent raising her children. A 22-year-old searches for a job after graduating from college. In both of these cases, it may take some time to find a job, and during that time, the job seeker is *frictionally* unemployed.

Because frictional unemployment is, by definition, short term, it causes little hardship to those affected by it. In most cases, people have enough savings to support themselves through a short spell of joblessness, or else they can borrow on their credit card or from friends or family to tide them over. Moreover, this kind of unemployment has important benefits: By spending time searching—rather than jumping at the first opening that comes their way—people find jobs for which they are better suited and in which they will ultimately be more productive. As a result, workers earn higher incomes, firms have more productive employees, and society has more goods and services.

SEASONAL UNEMPLOYMENT. Seasonal unemployment is joblessness related to changes in weather, tourist patterns, or other seasonal factors. For example, most ski instructors lose their jobs in April or May, and many construction workers are laid off each winter.

SEASONAL UNEMPLOYMENT Joblessness related to changes in weather, tourist patterns, or other seasonal factors.

Seasonal unemployment, like frictional unemployment, is rather benign: It is short term, and, because it is entirely predictable, workers are often compensated in advance for the unemployment they experience in the off-season. Construction workers, for example, are paid higher-than-average hourly wages, in part to compensate them for their high probability of joblessness in the winter.

Seasonal unemployment complicates the interpretation of unemployment data. Seasonal factors push the unemployment rate up in certain months of the year and pull it down in others, even when overall conditions in the economy remain unchanged. For example, each June, unemployment rises as millions of high school and college students—who do not want to work during the school year—begin looking for summer jobs. If the government reported the actual rise in unemployment in June, it would *seem* as if labor market conditions were deteriorating, when in fact, the rise is just a predictable and temporary seasonal change. To prevent any misunderstandings, the government usually reports the *seasonally adjusted* rate of unemployment, a rate that reflects only those changes beyond normal for the month. For example, if the unemployment rate in June is typically one percentage point higher than during the rest of the year, then the seasonally adjusted rate for June will be the actual rate minus one percentage point.

STRUCTURAL UNEMPLOYMENT. Sometimes, there are jobs available and workers who would be delighted to have them, but job seekers and employers are *mismatched* in some way. For example, in the 1990s, there have been plenty of job openings in high-tech industries such as computer hardware and software design, satellite technology, and communications. Many of the unemployed, however, do not have the skills and training to work in these industries—there is a mismatch between the skills they have and those that are needed. The mismatch can also be geographic, as when construction jobs go begging in Northern California, Oregon, and Washington, but unemployed construction workers live in other states.

STRUCTURAL UNEMPLOYMENT Joblessness arising from mismatches between workers' skills and employers' requirements or between workers' locations and employers' locations.

Unemployment that results from these kinds of mismatches is called **structural unemployment,** because it arises from *structural change* in the economy: when old, dying industries are replaced with new ones that require different skills and are located in different areas of the country. Structural unemployment is generally a stubborn, *long-term* problem, often lasting several years or more. Why? Because it can take considerable time for the structurally unemployed to find jobs—time to relocate in another part of the country or time to acquire new skills. The problem is exacerbated when workers need financial assistance for job training or relocation, but—because they are unemployed—are unable to get loans.

Structural unemployment is a much bigger problem in other countries, especially in Europe, than it is in the United States. In early 1997, when the U.S. unemployment rate was 5.0 percent, the rate in France was 12.8 percent, in Italy 12.8 percent, and in Spain 21.7 percent. All three countries have large groups of lower skilled workers who are unqualified for the jobs that are available. Even Canada suffers from much more structural unemployment than does the United States—its unemployment rate in early 1997 was 9.5 percent, much of it concentrated in the maritime provinces.

The types of unemployment we've considered so far—frictional, structural, and seasonal—arise from *microeconomic* causes; that is, they are attributable to changes in specific industries and specific labor markets, rather than to conditions in the overall economy. There will always be some unemployment of these types—some people will always be spending time searching for new jobs, there will always be seasonal industries in the economy, and structural changes will, from time to time, require workers to move to new locations or gain new job skills. Some amount of microeconomic employment is a sign of a dynamic economy. It allows workers to sort themselves into the best possible jobs, enables us to enjoy seasonal goods and services like winter skiing and summers at the beach, and permits the economy to go through structural changes when needed.

Nevertheless, many economists feel that the levels of microeconomic unemployment in the United States are too high and that we can continue to enjoy the benefits of a fast-changing and flexible economy with a lower unemployment rate. To achieve this goal, they advocate government programs to help match the unemployed with employers and to help the jobless relocate and learn new skills. Note, however, that these are *microeconomic* policies—government intervention in par-

U.S. QUARTERLY UNEMPLOYMENT RATE, 1960–1996

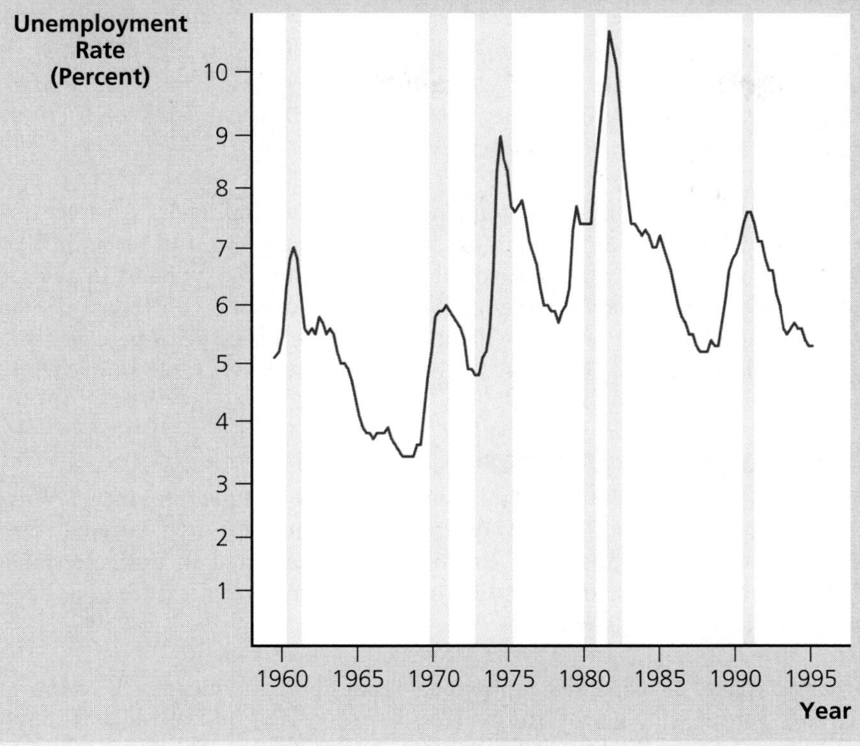

FIGURE 3

The unemployment rate rises during recessions (shaded) and falls during expansions.

ticular labor markets or to help particular kinds of workers. This makes good sense: Since frictional, seasonal, and structural unemployment have microeconomic causes, we cannot solve them with macroeconomic policy.

Our fourth and last type of unemployment, however, has an entirely *macro*economic cause.

CYCLICAL UNEMPLOYMENT. When the economy goes into a recession and total output falls, the unemployment rate rises: Many previously employed workers lose their jobs and have difficulty finding new ones, and—with fewer openings—new entrants to the labor force must spend more time searching before they are hired. This type of unemployment—because it is caused by the business cycle—is called **cyclical unemployment.**

CYCLICAL UNEMPLOYMENT Joblessness arising from changes in production over the business cycle.

Look at Figure 3, which shows the unemployment rate in the United States for each quarter since 1960, and notice the rises that occurred during periods of recession (shaded). For example, in the recessions of the early 1980s, the unemployment rate rose from about 6 percent to more than 10 percent; in the more recent recession of 1990–1991, it rose from 5.7 percent to almost 7 percent. These were rises in cyclical unemployment.

Since it arises from conditions in the overall economy, cyclical unemployment is a problem for *macro*economic policy. This is why, when we study macroeconomics, we are almost exclusively concerned with cyclical unemployment. Reflecting this emphasis, macroeconomists say we have reached **full employment** when we come out of a recession and *cyclical unemployment is reduced to zero,* even

FULL EMPLOYMENT A situation in which there is no cyclical unemployment.

though substantial amounts of frictional, seasonal, and structural unemployment may remain:

> *In macroeconomics, full employment is achieved when* cyclical *unemployment has been reduced to zero. But the overall unemployment rate at full employment is greater than zero, because there are still positive levels of frictional, seasonal, and structural unemployment.*

How do we tell how much of our unemployment is cyclical? Most economists believe that today, normal amounts of frictional, seasonal, and structural unemployment account for an unemployment rate of about 5.5 percent in the United States. Therefore, any unemployment beyond this is considered cyclical unemployment. For example, if the unemployment rate rises from, say, 5.5 percent to 7 percent, we would identify $7 - 5.5 = 1.5$ percent of the labor force as cyclically unemployed.

THE COSTS OF UNEMPLOYMENT

Why are we so concerned about achieving a low rate of unemployment? What are the *costs* of unemployment to our society? We can identify two different types of costs: economic costs—those that can be readily measured in dollar terms—and noneconomic costs—those that are difficult or impossible to measure in dollars, but still affect us in important ways.

Economic Costs. The chief economic cost of unemployment is the *opportunity cost* of lost output—the goods and services the jobless *would* produce if they were working, but do not produce because they cannot find work. This cost must be paid by society, although the burden of paying it may fall mostly on one group or another. If, for example, the unemployed were simply left to fend for themselves, then *they* would bear most of the cost. If they turned to crime in order to survive, then crime victims would share the burden. In fact, the unemployed are often given government assistance, so that the costs are spread among citizens in general. But there is no escaping this central fact:

Opportunity Cost

> *When there is cyclical unemployment, the nation* produces *less output, and so some group or groups within society must* consume *less output.*

There are, of course, benefits to unemployment, which must be compared with these costs. First, there is the value of additional leisure time for the unemployed, which—even though the jobless may prefer to work and earn income—is not zero.

Second, as we've seen, certain types of unemployment provide benefits for society as a whole. Frictional unemployment contributes to better matches between workers and jobs; in the long run, this can result in *higher* output. Structural unemployment is the by-product of a flexible economy that responds to changing consumer desires and technological progress; this, too, can mean greater output in the long run.

But cyclical unemployment is a different story: The economic costs are substantial, and there are no significant benefits to society as a whole.[6] One way of

6 Some would argue that cyclical unemployment *does* benefit the economy, by reducing the rate of inflation. (We'll see how this happens in later chapters.) But since high inflation is most often the result of an earlier error in macroeconomic policy, a better way to achieve low inflation is to prevent the high inflation in the first place.

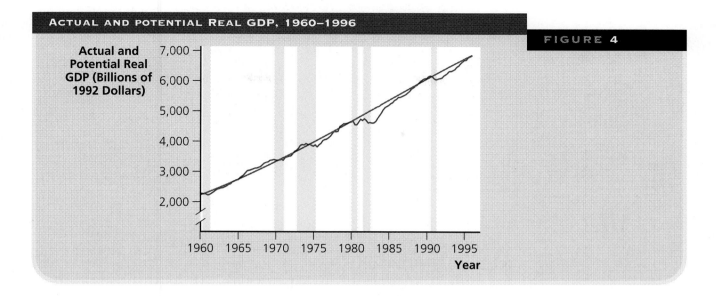

ACTUAL AND POTENTIAL REAL GDP, 1960–1996

FIGURE 4

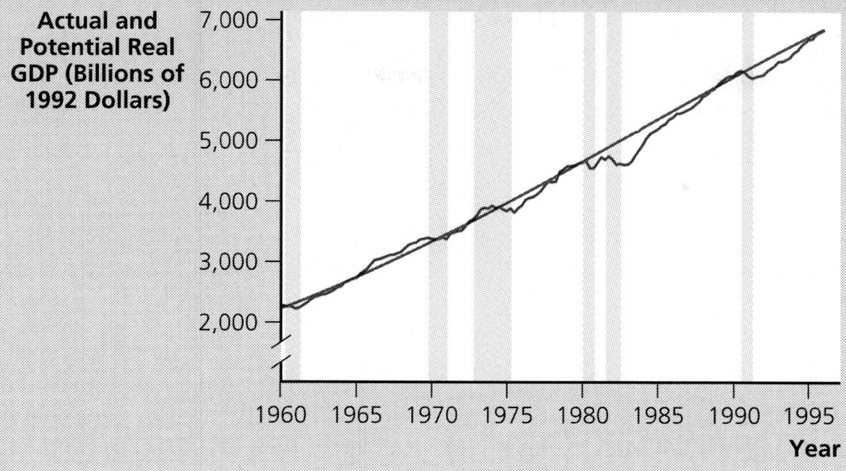

viewing the cost of cyclical unemployment is illustrated in Figure 4. The blue line shows real GDP over time, while the red line shows the path of our **potential output**—the output we *could* have produced if the economy were operating at full employment. (Remember that full employment means zero cyclical, and normal amounts of frictional, seasonal, and structural unemployment.)

POTENTIAL OUTPUT The level of output the economy could produce if operating at full employment.

Notice that actual output is sometimes *above* potential output. At these times, unemployment is *below* the full-employment rate. For example, during the expansion in the late 1960s, cyclical unemployment was eliminated, and the sum of frictional, seasonal, and structural unemployment dropped below 4.5 percent, its normal level for those years. At other times, real GDP is *below* potential output, most often during and immediately following a recession. At these times, unemployment rises above the full-employment rate. In the 1982–83 recession, the average unemployment rate exceeded 9.5 percent.

In the figure, you can see that we have spent more of the last 35 years operating *below* our potential than above it. That is, the cyclical ups and downs of the economy have, on balance, led to lower living standards than we would have had if the economy had always operated just at potential output.

BROADER COSTS. There are also costs of unemployment that go beyond lost output—the *human* costs that we do not measure in dollars, but are significant nonetheless. Unemployment—especially when it lasts for many months or years—can have serious psychological and physical effects. Some studies have found that increases in unemployment cause noticeable rises in the number of heart attack deaths, suicides, and admissions to state prisons and psychiatric hosptals. The jobless are more likely to suffer a variety of health problems, including high blood pressure, heart disorders, troubled sleep, and back pain. There may be other problems—such as domestic violence, depression, and alcoholism—that are more difficult to document. And, tragically, most of those who lose their jobs also lose their health insurance, increasing the likelihood that these problems will have serious consequences.

TABLE 3

UNEMPLOYMENT RATES FOR VARIOUS GROUPS DECEMBER, 1996

Group	Rate
Whites	4.6%
Hispanics	7.7%
Blacks	10.5%
White Teenagers	13.7%
Black Teenagers	34.7%

Source: *The Employment Situation: December 1996,* Bureau of Labor Statistics News Release, January 10, 1997.

Unemployment also causes setbacks in achieving important social goals. For example, most of us want a fair and just society where all have an equal chance to better themselves. But our citizens do not bear the burden of unemployment equally. In a recession, we do not reduce everyone's work hours by some fraction; instead, some people are laid off entirely, while others continue to work roughly the same hours.

Moreover, the burden of unemployment is not shared equally among different groups in the population, but tends to fall most heavily on minorities, especially minority youth. As a rough rule of thumb, the unemployment rate for blacks is twice that for whites; and the rate for *teenage* blacks is triple the rate for blacks overall. Table 3 shows that the unemployment rates for December 1996 are consistent with this general experience. Notice the extremely high unemployment rate for black teenagers: 34.7%. This contributes to a vicious cycle of poverty and discrimination: When minority youths are deprived of that all-important first job, they remain at a disadvantage in the labor market for years to come.

HOW UNEMPLOYMENT IS MEASURED

In December 1996, the official U.S. unemployment rate was 5.3 percent. Where did this number come from?

Let's start by noting that about 140 million Americans did not have jobs at the time. Were all of these people unemployed? Absolutely not. The unemployed are those *willing and able* to work, but who do not have jobs. Most of the 140 million nonworking Americans were either *un*able or *un*willing to work. For example, the very old, the very young, and the very ill were unable to work, as were those serving prison terms. Others were able to work, but preferred not to, including millions of college students, homemakers, and retired people.

But how, in practice, can we determine who is willing and able? This is a thorny problem, and there is no perfect solution to it. In the United States, we determine whether a person is willing and able to work by his or her *behavior*. More specifically, to be counted as unemployed, you must have recently *searched* for work. But how can we tell who has, and who has not, recently searched for work?

THE CENSUS BUREAU'S HOUSEHOLD SURVEY. Every month, thousands of interviewers from the United States Census Bureau—acting on behalf of the U.S. Bureau of Labor Statistics (BLS)—knock on the doors of 65,000 households across America. This sample of households is carefully selected to give information about the entire population.

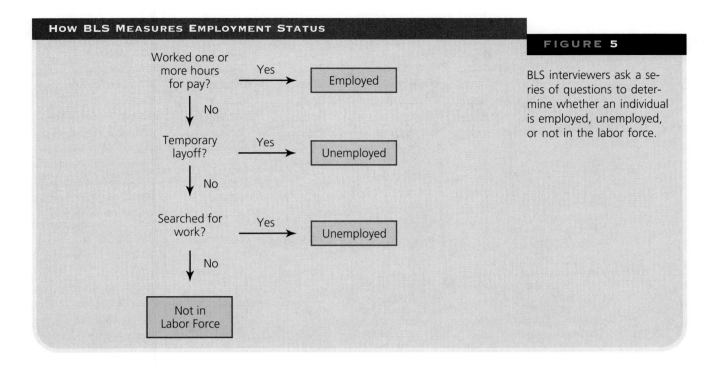

HOW BLS MEASURES EMPLOYMENT STATUS

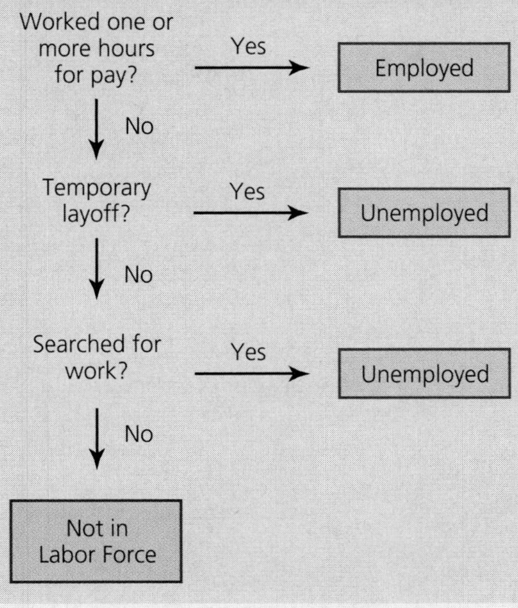

FIGURE 5

BLS interviewers ask a series of questions to determine whether an individual is employed, unemployed, or not in the labor force.

Household members who are under 16, in the military, or currently residing in an institution like a prison or hospital are excluded. The interviewer will then ask questions to determine what the remaining household members did during the *previous week*.

Figure 5 shows roughly how this works. First, the interviewer asks whether the household member has worked one or more hours for pay or profit. If the answer is yes, the person is considered employed; if no, another question is asked: Has she been *temporarily* laid off from a job from which she is waiting to be recalled? A yes means the person is unemployed; a no leads to one more question: Did the person *search* for work actively during the previous four weeks. If yes, the person is unemployed; if no, she is not in the labor force.

Figure 6 illustrates how the BLS, extrapolating from its 65,000-household sample, classified the U.S. population in December 1996. First, note that 65 million people were ruled out from consideration because they were under 16 years of age, living in institutions, or in the military. The remaining 201.6 million people made up the civilian, noninstitutional population, and of these, 127.8 million were employed, and 7.2 million were unemployed. Adding the employed and unemployed together gives us the **labor force,** equal to 127.8 million + 7.2 million = 135.0 million.

LABOR FORCE Those people who have a job or who are looking for one.

Finally, we come to the official **unemployment rate,** which is defined as the percentage of the labor force that is unemployed:

UNEMPLOYMENT RATE The fraction of the labor force that is without a job.

$$\begin{aligned}\text{Unemployment rate} &= \text{Unemployed/Labor Force}\\ &= \text{Unemployed/(Unemployed + Employed)}\end{aligned}$$

Using the numbers in Figure 6, the unemployment rate in December 1996 was 7.2/(7.2 + 127.8) = 0.053, or 5.3 percent. This was the number released to jour-

FIGURE 6

EMPLOYMENT STATUS OF THE U.S. POPULATION, (DECEMBER 1996)

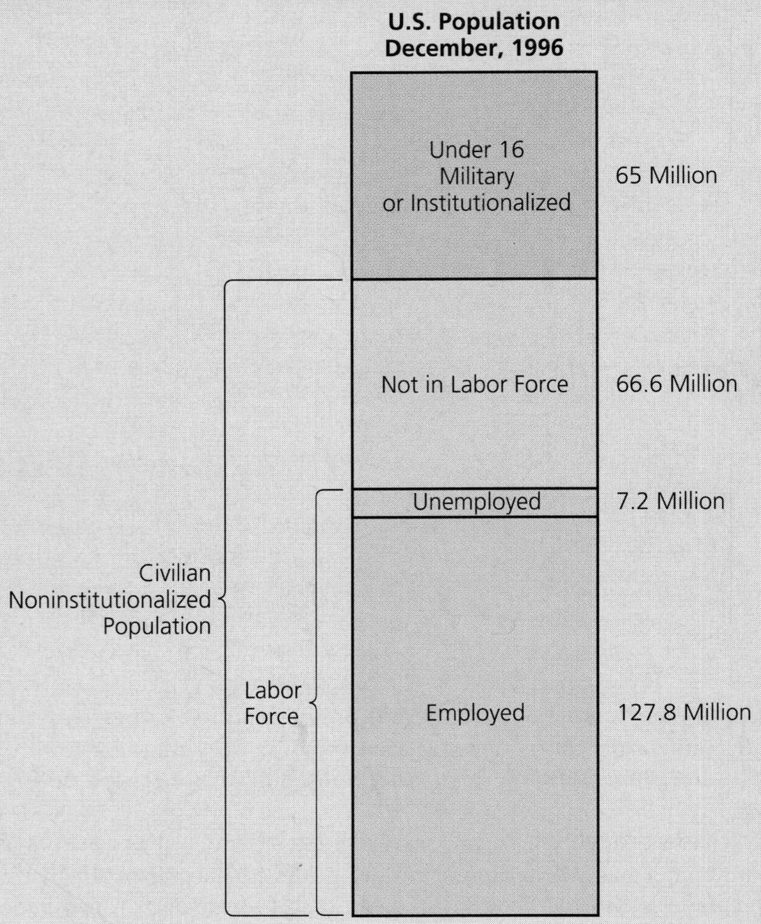

nalists at 8:00 A.M. on the first Friday of January 1997, and the number that appeared in the headlines of your local newspaper the next day.

PROBLEMS IN MEASURING UNEMPLOYMENT

The Bureau of the Census earns very high marks from economists for both its sample size—65,000 households—and the characteristics of its sample, which very closely match the characteristics of the U.S. population. Still, the official unemployment rate suffers from some important measurement problems.

Many economists believe that our official measure seriously underestimates the extent of unemployment in our society. There are two reasons for this belief: the treatment of *involuntary part-time workers,* and the treatment of *discouraged workers.* As you can see in Figure 5, anyone working one hour or more for pay during the survey week is treated as employed. This includes many people who would like a full-time job—who may even be actively searching for one—but who did some part-time work during the week. Some economists have suggested that these people—called **involuntary part-time workers**—should be regarded as partially employed and partially unemployed.

INVOLUNTARY PART-TIME WORKERS Individuals who would like a full-time job, but who are working only part time.

How many involuntary part-time workers are there? At the end of 1996, the BLS estimated that there were about 4.3 million.[7] If each of these workers were considered half employed and half unemployed, the unemployment rate at the end of 1996 would have been 6.9 percent, instead of the officially reported 5.3 percent.

DISCOURAGED WORKERS Individuals who would like a job, but have given up searching for one.

Another problem is the treatment of **discouraged workers**—individuals who would like to work but, because they feel little hope of finding a job, have given up searching. Because they are not actually taking active steps to find work, they are counted as not in the labor force. (See Figures 5 and 6.) Some observers feel that all discouraged workers should be included among the unemployed. After all, these people are telling us that they are willing and able to work, but they are not working; it seems wrong to exclude them just because they are not actively seeking work. Others argue that counting discouraged workers as unemployed would reduce the objectivity of our unemployment measure. Talk is cheap, they believe, and people may *say* anything when asked whether they would like a job; the real test is what people *do*. Yet even the staunchest defenders of the current method of measuring employment would agree that *some* discouraged workers are, in fact, willing and able to work and should be considered unemployed. The problem, in their view, is determining which ones.

How many discouraged workers are there? No one knows for sure. The BLS tries to count them periodically, but defining who is genuinely discouraged is a thorny problem. Still, using the BLS's rather strict criteria, there were about 334,000 discouraged workers at the end of 1996. With more relaxed definitions of discouragement, the number rises to almost 1 million. Counting some or all of these people as unemployed could raise the unemployment rate significantly.

There are also reasons to believe that the unemployment rate overstates the amount of joblessness as we usually think of it. Remember that a person is counted as unemployed if he or she did not work in the past week, but took some active steps to look for work in the past month. A fair number of the unemployed did work earlier in the month, even though they were not at work in the survey week. Many people whose principal activities are outside the labor market—going to school, keeping house, or being retired—are counted as unemployed because they checked the help-wanted ads in the past month or talked to friends about what jobs might be available.

Still, the unemployment rate—as currently measured—tells us something important: the number of people who are *searching* for jobs, but have not yet found them. It is not exactly the same as the percentage of the labor force that is jobless even though willing and able to work. But if we could obtain a perfect measure of the latter, the unemployment rate—as currently measured—would be highly correlated with it.

Moreover, the unemployment rate tells us something unique about conditions in the macroeconomy. When the unemployment rate is relatively low—so that few people are actively seeking work—a firm that wants to increase its employment may be forced to hire its workers from other firms, by offering a higher wage rate. This will tend to put upward pressure on wages and can lead to future inflation. A high unemployment rate, by contrast, tells us that firms can more easily expand by hiring those who are actively seeking work, without having to lure new workers from another firm and without having to offer higher wages. This suggests little inflationary danger. A bit later in the book, we will discuss the connection between unemployment and inflation more fully.

---

7 This and other information about unemployment in December 1996 comes from *The Employment Situation: December 1996*, Bureau of Labor Statistics News Release, January 10, 1997.

USING THE THEORY

SOCIETY'S CHOICE OF GDP

The title of this section might seem absurd: How can we say that society chooses its level of GDP? Wouldn't the citizens of any nation want their GDP to be as large as possible—and certainly larger than it currently is? The answer is yes. After all, GDP is certainly important to our economic well-being. Few of us would want to live at the levels of output per capita that prevailed 100, 50, or even 25 years ago. Increased output of medical care, restaurant meals, entertainment, transportation services, and education have all contributed to a higher standard of living and an overall improvement in our economic well-being.

But there is more to economic well-being than *just* GDP. Suppose that, over the next 10 years, real GDP per capita were to double. Further, suppose that our measure is entirely accurate (not plagued by the measurement problems discussed in the previous section). Would the average person be twice as well off in 10 years? Maybe. But maybe not. We cannot say, because our GDP statistic ignores so many *other* things that are important to our economic well-being besides the quantity of goods and services at our disposal, and these things may be changing at the same time that GDP is changing.

What are these other things that affect our economic well-being? They include the leisure time we have to spend with family and friends; the cleanliness of our environment; the safety of our workplaces, homes, and streets; the fairness of our society; and more. None of these are included in GDP, which is, after all, just a measure of our output of goods and services.

But what does this have to do with society's choice of GDP? Remember that economics is the study of choice under conditions of scarcity, and just as individuals are constrained by a scarcity of time or income or wealth, society as a whole is constrained by the resources at its disposal. In many cases, we must choose between using our resources to have more of the output that is included in GDP or more of those other things that we care about.

For example, look at Figure 7, which shows the familiar production possibility frontier, or PPF, from Chapter 2, but with a new twist. Instead of looking at the tradeoff between two different *goods*—such as movies and medical care—we explore the tradeoff between real GDP on the horizontal axis and some other thing that we care about—in this example, leisure time—on the vertical axis.

Why is there a tradeoff between real GDP and leisure? Because with a given state of technology for producing output, a given population, and given quantities of other resources, the more labor time we devote to production, the more goods and services we will have. But more labor time means less leisure time: Either more people must become employed, or the employed must work longer hours. In either case, the total amount of leisure time enjoyed by the population will decrease.

Let's first identify the two extremes of the PPF in the figure. The maximum leisure time achievable would occur at point *A*—zero output. Here, people would have to survive by eating fruit and nuts that fell to the ground—even climbing trees or hunting animals would involve "work." On the other hand, the maximum GDP achievable would require the lowest possible level of leisure—every able-bodied person working 16 hours per day, 365 days per year. This is indicated by point *D* in the figure. The curve which connects points *A* and *D* is the PPF that shows the maximum combinations of output and leisure achievable. (Why does the curve bow out from the origin? Review the material on PPFs in Chapter 2 if you need to.)

THE TRADEOFF BETWEEN REAL GDP AND LEISURE

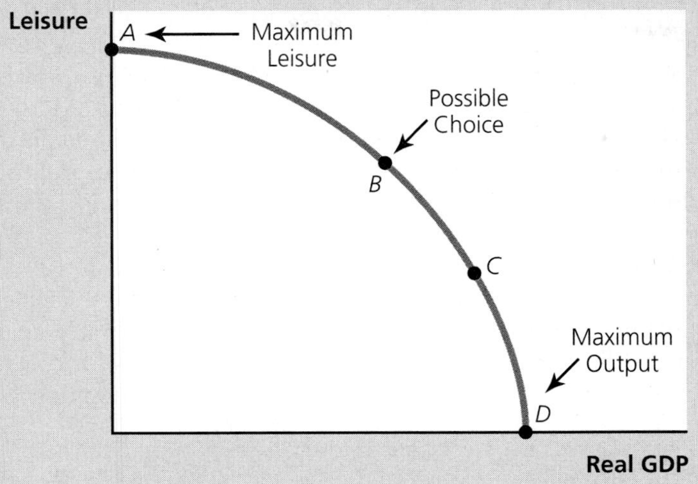

FIGURE 7

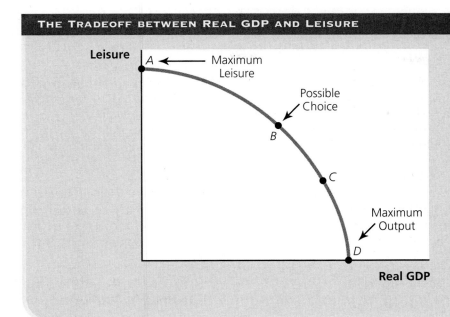

The production possibilities frontier shows that, for a given population and state of technology, a fully employed economy must choose between the level of real GDP and the time available for leisure. At point *A*, people devote all their time to leisure, so GDP is zero. Point *D*, by contrast, represents the maximum GDP attainable if everyone works the maximum hours, year-round. *B* and *C* represent intermediate possibilities.

The PPF in the figure makes it clear that society faces a tradeoff and that, in any year, we choose our level of GDP subject to the constraints of this tradeoff. We could draw a similar PPF illustrating the tradeoff between a high GDP on the one hand and a clean environment or workplace safety on the other.

How does society choose its location on this kind of PPF?

In a market economy, the choice is made partly by individual households and firms. Suppose that most workers' tastes began to shift toward having more leisure and that they were willing to sacrifice income in order to have it. For example, workers might prefer a 20-percent cut in work hours, with a 20-percent cut in total compensation. Suppose, too, that there were no loss of efficiency from having people work shorter hours. Then any firm that refused to match these new worker preferences—cutting pay and work hours by 20 percent—would have to pay a wage premium in order to attract workers and would have to charge a higher price for its output to cover its higher labor costs. Such a firm would not be able to compete with other firms that were offering jobs with the shorter workweek. As firms in general began moving toward a shorter workweek, society as a whole would be moving from a point like *C* in Figure 7 to a point like *B*—more leisure and a lower GDP.

Thus, at least to some extent, we can expect market pressures to adjust work hours to worker preferences for leisure on the one hand and income on the other. The result of these individual decisions will determine, in large measure, where we will be on the PPF in Figure 7.

Interestingly, the United States is farther down and to the right on this PPF (a point like *C*) than most European countries (which are at points like *B*). For example, the average workweek in manufacturing is 37.7 hours in the United States, but only 30 hours in Germany. In addition, the typical U.S. worker takes two weeks of vacation each year, while the typical German worker takes five weeks. To a great extent, these differences in labor hours reflect differences in worker tastes. For example, when Germany introduced Thursday night shopping in 1989, retail workers—who didn't want to work the additional two hours even for additional pay—

went on strike. As a result of his greater taste for leisure, the typical German—and the typical French person, Italian, and Spaniard—enjoys more leisure each year than the typical American does—and pays the cost of having a lower GDP than he would otherwise have.

But our location on the PPF is also determined by society as a whole, as a matter of public policy. We vote for our representatives, who make rules and regulations under which our firms must operate. If, for example, the majority prefers a higher GDP and less leisure, it can vote for representatives who promise to change work rules. In Germany, for example, it is *illegal* for workers to take another job during their five-weeks of annual vacation.[8]

There are also other dimensions to our choice of GDP, which will become clear in later chapters. For example, a nation can enjoy a greater GDP in the future *and* more of other things—say, workplace safety or leisure—but once again, only by paying a cost. In this case (as you will see in a few chapters), the cost of having more of what we value in the future is the sacrifice of consumption goods in the present.

8 Benjamin, Daniel and Tony Horwitz, "German View: You Americans Work Too Hard—And For What?" *The Wall Street Journal,* July 14, 1994, p. B1.

SUMMARY

This chapter discusses how some key macroeconomic aggregates are measured and reported. One important economic aggregate is *gross domestic product*—the total value of all final goods and services produced for the marketplace during a given year, within a nation's borders. GDP is a measure of an economy's total production. It is a flow variable that measures sales, to final users, of newly produced output. In the *expenditure approach,* GDP is calculated as the sum of spending by households, businesses, governments, and foreigners on domestically produced goods and services. The *value-added approach* computes GDP by adding up each firm's contributions to total product as it is being produced. Value added at each stage of production is the revenue a firm receives minus the cost of the intermediate inputs it uses. Finally, the *factor payments approach* sums the payments to all resource owners. The three approaches reflect three different ways of viewing GDP.

Since nominal GDP is measured in current dollars, it changes when either production or prices change. *Real GDP* is nominal GDP adjusted for price changes; it rises only when production rises.

Real GDP is useful in the short run for giving warnings about impending recessions, and in the long run for indicating how fast the economy is growing. Unfortunately, it is plagued by important inaccuracies. It does not fully reflect quality changes or production in the underground economy, and it does not include many types of nonmarket production.

When real GDP grows, employment tends to rise and unemployment tends to fall. In the United States, a person is considered unemployed if he or she does not have a job but wants to have one. Economists have found it useful to classify unemployment into four different categories. *Frictional unemployment* is short-term unemployment experienced by people between jobs or by those who are just entering the job market. *Seasonal unemployment* is related to changes in the weather, tourist patterns, or other predictable seasonal changes. *Structural unemployment* results from mismatches—in skills or location—between jobs and workers. Finally, *cyclical unemployment* occurs because of the business cycle. Unemployment, particularly the structural and cyclical forms, involves costs. From a social perspective, unemployment means lost production. From the individual viewpoint, unemployment often involves financial, psychological, and physical harm.

KEY TERMS

gross domestic product (GDP)
intermediate goods
final good
flow variable
stock variable
expenditure approach
consumption
capital stock
private-investment spending
net investment spending
government purchases
net exports
value added
value-added approach
factor payments

factor payments approach	frictional unemployment	full employment	involuntary part-time workers
nominal variable	seasonal unemployment	potential output	discouraged workers
real variable	structural unemployment	labor force	
nonmarket production	cyclical unemployment	unemployment rate	

REVIEW QUESTIONS

1. What is the difference between final goods and intermediate goods? Why is it that only the value of final goods and services is counted in GDP?

2. Which of the following are stock variables, and which are flow variables?
   a. Microsoft's revenues
   b. Microsoft's market value
   c. A household's spending
   d. The value of a stock portfolio

3. Which of the following would be directly counted as part of 1998 U.S. GDP using the expenditure approach? For each item counted, state whether it is *I, C, G,* or *NX*.
   a. A new personal computer produced by IBM, which remained unsold at the year's end
   b. A physician's services
   c. Produce bought by a restaurant to serve to customers
   d. The purchase of 1,000 shares of Disney stock
   e. The sale of 50 acres of commercial property
   f. The real estate agent's commission from the sale of property
   g. A transaction in which you type your roommate's term paper in exchange for his working on your car
   h. Salaries paid to workers at a General Motors plant in Michigan
   i. The government's Social Security payments to retired people

4. How is the word "investment" used differently in economics than in ordinary language? Explain each of the three categories of investment.

5. Describe the different kinds of factor payments.

6. What is the difference between nominal and real variables? What is the main problem with using nominal variables?

7. Discuss the value and reliability of GDP statistics in both short-run and long-run analyses of the economy.

8. GDP was measured at around $7.2 trillion in 1995. Was the actual value of goods and services produced in the United States in 1995 likely to have been higher or lower than that? Why?

9. In later chapters, you will learn about policies the government can pursue to reduce cyclical unemployment. What, if anything, could the government do to reduce frictional and structural unemployment?

10. Categorize each of the following according to the type of unemployment it reflects. Justify your answers.
    a. Workers are laid off when a GM factory closes due to a recession.
    b. Workers making typewriters are laid off when their firm goes bankrupt due to competition from personal computers.
    c. Migrant farm workers' jobs end when the harvest is finished.
    d. Lost jobs resulted from the movement of textile plants from Massachusetts to the South and overseas.

11. In what sense can unemployment sometimes be considered a constructive aspect of economic life?

12. What are some of the different types of costs associated with unemployment?

13. Discuss some of the problems with the way the Bureau of Labor Statistics computes the unemployment rate. In what ways might official criteria lead to an overestimate or underestimate of the actual unemployment figure?

PROBLEMS AND EXERCISES

1. Calculate the total change in a year's GDP for each of the following scenarios:
   a. A family sells a home, without using a broker, for $150,000. They could have rented it on the open market for $700 per month. They buy a 10-year-old condominium for $200,000; the broker's fee on the transaction is 6 percent of the selling price. The condo's owner was formerly renting the unit at $500 per month.
   b. General Electric uses $10 million worth of steel, glass, and plastic to produce its dishwashers. Wages and salaries in the dishwasher division are $40 million; the

division's only other expense is $15 million in interest that it pays on its bonds. The division's revenue for the year is $75 million.

c. On March 31, you decide to stop throwing away $50 a month on convenience store nachos. You buy $200 worth of equipment, corn meal, and cheese, and make your own nachos for the rest of the year.

d. You win $25,000 in your state's lottery. Ever the entrepreneur, you decide to open a Ping Pong ball washing service, buying $15,000 worth of equipment from SpiffyBall Ltd. of Hong Kong and $10,000 from Ball-B-Kleen of Toledo, Ohio.

e. Tone-Deaf Artists, Inc. produces 100,000 new White Snake CDs that it prices at $15 apiece. Ten thousand CDs are sold abroad, but, alas, the rest remain unsold on warehouse shelves.

2. The country of Freedonia uses the same method to calculate the unemployment rate as the U.S. Bureau of Labor Statistics uses. From the data below, compute Freedonia's unemployment rate.

Population	10,000,000
Under 16	3,000,000
Over 16	
In military service	500,000
In hospitals	200,000
In prison	100,000
Worked one hour or more in previous week	4,000,000
Searched for work during previous four weeks	1,000,000

CHALLENGE QUESTION

Look back at Figure 7. Consider similar tradeoffs between GDP and some other aspects of our quality of life—environmental quality and leisure. Draw the relevant PPFs and identify a point on each indicating where you believe the United States to be located now. Then indicate a point on each PPF showing where you think the country *ought* to be in the best of all possible worlds. Discuss your choice of points, and offer evidence from your own reading and research to support your arguments.

WWW

Review the information on the Bureau of Economic Analysis' national programs (http://www.bea.doc.gov/bea/data-n2.htm). Locate the most recent summary estimates for the income and product accounts. Using this information, answer the following questions:

Has GDP been increasing or decreasing lately? For how long? What was the rate of growth for the most recent quarter? Does the growth rate appear to be increasing or decreasing lately?

CHAPTER

6

THE MONETARY SYSTEM, PRICES, AND INFLATION

You pull into a gas station deep in the interior of the distant nation of Chaotica. The numbers on the gas pump don't make sense to you, and you can't figure out how much to pay. Luckily, the national language of Chaotica is English, so you can ask the cashier how much the gas costs. He replies, "Here in Chaotica, we don't have any standard system for measuring quantities of gas, and we don't have any standard way to quote prices. My pump here measures in my own unit, called the Slurp, and I will sell you 6 Slurps for that watch you are wearing, or a dozen Slurps for your camera." You spend the next half hour trying to determine how many Slurps there are in a gallon and what form of payment you can use besides your watch and camera.

Life in the imaginary nation of Chaotica would be difficult. People would spend a lot of time figuring out how to trade with each other, time that could otherwise be spent producing things or enjoying leisure activities. Luckily, in the real world, virtually every nation has a *monetary system* that helps to organize and simplify our economic transactions.

THE MONETARY SYSTEM

A monetary system establishes two different types of standardization in the economy. First, it establishes a **unit of value**—a common unit for measuring how much something is worth. A standard unit of value permits us to compare the costs of different goods and services and to communicate these costs when we trade. The dollar is the unit of value in the United States. If a college textbook costs $75, while a one-way flight from Phoenix to Minneapolis costs $300, we know immediately that the ticket costs the same as (is worth) four college textbooks.

The second type of standardization concerns the **means of payment**—the things we can use as payment when we buy goods and services. In the United States, the

UNIT OF VALUE A common unit for measuring how much something is worth.

MEANS OF PAYMENT Anything acceptable as payment for goods and services.

means of payment include dollar bills, personal checks, travelers' checks, credit cards like Visa and American Express, and, in some experimental locations, prepaid cash cards with magnetic strips.

These two functions of a monetary system—establishing a unit of value and a standard means of payment—are closely related, but they are not the same thing. The unit-of-value function refers to the way we *think* about and record transactions; the means-of-payment function refers to how payment is actually made.

The unit of value works in the same way as units of weight, volume, distance, and time. In fact, the same sentence in Article I of the U.S. Constitution gives Congress the power to create a unit of value along with units of weights and measures. All of these units help us determine clearly and precisely what is being traded for what. Think about buying gas in the United States—you exchange dollars for gallons. The transaction will go smoothly and quickly only if there is clarity about both the unit of fluid volume (gallons) *and* the unit of purchasing power (dollars).

The means of payment can be different from the unit of value. For example, in some countries where local currency prices change very rapidly, it is common to use the U.S. dollar as the unit of value—to specify prices in dollars—while the local currency remains the means of payment. Even in the United States, when you use a check to buy something, the unit of value is the dollar, but the means of payment is a piece of paper with your signature on it.

In the United States, the dollar is the centerpiece of our monetary system. It is the unit of value in virtually every economic transaction, and dollar bills are very often the means of payment as well. How did the dollar come to play such an important role in the economy?

HISTORY OF THE DOLLAR

Prior to 1790, each colony had its own currency. It was named the "pound" in every colony, but it had a different purchasing power in each of them. In 1790, soon after the Constitution went into effect, Congress created a new unit of value called the dollar. Historical documents show that merchants and businesses switched immediately to the new dollar, thereby ending the chaos of the colonial monetary systems. Prices began to be quoted in dollars, and accounts were kept in dollars. The dollar rapidly became the standard unit of value.

But the primary means of payment in the United States until the Civil War was paper currency issued by private banks. Just as the government defined the length of the yard, but did not sell yardsticks, the government defined the unit of value, but let private organizations provide the means of payment.

FEDERAL RESERVE SYSTEM The central bank and national monetary authority of the United States.

During the Civil War, however, the government issued the first federal paper currency, the greenback. It functioned as both the unit of value and the major means of payment until 1879. Then the government got out of the business of money creation for a few decades. During that time, currency was once again issued by private banks. Then, in 1913, a new institution called the **Federal Reserve System** was created to be the national monetary authority in the United States. The Federal Reserve was charged with creating and regulating the supply of money in the nations and it continues to do so today.

WHY PAPER CURRENCY IS ACCEPTED AS A MEANS OF PAYMENT

You may be wondering why people are willing to accept paper dollars as a means of payment. Why should a farmer give up a chicken, or a manufacturer give up a new car, just to receive a bunch of green rectangles with words printed on them? In fact, paper currency is a relatively recent development in the history of the means of payment.

The earliest means of payment were precious metals and other valuable commodities such as furs or jewels. These were called *commodity money* because they had important uses other than as a means of payment. The nonmoney use is what gave commodity money its ultimate value. For example, people would accept furs as payment because furs could be used to keep warm. Similarly, gold and silver had a variety of uses in industry, as religious artifacts, and for ornamentation.

Precious metals were an especially popular form of commodity money. Eventually, to make it easier to identify the value of precious metals, they were minted into coins whose weight was declared on their faces. Because gold and silver coins could be melted down into pure metal and used in other ways, they were still commodity money.

At some point in history, commodity money gave way to paper currency. Initially, the paper currency was just a certificate representing a certain amount of gold or silver. At any time, the holder of a certificate could go to a bank and trade the certificate for the stated amount of gold or silver. People were willing to accept paper money as a means of payment for two reasons. First, it could be exchanged for a valuable commodity like gold or silver. Second, because the issuer—either a government or a bank—could not print as much money as it wanted, people believed that paper money would retain its value in the marketplace.

Indeed, when the United States government printed greenbacks during the Civil War, they were not exchangeable into gold and quickly began to lose value in relation to gold. On the other hand, when the U.S. Federal Reserve began printing paper currency in 1913, it was fully exchangeable into gold and retained its value.

But today, paper currency is no longer backed by gold or any other physical commodity. If you have a dollar handy, put this book down and take a close look at the bill. You will not find on it anywhere a promise that you can trade your dollar for gold, silver, furs, or anything else. Yet we all accept it as a means of payment. Why? A clue is provided by the statement in the upper left-hand corner of every bill: *This note is legal tender for all debts, public and private.* The statement affirms that the piece of paper in your hands must be accepted as a means of payment (you can "tender" it to settle any "debt, public or private") by any American because the government says so. This type of currency is called **fiat money.** *Fiat,* in Latin, means "let there be" and fiat money serves as a means of payment by government declaration.

FIAT MONEY Anything that serves as a means of payment by government declaration.

But the government need not work very hard to enforce this declaration: The real force behind the dollar is its long-standing acceptability by *others.* As long as you have confidence that you can exchange your dollars for goods and services, you won't mind giving up goods and services for dollars. And because everyone else feels the same way, the circle of acceptability is completed.

But while the government can declare that paper currency be accepted as a means of payment, it cannot declare the terms. Whether 10 gallons of gas will cost you 1 dollar, 10 dollars or 20 dollars is up to the marketplace. The value of the dollar—its purchasing power—does change from year to year, as reflected in the changing prices of the things we buy. In the rest of this chapter, we will discuss some of the problems created by the dollar's changing value and the difficulty economists have measuring and monitoring the changes. In later chapters, you will learn *why* the value of the dollar changes from year to year.

MEASURING THE PRICE LEVEL AND INFLATION

PRICE LEVEL The average level of dollar prices in the economy.

While microeconomists are interested in prices in individual markets, macroeconomists are concerned with the **price level**—the average level of dollar prices in the economy. Consider this: One hundred years ago, you could buy a pound of coffee for 15 cents, see a Broadway play for 40 cents, buy a new suit for $6, and attend a private college for $200 in yearly tuition.[1] Needless to say, the price of each of these items has gone up considerably since then. Microeconomic causes—changes in individual markets—can explain only a tiny fraction of these price changes; the rest is *inflation*—an ongoing rise in the overall price level. In this section, we begin to explore how the price level and inflation are measured and how the measurements are used.

INDEX NUMBERS

INDEX A series of numbers used to track a variable's rise or fall over time.

Most measures of the price level are reported in the form of an **index**—a series of numbers, each one representing a different period. Index numbers are meaningful only in a *relative* sense: We compare one period's index number with that of another period and can quickly see which one is larger and by how much. The actual number for a particular period has no meaning in and of itself.

In general, an index number for any measure is calculated as

(Value of measure in current period/Value of measure in base period) × 100.

Let's see how index numbers work with a simple example. Suppose we want to measure how violence on TV has changed over time, and we have data on the number of violent acts shown in each of several years. We could then construct a TV-violence index. Our first step would be to choose a *base period*—a period to be used as a benchmark. Let's choose 1993 as our base period, and suppose that there were 10,433 violent acts on television in that year. Then our violence index in any current year would be calculated as

(Number of violent acts in current year/10,433) × 100.

In 1993—the base year—the index will have the value (10,433/10,433) × 100 = 100. Look again at the general formula for index numbers, and you will see that this is always true: *An index will always equal 100 in the base period.*

Now let's calculate the value of our index in another year. If there were 14,534 violent acts in 1996, then the index that year would have the value

(14,534/10,433) × 100 = 139.3

Index numbers compress and simplify information, so that we can see how things are changing at a glance. Our media violence index, for example, tells us at a glance that the number of violent acts in 1996 was 139.3 percent of the number in 1993. More simply, the number grew by 39.3 percent between 1993 and 1996.

---

1 Scott Derks: ed., *The Value of the Dollar: Prices and Incomes in the United States: 1860–1989* (Detroit, MI: Gale Research Inc., 1994), various pages.

THE CONSUMER PRICE INDEX

The most widely used measure of the price level in the United States is the **Consumer Price Index (CPI).** This index—which is designed to track the prices paid by the typical consumer—is compiled and reported by the Bureau of Labor Statistics (BLS).

CONSUMER PRICE INDEX An index of the cost, through time, of a fixed market basket of goods purchased by a typical household in some base period.

Measuring the prices paid by the typical consumer is not easy. In any given month, the average price of doctor's visits might rise by 1 percent, the price of blue jeans might rise by a tenth of a percent, and the price of milk might fall by a half of a percent. When prices change at different rates, and when some are rising while others are falling, how can we measure changes in the price level?

Two problems must be solved before we even begin. The first problem is to decide which goods and services should we include in our average. The CPI tracks only consumer prices; it excludes goods and services that are not directly purchased by consumers. Thus, the CPI excludes raw materials, wholesale goods, and machinery that firms buy from other firms, as well as goods and services purchased by government agencies, such as fighter–bombers and the services of police officers.

The CPI incorporates a wide array of goods and services purchased by the typical consumer. These include not only newly produced consumer goods and services that are part of our GDP—things such as new clothes, new furniture, new cars, haircuts, and restaurant meals—but also some things that are *not* included in GDP. For example, the CPI includes prices for *used* goods like used cars or used books. Also, since some of what we buy is imported from other countries—for example, French cheese, Japanese cars, and Mexican tomatoes—the CPI includes a wide variety of consumer imports. The second problem is how to combine all the different prices into an average price level. We would not want to use a simple average of all prices—adding them up and dividing by the number of goods. A proper measure would recognize that we spend very little of our incomes on some goods—such as Tabasco sauce—and much more on others—like car repairs or electricity. The CPI's approach is to measure what it costs to buy the goods that the typical consumer bought in some base period—called the CPI *market basket.* If the basket's cost rises by 10 percent over some period, then the price level, as reported by the CPI, will rise by 10 percent. This way, goods and services that are relatively unimportant in the typical consumer's budget will have little weight in the CPI. Tabasco sauce could triple in price and have no noticeable impact on the market basket's cost. Goods that are more important—such as electricity and auto repairs—will have more weight. The appendix to this chapter discusses the calculation of the CPI in more detail.

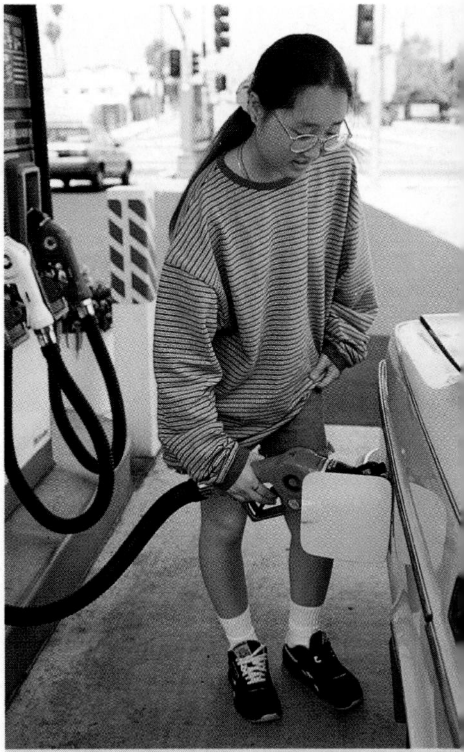

Name:
U.S. Department of Labor, Bureau of Labor Statistics (BLS) Consumer Price Index Page
Description:
Information about the nature, calculation of, and current issues regarding the Consumer Price Index
Resources:
The Bureau of Labor Statistics provides Consumer Price Indexes (CPIs) for the United States, the four Census regions, and some local areas. BLS also provides indexes for major groups of consumer expenditures as well as publications and news releases.
Address:
http://stats.bls.gov/cpihome.htm

HOW THE CPI HAS BEHAVED

In recent years, the base period for the CPI has been the period 1982–1984, so, following our general formula for price indexes, the CPI is calculated as

(Cost of market basket in current year/
Cost of market basket in 1982–1984) × 100.

Table 1 shows the actual value of the CPI for selected years. Because it is reported in index number form, we can easily see how much the price level has changed over different time intervals. In 1995, for example, the CPI had an average value of 152.4, telling us that the typical market basket in that year cost 52.4 percent more than it did in the 1982–84 base period. In 1960, the CPI was 29.6, so the cost of the market basket in that year was only 29.6 percent of its cost in 1982–84.

TABLE 1 CONSUMER PRICE INDEX, FIVE-YEAR INTERVALS, 1960–1995

Year	Consumer Price Index
1960	29.6
1965	31.5
1970	38.8
1975	53.8
1980	82.4
1985	107.6
1990	130.7
1995	152.4

FROM PRICE INDEX TO INFLATION RATE

INFLATION RATE The percent change in the price level from one period to the next.

DEFLATION A period during which the price level is falling.

The Consumer Price Index is a measure of the price *level* in the economy. The **inflation rate** measures how fast the price level is changing, in percentage terms. When the price level is rising, as it almost always is, the inflation rate is positive. When the price level is falling, as it did during the Great Depression, we have **deflation**—a negative inflation rate.

Figure 1 shows the U.S. rate of inflation—as measured by the CPI—since 1950. Notice that inflation was low in the 1950s and 1960s, was high in the 1970s and early 1980s, and has been low since then. In later chapters, you will learn what causes the inflation rate to rise and fall.

HOW THE CPI IS USED

The CPI is one of the most important measures of the performance of the economy. It is used in three major ways:

INDEXATION Adjusting the value of some payment in proportion to a price index.

To Index Payments. A payment is **indexed** when its value is adjusted in proportion to a price index. An indexed payment makes up for the loss in purchasing power that occurs when the price level rises. In the United States, millions of government retirees and Social Security recipients have their benefits indexed to the CPI. About one-quarter of all union members—more than 5 million workers—have labor contracts that index their wages to the CPI. Since the 1980s, the U.S. income tax has been indexed as well—the threshold income levels at which tax rates change automatically rise at the same rate as the CPI. And the government now sells bonds that are indexed to the CPI—the owner of an indexed bond receives a payment each year to make up for the loss of purchasing power when the CPI rises.

DANGEROUS CURVES

People often confuse the statement "prices are rising" with the statement "inflation is rising," but they do not mean the same thing. Remember that the inflation rate tells us the rate of *change* of the price level. To have rising inflation, the price level not only must rise, but must rise by a greater and greater percentage each period. But we can also have rising prices and *falling* inflation. For example, from 1979 to 1983, the CPI rose each year—"prices were rising." But they rose more slowly each year than the year before, so "inflation was falling"—from 13.3 percent, to 12.5 percent, to 8.9 percent, and, finally, to 3.8 percent.

As a Policy Target. In Chapter 17, we identified price stability—or a low inflation rate—as one of the nation's important macroeconomic goals. The CPI

THE RATE OF INFLATION USING THE CONSUMER PRICE INDEX

FIGURE 1

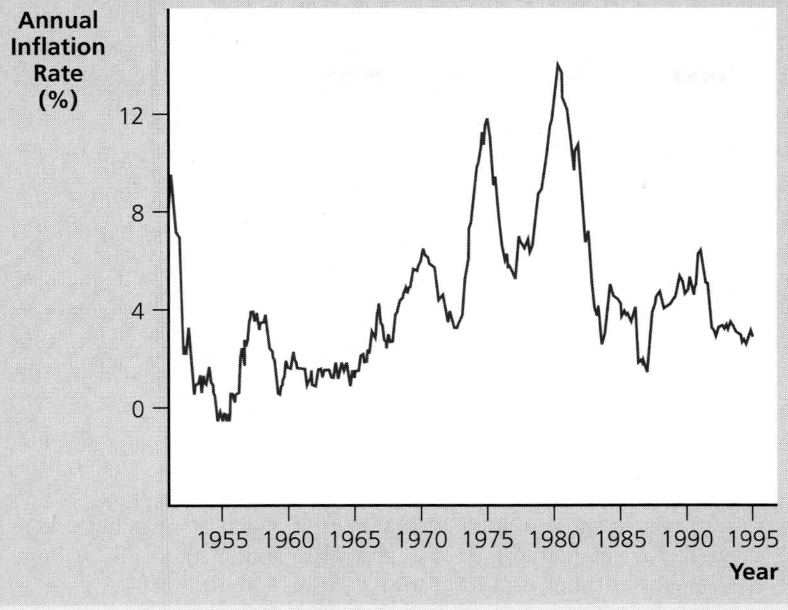

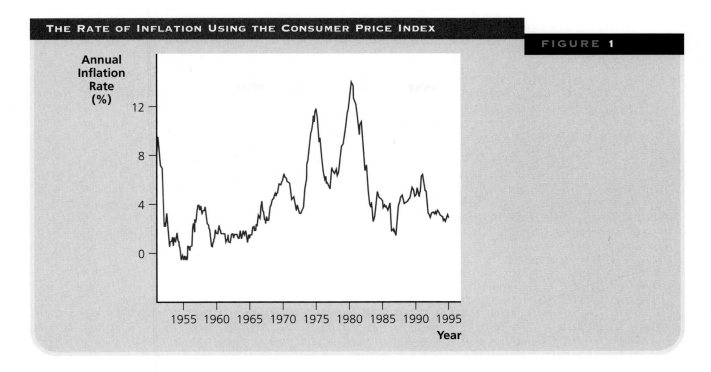

is usually the measure of choice for gauging our success in achieving low inflation. A rise in the inflation rate can cause—and often has caused—the government to engineer a recession to slow down the economy.

To Translate from Nominal to Real Values. In order to compare economic values from different periods, we must translate *nominal variables*—measured in the number of dollars—into *real variables,* which are measured in terms of purchasing power. The CPI is often used for this translation. Since calculating real variables is one of the most important uses of the CPI, we devote the next section to that topic.

REAL VARIABLES AND ADJUSTMENT FOR INFLATION

Suppose that from 1998 to 1999, your nominal wage—what you are paid in dollars—rises from $15 to $30 per hour. Are you better off? That depends. You are earning twice as many dollars. But you should care not about how many green pieces of paper you earn, but how many goods and services you can buy with what you earn. How, then, can we tell what happened to your purchasing power? By focusing not on the **nominal wage**—the number of *dollars* you earn—but on the **real wage**—the purchasing power of your wage. To track your real wage, we need to look at the number of dollars you earn *relative to the price level.*

NOMINAL WAGE A wage measured in current dollars.

REAL WAGE A wage measured in terms of purchasing power.

Since the "typical worker" and the "typical consumer" are pretty much the same, the CPI is usually the price index used to calculate the real wage. The real-wage formula is as follows:

Real wage in any year = (Nominal wage in that year/CPI in that year) × 100

TABLE 2

NOMINAL AND REAL WAGES

Year	Nominal Wage, Dollars per Hour	CPI	Real Wage in 1982–84 Dollars per Hour
1960	2.09	29.6	7.06
1965	2.46	31.5	7.81
1970	3.23	38.8	8.32
1975	4.53	53.8	8.42
1980	6.66	82.4	8.08
1985	8.57	107.6	7.96
1990	10.01	130.7	7.66
1995	11.46	152.4	7.52

To see that this formula makes sense, let's go back to our fictional example: From 1998 to 1999, your nominal wage doubles from \$15 to \$30. Now, suppose the price of everything that you buy doubles at the same time. It is easy to see that in this case, your purchasing power would remain unchanged. And that is just what our formula tells us: If prices double, the CPI doubles as well. With 1998 as our base year, the CPI would increase from 100 in 1998 to 200 in 1999. The *real* wage would be (\$15/100) × 100 = \$15 in 1998 and (\$30/200) × 100 = \$15 in 1999. The real wage would remain unchanged.

Now suppose that prices doubled between 1998 and 1999, but your nominal wage remained unchanged at \$15. In this case, your purchasing power would be cut in half. You'd have the same number of dollars, but each one would buy half as much as it did before. Our formula gives us a real wage of (\$15/100) × 100 = \$15 in 1998 and (\$15/200) × 100 = \$7.50 in 1999. The real wage, like your purchasing power, falls by half.

Now look at Table 2, which shows the average hourly earnings of wage earners over the past 35 years. In the first two columns, you can see that the average American wage earner was paid about \$4.53 per hour in 1975 and more than twice as much—\$11.46—in 1995. Does this mean the average hourly worker was paid more in 1995 than in 1975? In *dollars,* the answer is clearly yes. But what about in *purchasing power?* Or, using the new terminology you've learned, What happened to the *real wage* over this period?

We know that the *nominal* wage rose from \$4.53 in 1975 to \$11.46 in 1995. But—from the table—we also know that the CPI rose from 53.8 to 152.4. Using our formula, we find that

Real wage in 1975 = (\$4.53/53.8) × 100 = \$8.42
Real wage in 1995 = (\$11.46/152.4) × 100 = \$7.52

Thus, although the average worker earned more *dollars* in 1995 than in 1975, her purchasing power actually fell over those years. *Why* did purchasing power fall? This is an interesting and important question, and one we'll begin to answer later in the chapter. The important point to remember here is that

When we measure changes in the macroeconomy, we usually care not about the number of dollars we are counting, but the purchasing power those dollars represent. Thus, we translate nominal values into real values using the formula

$$\text{real value} = (\text{nominal value}/\text{price index}) \times 100$$

THE IMPORTANCE OF REAL VALUES

This formula, usually using the CPI as the price index, is how most real values in the economy are calculated. But there is one important exception: To calculate real GDP, the government uses a different procedure, to which we now turn.

INFLATION AND THE MEASUREMENT OF REAL GDP

In the previous chapter, we discussed the difference between nominal GDP and real GDP. After reading this chapter, you might think that real GDP is calculated just like the real wage: dividing nominal GDP by the consumer price index. But the consumer price index is *not* used to translate nominal GDP figures into real GDP figures. Why not?

There are several reasons. First, the CPI tracks only the prices of goods bought by American *consumers* and therefore excludes some prices that are needed for adjusting the GDP. Specifically, the CPI *excludes* the prices of (a) goods and services purchased by the government, (b) investment goods purchased by businesses, and (c) exports, which are purchased by foreigners. All of these categories of goods are included in the GDP, but their prices are ignored by the CPI.

The CPI also *includes* some prices that are *not* relevant for adjusting the GDP, such as prices for used goods, which are not part of the current year's GDP, and imports, which are not part of our GDP. Finally, the CPI suffers from some serious measurement problems (see the "Using the Theory"section at the end of the chapter), some of which the government has managed to avoid when calculating real GDP.

As part of the calculation of real GDP, the government produces a special price index. The index's official name is the *chain-type annual weights GDP price index*, but we will call it, more simply, the **GDP price index.** The GDP price index is a different measure of inflation than the CPI, because it includes the prices of *all* final goods and services produced in the United States, and *only* these goods and services.

GDP PRICE INDEX An index of the price level for all final goods and services included in GDP.

The GDP price index measures the prices of goods and services produced in the United States, while the CPI measures the prices of all goods and services bought by households.

The appendix to this chapter discusses the calculation of real GDP and the GDP price index more fully.

THE COSTS OF INFLATION

What's so bad about inflation? As we've seen, it certainly makes your task as an economics student more difficult: Instead of taking nominal variables at face value, you must do those troublesome calculations to convert them into real variables. But inflation causes much more trouble than this. It imposes important costs on society and on each of us as individuals. Yet when most people are asked what this cost is, they come up with an incorrect answer.

THE INFLATION MYTH

Most people think that inflation—merely by making goods and services more expensive—erodes the average purchasing power of income. The reason for this belief is easy to see: The higher the price level, the fewer goods and services a given income will buy. It stands to reason, then, that inflation—which raises prices—must be destroying the purchasing power of our incomes. Right?

Actually, this statement is mostly wrong. It is true that when the price level rises, the average family will be able to buy fewer goods ... *if* its income remains unchanged. The "if," however, is crucial. In general, incomes do not remain unchanged when prices rise.

To see why, let's consider a simple example: Suppose that we can divide the economy into two distinct groups of people: wage earners and goods sellers. (In the real world, people are often both, but not in this example.) Now suppose the price level doubles, but all wages remain unchanged. The average wage earner would then see the purchasing power of his income cut in half.

But that is only part of the story. Remember that every market transaction involves *two* parties—a buyer and a seller. If wages were to remain constant as prices doubled, then sellers of goods and services would have a field day—selling their goods at higher prices, yet paying their workers the same wages as before. Sellers' profits—which are part of their incomes—would rise. In fact, the real incomes of sellers would rise by as much as the real incomes of wage earners fell. Inflation would have *redistributed* purchasing power among the population, but the average purchasing power (including that of both buyers and sellers) would remain unchanged.

In fact, it is rare for wages to remain constant when the price level rises. And when nominal wages rise along with prices, wage earners will see a smaller decline in their real incomes. Indeed, if nominal wages rise by the same proportion as prices, wage earners will not suffer at all:

> *Inflation can redistribute purchasing power from one group to another, but it cannot—by itself—decrease the average real income in the economy.*

Why, then, do people continue to believe that inflation robs the average citizen of real income? Largely because real incomes can indeed decline—for *other* reasons. Inflation—while not the *cause* of the decline—will often be the *mechanism* that brings it about. Just as we often blame the messenger for bringing bad news, so too, we often blame inflation for lowering our purchasing power when the real cause lies elsewhere.

Let's consider an example. In Table 2, notice the decline in real wages during the late 1970s. The real wage fell from \$8.42 in 1975 to \$8.08 in 1980—a decline of more than 4 percent. During this period, not only wage earners, but also salaried workers, small-business owners, and corporate shareholders all suffered a decline in their real incomes. What caused the decline?

There were several reasons, but one of the most important was the dramatic rise in the price of imported oil—from \$3 per barrel in 1973 to \$34 in 1981, an increase of more than 1,000 percent. The higher price for oil meant that oil-exporting countries, like Saudi Arabia, Kuwait, and Iraq, got more goods and services for each barrel of oil they supplied to the rest of the world, including the United States. But with these nations claiming more of America's output, less remained for the typical American—that is, the typical American family had to suffer a decline in real income. The rise in price shifted income from buyers to sellers, but in this case, the sellers were outside the U.S. economy, while the buyers were Americans.

But what was the mechanism that caused the average person's real income to decline? Since real income is equal to (nominal income/price index) × 100, a decline can occur in one of two ways: a fall in the numerator (nominal income) or a rise in the denominator (the price index). The decline in real income in the 1970s was all from the denominator. Look back at Figure 1. You can see that this period of declining real wages in the United States was also a period of unusually high inflation; at its peak in 1979, the inflation rate exceeded 13 percent. As a result, most workers blamed *inflation* for their lower real incomes. But inflation was not the *cause* of the decline in purchasing power; it was just the *mechanism* that brought it about. The cause was mainly higher oil prices.

To summarize, the common idea that inflation imposes a cost on society by decreasing the average level of income in the economy is incorrect. But inflation *does* impose costs on society, as the next section shows.

THE REDISTRIBUTIVE COST OF INFLATION

One cost of inflation is that it often redistributes purchasing power *within* society. Because the winners and losers are chosen haphazardly—rather than by conscious social policy—the redistribution of purchasing power is not generally desirable. In some cases, the shift in purchasing power is downright perverse—harming the needy and helping those who are already well off.

How does inflation sometimes redistribute real income? An increase in the price level reduces the purchasing power of any *promise to pay* that is stated in nominal terms. For example, some workers have contracts that promise them a future wage, in dollars; retired people receive pensions that, in many cases, are specified in dollars. Unless payments like these are indexed to the CPI, ordinary people will be harmed by inflation, since it erodes the purchasing power of the promised payment. But the effect can also work the other way: Many homeowners sign fixed-dollar mortgage agreements with a bank. These are promises to pay the bank a nominal sum each month. Inflation can reduce the *real* value of these payments, thus benefiting the average homeowner:

> *Inflation can shift purchasing power away from those who are awaiting future dollar payments and toward those who are obligated to make such payments.*

But does inflation *always* redistribute income from one party in a contract to another? Actually, no; if the inflation is *expected* by both parties, it should not redistribute income. The next section explains why.

EXPECTED *INFLATION* DOES NOT *SHIFT PURCHASING POWER*. Suppose a labor union is negotiating a three-year contract with an employer, and both sides agree that workers will get a 3-percent increase in their real wage. If neither side anticipates any inflation, they could simply negotiate a 3-percent *nominal* wage hike. With an unchanged price level, the *real* wage would then also rise by 3 percent.

Now suppose that both sides anticipate 10-percent inflation each year for the next three years. Then, they must agree to *more* than a 3-percent nominal wage increase in order to raise the real wage by 3 percent. How much more?

We can answer this question with a simple mathematical rule:

THE IMPORTANCE OF REAL VALUES

Over any period, the percentage change in a real value (%ΔReal) is approximately equal to the percentage change in the associated nominal value (%ΔNominal) minus the rate of inflation:

$$\%\Delta\text{Real} = \%\Delta\text{Nominal} - \text{Rate of inflation}$$

If the inflation rate is 10 percent, and the real wage is to rise by 3 percent, then the change in the nominal wage must satisfy the equation

$$3\text{ percent} = \%\Delta\text{Nominal} - 10\text{ percent} \rightarrow \%\Delta\text{Nominal} = 13\text{ percent}$$

The required nominal wage hike is 13 percent.

You can see that as long as both sides correctly anticipate the inflation, and no one stops them from negotiating a 13-percent nominal wage hike, inflation will not cause either party to gain or lose in real terms:

If inflation is fully anticipated, and if there are no restrictions on contracts, then inflation will not *redistribute purchasing power.*

We come to a similar conclusion about contracts between lenders and borrowers. When you lend someone money, you receive a reward—an interest payment—for letting that person use your money instead of spending it yourself. The annual *interest rate* is the interest payment divided by the amount of money you have lent. For example, if you lend someone $1,000 and receive back $1,040 in one year, then your interest payment is $40, and the interest *rate* on the loan is $40/$1,000 = 0.04, or 4 percent.

NOMINAL INTEREST RATE The annual percent increase in a lender's *dollars* from making a loan.

REAL INTEREST RATE The annual increase in a lender's *purchasing power* from making a loan.

But there are actually *two* interest rates associated with every loan. One is the **nominal interest rate**—the percentage increase in the lender's *dollars* from making the loan. The other is the **real interest rate**—the percentage increase in the lender's *purchasing power* from making the loan. It is the *real* rate—the change in purchasing power—that lenders and borrowers should care about.

In the absence of inflation, real and nominal interest rates would always be equal. A 4-percent increase in the lender's *dollars* would always imply a 4-percent increase in her purchasing power. But if there is inflation, it will reduce the purchasing power of the money paid back. Does this mean that inflation redistributes purchasing power? Not if the inflation is correctly anticipated and if there are no restrictions on making loan contracts.

For example, suppose both parties anticipate inflation of 5 percent and want to arrange a contract whereby the lender will be paid a 4-percent *real* interest rate. What *nominal* interest rate should they choose? Since an interest rate is the *percentage change* in the lender's funds, we can use our approximation rule,

$$\%\Delta\text{Real} = \%\Delta\text{Nominal} - \text{Rate of inflation}$$

which here becomes

Real interest rate = Nominal interest rate − Rate of inflation

In our example, where we want the real interest rate to equal 4 percent when the inflation rate is 5 percent, we must have

4 percent = Nominal interest rate − 5 percent
→ Nominal interest rate = 9 percent

Once again, we see that as long as both parties correctly anticipate the inflation rate and are free to set the nominal interest rate at 9 percent, no one gains or loses.

When inflation is *not* correctly anticipated, however, our conclusion is very different.

***Unexpected Inflation* Does *Shift Purchasing Power*.** Suppose that, expecting no inflation, you agree to lend money at a 4-percent nominal interest rate for one year. You and the borrower think that this will translate into a 4-percent real rate. But it turns out you are both wrong: The price level rises by 3 percent, and the *real* interest rate ends up at 4 percent − 3 percent = 1 percent. As a lender, you have given up the use of your money for the year, expecting to be rewarded with a 4-percent increase in purchasing power. But you get only a 1-percent increase. Your borrower was willing to pay 4 percent in purchasing power, but ends up only paying 1 percent. *Unexpected* inflation has led to a better deal for your borrower and a worse deal for you.

That will not make you happy. But it could have been even worse. If the inflation rate had been higher—say, 6 percent—your real interest rate would have been 4 percent − 6 percent = −2 percent—a negative real interest rate. You would get back *less* in purchasing power than you lent out—*paying* (in purchasing power) for the privilege of lending out your money. The borrower would have been *rewarded* (in purchasing power) for borrowing! Negative real interest rates are more than a theoretical possibility. In the late 1970s, when inflation turned out higher than expected for several years in a row, many borrowers ending up paying negative rates to lenders.

Now, let's consider one more possibility: Expected inflation is 6 percent, so you negotiate a 10-percent nominal rate. But the actual inflation rate turns out to be zero, so the real interest rate is 10 percent − 0 percent = 10 percent—higher than either of you anticipated. Here is a case where inflation turns out to be *less* than expected, harming your borrower and benefiting you.

These examples apply, more generally, to any agreement on future payments: to a worker waiting to get a raise and the employer who has promised to pay it; to a doctor who has sent out a bill and the patient who has not yet paid it; or to a supplier who has delivered goods and his customer who hasn't yet paid for them.

When inflationary expectations are inaccurate, purchasing power is shifted between those obliged to make future payments and those waiting to be paid. An inflation rate higher than expected harms those awaiting payment and benefits the payers; an inflation rate lower than expected harms the payers and benefits those awaiting payment.

THE RESOURCE COST OF INFLATION

In addition to its possible redistribution of income, inflation imposes another cost upon society. To cope with inflation, we are forced to use up time and other resources as we go about our daily economic activities (shopping, selling, saving, investing)—resources that we could otherwise have devoted to productive activities. Thus, inflation imposes an *opportunity cost* on society as a whole and on each of its members:

OPPORTUNITY COST

When people must spend time and other resources coping with inflation, they pay an opportunity cost—they sacrifice the goods and services those resources could have produced instead.

Let's first consider the resources used by consumers. Suppose you shop for clothes twice a year. You've discovered that both The Gap and Banana Republic sell clothing of similar quality and have similar service, and you naturally want to shop at the one with the lower prices. If there is no inflation, your task is easy: You shop first at the Gap and then at Banana Republic; thereafter, you rely on your memory to determine which is less expensive.

With inflation, however, things are more difficult. If you find that prices at Banana Republic are higher than you remember them to be at The Gap, it may be that Banana Republic is the more expensive store, or it may be that prices have risen at *both* stores. How can you tell? Only a trip back to The Gap will answer the question—a trip that will cost you extra time and trouble. If prices are rising very rapidly, you may have to visit both stores in the same day to find which one is cheaper. Now, multiply this time and trouble by all the different types of shopping you must do on a regular or occasional basis—for groceries, an apartment, a car, concert tickets, compact discs, restaurant meals, and more. Inflation can make you use up valuable time—time you could have spent earning income or enjoying leisure activities.

Inflation also forces sellers to use up resources. First, remember that sellers of goods and services are also buyers of resources and intermediate goods. They, too, must devote labor time to comparison shopping when there is inflation. Second, each time sellers raise their own prices, they must use labor to put new price tags on merchandise, or enter new prices into a computer scanning system, or change the prices on advertising brochures, menus, and so on.

Finally, inflation makes us all use up resources managing our financial affairs. We will try to keep our funds in accounts that pay high nominal interest rates, to preserve our purchasing power, and minimize what we keep as cash or in low-interest checking accounts. Of course, this means we must take more frequent trips to the bank or the automatic teller machine, to transfer money into our checking accounts or get cash each time we need it.

All of these additional activities—inspecting prices at several stores, changing price tags or price entries, going back and forth to the automatic teller machine—use up time and other resources, such as gasoline or paper. From society's point of view, these resources could have been used to produce additional goods and services that we would all enjoy. Recall our discussion at the beginning of the chapter about the large benefits of standardization in the unit of value. Some of these benefits diminish if inflation is high, because the unit of value becomes so unstable.

You may not have thought much about the resource cost of inflation, because in recent years, U.S. inflation has been so low—under 3 percent per year in the

1990s. Such low rates of inflation are often called *creeping inflation*—from week to week or month to month, the price level creeps up so slowly that we hardly notice the change, and the cost of coping with it is negligible.

But it has not always been this way. Three times during the last 50 years, we have had double-digit inflation—about 14 percent during 1947–48, 12 percent in 1974, and 13 percent during 1979 and 1980. Going back farther, the annual inflation rate reached almost 20 percent during World War I and rose above 25 percent during the Civil War. And as serious as these episodes of American inflation have been, they pale in comparison to the experiences of other countries. In Germany in the early 1920s, the inflation rate hit thousands of percent *per month*. Under these conditions, the monetary system breaks down almost completely. Economic life is almost as difficult as in Chaotica.

IS THE CPI ACCURATE?

USING THE THEORY

The Bureau of Labor Statistics spends millions of dollars gathering data to ensure that its measure of inflation is accurate. To determine the market basket of the typical consumer every 10 years or so, the BLS randomly selects thousands of households and analyzes their spending habits. In the last household survey—completed in 1982–84—each of 20,000 families kept diaries of their purchases for two weeks.

But that is just the beginning. Every month, the bureau's shoppers visit 24,000 retail stores, 18,000 rental apartments, and 18,000 owner-occupied homes to record 71,000 different prices. Finally, all of the prices are combined according to their relative importance in the typical consumer's market basket, to obtain the CPI for the current month.

The BLS is a highly professional agency, typically headed by an economist. Even though billions of dollars are at stake for each 1-percent change in the CPI, the BLS has kept its measurement honest and free of political manipulation. Nevertheless, conceptual problems and resource limitations make the CPI fall short of the ideal measure of inflation. Economists—even those who work in the BLS—widely agree that the CPI seriously overstates the U.S. inflation rate. By how much?

According to a report by an advisory committee of economists appointed by the Senate Finance Committee in 1996, the overall bias is at least 1.1 percent per year.[2] That is, in a typical year, the reported rise in the CPI is about 1 percentage point greater than the true rise in the price level.

SOURCES OF BIAS IN THE CPI

SUBSTITUTION BIAS. The CPI ignores a general principle of consumer behavior: People tend to *substitute* goods that have become relatively cheaper for those that have become relatively more expensive. For example, from 1973 to 1980, the price of oil-related products—like gasoline and home heating oil—increased by more than 300 percent, while the prices of most other goods and services rose by less than 100 percent. As a result, people found ways to conserve on oil products: They joined carpools, used public transportation, insulated their homes, and in many

2 See *Toward a More Accurate Measure of the Cost of Living*, Report to the Senate Finance committee from the Advisory Commission to Study the Consumer Price Index, December 1996.

cases moved closer to their workplaces to shorten their commute. Yet throughout this period, the CPI basket—based on the 1972–73 household survey—assumed that consumers were buying unchanged quantities of oil products.

For a more extreme case, consider the following example. One of the authors of this book eats a lot of raspberries, in an effort to include fiber in his diet. But the cost of raspberries can vary widely. When raspberries are cheap—say, $0.99 per box—he may buy four boxes in a week. But he will not buy any raspberries at all when the price reaches $2.99. Any further price increase beyond $2.99 has no impact on the overall cost of the goods that he buys. Now suppose that the typical consumer behaves like the author does. Even though the cost of the typical consumer's market basket wouldn't rise at all after the price of raspberries went beyond $2.99, the CPI would keep on counting the price increases, as if people were continuing to buy their usual quantity of raspberries.

These two examples illustrate the following general principle:

Because the CPI updates its market basket only every 10 years or so, it routinely overestimates the relative importance of the goods whose prices are rising most rapidly and underestimates the relative importance of goods whose prices are falling or rising more slowly. The result is an overestimate of the inflation rate.

NEW TECHNOLOGIES. A brand-new technology often makes it cheaper to achieve a given standard of living, but the CPI is not able to take that factor into account. One problem is that goods using new technologies are introduced into the BLS market basket only after a long lag. These goods often drop rapidly in price after they are introduced, helping to balance out price rises in other goods. By excluding a category of goods whose prices are dropping, the CPI overstates the rate of inflation. For example, as of 1996, the cellular phone was *still* not included in the BLS sample of goods, so the rapid decline in its price is being missed by the CPI.

But there is another problem with new technologies: They often offer consumers a lower cost alternative for obtaining the same service. For example, the introduction of cable television lowered the cost of entertainment significantly by offering a new, cheaper alternative to going out to see movies. This should have registered as a drop in the price of "seeing movies." But the CPI does not have any good way to measure this reduction in the cost of living. Instead, it treats cable television as an entirely separate service.

Because the CPI excludes new products that lower the cost of living when they come on the market, it overestimates the overall rise in the price level in any given year.

CHANGES IN QUALITY. Many products are improving over time. Cars are much more reliable than they used to be and require much less routine maintenance. They have features like air bags and antilock brakes that were unknown in the early 1980s. The CPI struggles to deal with these changes, since some of the rise in price is not really inflation, but rather charging more because the consumer is *getting* more. But many improvements in quality are not considered in the CPI at all. For example, when prices rise due to better nutritional quality in foods, to better performance and convenience of VCRs, or to greater success rates in surgery, the BLS merely records a price increase, as if the same thing is costing more.

The CPI fails to recognize that, in many cases, prices rise because of improvements in quality, not because the cost of living has risen. This causes the CPI to overstate the inflation rate.

Growth in Discounting. The CPI treats toothpaste bought at a high-priced drugstore and toothpaste bought at Wal-Mart as different products. In fact, Americans are buying more and more of their toothpaste and other products from discounters, but the CPI does not consider this in measuring inflation. The purchasing power you have lost from inflation is not as great as the CPI says if you, like most Americans, are stretching your dollar by going more often to discount outlets and warehouse stores.

The CPI omits reductions in the prices people pay from more frequent shopping at discount stores and so overstates the inflation rate.

THE CONSEQUENCES OF OVERSTATING INFLATION

The impact of overstating the inflation rate by 1.1 percent per year is both serious and wide ranging. First, it means that many real variables are rising more rapidly than the official numbers suggest. For example, we've seen that, based on the CPI measure of inflation, the average real wage *fell* by about 7 percent between 1980 and 1995. But if the CPI has overstated the inflation rate by just 1.1 percentage points in each of those years, as the government's advisory commission has suggested, then the real wage has not fallen at all over this period, but has actually *risen* by about 7 percent.

Second, remember that low inflation is itself an important goal. As you'll learn in future chapters, this goal is not always easy to achieve and may require large—if temporary—sacrifices. If the CPI overstates inflation, we may be making these sacrifices unnecessarily: We may think inflation is too high when the real problem is that our official inflation measure is exaggerating the problem. Finally, since many payments are indexed to the CPI, an overstatement of inflation results in overindexing—payments that rise *faster* than the true price level. For example, suppose a Social Security recipient's payment of $1,000 per month is indexed to the CPI in order to keep the real payment constant as prices rise. Suppose, too, that over 10 years, the CPI reports annual inflation of 3 percent. By the end of the period, the nominal payment will rise to $1,350.[3] But what if the CPI is wrong, and the actual inflation rate was just 1.9 percent per year during the period? Then the true price index would have risen from 100 to 120.7, and the *real* Social Security payment would have risen from $1,000 to ($1,350/120.7) × 100 = $1,118—an increase of about 11 percent. This "overpayment" of $118 per month at the end of the period may suit the Social Security recipient just fine, but remember that this greater purchasing power is financed with greater real tax payments by the rest of

3 Over 10 years, 3 percent annual inflation raises the CPI by a factor of $(1.03)^{10} = 1.35$.

society. The same general principle applies to union workers, government pensioners, or anyone else who is overindexed due to errors in the CPI:

THE IMPORTANCE OF REAL VALUES

When a payment is indexed, and the price index overstates inflation, inflation will increase the real payment, shifting purchasing power toward those who are indexed and away from the rest of society.

WILL WE CHANGE THE CPI?

We have, in the past, significantly changed how the CPI is measured. Most recently, in 1983, the BLS corrected a serious error in the measurement of housing costs and then revised the CPI back to 1968 to reflect the change. The result was a lower official inflation rate through the 1970s and 1980s—in some years, more than two percentage points lower. But fixing the CPI today would be different, for two reasons.

First, the 1983 fix was cheap: Mostly, it required the BLS to change its computer software. Fixing the remaining problems, however, would be expensive. For example, to estimate changes in quality for more goods and services, the BLS would have to hire more economists and data gatherers. To reduce the bias caused by substitution and new technology, the BLS would have to measure the typical consumer's market basket more frequently—say, once a year instead of once every 10 years. This would require more frequent household surveys, which are very expensive to conduct. In an era of tight budgets, such expenses are not popular.

Second, fixing the CPI's current problems would require us to look at the CPI in an entirely new way. At present, the CPI mostly tracks the cost of a fixed basket of goods, and it does a reasonably good job of doing so. But it does *not* do a good job tracking what many people call the *cost of living*—the number of dollars a person must pay in order to enjoy a given level of satisfaction. When people substitute cheaper goods, take advantage of new technologies, enjoy quality improvements, and shop at discount stores, they are either getting more satisfaction for a given cost, or else attempting to prevent price hikes from decreasing their level of satisfaction. And to some extent, they are successful. The CPI, by ignoring our ability to increase and preserve our satisfaction from a given amount of spending, does not accurately tell us what is happening to the cost of *living*.

On the other hand, once we try to measure the cost of living, rather than the price of a fixed basket of goods, we enter into some nebulous territory. How is the cost of living affected when our medical care is provided by an HMO that lowers the price, but gives us fewer options in choosing our own doctors? When the price of beef goes up, how much satisfaction do people lose when they substitute by buying more chicken? What about falling crime rates that enable us to protect our lives and property at lower cost? And what about other aspects of our society that affect the quality of our lives: leisure time, the state of the environment, the safety of our workplaces, the quality of our culture, and so on? Do we really want changes in these aspects of life to affect our cost-of-living measure?

For all of these reasons, fixing the CPI is controversial. Further, some groups—including Social Security recipients, union workers, and pensioners—stand to lose from any fix that will reduce the reported inflation rate. In early 1997, these groups viewed suggestions to correct the CPI—which might lower reported inflation by a full percentage point or more—as a backdoor effort to reduce their benefits.

Thus, the CPI has entered the realm of politics. The voices arguing for changing the CPI are getting stronger, but so are the voices of those opposed.

SUMMARY

Money serves two important functions. First, it is a *unit of value* that helps us measure how much something is worth and compare the costs of different goods and services. Second, it is a *means of payment* by being generally acceptable in exchange for goods and services. Without money, we would be reduced to barter, a very inefficient way of carrying out transactions.

Money and prices are intimately related. The overall trend of prices is measured using a price index, a weighted average of the prices of individual goods and services. Like any index number, a price index is calculated as: 100 × (value in current period/value in base period). The most widely used price index in the United States is the *Consumer Price Index (CPI),* which tracks the prices paid for a typical consumer's "market basket." The percent change in the CPI is the inflation rate.

The most common uses of the CPI are for indexing payments, as a policy target, and to translate from nominal to real variables. Many nominal variables, such as the nominal wage, can be corrected for price changes by dividing by the CPI. The result is a real variable, such as the real wage, that is measured in units of purchasing power. Another price index in common use is the GDP price index. It includes the prices of all final goods and services included in GDP.

Inflation—a rise over time in a price index—involves costs. One of these costs may be an arbitrary redistribution of income. Unanticipated inflation shifts purchasing power away from those awaiting future dollar payments and toward those obligated to make such payments. Another cost of inflation is the resource cost: People use valuable time and other resources trying to cope with inflation.

KEY TERMS

unit of value
means of payment
Federal Reserve System
fiat money
price level
index
Consumer Price Index
inflation rate
deflation
indexation
nominal wage
real wage
GDP price index
nominal interest rate
real interest rate

REVIEW QUESTIONS

1. Distinguish between the *unit of value* function of money and the *means of payment* function. Give examples of how the U.S. dollar has played each of these two roles.
2. How does the price level differ from, say, the price of a haircut or a Big Mac?
3. Explain how you might construct an index of bank deposits over time. What steps would be involved?
4. What is the CPI? What does it measure? How can it be used to calculate the inflation rate?
5. Can the inflation rate be decreasing at the same time the price level is rising? Can the inflation rate be increasing at the same time the price level is falling?
6. What are some of the main uses of the CPI? Give an example of each use.
7. Explain the logic of the formula that relates real values to nominal values.
8. What are the similarities between the CPI and the GDP price index? What are the differences?
9. What are the costs of inflation?
10. Under what circumstances would inflation redistribute purchasing power? How? When would it *not* redistribute purchasing power?
11. How is a nominal interest rate different from a real interest rate? Which do you think is the better measure of the rate of return on a loan?

PROBLEMS AND EXERCISES

1. Both gold and paper currency have served as money in the United States. What are some of the advantages of paper currency over gold?
2. Which would be more costly—a steady inflation rate of 3 percent per year, or an inflation rate that was sometimes high and sometimes low, but that averaged 3 percent per year? Justify your answer.

3. Given the following year-end data, calculate the inflation rate for years 2, 3, and 4. Calculate the real wage in each year:

Year	*CPI*	*Inflation Rate*	*Nominal Wage*	*Real Wage*
1	100	—	$10.00	____
2	110	____	12.00	____
3	120	____	13.00	____
4	115	____	12.75	____

4. The chapter discusses the costs of inflation. Would there be any costs to a *deflation*—a period of falling prices? If so, what would they be? Give examples.

5. Given the following data, calculate the real interest rate for years 2, 3, and 4. (Assume that each CPI number tells us the price level at the *end* of each year.)

Year	*CPI*	*Nominal Interest Rate*	*Real Interest Rate*
1	100	—	—
2	110	15%	____
3	120	13%	____
4	115	8%	____

If you lent $200 to a friend at the beginning of year 2 at the prevailing nominal interest rate of 15 percent, and your friend returned the money—with interest—at the end of year 2, did you benefit from the deal?

6. Your friend asks for a loan of $100 for one year and offers to pay you 5 percent interest. Your friend expects the inflation rate over that one-year period to be 6 percent; you expect it to be 4 percent. You agree to make the loan, and the actual inflation rate turns out to be 5 percent. Who benefits and who loses?

CHALLENGE QUESTIONS

1. Inflation is sometimes said to be a tax on nominal money holdings. If you hold $100 and the price level increases by 10 percent, the purchasing power of that $100 falls by about 10 percent. Who benefits from this inflation tax?

2. During the late 19th and early 20th centuries, many U.S. farmers favored inflationary government policies. Why might this have been the case?

The Bureau of Labor Statistics (BLS) provides Consumer Price Indexes (CPIs) for All Urban Consumers (CPI-U) and for Urban Wage Earners and Clerical Workers (CPI-W).

a. Visit the BLS "Most Requested Data Series" page (http://stats.bls.gov/cgi-bin/surveymost?bls). Under "Price and Living Conditions," choose "Consumer Price Index–All Urban Consumers" and select your home region for a period of 10 years. Do the same for "CPI for Urban Wage Earners and Clerical Workers." Are there any differences in the data time series?

b. Using the same procedure, choose a city you believe has the highest CPI-U and a city that you believe has the lowest CPI-U. Were your assumptions correct? What reasons guided your choice of these cities?

APPENDIX

CALCULATING THE CPI, THE GDP PRICE INDEX, AND REAL GDP

This appendix demonstrates how the government calculates its two major measures of inflation—the CPI and the GDP price index—as well as its measure of total production—real GDP. To help you see the differences between these measures, we'll base all of our calculations on the same hypothetical information. In particular, we'll imagine a very simple economy with just two goods: medical checkups and frozen burrito dinners (not a pleasant world, but a manageable one). Table 3 shows prices for each good, and the quantities produced and consumed, in two different years: 1997 and 1998.

CALCULATING THE CONSUMER PRICE INDEX

The Consumer Price Index (CPI) is the government's most popular measure of inflation. It tracks the cost of the collection of goods—called the *CPI market basket*—bought by a typical consumer in some *base year*. To keep our example simple, we'll select a base year of 1997—the first year for which we have data in Table 3. Then the market basket is given in the third column of the table: In 1997, the typical consumer buys 100 medical checkups and 1,000 frozen dinners. Our formula for the CPI in any year t is

CPI in year t

$$= \frac{\text{Cost of market basket at prices in year } t}{\text{Cost of market basket at 1997 prices}} \times 100$$

TABLE 3

PRICES AND QUANTITIES IN A TWO-GOOD ECONOMY

	1997		1998	
	Price	**Quantity**	**Price**	**Quantity**
Checkups	\$110	100	\$150	96
Frozen Dinners	\$ 5	1,000	\$ 6	1,200

Table 4 shows the calculations we must do to determine the CPI in 1997 and 1998.

In the table, you can see that the cost of the 1997 market basket at 1997 prices is \$16,000. The cost of the same market basket at 1998's higher prices is \$21,000. To determine the CPI in 1997, we use the formula with year t equal to 1997, giving us

CPI in 1997

$$= \frac{\text{Cost of 1997 basket at 1997 prices}}{\text{Cost of 1997 basket at 1997 prices}} \times 100$$

$$= \frac{\$16{,}000}{\$16{,}000} \times 100 = 100$$

That is, the CPI in 1997—the base year—is equal to 100. (The formula, as you can see, is set up so that the CPI will always equal 100 in the base year, regardless of which base year we choose.)

Now let's apply the formula again, to get the value of the CPI in 1998:

CPI in 1998

$$= \frac{\text{Cost of market basket at 1998 prices}}{\text{Cost of market basket at 1997 prices}} \times 100$$

$$= \frac{\$21{,}000}{\$16{,}000} \times 100 = 131.3$$

TABLE 4

CALCULATIONS FOR THE CPI

	At 1997 Prices	**At 1998 Prices**
Cost of 100 medical checkups	\$110 × 100 = \$11,000	\$150 × 100 = \$15,000
Cost of 1,000 frozen dinners	\$5 × 1,000 = \$5,000	\$6 × 1,000 = \$6,000
Cost of entire market basket	\$11,000 + \$5,000 = \$16,000	\$15,000 + \$6,000 = \$21,000

From 1997 to 1998, the CPI rises from 100 to 131.3. The rate of inflation over this period is 31.3 percent.

Notice that the CPI gives more weight to price changes to goods that are more important in the consumer's budget. In our example, the percentage rise in the CPI (31%) is closer to the percentage rise in the price of medical checkups (36%) than it is to the percentage price rise in the price of frozen dinners (20%). This is because a greater percentage of our budget is spent on medical checkups than frozen dinners, so medical checkups carry more weight in the CPI.

But one of the CPI's problems, discussed in the body of the chapter, is *substitution bias*. No matter how much the relative price of checkups rises, the CPI assumes that people will continue to buy the same quantity of them. Therefore, as the price of medical checkups rises, the CPI assumes that we spend a greater and greater percentage of our budgets on them; medical checkups get *increasing weight* in the CPI. In our example, spending on checkups is assumed to rise from $11,000/$16,000 = 0.69, or 69 percent of the typical budget, to $15,000/$21,000 = 0.71, or 71 percent. In fact, however, the rapid rise in price may cause many people to substitute *away* from medical checkups towards other goods. This is what occurs in the last column of Table 3, where, in 1998, the quantity of checkups purchased drops to 96, and the quantity of frozen dinners rises to 1,200. In an ideal measure, the decrease in the quantity of checkups would reduce their weight in determining the overall rate of inflation. But the CPI ignores this. Look back at how we've calculated the CPI in this example, and you will see that we have entirely ignored the information in the last column of Table 3, which shows the new quantities purchased in 1998. This failure to correct for substitution bias is one of the reasons the CPI overstates inflation.

CALCULATING THE GDP PRICE INDEX

The GDP price index—calculated by the government's Bureau of Economic Analysis (BEA)—measures inflation differently than the CPI does. One difference is in the coverage of goods, as discussed earlier: Recall that the GDP price index *includes* some prices that are not included in the CPI (such as prices for government purchases, investment goods, and exports). And the GDP price index also *excludes* some prices that *are* included in the CPI (such as prices for imports and used goods).

Another difference between the two measures is that the GDP price index is a bit more complicated to calculate than the CPI, as you are about to see. The added complexity helps to reduce the substitution bias that plagues the CPI.

Once again, we assume that the economy produces only two goods: medical checkups and frozen dinners, with the quantities and prices indicated in Table 3. This means that we ignore differences in the goods covered by the CPI and the GDP in our example and concentrate just on differences in calculation.

Our first step in computing the GDP price index is to compute a price index very much like the CPI, using 1997 quantities. We ask: How much more would 1997's output cost at 1998 prices than at 1997 prices? The relevant calculations are shown in the top part of Table 5, where, using 1997 quantities, we obtain a price index equal to 131.3. In other words, 1997's output would cost 31.3 percent more at 1998 prices than at 1997 prices.

Notice that the first price index listed is exactly like the CPI for 1998. That is, the first step to get to the GDP price index is to calculate a price index just like the CPI (except for differences in goods covered). Of course, if we stopped here, the GDP price index, like the CPI, would suffer from substitution bias: We have not yet taken account of the fact that people tend to buy less of goods that are rising relatively rapidly in price.

This is why the BEA goes on to calculate a *second* price index, using 1998's output (the last column of Table 4) instead of 1997's output. For this second price index, the relevant calculations are shown in the middle section of Table 5. The price index, using 1998 quantities, is equal to 130.4, telling us that 1998's output would cost 30.4 percent more using 1998 prices than using 1997 prices.

Now we have two different stories about inflation between 1997 and 1998. Using 1997 quantities, the price level rises by 31.3 percent; but using 1998 quantities, it grows by 30.4 percent. Which do we use? Both: The BEA takes an *average* of the two indexes, giving us an increase of about 30.9 percent.[4] This increase is then used to construct the GDP price index: With 1997 as the base year, the BEA would report 1997's GDP price index as 100.0 and 1998's index as 130.9, reflecting the 30.9-percent inflation between those two years.[5]

4 Typically, an average of two numbers is a mean or arithmetic average, where the numbers are summed and divided by two. For technical reasons, the BEA uses a geometric average instead, multiplying the two numbers and then taking the square root of the product. The two procedures give very similar results, as you can verify.

5 The formal name for this price index is the "chain-type price index for gross domestic product." You can see why we prefer the term "GDP price index."

TABLE 5

CALCULATING THE GDP PRICE INDEX

Using 1997 output quantities:

1997 output at 1997 prices
= ($110 × 100) + ($5 × 1,000) = $16,000
1997 output at 1998 prices
= ($150 × 100) + ($6 × 1,000) = $21,000
Price index using 1997 output quantities:
($21,000/$16,000) × 100 = 131.3
Percent increase in price level using 1997 output quantities: 31.3%

Using 1998 output quantities:

1998 output at 1997 prices
= ($110 × 96) + ($5 × 1,200) = $16,560
1998 output at 1998 prices =
= ($150 × 96) + ($6 × 1,200) = $21,600
Price index using 1998 output quantities:
($21,600/$16,560) × 100 = 130.4
Percent increase in price level using 1998 output quantities: 30.4%

Average of the increases under the two methods = 30.9%

Conclusion: GDP price index increased by 30.9% between 1997 and 1998
Final "chain-weighted GDP price index" (1997 base year):
1997 GDP price index = 100.0
1998 GDP price index = 130.9

Any GDP price index can be "spliced together" with another to create an index that tracks the price level over several years. For example, suppose we move on to the *next* year (1999), repeat all of our steps (using 1998 and 1999 to do our calculations), and find that the price level rose by 10 percent from 1998 to 1999, giving us index numbers for 1998 and 1999 of 100.0 and 110.0, respectively. To "splice" this index onto our previous index, keeping 1997 as the base year, we simply make the 1999 index number 10 percent greater than the 1998 index number (130.9 × 1.1 = 144.0). Thus, the GDP price index for all three years, with 1997 as the base year, would be as follows: 1997 = 100.0; 1998 = 130.9; 1999 = 144.0.

CALCULATING REAL GDP

As discussed in the previous chapter, nominal GDP can give us a misleading view of changes in production. For example, suppose nominal GDP rises by 3 percent between one year and the next. This could mean that the quantity of every good and service has increased by 3 percent—a true rise in production. Or it could mean that output hasn't changed at all, but that every good's price has risen by 3 percent. In most years, it would mean something in between—that both prices and quantities have changed.

Fortunately, the BEA provides a measure of our real GDP—a measure designed to increase in the same proportion as the economy's actual production of goods and services. The procedure shares much in common with the calculation of the GDP price index. In this case, though, we want to measure the increase in total production between one year and the next, rather than the increase in the price level.

As before, we assume that there are only two goods—medical checkups and frozen dinners, with the quantities and prices indicated in Table 3. As a first step, the BEA will calculate the nation's total output in 1997 using *1997* prices. Then, it calculates 1998's total output, *still* using 1997 prices. This way, a rise in prices will not affect the measure of total output. The calculations for this first step are shown in the top part of Table 6. Using 1997 prices, our index of total output rises from 100 to 103.5 from 1997 to 1998.

But why limit ourselves to using 1997 prices? We could just as easily have valued output at 1998 prices instead. In fact, the BEA uses *both* sets of prices. It calculates a second output index, wherein each good is valued at 1998 prices. The relevant calculations are shown in the middle section of Table 6. This time, using 1998 prices, our index number for total output is 102.9. In other words, using 1998 prices, 1998's output is 2.9 percent greater than 1997's output.

Now we have two different stories about the increase in output between the two years: Using 1997 prices, total output rises by 3.5 percent; but using 1998 prices, it grows by 2.9 percent. The BEA then takes an *average* of the two increases, giving us a final increase of about 3.2 percent.[6] This increase is then used to construct an index number: With 1997 as the base year, the BEA would report 1997's *real GDP index* as 100.0 and 1998's real GDP index as 103.2, reflecting the 3.2-percent increase in output between those two years.

A real GDP index can be "spliced together" with another to create an index that tracks real GDP over several years. For example, suppose we move on to the

6 Once again, the BEA uses a geometric average instead of an arithmetic average, multiplying the two numbers and then taking the square root of the product.

TABLE 6

CALCULATING THE REAL GDP INDEX AND REAL GDP

Using 1997 prices:

1997 output at 1997 prices
= ($110 × 100) + ($5 × 1,000) = $16,000
1998 output at 1997 prices
= ($110 × 96) + ($5 × 1,200) = $16,560
Output index using 1997 prices:
($16,560/$16,000) × 100 = 103.5
Percent increase in output using 1997 prices: 3.5%

Using 1998 prices:

1997 output at 1998 prices
= ($150 × 100) + ($6 × 1,000) = $21,000
1998 output at 1998 prices
= ($150 × 96) + ($6 × 1,200) = $21,600
Output index using 1998 prices:
($21,600/$21,000) × 100 = 102.9
Percent increase in output using 1998 prices: 2.9%

Average of the increases under the two methods = 3.2%

Conclusion: Real GDP increased by 3.2% between 1997 and 1998
Final chain-weighted GDP index (1997 base year):
1997 GDP index = 100.0
1998 GDP index = 103.2
Calculation of real GDP in 1997 dollars:
1997 real GDP = $16,000.
1998 real GDP = $16,000 × 1.032 = $16,512

next year (1999), repeat all of our steps (using 1998 and 1999 to do our calculations), and find that output rose by 4 percent from 1998 to 1999, giving us a real GDP index for 1998 and 1999 of 100.0 and 104.0, respectively. To "splice" this index onto our previous index, so that 1997 remains the base year, we simply set the 1999 index 4 percent higher than our 1998 index (103.2 × 1.04 = 107.3). Thus, the real GDP index for all three years, with 1997 as the base year, would be as follows: 1997 = 100.0; 1998 = 103.2; 1999 = 107.3.

Finally, the BEA does one more thing with its real GDP index: convert it to a *dollar* measure of real output, using the dollars of some base year. This is our *real GDP*. For example, suppose that 1997 is our base year. Then 1997 real GDP is $16,000—the same as nominal GDP in that year. Now remember that 1998's total output was found to be 3.2 percent greater than total output in 1997. (See Table 6.) If we add 3.2 percent to 1997's real GDP, we get $16,000 × 1.032 = $16,512. This last number is 1998's real GDP (measured in 1997 dollars).

Currently, the government uses 1992 as its base year for real GDP. Thus, all of the graphs and tables showing real GDP in this text give real GDP in 1992 dollars.[7]

7 The official term is "real GDP in chained (1992) dollars."

C H A P T E R

7

THE CLASSICAL LONG-RUN MODEL

CHAPTER OUTLINE

Economists disagree with each other. In news interviews, class lectures, and editorials, they give differing opinions about even the simplest matters. To the casual observer, it might seem that economics is little more than guesswork, where anyone's opinion is as good as anyone else's. But there is actually much more agreement among economists than there appears to be.

Take the following typical example: After some bad economic news (say, a drop in last quarter's GDP), two distinguished economists appear on "ABC News Nightline." In a somber tone, Ted Koppel asks each of them what should be done to improve the state of the economy. "We need to decrease government spending," replies the first economist. "This will free up funds for business firms to borrow and invest, boost productivity, and lead to more and better jobs for Americans." (Don't worry if this chain of logic isn't clear to you yet—it will be by the end of the next chapter.)

"No, no, no," the second economist interrupts. "A cut in government spending would be the *worst* thing for the economy right now. Think of all the businesses that would be forced to lay off workers because the government wouldn't be buying their products. This foolhardy policy might even push the economy into a recession." (You'll learn what's behind this argument a few chapters later.)

Which of these economists is correct? The answer—which may surprise you—is *both* of them. But how can this be? Aren't the two responses contradictory? Not really, because each economist is hearing—and answering—a different question. The first economist is addressing the *long-run* impact of a cut in government spending—the impact we can expect after several years have elapsed. The second economist is focusing on the *short-run* impact—the effects we'd see over the next few quarters.

When economists analyze a problem, they automatically think of the short run versus the long run and then choose the time period most appropriate for the question at hand. As you'll see, this way of thinking is applied again and again in economics. It is one of the basic principles you will learn in this book.

SHORT-RUN VERSUS LONG-RUN OUTCOMES

Markets behave differently in the short run and the long run. When studying a market, we can take a short-run or long-run perspective, and our choice will depend on the question we want to answer.

The short run/long run distinction is important in both microeconomics and macroeconomics. In microeconomics, it is applied to individual markets such as the market for maple syrup or crude oil. In macroeconomics, as you'll see in the chapters to come, we will apply this distinction in highly aggregated markets, such as the market for "labor" or the market for "loanable funds," as well as to the economy as a whole.

Once the distinction between the long run and the short run becomes clear, many apparent disagreements among macroeconomists dissolve. If Ted Koppel had asked our two economists about the long-run impact of cutting the deficit, both may well have agreed that it would be very positive. If asked about the short-run impact, both may have agreed about a possible loss of jobs and a risk of recession. If no time horizon is specified, however, an economist is likely to focus on the horizon he or she feels is most important—something about which economists *do* disagree. The real dispute, though, is less over how the economy *works* and more about what our priorities should be in guiding it.

Ideally, we would like our economy to do well in both the long run and the short run. Unfortunately, there is often a tradeoff between these two goals: Doing better in the short run can require some sacrifice of long-run goals, and vice versa. The problem for policymakers is much like that of the captain of a ship sailing through the North Atlantic: On the one hand, he wants to reach his destination (his long-run goal); on the other hand, he must avoid icebergs along the way (his short-run goal). As you might imagine, avoiding icebergs may require the captain to deviate from what might otherwise be the ideal long-run course. At the same time, achieving his long-run desire to reach port might require risking the occasional iceberg.

The same is true of the macroeconomy. If you flip back two chapters and look at Figure 4, you will see that there are two types of movements in total output—the long-run trajectory showing the growth of potential output and the short-run movements around that trajectory, which we call economic fluctuations or business cycles. Macroeconomists are concerned with both types of movements. But, as you will see, policies that can help us smooth out economic fluctuations may prove harmful to growth in the long run, while policies that promise a high rate of growth might require us to put up with more severe fluctuations in the short run.

MACROECONOMIC MODELS: CLASSICAL VERSUS KEYNESIAN

CLASSICAL MODEL A macroeconomic model that explains the long-run behavior of the economy, assuming that all markets clear.

The **classical model,** developed by economists in the 19th and early 20th centuries, was an attempt to explain a key observation about the economy: Over periods of several years or longer, the economy performs rather well. That is, if we step back from current conditions and view the economy over a long stretch of time, we see that it operates reasonably close to its potential output, and even when it deviates, it does not do so for very long. Business cycles may come and go, but the economy eventually returns to full employment. Indeed, if we think in terms of decades rather than years or quarters, the business cycle fades in significance much like the waves in a choppy sea disappear when viewed from a jet plane.

In the classical view, this behavior is no accident: Powerful forces are at work that drive the economy toward full employment. Many of the classical economists went even further, arguing that these forces operated within a reasonably short period of time. And even today, an important group of macroeconomists continues to believe that the classical model is useful even in the shorter run.

Until the Great Depression of the 1930s, there was little reason to question these classical ideas. True, output fluctuated around its trend, and from time to time there were serious recessions, but output always returned to its full-employment level within a few years or less, just as the classical economists predicted. But during the Great Depression, output was stuck far below its potential for many years. For some reason, the economy wasn't working the way the classical model said it should.

In 1936, in the midst of the Great Depression, the British economist John Maynard Keynes offered an explanation for the economy's poor performance. His new model of the economy—soon dubbed the *Keynesian model*—changed many economists' thinking.[1] Keynes and his followers argued that, while the classical model might explain the economy's operation in the long run, the long run could be very long indeed. In the meantime, production could be stuck below its full-employment level, as it seemed to be during the Great Depression.

Keynesian ideas became increasing popular in universities and government agencies during the 1940s and 1950s. By the mid-1960s, the entire profession had been won over: Macroeconomics *was* Keynesian economics, and the classical model was removed from virtually all introductory economics textbooks. You might be wondering, then, why we are bothering with the classical model here. After all, it's an older model of the economy, one that was largely discredited and replaced, just as the Ptolemaic view that the sun circled the earth was supplanted by the more modern, Copernican view. Right?

Not really. The classical model is, in fact, still very useful, in two different ways. First, in recent decades, there has been an active counterrevolution against Keynes's approach to understanding the macroeconomy. Many of the counterrevolutionary new theories—which we'll study in later chapters—are based largely on classical ideas. In some cases, the new theories are just classical economics in modern clothing, but in other cases significant new ideas have been added. By studying classical macroeconomics, we can better understand the controversies centering on these newer schools of thought.

The second—and more important—reason for us to study the classical model is its usefulness in understanding the economy over the long run. Even the many economists who find the classical model inadequate for understanding the economy in the short run find it extremely useful in analyzing the economy in the long run.

While Keynes's ideas and their further development help us understand economic fluctuations—movements in output around its long-run trend—the classical model has proven more useful in explaining the long-run trend itself.

This is why we will use the terms "classical view" and "long-run view" interchangeably in the rest of the book; in either case, we mean "the ideas of the classical model used to explain the economy's long-run behavior."

1 Keynes's attack on the classical model was presented in his book, *The General Theory of Employment, Interest and Money* (1936). Unfortunately, it's a very difficult book to read, though you may want to try. Keynes's assumptions were not always clear, and some of his text is open to multiple interpretations. As a result, economists have been arguing for decades about what Keynes really meant.

ASSUMPTIONS OF THE CLASSICAL VIEW

Remember from Chapter 1 that all models begin with *assumptions* about the world. The classical model is no exception. Many of the assumptions are merely simplifying—they make the model more manageable, enabling us to see the broad outlines of economic behavior without getting lost in the details. Typically, these assumptions involve aggregation, such as ignoring the many different interest rates in the economy and instead referring to a single interest rate, or ignoring the many different types of labor in the economy and analyzing instead a single aggregate labor market. These simplifications are usually harmless—adding more detail would make our work more difficult, but would not add much insight, nor would it change any of the central conclusions of the classical view.

There is, however, one assumption in the classical view that goes beyond mere simplification. This is an assumption about how the world works, and it is critical to the conclusions we will reach in this and the next chapter. We can state it in two words: *markets clear.*

MARKET CLEARING Adjustment of prices until quantities supplied and demanded are equal.

MARKETS AND EQUILIBRIUM

A critical assumption in the classical model is that ***markets clear:*** *The price in every market will adjust until quantity supplied and quantity demanded are equal.*

Does the market-clearing assumption sound familiar? It should: It was the basic idea behind our study of supply and demand. When we look at the economy through the classical lens, we assume that the forces of supply and demand work fairly well throughout the economy and that markets do reach equilibrium. An excess supply of anything traded will lead to a fall in its price; an excess demand will drive the price up.

The market-clearing assumption, which permeates classical thinking about the economy, provides an early hint about why the classical model does a better job over longer time periods (several years or more) than shorter ones. In many markets, prices might not fully adjust to their equilibrium values for many months or even years after some change in the economy. An excess supply or excess demand might persist for some time. Still, if we wait long enough, an excess supply in a market will eventually force the price down, and an excess demand will eventually drive the price up. That is, *eventually,* the market will clear. Therefore, when we are trying to explain the economy's behavior over the long run, market clearing seems to be a reasonable assumption.

In the remainder of the chapter, we'll use the classical model to answer a variety of important questions about the economy in the long run, such as:

- How is total employment determined?
- How much output will we produce?
- What is the role of *spending* in determining output?
- How is the price level determined?
- What happens when the government tries to change output or employment by changing total spending in the economy?

Keep in mind that, in our discussion of the classical model, we will focus on *real* variables: real GDP, the real wage, real saving, and so on. These variables are typically measured in the dollars of some base year, but they change only when the *purchasing power* of the underlying variable changes.

HOW MUCH OUTPUT WILL WE PRODUCE?

Over the last decade, the U.S. economy produced about $6 trillion worth of goods and services per year (valued in 1992 dollars). How was this average level of output determined? Why didn't we produce $10 trillion per year on average? Or just $2 trillion? There are so many things to consider when answering this question—variables you constantly hear about in the news—wages, interest rates, investment spending, government spending, taxes, and more. Each of these concepts plays an important role in determining total output, and our task in this chapter is to show how they all fit together.

But what a task! How can we hope to disentangle the complicated web of economic interactions we see around us? The best way is to begin at the beginning, with the *reason* for all this production in the first place. In the classical view, all production arises from one source: our desires for goods and services. More specifically,

> *in order to earn income so we can buy goods and services, we must supply labor and other resources to firms.*

The resources that households make available to firms—land, capital, and labor—are traded in different **resource markets.** For example, there is a market for industrial sites (land), a market for oil-drilling rigs (capital), and a market for pianists (labor). Although we could include hundreds or even thousands of different resource markets in a classical model of the economy, it would make the model needlessly complicated. This is why we concentrate our attention on just one type of resource—labor. In our classical world, we assume that firms are making use of all the capital and land available. We will not go into detail about how the prices of capital and land are determined. Moreover, since we are building a *macro*economic model, we'll aggregate all the different types of labor—office workers, construction workers, teachers, taxi drivers, waiters, writers, and more—into a single variable, called labor.

RESOURCE MARKETS Markets in which land, labor, and capital are traded.

THE LABOR MARKET

The labor market—where households sell, and firms buy, labor services—is illustrated in Figure 1. The number of workers is measured on the horizontal axis, and the real hourly wage rate is measured on the vertical axis. Remember that the *real wage*—which is measured in the dollars of some base year—tells us the amount of goods that workers can buy with an hour's earnings.

Now look at the two curves in the figure. These are supply and demand curves, similar to the supply and demand curves for maple syrup, but there is one key difference: for a *good* such as maple syrup, households are the demanders and firms the suppliers. But for labor, the roles are reversed: Households supply labor, and firms demand it.

The curve labeled L^S is the **labor supply curve** in this market; it tells us how many people will want to work at each wage. The upward slope tells us that the greater the real wage, the greater is the number of people who will want to work. The curve labeled L^D is the **labor demand curve,** which shows the number of workers firms will want to hire at any real wage. This curve slopes downward: The higher the wage, the fewer workers firms will want to employ.[2]

LABOR SUPPLY CURVE Indicates how many people will want to work at various wage rates.

LABOR DEMAND CURVE Indicates how many workers firms will want to hire at various wage rates.

2 If you have the microeconomics portion of this text or the comprehensive version, see the chapter on the labor market for a thorough explanation of why an increase in the wage rate tends to increase the quantity of labor supplied and decrease the quantity of labor demanded.

FIGURE 1

The equilibrium wage rate of $15 per hour is determined at point *E*, where the upward-sloping labor supply curve crosses the downward-sloping labor demand curve. At any other wage, an excess demand or excess supply of labor will cause the market to return to equilibrium.

THE LABOR MARKET

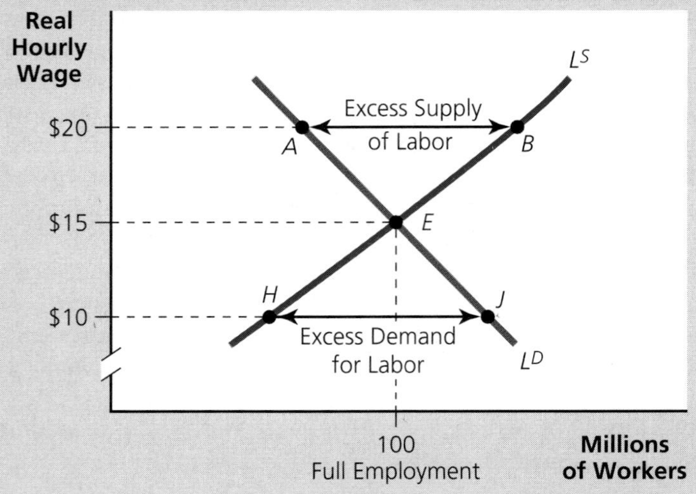

In the classical view, *all markets clear*—including the market for labor. That is, the real wage will adjust until the quantities of labor supplied and demanded are equal. In the labor market in Figure 1, the market-clearing wage is $15 per hour, since that is where the labor supply and labor demand curves intersect. While every worker would prefer to earn $20 rather than $15, at $20 there would be an excess supply of labor equal to the distance *AB*. With not enough jobs to go around, competition among workers would drive the wage downward. Similarly, firms might prefer to pay their workers $10 rather than $15, but at $10, the excess demand for labor (equal to the distance *HJ*) would drive the wage upward. When the wage is $15, however, there is neither an excess demand nor an excess supply of labor, so the wage will neither increase nor decrease. Thus, $15 is the equilibrium wage in the economy. Reading along the horizontal axis, we see that at this wage, 100 million people will be working.

Notice that, in the figure, labor is fully employed; that is, at the prevailing wage rate, the number of workers that firms want to hire is equal to the number of people who want jobs. Therefore, everyone who wants a job should be able to find one. Small amounts of frictional unemployment might exist, since it takes some time for new workers or job switchers to find jobs. And there might be structural unemployment, due to some mismatch between those who want jobs in the market and the types of jobs available. But there is no *cyclical* unemployment of the type we discussed two chapters ago.

Full employment of the labor force is an important feature of the classical model. As long as we can count on markets (including the labor market) to clear, government action is not needed to ensure full employment; it happens automatically:

In the classical view, the economy achieves full employment on its own.

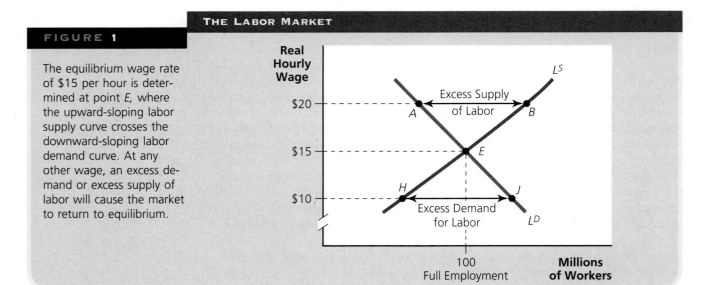

Automatic full employment may strike you as a bit odd, since it contradicts what we often see around us: substantial cyclical unemployment during recessions (as in the recession of the early 1990s). Remember, though, that the classical model takes the long-run view, and over long periods of time, full employment is a fairly accurate description of the U.S. labor market. Cyclical unemployment, by definition, lasts only as long as the current business cycle itself; it is not a permanent, long-run problem.

Determining the Economy's Output

So far, we've focused on the labor market to determine the economy's level of employment. In our example, 120 million people will have jobs. Now we ask, How much output will these 120 million workers produce? The answer depends on two things: (1) the amount of other resources (land and capital) available for labor to use; and (2) the state of *technology,* which determines how much output we can produce with given inputs, as well as the types of inputs available (horse-driven wagons or trucks; pencil and paper or a Pentium-chip computer).

In the classical model, we treat the quantities of land and capital, as well as the state of technology, as fixed during the period we are analyzing. This certainly makes sense in the case of land: Total acreage is pretty much fixed in a country, and there is little that anyone can do to increase it. But what about technology and capital? The state of technology changes with each new invention or discovery. We can already predict, for example, that over the next decade, gene splicing will lead to completely new drugs and other medical treatments and change the way many existing drugs are produced. And our capital stock changes rapidly as well, since we are constantly producing new capital—more shovels, irrigation pipes, tractors, computers, and factory buildings. How can we treat these as fixed, especially since the classical model is a long-run model?

The answer is: we assume that technology and the capital stock are constant *not* because we believe that they are, but because doing so helps us understand what happens when they change. We divide our classical analysis of the economy into two questions: (1) What would be the long-run equilibrium of the macroeconomy for a *given* state of technology and a *given* capital stock? and (2) What happens to this equilibrium when capital or technology *changes*? In this chapter, we focus on the first question only. In the next chapter, on economic growth, we'll address the second question. Since we are assuming, for now, a given state of technology, as well as given quantities of land and capital, there is only one variable left that can affect total output: labor. In the next section, we turn our attention to this all important variable and its impact on production.

The Production Function. The relationship between the quantity of labor employed in the economy and the total quantity of output produced is called the **aggregate production function:**

Aggregate production function The relationship showing how much total output can be produced with different quantities of labor, with land, capital, and technology held constant.

The aggregate production function shows the total output the economy can produce with different quantities of labor, holding constant the amounts of land and capital and the state of technology.

The bottom panel of Figure 2 shows what a nation's aggregate production function might look like. The upward slope tells us that an increase in the number of people working will increase the quantity of output produced. But notice the shape of the production function: It flattens out as we move rightward along it.

The declining slope of the aggregate production function is the result of *diminishing returns to labor:* Output rises when another worker is added, but the rise is smaller and smaller with each successive worker. Why does this happen? For one thing, as we keep adding workers, gains from specialization are harder and harder

FIGURE 2

OUTPUT DETERMINATION IN THE CLASSICAL MODEL

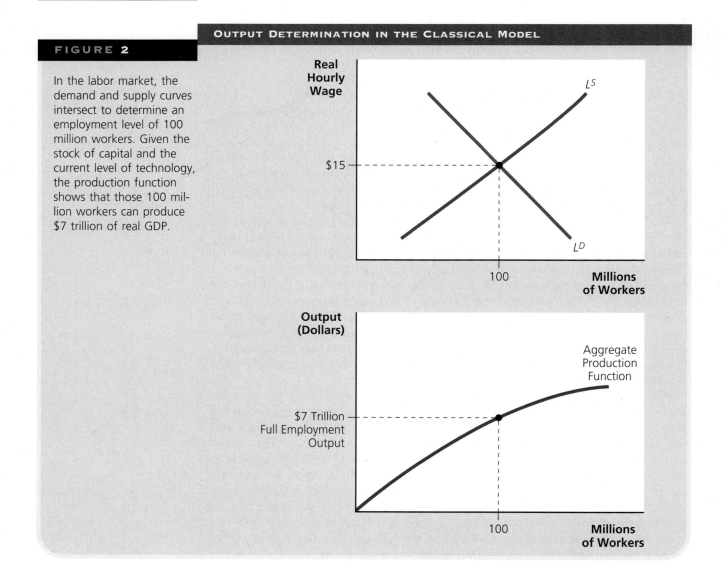

In the labor market, the demand and supply curves intersect to determine an employment level of 100 million workers. Given the stock of capital and the current level of technology, the production function shows that those 100 million workers can produce $7 trillion of real GDP.

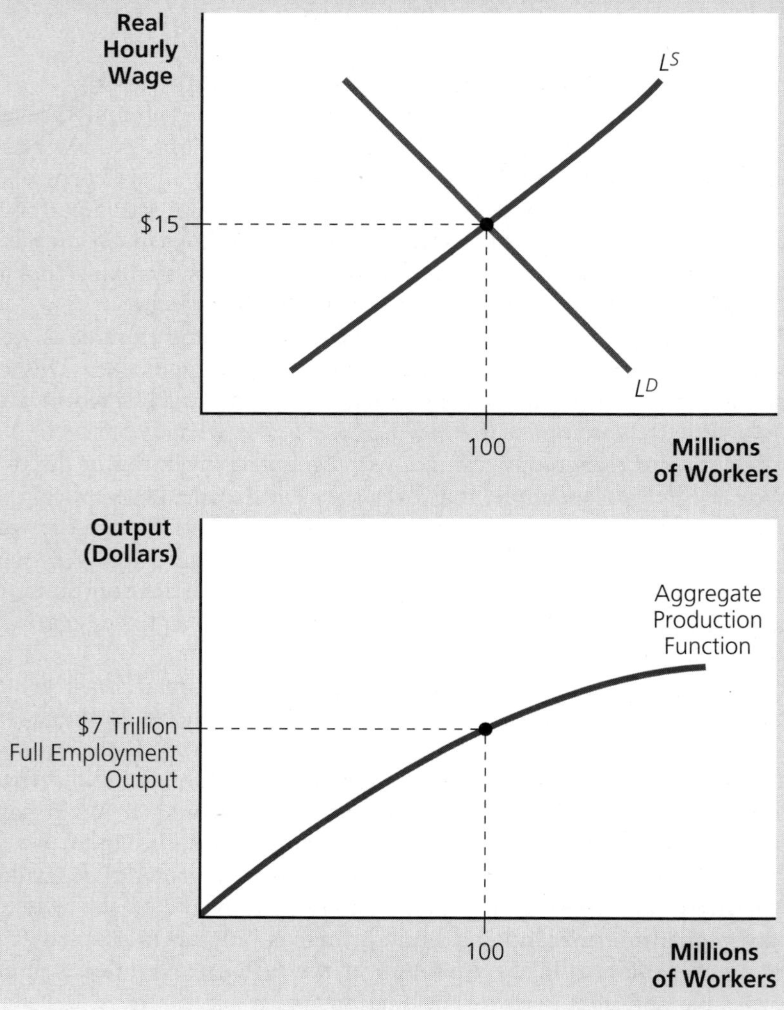

to come by. Moreover, as we continue to add workers, each one will have less and less capital and land with which to work.

Figure 2 also illustrates how the aggregate production function, together with the labor market, determines the economy's total output or real GDP. In our example, the labor market (upper panel) automatically generates full employment of 100 million workers, and the production function (lower panel) tells us that 100 million workers—together with the available capital and land and the current state of technology—can produce $7 trillion worth of output. Since $7 trillion is the output produced by a fully employed labor force, it is also the economy's potential output level. To stress that this output level results from market clearing in the labor market, we'll use the term **full-employment output level:**

FULL-EMPLOYMENT OUTPUT LEVEL The level of real GDP produced when the labor market clears.

In the classical, long-run view, the economy reaches its full-employment output level automatically.

This last statement is an important conclusion of the classical model and an important characteristic of the economy in the long run: Full-employment output tends to occur *on its own,* with no need for government to steer the economy toward it. And we have arrived at this conclusion merely by assuming that the labor market clears and observing the relationship between employment and output.

THE ROLE OF SPENDING

Something may be bothering you about the classical view of output determination—a potential problem we have so far carefully avoided: What if business firms are unable to sell all the output produced by a fully employed labor force? Then the economy would not be able to sustain full employment for very long. Thus, if we are asserting that full-employment output is an equilibrium for the economy, we had better be sure that *total spending* on output is equal to *total production* during the year. But can we be sure of this?

In the classical view, the answer is, absolutely yes! We'll demonstrate this in two stages: first, in a very simple (but very unrealistic) economy, and then, under more realistic conditions.

TOTAL SPENDING IN A VERY SIMPLE ECONOMY

Imagine a world much simpler than our own, a world with just two types of economic units: households and business firms. In this world, households spend all of their income on goods and services. They do not save any of their income, nor do they pay taxes. Such an economy is illustrated in the **circular flow** diagram of Figure 3.

CIRCULAR FLOW A diagram that shows how goods, resources, and dollar payments flow between households and firms.

The arrows on the right-hand side show that resources—labor, land, and capital—are supplied by households, and purchased by firms, in *resource markets.* In return, households receive payments—wages, rent, interest, and profit. For example, if you were working part time in a restaurant while attending college, you would be supplying a resource (labor) in a resource market (the market for waiters). In exchange, you would earn a wage. Similarly, the owner of the land on which the restaurant sits is a supplier in a resource market (the market for land) and will receive a payment (rent) in return. The payments received by resource owners are called *factor payments.*

On the left side of the diagram, the outer arrows show the flow of goods and services—food, new clothes, books, movies, and more—that firms supply, and households buy, in various *goods* markets. Of course, households must pay for these goods and services, and their payments provide revenue to firms—as shown by the inner arrows.

Now comes an important insight. As you learned two chapters ago, the total output of firms is equal to the total income of households. And in this simple economy—in which households spend all of their earnings—consumption spending will always equal total income. Putting all of this together, we find that in the simple economy, *total spending will always equal total output:*

> *In a simple economy with just households and firms, in which households spend all of their income, total spending must be equal to total output.*

SAY'S LAW The idea that total spending will be sufficient to purchase the total output produced.

This simple proposition is called **Say's law** after the classical economist, Jean Baptiste Say (1767–1832), who popularized the idea. Say noted that each time a good or

FIGURE 3

THE CIRCULAR FLOW

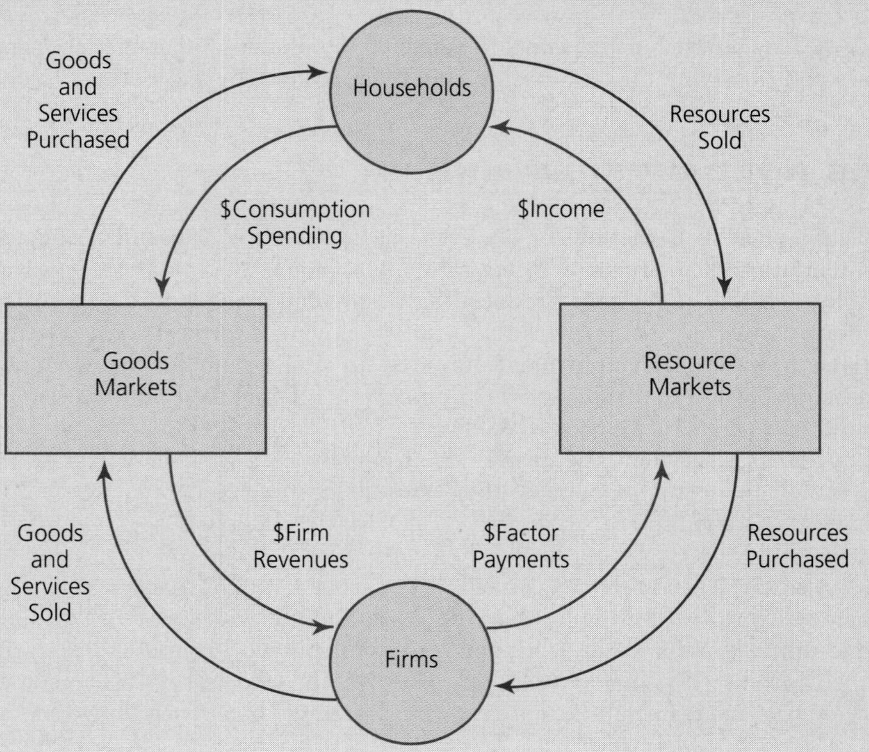

The outer loop of the diagram shows the flows of goods and resources. Households supply resources to firms, which use them to produce goods. The inner loop shows money flows. Firms' factor payments become income to households. Households use the income to purchase goods from firms.

service is produced, an equal amount of income is created. This income is spent—it comes back to the business sector to purchase its goods and services. In Say's own words:

A product is no sooner created than it, from that instant, affords a market for other products to the full extent of its own value . . . . Thus, the mere circumstance of the creation of one product immediately opens a vent for other products.[3]

For example, each time a shirt manufacturer produces a $25 shirt, it creates $25 in factor payments to households. (Forgot why? Go back two chapters.) But $25 in factor payments will lead to $25 in total spending—just enough to buy the very shirt produced. Of course, those households who receive the $25 in factor payments will not necessarily buy a shirt with it: The shirt manufacturer must still worry about selling its own output. But in the aggregate, we needn't worry about there being sufficient demand for the *total* output produced. Business firms—by producing output—also create a demand for goods and services equal to the value of that output. Or, to put it most simply, *supply creates its own demand*:

Say's law states that by producing goods and services, firms create a total demand for goods and services equal to what they have produced.

3 J. B. Say, *A Treatise on Political Economy,* 4th ed. (London: Longman, 1821), vol. I, p. 167.

Say's law is crucial to the classical view of the economy. Why? Remember that market clearing in resource markets assures us that firms will produce full-employment output. Say's law then assures us that, in the aggregate, firms will be able to *sell* this output, so that full employment can be sustained.

TOTAL SPENDING IN A MORE REALISTIC ECONOMY

The real world is more complicated than the imaginary one we've just considered. In the real world,

1. In addition to spending, households also *save* and *pay taxes;*
2. In addition to households, businesses and the government buy final goods and services; and
3. There is a *loanable funds* market where household saving is made available to borrowers in the business or government sectors.

All of these details complicate our picture of the economy. Can we have confidence that Say's law will hold under these more realistic conditions?

As you are about to see, yes we can.

Let's consider the economy of "Classica"—a fictional economy that behaves according to the classical model. Classica's economy in 1998 is described in Table 1. Notice that total output and total income are both equal to $7 trillion, which is assumed to be the full-employment output level.

Two entries in the table require a bit of explaining. First, **net taxes** are total tax revenue minus government transfer payments such as unemployment insurance, welfare payments, and social security benefits. As discussed two chapters ago, these transfer payments are the part of tax revenue that the government takes from one set of households and gives right back to another set of households. Since transfer payments stay within the household sector as a whole, we can treat them as if they were never paid to the government at all. Net taxes, then, are the funds that flow from the household sector as a whole to the government in any given year. Letting T represent net taxes, we have

NET TAXES Government tax revenues minus transfer payments.

$$T = \text{Total Taxes} - \text{Transfer Payments}$$

Second, **household saving** (often, just **saving**) is the after-tax income that the household sector, as a whole, earns and does *not* spend. Using the symbol S for household saving, Y for total income, and C for consumption spending, we can write

(HOUSEHOLD) SAVING The portion of after-tax income that households do not spend on consumption goods.

$$S = Y - T - C$$

FLOWS IN THE ECONOMY OF "CLASSICA," 1998

TABLE 1

Total Output	$7 trillion
Total Income	$7 trillion
Consumption Spending (*C*)	$4 trillion
Investment Spending (*I*)	$1 trillion
Government Spending (*G*)	$2 trillion
Net Tax Revenue (*T*)	$1.25 trillion
Household Saving (*S*)	$1.75 trillion

FIGURE 4

LEAKAGES AND INJECTIONS

By definition, total output equals total income. Leakages—net taxes and saving—reduce consumption spending below total income. Injections—government purchases plus investment—contribute to total spending. When leakages equal injections, total spending equals total income.

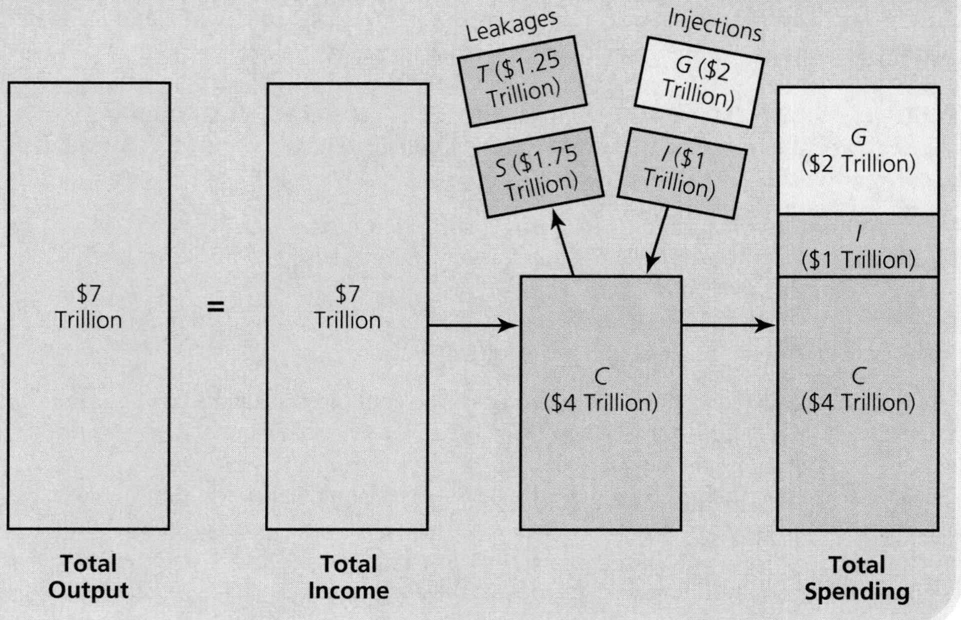

LEAKAGES AND INJECTIONS

As you can see in Table 1, Classica's households earn $7 trillion in income during the year, but they spend only $4 trillion. Part of the remaining $3 trillion goes to pay net taxes ($1.25 trillion), and whatever is left is, by definition, saved ($1.75 trillion). Saving and net taxes are called **leakages** out of the income–spending stream—income that households earn but do not spend. Leakages are important because they threaten our simple conclusion that total spending will always equal output.

LEAKAGES Income earned, but not spent, by households during a given year.

To see why, look at the rectangles in Figure 4. Total output (the first rectangle) is, by definition, always equal in value to total income (the second rectangle). As we've seen in Figure 3, if households spent all of this income, then consumption spending would equal total output. But leakages reduce consumption spending below total income, as you can see in the third, lower rectangle. In Classica, total leakages = $1.75 trillion + $1.25 trillion = $3 trillion, and this must be subtracted from income of $7 trillion to get consumption spending of $4 trillion. Thus, if consumption spending were the only spending in the economy, business firms would be unable to sell their entire full-employment output of $7 trillion.

INJECTIONS Spending from sources other than households.

Fortunately, in addition to leakages, there are **injections**—spending from sources other than households. More specifically, injections consist of the business sector's investment spending on new capital and the government's purchases of goods and services. Injections are the opposite of leakages: whereas leakages reduce total spending in the economy, injections increase it.

In Figure 4, the last rectangle shows how total injections—investment and government purchases—are added to consumption to obtain total spending. As you can see, total spending is the sum of consumption, investment, and government purchases. In Classica, using Table 1, we find that consumption spending is $4 trillion, investment spending is $1 trillion, and government purchases are $2 trillion, giving us total spending of $7 trillion.

This may strike you as suspiciously convenient: Total spending is exactly equal to total output, just as we would like it to be if we want firms to continue producing at full employment. And of course, we have cooked the numbers to make them come out that way. But do we have any reason to *expect* this result in an economy over the long run? Actually, we do.

Take another look at the rectangles in Figure 4. Notice that in going from total output to total spending, leakages are subtracted and injections are added. Clearly, total output and total spending will be equal only when leakages and injections are equal as well:

Total spending will equal total output if and only if total leakages in the economy are equal to total injections—that is, only if the sum of saving and net taxes is equal to the sum of investment spending and government purchases.

And here is a surprising result: This condition will automatically be satisfied. To see why, we must first take a detour through another important market. At the end of this detour, we'll come back to the all-important equality between leakages and injections.

The Loanable Funds Market

The **loanable funds market** is where households make their saving available to those who need additional funds. When you save—that is, when you have income leftover after paying taxes and buying consumption goods—you can put your surplus funds in a bank, buy a bond or a share of stock, or use the funds to buy a variety of other assets. In each of these cases, you would be a supplier in the loanable funds market.

Loanable funds market Arrangements through which households make their saving available to borrowers.

On the other side of the market are those who want to obtain funds—demanders in this market. Business firms are important demanders of funds. When Avis wants to add cars to its automobile-rental fleet, when McDonald's wants to build a new beef-processing plant, or when the local dry cleaner wants to buy new drycleaning machines, it will likely raise the funds in the loanable funds market. It may take out a bank loan, sell bonds, or sell new shares of stock. In each of these cases, a firm's investment spending would be equal to the funds it obtains from the loanable funds market.

Aside from business firms, the other major demander in the loanable funds market is the government. When government purchases of goods and services are greater than net taxes, the government runs a *deficit* for the year:

The government ***budget deficit*** *is the difference between government purchases (G) and net taxes (T):*

$$\text{Deficit} = G - T$$

Budget deficit The difference between government purchases and net taxes.

For example, Classica's budget deficit can be calculated from the information in Table 1. There, we see that government purchases are \$2 trillion, while net taxes are \$1.25 trillion, giving us a deficit of \$2 trillion − \$1.25 trillion = \$0.75 trillion. This deficit is financed by borrowing in the loanable funds market. In any year, the government's demand for funds is equal to its deficit.

Those who supply funds—households, in our model—receive a reward for doing so. Those who demand funds—business firms and the government—must pay

FIGURE 5

THE SUPPLY OF FUNDS

Interest is the reward for saving. The upward-sloping supply of funds curve shows that at higher interest rates, households consume less, save more, and supply more funds to the loanable funds market.

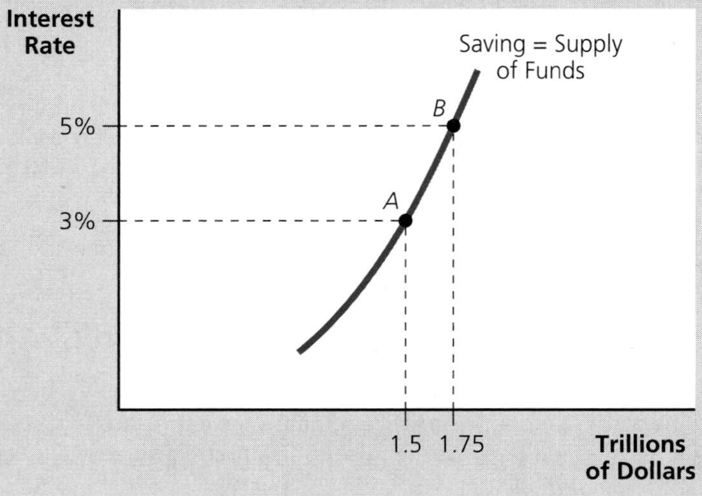

this reward. When funds are transferred from suppliers to demanders via banks or the bond market, the funds are *loaned* and the payment is called *interest*. When the funds are transferred via the stock market, the suppliers become part owners of the firm and their payment is called *dividends*. To keep our discussion simple, we'll assume that all funds transferred are *loaned* and that the payment is simply *interest*.

We can summarize our view of the loanable funds market so far with these three points:

- The supply of funds is household saving;
- The demand for funds is the sum of: (1) the business sector's investment spending and (2) the government sector's budget deficit.
- Demanders of funds pay interest to suppliers of funds.

The Supply of Funds Curve

SUPPLY OF FUNDS CURVE Indicates the level of household saving at various interest rates.

Since interest is the reward for saving and supplying funds to the financial market, a rise in the interest rate *increases* the quantity of funds supplied (household saving), while a drop in the interest rate decreases it. This relationship is illustrated by Classica's upward-sloping **supply of funds curve** in Figure 5. When the interest rate is 3 percent, households save $1.5 trillion, and if the interest rate rises to 5 percent, saving (and the supply of funds) rises to $1.75 trillion.

The quantity of funds supplied to the financial market depends positively on the interest rate. This is why saving, or the supply of funds curve, slopes upward.

Of course, other things can affect saving besides the interest rate—tax rates, expectations about the future, and the general willingness of households to postpone consumption, to name a few. In drawing the supply of funds curve, we hold each of these variables constant. In the next chapter, we'll explore what happens when some of these variables change.

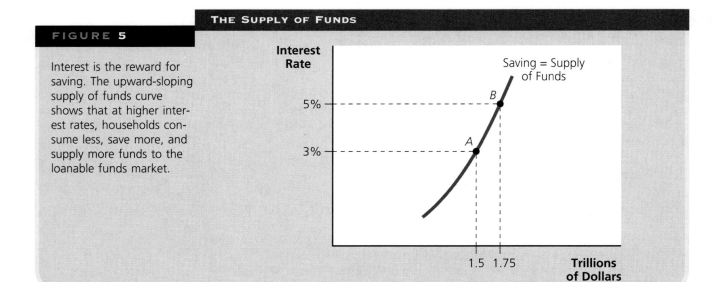

INVESTMENT SPENDING

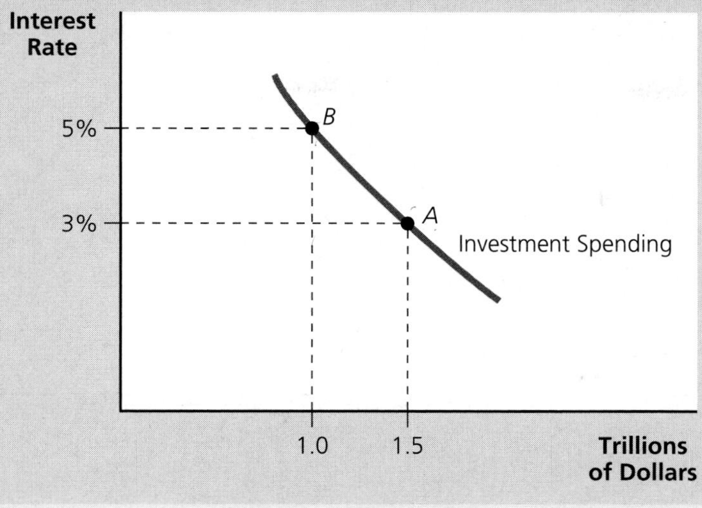

FIGURE 6

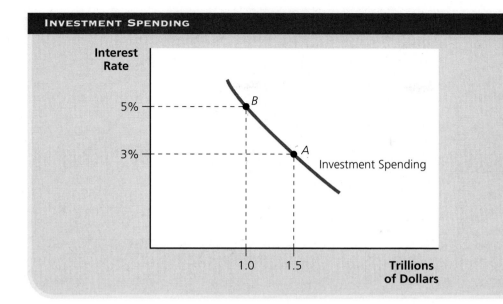

Businesses borrow in order to finance new investment, and the interest rate measures the cost of borrowing. The downward-sloping investment curve shows that more new projects will be financially attractive at low interest rates than at high rates.

THE DEMAND FOR FUNDS CURVE

Like saving, investment also depends on the interest rate. This is because businesses buy plant and equipment when the expected benefits of doing so exceed the costs. Since businesses obtain the funds for their investment spending from the loanable funds market, a key cost of any investment project is the interest rate that must be paid on borrowed funds. As the interest rate rises and investment costs increase, fewer projects will look attractive, and investment spending will decline. This is the logic of the downward-sloping **investment demand curve** in Figure 6. At a 5-percent interest rate, firms would borrow $1 trillion and spend it on capital equipment; at an interest rate of 3 percent, business borrowing and investment spending would rise to $1.5 trillion.

INVESTMENT DEMAND CURVE Indicates the level of investment spending firms plan at various interest rates.

When the interest rate falls, investment spending and the business borrowing needed to finance it rise. The investment demand curve slopes downward.

What about the government's demand for funds? Will it, too, be influenced by the interest rate? Probably not very much. Government seems to be cushioned from the cost–benefit considerations that haunt business decisions. Any company president who ignored interest rates in deciding how much to borrow would be quickly out of a job. U.S. presidents and legislators have often done so with little political cost.

For this reason, the classical model treats government borrowing as independent of the interest rate: No matter what the interest rate, the government sector's deficit—and its borrowing—remain constant. This is why we have graphed the **government's demand for funds curve** as a vertical line in panel (a) of Figure 7.

GOVERNMENT DEMAND FOR FUNDS CURVE Indicates the amount of government borrowing at various interest rates.

The government sector's deficit and, therefore, its demand for funds are independent of the interest rate.

FIGURE 7

THE DEMAND FOR FUNDS

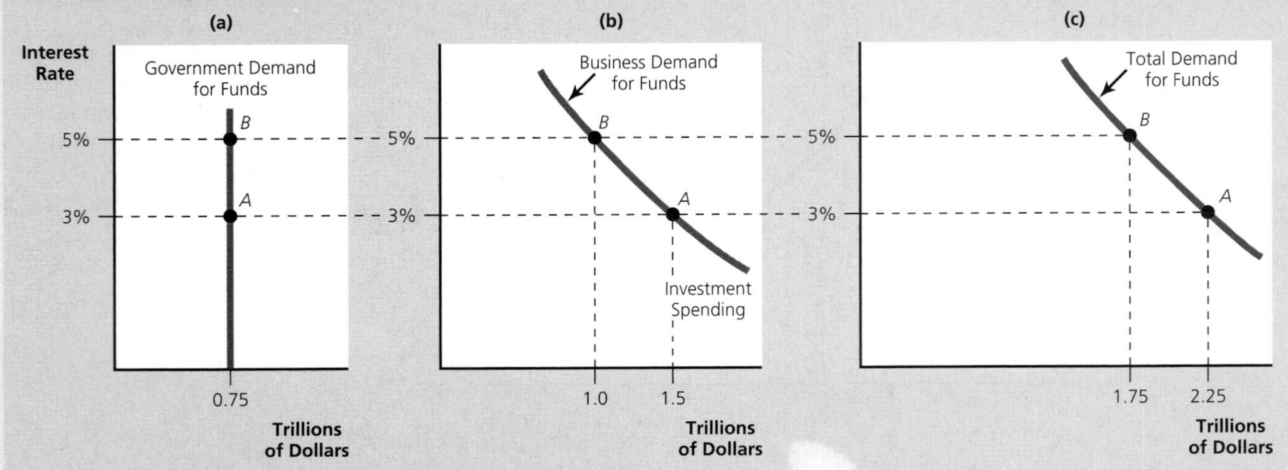

In panel (a), the government's demand for funds—to finance the budget deficit—is independent of the interest rate. Businesses' demand for funds—for investment—is inversely related to the interest rate in panel (b). The total demand for funds in panel (c) is the horizontal sum of government and business demand. At lower interest rates, more funds are demanded than at higher rates.

In the figure, the government deficit—and hence the government's demand for funds—is equal to $0.75 trillion at any interest rate.

TOTAL DEMAND FOR FUNDS CURVE Indicates the total amount of borrowing at various interest rates.

In Figure 7, the **total demand for funds curve** is found by horizontally summing the government demand curve (panel (a)) and the business demand curve (panel (b)). For example, if the interest rate is 5 percent, firms demand $1 trillion in funds, and the government demands $0.75 trillion, so that the total quantity of loanable funds demanded is $1.75 trillion. A drop in the interest rate—to 3 percent—increases business borrowing to $1.5 trillion, while the government's borrowing remains at $0.75 trillion, so the total demand for funds rises to $2.25 trillion.

As the interest rate decreases, the quantity of funds demanded by business firms increases, while the quantity demanded by the government remains unchanged. Therefore, the total quantity of funds demanded rises.

EQUILIBRIUM IN THE LOANABLE FUNDS MARKET

In the classical view, the loanable funds market—like all other markets—is assumed to clear: The price of funds will rise or fall until the quantities of funds supplied and demanded are equal. Figure 8 illustrates the financial market of Classica, our fictional economy. Equilibrium occurs at point *E*, with an interest rate of 5 percent and total saving equal to $1.75 trillion. Of the total saved, $1 trillion goes to business firms for capital purchases, and $0.75 trillion goes to the government to cover its deficit.

So far, our exploration of the loanable funds market has shown us how three important variables in the economy are determined: the interest rate, the level of

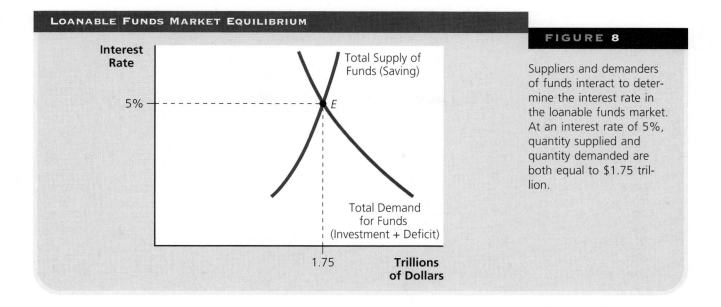

LOANABLE FUNDS MARKET EQUILIBRIUM

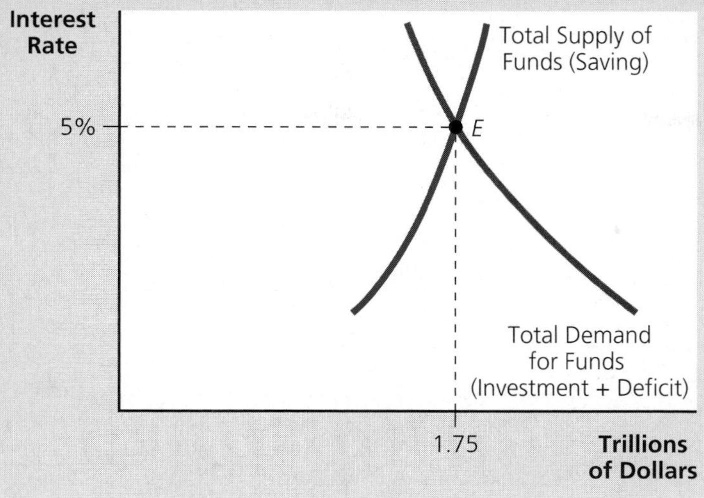

FIGURE 8

Suppliers and demanders of funds interact to determine the interest rate in the loanable funds market. At an interest rate of 5%, quantity supplied and quantity demanded are both equal to $1.75 trillion.

saving, and the level of investment. But it really tells us more. Remember the question that sent us on this detour into the loanable funds market in the first place: Can we be sure that all of the output produced at full employment will be purchased? We now have the tools to answer this question.

THE LOANABLE FUNDS MARKET AND SAY'S LAW

In Figure 4, you saw that total spending will equal total output if and only if *total leakages* in the economy (saving plus net taxes) are equal to *total injections* (planned investment plus government purchases). Now we can see how this requirement is satisfied automatically. Because the loanable funds market clears, we know that the interest rate—the price in this market—will rise or fall until the quantity of funds supplied (saving) and funds demanded (investment plus the deficit) are equal. Letting S stand for saving, I for investment, and $G - T$ for the deficit, we can state that the interest rate will adjust until

$$\underbrace{S}_{\substack{\text{Supply}\\\text{of}\\\text{funds}}} = \underbrace{I + G - T}_{\substack{\text{Demand}\\\text{for}\\\text{funds}}}$$

Rearranging this equation by moving T to the left side, we find that, when the loanable funds market clears,

$$\underbrace{S + T}_{\text{Leakages}} = \underbrace{I + G}_{\text{Injections}}$$

In other words, market clearing in the loanable funds market *assures us* that total leakages in the economy will equal total injections, which in turn *assures us* that

FIGURE 9

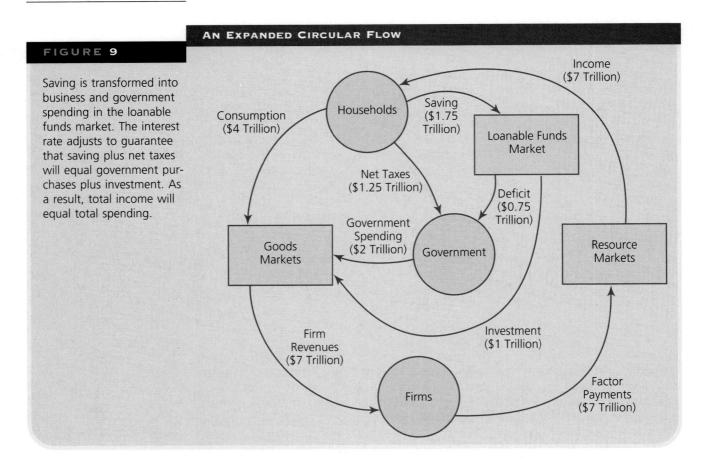

AN EXPANDED CIRCULAR FLOW

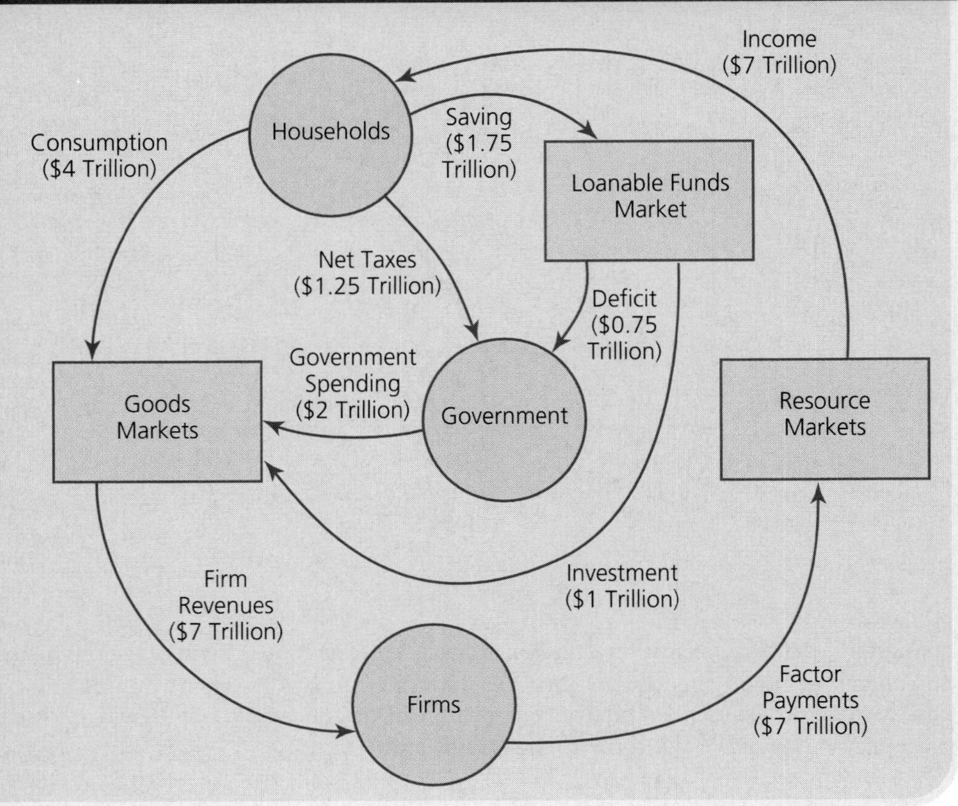

Saving is transformed into business and government spending in the loanable funds market. The interest rate adjusts to guarantee that saving plus net taxes will equal government purchases plus investment. As a result, total income will equal total spending.

there will be enough spending in the economy to purchase whatever output level is produced. Thus,

as long as the loanable funds market clears, Say's law holds even in a more realistic economy with saving, taxes, investment, and a government deficit.

To see the logic of this conclusion another way, go back to Figure 4. There, we saw that households spend only part of their income; the rest is either saved or paid as taxes. Now, taxes and saving do not just disappear from the economy: Tax payments go to the government, which spends them. Saving goes to the loanable funds market, where it will be passed along to the government or to business firms. In each case, the funds that households do not spend are simply passed along to another sector of the economy that *does* spend them. As long as the loanable funds market is working properly, income never escapes from the economy. Instead, every dollar in leakages is recycled back into the spending stream in the form of injections.

Figure 9 shows how leakages are transformed into injections. The dollar amounts are for the economy of Classica. In the figure, you can see that by producing $7 trillion in output, firms create $7 trillion in payments to inputs. Of this total, households spend $4 trillion. The rest goes to pay net taxes ($1.25 trillion) or is saved ($1.75 trillion). But taxes and saving do not escape from the economy:

The tax dollars of $1.25 trillion and part of the saving ($0.75 trillion) are spent by the government, whose purchases are $2 trillion. The rest of the saving ($1 trillion) is spent by business firms on new capital. In the end, the entire $7 trillion in output is purchased, just as Say's law asserts.

Say's law is a powerful concept. But be careful not to overinterpret it. Say's law shows that the *total* value of spending in the economy will equal the *total* value of output, which rules out a general overproduction or underproduction of goods in the economy. It does not promise us that each firm in the economy will be able to sell all of its output. It is perfectly consistent with Say's law that there be excess supplies in some markets, as long as they are balanced by excess demands in other markets.

But lest you begin to think that the classical economy might be a chaotic mess, with excess supplies and demands in lots of markets—don't forget about the *market-clearing* assumption. In each market, prices adjust until supplies and demands are equal. For this reason, the classical, long-run view rules out over- or underproduction in individual markets, as well as the generalized overproduction ruled out by Say's law.

MONEY AND PRICES IN THE CLASSICAL MODEL

So far, we've said very little about the price level in the economy. Now we turn our attention to this neglected variable. What determines the price level? What makes it change? And what happens in the economy when the price level *does* change?

In the classical, long-run view, the overall level of prices is determined by the quantity of money in circulation relative to the quantity of goods produced at full employment. Because of its emphasis on these two quantities, the classical economists called their theory of the price level the **quantity theory of money.**

QUANTITY THEORY OF MONEY The idea that the long-run price level depends on the supply of money.

The theory centers on the idea that there is a supply of money and a demand for money, and that the price level will adjust until the two are equal. For now, you can think of the supply of money as the total value of coins and bills in circulation, which is controlled by the government. (In a few chapters, you'll learn that the money supply—and the government's control of it—is a bit more complicated than that.) The demand for money, to which we now turn, depends on the public's behavior.

THE DEMAND FOR MONEY

What do we mean when we refer to the *demand* for money? Doesn't everyone want to have as much money as possible?

Indeed, everyone does. But when we speak about the *demand* for something, we don't mean the amount that people would desire if they could have all they wanted, without having to sacrifice anything for it. Instead, economic decision makers always face constraints: They must sacrifice one thing in order to have more of another. In the case of the demand for money, there is an important constraint: Households have only a given amount of *wealth*. The more of its wealth that a household holds in the form of money, the less it holds in other forms. Some of these other assets (such as housing or furniture) provide direct pleasure to their holders; some (such as livestock or land) earn income for their holders. But wealth in the form of money offers its holder neither direct pleasure nor additional income. Why, then, would anyone want to hold their wealth as money? To the classical economists, there was only one reason: Money is a *means of payment,* and therefore, it makes life more *convenient.* Simply put, money allows its possessor to make purchases with a minimum of fuss.

Since money's only value is to facilitate making purchases, it follows that the greater the value of total purchases, the greater the quantity of money people would want to hold. And since purchases tend to be more or less proportional to one's income, we can postulate, as the classical economists did, that the quantity of money people want to hold is equal to some proportion of their yearly nominal income.

To see this more clearly, suppose that the typical household wants to hold money equal to one-fifth of its yearly income. Then a household with an income of \$25,000 per year would want to hold \$5,000 worth of money, while a household with an income of \$100,000 per year would want to possess \$20,000 of money. If we add up the quantity of money that all households in the economy want to hold, we would find that it is the same proportion—one-fifth—of total nominal income in the economy.

It will be helpful to express the demand for money in equation form. If we let Y represent the quantity of goods produced (real output, which equals real income) and P represent the average price of goods in the economy, then PY will be the current dollar value of total production—nominal output and nominal income. Letting k represent the ratio of money to income that the public desires, we can state that

$$\text{Demand for money} = kPY$$

For example, if $k = 0.2$, $P = 1.0$, and $Y = \$7$ trillion, then the public would want to hold $0.2 \times 1.0 \times \$7$ trillion $= \$1.4$ trillion in money.

MONETARY EQUILIBRIUM

The term kPY tells us how much money people *want* to hold. But the amount of money that they *actually* hold is whatever amount the government has created. Let M represent the quantity of money in circulation. In order for people to be satisfied holding this quantity of money (that is, in order for the demand for money and the supply of money to be equal), the following must be true:

$$M = kPY$$

This is the *condition for monetary equilibrium*—a situation in which the entire money supply is being willingly held.

Notice that the condition for monetary equilibrium has four variables: M, k, P, and Y. But the values of three of these variables—M, k, and Y—are treated as givens when we consider monetary equilibrium. It's worthwhile to spend a moment discussing why.

The desired ratio of money to income (k) in the economy is determined in part by public attitudes. For example, if a decrease in the crime rate leads people to estimate a lower probability of being mugged or having their pocket picked, they might prefer to hold more of their wealth in the form of money, increasing the value of k. The ratio k is also influenced by the availability of substitutes for money in making purchases. For instance, the introduction of credit cards into an economy would decrease the desired cash holdings of the public—since people could make many of their purchases without cash. This would reduce the value of k.

But while the value of k may change, it is *not* affected by any of the variables that appear in the condition for monetary equilibrium. In particular, a change in M, P, or Y will not change either public tastes toward holding money or the availability of money substitutes, so the value of k will remain unchanged:

In the condition for monetary equilibrium, k *is a constant; it is not affected by changes in any of the other variables in the equation.*

What about the level of real output, Y? You've already learned how this is determined in the classical model: First, we find the equilibrium level of employment in the labor market (100 million workers in our example); then, we use the production function to tells us how much output this number of workers can produce ($7 trillion worth of output in our example). Since Y has already been determined by other forces—forces that have nothing to do with monetary equilibrium—by the time we get to the equation $M = kPY$, we can treat Y as given as well as k.

Finally, we treat the money supply, M, as given. The government can fix the money supply at whatever value it chooses, and there is no reason for that value to change unless the government wants it to change.

To recap:

In the condition for monetary equilibrium M = kPY, *we treat* k, Y, *and* M *as givens. Therefore, the condition for monetary equilibrium determines the value of just one variable: the price level* P.

To make this more concrete, let's suppose that in the economy of Classica, there is just one good. (This will allow us to express the price level as the price of the single good.) Suppose that total output of this good is 7 trillion units. Let's also suppose that the desired money–income ratio, k, is 0.2, and that the quantity of money in circulation is $2 trillion. Plugging these values into the monetary equilibrium equation, we have

$$0.2 \times P \times \$7 \text{ trillion} = \$2 \text{ trillion}$$

Solving for the price of output, we obtain

$$P = \$2 \text{ trillion}/(0.2 \times \$7 \text{ trillion}) = \$1.43$$

This last equation states that, in order for all $2 trillion in money in the economy to be willingly held, the price of output must equal $1.43—no more and no less.

But what would happen if this monetary equilibrium condition were *not* satisfied? Suppose that output actually cost only $1.00 per unit? In that case, money demand would be $kPY = 0.2 \times \$1.00 \times 7$ trillion $= \$1.4$ trillion. But *actual* money holdings—the quantity of money in circulation—would still be $2 trillion. That is, households would actually be holding more money than they wanted to hold. What would they do?

The classical economists argued that households would get rid of their money holdings by *spending* the excess. The increase in spending would create excess demand in markets for goods and services, raising prices throughout the economy. As the price level rose, desired money holdings (kPY) would rise also, and this

Name:
U.S. Department of Labor, Bureau of Labor Statistics (BLS) Data Page
Description:
Current and historical federal, state, and regional labor force data
Resources:
BLS provides recent and historical data on national employment and unemployment, consumer prices, labor costs, consumer expenditures, and labor productivity. It also provides regional and international labor data.
Address:
http://stats.bls.gov/datahome.htm

would continue until the public was satisfied holding the entire $2 trillion in money. As we know, this occurs when the price level is $1.43. Thus,

if the price level is below its equilibrium value, the public finds itself holding more money than it wishes to hold in that form. Increased spending will then drive the price level upward until it reaches equilibrium—that is, until the public is satisfied holding the quantity of money it is actually holding.

What if the price level were too *high,* above $1.43 in our example? As you can verify, if the price of output were, say, $2.00, the quantity of money demanded would equal $2.8 trillion, while actual money holdings would still be only $2 trillion. Households would want to hold a greater quantity of money than they were currently holding, so they would *decrease* spending in an attempt to acquire the money. This, in turn, would cause the price level to drop, decreasing the demand for money. The process would continue until the demand for money had decreased all the way to $2 trillion—the quantity of money that is actually circulating.

If the price level is greater than its equilibrium value, the public finds itself holding less money than it wishes to hold. Decreased spending will then drive the price level downward until it reaches equilibrium—that is, until the public is satisfied holding the quantity of money it is actually holding.

As you can see, whenever the price level departs from the level that creates monetary equilibrium, there are forces in the economy that push it back to its equilibrium value.

THE CLASSICAL MODEL: A SUMMARY

You've just completed a first tour of the classical model, our framework for understanding the economy in the long run. Before we begin to use this model, this is a good time to go back and review what we've done.

We began with a critical assumption: All markets clear. When applied to the labor market, market clearing guarantees that the economy will generate full employment. The production function tells how much output a fully employed labor force will produce. Then, market clearing in the loanable funds market assures us that total spending will be just sufficient to purchase the full-employment output level. Finally, the price level is determined by the condition for monetary equilibrium: The entire money supply must be willingly held.

In our excursion through the classical model, we've come to some important conclusions. First, we've seen that *the economy will achieve and sustain full-employment output on its own.* We have also reached an interesting conclusion about the role of spending in the economy: *We need never worry about there being too little or too much spending; Say's law assures us that total spending is always just right to purchase the economy's total output.*

All of this tells us that the government needn't worry much about the economy: It does fine on its own. But suppose the government wanted to stimulate the level of economic activity, in order to increase employment and output. Could the government do so by engineering an *increase* in total spending?

Let's be more specific: How would the government engineer an increase in spending? Two ideas come to mind. First, the government could simply spend more itself—purchasing more goods, like tanks and police cars, and more services, like those provided by high school teachers and judges. Alternatively, it could increase the money supply—say, by printing up new bills and circulating them among the public. In either case, spending would rise and business firms—able to sell more—would surely hire more workers and produce more goods and services. Right?

In the classical model, this is dead wrong. Government policies designed to change total spending in the economy, and thereby change output and employment, are called **demand management policies.** And in the classical model, demand management policies are completely ineffective: They cannot change total output or employment in the economy. Moreover, demand management policy is *unnecessary,* since the economy achieves and sustains full employment on its own.

DEMAND MANAGEMENT POLICIES Government policies designed to change the level of spending in the economy.

In the classical view, demand management policy is both ineffective and unnecessary.

But how can we know for certain that demand management policy is *ineffective* in the classical model? That is the subject of the "Using the Theory" section that follows.

FISCAL AND MONETARY POLICY IN THE CLASSICAL MODEL

USING THE THEORY

Although we will not study the Keynesian model until later, your thinking about the economy may already have been influenced by Keynesian ideas. This influence comes from the media, from public debates, and even from informal conversations about current issues. For example, it may seem quite natural to you that the government can use demand management policies—say, a change in government spending or taxes, or a change in the money supply—to influence the level of output and employment in the economy. In the classical model, however, demand management policies cannot work. In this final section of the chapter, we demonstrate why two types of demand management policy—a change in government purchases and a change in the money supply—cannot succeed in the classical, long-run model.

An Increase in Government Purchases

When the government either increases its spending or reduces taxes in order to influence the level of economic activity, it is engaging in *fiscal policy:*

Fiscal policy *is a change in government purchases or in net taxes designed to change total spending in the economy and thereby influence the levels of employment and output.*

FISCAL POLICY A change in government purchases or net taxes designed to change total spending and total output.

Let's see what would happen if the government of Classica attempted to increase employment and output by increasing its purchases. More specifically, suppose its purchases rise from the current \$2 trillion to \$2.5 trillion annually, while net taxes remain unchanged. What will happen?

To answer this, we must first answer another question: Where will Classica's government get the additional \$0.5 trillion it spends? If net taxes are unchanged (as we are assuming), then the government must dip into the loanable funds market to borrow the additional funds. Figure 10 illustrates the effects. Initially, with government purchases equal to \$2 trillion, the demand for funds curve is D_1, and

FIGURE 10

CROWDING OUT

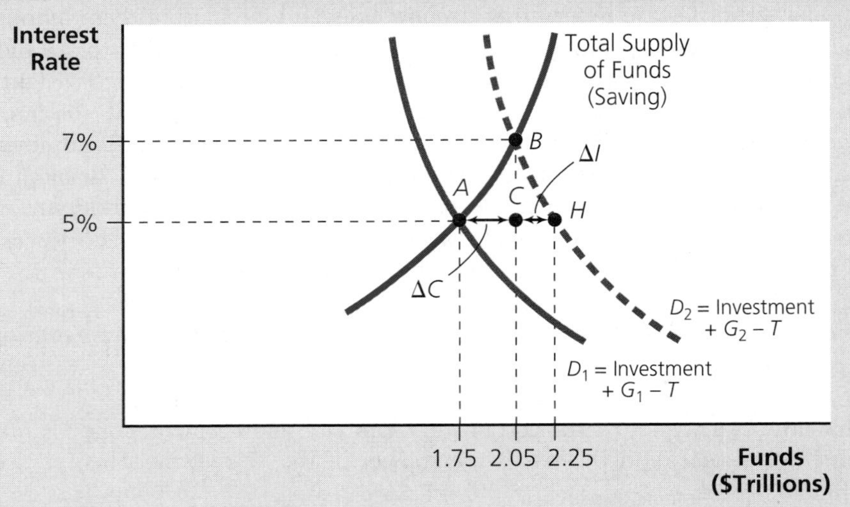

Beginning from equilibrium at point *A*, a budget deficit created to finance additional government purchases shifts the demand for funds curve from D_1 to D_2. At point *H*, the quantity of funds demanded exceeds the quantity supplied, so the interest rate begins to rise. As it rises, households are led to save more, and business firms invest less. In the new equilibrium at point *B*, both consumption and investment spending have been crowded out by the increased government spending.

equilibrium occurs at point *A* with the interest rate equal to 5 percent. If government purchases increase by $0.5 trillion, with no change in taxes, the budget deficit increases by $0.5 trillion, and so does the government's demand for funds. The demand for funds curve shifts rightward by $0.5 trillion to D_2, since total borrowing will now be $0.5 trillion greater at *any* interest rate. After the shift, there would be an excess demand for funds at the original interest rate of 5 percent. The total quantity of funds demanded would be $2.25 trillion (point *H*), while the quantity supplied would continue to be $1.75 trillion (point *A*). Thus, the excess demand for funds would be equal to the distance *AH* in the figure, or $0.5 trillion. This excess demand drives up the interest rate to 7 percent. As the interest rate rises, two things happen.

First, a higher interest rate chokes off some investment spending, as business firms decide that certain investment projects no longer make sense. For example, the local dry cleaner might wish to borrow funds for that new machine at an interest rate of 5 percent, but not at 7 percent. In the figure, as investment declines by $0.2 trillion (from $2.25 trillion to $2.05 trillion), we move along the new demand-for-funds curve D_2, from point *H* to point *B*. (Question: How do we know that only business borrowing, and not also government borrowing, adjusts as we move from point *H* to point *B*?) Thus, one consequence of the rise in government purchases is a *decrease in investment spending*.

But that's not all: The rise in the interest rate also causes saving to increase. Of course, when people save more of their incomes, they spend less, so another consequence of the rise in government purchases is a *decrease in consumption spending*. In the figure, we move from point *A* to point *B* along the saving curve, as saving increases (and consumption decreases) by \$0.3 trillion—rising from \$1.75 trillion to \$2.05 trillion.

Let's recap: As a result of the increase in government purchases, both investment spending and consumption spending decline. The government's purchases have *crowded out* the spending of households (C) and businesses (I).

Crowding out is a decline in one sector's spending caused by an increase in some other sector's spending.

Crowding out A decline in one sector's spending caused by an increase in some other sector's spending.

But we are not quite finished. If we sum the drop in C and the drop in I, we find that total private sector spending has fallen by \$0.3 trillion + \$0.2 trillion = \$0.5 trillion. That is, the drop in private sector spending is precisely equal to the rise in public sector spending, G. Not only is there crowding out, there is **complete crowding out**—each dollar of government purchases causes private sector spending to decline by a full dollar. The net effect is that total spending ($C + I + G$) does not change at all!

Complete crowding out A dollar-for-dollar decline in one sector's spending caused by an increase in some other sector's spending.

In the classical model, a rise in government purchases completely crowds out private sector spending, so total spending remains unchanged.

A closer look at Figure 10 shows that this conclusion always holds, regardless of the particular numbers used or the shapes of the curves. When G increases, the demand-for-funds curve shifts rightward by the amount that G increases, or the distance from point A to point H. Then the interest rate rises, causing two things to happen. First, we move along the supply of funds curve, from point A to point B, showing that saving rises (consumption falls) by the distance AC. Second, we move along the demand for funds curve, from point H to point B, showing that investment spending falls by the amount CH. The impact can be summarized as follows:

- Increase in $G = AH$
- Decrease in $C = AC$
- Decrease in $I = CH$

And since $AC + CH = AH$, we know that the combined decrease in C and I is precisely equal to the increase in G.

Because there is complete crowding out in the classical model, a rise in government purchases cannot change total spending. And the logic behind this result is straightforward. Each additional dollar the government spends is obtained from the financial market, where it would have been spent by someone else if the government hadn't borrowed it. How do we know this? Because the financial market funnels every dollar of household saving—no more and no less—to either the government or business firms. If the government borrows more, it just removes funds that would have been spent by businesses (the drop in I) or by consumers (the drop in C).

An increase in government purchases has no impact on total spending and no impact on total output or total employment.

Of course, the opposite sequence of events would happen if government purchases decreased: The drop in G would shrink the deficit. The interest rate would decline, and private sector spending (C and I) would rise by the same amount that government purchases had fallen. (See if you can draw the graphs to prove this to yourself.) Once again, total spending and total output would remain unchanged.

An Increase in the Money Supply

MONETARY POLICY Manipulation of the money supply to achieve some macroeconomic goal.

When a government attempts to achieve a macroeconomic goal by controlling or manipulating its money supply, it is engaging in **monetary policy.** We will have much to say about monetary policy in later chapters of this book. Here we ask just one question about it: Can monetary policy work as a *demand management policy*? That is, can the government, by changing the money supply, change total spending and thereby change employment or output? On the face of it, the answer would seem to be yes: Print up more money and put it into circulation, and households—finding themselves holding excess cash—will surely increase their spending as they reduce their cash holdings. This, in turn, will surely stimulate firms to produce more output and hire more workers. Right? Actually, the classical model suggests otherwise. Let's see why.

Suppose the government were to print more money and put it into circulation. (In later chapters, you'll learn precisely how the government puts money into circulation.) Immediately, the condition for monetary equilibrium—$M = kPY$—is thrown out of balance. For given values of k and Y, and a given price level P, people are now holding more cash than they want to hold, given their incomes. What will they do? As discussed earlier in the chapter, the public will attempt to reduce its excess cash holding by increasing its spending. This, in turn, will increase the demand for goods and services, and cause prices to rise throughout the economy.

But the increase in demand will be only temporary. As the price level rises, people will discover that they want to hold *more* cash, since their purchases cost them more. The price level will continue to rise until the condition for monetary equilibrium—$M = kPY$—once again holds. At this point, the public will be content to hold the new, greater money supply, and the temporary burst of additional spending caused by the increase in the money supply will come to a halt. In the end, after the increase in the money supply, the price level is higher, but the total demand for goods and services, as well as total output and employment, all return to their original values.

But something about this analysis might be bothering you. Since prices are higher, won't business firms respond by producing more goods and services? After all, in Chapter 3 you learned that supply curves slope upward: A rise in price will induce a firm to produce more output. As the price level rises, so that prices are rising throughout the economy, won't *all* firms increase their output? And wouldn't that mean that Y increases?

The answer is no: In the classical view, output does not change in response to a rise in the price level. In Chapter 3, when we moved along the supply curve in a single market, we assumed that many things remained constant, including the wage rate that firms pay their workers. But there is no reason for the wage to remain constant when prices are rising throughout the economy. In fact, as you are about to see, a rise in the price level will *cause* the wage to rise—by just enough to prevent any change in output.

WHY PRICE LEVEL CHANGES DON'T CHANGE EMPLOYMENT OR OUTPUT. Look back at Figure 1, which shows how labor demand and labor supply both depend on the real wage. Initially, the real wage is $15, and the economy is operating at full employment.

Now suppose that the price level rises, and imagine—for the moment—that the nominal wage were to remain unchanged. Then the real wage, by definition, would fall *below* \$15. For example, if the price level rose by 50 percent, then the real wage would fall from \$15 to \$10. But, as Figure 1 shows, with a real wage of \$10, there would be an excess demand for labor. Firms—competing with each other to hire more workers—would start paying higher wages. Thus, *a rise in the price level causes a rise in the nominal wage.*

When will the nominal wage rate stop rising? Only when the excess demand for labor is eliminated, which occurs only when the real wage is restored to \$15. Since the price level rose by 50 percent, the nominal wage will have to rise by 50 percent as well. Thus, the nominal wage will rise from \$15 to \$22.50.

When the price level rises, the nominal wage will rise by the same percentage as the price level. As a result, a rise in the price level causes no change in the real wage.

Now you can see why a rise in the price level causes no change in output in the classical model. With the real wage unchanged, employment remains unchanged as well. And since output depends on employment, output remains unaffected as well.

A rise in the price level causes the nominal wage to change, but causes no change in the real wage, employment, or output.

THE CLASSICAL DICHOTOMY. This notion—that changes in the quantity of money can affect nominal, but not real, variables in the economy—was a central idea of the classical economists. The line of causation going from the money supply to the price level works via a temporary increase in spending. But the causal link determining employment, production, and income is entirely separate: It involves only the labor market and the production function. This causal separation has been called the *classical dichotomy*:

CLASSICAL DICHOTOMY The classical idea that real variables are independent of the quantity of money in the economy.

THE IMPORTANCE OF REAL VALUES

The **classical dichotomy** *states that real variables—such as employment and output—are independent of the quantity of money circulating in the economy. Monetary policy can affect the price level and nominal variables, like the nominal wage, but it cannot affect real variables such as real output or the real wage.*

The classical dichotomy is an important property of the classical, long-run view. It means that monetary policy is completely ineffective as a tool to manage the economy in the long run. In the classical view, changing the money supply will change the price level, but it cannot change the overall level of economic activity.

Our exploration of monetary and fiscal policy supports the conclusion stated in the body of this chapter: In the long run, demand management policy by the government is not only unnecessary, it is also ineffective in changing output and employment. What, then, *should* a government do to help manage the macroeconomy in the long run? And what *can* it do? These are questions we explore in the next chapter, where we use the classical model to analyze how the economy grows and what governments can do to help or hinder that growth.

SUMMARY

The classical model is an attempt to explain the behavior of the economy over long time periods. Its most critical assumption is that markets clear—that prices adjust in every market to equate quantities demanded and supplied. The labor market is perhaps the most important part of the classical model. The quantity of labor employed when the labor market clears is termed the *full-employment* level of employment.

Another important concept is the production function. It shows the total output the economy can produce with different quantities of labor and for given amounts of land and capital and a given state of technology. When the labor market is at full employment, the production function can be used to determine the economy's full-employment level of output.

According to Say's law, total spending in the economy will always be just sufficient to purchase the amount of total output produced. By producing and selling goods and services, firms create a total demand equal to what they have produced. If households do not spend their entire incomes, the excess is channeled—as saving—into the loanable funds market, where it is borrowed and spent by businesses and government.

In the loanable funds market, the supply of funds equals household saving, which is directly related to the interest rate. The demand for funds arises from business firms that wish to use the funds to invest in new capital and from governments that need the funds to finance their budget deficits. The demand for funds is inversely related to the interest rate. The interest rate adjusts so that the quantity of funds supplied always equals the quantity demanded. Equivalently, it adjusts so that saving (S) equals the sum of investment spending (I) and the government budget deficit ($G - T$).

In the classical model, the overall price level is determined by the quantity of money in circulation relative to the amount of goods produced. The supply of money is set by the government. The demand for money is proportional to nominal income: $M = kPY$. For a given value of k and with Y at its full-employment level, the price level rises and falls whenever the money supply rises and falls.

Neither fiscal nor monetary policy can affect total output in the classical model. An increase in goverment purchases results in complete crowding out of investment and consumption spending, leaving total spending and total output unchanged. An increase in the money supply causes a rise in the price level but no change in total output.

KEY TERMS

classical model
market clearing
resource markets
labor supply curve
labor demand curve
aggregate production function
full-employment output level
circular flow
Say's law
net taxes
(household) saving
leakages
injections
loanable funds market
budget deficit
supply of funds curve
investment demand curve
government demand for funds curve
total demand for funds curve
quantity theory of money
demand management policies
fiscal policy
crowding out
complete crowding out
monetary policy
classical dichotomy

REVIEW QUESTIONS

1. Discuss the critical assumption on which the classical model is based. How does it relate to the length of time over which we are analyzing the economy?
2. Describe how, in the classical model, the economy reaches full employment automatically. Is this a "realistic" depiction of how the economy behaves?
3. Why does the classical model treat technology and the capital stock as constant?
4. Explain why the slope of the aggregate production function diminishes as more labor is employed.
5. "Say's law implies that all markets always clear." True or False. Explain.
6. What is the difference between net taxes and total tax revenue? Why is the distinction important?
7. Who are the two major players on the demand side of the loanable funds market? Why does each seek funds there? What is the "price" of these funds?
8. What is the source of funds supplied to the loanable funds market? Explain why the supply of funds curve slopes up, and why the curve depicting business demand for funds slopes down.

9. How will the slope of the demand for funds curve be affected if the government runs a deficit? Why?

10. Why does Say's law hold even after household saving and taxes are taken into account?

11. Explain the implications of the classical model for government economic policy. What are the two consequences of an increase in government spending that the model predicts?

12. A senator asserts that deficit spending reduces business investment dollar for dollar—every dollar the government borrows means that business investment must fall by a dollar. Is he correct? Why or why not?

13. What determines the price level in the classical model?

14. What are the disadvantages of holding your wealth in the form of money? What is the primary advantage?

15. What variables are assumed as given in the monetary equilibrium condition? Why can they be treated in this way?

16. Describe the forces that drive the price level to its equilibrium value.

17. What is the classical dichotomy? What, specifically, does it imply about macroeconomic policy?

PROBLEMS AND EXERCISES

1. The following data give a complete picture of the household, business, and government sectors for 1998 in the small nation of Sylvania. (All figures are in billions.)

Consumption spending	\$ 50
Capital stock (end of 1997)	\$100
Capital stock (end of 1998)	\$103
Government welfare payments	\$ 5
Government unemployment insurance payments	\$ 2
Government payroll	\$ 3
Government outlays for equipment and material	\$ 2
Depreciation rate	7%
Interest rate	6%

   a. Assuming the government budget for 1998 was in balance, calculate total investment, goverment purchases, real GDP, total saving, and net taxes for this economy.
   b. Calculate total leakages and total injections.
   c. Now suppose, instead, that the government increased its spending by \$2 billion for the year, with no change in taxes. Explain how the variables from (a) will be affected (i.e., will they increase or decrease?).
   d. Draw a graph depicting the situation in the loanable funds market reflecting the assumption of a balanced budget. Clearly label the equilibrium interest rate, saving, and demand for funds, Now, add another curve reflecting any change that occurs when the government runs a deficit; show what happens to the variables you discussed in (c).
   e. Under the assumption in (c), suppose Sylvania has a usury law that prohibits interest rates from going above 6 percent. Explain what will happen now in the loanable funds market, and in the economy as a whole.

2. The country of Marginalia is seething with discontent due to a recent economic downturn. The king, feeling his throne to be in peril, has come upon what he is convinced is the perfect solution: helicopter drops of additional currency across his realm.

   Only one good, kumquats, is bought and sold in the country. They cost 2 semis apiece (the semi is the local currency), and 1 million are produced each year. Prior to the helicopter drop, there are 400,000 semis circulating in the country.

   a. Assuming the country is in monetary equilibrium prior to the helicopter drop, what is the ratio of desired money holdings to income?
   b. If the king drops 200,000 more semis on the country, what variable will most likely change and by how much? Why does this effect arise? What will happen to the nominal wage? The real wage? Are the people of Marginalia any better off?
   c. One of the king's advisors, dissuades him from the helicopter drop idea. He recommends that the king increase government spending on roads and bridges, and pay for the increase by enlarging the kingdom's deficit. He claims this will improve the lot of the average citizen. Another advisor recommends against the policy, claiming it will lower living standards. What information would we need to determine which advisor is correct?

3. Use graphs to depict the effect on saving, investment, and the interest rate of a *decrease* in the government deficit.

CHALLENGE QUESTIONS

1. If Say's law holds, speculate as to why there are periods of recession and cyclical unemployment. Does this necessarily mean that the classical model is unvalid? Why or why not?

2. Assume the loanable funds market is in equilibrium. Influential media pundits begin to warn about impending economic doom—recession, layoffs, and so forth. Using graphs, discuss what might happen to the equilibrium interest rate and the equilibrium quantity of funds.

3. Will crowding out be more severe if the investment is more sensitive to the interest rate, or less sensitive? Explain, using graphs in your answer.

4. In the real world, can you think of another leakage out of the circular flow besides taxes and saving? Conversely, what is another injection besides investment and government spending? (*Hint:* Think about spending on *domestic* output.)

Visit the data page for the Bureau of Labor Statistics. Within "Selective Access," then within "Local Area Unemployment Statistics," retrieve the seasonally adjusted unemployment rate for your home state for the last 10 years. Review the discussion of full employment in this chapter, and answer the following questions. Assuming that that full employment requires that the unemployment rate be 5.5 percent or lower:

a. How many years was your state at or above full employment?
b. How many years was it below full employment?

CHAPTER

8

ECONOMIC GROWTH AND RISING LIVING STANDARDS

Economist Thomas Malthus, writing in 1798, came to a striking conclusion: "Population, when unchecked, goes on doubling itself every twenty-five years, or increases in a geometrical ratio. . . . The means of subsistence . . . could not possibly be made to increase faster than in an arithmetic ratio."[1] From this simple logic, Malthus forecast the long-run economic fate of the human race: repeated famines and wars to keep the population in balance with the supply of food and other necessities. The prognosis was so pessimistic that it led Thomas Carlyle, one of Malthus's contemporaries, to label economics "the dismal science."

But history has proven Malthus wrong . . . at least in part. In the industrialized nations, living standards have increased beyond the wildest dreams of anyone alive in Malthus's time, and economists today are optimistic about these nations' long-run material prospects. At the same time, living standards in many of the less developed countries have remained stubbornly close to survival level and, in some cases, have fallen below it.

What are we to make of this? Why have living standards steadily increased in some nations but not in others? And what, if anything, can governments do to speed the rise in living standards? These are questions about economic growth—the long-run increase in an economy's output of goods and services.

In this chapter, you will learn what makes economies grow. You will also see that increasing the rate of economic growth is not easy. While nations can take measures to speed growth, each measure carries an opportunity cost. As you'll see,

achieving a higher rate of growth in the long run generally requires some sacrifice in the short run.

1 Thomas Robert Malthus, *Essay on the Principle of Population,* 1798.

CHAPTER OUTLINE

THE IMPORTANCE OF GROWTH

Why should we be concerned about economic growth? For one simple reason:

*When output grows faster than the population, GDP per capita—which we call the **average standard of living**—will rise. When output grows more slowly than the population, GDP per capita, or the average living standard, will fall.*

AVERAGE STANDARD OF LIVING Total output (real GDP) per person.

Measuring the standard of living by GDP per capita may seem limiting. After all, as we saw two chapters ago, many important aspects of our quality of life are not captured in GDP. Leisure time, workplace safety, good health, a clean environment—we care about all of these. Yet they are not considered in GDP. Still, many aspects of our quality of life *are* counted in GDP: food, housing, medical care, education, transportation services, and movies and video games, to name a few. It is not surprising, then, that economic growth—measured by increases in GDP—remains a vital concern in every nation.

Economic growth is especially important in countries with income levels far below those of Europe, Japan, and the United States. The average standard of living in some third-world nations is so low that many families can barely acquire the basic necessities of life, and many others perish from disease or starvation. Table 1 lists GDP per capita, infant mortality rates, life expectancies, and adult literacy rates for some of the richest and poorest countries. The statistics for the poor countries are grim enough, but even they capture only part of the story. Unsafe and unclean workplaces, inadequate housing, and other sources of misery are part of daily life for most people in these countries. Other than emigration, economic growth is their only hope.

TABLE 1

SOME INDICATORS OF ECONOMIC WELL-BEING IN RICH AND POOR COUNTRIES, 1993

Country	GDP per Capita	Infant Mortality Rate (per 1,000 live births)	Life Expectancy at Birth	Adult Literacy Rate
RICH COUNTRIES				
United States	$24,680	8.4	76.1	Greater than 99%
Japan	$20,660	4.3	79.6	Greater than 99%
France	$19,140	6.8	77.0	Greater than 99%
Italy	$18,160	7.8	77.6	97.4%
United Kingdom	$17,230	7.4	76.3	Greater than 99%
POOR COUNTRIES				
Pakistan	$ 2,160	89	61.8	36.4%
Ghana	$ 2,000	80	56.2	62.0%
Cambodia	$ 1,250	115	51.9	35.0%
Afghanistan	$ 800	163	43.7	29.8%
Ethiopia	$ 420	118	47.8	33.6%
Zaire	$ 300	92	52.0	75.2%

Sources: United Nations Development Program, *Human Development Report, 1996* (Oxford: Oxford University Press, 1996), Tables 1, 6, 26; U.S. Department of Commerce, *Statistical Abstract of the United States, 1996* (Washington, U.S. Government Printing Office, 1996).

AVERAGE ANNUAL GROWTH OF OUTPUT PER CAPITA (PERCENT PER YEAR)

TABLE 2

Country	1948–1972	1972–1988	1988–1995
United States	2.2	1.7	1.0
United Kingdom	2.4	2.1	0.9
Canada	2.9	2.6	0.6
France	4.3	2.1	1.2
Italy	4.9	2.8	1.6
West Germany	5.7	2.2	1.3
Japan	8.2	3.3	2.1

Source: Angus Maddison, *Phases of Capitalist Development* (Oxford: Oxford University Press, 1982), and various World Bank publications.

Growth is a high priority in prosperous nations, too. As we know, resources are scarce, and we cannot produce enough of everything to satisfy all of our desires simultaneously. We want more and better medical care, education, vacations, compact discs . . . the list is endless. When output per capita is growing, everyone can enjoy an increase in material well-being without anyone having to cut back. We can also accomplish important social goals—helping the poor, improving education, cleaning up the environment—by sacrificing part of the rise in our material well-being, rather than suffering a drop.

But when output per capita stagnates, material gains become a fight over a fixed pie: The more purchasing power my neighbor has, the less is left for me. With everyone struggling for a larger piece of this fixed pie, strife replaces cooperation. Efforts to help the less fortunate, wipe out illiteracy, reduce air pollution—all are seen as threats, rather than opportunities.

In the 1950s and 1960s, economic growth in the wealthier nations seemed to be taking care of itself. Economists and policy makers focused their attention on short-run movements around full-employment output, rather than on the growth of full-employment output itself. The real payoff for government seemed to be in preventing recessions and depressions—in keeping the economy operating as close to its potential as possible.

All of that changed starting in the 1970s, and since then economic growth has become a national and international preoccupation. Like most changes in perception and thought, this one was driven by experience. Table 2 tells the story. It gives the average yearly growth rates of real GDP per capita for the United States and some of our key trading partners.

Over most of the postwar period, output in the more prosperous industrialized countries (such as the United States, the United Kingdom, and Canada) grew by 2 or 3 percent per year, while output in the less wealthy ones—those with some catching up to do—grew even faster. But beginning in the mid-1970s, all of these nations saw their growth rates slip.

Looking at the table, you might think that this slowing in growth was rather insignificant. Does the tiny difference between the pre-1972 and the post-1972 growth rates in the United States really matter? Indeed, it does. Recall our example a few chapters ago in which a 1-percentage-point increase in the growth rate would, over 23 years, mean an additional $16,000 worth of output at today's prices for every American. Seemingly small differences in growth rates matter a great deal.

WHAT MAKES ECONOMIES GROW

Today we understand much more about economic growth than we did in the days of Thomas Malthus. Yet virtually all of our modern ideas about growth are based on the classical model you studied in the previous chapter—and for good reason: Economic growth is a *long-run* phenomenon. The classical model is particularly well suited to analyze long-run economic problems, including the problem of growth.

From the classical model, we know that the economy tends to operate at its full-employment output level over the long run. When we think about the causes of economic growth, then, we should think about changes that would cause full-employment output to increase. In virtually all countries enjoying economic growth, the three most important causes are increases in employment, increases in the capital stock, and changes in technology. In the next several pages, we'll look at each of these in turn.

GROWTH IN EMPLOYMENT

In the long run, as the classical model shows, the economy tends to generate a job for just about everyone who wants to work. Therefore, total employment will rise whenever the *labor force*—the number of people who have or want jobs—increases. But what causes the labor force to increase?

One possibility is an increase in labor *supply:* a rise in the number of people who would like to work at any given wage. This is illustrated, in Figure 1, by a rightward shift in the labor supply curve. We'll discuss *why* the labor supply curve might shift a bit later; here, we'll concentrate on the consequences of the shift.

Before the shift, the labor supply curve is L_1^S, the market clears at a wage of \$15 per hour, and the fully employed labor force is 100 million workers. The aggregate production function tells us that, with the given amounts of capital and land in the economy, and the given state of technology, 100 million workers can produce \$7 trillion in goods and services—the initial value of full-employment output, Y_{FE}. When the labor supply curve shifts to L_2^S, the market-clearing wage drops to \$12. Business firms—finding labor cheaper to hire—increase the quantity of workers employed along the labor demand curve, from point *A* to point *B*. The labor force increases to 120 million workers, and full-employment output rises to \$8 trillion.

But growth in employment can also arise from an increase in labor demand: a rise in the number of workers firms would like to hire at any given wage. Once again, we'll consider the *causes* of labor demand changes momentarily; here, we focus on the *consequences.*

Graphically, an increase in labor demand is represented by a rightward shift in the labor demand curve, as in Figure 2. As the wage rate rises from \$15 to its new equilibrium of \$17, we move along the labor supply curve from point *A* to point *B:* More people decide they want to work as the wage rises. Equilibrium employment once again rises from 100 million to 120 million workers, and full-employment output rises from \$7 trillion to \$8 trillion. Thus,

MARKETS AND EQUILIBRIUM

growth in employment can arise from an increase in labor supply (a rightward shift in the labor supply curve) or an increase in labor demand (a rightward shift of the labor demand curve).

AN INCREASE IN LABOR SUPPLY

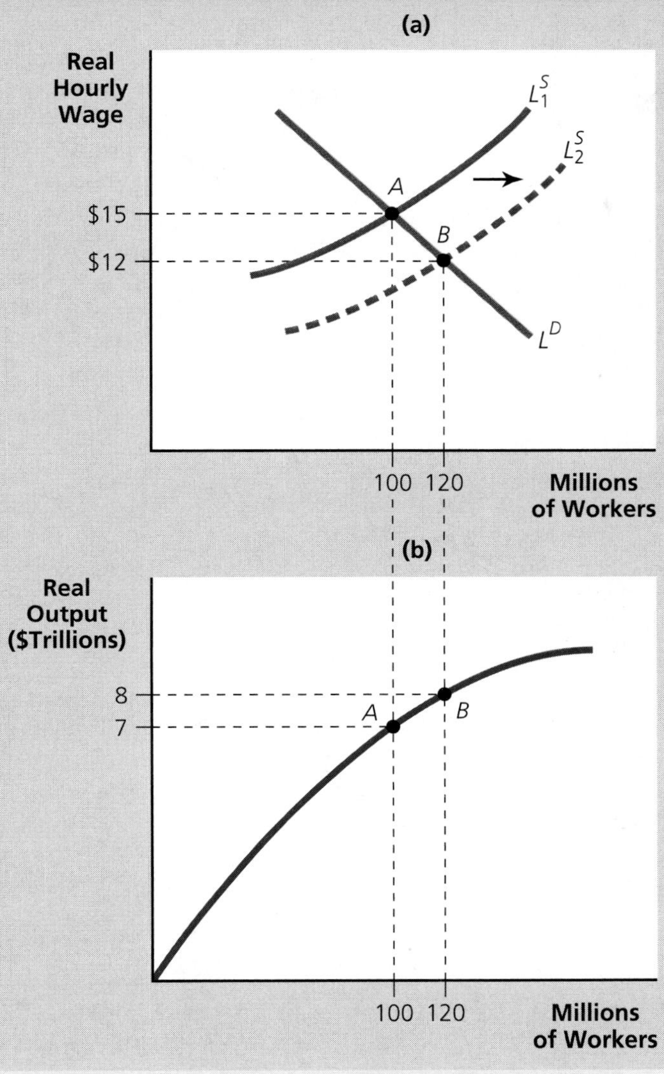

FIGURE 1

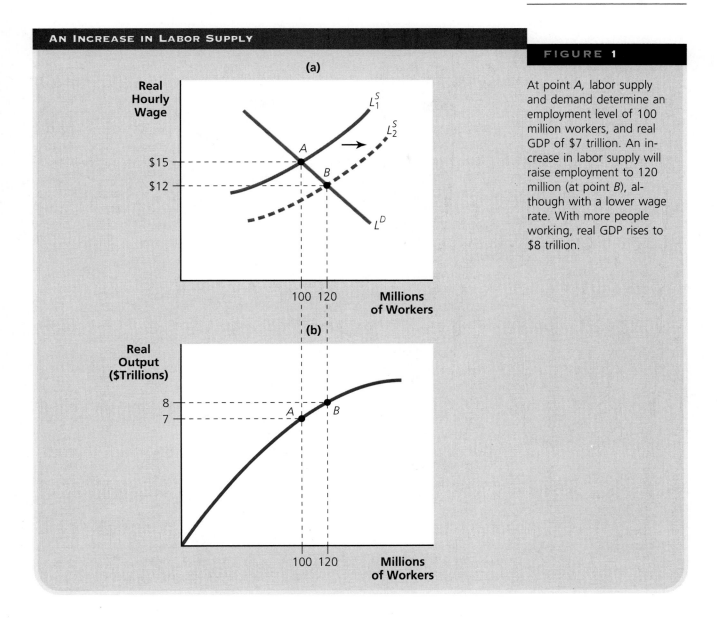

At point *A,* labor supply and demand determine an employment level of 100 million workers, and real GDP of $7 trillion. An increase in labor supply will raise employment to 120 million (at point *B*), although with a lower wage rate. With more people working, real GDP rises to $8 trillion.

You may have noticed one very important difference between the labor market outcomes in Figures 1 and 2: When labor *supply* increases, the wage rate falls (from $15 to $12 in Figure 1); when labor *demand* increases, the wage rate rises (from $15 to $17 in Figure 2). Which of the figures describes the actual experience of the U.S. labor market?

Actually, a combination of both: Over the past 50 years, the U.S. labor supply curve has shifted steadily rightward, sometimes slowly, sometimes more rapidly. Why the shift in labor supply? In part, the reason has been steady population growth: The more people there are, the more will want to work at any wage. But another reason has been an important change in tastes: an increase in the desire of women (especially married women) to work.

Over the past 50 years, as the labor supply curve has shifted rightward, the labor demand curve has shifted rightward as well. Why? Throughout this period,

FIGURE 2

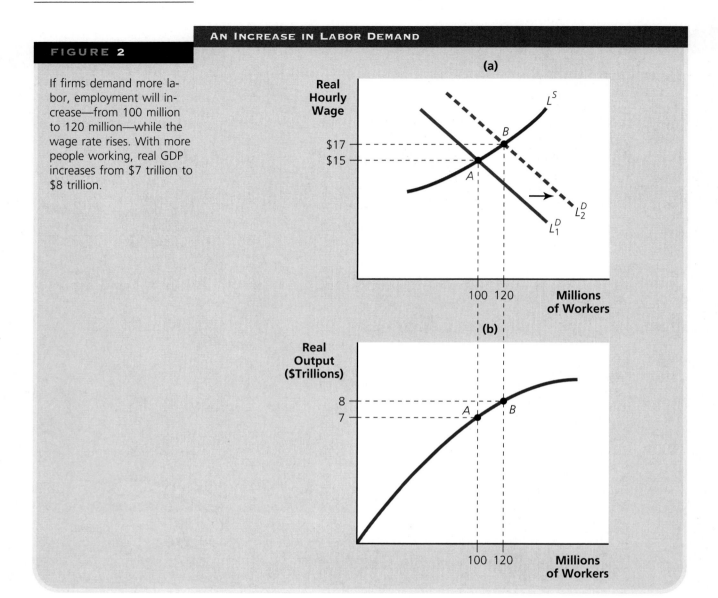

AN INCREASE IN LABOR DEMAND

If firms demand more labor, employment will increase—from 100 million to 120 million—while the wage rate rises. With more people working, real GDP increases from $7 trillion to $8 trillion.

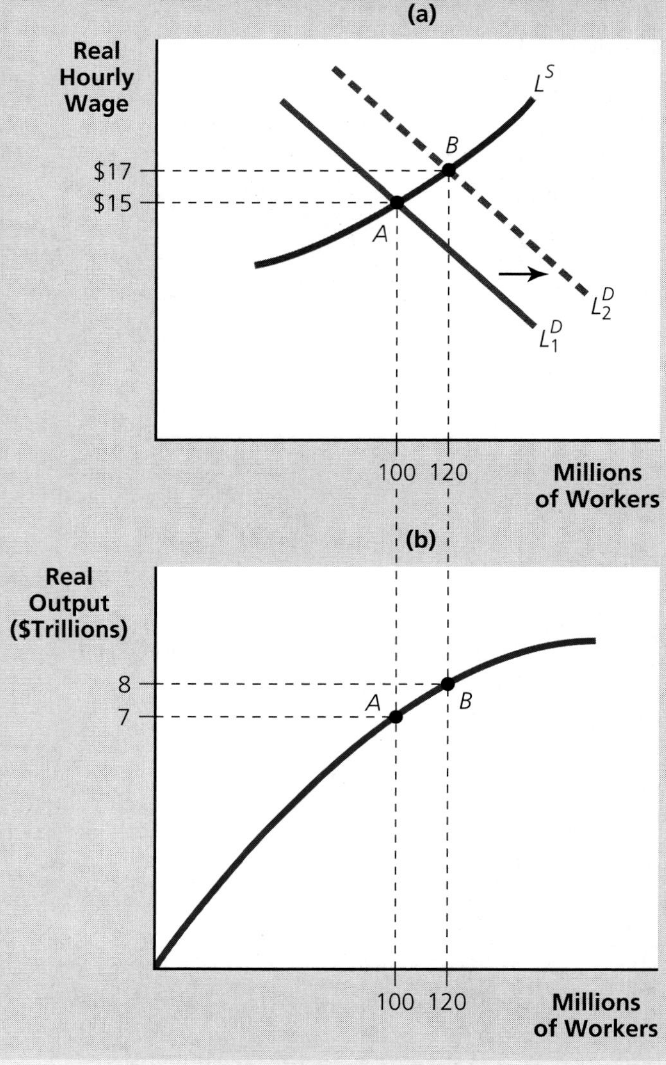

firms have been acquiring more and better capital equipment for their employees to use. Secretaries now work with word processors instead of typewriters, accountants use lightning-fast computer software instead of account ledgers, and supermarket clerks use electronic scanners instead of hand-entry cash registers. At the same time, workers have become better educated and better trained. These changes have increased the amount of output a worker can produce in any given period, so firms have wanted to hire more of them at any wage.

In fact, over the past century, increases in labor demand have outpaced increases in labor supply, so that, on balance, the average wage has risen and employment has increased. This is illustrated in Figure 3, which shows a shift in the labor supply curve from L_1^S to L_2^S, and an even greater shift in the labor demand curve from L_1^D to L_2^D.

THE U.S. LABOR MARKET OVER A CENTURY

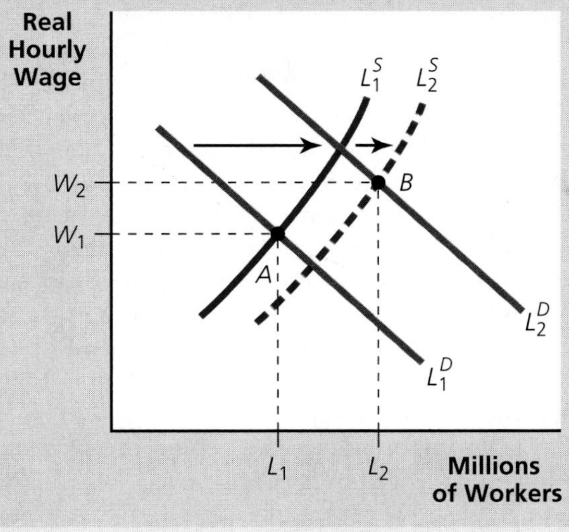

FIGURE 3

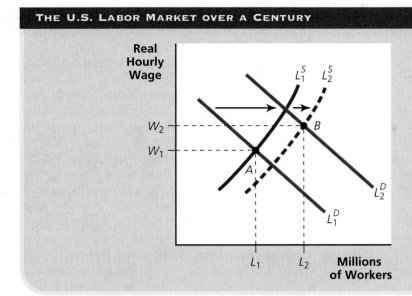

Over the past century, increases in labor demand have outpaced increases in supply. As a result, both the level of employment and the average wage have risen.

The impact of these changes on total employment has been dramatic. Between 1947 and 1995, the *labor force participation rate*—the fraction of the adult population that is either working or looking for work—rose from 58.3 percent to 66.6 percent. The increased participation rate was due partly to women's increased tastes for working, as mentioned, and partly to the increase in the average wage rate that made work more rewarding. Together, growth in the population and in the participation rate have increased the U.S. labor force from 59.5 million workers in 1947 to 132 million workers in 1995.

Currently, the U.S. Bureau of Labor Statistics predicts employment growth of 1 percent per year until the year 2010. Is there anything we can do to make employment grow even faster and thus increase our rate of economic growth? Can we speed up the rightward shifts in labor supply and labor demand? Yes, we can. But as you read on, keep in mind that these measures to increase employment are not necessarily socially desirable. They, would, most likely, accomplish the goal, but they would also have costs—costs that Americans may or may not be willing to pay. Later, we'll discuss these costs.

HOW TO INCREASE EMPLOYMENT. One set of policies to increase employment focuses on changing labor supply. And an often-proposed example of this type of policy is a decrease in income tax rates. Imagine that you have a professional degree in accounting, physical therapy, or some other field, and you are considering whether to take a job. Suppose the going rate for your professional services is $30 per hour. If your average tax rate is 33 percent, then one-third of your income will be taxed away, so your take-home pay would be only $20 per hour. But if your tax rate were cut to 20 percent, you would take home $24 per hour. Since you care about your take-home pay, you will respond to a tax cut in the same way you would respond to a wage increase—even if the wage your potential employer pays does not change at all. If you would be willing to take a job that offers a take home pay of $24, but not one that offers $20, then the tax cut would be just what was needed to get you to seek work.

When we extend your reaction to the population as a whole, we can see that a cut in the income tax rate can convince more people to seek jobs at any given wage, shifting the labor supply curve rightward. This is why economists and politicians who focus on the economy's long-run growth often recommend lower taxes on labor income to encourage more rapid growth in employment. They point out that many American workers must pay combined federal, state, and local taxes of more than 40 cents out of each additional dollar they earn, and that this may be discouraging work effort in the United States.

In addition to tax rate changes, some economists advocate changes in government transfer programs to speed the growth in employment. They argue that the current structure of many government programs creates disincentives to work. For example, families receiving welfare payments, food stamps, unemployment benefits, and Social Security retirement payments all face steep losses in their benefits if they go to work or increase their work effort. Redesigning these programs might therefore stimulate growth in labor supply.

This reasoning was an important motive behind the sweeping and highly controversial reforms in the U.S. welfare system passed by Congress, and signed by President Clinton, in August 1996. Among other things, the reforms reduced the number of people who were eligible for benefits, cut the benefit amount for many of those still eligible, and set a maximum coverage period of five years for most welfare recipients. Later in this chapter, we'll discuss some of the costs of potentially growth-enhancing measures like this. Here, we only point out that changes in benefit programs, whether "right" or "wrong," have the potential to change labor supply.

A cut in tax rates increases the reward for working, while a cut in benefits to the needy increases the hardship of not *working. Either policy can cause a greater rightward shift in the economy's labor supply curve than would otherwise occur and speed the growth in employment and output.*

Government policies can also affect the labor demand curve. In recent decades, subsidies for education and training, such as government-guaranteed loans for college students or special training programs for the unemployed, have helped to increase the skills of the labor force and made workers more valuable to potential employers. Government also subsidizes employment more directly—by contributing part of the wage when certain categories of workers are hired—the disabled, college work-study participants, and, in some experimental programs, inner-city youth. By enlarging these programs, government could increase the number of workers hired at any given wage and thus shift the labor demand curve to the right:

Government policies that help increase the skills of the workforce or that subsidize employment more directly shift the economy's labor demand curve to the right, increasing employment and output.

Efforts to speed employment growth are controversial. In recent decades, those who prefer an activist government have favored policies to increase labor *demand* through government-sponsored training programs, more aid to college students, employment subsidies to firms, and similar programs. Those who prefer a more *laissez-faire* approach have generally favored policies to increase the labor *supply* by *decreasing* government involvement—lower taxes or a less generous social safety net.

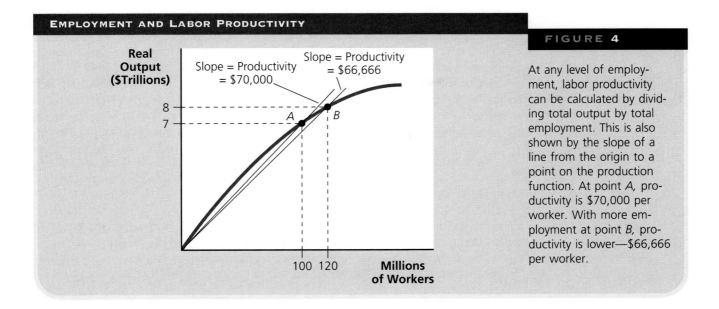

EMPLOYMENT AND LABOR PRODUCTIVITY

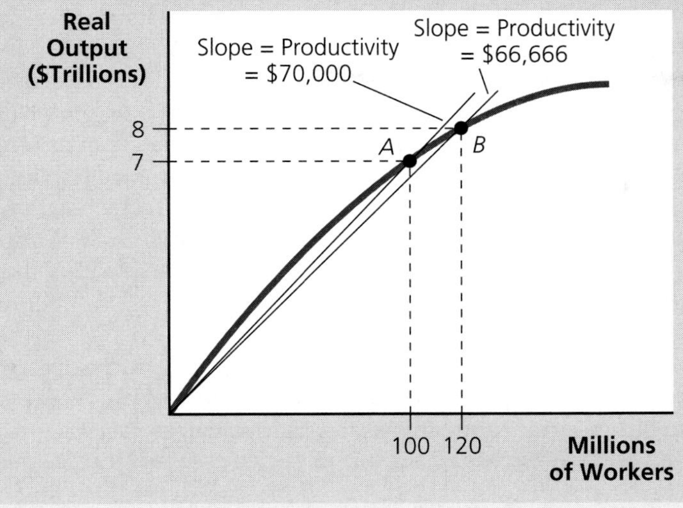

FIGURE 4

At any level of employment, labor productivity can be calculated by dividing total output by total employment. This is also shown by the slope of a line from the origin to a point on the production function. At point *A,* productivity is $70,000 per worker. With more employment at point *B,* productivity is lower—$66,666 per worker.

EMPLOYMENT GROWTH AND PRODUCTIVITY. Increases in employment have been an important source of economic growth in the United States and many other countries. But growth from this source has a serious drawback: It does not necessarily raise a nation's standard of living. Indeed, it can even cause living standards to fall. Why? Because living standards are closely tied to **labor productivity** (sometimes just called **productivity**)—the nation's total output divided by the total number of workers that produce it. Productivity is the output produced by the average worker in a year.[2]

LABOR PRODUCTIVITY Total output, real GDP, per worker.

Figure 4 illustrates the relationship between labor productivity and the economy's production function. At any level of employment, productivity is calculated by dividing total yearly output (on the vertical axis) by the total number of workers (on the horizontal axis):

Productivity = output/employment = vertical measure/horizontal measure

For example, in the figure, 100 million workers can produce $7 trillion in output. Productivity at this level of employment is thus $7 trillion/100 million = $70,000 per worker, which is the slope of the line drawn from the origin to point *A* on the production function.[3]

Now look at what happens when employment rises to 120 million workers: Labor productivity falls to $8 trillion/120 million = $66,666 per worker, the slope of the line drawn from the origin to point *B* on the production function. In fact, as you can see in the figure, as employment rises, labor productivity drops.

2 Productivity is more often defined as total output divided by total *labor hours*—the output produced by the average worker in an hour. But our calculations will be easier if we use the definition given in the text. As long as the typical worker's hours remain unchanged, the two definitions of productivity—output per hour or output per worker per year—will rise or fall by the same percentage.

3 The slope of a straight line is always "rise over run," or the change along the vertical axis divided by the change along the horizontal axis between any two points. Since our straight line begins at the origin, we can use the origin as our first point, so that the change in the vertical axis is just total output and the change in the horizontal axis is total employment. This gives us total output/total employment as the slope of the line.

Why? The answer lies with the assumption that the production function remains unchanged. As we move rightward along a given production function, like the one in Figure 4, we are holding the nation's capital stock constant. As a consequence, as employment increases, each worker has less and less capital equipment with which to work, and the average worker's output falls. If 100 ditchdiggers have 100 shovels, then each has his own shovel. If we double the number of ditchdiggers, but hold constant the number of shovels, then each worker must share his shovel with another and digs fewer ditches in any period. Labor productivity decreases:

When employment increases, while the capital stock remains constant, the amount of capital available to the average worker will decrease, and labor productivity will fall.

Falling labor productivity is bad news for a society. If output per worker falls, then the average standard of living will ordinarily fall as well. What can be done to prevent the fall in labor productivity as employment grows? Or—even better—can anything be done to *increase* labor productivity even as more people are working? The answer is yes.

GROWTH OF THE CAPITAL STOCK

The key to increasing labor productivity is to increase the nation's stock of capital. Has your college or university acquired more computers, desks, or campus-patrol vehicles in the past year? Did it install a new phone system? Build a new classroom or dormitory? If the answer to any of these questions is yes, then your institution has participated in the growth of the U.S. capital stock. With more capital—more assembly lines, bulldozers, computers, factory buildings, and the like—a given number of workers can produce more output than before, so the production function will *shift upward.*

Figure 5 shows the shift. With the initial amount of capital, the economy operates at point *A* on the lower aggregate production function, where 100 million workers produce $7 trillion in output. The increase in capital shifts the production function upward, and—with the same employment level—the economy now operates at point *D,* where 100 million workers produce $8 trillion in output.[4]

Looking back to Figure 4, and comparing it with Figure 5, you'll notice that output increases by the same amount in both cases; but the consequences for productivity are very different. In Figure 4, an increase in employment causes labor productivity to fall; in Figure 5, an increase in capital causes labor productivity to rise. (How do we know that productivity rises in Figure 5? *Hint:* compare the slopes of the line through point *A* and the line through point *D.*)

An increase in the capital stock causes labor productivity and living standards to increase.

To summarize, when the labor force grows (with a constant capital stock), labor productivity falls; and when the capital stock grows (with a constant labor

4 In order to focus on the pure effects of an increase in capital, Figure 5 holds the level of employment constant. But as you learned earlier in this chapter, an increase in capital will make workers more productive, and firms will want to hire more of them at any given wage. Thus, a complete analysis of capital growth would show the labor demand curve shifting rightward at the same time as the production function shifts upward.

CAPITAL ACCUMULATION AND LABOR PRODUCTIVITY

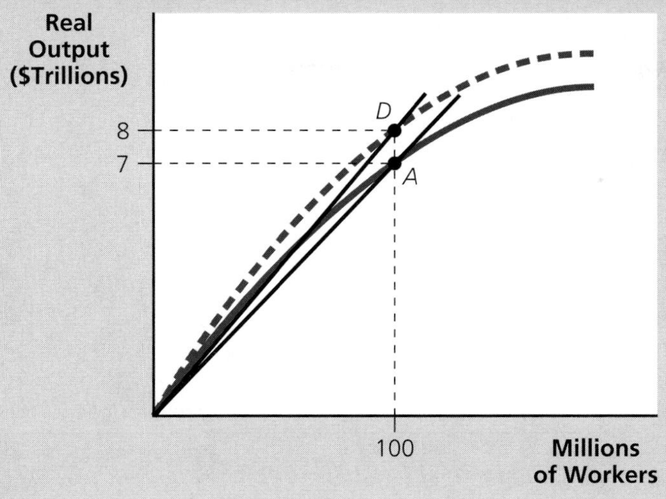

FIGURE 5

An increase in the capital stock shifts the production function upward. At point *A*, 100 million workers could produce $7 trillion of real GDP; labor productivity is $70,000 per worker. With more capital, those same workers could produce $8 trillion of real GDP; productivity is then higher, at $66,666 per worker.

force), productivity rises. These are interesting hypothetical cases. But in the real world, both the capital stock and the labor force grow from year to year. What happens to labor productivity when both changes occur simultaneously? That depends on what happens to **capital per worker**—the total quantity of capital divided by total employment. Greater capital per worker means greater productivity: You can dig more ditches with a shovel than with your bare hands, and even more with a backhoe.

CAPITAL PER WORKER The total capital stock divided by total employment.

If the capital stock grows faster than employment, then capital per worker will rise, and labor productivity will increase along with it. But if the capital stock grows more slowly than employment, then capital per worker will fall, and labor productivity will fall as well.

In the United States and most other developed countries, the capital stock has grown more rapidly than the labor force. As a result, labor productivity has risen over time. But in some developing countries, the capital stock has grown at about the same rate, or even more slowly than, the population, and labor productivity has remained stagnant or fallen. We will return to this problem in the "Using the Theory" section of the chapter.

INVESTMENT AND THE CAPITAL STOCK. Now you can see why an increase in the capital stock plays such a central role in economists' thinking about growth: It works by raising labor productivity and thus unambiguously helps to raise living standards. But how does a nation's capital stock grow?

Remember that capital is a *stock* variable—it represents the total amount of plant and equipment that exists at any moment in time. Investment, on the other hand, is a flow variable, telling us how rapidly we are producing *new* plant and equipment over some period. The relationship between the two is similar to that between the flow of water into a bathtub and the total amount of water in the tub itself. As long as investment is greater than depreciation (more water flows into the

FIGURE 6

INVESTMENT-ORIENTED PUBLIC POLICY

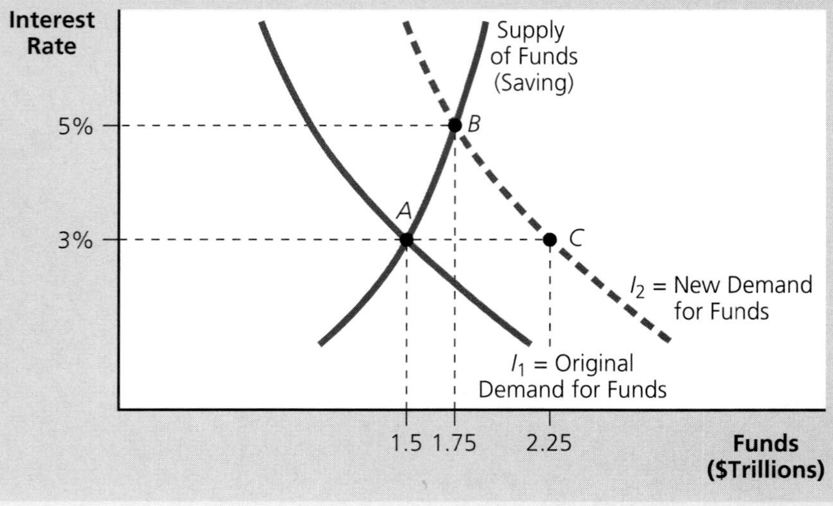

Government policies that make investment more profitable will increase investment spending at each interest rate. The resulting rightward shift of the investment demand curve leads to a higher level of investment spending, at point *B*.

tub than drains out), the total stock of capital (the quantity of water in the tub) will rise. Moreover, the greater the flow of investment, the faster will be the rise in the capital stock.

A government seeking to spur investment has more than one weapon in its arsenal. It can direct its efforts toward businesses themselves, toward the household sector, or toward its own budget.

INCREASING INCENTIVES FOR INVESTMENT. One kind of policy to increase investment targets the business sector itself, with the goal of increasing planned investment spending. Figure 6 shows how this works. The figure shows a simplified view of the loanable funds market where—to focus on investment—we assume that there is no budget deficit, so there is no government demand for funds. The initial equilibrium in the market is at point *A*, where household saving (the supply of funds) and investment (the demand for funds) are both equal to $1.5 trillion and the interest rate is 3 percent. Now suppose that the government takes steps to make investment more profitable, so that—at any interest rate—firms will want to purchase $0.75 trillion more in capital equipment than before. Then the investment curve would shift rightward by $0.75 trillion—from I_1 to I_2, and the interest rate would rise from 3 percent to 5 percent. Note that, as the interest rate rises, some—but not all—of the original increase in investment is choked off. In the end, investment rises from $1.5 trillion to $1.75 trillion, and so each year $0.25 trillion more is added to the capital stock than would otherwise be added.

CORPORATE PROFITS TAX A tax on the profits earned by corporations.

INVESTMENT TAX CREDIT A reduction in taxes for firms that invest in certain favored types of capital.

These are the mechanics of a rightward shift in the investment curve. But what government measures would *cause* such a shift in the first place? That is, how could the government help to make investment spending more profitable for firms?

One such measure would be a reduction in the **corporate profits tax,** which would allow firms to keep more of the profits they earn from investment projects. Another, even more direct, policy is an **investment tax credit,** which subsidizes corporate investment in new capital equipment.

SAVING AND INVESTMENT

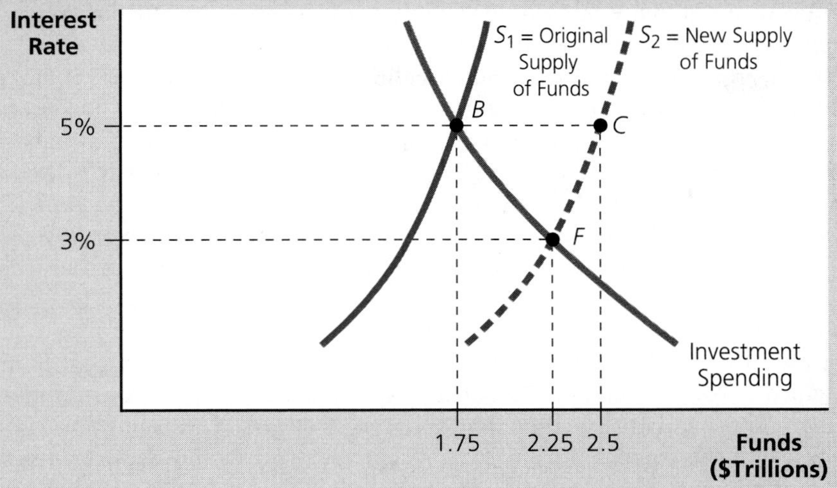

FIGURE 7

If households decide to save more of their incomes, the supply of funds will increase. With more funds available, the interest rate will fall. Businesses will respond by increasing their borrowing, and investment will increase from $1.75 trillion to $2.25 trillion.

Reducing business taxes or providing specific investment incentives can shift the investment curve rightward, speed growth in physical capital, and increase the growth rate of living standards.

Of course, the same reasoning applies in reverse: An *increase* in the corporate profits tax or the *elimination* of an investment tax credit would shift the investment curve to the left, slowing the rate of investment, the growth of the capital stock, and the rise in living standards.

Increasing Incentives for Savings. While firms make decisions to purchase new capital, it is largely households that supply the firms with funds, via personal saving. Thus, an increase in investment spending can originate in the household sector, through an increase in the desire to save. This is illustrated in Figure 7. If households decide to save more of their incomes at any given interest rate, the supply of funds curve will shift rightward, from S_1 to S_2. The increase in saving drives down the interest rate, from 5 percent to 3 percent, which, in turn, causes investment to increase. With a lower interest rate, NBC might decide to borrow funds to build another production studio, or the corner grocery store may finally decide to borrow the funds it needs for a new electronic scanner at the checkout stand. In this way, an increase in the desire to save is translated—via the financial market—into an increase in investment and faster growth in the capital stock.

What might cause households to increase their saving? The answer is found in the reasons people save in the first place. And to understand these reasons, you needn't look further than yourself or your own family. You might currently be saving for a large purchase (a car, a house, a vacation, college tuition) or to build a financial cushion in case of hard times ahead. You might even be saving to support yourself during retirement, though this may be a distant thought for most college students. Given these motives, what would make you increase your saving? Several things: greater uncertainty about your economic future, an increase in your life expectancy, anticipation of an earlier retirement, a change in tastes toward big-ticket items, or even just a change in your attitude about saving. Any of these changes—if they occurred in many households simultaneously—would shift the saving curve (the supply of funds curve) to the right, as in Figure 7.

CAPITAL GAINS TAX A tax on profits earned when a financial asset is sold at more than its acquisition price.

But government policy can increase household saving as well. One often-proposed idea is to decrease the **capital gains tax**. A capital gain is the profit you earn when you sell an asset, such as a share of stock or a bond, at a higher price than you paid for it. Through a special tax rate for capital gains that is lower than the income tax rate, households would be able to keep more of the capital gains they earn. As a result, stocks and bonds would become more rewarding to own, and you might decide to reduce your current spending in order to buy them. If other households react in the same way, total saving would rise, and the supply of funds to the financial market would increase.

CONSUMPTION TAX A tax on the part of their income that households spend.

Another frequently proposed measure is to switch from the current U.S. income tax—which taxes all income whether it is spent or saved—to a **consumption tax,** which would tax only the income that households spend. A consumption tax could work just like the current income tax, except that you would deduct your saving from your income and pay taxes on the remainder. This would increase the reward for saving, since, by saving, you would earn additional interest on the part of your income that would have been taxed away under an income tax. Individual retirement accounts, or IRAs, allow households to deduct limited amounts of saving from their incomes before paying taxes. A general consumption tax would go much further and allow *all* saving to be deducted.

Another proposal to increase household saving is to restructure the U.S. Social Security system, which provides support for retired workers who have contributed funds to the system during their working years. Because Social Security encourages people to rely on the government for income during retirement, they have less incentive to save for retirement themselves. The proposed restructuring would link workers' Social Security benefits to their actual contributions to the system, whereas under the current system some people receive benefits worth far more than the amount they have contributed.

> *Government can alter the tax and transfer system to increase incentives for saving. If successful, these policies would make more funds available for investment, speed growth in the capital stock, and speed the rise in living standards.*

(Do any of these methods of increasing saving disturb you? Remember, we are not advocating any measures here; rather, we are merely noting that such measures would increase saving and promote economic growth. We'll discuss the *costs* of growth-promoting measures later.)

SHRINKING THE BUDGET DEFICIT. A final pro-investment measure is directed at the government sector itself. The previous chapter showed that an increase in government purchases, financed by borrowing in the financial market, completely crowds out private-sector consumption and investment. A *decrease* in government purchases has the opposite effect: raising consumption and investment.

Figure 8 reintroduces government borrowing to the financial market to show how this works. Initially, the government is running a deficit of \$0.75 trillion, equal to the distance *EA*. The total demand for funds is now the sum of investment and the government's budget deficit, given by the curve labeled "Investment

DEFICIT REDUCTION AND INVESTMENT SPENDING

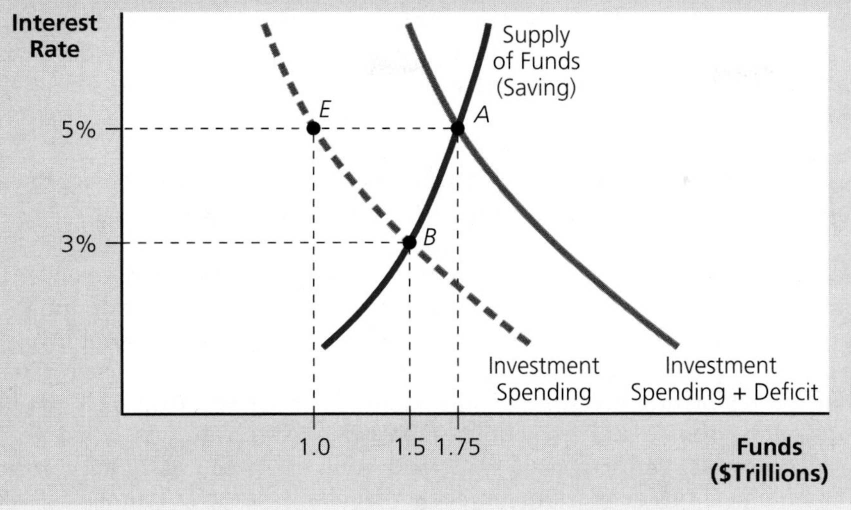

FIGURE 8

A reduction in the government's budget deficit will reduce government borrowing in the loanable funds market. As a result, the total demand for funds will fall, as will the interest rate. At a lower interest rate, businesses will increase their investment spending from $1 trillion (point *E*) to $1.5 trillion (point *B*).

Spending + Deficit." The demand for funds curve intersects the supply of funds curve at point *A*, creating an equilibrium interest rate of 5 percent and equilibrium saving of $1.75 trillion. At this interest rate, investment is only $1 trillion. The part of saving not going to finance investment spending ($1.75 trillion − $1 trillion = $0.75 trillion) is being used to finance the budget deficit.

Now consider what happens if the government eliminates the deficit—say, by reducing its spending by $0.75 trillion. The demand for funds would consist of planned investment only. Since there would be no other borrowing, the new equilibrium would be point *B*, with an interest rate of 3 percent and investment equal to $1.5 trillion—greater than before. By balancing its budget, the government no longer needs to borrow in the loanable funds market, which frees up funds to flow to the business sector instead. Initially, this creates a surplus of funds. But—as the loanable funds market clears—the interest rate drops, and the surplus of funds disappears. (Why does a drop in the interest rate make the surplus disappear? *Hint:* What happens to saving and to investment as the interest rate declines?)

The link between the budget deficit, the interest rate, and investment spending is the major reason why the U.S. government, and governments around the world, keep a watchful eye on their budget deficits. They have learned that

a shrinking deficit tends to reduce interest rates and increase investment, thus speeding the growth in the capital stock.

AN IMPORTANT PROVISO ABOUT DEFICIT REDUCTION. Deficit reduction, even if it stimulates private investment, is not necessarily a pro-growth measure. It depends on *how* the deficit is reduced. By an increase in taxes? A cut in government spending? And if the latter, which government programs will be cut? Welfare? National defense? Highway repair? The answers can make a big difference to the impact on growth.

For example, in our discussions of the capital stock so far, we've ignored government capital—roads, communication lines, bridges, and dams. To understand the importance of government capital, just imagine what life would be like without it. How would factories obtain their raw materials or distribute their goods if no one repaired the roads? How would contracts between buyers and sellers be enforced if there were no public buildings to house courts and police departments? Government capital supports private economic activity in more ways than we can list here.

Government investment in new capital and in the maintenance of existing capital makes an important contribution to economic growth.

This important observation complicates our view of deficit reduction. It is still true that a decrease in government spending will lower the interest rate and increase private investment. But if the budget cutting falls largely on government investment, the negative effect of smaller public investment will offset some of the positive impact of greater private investment. Shrinking the deficit will then alter the *mix* of capital—more private and less public—and the effect on growth could go either way. A society rife with lawlessness, deteriorating roads and bridges, or an unreliable communications network might benefit from a shift toward public capital. For example, a study of public budgets in African nations—which are notorious for having poor road conditions—found that each one-dollar-per-year cut in the road-maintenance budget increased vehicle operating costs by between \$2 and \$3 per year, and in one case, by as much as \$22 per year.[5] This is an example where a cut in government spending—even if it reduces the deficit—probably hinders growth. By contrast, a stable society (Sweden comes to mind) with a fully developed and well-maintained public infrastructure might benefit from shifting the mix toward private capital.

The impact of deficit reduction on economic growth depends on which government programs are cut. Shrinking the deficit by cutting government investment will not stimulate growth as much as would cutting spending that does not contribute to capital formation.

HUMAN CAPITAL AND ECONOMIC GROWTH

HUMAN CAPITAL Skills and knowledge possessed by workers.

So far, the only type of capital we've discussed is physical capital—the plant and equipment workers use to produce output. But when we think of the capital stock most broadly, we include *human capital* as well. **Human capital**—the skills and knowledge possessed by workers—is as central to economic growth as is physical capital. After all, most types of physical capital—computers, CAT scanners, and even shovels—will contribute little to output unless workers know how to use them. And when more workers gain skills or improve their existing skills, output rises just as it does when workers have more physical capital:

An increase in human capital works much like an increase in physical capital to increase output: It causes the production function to shift upward, raises productivity, and increases the average standard of living.

5 This World Bank study was cited in *The Economist,* June 10, 1995, p. 72.

There is another similarity between human and physical capital: Both are *stocks* that are increased by *flows* of investment. The stock of human capital increases whenever investment in new skills during some period, through education and training, exceeds the depreciation of existing skills over the same period, through retirement, death, or deterioration. Therefore, greater investment in human capital will speed the growth of the human capital stock, the growth in productivity, and the growth in living standards.

Human capital investments are made by business firms (when they help to train their employees), by government (through public education and subsidized training), and by households (when they pay for general education or professional training). Human capital investments have played an important role in recent U.S. economic growth. Can we do anything to increase our rate of investment in human capital?

In part, we've already answered this question: Some of the same policies that increase investment in *physical* capital also work to raise investment in human capital. For example, a decrease in the budget deficit would lower the interest rate and make it cheaper for households to borrow for college loans and training programs. A change in the tax system that increases the incentive to save would have the same impact, since this, too, would lower interest rates. And an easing of the tax burden on business firms could increase the profitability of *their* human capital investments, leading to more and better worker training programs.

Is infrastructure investment important to economic growth? Learn more about this issue in the Policy Debates portion of the ECONOMICS web site.
Address:
http://hall–lieb.swcollege.com

But there is more: Human capital, unlike physical capital, cannot be separated from the person who provides it. If you own a building, you can rent it out to one firm and sell your labor to another. But if you have training as a doctor, your labor and your human capital must be sold together, as a package. Moreover, your wage or salary will be payment for both your labor and your human capital. This means that income tax reductions—which we discussed earlier as a means of increasing labor supply—can also increase the profitability of human capital to households, and increase their rate of investment in their own skills and training. For example, suppose an accountant is considering whether to attend a course in corporate financial reporting, which would increase her professional skills. The course costs $4,000, and will increase the accountant's income by $1,000 per year for the rest of her career. With a tax rate of 40 percent, her take-home pay would increase by $600 per year, so her annual rate of return on her investment would be $600/$4,000 = 15 percent. But with a lower tax rate—say, 20 percent—her take-home pay would rise by $800 per year, so her rate of return would be $800/$4,000 = 20 percent. The lower the tax rate, the greater is the rate of return on our accountant's human capital investment, and the more likely she will be to acquire new skills. Thus,

> *many of the pro-growth policies discussed earlier—policies that increase employment or increase investment in physical capital—are also effective in promoting investment in human capital.*

Technological Change

So far, we've discussed how economic growth arises from greater quantities of resources—more labor, more physical capital, or more human capital. But another important source of growth is **technological change**—the invention or discovery of new inputs, new outputs, or new methods of production. Indeed, it is largely because of technological change that Malthus's horrible prediction (cited at the be-

Technological change The invention or discovery of new inputs, new outputs, or new production methods.

ginning of this chapter) has not come true. In the last 60 years, for example, the inventions of synthetic fertilizers, hybrid corn, and chemical pesticides have enabled world food production to rise faster than population.

New technology affects the economy in much the same way as do increases in the capital stock. Look back at Figure 5. There, we saw that an increase in the capital stock would shift the production function upward and increase output. New technology, too, shifts the production function upward, since it enables any given number of workers to produce more output. In many cases, the new technology requires the acquisition of physical and human capital before it can be used. For example, a new technique for destroying kidney stones with ultrasound, rather than time-consuming surgery, can make doctors more productive—but not until they spend several thousand dollars to buy the ultrasound machine and take a course on how to use it. In other cases, a new technology can be used without any additional equipment or training, as when a factory manager discovers a more efficient way to organize workers on the factory floor. In either case, technological change will shift the production function upward and increase productivity. It follows that

the faster the rate of technological change, the greater the growth rate of productivity, and the faster the rise in living standards.

It might seem that technological change is one of those things that just happens. Thomas Edison invents electricity, or Steve Jobs and Steve Wozniak develop the first practical personal computer in their garage. But the pace of technological change is not as haphazard as it seems. The transistor was invented as part of a massive research and development effort by AT&T and intended to improve the performance of communications electronics. Similarly, the next developments in computer technology, transportation, and more will depend on how much money is spent on research and development (R&D) by the leading technology firms:

The rate of technological change in the economy depends largely on firms' total spending on R&D. Policies that increase R&D spending will increase the pace of technological change.

What can the government do to increase spending on R&D? First, it can increase its own direct support for R&D by carrying out more research in its own laboratories or increasing funding for universities and tax incentives to private research labs.

PATENT PROTECTION A government grant of exclusive rights to use or sell a new technology.

Second, the government can enhance **patent protection,** which increases rewards for those who create new technology by giving them exclusive rights to use it or sell it. For example, when the DuPont Corporation discovered a unique way to manufacture Spandex, it obtained a patent to prevent other firms from copying its technique. This patent has enabled DuPont to earn millions of dollars from its invention. Without the patent, other firms would have copied the technique, competed with DuPont, and taken much of its profit away. Hundreds of thousands of new patents are issued every year in the United States: to pharmaceutical companies for new prescription drugs, to telephone companies for new cellular technologies, and to the producers of a variety of household goods ranging from can openers to microwave ovens.

Since patent protection increases the rewards that developers can expect from new inventions, it encourages them to spend more on R&D. By broadening patent protection—issuing patents on a wider variety of discoveries—or by lengthening patent protection—increasing the number of years during which the developer has exclusive rights to market the invention—the government could increase the expected profits from new technologies. That would increase total spending on R&D and increase the pace of technological change. Currently in the United States, patents give inventors and developers exclusive marketing rights over their products for a period of about 20 years. Increasing patent protection to 30 years would certainly increase R&D spending at many firms.

Finally, R&D spending is in many ways just like other types of investment spending: The funds are drawn from the financial market, and R&D programs require firms to buy something now (laboratories, the services of research scientists, materials to build prototypes) for the uncertain prospect of profits in the future. Therefore, almost any policy that stimulates investment spending in general will also increase spending on R&D. Cutting the tax rate on capital gains or on corporate profits, and lowering interest rates by encouraging greater saving or by reducing the budget deficit, can both help to increase spending on R&D and increase the rate of technological change.

ECONOMIC GROWTH IN THE UNITED STATES

In the preceding sections, we have discussed several potential contributors to a nation's economic growth. In practice, which of these causes have been most important to growth in the United States? In a well-known study, the late Edward F. Denison addressed this question, using data over the period 1929 to 1982. During these years, total output grew, on average, by 2.92 percent per year. Denison attributed this growth to the various factors shown in Table 3.

What is important in this table? First, it shows that most of the average yearly growth rate over the period studied (2.46 percent out of 2.92 percent) can be explained by the leading causes discussed in this chapter: increases in employment, increases in the capital stock (physical and human), and technological change. But notice also that these three cannot explain *all* growth. The most important components of the 0.46 percent of our growth in the category "other" are improvements in the allocation of resources (such as the movement of workers to industries and geographic areas where their productivity is higher) and economies of scale (greater productivity made possible by growth in the *size* of firms.) In both cases, productivity rises because of an increase in the economy's operating efficiency.

PERCENTAGE POINTS OF TOTAL GROWTH IN REAL GNP EXPLAINED BY VARIOUS FACTORS, 1929–1982

TABLE 3

Factor	Percentage Points per Year
Increases in employment	1.24
Increases in physical capital	0.56
Increases in human capital and technological change	0.66
Other	0.46

Source: *Trends in American Economic Growth, 1929–1982* (Washington: Brookings Institution, 1985)

Notice, too, that most of our economic growth comes from sources that increase productivity. Indeed, only growth from increases in employment tends to decrease productivity, leaving the productivity-increasing sources responsible for 0.56 + 0.66 + 0.46 = 1.68 percentage points out of the total 2.92 percentage points of yearly output growth.

This highlights the role of productivity in economic growth. Earlier, you learned that increases in productivity help to raise living standards. Now you can see that most of the rise in our living standard has been caused by increases in productivity. It is not surprising, then, that higher productivity is usually viewed as the most direct route to higher living standards, both in the wealthy industrialized countries and in the poorer, less developed countries. In the "Using the Theory" section we will focus our attention on the special problems of increasing productivity and living standards in the less-developed countries.

THE COST OF ECONOMIC GROWTH

So far in this chapter, we've discussed a variety of policies that could increase the rate of economic growth and speed the rise in living standards. Why don't all nations pursue these policies and push their rates of economic growth to the maximum? Why did the United States grow by 2.92 percent per year between 1929 and 1982? Why not 5 percent per year? Or 10 percent? Or even more?

The answer hinges on one of the basic principles of economics:

POLICY TRADEOFFS

Government policy is constrained by the reactions of private decisionmakers. As a result, policymakers face tradeoffs: Making progress toward one goal often requires some sacrifice of another goal.

Economics is famous for making the public aware of policy tradeoffs. One of the most important things you will learn in your introductory economics course is that there are no costless solutions to society's problems. Just as individuals face an opportunity cost when they take an action (they must give up something else that they value), so, too, policymakers face an opportunity cost whenever they pursue a policy: They must compromise on achieving some other social goal.

Economic models can help us identify the tradeoffs associated with different policy choices. Although facing a tradeoff is rarely pleasant, doing so helps us formulate wiser policies and avoid unpleasant surprises. In this section, you will see that while a variety of policies can increase a nation's rate of economic growth, each of these policies involves a tradeoff: It imposes a cost on some group or requires some sacrifice of other social goals.

Promoting economic growth involves unavoidable tradeoffs: It requires some groups, or the nation as a whole, to give up something else that is valued. In order to decide how fast we want our economy to grow, we must consider growth's costs as well as its benefits.

What are the costs of growth?

BUDGETARY COSTS

If you look back over this chapter, you'll see that many of the pro-growth policies we've analyzed involve some kind of tax cut. Cutting the income tax rate will likely increase the labor supply; cutting taxes on capital gains or corporate profits will increase investment directly; and cutting taxes on saving will increase household saving, lower interest rates, and thus increase investment spending indirectly. Unfortunately, implementing any of these tax cuts would force the government to choose among three unpleasant alternatives: increase some other tax to regain the lost revenue, cut government spending, or permit the budget deficit to rise.

Who will bear the burden of this budgetary cost? That depends on which alternative is chosen. Under the first option—increasing some other tax—the burden falls on those who pay the other tax. For example, if income taxes are cut, real estate taxes might be increased. A family might pay lower income taxes, but higher property taxes. Whether it comes out ahead or behind will depend on how much income the family earns relative to how much property it owns.

The second option, cutting government spending, imposes the burden on those who currently benefit from government programs. These include not only those who directly benefit from a program—like welfare recipients or farmers—but also those who benefit from government spending more indirectly. Even though you may earn your income in the private sector, if government spending is cut, you may suffer from a deterioration of public roads, decreased police protection, or poorer schools for your children.

The third option—a larger budget deficit—is more complicated. Under this option, greater government borrowing will increase the total amount of government debt outstanding—called the **national debt**—and lead to greater interest payments to be made by future generations, in the form of higher taxes. But that is not all. From the previous chapter, we know that a rise in the deficit increases the demand for funds and drives up the interest rate. The higher interest rate will reduce investment in physical capital by businesses, as well as investment in human capital by households, and both effects will work to decrease economic growth. It is even possible that so much private investment will be crowded out, that the tax cut, originally designed to boost economic growth, ends up slowing growth instead. At best, the growth-enhancing effects of the tax cut will be weakened. This is why advocates of high growth rates usually propose one of the other options—a rise in some other tax or a cut in government spending—as part of a pro-growth tax cut.

NATIONAL DEBT The total amount of government debt outstanding as a result of financing earlier budget deficits.

In sum,

properly targeted tax cuts can increase the rate of economic growth, but will force us to either redistribute the tax burden or cut government programs.

POLICY TRADEOFFS

CONSUMPTION COSTS

Any pro-growth policy that works by increasing investment—private or government, in physical capital, human capital, or R&D—requires a sacrifice of current consumption spending. The land, labor, and capital we use to produce new cloth-cutting machines, oil rigs, assembly lines, training facilities, college classrooms, or research laboratories could have been used instead to produce clothing, automobiles, video games, and other consumer goods. In other words, we face a tradeoff: The more capital goods we produce in any given year, the fewer consumption goods we can enjoy in that year.

The role of this tradeoff in economic growth can be clearly seen with a familiar tool from Chapter 2: the production possibilities frontier (PPF). Figure 9 shows the PPF for a nation with some given amount of land, labor, and capital that must be allocated to the production of two types of output: capital goods and con-

FIGURE 9

CONSUMPTION, INVESTMENT, AND ECONOMIC GROWTH

In the current period, a nation can choose to produce only consumer goods (point *C*), or it can produce some capital goods by sacrificing some current consumption. If investment at point *A* exceeds capital depreciation, the capital stock will grow, and the production possibilities frontier will shift outward. After it does, the nation can produce more consumption goods (point *B*), more capital goods (point *D*), or more of both (point *E*).

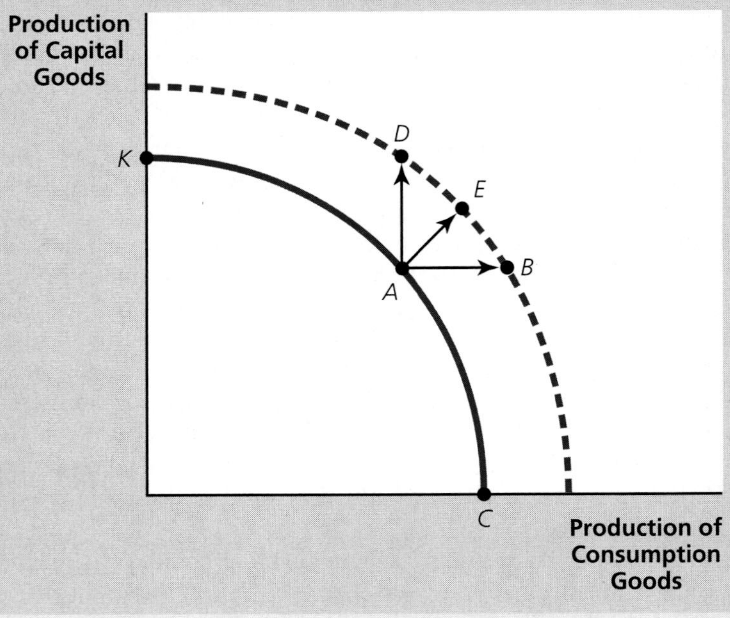

sumption goods. At point *K*, the nation is using all of its resources to produce capital goods and none to produce consumption goods. Point *C* represents the opposite extreme—all resources used to produce consumption goods and none for capital goods. Ordinarily, a nation will operate at an intermediate point such as *A*, where it is producing both capital and consumption goods.

Now, as long as capital production at point *A* is greater than the depreciation of existing capital, the capital stock will grow. In future periods, the economy—with more capital—can produce more output, as shown by the outward shift of the PPF to the dashed line in the figure. If a nation can produce more output, then it can produce more consumption goods for the same quantity of capital goods (moving from point *A* to point *B*) or more capital goods for the same quantity of consumption goods (from point *A* to point *D*) or more of both (from point *A* to point *E*).

Let's take a closer look at how this sacrifice of current consumption goods might come about. Suppose that some change in government policy—an investment tax credit or a lengthening of the patent period for new inventions—successfully shifts the investment curve to the right. (Go back to Figure 6.) What will happen? Businesses—desiring more funds for investment—will drive up the interest rate, and households all over the country will find that saving has become more attractive. As families increase their saving, we move rightward along the economy's supply of funds curve. In this way, firms get the funds they need to purchase new capital. But a decision to *save more* is also a decision to *spend less*. As current saving rises, current consumption spending necessarily falls. By driving up the interest rate, *the increase in investment spending causes a voluntary decrease in consumption spending by households.* Resources are freed from producing consumption goods and diverted to producing capital goods instead.

Although this decrease in consumption spending is voluntary, it is still a cost that we pay. And in some cases, a painful cost: Some of the increase in the household sector's net saving results from a decrease in borrowing by households that—at higher interest rates—can no longer afford to finance purchases of homes, cars, or furniture. In sum,

greater investment in physical capital, human capital, or R&D will lead to faster economic growth and higher living standards in the future, but we will have fewer consumer goods to enjoy in the present.

POLICY TRADEOFFS

OPPORTUNITY COSTS OF WORKERS' TIME

Living standards will also rise if a greater fraction of the population works or if those who already have jobs begin working longer hours. In either case, there will be more output to divide among the same population.[6] But this increase in living standards comes at a cost: a decrease in time spent in nonmarket activities. For example, with a greater fraction of the population working, a smaller fraction is spending time at home. This might mean that more students have summer jobs instead of studying, more elderly workers are postponing their retirement, or more previously nonworking spouses are entering the labor force. Similarly, an increase in average working hours means that the average worker will have less time for other activities—less time to watch television, read novels, garden, fix up the house, teach his or her children, or do volunteer work.

Thus, when economic growth comes about from increases in employment, we face a tradeoff: On the one hand, we can enjoy higher incomes and more goods and services; on the other hand, we will have less time to do things other than work in the market. In a market economy, where choices are voluntary, the value of the income gained must be greater than the value of the time given up. No one forces a worker to re-enter the labor force or to increase her working hours. Any worker who takes either of these actions must be better off for doing so. Still, we must recognize that *something* of value is always given up when employment increases:

An increase in the fraction of the population with jobs or a rise in working hours will increase output and raise living standards, but also requires us to sacrifice time previously spent in nonmarket activities.

POLICY TRADEOFFS

SACRIFICE OF OTHER SOCIAL GOALS

Rapid economic growth is an important social goal, but it's not the only one. Some of the policies that quicken the pace of growth require us to sacrifice other goals that we care about. For example, you've seen that restructuring Social Security benefits would increase saving, leading to more investment and faster growth. But such a move would cut the incomes of those who benefit from the current system and increase the burden on other social programs, such as welfare and food stamps. Extending patent protection would increase incentives for research and development. But it would also extend the monopoly power exercised by patent holders and force consumers to pay higher prices for drugs, electronic equipment, and even packaged foods.

6 You might be wondering how a rise in average hours would be represented in the classical model we've been using. This is left to you as an exercise. But here's a hint: An increase in average hours enables the same number of workers to produce more output.

Of course, the argument cuts both ways: Just as government policies to stimulate investment require us to sacrifice other goals, so, too, can the pursuit of other goals impede investment spending and economic growth. Most of us would like to see a cleaner environment and safer workplaces. But government safety and environmental regulations have increased in severity, complexity, and cost over time, reducing the rate of profit on new capital and shrinking investment spending.

Does this mean that business taxes and government regulations should be reduced to the absolute minimum? Not at all. As in most matters of economic policy, we face a tradeoff:

POLICY TRADEOFFS

We can achieve greater worker safety, a cleaner environment, and other social goals, but we may have to sacrifice some economic growth along the way. Alternatively, we can achieve greater economic growth, but we will have to compromise on other things we care about.

When values differ, people will disagree on just how much we should sacrifice for economic growth or how much growth we should sacrifice for other goals.

USING THE THEORY

ECONOMIC GROWTH IN THE LESS DEVELOPED COUNTRIES

In most countries, Malthus's dire predictions have not come true. An important part of the reason is that increases in the capital stock have raised productivity and increased the average standard of living. Increases in the capital stock are even more important in the less developed countries (LDCs), which have relatively little capital to begin with and where even small increases in capital formation can have dramatic effects on living standards.

But how does a nation go about increasing its capital stock? As you've learned, there are a variety of measures, all designed to accomplish the same goal: shifting resources away from consumer-goods production toward capital-goods production. A very simple formula.

Some countries that were once LDCs—like the four Asian tigers (Hong Kong, Singapore, South Korea, and Taiwan)—have applied the formula very effectively. Output per capita in these counties has grown by an average of 5.5 percent per year over the past 25 years. They were able to shift resources from consumption goods into capital goods in part by pursuing many of the growth-enhancing measures discussed in this chapter: large subsidies for human and physical capital investments, pro-growth tax cuts to encourage saving and investment, and the willingness to sacrifice other social goals—especially a clean environment—for growth.[7] These economies gave up large amounts of potential consumption during a period of intensive capital formation.

But other LDCs have had great difficulty raising living standards. Table 4 shows growth rates for several of them. In some cases—such as Pakistan—growth is slow, but picking up steam. In others—like Ghana—the standard of living has remained stagnant at very low levels for years. In still other cases—for example, Zaire and, more recently, Ethiopia—output per capita has been falling steadily. Why do some LDCs have such difficulty achieving economic growth?

7 The Asian tigers also had some special advantages—such as a high level of human capital to start with.

ECONOMIC GROWTH IN SELECTED POOR COUNTRIES

TABLE 4

	Average Annual Growth in Output per Capita	
Country	**1965–80**	**1980–1993**
Pakistan	1.8%	3.1%
Ghana	−0.8%	0.1%
Bangladesh	−0.3%	2.1%
Ethiopia	0.4%	−1.9%
Zaire	−1.3%	−1.8%
All of Sub-Saharan Africa	1.5%	−0.6%

Source: United Nations Development Program, *Human Development Reports, 1995–1997* (Oxford: Oxford University Press, 1995–97), Table 25.

Much of the explanation for the low growth rates of many LDCs lies with three characteristics that they share:

1. *Very low current output per capita.* Living standards are already so low in some LDCs, that they cannot take advantage of the trade-off between producing consumption goods and producing capital goods. In these countries, pulling resources out of consumption would threaten the survival of many households. In the individual household, the problem is an inability to save: Incomes are so low, that households must spend all they earn on consumption.
2. *High population growth rates.* Low living standards and high population growth rates are linked together in a cruel circle of logic. On the one hand, population growth by itself tends to reduce living standards; on the other hand, a low standard of living tends to increase population growth. Why? First, the poor are often uneducated in matters of family planning. Second, high mortality rates among infants and children encourage families to have many offspring, to ensure the survival of at least a few to care for parents in their old age. As a result, while the average woman in the United States will have fewer than two children in her lifetime, the average woman in Haiti will have about five children, and the average woman in Rwanda will have more than six.
3. *Poor infrastructure.* Political instability, poor law enforcement, corruption, and adverse government regulations make many LDCs unprofitable places to invest. Low rates of investment mean a smaller capital stock and lower productivity. Infrastructure problems also harm worker productivity in another way: Citizens must spend time guarding against thievery and trying to induce the government to let them operate businesses—time they could otherwise spend producing output.

These three characteristics—low current production, high population growth, and poor infrastructure—interact to create a vicious circle of continuing poverty, which we can understand with the help of the familiar PPF between capital goods and consumption goods. Look back at Figure 9, and now imagine that it applies to a poor, developing country. In this case, an outward shift of the PPF does not, in itself, guarantee an increase in the standard of living. In the LDCs, the population growth rate is often very high, and—with a constant labor force participation ratio—employment grows at the same rate as the population. If employment grows

FIGURE 10

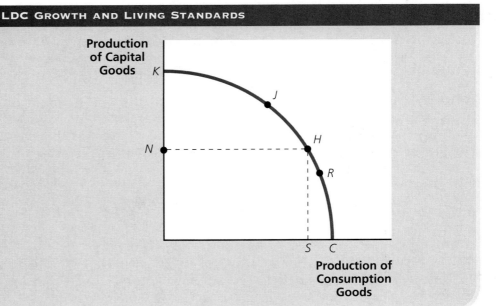

LDC GROWTH AND LIVING STANDARDS

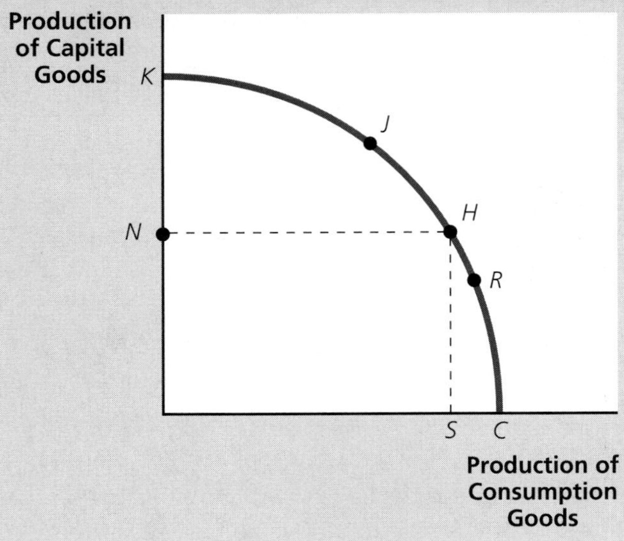

In order to increase capital per worker when population is growing, yearly investment spending must exceed some minimum level *N*. In any year, there is a minimum level of consumption, *S*, needed to support the population. If output is currently at point *H*, capital per worker and living standards are stagnant. But movement to a point like *J* would require an unacceptably low level of consumption.

more rapidly than the capital stock, then even though the PPF is shifting outward, capital per worker will decline. The result is falling labor productivity and a general decline in living standards.

In order to have rising living standards, a nation's stock of capital must not only grow, but grow faster than its population.

Point *N* in Figure 10 shows the minimum amount of investment needed to increase capital per worker, labor productivity, and living standards for a given rate of population growth. For example, if the population is growing at 4 percent per year, then point *N* indicates the investment needed to increase the total capital stock by 4 percent per year. If investment is just equal to *N*, then capital per worker—and living standards—remains constant. If investment exceeds *N*, then capital per worker—and living standards—will rise. Of course, the greater the growth in population, the higher point *N* will be on the vertical axis, since greater investment will be needed just to keep up with population growth.

The PPF in Figure 10 has an added feature: Point *S* shows the minimum acceptable level of consumption—the amount of consumer goods the economy *must* produce in a year. For example, *S* might represent the consumption goods needed to prevent starvation among the least well off, or to prevent unacceptable social consequences, such as violent revolution.

Now we can see the problem faced by the most desperate of the less developed economies. Output is currently at a point like *H* in Figure 10, with investment just equal to *N*. The capital stock is not growing fast enough to increase capital per worker, and so labor productivity and living standards are stagnant. In this situation, the PPF shifts outward each year, but not quickly enough to improve people's lives. It could be even worse: Convince yourself that, at a point like *R*, the average standard of living declines even though the capital stock is growing—that is, even though the PPF will shift outward in future periods.

The solution to this problem appears to be an increase in capital production beyond point *N*—a movement *along* the PPF from point *H* to a point such as *J*. As investment rises above *N*, capital per worker rises, and the PPF shifts outward rapidly enough over time to raise living standards. In a wealthy country, like the United States, such a move could be engineered by changes in taxes or other government policies. But in the LDCs depicted here, such a move would be intolerable: At point *H*, consumption is already equal to *S*, the lowest acceptable level. Moving to point *J* would require reducing consumption *below S*.

The poorest LDCs are too poor to take advantage of the trade-off between consumption and capital production in order to increase their living standards. Since they cannot reduce consumption below current levels, they cannot produce enough capital to keep up with their rising populations.

In recent history, countries have attempted several methods to break out of this vicious circle of poverty. During the 1930s, the dictator Joseph Stalin simply *forced* the Soviet economy from a point like *H* to one like *J*. His goal was to shift the Soviet Union's PPF outward as rapidly as possible. But, as you can see, this reduced consumption below the minimum level *S*, and Stalin resorted to brutal measures to enforce his will. Many farmers were ordered into the city to produce capital equipment. With fewer people working on farms, agricultural production declined, and there was not enough food to go around. Stalin's solution was to confiscate food from the remaining farmers and give it to the urban workforce. Of course, this meant starvation for millions of farmers. Millions more who complained too loudly, or who otherwise represented a political threat, were rounded up and executed.

A less brutal solution to the problem of the LDCs is to make the wealthy bear more of the burden of increasing growth. If the decrease in consumption can be limited to the rich, then total consumption can be significantly reduced—freeing up resources for investment—without threatening the survival of the poor. This, however, is not often practical, since the wealthy have the most influence with government in LDCs. Being more mobile, they can easily relocate to other countries, taking their savings with them. This is why efforts to shift the sacrifice to the wealthy are often combined with restrictions on personal liberties, such as the freedom to travel or to invest abroad. These moves often backfire in the long run, since restrictions on personal and economic freedom are remembered long after they are removed and make the public—especially foreigners—hesitant to invest in that country.

A third alternative—and the one used increasingly since the 1940s—is *foreign investment* or *foreign assistance*. If the wealthier nations, individually or through international organizations such as the World Bank or the International Monetary Fund—provide the LDCs with capital, then the capital *available* to them can increase, with *no* cutbacks in consumption. This permits an LDC to make *use* of capital and consumption goods at a point like *F* in Figure 11(a), even though its *production* remains—for the moment—at point *H*.

A variation of this strategy is for foreign nations to provide consumer goods so that the poorer nation can shift its *own* resources out of producing them (and into capital production) without causing consumption levels to fall. Once again, if capital production exceeds point *N* during the year, capital per worker will grow, setting the stage for continual growth to higher standards of living.

Finally, there is a fourth alternative. Consider a nation producing at point *T* in Figure 11(b). Capital production is just sufficient to keep up with a rising popula-

FIGURE 11 **GROWTH OPTIONS FOR LDCs**

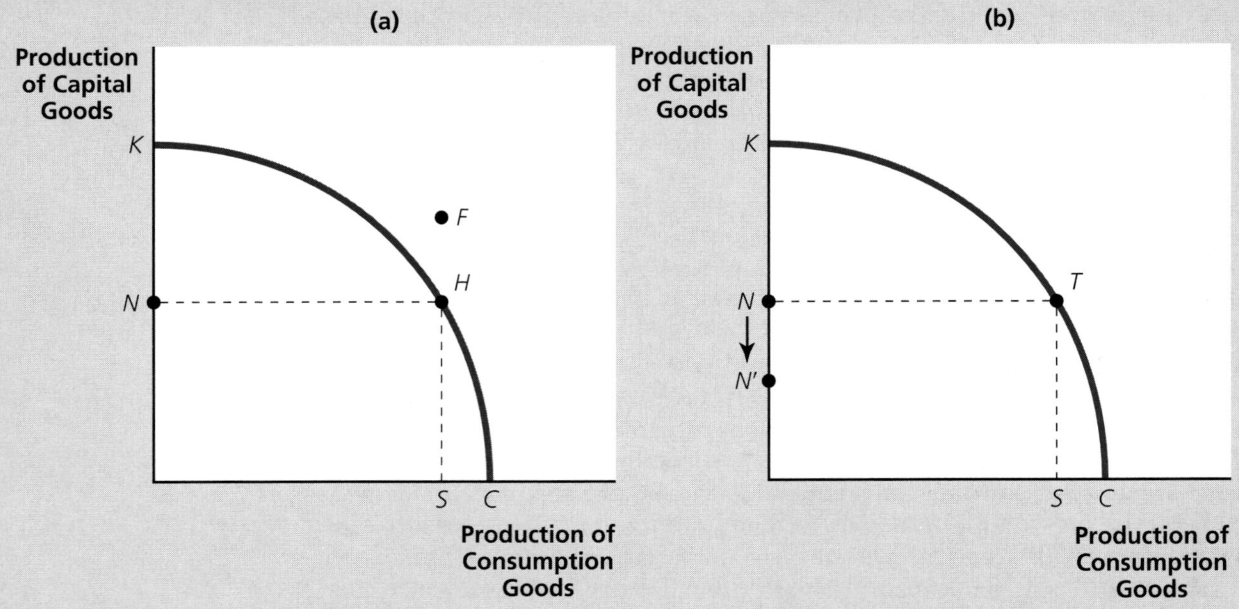

Panel (a) shows an LDC producing at point *H,* where the available consumption goods are just sufficient to meet minimum standards (point *S*). If the nation can obtain goods externally—through foreign investment or foreign assistance—it can *make use* of capital and consumption goods at a point like *F*—outside of its PPF.

Panel (b) shows a case where capital production at point *T* is just sufficient to keep up with a rising population, but not great enough to raise capital per worker and living standards. If this nation can reduce its population growth rate, then the same rate of capital production will increase capital per worker and shift the PPF outward.

tion, so the PPF shifts outward each year, but not rapidly enough to raise living standards. If this nation can reduce its population growth rate, however, then less capital production will be needed just to keep up with population growth. In the figure, point *N* will move downward to *N′*. If production remains at point *T,* the PPF will continue to shift outward as before, but now—with slower population growth—productivity and living standards will rise. Slowing the growth in population has been an important (and successful) part of China's growth strategy, although it has required severe restrictions on the rights of individual families to have children. Policy tradeoffs, once again.

SUMMARY

The growth rate of real GDP is a key determinant of economic well-being. If output grows faster than the population, then the average standard of living will rise. Output can grow because of increases in employment, increases in capital, and improvements in technology.

Employment will increase if there is an increase in either labor supply or labor demand. Labor supply is determined by the size of the working-age population and by individuals' willingness to forgo leisure in return for a wage. Population growth is something that occurs naturally, but the amount of work effort supplied by a given population in sensitive to after-tax labor earnings. A decrease in the income tax rate would stimulate labor supply.

Labor demand is influenced by productivity. Any factor that makes labor more productive will increase the demand for labor, raise employment, and contribute to economic growth. If employees become better trained, or if they are given more capital to work with, their productivity will increase.

An increase in the capital stock will shift the production function upward and contribute to economic growth. Whenever investment exceeds depreciation, the capital stock will grow. And if the capital stock grows faster than the labor force, then labor productivity will rise.

Investment can be encouraged by government policies. If the government reduces its budget deficit, the demand for loanable funds will fall, the interest rate will decline, and investment will increase. Investment can also be stimulated directly through reductions in the corporate profits tax or through subsidies to new capital. Finally, policies that encourage household saving can also lower the interest rate and contribute to capital formation.

The third factor that contributes to economic growth is technological change—the application of new inputs or new methods of production. Technological change increases productivity and raises living standards by permitting us to produce more output from a given set of inputs. Technological improvements can be traced back to spending on research and development, either by the government or by private firms.

Economic growth is not costless. Government policies that stimulate employment, capital formation, or technological progress require either tax increases, cuts in other spending programs, or an increase in the national debt. More broadly, any increase in investment requires the sacrifice of consumption today. Any increase in employment from a given population requires a sacrifice of leisure time and other nonmarket activities.

KEY TERMS

average standard of living
labor productivity
capital per worker
corporate profits tax
investment tax credit
capital gains tax
consumption tax
human capital
technological change
patent protection
national debt

REVIEW QUESTIONS

1. Discuss the three ways a country can increase its equilibrium level of output.
2. Why can population growth be a mixed blessing in terms of economic growth?
3. Explain how a tax cut could lead to *slower* economic growth.
4. Given that a country's PPF is shifting outward, is it necessarily the case that the country's standard of living is rising? Why or why not?
5. Why did Malthus's dire prediction fail to materialize? Do you think it could still come true? Explain your reasoning.
6. "Faster economic growth can benefit everyone and need not harm anyone. This is a rare violation of the basic principle of policy tradeoffs." True or false? Explain.
7. Discuss some of the factors that contribute to high population growth in LDCs.
8. Explain the following statement: "In some LDCs, it can be said that a significant cause of continued poverty is poverty itself."
9. Describe four ways in which LDCs have tried to improve their growth performance. Discuss the opportunity cost that must be borne in each case and identify the group that is most likely to bear it.

PROBLEMS AND EXERCISES

1. Discuss the effect (holding everything else constant) each of the following would have on full-employment output, productivity, and the average standard of living. Use the appropriate graphs (e.g., labor market, loanable funds market, production function), and state your assumptions when necessary.
   a. Increased immigration.
   b. An aging population with an increasing proportion of retirees
   c. A baby boom
   d. A decline in the tax rate on corporate profits
   e. Reduction of unemployment compensation benefits
   f. A balanced budget amendment to the U.S. Constitution
   g. Expanding the scope of the federal student loan program
   h. Easier access to technical information on the Internet

2. Below are GDP and growth data for the U.S. and four other countries:

	1950 per Capita GDP (in constant dollars)	*1990 per Capita GDP (in constant dollars)*	*Average Yearly Growth Rate*
United States	$9,573	$21,558	2.0%
France	$5,221	$17,959	3.0%
Japan	$1,873	$19,425	5.7%
Kenya	$ 609	$ 1,055	1.3%
India	$ 597	$ 1,348	2.0%

Source: Angus Maddison, *Monitoring the World Economy, 1820–1992.* Paris, OECD, 1995.

a. For both years, calculate each country's per capita GDP as a percentage of U.S. per capita GDP. Which countries appear to be catching up to the United States, and which are lagging behind?
b. If these countries continue to grow at the average growth rates given, how long will it take France to catch up to the U.S.? How long will it take India? Kenya?

3. Below are data for the country of Barrovia, which has long been concerned with economic growth.

	Population (millions)	*Employment (millions)*	*Labor Productivity*	*Total Output*
1991	100	50	$ 9,500	______
1992	104	51	$ 9,500	______
1993	107	53	$ 9,750	______
1994	108	57	$ 9,750	______
1995	110	57	$10,000	______

a. Fill in the entries for total output in each of the five years.
b. Calculate the following for each year (except 1991):
(1) Population growth rate (from previous year)
(2) Growth rate of output (from previous year)
(3) Growth rate of per capita output (from previous year)

CHALLENGE QUESTIONS

1. Harvard economist Amartya Sen has argued that famines in underdeveloped countries are not simply the result of crop failures or natural disasters. Instead, he suggests that wars, especially civil wars, are linked to most famine episodes in recent history. Using a framework similar to Figure 11, discuss the probable effect of war on a country's PPF. Explain what would happen if the country were initially operating at or near a point like *S*, the minimum acceptable level of consumption.

2. All else equal, why might a country with a small capital stock actually attract more investment than a country with more capital?

Visit the Economic Statistics Briefing Room (http://www.whitehouse.gov/fsbr/esbr.html) and review the data on output. Answer the following questions.
a. Did the U. S. economy experience economic growth in the most recent quarter? What data can you cite to support your answer?
b. Now review the data on income. Is the standard of living rising or falling for households? What data can you cite to support your answer?

CHAPTER

9

BOOMS AND RECESSIONS

If you are like most college students, you will be looking for a job when you graduate, or you will already have one and want to keep it for a while. In either case, your fate is not entirely in your own hands. Your job prospects will depend, at least in part, on the overall level of economic activity in the country.

If the classical model of the last two chapters described the economy at every point in time, you'd have nothing to worry about. Full employment would be achieved automatically, so you could be confident of getting a job at the going wage for someone with your skills and characteristics. Unfortunately, this is not how the world works: Neither output nor employment grows as smoothly and steadily as the classical model predicts. Instead, as far back as we have data, the United States and similar countries have experienced *economic fluctuations.*

In Figure 1, look first at the red line. It shows full-employment or potential output since 1960—the level of real GDP predicted by the classical model. As a result of technological change and growth in the capital stock and population, full-employment output rises steadily. But now look at the blue line, which shows *actual* output. You can see that actual GDP fluctuates above and below the classical model's predictions. During *contractions,* which are shaded in the figure, output declines, occasionally sharply. During *expansions,* the unshaded periods, output rises quickly—usually faster than potential output is rising.

Figure 2 shows another characteristic of expansions and contractions: fluctuations in employment. During expansions, such as the period from 1983 to 1990, employment grows rapidly. During contractions (shaded), such as 1990–91, employment declines.

Finally, look at Figure 3, which presents the unemployment rate over the same period as in Figure 2. Figure 3 shows a critical aspect of fluctuations—the bulge of unemployment that occurs during each contraction. When GDP falls, the unemployment rate increases. The worst bulge in unemployment was in 1982, when more

CHAPTER OUTLINE

FIGURE 1

POTENTIAL AND ACTUAL REAL GDP, 1960–

The red line shows full-employment, or potential, real GDP since 1960. It indicates how much output would be produced if the economy were always at full employment. The blue lines shows actual real GDP. During contractions (shaded), output declines; during expansions, it rises quickly.

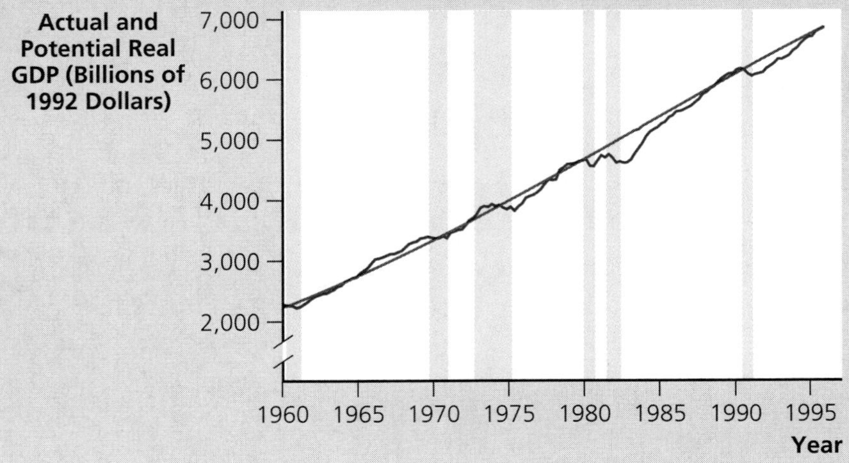

than 10 percent of the labor force was looking for work. In expansions, on the other hand, the unemployment rate falls. During the expansions of the late 1980s and mid-1990s, for example, unemployment reached a low of about 5 percent. In some expansions, the unemployment rate can drop even lower than the full-employment level. In the sustained expansion of the late 1960s, for example, it reached a low of just over 3 percent. At the same time, output exceeded its potential, as you can verify in Figure 1.

The terms "expansion" and "contraction" refer to *changes* in GDP: GDP *rises* in an expansion and *falls* in a contraction. But it is also useful to label periods when output is above and below its potential. In this book, we'll use the term **boom** to indicate a period during which GDP *exceeds* its full-employment, potential level. During a boom, employment is unusually high, and the *un*employment rate is un-

BOOM A period of time during which real GDP exceeds full-employment, potential GDP

FIGURE 2

U.S. EMPLOYMENT, 1960–

Employment fluctuates over the business cycle. During expansions, employment grows rapidly. During recessions (shaded), employment declines.

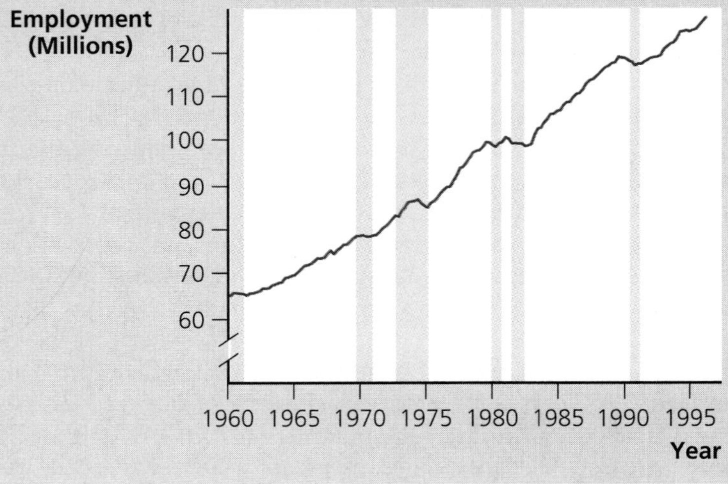

LABOR MARKET EQUILIBRIUM

FIGURE 8

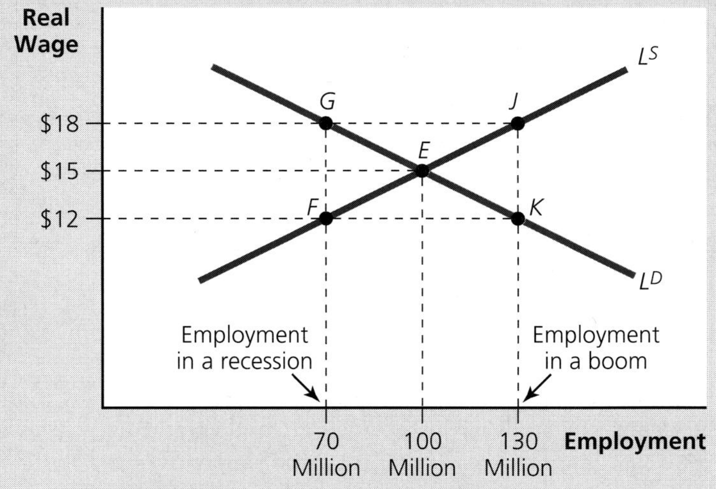

The labor supply and labor demand curves intersect at point *E* to determine an equilibrium employment of 100 million and an equilibrium real wage of $15 per hour. At any lower level of employment, such as 70 million, the benefit firms would gain from hiring an additional 30 million workers exceeds the opportunity cost to those workers. For example, the 70-millionth worker would benefit some firm by $18 per hour, but her opportunity cost of working is only $12 per hour. Mutually beneficial gains are possible for both parties. Only at equilibrium (*E*) are there no further gains to be exploited.

If employment *exceeds* the equilibrium at point *E,* firms would be hiring workers whose opportunity cost exceeded firms' benefit from hiring them. For example, the 130-millionth worker would benefit some firm by only $12 per hour, but her cost of working is $18 per hour. Employment has increased beyond the level of mutual gain, and there are incentives to reduce it.

from that person's work of just under $18 per hour, as shown by point *G*. At any wage between $12 and $18, both parties would gain if that worker were hired. For example, if the firm hired the worker for $15 per hour, the worker would gain: Her opportunity cost of working is only about $12, but she would actually get $15. The firm would also gain, since the benefit of hiring the worker is about $18, but the firm would pay only $15. Similar gains would be possible for any increase in hiring, until total employment reached 100 million.

Now suppose that employment has already reached 100 million. What would happen if the *next* worker (the 100,000,001st) were hired? This person would have an opportunity cost a tiny bit more than $15 per hour, but the benefit from hiring him would be a bit less than $15 per hour. There is no wage at which this worker could be hired for mutual gain. The same would be true of all other workers beyond 100 million. For example, if employment were to rise all the way to 130 million, the opportunity cost for the 130-millionth worker would be $18 (point *J*), but a firm could benefit by only $12 (point *K*) from hiring him.

In sum, there is only one level of employment that exhausts all of the mutually beneficial opportunities for trade among workers and firms, and this is where the labor supply and demand curves intersect:

At the equilibrium level of employment, all opportunities for mutually beneficial trade in the labor market have been exploited.

THE LABOR MARKET IN A RECESSION

Now we can see what happens in the labor market during a recession. When employment falls below the classical, full-employment level at point *E*, both firms and workers could gain if employment increased. But employment *doesn't* increase. Something in the overall economic system isn't working right, and the opportunities for mutual gain are not exploited as they should be. In Figure 8, for example, employment might fall to 70 million, where the opportunity cost for the next worker would be just $12, while the benefit to some firm from hiring this worker would be $18. A mutually beneficial deal between them is certainly possible . . . but it doesn't happen. The labor market is in *disequilibrium:*

> *During a recession, the labor market is in disequilibrium, and the benefit from hiring another worker exceeds the opportunity cost to that worker.*

What *causes* disequilibrium in the labor market? We'll discuss that a bit later in this chapter. But our analysis so far helps us understand why recessions—once they occur—do not last forever. There are strong incentives for the labor market to return to equilibrium, namely, the benefits workers and firms would enjoy from an increase in employment. Until employment returns to the level at which the labor demand and supply curves intersect, these opportunities for mutual gain are not being fully exploited.

> *In recessions, there are incentives to increase the level of employment, because the benefit to firms from additional employment exceeds the opportunity cost to workers. These incentives help explain why recessions do not last forever.*

THE LABOR MARKET IN A BOOM

What about booms? They are just as temporary as are recessions and recoveries. Once again, Figure 8 shows why. Suppose the economy is experiencing a boom in which 130 million people are working. Then there are workers whose opportunity cost of working exceeds the benefit of their work to firms. The 130-millionth worker, for example, has an opportunity cost of $18, but his firm benefits by only $12. No matter what wage we choose, one side of the deal—either the worker or the firm—loses out when that worker is hired. Suppose the 130-millionth worker is paid $18 in order to convince him to take a job. Then the firm has an incentive to let that worker go. The same is true for every level of employment beyond 100 million workers: If workers are paid their opportunity cost, firms will have an incentive to reduce employment.

> *In booms, there are incentives to decrease the level of employment, because the benefit to firms from some who have been hired is smaller than the opportunity cost to those workers. These incentives help explain why booms do not last forever.*

Now you can understand one of the observations about booms and recessions that we set out to explain: that they do not last forever. But why do they occur in the first place?

WHAT TRIGGERS BOOMS AND RECESSIONS?

You can see that recessions and booms are periods during which the economy is going a bit haywire: Opportunities for mutual gain are not being exploited. But why? In particular, why does the labor market move away from its equilibrium in the short run? Let's start to answer this question by looking at a world that is much simpler than our own.

A VERY SIMPLE ECONOMY

Imagine an economy with just two people: Yasmin and Pepe. Yasmin is especially good at making popcorn, but she eats only yogurt. Pepe, by contrast, is very good at making yogurt, but eats only popcorn. If things are going well, Yasmin and Pepe will make suitable amounts of popcorn and yogurt and trade with each other. Because of the gains from specialization, their trade will make them both better off than if they tried to function without trading. And under ordinary circumstances, Yasmin and Pepe will take advantage of all mutually beneficial opportunities for trading. Our two-person economy will thus operate at full employment, since both individuals will be fully engaged in making products for the other. You can think of their trading equilibrium as being like the labor market equilibrium in the classical model (such as point *E* in Figure 8), where workers and firms are taking advantage of all mutually beneficial opportunities for hiring and producing.

Now, suppose there is a breakdown in communication. For example, Yasmin may get the impression that Pepe is not going to want as much popcorn as before. She would then decide to make less popcorn for Pepe. At their next trading session, Pepe will be offered less popcorn, so he will decide to produce less yogurt. The result: Total production in the economy declines, and our two traders will lose some of the benefits of trading. This corresponds to a recession.

In reading the previous paragraph, you might be thinking, "Wait a minute. If either Yasmin or Pepe got the impression that the other might want less of the other's product, wouldn't a simple conversation between them straighten things out?" If these are your thoughts, you are absolutely right. A breakdown in communication and a drop in production would be extremely unlikely . . . *in a simple economy with just two people.* And therein lies the problem: The real-world economy is much more complex than the world of Yasmin and Pepe.

THE REAL-WORLD ECONOMY

Think about the U.S. economy, with its tens of millions of businesses producing goods and services for hundreds of millions of people. In many cases, production must be planned long before goods are actually sold. For example, from inception to final production, it takes close to a year to build a house and two years to develop a new automobile model or produce a Hollywood film. If one firm—say, General Motors—believes that consumers will buy fewer of its cars next year, it cannot simply call a meeting of all potential customers and find out whether its fears are justified. Nor can it convince people, as Yasmin can convince Pepe, that their own jobs depend on their buying a GM car. Most potential car buyers do *not* work for General Motors and don't perceive any connection between buying a car and keeping their own job. Under the circumstances, it may be entirely logical for General Motors to plan for a lower production level and lay off some of its workers.

Of course, this would not be the end of the story. By decreasing its workforce, GM would create further problems for the economy. The workers it has laid off,

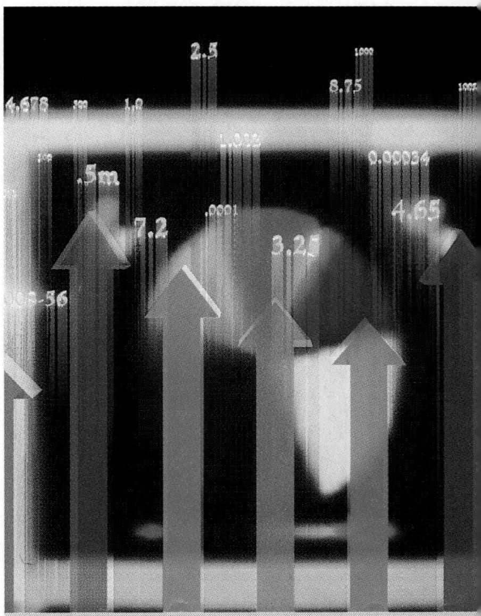

Name:
Economic Chart Dispenser
Description:
Collection of economic graphs and data provided by the University of Alabama that enables users to create custom charts
Resources:
The Economic Chart Dispenser contains a multitude of economic time series data files and graphs. If you cannot find exactly what you are looking for, use the Chart Maker to customize the data and corresponding charts.
Address:
http://bos.business.uab.edu/charts.htm

who will earn less income or none at all, will cut back on *their* spending for a variety of consumer goods—restaurant meals, movies, vacation travel—and they will certainly postpone any large purchases they'd been planning, such as a new large-screen television or that family trip to Disney World. This will cause other firms—the firms producing these consumer goods and services—to cut back on *their* production, laying off *their* workers, and so on. In other words, what began as a simple decrease in spending in one sector of the economy can work its way through other sectors, causing a full-blown recession.

This example illustrates a theme that we will revisit in the next chapter: There is an interdependence between production and income. People need income to purchase goods. When they spend their incomes, they give firms the revenue they need to hire workers . . . and pay the workers income! If any link in this chain is broken, output and income may both decline. In our example, the link was broken because of incorrect expectations by firms in one sector of the economy. But there are other causes of recessions as well, also centering on the interdependence between production and income, and a failure to coordinate the decisions of millions of firms and households.

The classical model, however, waves these potential problems aside. It assumes that workers and firms, with the aid of markets, can work things out—like Yasmin and Pepe—and enjoy the benefits of producing and trading. And the classical model is right: People *will* work things out . . . eventually. But in the short run, we need to look carefully at the problems of coordinating production, trade, and consumption in an economy with hundreds of millions of people and tens of millions of businesses.

A boom can arise in much the same way as a recession. It might start because of an increase in production in one sector of the economy—say, the housing sector. With more production, and more workers earning higher incomes, spending increases in other sectors as well, until output rises above the classical, full-employment level.

Shocks That Push the Economy Away from Equilibrium

In our discussion above, General Motors decided to cut back on its production of cars because its managers believed, rightly or wrongly, that the demand for GM cars had decreased. In the real world, a decision to decrease production is often made by many firms at the same time. We call this a **spending shock** to the economy—a change in spending that initially affects one or more sectors and ultimately works its way through the entire economy.

Spending shock A change in spending that ultimately affects the entire economy.

In the real world, the economy is constantly buffeted by shocks, and they often cause full-fledged recessions and booms. Table 1 lists some of the recessions and booms of the last fifty years, along with the shocks that are thought to have caused them, or at least contributed heavily. You can see that each of these shocks first affected spending in one or more sectors of the economy. For example, several recessions have been set off by increases in oil prices, which caused a decrease in spending on products that depend on oil and energy, such as automobiles, trucks, and new factory buildings. Other recessions were precipitated by military cutbacks and by financial crises—sudden increases in interest rates—that led to decreased spending on new homes. Booms, on the other hand, have been caused by military buildups, and by falling oil prices that stimulated spending on energy-related products.

In addition to these identifiable spending shocks, the economy is buffeted by other shocks whose origins are harder to spot. For example, consumption was higher

Booms, Recessions, and Shocks that Caused Them

TABLE 1

Period		Event	Spending Shock
Early 1950s	Boom	Korean War	Defense Spending ↑
1953	Recession	End of Korean War	Defense Spending ↓
Late 1960s	Boom	Vietnam War	Defense Spending ↑
1970	Recession	Financial Crisis	Spending on New Homes ↓
1974	Recession	Dramatic Increase in Oil Prices	Spending on Cars and other Energy-using Products ↓
1980	Recession	Dramatic Increase in Oil Prices	Spending on Cars and other Energy-using Products ↓
1981–82	Recession	Financial Crisis	Spending on New Homes, Cars, and Business Investment ↓
Early 1980s	Boom	Military Buildup	Defense Spending ↑
Late 1980s	Boom	Huge Decline in Oil Prices	Spending on Energy-using Products ↑
1990	Recession	Large Increase in Oil Prices; Collapse of Soviet Union	Spending on Cars and other Energy-using Products ↓; Defense Spending ↓

than expected in the late 1980s, contributing to the boom that occurred in those years. In the early 1990s, consumption fell back to normal, helping to cause the recession of that period. There was no obvious event that caused these changes in consumption.

As you can see in Table 1, the economy barely has time to adjust to one shock before it is hit by another. But we can usually see the beginnings of the adjustment process, and sometimes we can follow it through to its end. In the case of an adverse shock, large numbers of workers lose their jobs. The shock puts the labor market into the situation like that depicted in Figure 8, with employment at 70 million workers. At recession levels of employment, the benefit from working exceeds the opportunity cost of working, providing an incentive for firms to increase their hiring. This incentive guides the economy through a long and gradual period of **recovery**, during which output and employment rise to their equilibrium levels. Unemployed workers are gradually reabsorbed into the economy until full employment is restored.

Recovery The period after a recession during which output and employment return to their full-employment levels.

But notice the word "gradually." The process of adjustment back to equilibrium in the labor market can take surprisingly long. This is in sharp contrast to what happens in other markets. In microeconomic markets, like the one for maple syrup, or macroeconomic markets, like the stock market, the response is speedy to the incentives to return to equilibrium. If quantity supplied does not equal quantity demanded, equilibrium will be restored within hours, days, or weeks. In the labor market, the *incentives* to get to equilibrium are similar to those in other markets, but the process of getting there takes much longer. It can take—and has taken—years for the economy to return to full employment after a recession, as we saw in Figures 1, 2, and 3. For example, the unemployment rate exceeded 10 percent in 1982 and did not fall below 6 percent until 1986.

A positive shock triggers a boom, and puts the labor market in the situation like the one in Figure 8 in which employment rises to 130 million. Again, there is an incentive to return to normal conditions. In this case, cutting the workforce re-

FIGURE 9

JOB DESTRUCTION AND CREATION, 1972–1988

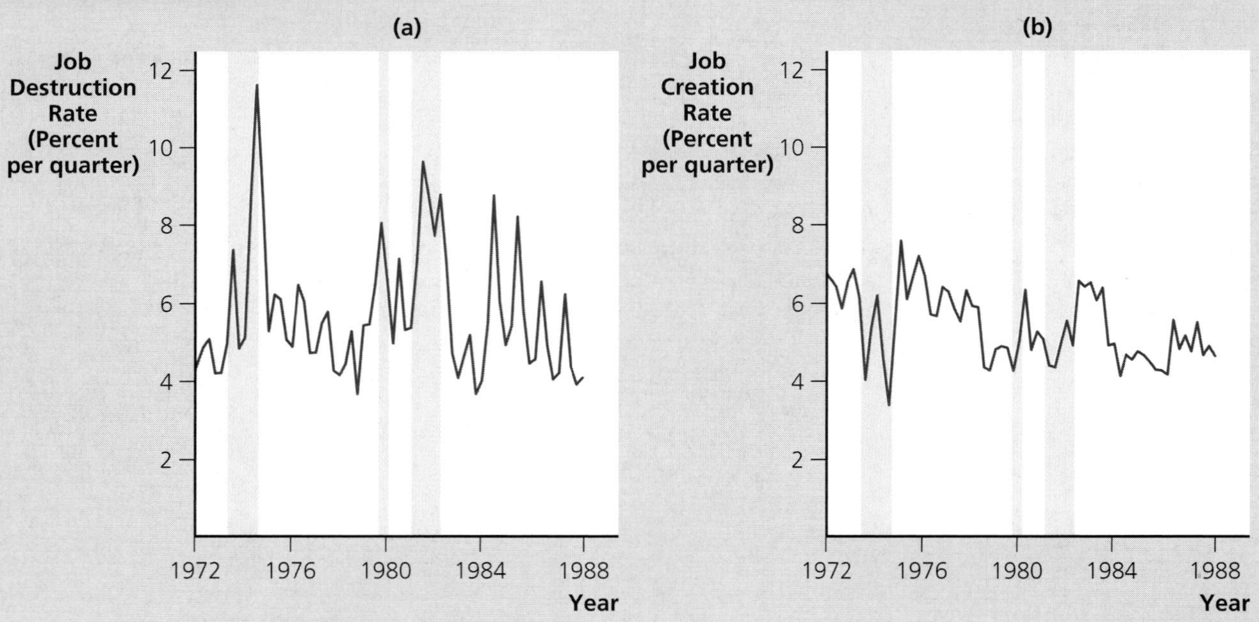

Panel (a) shows the number of manufacturing jobs destroyed, as a percentage of employment. Recessions (shaded) are periods of sharp increases in job destruction. Panel (b) shows job creation. There are sharp increases in job creation during and shortly after recessions.

leases workers whose opportunity cost of working is greater than the benefits firms get from their work. As firms respond to these incentives, employment and output will gradually fall back to their full-employment levels. But once again, the process of adjustment back to equilibrium can take years.

JOB DESTRUCTION AND JOB CREATION

JOB DESTRUCTION Decreases in employment at contracting firms.

Economists use the terms *job destruction* and *job creation* to describe the events in the labor market that occur when a shock pushes the economy away from full employment. **Job destruction** occurs when employers cut back employment. Workers lose their jobs and must find positions with other employers, often in other industries. When an adverse shock hits the economy—an oil price increase or a financial crisis, for example—there is a burst of job destruction in the industries directly affected, such as the auto and construction industries. As you'll see in the next chapter, job destruction that starts in a few hard-hit industries can spread throughout the entire economy.

Job destruction is measured from the employment records of individual factories and plants. The total amount of job destruction is the reduction in employment in all plants in which employment fell. Panel (a) of Figure 9 shows job destruction in U.S. manufacturing industries for the period 1972–1988, stated as a percent of total employment. In normal times, about 6 percent of all manufacturing jobs are destroyed each quarter. Immediately after adverse shocks, as in 1975, 1980, and 1982, job destruction soars to levels of 9 percent or higher. Jobs are destroyed in short, sharp episodes. During these episodes, total employment falls. Over the next two or more years, employment gradually recovers, but unemployment remains high for some time longer. In 1983 and 1984, for example, job destruction was at normal levels, but unemployment remained high.

Job creation is the other side of the coin. It is the sum of the increases in employment in all plants in which employment increased. Job creation rates are above normal during booms, but the biggest bursts of job creation occur not in booms, but toward the end of and right after recessions. At these times, job creation absorbs many of the workers released by job destruction, as they find new jobs; it is an essential part of the process of recovery from a recession. Panel (b) of Figure 9 shows the U.S. job creation rate, again as a percent of total employment. Note the spikes of job creation just after the spikes of job destruction in the two panels.

JOB CREATION Increases in employment at expanding firms.

The behavior of job destruction and creation helps us understand some aspects of recessions. An adverse shock causes a burst of job destruction as plants are shut down and production is cut back in the industries immediately affected by the shock. Further rounds of job destruction will occur in other, related industries. For example, a shock that begins with new-housing construction might spread to other industries, such as cement, lumber, and copper, and then on to still more industries.

The process of recovery starts immediately. Many of the workers released as a result of the shock and recession find work soon in other industries—that is why job creation reaches its highest levels just after recessions. But unemployment remains high for two or more years after the original shock that triggers the recession. Why? Because job creation is usually not high enough to absorb all of the workers released during the initial contraction. The process of rebuilding the level of employment—by taking advantage of situations in which the benefit to firms exceeds the opportunity cost to workers—takes years, not days or weeks.

A boom is a period when job creation consistently exceeds job destruction, so employment rises and unemployment falls. During a boom, the economy does an unusually good job of utilizing available labor. Only a small fraction of the labor force is unemployed—below the fraction that is considered normal.

Our description of the job creation and job destruction processes raises an important question: Why does it take so long for employment to return to normal after a shock? After an adverse shock, why does it take years before job creation fully compensates for job destruction? After a positive shock and a burst of job creation, why does it take years before job destruction brings employment back to normal?

THE ECONOMICS OF SLOW ADJUSTMENT

To see why the economy does not adjust immediately and fully to a shock, let's take a close look at a representative firm—say, a hotel. Imagine that you manage a hotel with 100 rooms. You would learn, as do most hotel operators, that you do *not* want to fill all 100 rooms night after night. Instead, you do better with some excess capacity—enough vacant rooms to enable some early arrivals to move in when they first show up, to permit some flexibility in case of problems like broken telephones or leaky faucets, and to accommodate the occasional surge in demand without turning away your regular customers and losing their business to another hotel. We'll suppose that you try to manage your operation so that, on an average night, you will fill 70 of the 100 rooms. (In fact, the hotel industry, like the airline industry, tends to operate at around 70 percent of capacity.)

Of course, if you are aiming to fill 70 percent of your rooms, on average, then you will hire the appropriate number of workers to clean the rooms, provide room service, wash dishes and towels, and so on. This is your normal employment level.

ADJUSTMENT IN A BOOM

Now suppose the economy experiences a boom. Output is above its potential, income is high, and so there is an increase in the number of travelers who want to stay at your hotel. As a result, you begin to find that all 100 rooms are filled. What will you do? Eventually, you will take steps to restore normal utilization, such as reducing the amount of advertising or changing your directory listings to show higher prices. But these changes take time, and it would not make sense to make them until you were sure they were necessary. After all, the jump in utilization may not last more than a few weeks. Reversing any changes you make would be costly, and you might regret having made them in haste. For a while, therefore, you will likely hold off making changes. That is, in the short run, you would probably accept unusually high utilization of your hotel.

But what about the additional work that must be done with higher occupancy? For a day or two, you might get your employees to work longer hours and work harder on the job, but you cannot expect them to do so for very long. Soon you will have to hire more workers, even if just temporarily. As we saw earlier, it will take time to bring utilization down to normal levels. In the meantime, your best choice is to increase employment above its normal level. Thus, in the short run, the increase in demand for rooms will lead to higher-than-normal employment.

What is true for your hotel will also be true of other firms in the economy. As they experience the immediate effects of a positive spending shock, they will temporarily operate their factories, stores, or offices at above-normal rates of utilization. As a consequence, they will increase employment to higher-than-normal levels. At these employment levels, the benefits firms get from hiring the additional workers will be smaller than the opportunity cost of their work, but—when all options are considered—this is the sensible thing for firms to do.

When a positive shock causes a boom, firms operate—temporarily—at above-normal rates of utilization. As a consequence, employment rises above its normal, full-employment level.

Now let's go back to your hotel. Suppose that the increase in demand turns out to be long lasting: Month after month, you find yourself filling all 100 rooms. Eventually, you will decide to start making the changes that will restore your normal rate of utilization. You might raise prices, cut back on your advertising, offer fewer frills, or take some combination of steps to get you back to your normal 70-percent occupancy rate.

As your occupancy rate falls back to normal, you will lay off those additional employees you hired, so your level of employment, too, will fall back to normal. Of course, you are not the only firm in the economy behaving this way. Other firms, too, are laying off workers as they bring their businesses back to normal operating ranges. When these adjustments are completed, employment in the nation as a whole will be back at its normal, full-employment level:

Over time, firms that have experienced an increase in demand will return to normal utilization rates, and employment will fall back to its normal, full-employment level.

Adjustment in a Recession

Now consider a quite different situation. The economy enters a recession, and you begin to find that only 30 of your rooms are rented. Do you take action on the spot to get to your normal 70 guests? Probably not, for two reasons. First, you cannot immediately bring your utilization rate back to normal: Most of the steps you could take to make your hotel more attractive (offer lower prices, more frills, and so on) will benefit the 30 guests who are renting your rooms already, but it takes time for the word to get out and attract *additional* guests. Second, you don't want to change your policies in haste, only to make costly reversals in a few weeks. You will probably wait a while, operating at below-normal capacity for several weeks or even months, meanwhile laying off some of your workers because they are no longer needed. As a result, you—and managers at thousands of other firms—will find yourself laying off some workers whose benefits to you are greater than their opportunity cost of working. Yet, considering all of your options, it's a sensible thing to do.

When an adverse shock causes a recession, firms operate—temporarily—at below-normal rates of utilization. As a consequence, employment drops below its normal, full-employment level

But what if the decrease in demand turns out to be long lasting? After several months, you—and other firms—will realize that it is time to make the changes necessary to bring rates of utilization back up. This might mean lowering prices, offering better amenities, stepping up advertising, and more. As you take these steps, and your occupancy rate rises back to normal, you will hire additional employees, since the benefits of hiring them exceed the opportunity cost of their work. Your employment level will rise back to normal. As other firms behave the same way, employment in the nation will rise back to its normal, full-employment level.

Over time, firms that have experienced a decrease in demand will return to normal utilization rates, and employment will rise back to its normal, full-employment level.

The Speed of Adjustment

The way we have told our story, it seems that the labor market should adjust fully to a shock—and return to full employment—in a few weeks or months, not the years it often actually takes in the real world. What accounts for the slow adjustment of employment? There is some controversy about this issue, but one of the likely explanations has to do with a realistic view of how jobs are destroyed and created. Think about what happens in a recession: Workers are laid off, temporarily, until firms decide to return to normal capacity. But unemployed workers don't necessarily wait around for their original employers to rehire them. Instead, many will look for other jobs, and some will find them. Remember, the rate of job creation remains high in a recession, suggesting that many of those whose jobs are destroyed in contracting sectors find jobs in other sectors, even during a recession. This means that when you, as hotel manager, decide to return to normal employment levels, many of those you laid off will have found jobs elsewhere. You will have to search once again for people suitable for hotel work, and you will have to train them. This searching and training is both costly *and time consuming*. We shouldn't be surprised, then, that it can take considerable time—even a few years—for employment to recover fully from a recession.

Job-searching behavior by firms and workers is just one explanation for the slow pace of adjustment back to full employment. In later chapters, we'll carefully examine other explanations.

WHERE DO WE GO FROM HERE?

The classical model that you've learned in previous chapters is certainly useful: It helps us understand economic growth over time, and how economic events and economic policies affect the economy over the long run. But in trying to understand booms and recessions—where they come from, and why they last for one or more years—we've had to depart from the strict framework of the classical model. In particular, you've seen that *the labor market will not always clear in the short run,* and you've learned why. As we saw with our hotel example, in order to maintain normal employment at every moment in time—which would add up nationally to the classical, market-clearing employment level—firms would have to adjust more quickly than it makes sense for them to do.

You've also seen how a shock to the economy can affect spending and production in one sector and spread to other sectors, causing a recession or a boom. And you've seen why it can take a year or more to return to full employment after a shock.

One theme of our discussion has been the central role of spending in understanding economic fluctuations. In the classical model, spending could be safely ignored. First, Say's law assured us that total spending would always be sufficient to buy the output produced at full employment. Second, a change in spending—for example, an increase in military spending by the government—causes other categories of spending to fall by just the right amount to free up the additional resources being used by the government. In the long run, we can have faith in the classical perspective on spending.

But in the short run, we've seen that shocks to the economy affect spending—usually in one specific sector. When employment changes in that sector, the spending of workers *there* will change as well, affecting demand in still other sectors. Clearly, if we want to understand booms and recessions, we need to take a close look at spending. This is what we will do in the next chapter, when we study the *short-run Keynesian model.*

SUMMARY

The classical model does not always do a good job of describing the economy over short time periods. Over periods of a few years, national economies experience economic fluctuations in which output rises above or falls below its long-term growth path. And when real GDP fluctuates, the level of employment and the unemployment rate fluctuate as well.

The classical model cannot explain economic fluctuations because it assumes that the labor market always clears—that is, it always operates at the point where the labor supply and demand curves intersect. Evidence suggests that this market-clearing assumption is not always valid over short time periods. Instead, the labor market is sometimes characterized by *disequilibrium* in which employment is above or below the level at which the supply and demand curves intersect.

Whenever the labor market—or any market—is out of equilibrium, there are forces operating that tend to drive it back to equilibrium. If employment is below equilibrium, then there are opportunities for mutually beneficial deals between employers and unemployed workers. If these deals go through, then employment—and output—will increase. But sometimes it takes time for these mutually beneficial agreements to be discovered and negotiated. During that time period, the economy can remain in recession. When employment is above equilibrium, firms have incentives to cut back employment, and eventually they will do so. But in the meantime, the economy will experience a boom.

Deviations from the full-employment level of output are often caused by *spending shocks*—changes in spending that initially affect one sector, and then work their way through the entire economy. Negative shocks can cause recessions, while positive shocks can cause booms. Eventually, output will return to its equilibrium level, but it does not do so immediately. The speed of adjustment has to do with how jobs are created and destroyed. Workers laid off in a recession, for example, will seek work elsewhere—a process that takes time. Similarly, it takes time for employers to find new employees to replace those laid off. The origins of economic fluctuations can be described more fully with the short-run Keynesian model, which we will study in the next chapter.

KEY TERMS

boom
spending shock
recovery
job destruction
job creation
disequilibrium

REVIEW QUESTIONS

1. How does a *recession* differ from a *boom*? Describe the typical behavior of GDP and the unemployment rate during these periods?

2. Why can't a recession be explained in terms of a reduction in labor demand? In terms of a reduction in labor supply?

3. In an economy with just two people, recessions and booms would be unlikely to occur. Why? What is the key difference in the real-world economy that makes economic fluctuations more likely?

4. "During the last half-century economic fluctuations in the United States have been caused entirely by changes in military spending." True or false? Explain.

5. Describe the typical pattern of job destruction during booms and during recessions. Do the same for job creation.

6. Suppose the economy is disturbed by a negative shock. Describe a typical pattern of adjustment to that shock. What will happen to real GDP and the unemployment rate over time?

7. In what sense are mutual opportunities for gain not being exploited during a recession?

PROBLEMS AND EXERCISES

1. Use the following data to construct a labor demand and supply diagram.

Wage Rate	*Quantity of Labor Demanded*	*Quantity of Labor Supplied*
$ 9	95 million	65 million
10	90	70
11	85	75
12	80	80
13	75	85
14	70	90

   a. What are the equilibrium wage rate and level of employment?
   b. Explain the opportunity for mutually beneficial trade that exists when employment is 70,000,000.

2. Suppose you run a photocopy shop and for one month you experience a surge in business above normal levels. What steps would you take during the month? What additional steps would you take if the surge lasted for two years? How do your answers help explain why booms occur and why they are temporary?

3. In the chapter, you learned that job creation rates are high toward the end of recessions. Why, then, is the unemployment rate unusually high during such periods?

Visit the University of Alabama's Economic Chart Dispenser (http://bos.business.uab.edu/charts.htm).

a. Locate the "Gross Domestic Product Fixed in 1992 Dollars" data series within "Quarterly Gross Domestic Product and Components." Review the discussion of economic contractions and expansions in the chapter. Using the data and chart from the Economic Chart Dispenser, when did the contraction of the 1990s begin? (*Hint:* Find the quarter and year in which real GDP peaked during the early 1990s.)

b. Return to the opening page for the Economic Chart Dispenser and visit the Economic Chart Maker (http://bos.business.uab.edu/~wsapi/cfusion?template=chart.dbm). Type in "domestic product," change the date to 1980, and click on "find matching series." Choose "Real Gross Domestic Product; Billions of Fixed 1992 Dollars, SAAR." How many contractions have there been since 1980? How many expansions?

CHAPTER 10

THE SHORT-RUN KEYNESIAN MODEL

CHAPTER OUTLINE

Every December, newspapers and television news broadcasts focus their attention on spending. You might see a reporter standing in front of a Toys-Я-Us outlet, warning that unless holiday shoppers loosen their wallets and spend big on toys, computers, vacation trips, dishwashers, and new cars, the economy is in for trouble.

Of course, spending matters during the rest of the year, too. But holiday spending attracts our attention because the normal forces at work during the rest of the year become more concentrated in late November and December. Factories churn out merchandise and stores stock up at higher than normal rates. If consumers are in scroogelike moods, unsold goods will pile up in stores. In the months that follow, these stores will cut back on their orders for new goods. As a result, factories will decrease production and lay off workers.

And the story will not end there. The laid-off workers—even those who collect some unemployment benefits—will see their incomes decline. As a consequence, they will spend less on a variety of consumer goods. This will cause other firms—the ones that produce those consumer goods—to cut back on *their* production.

This hypothetical example reinforces a conclusion we reached in the last chapter: Spending is very important in the short run. And it points out an interesting circularity: The more income households have, the more they will spend. That is, *spending depends on income.* But the more households spend, the more output firms will produce—and the more income they will pay to their workers. Thus, *income depends on spending.*

In the short run, spending depends on income, and income depends on spending.

In this chapter, we will explore this circular connection between spending and income. We will do so with a very simple macroeconomic model, commonly known as the *short-run Keynesian model,* named after the British economist John Maynard

DANGEROUS CURVES

Don't confuse the two different meanings of the term "Keynesian economics." To economists, this label refers to the scientific contributions of Keynes and his followers in explaining economic fluctuations. Among the most important of these contributions is the short-run Keynesian model you will learn about in this chapter. But in the media, the label "Keynesian economics" is often applied to Keynes's most famous policy recommendation: that the government should actively try to prevent recessions, and try to cure them once they have occurred. While the short-run Keynesian model helps us *understand* the call for an activist macroeconomic policy, it does not automatically lead to that conclusion.

Keynes, who originally developed the ideas behind the model in the 1930s. The **short-run Keynesian model** focuses on the role of spending in explaining economic fluctuations. It explains how shocks that initially affect one sector of the economy quickly influence other sectors, causing changes in total output and employment.

SHORT-RUN KEYNESIAN MODEL A macroeconomic model that explains how changes in spending can affect real GDP in the short run.

To keep the model as simple as possible, we will—for the time being—ignore all influences on production *besides* spending. As a result, the short-run Keynesian model may appear strange to you at first, like a drive along an unfamiliar highway. You may wonder: Where is all the scenery you are used to seeing along the classical road? Where are the labor market, the production function, the financial markets, and the market-clearing assumption? Rest assured that many of these concepts are still with us, lurking in the background and waiting to be exposed, and we will come back to them in later chapters. But in this chapter, we assume that spending—and *only* spending—determines how much output the economy will produce.

THINKING ABOUT SPENDING. Before we begin our analysis of spending, we have two choices to make. The first concerns our basic approach. There are so many different types of spenders in the economy: city dwellers and suburbanites; government agencies like the Department of Defense and the local school board; and businesses of all types, ranging from the corner grocery store to a huge corporation such as AT&T. How should we organize our thinking about spending? Macroeconomists have found that the most useful approach is to divide spending into three broad *aggregates:*

- Consumption spending (C)
- Investment spending (I)
- Government purchases (G)

After looking at each of these aggregates separately, we will combine them to explore the behavior of total spending in the economy.[1]

Our second choice in analyzing spending is whether to look at *nominal* or *real* spending. (Recall that a nominal variable is measured in current dollars, while a real variable is measured in the constant dollars of some base year.) Ultimately, we care more about real variables, such as real output and real income, because they are the more closely related to our economic well-being. For example, a rise in *nominal* output might mean that we are producing more goods and services, or it might just mean that prices have risen and production has remained the same or fallen. But a rise in *real* output always means that production has increased. For this reason, we will think about real variables right from the beginning. When we discuss "consumption spending," we mean "real consumption spending," "investment spending" means "real investment spending," and so on.

1 We are temporarily excluding net exports (NX), which means that we are not yet taking account of the foreign sector's spending on U.S. output. We'll introduce net exports in a later chapter.

CONSUMPTION SPENDING

A natural place for us to begin our look at spending is with its largest component: *consumption spending*. In all, household spending on consumer goods—groceries, restaurant meals, rent, car repairs, movies, telephone calls, and furniture—is about two-thirds of total spending in the economy. Because we are interested in the macroeconomy, we don't concern ourselves with the differences between one consumer good and another. Instead, we want to know: What determines the *total* amount of consumption spending?

The answer is, a lot of different things. Think about yourself: What determines how much you spend in a given year? The most obvious determinant is your income, or—more precisely—your **disposable income,** the part of your income left over after you pay taxes:[2]

DISPOSABLE INCOME The part of household income that remains after paying taxes.

$$\text{Disposable Income} = \text{Income} - \text{Taxes}$$

All else equal, you'd certainly spend more on consumer goods with a disposable income of $50,000 per year than with a disposable income of $20,000 per year. (Here, as elsewhere, we are speaking about *real* variables: *real* consumption and *real* disposable income.)

But other factors besides your disposable income influence how much you spend. For example, suppose your disposable income is $50,000 per year. How much of that sum will you spend, and how much will you save? Since the *interest rate* determines your reward for saving, you would probably save more at a higher interest rate like 10 percent than at a lower interest rate like 2 percent. But since you'd be saving more, you'd be spending less. So we can expect consumption spending to be smaller at higher interest rates, and greater at lower interest rates.

Another determinant of consumption is *wealth*—the total value of your assets (home, stocks, bonds, bank accounts, and the like) minus your outstanding liabilities (mortgage loans, credit card debt, student loans, and so on). Even if your disposable income stayed the same, an increase in your wealth—say, because your stocks or bonds became more valuable—would probably induce you to spend more.

Expectations about your future would affect your spending as well. If you become more optimistic about your job security or expect a big raise, you might spend more of your income now. Similarly, increased pessimism, such as greater worries about losing your job, would lead you to decrease spending now.

We could list many other variables that would influence your consumption spending—how long you expect to live, inheritances you expect to receive over your lifetime, and more.

What do these personal observations tell us about *aggregate* consumption spending? Just as your own consumption spending would be influenced by a variety of variables in the economy, so, too, would the consumption spending of other households. Each of the variables we've discussed will therefore influence aggregate consumption spending in predictable ways. We would expect a rise in aggregate disposable income—the total of every household's disposable income in the economy—to cause a rise in aggregate consumption spending. Similarly, a rise in the overall level of interest rates should cause a decrease in aggregate consumption spending.

2 Strictly speaking, we deduct *net* taxes from income to obtain disposable income. Net taxes are the taxes households pay *minus* the transfer payments households receive from the government.

FIGURE 1

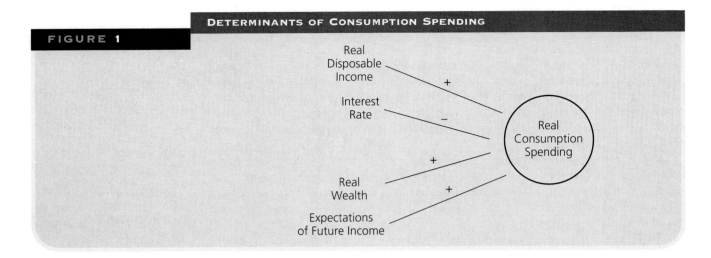

DETERMINANTS OF CONSUMPTION SPENDING

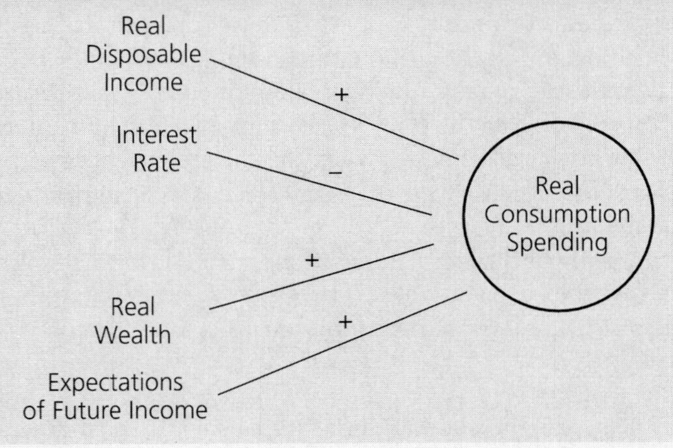

Figure 1 summarizes some of the important variables that influence consumption spending, and the direction of their effects. A plus sign indicates that consumption spending moves in the same direction as the variable; for example, a rise in disposable income will cause a rise in consumption. A minus sign indicates that the variables are negatively related—a rise in the interest rate will cause consumption spending to fall.

THE RELATIONSHIP BETWEEN CONSUMPTION AND DISPOSABLE INCOME

Of all the factors that might influence consumption spending, the most important is disposable income. Figure 2 shows the relationship between real consumption spending and real disposable income in the United States from 1960 to 1996. Each point in the diagram represents a different year. For example, the point labeled "1982" represents a disposable income in that year of $3,483 billion and consumption spending of $3,082 billion. Notice that each time disposable income rises, consumption spending rises as well. Indeed, almost all of the variation in consumption spending from year to year can be explained by variations in disposable income. Although the other factors in Figure 1 do affect consumption spending, their impact appears to be relatively minor.

There is something even more interesting about Figure 2: The relationship between consumption and disposable income is almost perfectly *linear*—the points lie remarkably close to a straight line. This almost-linear relationship between consumption and disposable income has been observed in a wide variety of historical periods and a wide variety of nations. This is why, when we represent the relationship between disposable income and consumption with a diagram or an equation, we use a straight line.

Our discussion will be clearer if we move from the actual data in Figure 2 to the hypothetical example in Table 1. Each row in the table represents a combination of real disposable income and consumption we might observe in an economy. For example, the table shows us that if disposable income were equal to $7,000 billion in some year, consumption spending would equal $6,200 billion in that year. When we plot this data on a graph, we obtain the straight line in Figure 3. This

U.S. CONSUMPTION AND DISPOSABLE INCOME, 1960–

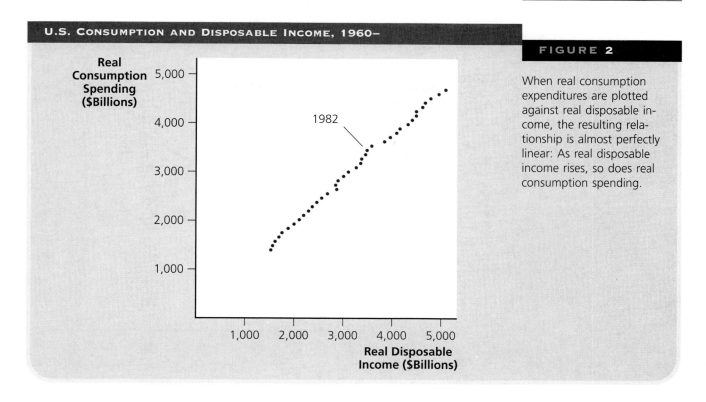

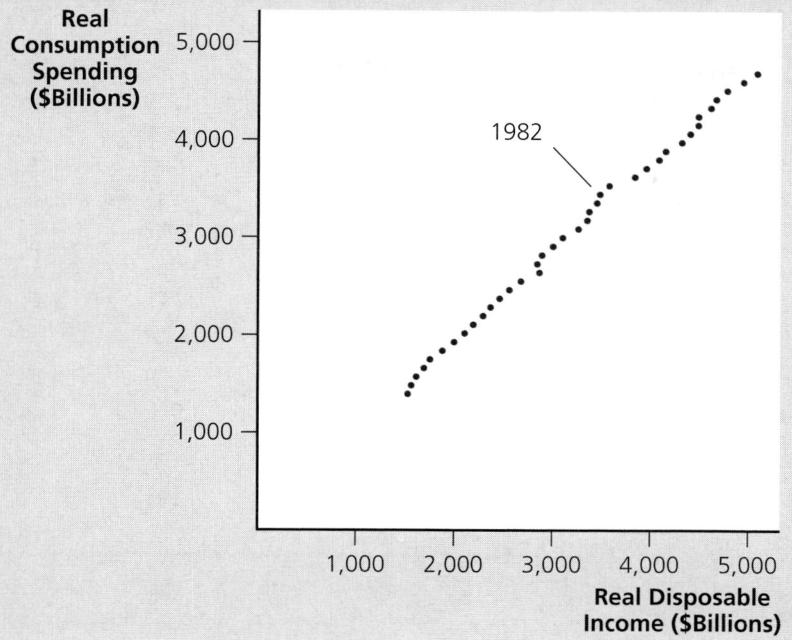

FIGURE 2

When real consumption expenditures are plotted against real disposable income, the resulting relationship is almost perfectly linear: As real disposable income rises, so does real consumption spending.

line is called the **consumption function,** because it illustrates the functional relationship between consumption and disposable income.

CONSUMPTION FUNCTION A positively-sloped relationship between real consumption spending and real disposable income.

Like every straight line, the consumption function in Figure 3 has two main features: a vertical intercept and a slope. Mathematically, the intercept—in this case, $2,000 billion—tells us how much consumption spending there would be in the economy if disposable income were zero. However, the real purpose of the vertical intercept is not to identify what would actually happen at zero disposable income, but rather to help us determine which particular line represents consumption spend-

HYPOTHETICAL DATA ON DISPOSABLE INCOME AND CONSUMPTION

TABLE 1

Disposable Income (Billions of dollars per year)	Consumption Spending (Billions of dollars per year)
0	2,000
1,000	2,600
2,000	3,200
3,000	3,800
4,000	4,400
5,000	5,000
6,000	5,600
7,000	6,200
8,000	6,800

THE CONSUMPTION FUNCTION

FIGURE 3

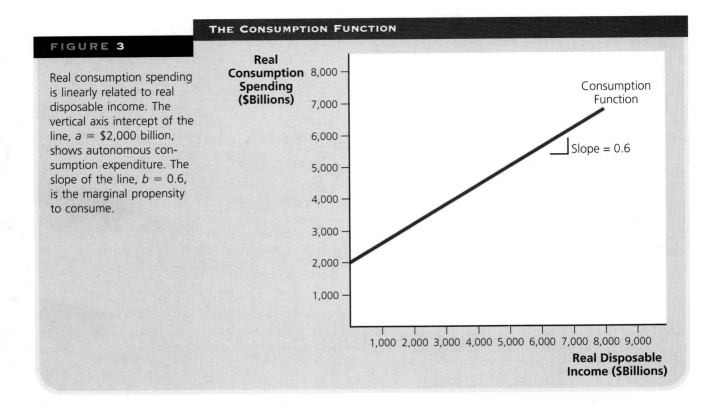

Real consumption spending is linearly related to real disposable income. The vertical axis intercept of the line, a = \$2,000 billion, shows autonomous consumption expenditure. The slope of the line, b = 0.6, is the marginal propensity to consume.

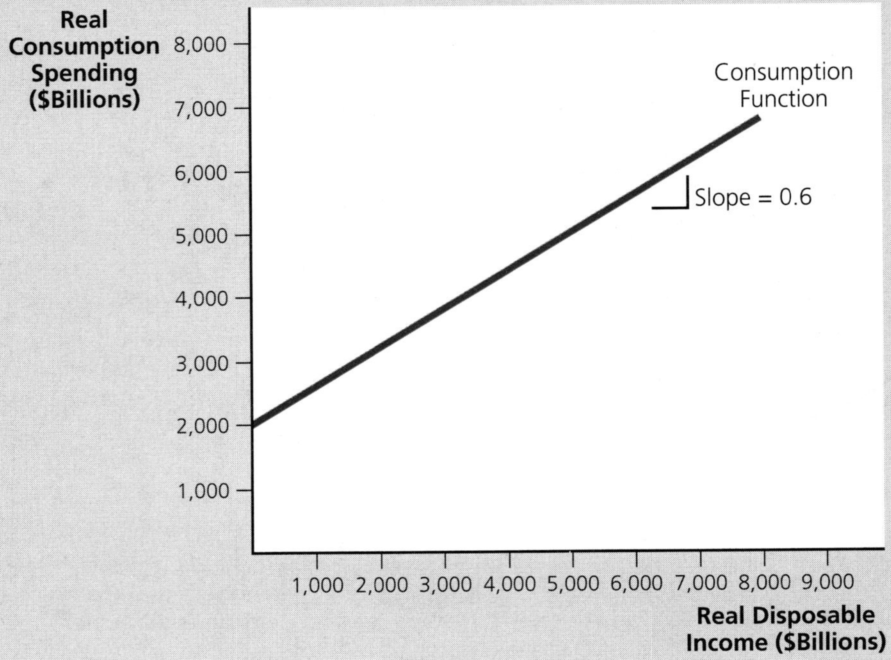

ing in the diagram. After all, there are many lines we could draw that have the same slope as the one in the figure. But only one of them has a vertical intercept of \$2,000.

AUTONOMOUS CONSUMPTION SPENDING The part of consumption spending that is independent of income; also, the vertical intercept of the consumption function.

The vertical intercept in the figure also has a name: **autonomous consumption spending.** It represents the combined impact on consumption spending of everything *other than* disposable income. For example, if household wealth were to increase, or the interest rate were to decrease, consumption would be greater at any level of disposable income. The entire consumption function in the figure would shift upward, so its vertical intercept would increase. We would call this *an increase in autonomous consumption spending.* Similarly, a decrease in wealth, or a rise in interest rates, would cause a *decrease in autonomous consumption spending,* and shift the consumption function downward.

The second important feature of Figure 3 is the slope, which shows the change along the vertical axis divided by the change along the horizontal axis as we go from one point to another on the line. If we use ΔC to represent the change in real consumption spending, and ΔDI to represent the change in real disposable income, then the slope of the consumption function is given by

$$\text{slope} = \Delta C/\Delta DI$$

As you can see in the table, each time disposable income rises by \$1,000 billion, consumption spending rises by \$600 billion, so that the slope is $\Delta C/\Delta DI$ = \$600 billion/\$1,000 billion = 0.6.

The slope in Figure 3 is an important feature not just of the consumption function itself, but of the macroeconomic analysis we will build from it. This is why economists have given this slope a special name, the *marginal propensity to consume,* abbreviated *MPC*. In our example, the *MPC* is 0.6.

We can think of the *MPC* in three different ways, but each of them has the same meaning:

> *The **marginal propensity to consume** (MPC) is (1) the slope of the consumption function; (2) the change in consumption divided by the change in disposable income (ΔC/ΔDI); or (3) the amount by which consumption spending rises when disposable income rises by one dollar.*

Logic suggests that the *MPC* should be larger than zero (when income rises, consumption spending will rise), but less than 1 (the rise in consumption will be *smaller* than the rise in disposable income). This is certainly true in our example: With an *MPC* of 0.6, a one-dollar rise in disposable income causes spending to rise by 60 cents. It is also observed to be true in economies throughout the world. Accordingly,

> *We will always assume that* $0 < \text{MPC} < 1$.

Name:
U.S. Department of Labor, Bureau of Labor Statistics Consumer Expenditure Survey
Description:
Information on the buying habits of U.S. consumers, including their expenditures and income
Resources:
The BLS Consumer Expenditure Survey page provides an overview of the types of data collected and the methods used to collect the income and expenditure data for this survey. Data from these surveys are included at http://stats.bls.gov/cgi-bin/dsrv?cx
Address:
http://stats.bls.gov/csxhome.htm

REPRESENTING CONSUMPTION WITH AN EQUATION. Sometimes, we'll want to use an equation to represent the straight-line consumption function. The most general form of the equation is

$$C = a + bDI$$

The term *a* is the vertical intercept of the consumption function. It represents the theoretical level of consumption spending at $DI = 0$, which you've learned is called *autonomous consumption spending*. In the equation, you can see clearly that autonomous consumption (*a*) is the part of consumption that does *not* depend on disposable income. In our example in Figure 3, *a* is equal to $2,000 billion.

The other term, *b,* is the slope of the consumption function. This is our familiar marginal propensity to consume (*MPC*), telling us how much consumption *increases* each time disposable income rises by a dollar. In our example in Figure 3, *b* is equal to 0.6.

THE RELATIONSHIP BETWEEN CONSUMPTION AND INCOME

The consumption function is an important building block of our analysis. Consumption is the largest component of spending, and disposable income is the most important determinant of consumption. But there is one limitation of the line as we've drawn it in Figure 3: It shows us the value of consumption at each level of *disposable* income, whereas we will need to know the value of consumption spending at each level of *income*. Disposable income, you remember, is the income that people have left over after taxes: $DI = Y - \text{Taxes}$. How can we convert the line in Figure 3 into a relationship between consumption and income?

MARGINAL PROPENSITY TO CONSUME The amount by which consumption spending changes when disposable income changes by one dollar.

If the government collected no taxes, total income and disposable income would be equal, so that the relationship between consumption and income on the one hand, and consumption and disposable income on the other hand, would be identical. In that case, the line in Figure 3 would show the relationship between consumption and income. But what about when taxes are not zero?

TABLE 2

THE RELATIONSHIP BETWEEN CONSUMPTION AND INCOME

Income or GDP (Billions of dollars per year)	Tax Collections (Billions of dollars per year)	Disposable Income (Billions of dollars per year)	Consumption Spending (Billions of dollars per year)
2,000	2,000	0	2,000
3,000	2,000	1,000	2,600
4,000	2,000	2,000	3,200
5,000	2,000	3,000	3,800
6,000	2,000	4,000	4,400
7,000	2,000	5,000	5,000
8,000	2,000	6,000	5,600
9,000	2,000	7,000	6,200
10,000	2,000	8,000	6,800

Table 2 illustrates the consumption–income relationship when households must pay taxes. In the table, we treat taxes as a fixed amount—in this case, $2,000 billion. Some taxes are, indeed, fixed in this way, such as the taxes assessed on real estate by local governments. Other taxes, like the personal income tax and the sales tax, rise and fall with income in the economy. Treating all taxes as if they are independent of income, as in Table 2, will simplify our discussion, without changing our results in any important way.

Notice that the last two columns of the table are identical to the columns in Table 1: In both tables, we assume that the relationship between consumption spending and disposable income is the same. For example, both tables show us that, when disposable income is $7,000 billion, consumption spending is $6,200 billion. But in Table 2, we see that a disposable income of $7,000 is associated with an income of $9,000. Thus, when income is $9,000, consumption spending is $6,200. By comparing the first and last columns of Table 2, we can trace out the relationship between consumption and income. This relationship—which we call the **consumption-income line**—is graphed in Figure 4.

CONSUMPTION–INCOME LINE A line showing aggregate consumption spending at each level of income or GDP.

If you compare the consumption–income line in Figure 4 with the line in Figure 3, you will notice that both have the same slope of 0.6, but the consumption income line is lower by $1,200 billion. This raises three important questions. First, why do taxes lower the consumption–income line? Because at any level of income, taxes reduce disposable income and therefore reduce consumption spending.

Second, why is the consumption–income line lower by precisely $1,200 billion? Because any decrease in disposable income (DI) will cause consumption spending to fall by $MPC \times \Delta DI$. In our example, when we impose taxes of $2,000 billion on the population, disposable income will drop by $2,000 billion at any level of income. With an MPC of 0.6, consumption at any level of income falls by $0.6 \times$ $2,000 billion = $1,200 billion.

Finally, why is the *slope* of the consumption–income line unaffected by taxes? Because when taxes are a fixed amount, disposable income rises dollar-for-dollar with income. With an MPC of 0.6, consumption spending will rise by 60 cents each time income rises by a dollar, just as it would if there were no taxes at all. In other words, while a fixed amount of taxes affects the relationship between the *level* of

THE CONSUMPTION–INCOME LINE

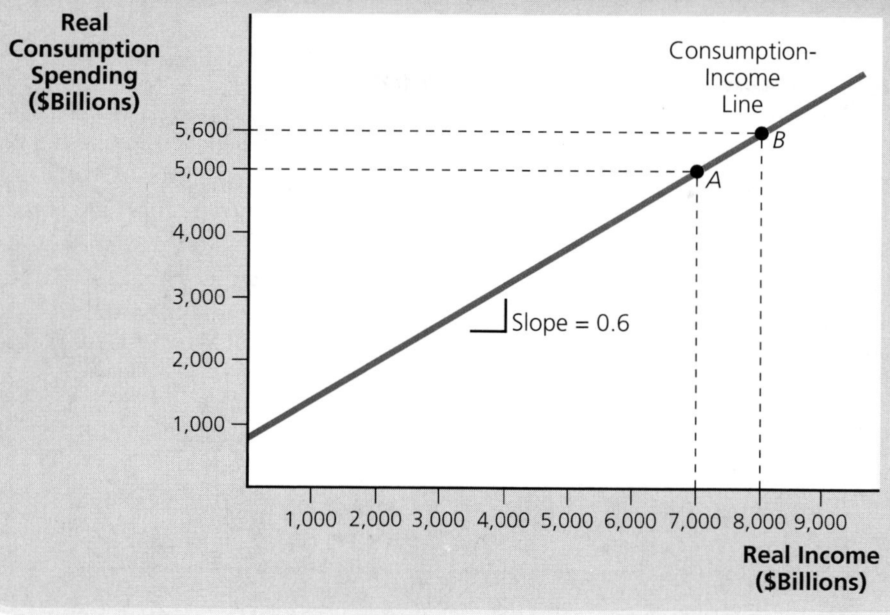

FIGURE 4

Real consumption spending is linearly related to real income. The slope of the line, $b = 0.6$, is the marginal propensity to consume.

income and the *level* of consumption spending, it does not affect the relationship between a *change* in income and a *change* in consumption spending. You can verify this in Table 2: Each time income rises by $1,000 billion, consumption spending rises by $600 billion, giving a slope of ΔC/ΔIncome = $600 billion/$1,000 billion = 0.6, just as in the case with no taxes.

More generally,

> *When the government collects a fixed amount of taxes from households, the line representing the relationship between consumption and income is shifted downward by the amount of the tax times the marginal propensity to consume (*MPC*). The slope of this line, however, is unaffected by taxes, and is equal to the* MPC.

SHIFTS IN THE CONSUMPTION–INCOME LINE

As you've learned, consumption spending depends positively on income: If income increases and taxes remain unchanged, disposable income will rise, and consumption spending will rise with it. The chain of causation can be represented this way:

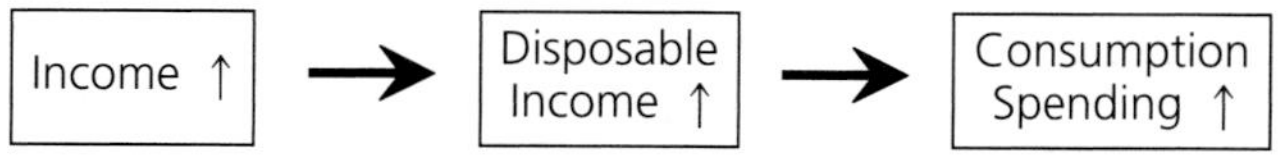

In Figure 4, this change in consumption spending would be represented by a *movement along* the consumption–income line. For example, a rise in income from $7,000 billion to $8,000 billion would cause consumption spending to increase from $5,000 billion to $5,600 billion, moving us from point *A* to point *B* along the consumption–income line.

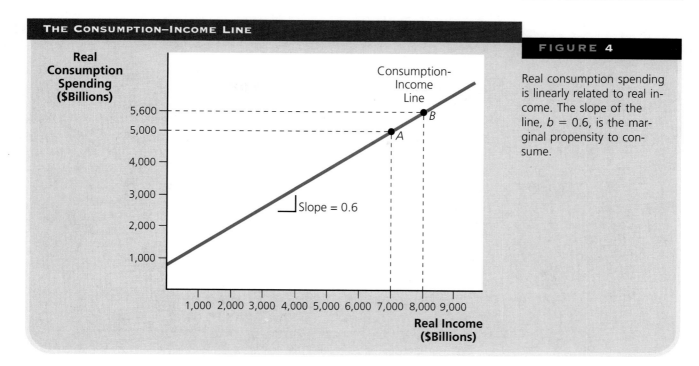

FIGURE 5

A SHIFT IN THE CONSUMPTION–INCOME LINE

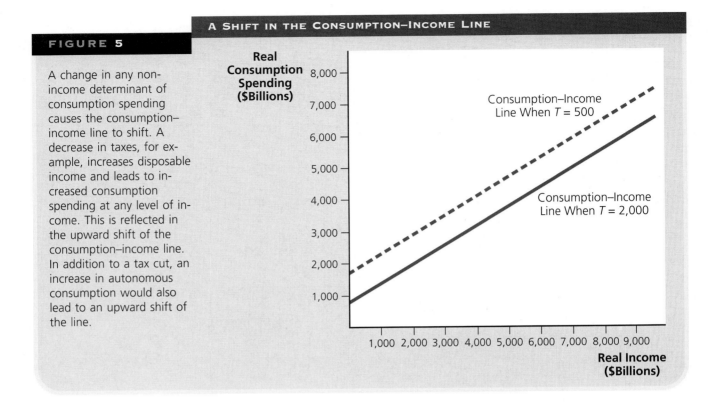

A change in any non-income determinant of consumption spending causes the consumption–income line to shift. A decrease in taxes, for example, increases disposable income and leads to increased consumption spending at any level of income. This is reflected in the upward shift of the consumption–income line. In addition to a tax cut, an increase in autonomous consumption would also lead to an upward shift of the line.

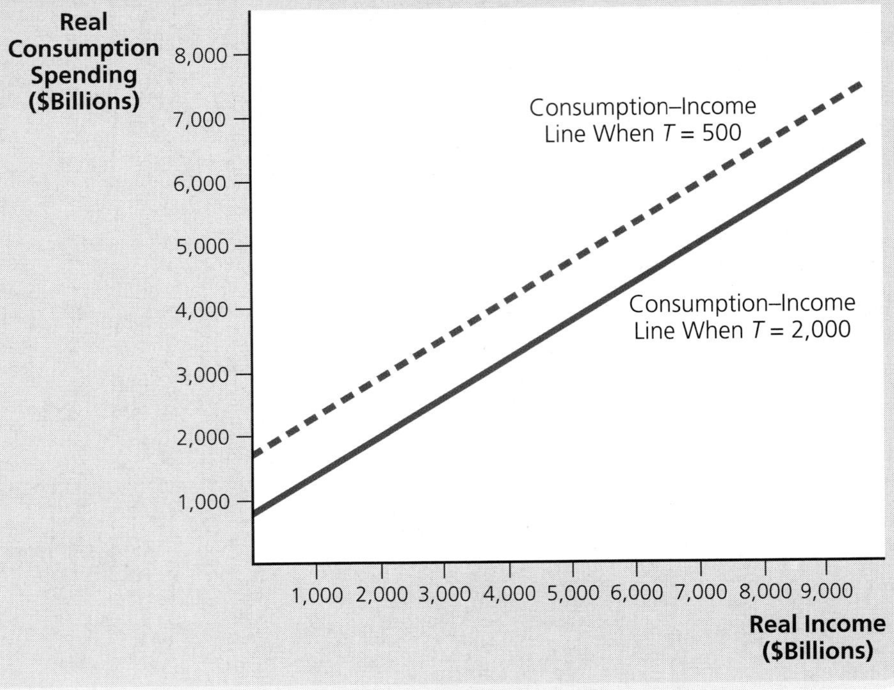

But consumption spending can also change for reasons other than a change in income, causing the consumption–income line itself to shift. For example, a decrease in taxes will increase disposable income at each level of income. Consumption spending will then increase at any income level, shifting the entire line upward. The mechanism works like this:

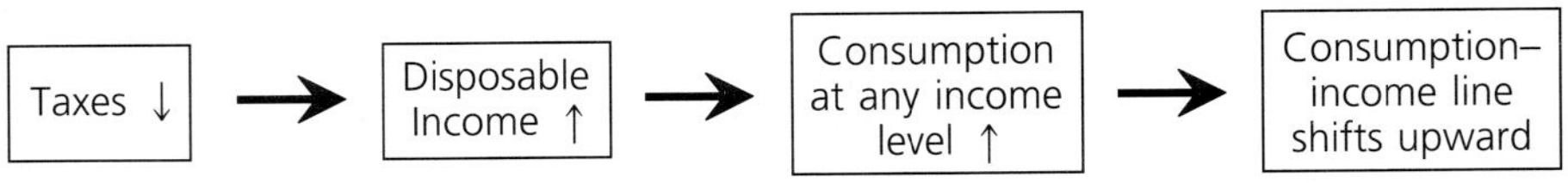

In Figure 5, a decrease in taxes from \$2,000 billion to \$500 billion increases disposable income at each income level by \$1,500 billion, and causes consumption at each income level to increase by $0.6 \times$ \$1,500 billion = \$900 billion. This means that the consumption line shifts upward, to the upper dashed line in the figure.

Other changes besides increases or decreases in taxes can shift the consumption–income line as well. All of these other changes work by changing *autonomous consumption*—the vertical intercept of the consumption function in Figure 3. By shifting the relationship between consumption and disposable income, we shift the relationship between consumption and income as well. For example, an increase in household wealth would increase autonomous consumption, and shift the consumption–income line upward, as in Figure 5. Other increases in autonomous consumption could occur if the interest rate decreased, if households developed a taste for spending more of their disposable incomes, or if they became more optimistic about the future. In general, increases in autonomous consumption work this way:

TABLE 3

CHANGES IN CONSUMPTION SPENDING AND THE CONSUMPTION–INCOME LINE

Rightward Movement along the Line	Leftward Movement along the Line	Entire Line Shifts Upward	Entire Line Shifts Downward
Income ↑	Income ↓	Taxes ↓	Taxes ↑
		Household wealth ↑	Household wealth ↓
		Interest rate ↓	Interest rate ↑
		Greater optimism	Greater pessimism

Autonomous consumption (a) ↑ → Consumption at each level of disposable income ↑ → Consumption spending at each level of income ↑ → Consumption–income line shifts upward

We can summarize our discussion of changes in consumption spending as follows:

> *When a change in income causes consumption spending to change, we move* along *the consumption–income line. When a change in anything else besides income causes consumption spending to change, the line will shift.*

Table 3 provides a more specific summary of how different types of changes in consumption spending are represented with the consumption–income line. Remember that all of the changes that *shift* the line—other than a change in taxes—work by increasing or decreasing autonomous consumption (a).

INVESTMENT SPENDING

Now we turn from spending by households to spending by business firms. Remember that in the definition of GDP, we used the term *actual investment* (I^{actual}), which consists of three components: (1) business spending on plant and equipment; (2) purchases of new homes; and (3) accumulation of unsold inventories. In this chapter, we focus not on actual investment, but on investment spending (I)—business purchases of plant and equipment, and construction of new homes. Why do we leave out inventory accumulation?

When we look at how spending influences the economy, we are interested in the purchases households, firms, and the government *want* to make. Inventory changes, however, are most often an *un*planned and undesired occurrence that firms try to avoid. While firms want to have *some* inventories on hand, sudden *changes* in inventories are not desirable. Accordingly, we exclude inventory investment when we measure spending in the economy. But even though they are excluded from spending, inventory changes will play an important part in our analysis, as you will see below.

In the short-run Keynesian model, we define investment spending as plant and equipment purchases by business firms, and new home construction. Inventory investment is treated as unintentional and undesired, and is therefore excluded from our definition of investment spending.

What determines the level of investment spending in a given year? In this chapter, we will regard investment spending as a *fixed value,* determined by forces outside of our analysis. This may seem a bit surprising. After all, aren't there variables that affect investment spending in predictable ways? Indeed, there are.

For example, in the classical model, you learned that investment is likely to be affected by the interest rate. Indeed, in the real world, the investment–interest rate relationship is quite strong. Investment is also influenced by the general level of optimism or pessimism about the economy and by new technological developments. But if we introduce all of these other variables into our analysis, we would find ourselves working with a very complex framework, and much too soon. In future chapters, we'll explore some of the determinants of investment spending, but in this chapter, to keep things simple, we assume that investment spending is some given amount. We'll explore what happens when that amount changes, but we will not, in this chapter, try to explain what causes investment spending to change.

For now, we regard investment spending as a given value, determined by forces outside of our model.

GOVERNMENT PURCHASES

Government purchases include all of the goods and services that government agencies—federal, state, and local—buy during the year. We treat government purchases in the same way as investment spending: as a given value, determined by forces outside of our analysis. Why?

The relationship between government purchases and other macroeconomic variables—particularly income—is rather weak. In recent decades, the biggest changes in government purchases have involved military spending. These changes have been based on world politics, rather than macroeconomic conditions. So when we assume that government spending is a given value, independent of the other variables in our model, our assumption is actually realistic.

In the short-run Keynesian model, government purchases are treated as a given value, determined by forces outside of the model.

As with investment spending, we'll be exploring what happens when the "given value" of government purchases changes. But we will not try to explain what causes it to change.

INCOME AND AGGREGATE EXPENDITURE

AGGREGATE EXPENDITURE (*AE*) The sum of spending by households, business firms, and the government on final goods and services.

Aggregate expenditure (*AE*) is the sum of spending by households, businesses, and the government on final goods and services. Remembering that *C* stands for household consumption spending, *I* for investment spending, and *G* for government purchases, we have

$$AE = C + I + G$$

THE RELATIONSHIP BETWEEN INCOME AND AGGREGATE EXPENDITURE

TABLE 4

(1) Income or GDP (Billions of dollars per year)	(2) Consumption Spending (Billions of dollars per year)	(3) Investment Spending (Billions of dollars per year)	(4) Government Purchases (Billions of dollars per year)	(5) Aggregate Expenditure (*AE*) (Billions of dollars per year)	(6) Change in Inventories (*GDP* − *AE*) (Billions of dollars per year)
2,000	2,000	1,000	600	3,600	−1,600
3,000	2,600	1,000	600	4,200	−1,200
4,000	3,200	1,000	600	4,800	−800
5,000	3,800	1,000	600	5,400	−400
6,000	**4,400**	**1,000**	**600**	**6,000**	**0**
7,000	5,200	1,000	600	6,600	400
8,000	5,600	1,000	600	7,200	800
9,000	6,200	1,000	600	7,800	1,200
10,000	6,800	1,000	600	8,400	1,600

As we discussed earlier, the relationship between income and spending is circular: Spending depends on income, and income depends on spending. In Table 4, we take up the first part of that circle: how total spending depends upon income. In the table, column 1 lists different income levels, and column 2 shows the level of consumption spending we can expect at each income level. These two columns are just the consumption-income relationship we introduced earlier, in Table 2.

Column 3 shows that business firms in this economy buy $1,000 billion per year in plant and equipment, regardless of the level of income. Government purchases are also fixed in value, as shown by column 4: At every level of income, the government buys $600 billion in goods and services. Finally, if we add together the entries in columns 2, 3, and 4, we get $C + I + G$, or aggregate expenditure, shown in column 5. (For now, ignore column 6.)

Notice that aggregate expenditure increases as income rises. But notice also that the rise in aggregate expenditure is *smaller* than the rise in income. For example, you can see that when income rises from $5,000 billion to $6,000 billion (column 1), aggregate expenditure rises from $5,400 billion to $6,000 billion (column 5). Thus, a $1,000 billion increase in income is associated with a $600 billion increase in aggregate expenditure. This is because, in our analysis, consumption is the only component of spending that depends on income, and consumption

DANGEROUS CURVES

The definition of aggregate expenditure ($C + I + G$) should look familiar to you. It looks very close to the expression used to define GDP that you learned a few chapters ago ($GDP = C + I^{actual} + G + NX$). But don't forget the all-important differences you read about earlier. First, in defining aggregate expenditure, we are excluding the foreign sector's spending until a later chapter. Second, in aggregate expenditure, we use investment spending (I) instead of actual investment (I^{actual}). The reason? When measuring GDP, we want to include all production, whether it is sold during the year or not. The definition of GDP therefore uses I^{actual}, which includes the change in inventories—goods produced but not sold. But when we think about aggregate expenditure, we want to include only goods that households, business firms, and the government want to buy during the year. So in measuring aggregate expenditure, we use I – investment spending.

spending always increases according to the marginal propensity to consume, here equal to 0.6. More generally,

*When income increases, aggregate expenditure (*AE*) will rise by the* MPC *times the change in income:* $\Delta AE = MPC \times \Delta Y$.

FINDING EQUILIBRIUM GDP

Table 4 shows how spending depends on income. In this section, you will see how income depends on spending—that is, how the spending behavior of households, firms, and government agencies determines the economy's *equilibrium income* or *equilibrium GDP*—a level of GDP that represents, at least in the short run, a point of rest for the economy.

The easiest way to find the equilibrium GDP is to ask ourselves what would happen, hypothetically, if the economy were operating at different levels of output. Let's start with a GDP of $9,000 billion. Could this be the equilibrium value? That is, if firms were producing this level of output, would they keep doing so? Let's see.

Table 4 tells us that when GDP is equal to $9,000 billion, aggregate expenditure is equal to $7,800 billion. Business firms are *producing* $1,200 billion more than they are *selling*. Since firms will certainly not be willing to continue producing output they cannot sell, we can infer that, in future periods, they will slow their production. Thus, if the economy finds itself at a GDP of $9,000 billion, it will not stay there. In other words, $9,000 billion is *not* where the economy will settle in the short run, so it is *not* our equilibrium GDP. More generally,

When aggregate expenditure is less than GDP, output will decline in the future. Thus, any level of output at which aggregate expenditure is less than GDP cannot be the equilibrium GDP.

Now let's consider the opposite case: a level of GDP of $3,000 billion. At this level of output, the table shows aggregate expenditure of $4,200 billion—spending is actually *greater* than output by $1,200 billion. What will business firms do as a response? Since they are selling more output than they are currently producing, we can expect them to *increase* their production in future months. Thus, if GDP is $3,000 billion, it will tend to rise in the future. So $3,000 is *not* our equilibrium GDP.

When aggregate expenditure is greater than GDP, output will tend to rise in the future. Thus, any level of output at which aggregate expenditure exceeds GDP cannot be the equilibrium GDP.

Now consider a GDP of $6,000 billion. At this level of output, our table shows that aggregate expenditure is precisely equal to $6,000: Output and aggregate expenditure are equal. Since firms, on the whole, are selling just what they produce—no more and no less—they should be content to produce that same amount in the future. We have found our equilibrium GDP:

In the short run, ***equilibrium GDP*** *is the level of output at which output and aggregate expenditure are equal.*

Inventories and Equilibrium GDP

When firms *produce* more goods than they sell, what happens to the unsold output? It is added to their inventory stocks. When firms *sell* more goods than they produce, where do the additional goods come from? They come from firms' inventory stocks. You can see that the gap between output and spending determines what will happen to inventories during the year.

More specifically,

> *the change in inventories during any period will always equal output minus aggregate expenditure.*

For example, Table 4 tells us that if GDP is equal to $9,000 billion, aggregate expenditure is equal to $7,800 billion. In this case, we can find that the change in inventories is

$$\begin{aligned}\Delta\text{Inventories} &= GDP - AE \\ &= \$9{,}000 \text{ billion} - \$7{,}800 \text{ billion} = \$1{,}200 \text{ billion.}\end{aligned}$$

When GDP is equal to $3,000 billion, aggregate expenditure is equal to $4,200 billion, so that the change in inventories is

$$\begin{aligned}\Delta\text{Inventories} &= GDP - AE \\ &= \$3{,}000 \text{ billion} - \$4{,}800 \text{ billion} = -\$1{,}200 \text{ billion.}\end{aligned}$$

Notice the negative sign in front of the $1,200 billion; if output is $3,000 billion, then inventory stocks will *shrink* by $1,200 billion.

Only when output and total sales are equal—that is, when GDP is at its equilibrium value—will the change in inventories be zero. In our example, when GDP is at its equilibrium value of $6,000 billion, so that aggregate expenditure is also $6,000 billion, the change in inventories is equal to zero. At this output level, we have

$$\begin{aligned}\Delta\text{Inventories} &= GDP - AE \\ &= \$6{,}000 \text{ billion} - \$6{,}000 \text{ billion} = \$0\end{aligned}$$

What you have just learned about inventories suggests another way to find the equilibrium GDP in the economy: Find the output level at which the change in inventories is equal to zero. Firms cannot allow their inventories of unsold goods to keep growing for very long (they would go out of business), nor can they continue to sell goods out of inventory for very long (they would run out of goods). Instead, they will desire to keep their production in line with their sales, so that their inventories do not change.

Dangerous Curves

You may be wondering why, in the short-run Keynesian model, a firm that produces more output than it sells wouldn't just lower the price of its goods. That way, it could sell more of them, and not have to lower its output as much. Similarly, a firm whose sales exceeded its production could take advantage of the opportunity to raise its prices, which would result in lower sales.

To some extent, firms *do* change prices—even in the short run. But they change their output levels, too. To remain as simple as possible, the short-run Keynesian model assumes that firms adjust *only* their output to match aggregate expenditure. That is, *in the short-run Keynesian model, prices don't change at all.* In a later chapter, we'll make the more realistic assumption that firms adjust both prices and output.

FIGURE 6

DERIVING THE AGGREGATE EXPENDITURE LINE

Aggregate expenditure is the total of consumption, investment, and government spending at a given level of real income. The aggregate expenditure line is derived by adding fixed amounts of investment and government spending to consumption, as determined by the consumption-income line. The slope of the aggregate expenditure line is the marginal propensity to consume.

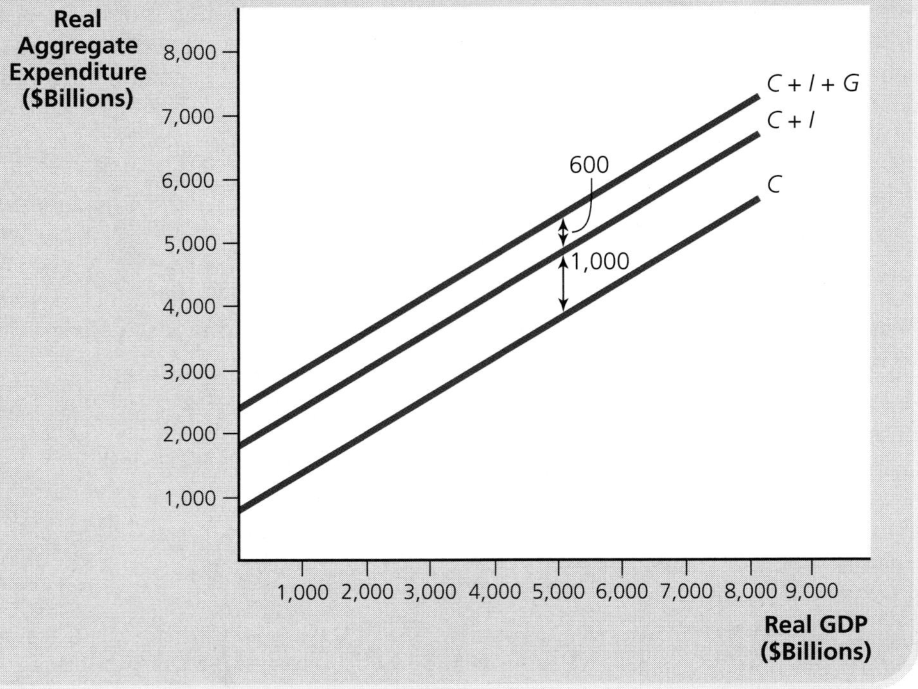

To recap,

$AE < GDP$	→	ΔInventories > 0	→	GDP ↓ in future periods
$AE > GDP$	→	ΔInventories < 0	→	GDP ↑ in future periods
$AE = GDP$	→	ΔInventories = 0	→	GDP will not change

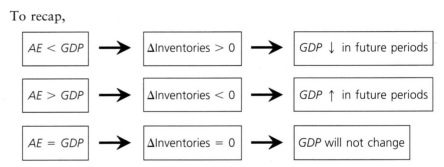

Now look at the last column in Table 4, which lists the change in inventories at different levels of output. This column is obtained by subtracting column 5 from column 1. The equilibrium output level is the one at which the change in inventories equals zero, which, as we've already found, is $6,000 billion.

FINDING EQUILIBRIUM GDP WITH A GRAPH

To get an even clearer picture of how equilibrium GDP is determined, we'll illustrate it with a graph, although it will take us a few steps to get there. Figure 6 begins the process by showing how we can construct a graph of aggregate expenditure. The lowest line in the figure, labeled *C*, is our familiar consumption–income line, obtained from the data in the first two columns of Table 4.

The next line, labeled $C + I$, shows the *sum* of consumption and investment spending at each income level. Notice that this line is parallel to the *C* line, which means that the vertical difference between them—$1,000 billion—is the same at any income level. This vertical difference is investment spending, which remains the same at all income levels.

THE 45° LINE

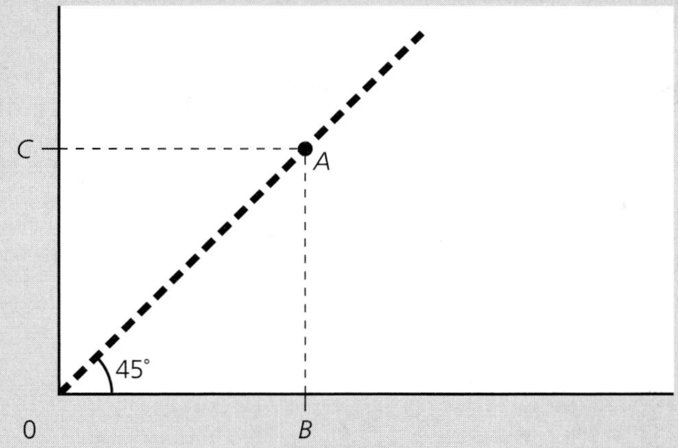

FIGURE 7

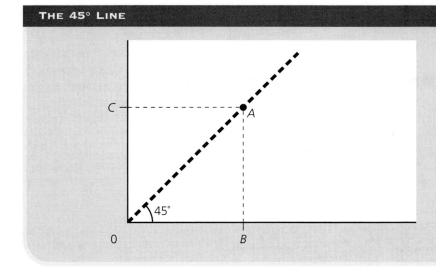

When both axes are measured in the same units, the 45° line can be used to show all points at which the value measured on the horizontal axis equals the value measured on the vertical axis. In the figure, the distances 0*C*, 0*B*, and *BA* are all equal.

Finally, the top line adds government purchases to consumption and investment spending, giving us $C + I + G$, or aggregate expenditure. The $C + I + G$ line is parallel to the $C + I$ line. The vertical difference between them—\$600 billion—represents government purchases. Like investment, government purchases are the same at all income levels.

Now look just at the aggregate expenditure line—the top line—in Figure 6. Notice that it slopes upward, telling us that as income increases, so does aggregate expenditure. And the slope of the aggregate expenditure line is less than 1: When income increases, the rise in aggregate expenditure is *smaller* than the rise in income. In fact, the slope of the aggregate expenditure line is equal to the *MPC,* or 0.6 in this example. This tells us that a one-dollar rise in income causes a 60-cent increase in aggregate expenditure. (Question: Which of the three components of aggregate expenditure rises when income rises? Which remain the same?)

Now we're almost ready to use a graph like the one in Figure 6 to locate equilibrium GDP, but first we must develop a little geometric trick.

Figure 7 shows a graph in which the horizontal and vertical axes are both measured in dollar units. It also shows a 45° line that begins at the origin. This 45° line has a useful property: Any point along it will have the same value along the vertical axis and along the horizontal axis. For example, consider point *A* on the line. Point *A* corresponds to the horizontal distance 0*B*, and it also corresponds to the vertical distance 0*C*. But because the line is a 45° line, we know that these two distances are equal: $0B = 0C$. Moreover, a glance at the figure shows that that 0*B* and *BA* are equal as well. Now we have two choices for measuring the distance 0*B:* We can measure it horizontally, or we can measure it as the vertical distance *BA*. In fact, *any* horizontal distance can also be read vertically, merely by going from the horizontal value (point *B* in our example) up to the 45° line.

A 45° line is a translator line: It allows us to measure any horizontal distance as a vertical distance instead.

Now we can apply this geometric trick to help us find the equilibrium GDP. In our aggregate expenditure diagram, we want to compare output with aggregate ex-

FIGURE 8

DETERMINING EQUILIBRIUM REAL GDP

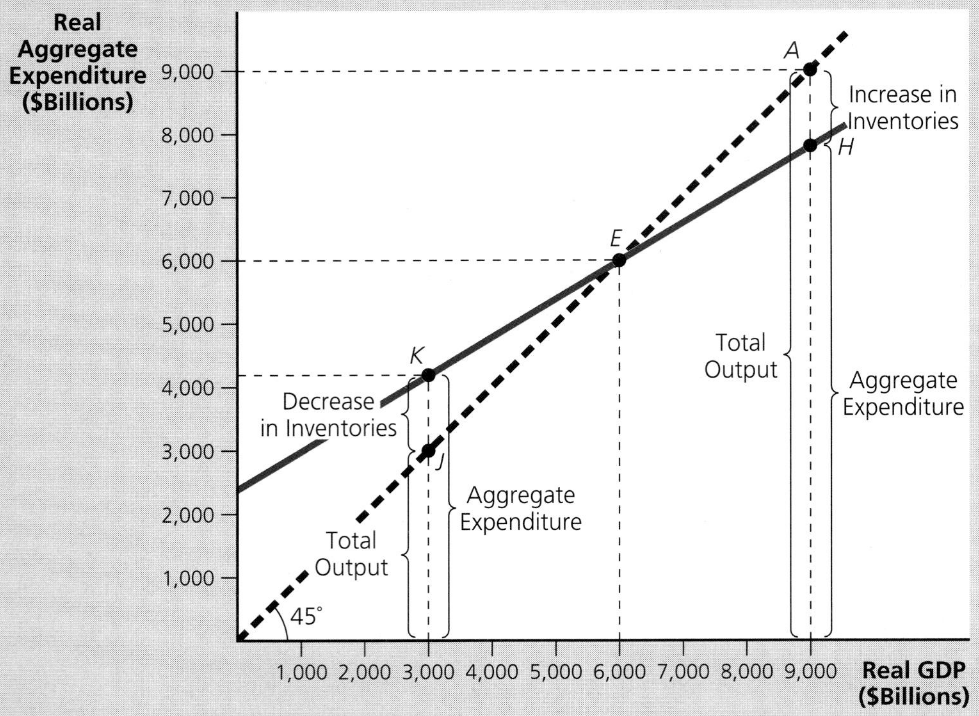

At point *E,* where the aggregate expenditure line crosses the 45° line, the economy is in short-run equilibrium. With real GDP equal to $6,000 billion, aggregate expenditure equals real GDP. At higher levels of real GDP—such as $9,000 billion—total production exceeds aggregate expenditures. At point *A,* firms will be unable to sell all they produce. Unplanned inventory increases equal to *HA* will lead them to reduce production. At lower levels of real GDP—such as $3,000 billion—aggregate expenditure exceeds total production. Firms find their inventories falling, and they will respond by increasing production.

penditure. But output is measured horizontally, while aggregate expenditure is measured vertically. Our 45° line, however, enables us to measure output vertically as well as horizontally, and thus permits us to compare two vertical distances.

Figure 8 shows how this is done. The solid line is the aggregate expenditure line ($C + I + G$) from Figure 6. We've dispensed with the other two lines, C and $C + I$, because we no longer need them. The dashed line is our 45° translator line. Now, let's search for the equilibrium GDP by considering a number of possibilities. For example, could the output level $9,000 billion be our sought-after equilibrium? Let's see. We can measure the output level $9,000 as the vertical distance from the horizontal axis up to point *A* on the 45° line. But when output is $9,000 billion, aggregate expenditure is the vertical distance from the horizontal axis to point *H* on the aggregate expenditure line. Notice that, since point *H* lies below point *A,* aggregate expenditure is less than output. If firms *did* produce $9,000 worth of output, they would accumulate inventories equal to the vertical distance *HA* (the excess of output over spending). We conclude graphically (as we did earlier, using our table) that if output is $9,000 billion, firms will accumulate inventories of unsold goods and reduce output in the future. Thus, $9,000 billion is not our equilibrium. In general,

At any output level at which the aggregate expenditure line lies below *the 45° line, aggregate expenditure is less than GDP. If firms produce any of these output levels, their inventories will grow, and they will reduce output in the future.*

Now let's see if an output of $3,000 billion could be our equilibrium. First, we read this output level as the vertical distance up to point *J* on the 45° line. Next, we note that when output is $3,000 billion, aggregate expenditure is the vertical distance up to point *K* on the aggregate expenditure line. Point *K* lies *above* point *J*, so aggregate expenditure is greater than output. If firms *did* produce $3,000 in output, inventories would *decrease* by the vertical distance *JK*. With declining inventories, firms would want to increase their output in the future, so $3,000 billion is not our equilibrium. More generally,

at any output level at which the aggregate expenditure line lies above *the 45° line, aggregate expenditure exceeds GDP. If firms produce any of these output levels, their inventories will decline, and they will increase their output in the future.*

Finally, consider an output of $6,000. At this output level, the aggregate expenditure line and the 45° line cross. As a result, the vertical distance up to point *E* on the 45° line (representing output) is the same as the vertical distance up to point *E* on the aggregate expenditure line. If firms produce an output level of $6,000 billion, aggregate expenditure and output will be precisely equal, inventories will remain unchanged, and firms would have no incentive to increase or decrease output in the future. We have thus found our equilibrium on the graph: $6,000 billion.

Equilibrium GDP is the output level at which the aggregate expenditure line intersects the 45° line. If firms produce this output level, their inventories will not change, and they will be content to continue producing the same level of output in the future.

Equilibrium GDP and Employment

Now that you've learned how to find the economy's equilibrium GDP in the short run, a question may have occurred to you: When the economy operates at equilibrium, will it also be operating at full employment? The answer is: *not necessarily*. Let's see why.

If you look back over the two methods we've employed to find equilibrium GDP—using columns of numbers as in Table 4, and using a graph as in Figure 8—you will see that in both cases we ask only one question: How much will households, businesses, and the government *spend*. We do not ask any questions about the number of people who want to work. Therefore, it would be quite a coincidence if our equilibrium GDP happened to be the output level at which the entire labor force were employed.

Figure 9 shows how we can find total employment in the economy. In the lower panel, we show the economy's production function—the relationship between employment and output for a given capital stock and technology. This production function is similar to the one we used a few chapters ago in the classical model. But there is one important difference: The axes are reversed. Instead of measuring

FIGURE 9

EQUILIBRIUM GDP CAN FALL SHORT OF FULL-EMPLOYMENT GDP

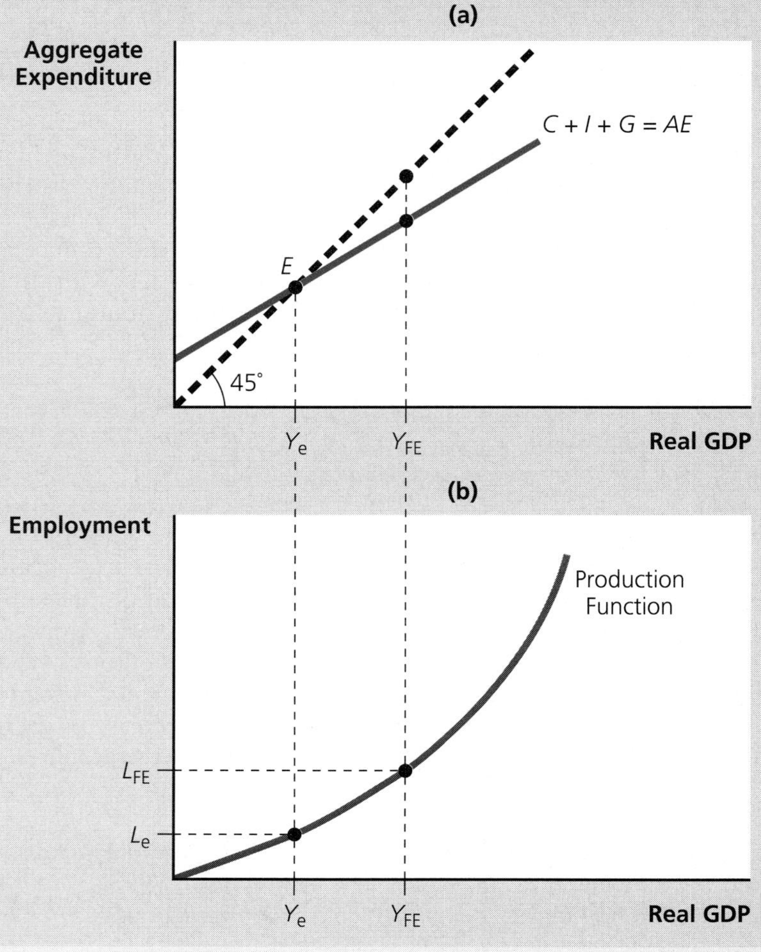

In the short run, there is no guarantee that the economy will end up in equilibrium at full employment. At point *E*, the aggregate expenditure line crosses the 45° line to determine an equilibrium GDP of Y_e, which is below full-employment equilibrium, Y_{FE}. The production function in panel (b) shows that employment is L_e, which lies below the full-employment level, L_{FE}.

labor on the horizontal axis and output on the vertical axis, the production function in Figure 9 is turned on its side, with labor measured vertically and output measured horizontally. On the vertical axis, L_{FE} is the number of people who *would* be working if the economy were operating at full employment. The production function tells us that, at full employment, GDP would be Y_{FE} (full-employment output). This is the long-run equilibrium from the classical model. But will Y_{FE} be the equilibrium in the short run? Not necessarily—and not in our diagram. Here, the aggregate expenditure line and the 45° line intersect at point *E*. Equilibrium GDP in the short run is Y_e. But to produce an output of Y_e requires employment of only L_e. Since L_e is less than L_{FE}, we will have abnormally low employment. Or, looked at another way, the level of *un*employment will be higher than normal. We will be in a *recession*.

But why? What prevents firms from hiring the extra people who want jobs? After all, with more people working, producing more output, wouldn't there be more income in the economy and therefore more spending? Indeed, there would be. But not *enough* additional spending to justify the additional employment. To prove this, just look at what would happen if firms *did* hire L_{FE} workers. Output

EQUILIBRIUM GDP CAN BE ABOVE FULL-EMPLOYMENT GDP

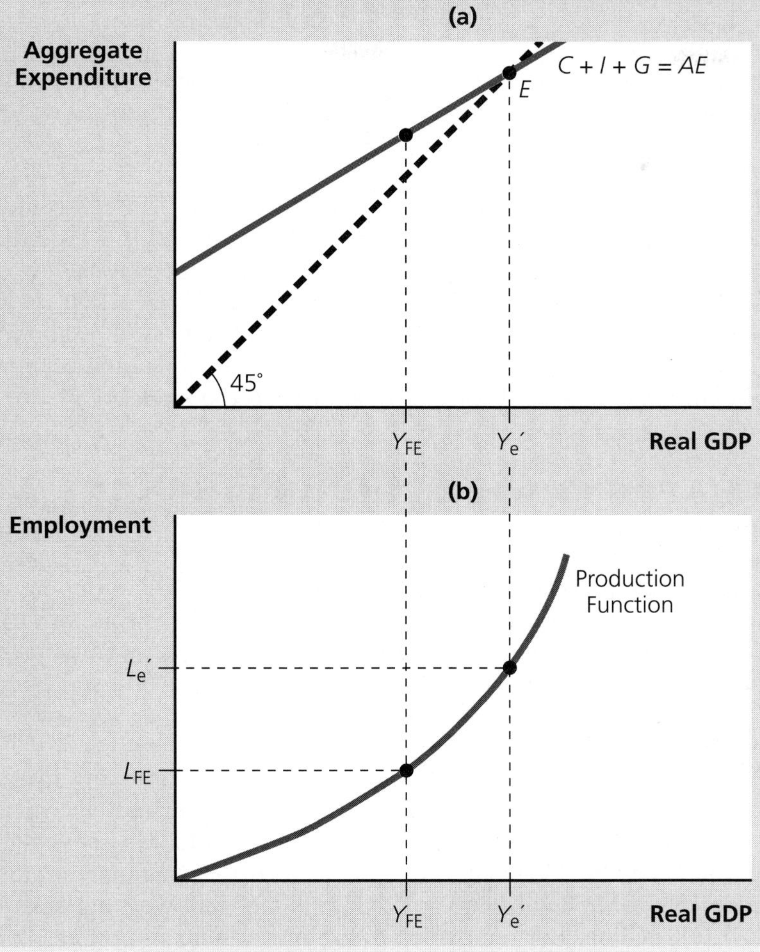

FIGURE 10

In the short run, the economy can end up in equilibrium with GDP above its full-employment level. At point E', the aggregate expenditure line crosses the 45° line to determine an equilibrium GDP of Y_e', which exceeds full-employment equilibrium, Y_{FE}. The production function in panel (b) shows that employment is L_e', which lies above the full-employment level, L_{FE}.

would rise to Y_{FE}, but at this output level, the aggregate expenditure line would lie below the 45° line, so *firms would be unable to sell all their output.* Unsold goods would pile up in inventories, and firms would cut back on production until output reached Y_e again, with employment back at L_e.

Figure 9 shows that we can be in short-run equilibrium and yet have abnormally high unemployment. The reason: the aggregate expenditure line is *too low* to create an intersection at full-employment output.

In the short-run Keynesian model, cyclical unemployment is caused by insufficient spending. As long as spending remains low, production will remain low, and unemployment will remain high.

What about the opposite possibility? In the short run, is it possible for spending to be too *high,* causing unemployment to be too *low*? Absolutely. Figure 10 illustrates such a case. Here, the aggregate expenditure line and the 45° line intersect at point E', giving us a short-run equilibrium GDP at Y_e'. According to the production function, producing an output of Y_e' requires employment of L_e'. Since

L_e' is greater than the economy's normal employment L_{FE}, we will have abnormally high employment, and abnormally low unemployment. That is, we will be in a *boom.*

In the short-run Keynesian model, the economy can overheat because spending is too high. As long as spending remains high, production will exceed potential output, and unemployment will be unusually low.

In the previous chapter, we concluded that the classical model could not explain booms and recessions. The short-run Keynesian model, on the other hand, does provide an explanation: The aggregate expenditure line may be low, meaning that in the short run, equilibrium GDP is below full employment. Or the spending line may be high, meaning that in the short run, equilibrium GDP is above the full-employment level. (Of course, this is just a first step in explaining economic fluctuations. In later chapters, we'll add more realism to the model.)

WHAT HAPPENS WHEN THINGS CHANGE?

So far, you've seen that spending can be very important in the short run: It determines the equilibrium levels of output and employment in the economy. Now we will see how a spending shock—a sudden change in spending—can affect the overall economy. The shocks we will consider in detail are a change in investment spending, a change in consumption spending, and a change in government purchases.

A CHANGE IN INVESTMENT SPENDING

Suppose the equilibrium GDP in an economy is \$6,000 billion, and then business firms increase their investment spending on plant and equipment. Specifically, they decide to increase yearly investment purchases by \$1,000 billion above the original level. What will happen? First, sales revenue at firms that manufacture investment goods—firms like IBM, Bethlehem Steel, Caterpillar, and Westinghouse—will increase by \$1,000 billion. But remember, each time a dollar in output is produced, a dollar of income (factor payments) is created. Thus, the \$1,000 billion in additional sales revenue will become \$1,000 billion in additional income. This income will be paid out as wages, rent, interest, and profit to the households who own the resources these firms have purchased.[3]

What will households—as consumers—do with their \$1,000 billion in additional income? Remember that taxes are fixed, so that households are free to spend or save their additional income as they desire. What they will do depends crucially on the *marginal propensity to consume* (MPC) *in the economy.* If the *MPC* is 0.6, then consumption spending will rise by $0.6 \times \$1{,}000$ billion $=$ \$600 billion. Households will save the remaining \$400 billion.

But that is not the end of the story. When households spend an additional \$600 billion, firms that produce consumption goods and services—firms such as McDonald's, Coca Cola, American Airlines, and Disney—will receive an additional \$600 billion in sales revenue, which, in turn, will become income for the households that supply resources to these firms. And when *these* households see *their* in-

3 Some of the sales revenue will also go to pay for intermediate goods, such as raw materials, electricity, and supplies. But then these intermediate-goods manufacturers will pay wages, rent, interest, and profit for *their* resources, so that household income will still rise by the full \$1,000 billion.

THE EFFECT OF A CHANGE IN INVESTMENT SPENDING

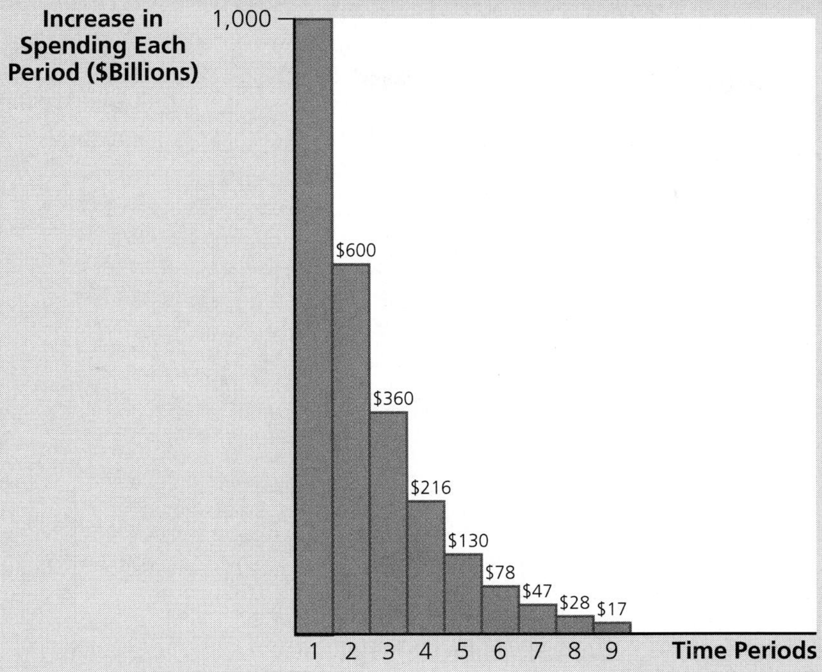

FIGURE 11

An increase in investment spending sets off a chain reaction, leading to successive rounds of increased spending and income. As shown here, a $1000 billion increase in investment first causes real GDP to increase by $1,000 billion. Then, with higher incomes, households increase consumption spending by the *MPC* times the change in disposable income. In round 2, spending and GDP increase by $600 billion. In succeeding rounds, increases in income lead to further changes in spending, but in each round the increase in income is smaller than in the preceding round.

comes rise by $600 billion, they will spend part of it as well. With an *MPC* of 0.6, consumption spending will rise by $0.6 \times \$600$ billion = $360 billion, creating still more sales revenue for firms, and so on and so on . . . .

As you can see, an increase in investment spending will set off a chain reaction, leading to successive rounds of increased spending and income. The process is illustrated in Figure 11: After the $1,000 billion increase in investment spending, there is a $600 billion increase in consumption, then a $360 billion increase in consumption, and on and on. Each successive round of additional spending is 60 percent of the round before. Each time spending increases, output rises to match it. These successive increases in spending and output occur quickly—the process is largely completed within a year. At the end of the process, when the economy has reached its new equilibrium, spending and output will have increased considerably. But by how much?

Table 5 gives us the answer. The second column shows us the additional spending in each round, while the third column shows the cumulative rise in spending. As you can see, the cumulative increase gets larger and larger with each successive round, but it grows by less and less each time. Eventually, the additional spending in a given round is so small that we can safely ignore it. At this point, the cumulative increase in spending and output will be very close to $2,500 billion—so close that we can ignore any difference.

THE EXPENDITURE MULTIPLIER

Let's go back and summarize what happened in our example: Business firms increased their investment spending by $1,000 billion, and as a result, spending and

TABLE 5

CUMULATIVE INCREASES IN SPENDING WHEN INVESTMENT INCREASES BY $1,000 BILLION

Round	Additional Spending in This Round (billions of dollars)	Additional Spending in All Rounds (billions of dollars)
Initial Increase in Investment	1,000	1,000
Round 2	600	1,600
Round 3	360	1,960
Round 4	216	2,176
Round 5	130	2,306
Round 6	78	2,384
Round 7	47	2,431
Round 8	28	2,459
Round 9	17	2,476
Round 10	10	2,486
.	.	.
.	.	.
.	.	.
All other rounds	Very close to 14	Very close to 2,500

output rose by $2,500 billion. Equilibrium GDP increased by *more* than the initial increase in investment spending. In our example, the increase in equilibrium GDP ($2,500 billion) was two-and-a-half times the initial increase in investment spending ($1,000 billion). As you can verify, if investment spending had increased by half as much ($500 billion), GDP would have increased by 2.5 times *that* amount ($1,250 billion). In fact, *whatever* the rise in investment spending, equilibrium GDP would increase by a factor of 2.5, so we can write

$$\Delta GDP = 2.5 \times \Delta I$$

The change in investment spending must be *multiplied by* the number 2.5 in order to get the change in GDP that it causes. For this reason, 2.5 is called the *expenditure multiplier* in this example.

EXPENDITURE MULTIPLIER The amount by which equilibrium real GDP changes as a result of a one-dollar change in autonomous consumption, investment, or government purchases.

*The **expenditure multiplier** is the number by which a change in spending (e.g., investment spending) must be multiplied to get the change in equilibrium GDP.*

The value of the expenditure multiplier depends on the value of the *MPC* in the economy. If you look back at Table 5, you will see that each round of additional spending would have been larger if the *MPC* had been larger. For example, with an *MPC* of 0.9 instead of 0.6, spending in round 2 would have risen by $900 billion, in round 3 by $810 billion, and so on. The result would have been a larger cumulative change in GDP, and a larger multiplier.

There is a very simple formula we can use to determine the multiplier for *any* value of the *MPC*. To obtain it, let's start with our numerical example in which the *MPC* is 0.6. When investment spending rises by $1,000, the change in equilibrium GDP can be written as follows:

$$\Delta GDP = \$1{,}000 \text{ billion} + \$600 \text{ billion} + \$360 \text{ billion} + \$216 \text{ billion} + \ldots$$

Factoring out the $1,000 billion change in investment, this becomes

$$\Delta GDP = \$1{,}000 \text{ billion } [1 + 0.6 + 0.36 + 0.216 + \ldots]$$
$$= \$1{,}000 \text{ billion } [1 + 0.6 + 0.6^2 + 0.6^3 + \ldots]$$

In this equation, $1,000 billion is the change in investment (ΔI), and 0.6 is the *MPC*. To find the change in GDP that applies to *any* ΔI and *any MPC,* we can write

$$\Delta GDP = \Delta I \times [1 + (MPC) + (MPC)^2 + (MPC)^3 + \ldots]$$

Now we can see that the term in brackets—the infinite sum $1 + MPC + (MPC)^2 + (MPC)^3 + \ldots$—is our multiplier. But what is its value?

The mathematical appendix at the back of this book shows that an infinite sum

$$1 + H + H^2 + H^3 + \ldots$$

always has the value $1/(1 - H)$ as long as H is a fraction between zero and 1. Thus, we replace H with the *MPC*—which is always between zero and 1—to obtain a value for the multiplier of $1/(1 - MPC)$.

For any value of the MPC, *the formula for the expenditure multiplier is 1/(1 –* MPC*).*

In our example, the *MPC* was equal to 0.6, so the expenditure multiplier had the value $1/(1 - 0.6) = 1/0.4 = 2.5$. If the *MPC* had been 0.9 instead, the expenditure multiplier would have been equal to $1/(1 - 0.9) = 1/0.1 = 10$. The formula $1/(1 - MPC)$ can be used to find the multiplier for any value of the *MPC* between zero and one.

Using the general formula for the expenditure multiplier, we can restate what happens when investment spending increases:

$$\Delta GDP = [1/(1 - MPC)] \times \Delta I$$

The multiplier effect is a rather surprising phenomenon. It tell us that an increase in investment spending ultimately affects GDP by *more* than the initial increase in investment. Moreover, the multiplier can work in the other direction, as you are about to see.

THE MULTIPLIER IN REVERSE

Suppose, in Table 5, that investment spending had *decreased* instead of increased. Then the initial change in spending would be –$1,000 billion ($\Delta I$ = –$1,000 billion). This would cause a $1,000 billion decrease in revenue for firms that produce investment goods, and they, in turn, would pay out $1,000 billion less in factor payments. In the next round, households—with $1,000 billion less in income—would spend $600 billion less on consumption goods, and so on. The final result would be a $2,500 billion *decrease* in equilibrium GDP.

Just as increases in spending cause equilibrium GDP to rise by a multiple of the change in spending, decreases in investment spending cause equilibrium GDP to fall by a multiple of the change in spending.

The multiplier formula we've already established will work whether the initial change in spending is positive or negative.

OTHER SPENDING SHOCKS

Shocks to the economy can come from other sources besides investment spending. In fact, when *any* sector's spending behavior changes, it will set off a chain of events similar to that in our investment example. Let's see how an increase in government spending could set off the same chain of events as an increase in investment spending.

Suppose that government agencies increased their purchases above previous levels. For example, the Department of Defense might raise its spending on new bombers, or state highway departments might hire more road-repair crews, or cities and towns might hire more teachers. If total government purchases rise by $1,000 billion, then, once again, household income will rise by $1,000 billion. As before, households will spend 60 percent of this increase, causing consumption—in the next round—to rise by $600 billion, and so on and so on. The chain of events is exactly like that of Table 5, with one exception: The first line in column 1 would read, "Initial Increase in Government Spending" instead of "Initial Increase in Investment." Once again, output would increase by $2,500 billion.

Finally, besides investment and government purchases, a change in autonomous consumption, *a*, can set off the same process. For example, after a $1,000 billion increase in autonomous consumption spending we would see further increases in consumption spending of $600 billion, then $360 billion, and so on. This time, the first line in column 1 of Table 5 would read, "Initial Increase in Autonomous Consumption," but every entry in the table would be the same.

> *Changes in investment, government purchases, or autonomous consumption lead to a multiplier effect on GDP. The expenditure multiplier—1/(1 −* MPC*)—is what we multiply the initial change in spending by in order to get the change in equilibrium GDP.*

The following three equations summarize how we use the expenditure multiplier to determine the effects of different spending shocks in the short-run Keynesian model. Keep in mind that these formulas work whether the initial change in spending is positive or negative.

$$\Delta GDP = [1/(1 - MPC)] \times \Delta I$$
$$\Delta GDP = [1/(1 - MPC)] \times \Delta G$$
$$\Delta GDP = [1/(1 - MPC)] \times \Delta a$$

A GRAPHICAL VIEW OF THE MULTIPLIER

Figure 12 illustrates the multiplier using our aggregate expenditure diagram. The solid line is the aggregate expenditure line from Figure 8. The aggregate expenditure line intersects the 45° line at point *E*, giving us an equilibrium GDP of $6,000 billion.

Now, suppose that either autonomous consumption, investment spending, or government spending rises by $1,000 billion. Regardless of which of these types of spending increases, the effect on our aggregate expenditure line is the same: It will *shift upward* by $1,000 billion, to the dashed line in the figure. The new aggregate

A GRAPHICAL VIEW OF THE MULTIPLIER

FIGURE 12

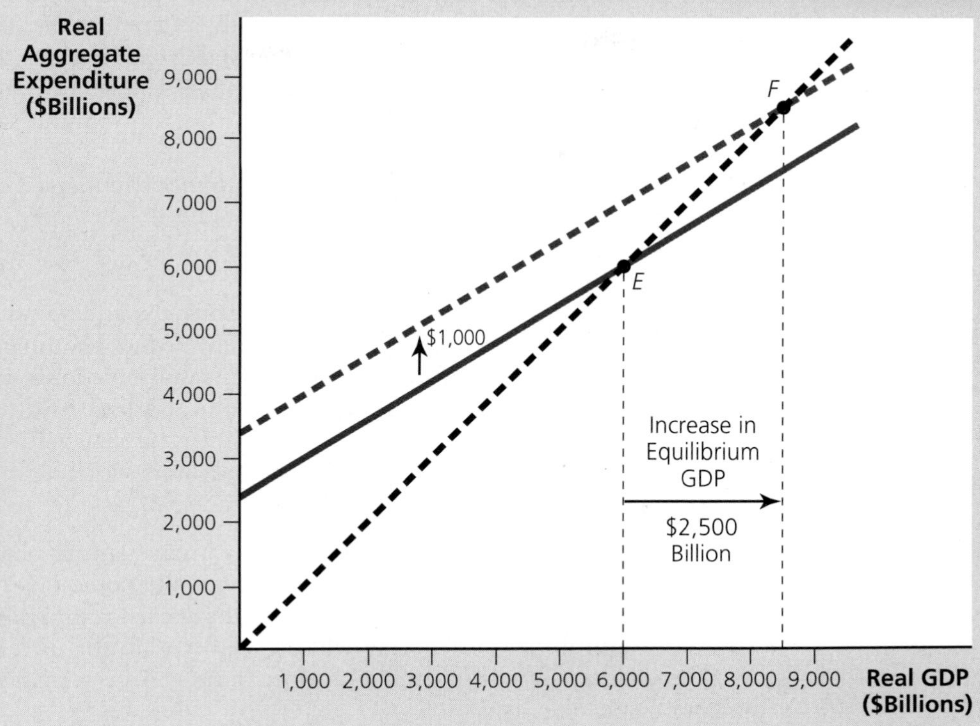

The economy starts off at point *E* with equilibrium real GDP of \$6,000 billion. A \$1,000 billion increase in spending shifts the aggregate expenditure line upward by \$1,000 billion, triggering the multiplier process. Eventually, the economy will reach a new equilibrium at point *F*, where the higher, dashed aggregate expenditure line crosses the 45° line. At *F*, real GDP is \$8,500 billion—an increase of \$2,500 billion.

expenditure line intersects the 45° line at point *F*, showing that our new equilibrium GDP is equal to \$8,500 billion.

What has happened? An initial spending increase of \$1,000 billion has caused equilibrium GDP to increase from \$6,000 billion to \$8,500 billion—an increase of \$2,500 billion. This is just what our multiplier of 2.5 suggests. In general,

$$\Delta GDP = [1/(1 - MPC)] \times \Delta \text{Spending}$$

and in this case,

$$\$2{,}500 \text{ billion} = 2.5 \times \$1{,}000 \text{ billion}$$

An increase in autonomous consumption spending, investment spending, or government spending will shift the aggregate expenditure line upward by the increase in spending, causing equilibrium GDP to rise. The increase in GDP will equal the initial increase in spending times the expenditure multiplier.

AN IMPORTANT PROVISO ABOUT THE MULTIPLIER

AUTOMATIC STABILIZERS Forces that reduce the size of the expenditure multiplier and diminish the impact of spending shocks.

In this chapter, we've presented a model to help us focus on the central relationship between spending and output. To keep the model as simple as possible, we've ignored many real-world factors that interfere with, and reduce the size of, the multiplier effect. These forces are called **automatic stabilizers** because, with a smaller multiplier, spending shocks will cause a much smaller change in GDP. As a result, booms and recessions will be milder.

Automatic stabilizers reduce the size of the multiplier and therefore reduce the impact of spending shocks on the economy. With milder booms and recessions, the economy is more stable.

How do automatic stabilizers work? They shrink the additional spending that occurs in each round of the multiplier, and thereby reduce the final multiplier effect on equilibrium GDP. In Table 5, automatic stabilizers would reduce each of the numerical entries after the first $1,000 billion, and lead to a final change in GDP smaller than $2,500 billion.

Here are some of the real-world automatic stabilizers we've ignored in the simple, short-run Keynesian model of this chapter:

Taxes. We've been assuming that taxes remain constant, so that a rise in income causes an equal rise in disposable income. But some taxes (like the personal income tax) rise with income. As a result, in each round of the multiplier, the increase in disposable income will be smaller than the increase in income. With a smaller rise in disposable income, there will be a smaller rise in consumption spending as well.

Transfer Payments. Some government transfer payments fall as income rises. For example, many laid-off workers receive unemployment benefits, which help support them for several months while they are unemployed. But when income and output rise, employment rises too, and newly hired workers must give up their unemployment benefits. As a result, a rise in income will cause a smaller rise in *disposable* income. Consumption will then rise by less in each round of the multiplier.

Interest Rates. In a later chapter, you'll learn that an increase in output often leads to rising interest rates as well. This will crowd out some investment spending, making the increase in aggregate expenditure smaller than our simple story suggests.

Prices. In a later chapter, you'll learn that the price level tends to rise as spending and production increase. This, in turn, tends to counteract any increase in spending.

Imports. Some additional spending is on goods and services imported from abroad. This will increase the revenue of foreign firms and the incomes of foreign workers, but will not contribute to higher incomes for U.S. workers. We'll bring imports into our model in the last chapter of the book.

Forward-looking Behavior. Consumers may be *forward looking.* If they realize that recessions and booms are temporary, their consumption spending may be less sensitive to changes in their current income. Therefore, any change in income will cause a smaller change in consumption spending, and lead to a smaller multiplier effect.

Remember that each of these automatic stabilizers reduces the size of the multiplier, making it smaller than the simple formulas given in this chapter. For example, the simple formula for the expenditure multiplier is 1/(1 − *MPC*). With an *MPC* of about 0.9—which is in the ballpark for the United States and many other countries—we would expect the multiplier to be about 10 . . . *if the simple formula were accurate.* In that case, a $1,000 billion increase in government spending would cause output to rise by $10,000 billion—quite a large multiplier effect.

DANGEROUS CURVES

It's easy to become confused about the relationship between consumption spending and the expenditure multiplier. Does a change in consumption spending *cause* a multiplier effect? Or does the multiplier effect create an increase in consumption spending? Actually, the causation runs in both directions. The key is to recognize that there are *two* kinds of changes in consumption spending.

One kind of change is a change in autonomous consumption spending (the term *a* in the consumption function). This change will *shift* the aggregate expenditure line up or down, telling us that total spending will be greater or smaller at *any* level of income. It is the kind of change that *causes* a multiplier effect.

But consumption also changes when something other than autonomous consumption sets off a multiplier effect. This is because consumption depends on income, and income always increases during the successive rounds of the multiplier effect. Such a change in consumption is represented by a movement *along* the aggregate expenditure line, rather than a shift.

Whenever you discuss a change in consumption spending, make sure you know whether it is a change in autonomous consumption (a shift of the curve) or a change in consumption caused by a change in income (movement along the curve).

But after we take account of all of the automatic stabilizers, the multiplier is considerably smaller. How much smaller? Most of the forecasting models used by economists in business and government predict that the multiplier effect takes about 3 or 4 quarters to work its way through the economy. At the end of the process, the multiplier has a value of about 1.5. This means that a $1,000 billion increase in, say, government spending should cause GDP to increase by only about $1,500 billion in a year. This is much less than the $10,000 billion increase predicted by the simple formula 1/(1 − *MPC*) when the *MPC* is equal to 0.9.

In the real world, due to automatic stabilizers, spending shocks have much weaker impacts on the economy than our simple multiplier formulas would suggest.

Finally, there is one more automatic stabilizer you should know about, perhaps the most important of all: the *passage of time.* Why is this an automatic stabilizer? Because, as you've learned, the impact of spending shocks on the economy are *temporary.* As time passes, the classical model—lurking in the background—stands ready to take over. A few months after a shock, the corrective mechanisms we discussed in the previous chapter begin to operate, and the economy begins to return to full employment. As time passes, the impact of the spending shock gradually disappears. And if we wait long enough—a few years or so—the effects of the shock will be gone entirely. That is, after a shock pulls us away from full-employment GDP, the economy will eventually return to full-employment GDP—right where it started. We thus conclude that

SHORT-RUN VERSUS LONG-RUN OUTCOMES

in the long run, our multipliers have a value of zero: No matter what the change in spending or taxes, output will return to full employment, so the change in equilibrium GDP will be zero.

Of course, the year or two we must wait can seem like an eternity to those left jobless in a recession. The short run is not to be overlooked. This is why, in the next several chapters, we will continue with our exploration of the short run, building on the Keynesian model you've learned in this chapter. However, we'll make the analysis more complete and more realistic by bringing in some of the real-world features that were not fully considered here.

COMPARING MODELS: CLASSICAL AND KEYNESIAN

Before leaving this chapter, it's important to note some startling differences between the long-run classical model you learned about a few chapters ago, and the short-run Keynesian model of this chapter. We've already discussed one of these differences: In the classical model, the economy operates *automatically* at full-employment, or potential, output. In the short-run Keynesian model, by contrast, the economy can operate above its potential (a boom) or below its potential (a recession). The reason for the difference is that, in the short run, spending affects output: A negative spending shock can cause a recession; a positive spending shock can cause a boom.

There are two other important contrasts between the predictions of the two models. One concerns the role of saving in the economy, and the other concerns the effectiveness of fiscal policy. Let's explore each of these issues in turn.

THE ROLE OF SAVING

In the long run, saving has positive effects on the economy. This was demonstrated two chapters ago, when—using the classical model—we discussed economic growth. Suppose, for example, that households decide to save more at any level of income. In the long run, the extra saving will flow into the loanable funds market, where it will be borrowed by business firms to purchase new plant and equipment. Thus, an increase in saving automatically leads to an increase in investment, faster growth in the capital stock, and a faster rise in living standards. Indeed, we can expect an increase in saving to have precisely these effects . . . in the long run.

But in the short run, the automatic mechanisms of the classical model do not keep the economy operating at its potential. On the contrary, *spending* influences output in the short run. If households decide to save more at each income level, they also—by definition—*spend less* at each income level. Or, putting it another way, an increase in saving is the same as a *decrease* in autonomous consumption spending, a. As you've learned in this chapter, a decrease in autonomous consumption spending causes a decrease in output through the multiplier process. If the economy is initially operating at full employment, the increase in saving will bring about a recession.

SHORT-RUN VERSUS LONG-RUN OUTCOMES

In the long run, an increase in the desire to save leads to faster economic growth and rising living standards. In the short run, however, it can cause a recession.

You can see that there are two sides to the "savings coin." The impact of increased saving is positive in the long run and potentially dangerous in the short run. Are you wondering how we get from the potentially harmful short-run effect of higher saving to the beneficial long-run effect? We'll address this question a few chapters later, when we examine how the economy adjusts from its short-run equilibrium to its long-run equilibrium.

THE EFFECT OF FISCAL POLICY

In the classical model, you learned that fiscal policy—changes in government spending or taxes designed to change equilibrium GDP—is completely ineffective. More specifically, an increase in government spending *crowds out* an equal amount of household and business spending: The rise in G is exactly matched by the decrease in C and I . . . in the long run.

But in the short run, once again, we cannot rely on the mechanisms of the classical model that are so effective in the long run. In the short run, *an increase in government spending causes a multiplied increase in equilibrium GDP.* Therefore, in the short run, fiscal policy can actually change equilibrium GDP!

This important observation suggests that fiscal policy could, in theory, play a role in altering the path of the economy. If we are entering a recession, couldn't we use fiscal policy to pull us out of it or even prevent the recession entirely? For example, if investment spending decreases by $100 billion, setting off a negative multiplier effect, couldn't we just increase government spending by $100 billion to set off an equal, positive multiplier effect? Why wait the many months or years it would take for the classical model to "kick in" and bring the economy back to full employment when we have such a powerful tool—fiscal policy—at our disposal?

Indeed, in the 1960s and early 1970s, this was the thinking of many economists. At that time, the view that fiscal policy could effectively smooth out economic fluctuations—perhaps even preventing recessions and booms entirely—was very popular. But very few economists believe this today. Why? In part, because of practical difficulties in executing the right fiscal policy at the right time. But more importantly, the rules of economic policy making have changed: The Federal Reserve now attempts to neutralize fiscal policy changes long before they can affect spending and output in the economy. In later chapters, we'll discuss the practical difficulties of executing fiscal policy and how the Federal Reserve has changed the "rules of the game."

THE RECESSION OF 1990–1991

USING THE THEORY

Our most recent recession began in the second half of 1990 and continued into 1991. Table 6 tells the story. The first column shows real GDP in 1992 dollars in each of several quarters. For example, "1990:2" denotes the second quarter of 1990, and during that three-month period, GDP was $6,174 billion at an annual rate. (That is, if we had continued producing that quarter's GDP for an entire year, we *would* have produced a total of $6,174 billion worth of goods and services in that year.)

As you can see, real GDP began to fall in the third quarter, and it continued to drop until the second quarter of 1991. In all, GDP fell for three consecutive quarters. During this time, real output fell by $100 billion, a drop of about 1.6 percent. At the same time, the unemployment rate rose, from 5.1 percent in June of 1990 to 7.7 percent in June of 1992. The economy had not completely recovered by the presidential election of November 1992, and many observers believe that the recession and slow recovery were the deciding factors in George Bush's loss to Bill Clinton.

Can our short-run Keynesian model help us understand what caused this recession? Very much so. In retrospect, we can see that there were two separate spending shocks to the economy in early 1990.

TABLE 6 THE RECESSION OF 1990–1991

Quarter	Real GDP (billions of 1992 dollars)	Change in Real GDP from Previous Quarter (billions of 1992 dollars)	Real Investment Spending (billions of 1992 dollars)	Consumer Confidence Index
1990:2	6,174		811	105
1990:3	6,145	−29	803	90
1990:4	6,081	−64	774	61
1991:1	6,048	−33	742	65
1991:2	6,074	+26	739	77

First, for a variety of reasons, a financial crisis had developed, in which some banks and savings and loan associations were near bankruptcy. Many banks, playing it safe, responded by cutting back on loans for new home purchases, as well as for business expansion. The media began to speak of a "credit crunch," in which homebuyers and businesses were forced to pay very high interest rates on loans, or were unable to borrow at all. The consequence was a sizable decrease in the demand for new housing and for plant and equipment—an investment spending shock. (Remember that investment spending includes new-housing construction as well as plant and equipment.)

The second shock resulted from global politics. In the summer of 1990, Iraqi troops invaded and occupied much of Kuwait. The United States responded by sending troops to Kuwait and, in early 1991, launched an attack on Iraqi troops. Americans began to fear a prolonged and costly war in the Middle East, one that would, among other things, cause a large increase in the price of oil. They remembered that in the early 1970s, the last time that oil prices had risen substantially, the U.S. economy plunged into recession. As a result, American households became less confident about the economy.

The fifth column of Table 6 shows the rapid decline in the *consumer confidence index* that was occurring at the time. The index is based on a survey of about 5,000 households. Each month, these households respond to questions about their job and career prospects in the months ahead, their expected income, their spending plans, and so forth. A drop in consumer confidence makes households spend less at *any* income level. Or, put another way, households wanted to *save more* at any income level. Viewed either way, the drop in consumer confidence caused a decrease in autonomous consumption, a. This was the second spending shock to the economy.

In sum, in early 1990, there were two spending shocks to the economy: a decline in investment and a decline in autonomous consumption. Each of these shocks had a multiplier effect on the economy, causing income and spending to decline in successive rounds for almost a year. Beginning in 1992, the credit crunch began to subside, increasing investment spending, and the Gulf War ended, increasing consumer confidence. At the same time, the long-run corrective forces of the classical model were beginning to work. Together, all of these factors helped the economy to recover in 1992 and on into 1993.

SUMMARY

In the short run, spending depends upon income and income depends upon spending. The short-run Keynesian model was developed to explore this circular connection between spending and income.

Total spending is the sum of three aggregates—consumption spending by households, investment spending by firms, and government purchases of goods and services. Consumption spending (C) depends primarily on disposable income—what households have left over after paying taxes. The consumption function is a linear relationship between disposable income and consumption spending. The marginal propensity to consume—a number between zero and 1—indicates the fraction of each additional dollar of disposable income that is consumed. For a given level of income, consumption spending can change as a result of changes in the interest rate, wealth, or expectations about the future. Each of these changes will shift the consumption function.

Investment spending (I) and government spending (G) are taken as given values, determined by forces outside our analysis. Aggregate expenditure (AE) is the sum $C + I + G$; it varies with income because consumption spending varies with income.

Equilibrium GDP is the level of output at which aggregate expenditure is just equal to GDP (Y). If AE exceeds Y, then firms will experience unplanned decreases in inventories. They will respond by increasing production. If Y exceeds AE, firms will find their inventories increasing and will respond by reducing production. Only when $AE = Y$ will there be no unplanned inventory changes and no reason for firms to change production. Graphically, this occurs at the point where the aggregate expenditure line intersects the 45° line.

Spending shocks will change the economy's short-run equilibrium. An increase in investment spending, for example, shifts the aggregate expenditure line upward and triggers the multiplier process. The initial increase in investment causes income to increase. That, in turn, leads to an increase in consumption spending, a further increase in income, more consumption spending, and so on. The economy eventually reaches a new equilibrium with a change in GDP that is a multiple of the original increase in spending. Other spending shocks would have similar effects. The size of the *expenditure multiplier* is determined by the marginal propensity to consume.

There are several important differences between the short-run Keynesian model and the long-run classical model. In the long run, the economy operates at potential output; in the short run, GDP can be above or below potential. In the long run, saving contributes to economic growth by making funds available for firms to invest in new capital. In the short run, increased saving means reduced spending and a lower level of output. Finally, fiscal policy is completely ineffective in the long run, but can have important effects on total demand and output in the short run.

KEY TERMS

short-run Keynesian model
disposable income
consumption function
autonomous consumption spending
marginal propensity to consume
consumption–income line
aggregate expenditure (AE)
equilibrium GDP
expenditure multiplier
automatic stabilizers

REVIEW QUESTIONS

1. Briefly describe the three main categories of spending.
2. List, and briefly explain, the main determinants of consumption spending. Indicate whether a change in each determinant causes a movement along, or a shift of, the consumption–income line.
3. What are the main components of investment spending? How does actual investment differ from planned investment?
4. What conditions must be satisfied at the economy's short-run equilibrium level of real GDP?
5. Suppose that a change in government expenditure (G) disturbs the economy's short-run equilibrium. Describe what happens as the economy adjusts to the change in spending.
6. Compare the macroeconomic role of saving in the short run and the long run.

PROBLEMS AND EXERCISES

1.

Y	C	I	G
3,000	2500	500	500
4,000	3250	500	500
5,000	4000	500	500
6,000	4750	500	500
7,000	5500	500	500
8,000	6250	500	500

a. What is the marginal propensity to consume implicit in this data?
b. Plot a 45° line, and then use the data to plot an aggregate expenditure line.
c. What is the equilibrium level of real GDP?

2.

Y	C	I	G
7,000	6,600	400	1,000
8,000	7,400	400	1,000
9,000	8,200	400	1,000
10,000	9,000	400	1,000
11,000	9,800	400	1,000
12,000	10,600	400	1,000
13,000	11,400	400	1,000

a. What is the marginal propensity to consume implicit in this data?
b. What is the numerical value of the multiplier for this economy?
c. What is the equilibrium level of real GDP?
d. Suppose that government spending (G) decreased from 1,000 to 400 at each level of income. What would happen to the equilibrium level of real GDP?

3. Using the data given in problem 2, construct a table similar to Table 5 in the chapter.
a. Show what would happen in the first five rounds following an increase in investment spending from 400 to 800.
b. What would be the ultimate effect of that increase in investment spending?
c. How much would households spend on consumption goods in the new equilibrium?

4. Suppose that households become more thrifty—that is, they now wish to save a larger proportion of their disposable income and spend a smaller proportion.
a. Draw an aggregate expenditure diagram and show how an economy that is initially in short-run equilibrium will respond to such an increase in thriftiness.
b. In the table in problem 2, which column of data would be affected? How?

CHALLENGE QUESTIONS

1. Read Appendix 1 (if you have not already done so). Then, suppose that $a = 600$, $b = 0.75$, $T = 400$, $I = 600$, and $G = 900$. Calculate the equilibrium level of real GDP. Then check that the equilibrium value equals the sum $C + I + G$.

2. The short-run equilibrium condition that $Y = C + I + G$ can be reinterpreted as follows. First, subtract C from both sides to get $Y - C = I + G$. Then, note that all income not spent on consumption goods is either taxed or saved, so that $Y - C = S + T$. Now, combine the two equations to obtain $S + T = I + G$.

Construct a diagram with real GDP measured on the horizontal axis. Draw two lines—one for $S + T$, and the other for $I + G$. How would you interpret the point where the two lines cross? What would happen if investment spending increased?

WWW

Visit the Bureau of Labor Statistics Consumer Expenditure Survey page (http://stats.bls.gov/csxhome.htm) and review the most current news release. Answer the following questions:
a. What was the rate of change for consumer expenditures between this year and last year?
b. Which category of expenditures had the largest rate of change? The smallest?
c. What are the eight major categories of expenditures reported in this survey?

APPENDIX 1

FINDING EQUILIBRIUM GDP ALGEBRAICALLY

The chapter showed how we can find equilibrium GDP using tables and graphs. This appendix demonstrates a more straightforward way of finding the equilibrium GDP: using algebraic equations.

Our starting point is the relationship between consumption and disposable income given in the chapter,

$$C = a + bDI$$

where a represents autonomous consumption spending, and b represents the marginal propensity to consume. Remember that disposable income (DI) is the income that the household sector has left after taxes. Letting T represent taxes, and Y represent total income or GDP, we have

$$DI = Y - T$$

If we now substitute $DI = Y - T$ into $C = a + bDI$, we get an equation showing consumption at each level of income:

$$C = a + b(Y - T)$$

we can rearrange this equation algebraically to read

$$C = (a - bT) + bY$$

This is the general equation for the consumption–income line. When graphed, the term in parentheses $(a - bT)$ will be the vertical intercept, and b will be the slope. (Figure 5 shows a specific example of this line in which a = \$2,000, b = 0.6, and T = \$2,000.)

As you've learned, total spending or aggregate expenditure (AE) is the sum of consumption spending (C), investment spending (I), and government spending (G):

$$AE = C + I + G$$

If we substitute for C the equation $C = (a - bT) + bY$, we get:

$$AE = a - bT + bY + I + G$$

Now we can use this equation to find the equilibrium GDP. Equilibrium occurs when output (Y) and aggregate expenditure (AE) are the same. That is,

$$Y = AE$$

or, substituting the equation for AE,

$$Y = a - bT + bY + I + G$$

This last equation will hold true only when Y is at its equilibrium value. We can solve for equilibrium Y by first bringing all terms involving Y to the left-hand side:

$$Y - bY = a - bT + I + G$$

Next, factoring out Y, we get

$$Y(1 - b) = a - bT + I + G$$

Finally, dividing both sides of this equation by $(1 - b)$ yields

$$Y = \frac{a - bT + I + G}{1 - b}$$

This last equation shows how equilibrium GDP depends on a (autonomous consumption), b (the MPC), T (taxes), I (investment spending), and G (government purchases). These variables are all determined "outside our model." That is, they are given values that we use to determine equilibrium output, but they are not themselves affected by the level of output. Whenever we use actual numbers for these given variables in the equation, we find the same equilibrium GDP we would find using a table or a graph.

In the example we used throughout the chapter, the given values (found in Tables 1, 2 and 4) are, in billions of dollars, $a = 2{,}000$; $b = 0.6$; $T = 2{,}000$; $I = 1{,}000$; and $G = 600$. Plugging these values into the equation for equilibrium GDP, we get

$$Y = \frac{2{,}000 - (0.6 \times 2{,}000) + 1{,}000 + 600}{1 - 0.6}$$

$$= \frac{2{,}400}{0.4}$$

$$= 6{,}000$$

This is the same value we found in Table 4 and Figure 8.

APPENDIX 2

THE SPECIAL CASE OF THE TAX MULTIPLIER

You learned in this chapter how changes in autonomous consumption, investment, and government purchases affect aggregate expenditure and equilibrium GDP. But there is another type of change that can influence equilibrium GDP: a change in taxes. For this type of change, the formula for the multiplier is a bit different from the one presented in the chapter.

Let's suppose that household taxes (T) *decrease* by $1,000 billion. The immediate impact is to increase households' *disposable income* (*DI*) by $1,000 billion at the current level of income. As a result, consumption spending will increase. But by how much?

The answer is, *less* than $1,000 billion. When households get a tax cut, they increase their spending *not* by the full amount of the cut, but only by a *part* of it. The amount by which spending initially increases depends on the *MPC*. In our example, in which the *MPC* is 0.6, and disposable income rises by $1,000 billion, the initial change in consumption spending is just $600 billion. *This is the first change in spending that occurs after the tax cut.* Of course, once consumption spending rises, every subsequent round of the multiplier will work just as in Table 5: In the next round, consumption spending will rise by $360 billion, and then $216 billion, and so on.

Now let's compare what happens when taxes are cut by $1,000 billion with what happens when spending rises by $1,000 billion. As you can see from Table 5, when investment rises by $1,000 billion, the initial change in spending is, by definition, $1,000 billion. But when taxes are cut by $1,000 billion, the initial change in spending is *not* $1,000 billion, but *$600 billion*. Thus, the first line of the table is missing in the case of a $1,000 billion tax cut. All subsequent rounds of the multiplier are the same, however. Therefore, we would expect the $1,000 billion tax cut to cause a $1,500 billion increase in equilibrium GDP—not the $2,500 billion increase listed in the table.

Another way to say this is: for each dollar that taxes are cut, equilibrium GDP will increase by $1.50 rather than $2.50—the increase is one dollar less in the case of the tax cut. This observation tells us that the tax multiplier must have a numerical value *1 less than* the spending multiplier of the chapter.

Finally, there is one more difference between the spending multiplier of the chapter and the tax multiplier: While the spending multiplier is a positive number (because an increase in spending causes an increase in equilibrium GDP), the tax multiplier is a negative number, since a tax cut (a negative change in taxes) must be multiplied by a *negative* number to give us a *positive* change in GDP. Putting all this together, we conclude that

> *the tax multiplier is one less than the spending multiplier, and negative in sign.*

Thus, if the *MPC* is 0.6 (as in the chapter), so that the spending multiplier is 2.5, then the tax multiplier will have a value of $-(2.5 - 1) = -1.5$.

More generally, since the tax multiplier is 1 less than the spending multiplier and is also negative, we can write

$$\text{Tax multiplier} = -(\text{spending multiplier} - 1)$$

Because the spending multiplier is $1/(1 - MPC)$, we can substitute to get

$$\text{Tax multiplier} = -\left[\frac{1}{1 - MPC} - 1\right]$$

$$= -\frac{1 - (1 - MPC)}{1 - MPC}$$

$$= \frac{-MPC}{1 - MPC}$$

Hence,

the general formula for the tax multiplier is

−MPC/(1 − MPC)

For any change in taxes, we can use the formula to find the change in equilibrium GDP as follows:

$$\Delta GDP = \left[\frac{-MPC}{1 - MPC}\right] \times \Delta T$$

In our example, in which taxes were cut by \$1,000 billion, we have $\Delta T = -\$1{,}000$ billion and $MPC = 0.6$. Plugging these values into the formula, we obtain

$$\Delta GDP = \left[\frac{-0.6}{1 - 0.6}\right] \times -\$1{,}000 \text{ billion}$$

$$= \$1{,}500 \text{ billion}$$

CHAPTER 11

THE BANKING SYSTEM AND THE MONEY SUPPLY

CHAPTER OUTLINE

What Is Counted as Money

Measuring the Money Stock
- Assets and Their Liquidity
- M1 and M2

The Banking System
- Financial Intermediaries
- Commercial Banks
- A Bank's Balance Sheet

The Federal Reserve System
- The Structure of the Fed
- The Federal Open Market Committee
- The Functions of the Federal Reserve

The Fed and the Money Supply
- How the Fed Increases the Money Supply
- The Demand Deposit Multiplier
- The Fed's Effect on the Banking System as a Whole
- How the Fed Decreases the Money Supply
- Some Important Provisos about the Demand Deposit Multiplier
- Other Tools for Controlling the Money Supply

Using the Theory: Bank Failures and Banking Panics

Everyone knows that money doesn't grow on trees. But where does it actually come from? You might think that the answer is simple: The government just prints it. Right?

Sort of. It is true that much of our money supply is, indeed, paper currency printed by our national monetary authority. But most of our money supply is not paper currency at all, and is not printed by anyone. Strictly speaking, the monetary authority in the United States—the Federal Reserve System—is not a part of the executive, legislative, or judicial branches of the government, but a quasi-independent agency that operates *along side* of the regular branches of the government.

This chapter is about money and the institutions that help create it: the private banking system and the Federal Reserve. What you learn here will, in future chapters, help add realism to the short-run Keynesian model, deepen your understanding of economic fluctuations, and help you understand our policy choices in dealing with them. We will begin by taking a close look at what money is and how it is measured. Then, we turn our attention to the private banking system and the U.S. Federal Reserve. Finally, we'll bring all of the pieces together and consider how the Federal Reserve works through the private banking system to change the money supply.

WHAT IS COUNTED AS MONEY

Money, loosely defined, is the means of payment in the economy. And as you will learn in the next chapter, the amount of money in circulation can affect the macroeconomy. This is why governments around the world like to know how much money is available to their citizens.

In practice, the standard definition of money is *currency, checking account balances,* and *travelers' checks.* What do these have in common and why are they included in the definition of money when other means of payment—such as credit cards—are not included?

First, only *assets*—things of value that people own—are regarded as money. Paper currency, travelers' checks, and funds held in checking accounts are all examples of assets. But *the right to borrow* is not considered an asset, so it is not part of the money supply. This is why the credit limit on your credit card, or your ability to go into a bank and borrow money, is not considered part of the money supply.

Second, only things that are widely *acceptable* as a means of payment are regarded as money. Currency, travelers' checks, and personal checks can all be used to buy things or pay bills. Other assets—such as the funds in your savings account—cannot generally be used to pay for goods and services, and so they fail the acceptability test.

Finally, only highly *liquid* assets are regarded as money.

> *An asset is considered* **liquid** *if it can be converted to cash quickly and at little cost. An illiquid asset, by contrast, can be converted to cash only after a delay, or at considerable cost.*

LIQUIDITY The property of being easily converted into cash.

Checking account balances are highly liquid because you can convert them to cash at the ATM or by cashing a check. Travelers' checks are also highly liquid. But stocks and bonds are *not* as liquid as checking accounts or travelers' checks. Stock and bondholders must go to some trouble and pay brokers' fees to convert these assets into cash.

MEASURING THE MONEY STOCK

In practice, governments have several alternative definitions of the money stock. These definitions include a selection of *assets* that are (1) generally acceptable as a means of payment and (2) relatively liquid.

Notice the phrase "*relatively* liquid." This does not sound like a hard and fast rule for measuring the money supply, and indeed it is not. This is why there are different measures of the money supply: Each interprets the phrase "relatively liquid" in a different way. To understand this better, let's look at the different kinds of liquid assets that people can hold.

ASSETS AND THEIR LIQUIDITY

Figure 1 lists a spectrum of assets, ranked according to their liquidity, along with the amounts of each asset in the U.S. public's hands on December, 2, 1996. The most liquid asset of all is **cash in the hands of the public.** It takes no time and zero expense to convert this asset into cash, since it's *already* cash. At the end of 1996, the public held about $396 billion in cash.

CASH IN THE HAND OF THE PUBLIC Currency and coins held outside of banks.

Next in line are three asset categories of about equal liquidity. **Demand deposits** are the checking accounts held by households and business firms at commercial banks, including huge ones like the Bank of America or Citibank, and smaller ones like Simmons National Bank in Arkansas. These checking accounts are called "demand" deposits because when you write a check to someone, that person can go into a bank and, on demand, be paid in cash. This is one reason that demand deposits are considered very liquid: The person who has your check can convert it into cash quickly and easily. Another reason is that you can withdraw cash from your own checking account very easily—24 hours a day with an ATM card, or dur-

DEMAND DEPOSITS Checking accounts that do not pay interest.

FIGURE 1

MONETARY ASSETS AND THEIR LIQUIDITY (DECEMBER, 1996)

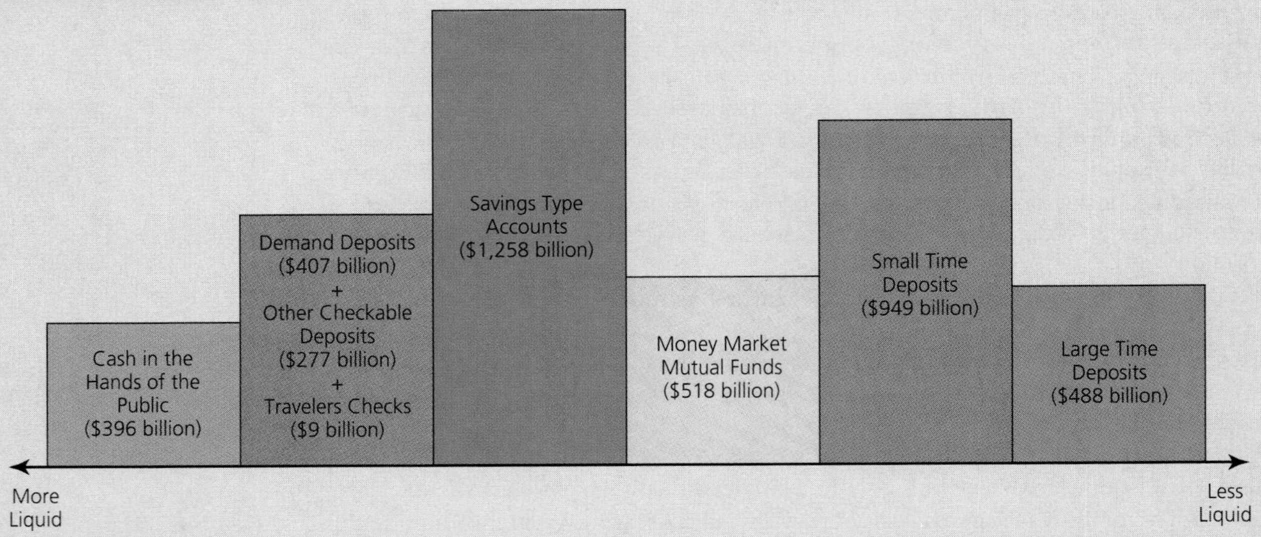

Assets vary according to the ease with which they can be converted into cash. Assets toward the left side of this figure are more liquid than those toward the right side.

ing banking hours if you want to speak to a teller. As you can see in the figure, the U.S. public held $407 billion in demand deposits at the end of 1996.

Other checkable deposits is a catchall category for several types of checking accounts that work very much like demand deposits. These include *negotiable order of withdrawal (NOW) accounts,* which work much like checking accounts but also pay interest, and *automatic transfer from savings accounts,* which are interest-paying savings accounts that automatically transfer funds into checking accounts when needed. At the end of 1996, the U.S. public held $277 billion of these types of checkable deposits.

Travelers' checks are specially printed checks that you can buy from banks or other private companies, like American Express. Travelers' checks can be easily spent at almost any hotel or store. You can often cash them at a bank. You need only show an I.D. and countersign the check. At the end of 1996 the public held about $9 billion in travelers' checks.

Savings-type accounts at banks and other financial institutions (such as *savings and loan* institutions) amounted to $1,258 billion at the end of 1996. These are less liquid than checking-type accounts, since they do not allow you to write checks. While it is easy to transfer funds from your savings account to your checking account, you must make the transfer yourself.

Next on the list are deposits in *money market mutual funds (MMMFs),* which use customer deposits to buy a variety of financial assets. Depositors can withdraw their money by writing checks. At the end of 1996, the general public held about $518 billion in MMMFs.

Time deposits (sometimes called *certificates of deposit,* or *CDs*) require you to keep your money in the bank for a specified period of time (usually 6 months or longer), and impose an interest penalty if you withdraw early. At the end of 1996, the public held \$949 billion in *small time deposits* (in amounts under \$100,000) and \$488 billion in *large time deposits* (in amounts over \$100,000).

Now let's see how these assets have been used to define "money" in different ways.

M1 AND M2

The standard measure of the money stock is called **M1.** It is the sum of the first four assets in our list: cash in the hands of the public, demand deposits, other checkable deposits, and travelers' checks. These are also the four most liquid assets in our list.

M1 A standard measure of the money supply, including cash in the hand of the public, checking account deposits, and travelers' checks.

M1 = cash in the hands of the public + checking account deposits + travelers' checks.

In the United States at the end of 1996, this amounted to:

$$\begin{aligned} \text{M1} &= \$396 \text{ billion} + \$684 \text{ billion} + \$9 \text{ billion} \\ &= \$1{,}089 \text{ billion.} \end{aligned}$$

When economists or government officials speak about "the money supply," they usually mean M1.

But what about the assets left out of M1? While savings accounts are not as liquid as any of the components of M1, for most of us there is hardly a difference. All it takes is an ATM card and *presto,* funds in your savings account become cash. Money market funds held by households and businesses are fairly liquid, even though there are sometimes restrictions or special risks involved in converting them into cash. And even time deposits—if they are not too large—can be cashed in early with only a small interest penalty. When you think of how much "means of payment" you have, you are very likely to include the amounts you have in these types of accounts. This is why another common measure of the money supply, **M2,** adds these and some other types of assets to M1:

M2 M1 plus savings account balances, noninstitutional money market mutual fund balances, and small time deposits.

$$\text{M2} = \text{M1} + \text{savings-type accounts} + \text{noninstitutional MMMF balances} + \text{small time deposits}$$

Using the numbers for the end of 1996 in the United States:

$$\begin{aligned} \text{M2} &= \$1{,}089 \text{ billion} + \$1{,}258 \text{ billion} + \$\ 518 \text{ billion} + \$949 \text{ billion} \\ &= \$3{,}814 \text{ billion} \end{aligned}$$

> **DANGEROUS CURVES**
>
> In our definitions of money—whether M1, M2, or some other measure—we include cash (coin and paper currency) only if it is *in the hands of the public*. The italicized words are important. Some of the nation's cash is stored in banks' vaults, and is released only when the public withdraws cash from their accounts. Other cash is in the hands of the Federal Reserve, which stores it for future release. But until this cash is released from bank vaults or the Fed, it is *not* part of the money supply. Only the cash possessed by households, businesses, or government agencies (other than the Fed) is considered part of the money supply.

There are other official measures of the money supply besides M1 and M2 that add in assets that are less liquid than those in M2. But M1 and M2 have been the most popular, and most commonly watched, definitions.

It is important to understand that the M1 and M2

money stock measures exclude many things that people use regularly as a means of payment. Although M1 and M2 give us important information about the activities of the Fed and of banks, they do not measure all the different ways that people hold their wealth or pay for things. Credit cards, for example, are not included in any of the official measures. But for most of us, unused credit is a means of payment, to be lumped together with our cash and our checking accounts. As credit cards were issued to more and more Americans over the last several decades, the available means of payment increased considerably, much more than the increase in M1 and M2 suggests.

Technological advances—now and in the future—will continue the trend toward new and more varied ways to make payments. For example, at the 1996 Olympics, people used electronic cash to make small transactions, smaller than would make sense with credit cards. You could buy a card worth \$5, \$10, or \$20 and use it in place of cash or checks. You could even put the card in a machine and add purchasing power to it by tapping into your Visa or Mastercard credit line. Electronic cash is clearly a means of payment, even though it is yet not included in any measure of the money supply. If electronic cash becomes important in the economy, it will probably be included in M1.

Fortunately, the details and complexities of measuring money are not important for understanding the monetary system and monetary policy. For the rest of our discussion, we will make a simplifying assumption:

We will assume the money supply consists of just two components: cash in the hands of the public and demand deposits.

Money supply = Cash in the hands of public + Demand deposits

As you will see later, our definition of the money supply corresponds closely to the liquid assets that our national monetary authority—the Federal Reserve—can control. While there is not much that the Federal Reserve can do directly about the amount of funds in savings accounts, MMMFs, or time deposits or about the development of electronic cash or the ability to borrow on credit cards, it can tightly control the sum of cash in the hands of the public and demand deposits.[1]

We will spend the rest of this chapter analyzing how money is created and what makes the money supply change. Our first step is to introduce a key player in the creation of money: the banking system.

THE BANKING SYSTEM

Think about the last time you went into a bank. Perhaps you deposited a paycheck, or withdrew cash to take care of your shopping needs for the week. We make these kinds of transactions dozens of times every year without ever thinking about what a bank really is, or how our own actions at the bank—and the actions of millions of other bank customers—might contribute to a change in the money supply.

1 The Fed can also control some other types of checkable deposits. To keep our analysis as simple as possible, we consider only demand deposits.

FINANCIAL INTERMEDIARIES

Let's begin at the beginning: What are banks? They are important examples of **financial intermediaries**—business firms that specialize in assembling loanable funds from households and firms whose revenues exceed their expenditures, and channeling those funds to households, firms, and government agencies whose expenditures exceed revenues. Financial intermediaries make the economy work much more efficiently than would be possible without them.

FINANCIAL INTERMEDIARY A business firm that specializes in brokering between savers and borrowers.

To understand this more clearly, imagine that Boeing, the U.S. aircraft maker, wants to borrow a billion dollars for three years. If there were no financial intermediaries, Boeing would have to make individual arrangements to borrow small amounts of money from thousands—perhaps millions—of households, each of which wants to lend money for, say, three months at a time. Every three months, Boeing would have to renegotiate the loans, and it would find borrowing money in this way to be quite cumbersome. Lenders, too, would find this arrangement troublesome. All of their funds would be lent to one firm. If that firm encountered difficulties, the funds might not be returned at the end of three months.

An intermediary helps to solve these problems by combining a large number of small savers' funds into custom-designed packages and then lending them to larger borrowers. The intermediary can do this because it can predict—from experience—the pattern of inflows of funds. While some deposited funds may be withdrawn, the overall total available for lending tends to be quite stable. The intermediary can also reduce the risk to depositors by spreading its loans among a number of different borrowers. If one borrower fails to repay its loan, that will have only a small effect on the intermediary and its depositors.

Of course, intermediaries must earn a profit for providing brokering services. They do so by charging a higher interest rate on the funds they lend than the rate they pay to depositors. But they are so efficient at brokering that both lenders and borrowers benefit. Lenders earn higher interest rates, with lower risk and greater liquidity, than if they had to deal directly with the ultimate users of funds. And borrowers end up paying lower interest rates on loans that are specially designed for their specific purposes.

The United States boasts a wide variety of financial intermediaries, including commercial banks, savings and loan associations, mutual savings banks, credit unions, insurance companies, and some government agencies. Some of these intermediaries—called *depository institutions*—accept deposits from the general public and lend the deposits to borrowers. There are four types of depository institutions:

1. *Savings and loan associations (S&Ls)* obtain funds through their customers' time, savings, and checkable deposits and use them primarily to make mortgage loans.
2. *Mutual savings banks* accept deposits (called *shares*) and use them primarily to make mortgage loans. They differ from S&Ls because they are owned by their depositors, rather than outside investors.
3. *Credit unions* specialize in working with particular groups of people, such as members of a labor union or employees in a specific field of business. They acquire funds through their members' deposits and make consumer and mortgage loans to other members.
4. *Commercial banks* are the largest group of depository institutions. They obtain funds mainly by issuing checkable deposits, savings deposits, and time deposits and use the funds to make business, mortgage, and consumer loans.

Since commercial banks will play a central role in the rest of this chapter, let's take a closer look at how they operate.

COMMERCIAL BANKS

A commercial bank (or just "bank" for short) is a private corporation, owned by its stockholders, that provides services to the public. For our purposes, the most important service is to provide checking accounts, which enable the bank's customers to pay bills and make purchases without holding large amounts of cash that could be lost or stolen. Checks are one of the most important means of payment in the economy. Every year, U.S. households and businesses write trillions of dollars worth of checks to pay their bills, and many wage and salary earners have their pay deposited directly into their checking accounts. And as you saw in Figure 1, the public holds about twice as much money in the form of demand deposits and other checking-type accounts than it holds in cash.

Banks provide checking account services in order to earn a profit. Where does a bank's profit come from? Mostly from lending out the funds that people deposit and charging interest on the loans; but also by charging for some services directly, such as check-printing fees or that annoying dollar or so sometimes charged for using an ATM.

A BANK'S BALANCE SHEET

BALANCE SHEET A financial statement showing assets, liabilities, and net worth at a point in time.

We can understand more clearly how a bank works by looking at its *balance sheet,* a tool used by accountants. A **balance sheet** is a two-column list that provides information about the financial condition of a bank at a particular point in time. In one column, the bank's *assets* are listed—everything of value that it *owns.* On the other side, the bank's *liabilities* are listed—the amounts that the bank *owes.*

Table 1 shows a simplified version of a commercial bank's balance sheet.

Why does the bank have these assets and liabilities? Let's start with the assets side. The first item, $20 million, is the value of the bank's real estate—the buildings and the land underneath them. This is the easiest to explain, because a bank must have one or more branch offices in order to do business with the public.

BOND An IOU issued by a corporation or government agency when it borrows funds.

LOAN An IOU issued by a household or noncorporate business when it borrows funds.

Next, comes $25 million in *bonds,* and $65 million in *loans.* **Bonds** are IOUs issued by a corporation or a government agency when it borrows money. A bond promises to pay back the loan either gradually (e.g., each month), or all at once at some future date. **Loans** are IOUs signed by households or noncorporate businesses. Examples are auto loans, student loans, small business loans, and home mortgages (where the funds lent out are used to buy a home). Both bonds and loans generate interest income for the bank.

Next come two categories that might seem curious: $2 million in "vault cash," and $8 million in "accounts with the Federal Reserve." Vault cash, just like it sounds, is the coin and currency that the bank has stored in its vault. In addition, banks maintain their own accounts with the Federal Reserve, and they add and subtract to these accounts when they make transactions with other banks. Neither vault cash nor accounts with the Federal Reserve pay interest. Why, then, does the bank hold them? After all, a profit-seeking bank should want to hold as much of its assets as possible in income-earning form—bonds and loans.

There are two explanations for vault cash and accounts with the Federal Reserve. First, on any given day, some of the bank's customers might want to withdraw more cash than other customers are depositing. The bank must always be prepared to honor its obligations for withdrawals, so it must have some cash on hand to meet these requirements. This explains why it holds vault cash.

TABLE 1

A Typical Commercial Bank's Balance Sheet

Assets		**Liabilities and Net Worth**	
Property and buildings	\$ 20 million	Demand deposit liabilities	\$100 million
Government and corporate bonds	\$ 25 million	Net worth	\$ 20 million
Loans	\$ 65 million		
Cash in vault	\$ 2 million		
In accounts with the Federal Reserve	\$ 8 million		
Total Assets	\$120 million	Total Liabilities plus Net Worth	\$120 million

Second, banks are required by law to hold **reserves,** which are defined as *the sum of cash in the vault and accounts with the Federal Reserve*. The amount of reserves a bank must hold are called **required reserves.** The more funds its customers hold in their checking accounts, the greater the amount of required reserves. The **required reserve ratio,** set by the Federal Reserve, tells banks the fraction of their checking accounts that they must hold as required reserves.

For example, the bank in Table 1 has \$100 million in demand deposits. If the required reserve ratio is 0.1, this bank's required reserves are $0.1 \times \$100$ million = \$10 million in reserves. The bank must hold *at least* this amount of its assets as reserves. Since our bank has \$2 million in vault cash, and \$8 million in its *reserve account* with the Federal Reserve, it has a total of \$10 million in reserves, the minimum required amount.

RESERVES Vault cash plus balances held at the Fed.

REQUIRED RESERVES The minimum amount of reserves a bank must hold, depending upon the amount of its deposit liabilities.

REQUIRED RESERVE RATIO The minimum fraction of checking account balances that banks must hold as reserves.

NET WORTH The difference between assets and liabilities.

Now skip to the right side of the balance sheet. This bank's only liability is its demand deposits. Why are demand deposits a *liability*? Because the bank's customers have the right to withdraw funds from their checking accounts. Until they do, the bank *owes* them these funds.

Finally, the last entry. When we total up both sides of the bank's balance sheet, we find that it has \$120 million in assets, and only \$100 million in liabilities. If the bank were to go out of business, selling all of its assets and using the proceeds to pay off all of its liabilities (its demand deposits), it would have \$20 million left over. Who would get this \$20 million? The bank's owners—its stockholders. The \$20 million is called the bank's **net worth.** More generally,

Net worth = Total assets − Total liabilities

DANGEROUS CURVES

Don't confuse a *balance sheet* with another accounting tool, called an *income statement* (or *profit and loss statement*). An income statement tells us how much a bank (or any firm) earns *over a period of time*. It does this by listing the bank's revenue from all sources and all of its expenditures over the period. Each item listed is a *flow variable*—dollars per month or dollars per year.

By contrast, a balance sheet tells us the bank's financial position *at a moment in time*. Every asset and liability on the balance sheet is a *stock variable*—a quantity that exists at a moment in time. (For example, the balance sheet in Table 1 shows that, *at the moment it was tabulated,* the bank held \$65 million in loans.)

There is a relationship between these two accounting statements, but they are not the same. A bank's balance sheet can show a positive net worth—a good financial position—and yet the bank's income statement could show a loss for the year. Or the balance sheet might show a negative net worth (total liabilities greater than total assets), and yet the income statement could show a profit for the year.

We include net worth on the liabilities side of the balance sheet because it is, in a sense, what the bank would owe to its owners if it went out of business. Notice that, because of the way net worth is defined, both sides of a balance sheet must always have the same total: *A balance sheet always balances.*

Private banks are just one of the players that help determine the money supply. Now we turn our attention to the other key player—the Federal Reserve System.

THE FEDERAL RESERVE SYSTEM

CENTRAL BANK A nation's principal monetary authority.

Every large nation controls its banking system with a **central bank.** Most of the developed countries established their central banks long ago. For example, England's central bank—the Bank of England—was created in 1694. France was one of the latest, waiting until 1800 to establish the Banque de France, but the United States was even later. Although we experimented with central banks at various times in our history, we did not get serious about a central bank until 1913, when Congress established the *Federal Reserve System.*

Why did it take the United States so long to take control of its monetary system? Part of the reason is the suspicion of central authority that has always been part of U.S. politics and culture. Another reason is the large size and extreme diversity of our country, and the fear that a powerful central bank might be dominated by the interests of one region to the detriment of others. These special American characteristics help explain why our own central bank is different in form from its European counterparts.

One major difference is indicated in the very name of the institution—the Federal Reserve System. It does not have the word "central" or "bank" anywhere in its title, making it less suggestive of centralized power.

Another difference is the way the system is organized. Instead of a single central bank, the United States is divided into 12 different Federal Reserve districts, each one served by its own Federal Reserve Bank. The 12 districts and the Federal Reserve Banks that serve them are shown in Figure 2. For example, the Federal Reserve Bank of Dallas serves a district consisting of Texas and parts of New Mexico and Louisiana, while the Federal Reserve Bank of Chicago serves a district including Iowa and parts of Illinois, Indiana, Wisconsin, and Michigan.

Another interesting feature of the Federal Reserve System is its peculiar status within the government. Strictly speaking, it is not even a *part* of the government, but rather a corporation whose stockholders are the private banks that it regulates. But it is unlike other corporations in several ways. First, the *Fed* (as the system is commonly called) was created by Congress, and could be eliminated by Congress if it so desired. Second, both the president and Congress exert some influence on the Fed through their appointments of key officials in the system. Finally, the Fed's mission is not to make a profit for its stockholders like an ordinary corporation, but rather to serve the general public.

THE STRUCTURE OF THE FED

Figure 3 shows the organizational structure of the Federal Reserve System. Near the top is the Board of Governors, consisting of seven members who are appointed by the president and confirmed by the Senate for a 14-year term. The most powerful person at the Fed is the chairman of the Board of Governors—one of the seven governors who is appointed by the president, with Senate approval, to a four-year term as chair. In order to keep any president or Congress from having too much

THE GEOGRAPHY OF THE FEDERAL RESERVE SYSTEM

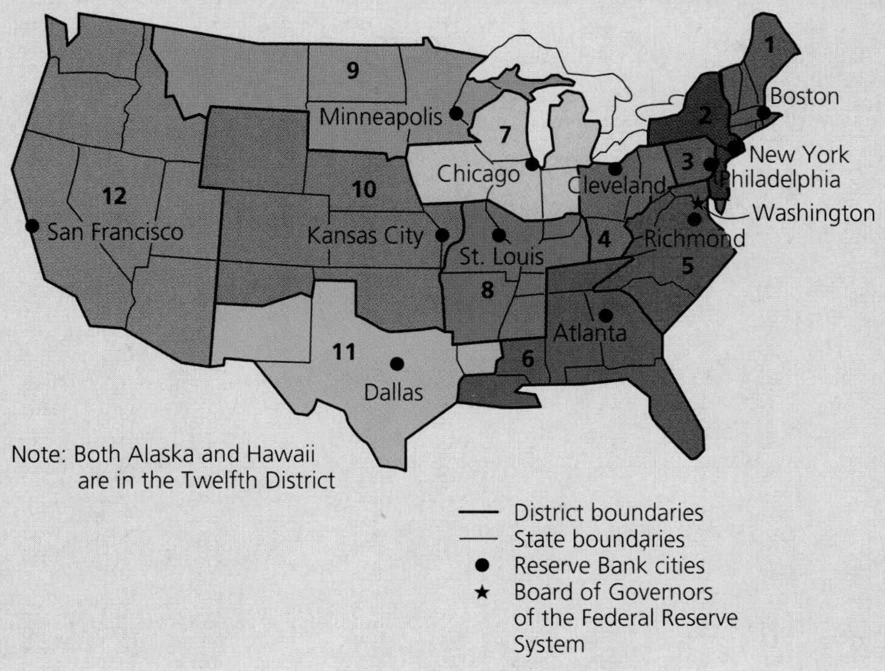

FIGURE 2

The United States is divided into 12 Federal Reserve districts, each with its own Federal Reserve Bank.

influence over the Fed, the four-year term of the chair is *not* coterminous with the four-year term of the president. As a result, every newly elected president inherits the Fed chair appointed by his predecessor, and may have to wait several years before making an appointment of his own.

For example, the current chairman of the Board of Governors is Alan Greenspan. He was originally appointed by President Reagan in 1987 for a term lasting until 1991, well into George Bush's term as president. In 1991, President Bush reappointed Greenspan to another four-year term, which included the first three years of Bill Clinton's administration. In 1995, President Clinton reappointed Greenspan yet again, for a term lasting until 1999.

Each of the 12 Federal Reserve Banks is supervised by nine directors, three of whom are appointed by the Board of Governors. The other six are elected by private commercial banks—the official stockholders of the system. The directors of each Federal Reserve Bank choose a president of that bank, who manages its day-to-day operations.

Notice that Figure 3 refers to "member banks." Only about 5,000 of the 12,000 or so commercial banks in the United States are members of the Federal Reserve System. But they include all *national banks* (those chartered by the federal government) and most *state banks* (chartered by their state governments). All of the largest banks in the United States (e.g., Citibank, Bank of America, and BankBoston) are nationally chartered banks and therefore member banks as well.

THE FEDERAL OPEN MARKET COMMITTEE

Finally, we come to what most economists regard as the most important part of the Fed—the **Federal Open Market Committee (FOMC)**. As you can see in Figure 3, the FOMC consists of all seven governors of the Fed, along with the 12 district

FEDERAL OPEN MARKET COMMITTEE A committee of Federal Reserve officials that establishes U.S. monetary policy.

FIGURE 3

THE STRUCTURE OF THE FEDERAL RESERVE SYSTEM

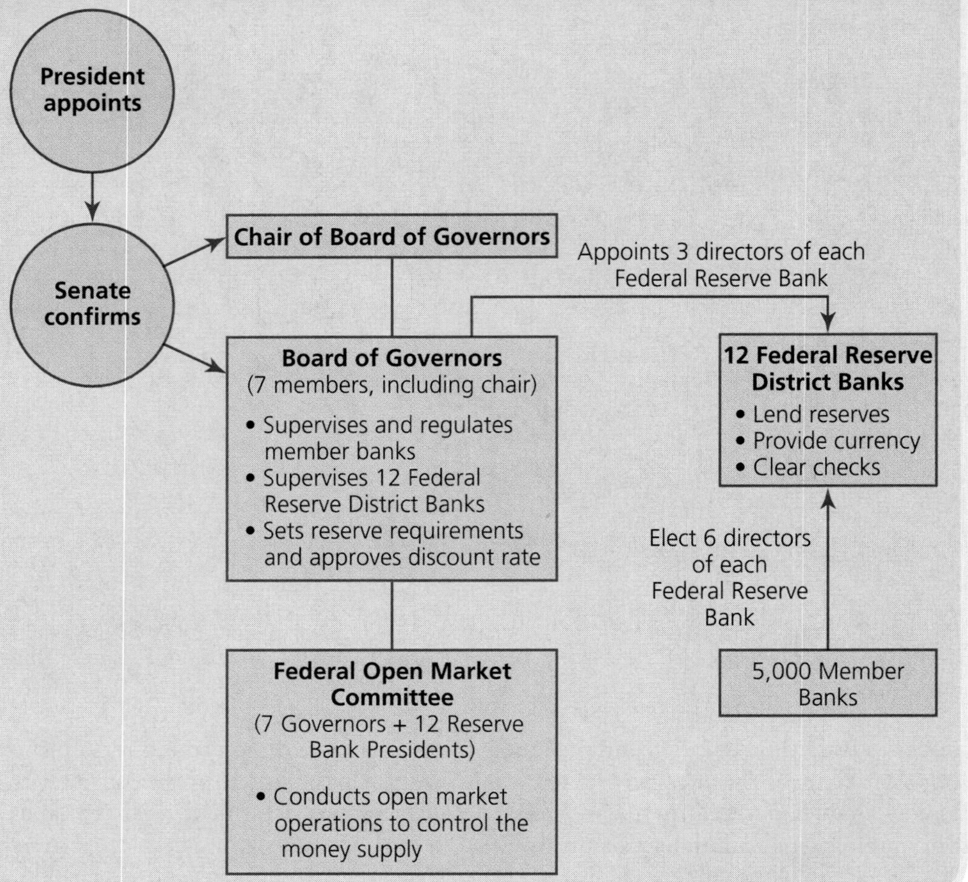

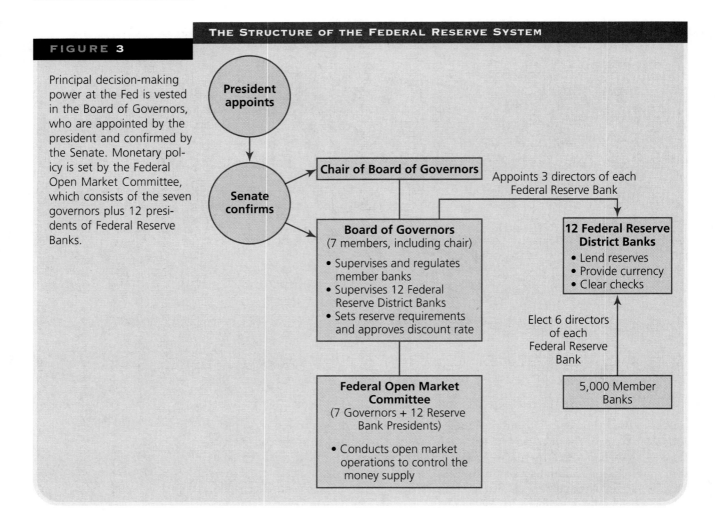

Principal decision-making power at the Fed is vested in the Board of Governors, who are appointed by the president and confirmed by the Senate. Monetary policy is set by the Federal Open Market Committee, which consists of the seven governors plus 12 presidents of Federal Reserve Banks.

bank presidents.[2] The committee meets about eight times a year to discuss current trends in inflation, unemployment, output, interest rates, and international exchange rates. After determining the current state of the economy, the FOMC sets the general course for the nation's money supply.

The word "open" in the FOMC's name is ironic, since the committee's deliberations are private. Summaries of its meetings are published only after a delay of a month or more. In some cases, the committee will release a brief public statement about its decisions on the day they are made. But not even the president of the United States knows the details behind the decisions, or what the FOMC actually discussed at its meeting, until the summary of the meeting is finally released. The reason for the word "open" is that the committee controls the nation's money supply by buying and selling bonds in the public ("open") bond market. Later, we will discuss how and why the FOMC does this.

2 Only five of the 12 presidents can vote on FOMC decisions. The president of the Federal Reserve Bank of New York has a permanent vote, because New York is such an important financial center. But the remaining four votes rotate among the other district presidents.

The Functions of the Federal Reserve

The Federal Reserve, as the overseer of the nation's monetary system, has a variety of important responsibilities. Some of the most important are:

Supervising and Regulating Banks. We've already seen that the Fed sets and enforces reserve requirements, which all banks—not just Fed members—must obey. The Fed also sets standards for establishing new banks, determines what sorts of loans and investments banks are allowed to make, and closely monitors banks' financial activities.

Acting as a "Bank for Banks." In many ways, commercial banks use the Fed in much the same way that ordinary citizens use commercial banks. For example, we've already seen that banks hold most of their reserves in reserve accounts with the Fed. In addition, banks can borrow from the Fed, just as we can borrow from our local bank. The Fed charges a special interest rate, called the **discount rate,** on loans that it makes to member banks. In times of financial crisis, the Fed is prepared to act as *lender of last resort,* to make sure that banks have enough reserves to meet their obligations to depositors.

Issuing Paper Currency. The Fed doesn't actually *print* currency; that is done by the government's Bureau of Engraving and Printing. But once printed, it is shipped to the Fed (under *very* heavy guard). The Fed, in turn, puts this currency into circulation. This is why every U.S. bill carries the label *Federal Reserve Note* on the top.

Check Clearing. Suppose you write a check for $500 to pay your rent. Your building's owner will deposit the check into *his* checking account, which is probably at a different bank than yours. Somehow, your rent payment must be transferred from your bank account to your landlord's account at the other bank—a process called *check clearing.* In some cases, the services are provided by private clearinghouses. But in many other cases—especially for clearing out-of-town checks—the Federal Reserve system performs the service by transferring funds from one bank's reserve account to another's.

Controlling the Money Supply. The Fed, as the nation's monetary authority, is responsible for controlling the money supply. Since this function is so important in macroeconomics, we explore it in detail in the next section.

Name:
Federal Reserve Bank of New York
Description:
One of 12 regional Reserve Banks that comprise the Federal Reserve System
Resources:
The Federal Reserve Bank of New York engages in currency market transactions on behalf of U.S. monetary authorities and its own customers (foreign central banks and international agencies). The New York Fed provides a wealth of data, publications, and educational materials.
Address:
http://www.ny.frb.org/

THE FED AND THE MONEY SUPPLY

Discount rate The interest rate the Fed charges on loans to banks.

Suppose the Fed wants to change the nation's money supply. (*Why* might the Fed want to do this? The answer will have to wait until the next chapter.) There are many ways this could be done. To increase the money supply, the Fed could print up currency and give it to Fed officials, letting them spend it as they wish. Or it could hold a lottery and give all of the newly printed money to the winner. To decrease the money supply, the Fed could require that all citizens turn over a portion of their cash to Fed officials who would then feed it into paper shredders.

These and other methods would certainly work, but they hardly seem fair or orderly. In practice, the Fed uses a more organized, less haphazard method to change the money supply: *open market operations.*

OPEN MARKET OPERATIONS Purchases or sales of bonds by the Federal Reserve System.

When the Fed wishes to increase or decrease the money supply, it buys or sells government bonds *to bond dealers, banks, or other financial institutions. These actions are called* ***open market operations.***

We'll make two special assumptions to keep our analysis of open market operations simple for now.

1. Households and businesses are satisfied holding the amount of cash they are currently holding. Any additional funds they might acquire are deposited in their checking accounts. Any decrease in their funds comes from their checking accounts.
2. Banks never hold reserves in excess of those legally required by law.

Later, we'll discuss what happens when these simplifying assumptions do not hold. We'll also assume that the required reserve ratio is 0.1, so that each time deposits rise by $1,000 at a bank, its required reserves rise by $100.

HOW THE FED INCREASES THE MONEY SUPPLY

To increase the money supply, the Fed will *buy* government bonds. This is called an *open market purchase.* Suppose the Fed buys a government bond worth $1,000 from a bond dealer, Salomon Brothers, that has a checking account at First National Bank.[3] The Fed will pay Salomon Brothers with a $1,000 check, which the firm will deposit into its account at First National. First National, in turn, will send the check to the Fed, which will credit First National's reserve account by $1,000.

These actions will change First National's balance sheet as follows:

CHANGES IN FIRST NATIONAL BANK'S BALANCE SHEET

Action	Changes in Assets	Changes in Liabilities
Fed buys $1,000 bond from Salomon Brothers, which deposits $1,000 check from Fed into its checking account:	**+$1,000 in reserves**	**+$1,000 in demand deposits**

Notice that here we show only *changes* in First National's balance sheet. Other balance-sheet items—such as property and buildings, loans, government bonds, or net worth—are not immediately affected by the open market purchase, so they are not listed here. As you can see, First National gains an asset—reserves—so we enter "+$1,000 in reserves" on the left side of the table. But there are also additional liabilities—the $1,000 that is now in Salomon Brothers' checking account and which First National owes to that firm. The additional liabilities are represented by the entry "+$1,000 in demand deposits" on the right side. Since First National's balance sheet was in balance before Salomon Brothers' deposit, and since assets and liabilities both grew by the same amount—$1,000—we know that the balance sheet is still in balance. Total assets are again equal to total liabilities plus net worth.

Before we go on, let's take note of two important things that have happened. First, the Fed, by conducting an open market purchase, has injected *reserves* into

3 We'll limit our analysis to commercial banks, which hold demand deposits, although our story would be similar if other types of depository institutions were involved.

the banking system. So far, these reserves are being held by First National, in its reserve account with the Fed.

The second thing to notice is something that is easy to miss: *The money supply has increased.* How do we know? Because demand deposits are part of the money supply, and they have increased by $1,000. As you are about to see, even more demand deposits will be created before our story ends.

To see what will happen next, let's take the point of view of First National Bank's manager. He might reason as follows: "My demand deposits have just increased by $1,000. Since the required reserve ratio is 0.1, I must now hold 0.1 × $1,000 = $100 in additional reserves. But my *actual* reserves have gone up by more than $100; in fact, they have gone up by $1,000. Therefore I have **excess reserves**—reserves above those I'm legally required to hold—equal to $1,000 − $100, or $900. Since these excess reserves are earning no interest, I should lend them out." Thus, we can expect First National, in its search for profit, to lend out $900 at the going rate of interest.

EXCESS RESERVES Reserves in excess of required reserves.

How will First National actually make the loan? It could lend out $900 in *cash* from its vault. It would be more typical, however, for the bank to issue a $900 *check* to the borrower. When the borrower deposits the $900 check into his own bank account (at some other bank), the Federal Reserve—which keeps track of these transactions for the banking system—will deduct $900 from First National's reserve account and transfer it to the other bank's reserve account. This will cause a further change in First National's balance sheet, as follows:

CHANGES IN FIRST NATIONAL BANK'S BALANCE SHEET

Action	Changes in Assets	Changes in Liabilities
Fed buys $1,000 bond from Salomon Brothers, which deposits $1,000 check from Fed into its checking account:	+$1,000 in reserves	+$1,000 in demand deposits
First National lends out $900 in excess reserves:	**−$ 900 in reserves** **+$ 900 in loans**	
The total effect on First National from beginning to end:	+$ 100 in reserves +$ 900 in loans	+$1,000 in demand deposits

Look at the boldface entries in the table. By making the loan, First National has given up an asset—$900 in reserves. This causes assets to change by −$900. But First National also gains an asset of equal value—the $900 loan. (Remember: while loans are liabilities to the borrower, they are assets to banks.) This causes assets to change by +$900. Both of these changes are seen on the assets side of the balance sheet.

Now look at the bottom row of the table. This tells us what has happened to First National from beginning to end. We see that, after making its loan, First National has $100 more in reserves than it started with, and $900 more in loans, for a total of $1,000 more in assets. But it also has $1,000 more in liabilities than it had before—the additional demand deposits that it owes to Salomon Brothers. Both assets and liabilities have gone up by the same amount. Notice, too, that First National is once again holding exactly the reserves it must legally hold. It now has $1,000 more in demand deposits than it had before, and it is holding $0.1 \times \$1{,}000 = \$100$ more in reserves than before. First National is finished ("loaned up") and cannot lend out any more reserves.

But there is still more to our story. Let's suppose that First National lends the $900 to the owner of a local business, Paula's Pizza, and that Paula deposits her loan check into *her* bank account at Second Federal Bank. Then, remembering that the Fed will transfer $900 in reserves from First National's reserve account to that of Second Federal, we'll see the following changes in Second Federal's balance sheet:

CHANGES IN SECOND FEDERAL'S BALANCE SHEET

Action	Changes in Assets	Changes in Liabilities
Paula deposits $900 loan check into her checking account:	**+$900 in reserves**	**+$900 in demand deposits**

Second Federal now has $900 more in assets—the increase in its reserve account with the Federal Reserve—and $900 in additional liabilities—the amount added to Paula's checking account.

Now consider Second Federal's situation from its manager's viewpoint. He reasons as follows: "My demand deposits have risen by $900, which means my required reserves have risen by $0.1 \times \$900 = \$90$. But my reserves have *actually* increased by $900. Thus, I have *excess reserves* of $\$900 - \$90 = \$810$, which I will lend out." After making the $810 loan, Second Federal's balance sheet will change once again (look at the boldface entries):

CHANGES IN SECOND FEDERAL'S BALANCE SHEET

Action	Changes in Assets	Changes in Liabilities
Paula deposits $900 loan check into her checking account:	+$900 in reserves	+$900 in demand deposits
Second Federal lends out $810 in excess reserves:	**−$810 in reserves** **+$810 in loans**	
The total effect on Second Federal from beginning to end:	+$ 90 in reserves +$810 in loans	+$900 in demand deposits

In the end, as you can see in the bottom row of the table, Second Federal has $90 more in reserves than it started with, and $810 more in loans. Its demand deposit liabilities have increased by $900. Notice, too, that demand deposits have increased once again—this time, by $900.

Are you starting to see a pattern? Let's carry it through one more step. Whoever borrowed the $810 from Second Federal will put it into his or her checking account at, say, Third State Bank. This will give Third State excess reserves that it will lend out. As a result, its balance sheet will change as shown at the top of the next page:

CHANGES IN THIRD STATE'S BALANCE SHEET

Action	Changes in Assets	Changes in Liabilities
Borrower from Second Federal deposits $810 loan check into checking account	**+$810 in reserves**	**+$810 in demand deposits**
Third State lends out $729 in excess reserves:	**−$729 in reserves** **+$729 in loans**	
The total effect on Third State from beginning to end:	+$ 81 in reserves +$729 in loans	+$810 in demand deposits

As you can see, demand deposits increase each time a bank lends out excess reserves. In the end, they will increase by a *multiple* of the original $1,000 in reserves injected into the banking system by the open market purchase. Does this process sound familiar? It should. It is very similar to the explanation of the *expenditure multiplier* in the previous chapter, where in each round, an increase in spending led to an increase in income, which caused spending to increase again in the next round. Here, instead of spending, it is the *money supply*—or more specifically, *demand deposits*—that increase in each round.

THE DEMAND DEPOSIT MULTIPLIER

By how much will demand deposits increase in total? If you look back at the balance sheet changes we've analyzed, you'll see each bank creates less in demand deposits than the bank before. When Salomon Brothers deposited its $1,000 check from the Fed at First National, $1,000 in demand deposits was created. This led to an additional $900 in demand deposits created by Second Federal, another $810 created by Third State, and so on. In each round, a bank lent 90 percent of the deposit it received. Eventually the additional demand deposits will become so small that we can safely ignore them. When the process is complete, how much in additional demand deposits have been created?

Table 2 provides the answer. Each row of the table shows the additional demand deposits created at each bank, as well as the running total. The last row shows that, in the end, $10,000 in new demand deposits has been created.

Let's go back and summarize what happened in our example. The Fed, through its open market purchase, injected $1,000 in reserves into the banking system. As a result, demand deposits rose by $10,000—10 times the injection in reserves. As you can verify, if the Fed had injected twice the amount of reserves ($2,000), demand deposits would have increased by 10 times *that* amount ($20,000). In fact, *whatever* the injection of reserves, demand deposits will increase by a factor of 10, so we can write:

$$\Delta DD = 10 \times \text{reserve injection}$$

where "*DD*" stands for demand deposits. The injection of reserves must be *multiplied by* the number 10 in order to get the change in demand deposits that it causes. For this reason, 10 is called the *demand deposit multiplier* in this example.

DEMAND DEPOSIT MULTIPLIER The number by which a change in reserves is multiplied to determine the resulting change in demand deposits.

*The **demand deposit multiplier** is the number by which we must multiply the injection of reserves to get the total change in demand deposits.*

TABLE 2

CUMULATIVE INCREASES IN DEMAND DEPOSITS AFTER A $1,000 CASH DEPOSIT

Round	Additional Demand Deposits Created by This Bank	Additional Demand Deposits Created by All Banks
First National Bank	$1,000	$ 1,000
Second Federal	$ 900	$ 1,900
Third State	$ 810	$ 2,710
Bank 4	$ 729	$ 3,439
Bank 5	$ 656	$ 4,095
Bank 6	$ 590	$ 4,685
Bank 7	$ 531	$ 5,216
Bank 8	$ 478	$ 5,694
Bank 9	$ 430	$ 6,124
Bank 10	$ 387	$ 6,511
Bank 11	$ 349	$ 6,860
Bank 12	$ 314	$ 7,174
. . .		
All Other Banks	very close to $2,826	
Total		$10,000

The size of the demand deposit multiplier depends on the value of the required reserve ratio set by the Fed. If you look back at Table 2, you will see that each round of additional deposit creation would have been smaller if the required reserve ratio had been larger. For example, with a required reserve ratio of 0.2 instead of 0.1, Second Federal would have created only $800 billion in deposits, Third State would have created only $640, and so on. The result would have been a smaller cumulative change in deposits, and a smaller multiplier.

Now let's derive the formula we can use to determine the demand deposit multiplier for *any* required reserve ratio. We'll start with our example in which the required reserve ratio is 0.1. If $1,000 in reserves are injected into the system, the total change in deposits can be written as follows:

$$\Delta DD = \$1{,}000 + \$900 + \$810 + \$729 + \ldots$$

Factoring out $1,000, this becomes:

$$\Delta DD = \$1{,}000 \times [1 + 0.9 + 0.9^2 + 0.9^3 + \ldots]$$

In this equation, $1,000 billion is the initial injection of reserves (ΔReserves), and 0.9 is the fraction of reserves that each bank loans out, which is 1 minus the required reserve ratio ($1 - 0.1 = 0.9$). To find the change in deposits that applies to *any* change in reserves and *any* required reserve ratio (*RRR*), we can write:

$$\Delta DD = \Delta\text{Reserves} \times [1 + (1 - RRR) + (1 - RRR)^2 + (1 - RRR)^3 + \ldots]$$

Now we can see that the term in brackets—the infinite sum $1 + (1 - RRR) + (1 - RRR)^2 + (1 - RRR)^3 + \ldots$—is our demand deposit multiplier. But what is its value?

From the mathematical appendix at the back of this book, we know that an infinite sum

$$1 + H + H^2 + H^3 + \ldots$$

always has the value $1/(1 - H)$ as long as H is a fraction between zero and 1. Replacing H with $1 - RRR$—which is always between zero and 1—we obtain a value for the deposit multiplier of $1/([1 - (1 - RRR)] = 1/RRR$.

*For any value of the required reserve ratio (*RRR*), the formula for the demand deposit multiplier is 1/*RRR.

In our example, the RRR was equal to 0.1, so the deposit multiplier had the value $1/0.1 = 10$. If the RRR had been 0.2 instead, the deposit multiplier would have been equal to $1/0.2 = 5$.

Using our general formula for the demand deposit multiplier, we can restate what happens when the Fed injects reserves into the banking system as follows:

$$\Delta DD = (1/RRR) \times \Delta\text{Reserves}$$

Since we've been assuming that the amount of cash in the hands of the public (the other component of the money supply) does not change, we can also write:

$$\Delta\text{Money Supply} = (1/RRR) \times \Delta\text{Reserves}$$

The Fed's Effect on the Banking System as a Whole

We can also look at what happened to total demand deposits and the money supply from another perspective. When the Fed bought the $1,000 bond from Salomon Brothers, it injected $1,000 in reserves into the banking system. That was the only increase in reserves that occurred in our story. Where did the additional $1,000 in reserves end up? If you go back through the changes in balance sheets, you'll see that First National ended up with $100 in additional reserves, Second Federal ended up with $90, Third Savings with $81, and so on. Each of these banks is required to hold more reserves than initially, because its demand deposits have increased. In the end, *the additional $1,000 in reserves is distributed among different banks in the system as required reserves.*

This observation helps us understand the demand deposit multiplier in another way. The deposit-creation process will continue as long as any bank has excess reserves, and it ends only when the entire injection of $1,000 becomes required reserves. But with a RRR of 0.1, each dollar of reserves entitles a bank to have $10 in demand deposits. Therefore, by injecting $1,000 of reserves into the system, the Fed has enabled banks, in total, to hold $10,000 in additional demand deposits. Only when $10,000 in deposits have been created will the process come to an end.

Just as we've looked at balance sheet changes for each bank, we can also look at the change in the balance sheet of the *entire banking system.* The Fed's open market purchase of $1,000 has caused the following changes:

Changes in the Balance Sheet of the Entire Banking System

Changes in Assets	Changes in Liabilities
+$1,000 in reserves +$9,000 in loans	+$10,000 in demand deposits

In the end, total reserves in the system have increased by $1,000—the amount of the open market purchase. Each dollar in reserves supports $10 in demand deposits, so we know that total deposits have increased by $10,000. Finally, we know that a balance sheet always balances. Since liabilities increased by $10,000, loans must have increased by $9,000 to increase total assets (loans and reserves) by $10,000.

DANGEROUS CURVES

Demand deposits are a means of payment, and banks create them. This is why we say that banks "create deposits" and "create money." But don't fall into the trap of thinking that banks create *wealth.* No one gains any additional wealth as a result of money creation.

To see why, think about what happened in our story when Salomon Brothers deposited the $1,000 check from the Fed into its account at First National. *Salomon Brothers* was no wealthier: It gave up a $1,000 check from the Fed and ended up with $1,000 more in its checking account, for a net gain of zero. Similarly, the *bank* gained no additional wealth: It had $1,000 more in cash, but it also *owed* Salomon Brothers $1,000—once again, a net gain of zero.

The same conclusion holds for any other step in the money-creation process. When Paula borrows $900 and deposits it into her checking account at Second Federal, she is no wealthier: She has $900 more in her account, but owes $900 to First National. And once again, the bank is no wealthier: It has $900 more in demand deposits, but owes this money to Paula.

Always remember that while banks can "create money," they cannot create wealth.

HOW THE FED DECREASES THE MONEY SUPPLY

Just as the Fed can increase the money supply by purchasing government bonds, it can also *decrease* the money supply by *selling* government bonds—an *open market sale.*

Where does the Fed get the government bonds to sell? It has trillions of dollars worth of government bonds from open market *purchases* it has conducted in the past. Since, on average, the Fed tends to increase the money supply each year, it conducts more open market purchases than open market sales, and its stock of bonds keeps growing. So we needn't worry that the Fed will run out of bonds to sell.

Suppose the Fed sells a $1,000 government bond to a bond dealer, Merrill Lynch, which—like Salomon Brothers in our earlier example—has a checking account at First National Bank. Merrill Lynch pays the Fed for the bond with a $1,000 check drawn on its account at First National. When the Fed gets Merrill Lynch's check, it will present the check to First National and deduct $1,000 from First National's reserve account. In turn, First National will deduct $1,000 from Merrill Lynch's checking account.

After all of this has taken place, First National's balance sheet will show the following changes:

CHANGES IN FIRST NATIONAL BANK'S BALANCE SHEET

Action	Changes in Assets	Changes in Liabilities
Fed sells $1,000 bond to Merrill Lynch, which pays with a $1,000 check drawn on First National:	**−$1,000 in reserves**	**−$1,000 in demand deposits**

Now First National has a problem. Since its demand deposits have decreased by $1,000, it can legally decrease its reserves by 10 percent of that, or $100. But its reserves have *actually* decreased by $1,000, which is $900 more than they are allowed to decrease. First National has *deficient reserves*—reserves smaller than those it is legally required to hold. How can it get the additional reserves it needs?

First National will have to *call in a loan*—that is, ask for repayment—in the amount of $900.[4] A loan is usually repaid with a check drawn on some other bank. When First National gets this check, the Federal Reserve will add $900 to its reserve account, and deduct $900 from the reserve account at the other bank. This is how First National brings its reserves up to the legal requirement. After it calls in the $900 loan, First National's balance sheet will change as follows:

CHANGES IN FIRST NATIONAL BANK'S BALANCE SHEET

Action	Changes in Assets	Changes in Liabilities
Fed sells $1,000 bond to Merrill Lynch, which pays with a $1,000 check drawn on First National:	−$1,000 in reserves	−$1,000 in demand deposits
First National calls in loans worth $900:	**+$ 900 in reserves** **−$ 900 in loans**	
The total effect on First National from beginning to end:	−$ 100 reserves −$ 900 in loans	−$1,000 in demand deposits

Look at the boldfaced terms. After First National calls in the loan, the composition of its assets will change: $900 more in reserves, and $900 less in loans. The last row of the table shows the changes to First National's balance sheet from beginning to end. Compared to its initial situation, First National has $100 less in reserves (it lost $1,000 and then gained $900), $900 less in loans, and $1,000 less in demand deposits.

As you might guess, this is not the end of the story. Remember that whoever paid back the loan to First National did so by a check drawn on another bank. That other bank, which we'll call Bank 2, will lose $900 in reserves and experience the following changes in its balance sheet:

CHANGES IN BANK 2'S BALANCE SHEET

Action	Changes in Assets	Changes in Liabilities
Someone with an account at Bank 2 writes a $900 check to First National:	−$900 in reserves	−$900 in Demand Deposits

Now Bank 2 is in the same fix that First National was in. Its demand deposits have decreased by $900, so its reserves can legally fall by $90. However, its actual reserves have decreased by $900—which is $810 too much. Now it is Bank 2's turn to call in a loan. (On your own, fill in the rest of the changes in Bank 2's balance sheet as it successfully brings its reserves up to the legal requirement.)

4 In reality, bank loans are for specified time periods, and a bank cannot actually demand that a loan be repaid early. But most banks have a large volume of loans outstanding, with some being repaid each day. Typically, the funds will be lent out again the very same day they are repaid. But a bank that needs additional reserves will simply reduce its rate of new lending on that day, thereby reducing its total amount of loans outstanding. This has the same effect as "calling in a loan."

DANGEROUS CURVES

In this section, you learned how the Fed sells government bonds to decrease the money supply. It's easy to confuse this with another type of government bond sale, which is done by the U.S. Treasury.

The U.S. Treasury is the branch of government that collects tax revenue, disburses money for government purchases and transfer payments, and borrows money to finance the government's budget deficit. The Treasury borrows funds by issuing *new* government bonds and selling them to the public—to banks, other financial institutions, and bond dealers. What the public pays for these bonds is what they are lending the government.

When the Fed conducts open market operations, however, it does not buy or sell *newly* issued bonds, but "second-hand bonds"—those already issued by the Treasury to finance the deficit. Thus, open market sales are *not* government borrowing; they are strictly an operation designed to change the money supply, and they have no direct effect on the government budget.

As you can see, the process of calling in loans will involve many banks. Each time a bank calls in a loan, demand deposits are destroyed—the same amount as were created in our earlier story, in which each bank *made* a new loan. The total decline in demand deposits will be a multiple of the initial withdrawal of reserves. Keeping in mind that a withdrawal of reserves is a *negative change in reserves,* we can still use our demand deposit multiplier—$1/(RRR)$—and our general formula:

$$\Delta DD = (1/RRR) \times \Delta\text{Reserves}$$

Applying it to our example, we have:

$$\Delta DD = [1/0.1] \times (-\$1{,}000) = -\$10{,}000$$

In words, the Fed's $1,000 open market sale causes a $10,000 decrease in demand deposits. Since we assume that the public's cash holdings do not change, the money supply decreases by $10,000 as well.

To the banking system as a whole, the Fed's bond sale has done the following:

CHANGES IN BALANCE SHEET FOR THE ENTIRE BANKING SYSTEM

Changes in Assets	Changes in Liabilities
−$1,000 in reserves	−$10,000 in demand deposits
−$9,000 in loans	

SOME IMPORTANT PROVISOS ABOUT THE DEMAND DEPOSIT MULTIPLIER

Although the process of money creation and destruction as we've described it illustrates the basic ideas, our formula for the demand deposit multiplier—$1/RRR$—is oversimplified. In reality, the multiplier is likely to be smaller than our formula suggests, for two reasons.

First, we've assumed that as the money supply changes, the public does *not* change its holdings of cash. But as the money supply increases, the public typically will want to hold part of the increase as demand deposits, and part of the increase as cash. As a result, in each round of the deposit-creation process, some reserves will be *withdrawn* in the form of cash. This will lead to a smaller increase in demand deposits than in our story.

Second, we've assumed that banks will always lend out all of their excess reserves. In reality, banks often *want* to hold excess reserves, for a variety of reasons.

For example, they may want some flexibility to increase their loans in case interest rates—their reward for lending—rise in the near future. Or they may prefer not to lend the maximum legal amount during a recession, because borrowers are more likely to declare bankruptcy and not repay their loans. If banks increase their holdings of excess reserves as the money supply expands, they will make smaller loans than in our story, and in each round, demand deposit creation will be smaller.

OTHER TOOLS FOR CONTROLLING THE MONEY SUPPLY

Open market operations are the Fed's primary means of controlling the money supply. But there are two other tools that the Fed can use to increase or decrease the money supply.

- *Changes in the required reserve ratio.* In theory, the Fed can set off the process of deposit creation, similar to that described earlier, by lowering the required reserve ratio. Look back at Table 1, which showed the balance sheet of a bank facing a required reserve ratio of 0.1 and holding exactly the amount of reserves required by law—$10 million. Now suppose the Fed lowered the required reserve ratio to 0.05. Suddenly, the bank would find that its required reserves were only $5 million; the other $5 million in reserves it holds would become excess reserves. To earn the highest profit possible, the bank would increase its lending by $5 million. At the same time, all other banks in the country would find that some of their formerly required reserves were now excess reserves, and they would increase their lending. The money supply would increase.

  On the other side, if the Fed *raised* the required reserve ratio, the process would work in reverse: All banks would suddenly have reserve deficiencies and be forced to call in loans. The money supply would decrease.
- *Changes in the discount rate.* The discount rate, mentioned earlier, is the rate the Fed charges banks when it lends them reserves. In principle, a lower discount rate—enabling banks to borrow reserves from the Fed more cheaply—might encourage banks to borrow more. An increase in borrowed reserves works just like any other injection of reserves into the banking system: It increases the money supply.

  On the other side, a rise in the discount rate would make it more expensive for banks to borrow from the Fed, and decrease the amount of borrowed reserves in the system. This withdrawal of reserves from the banking system would lead to a decrease in the money supply.

Changes in either the required reserve ratio or the discount rate *could* set off the process of deposit creation or deposit destruction in much the same way outlined in this chapter. In reality, neither of these policy tools is used very often. The most recent change in the required reserve ratio was in April 1992, when the Fed lowered the required reserve ratio for most demand deposits from 12 percent to 10 percent. Changes in the discount rate are more frequent, but it is not unusual for the Fed to leave the discount rate unchanged for a year or more.

Why are these other tools used so seldom? Part of the reason is that they can have such unpredictable effects. When the required reserve ratio changes, all banks in the system are affected simultaneously. Even a tiny error in predicting how a typical bank will respond can translate into a huge difference for the money supply.

A change in the discount rate has uncertain effects as well. Many bank managers do not like to borrow reserves from the Fed, since it puts them under closer Fed scrutiny. And the Fed discourages borrowing of reserves unless the bank is in difficulty. Thus, a small change in the discount rate is unlikely to have much of an impact on bank borrowing of reserves, and therefore on the money supply.

Open market operations, by contrast, have more predictable impacts on the money supply. They can be fine-tuned to any level desired. Another advantage is that they are covert. No one knows exactly what the FOMC decided to do to the money supply at its last meeting. And no one knows whether it is conducting more open market purchases or more open market sales on any given day (it always does a certain amount of both to keep bond traders guessing). By maintaining secrecy, the Fed can often change its policies without destabilizing financial markets, and also avoid the pressure that Congress or the president might bring to bear if its policies are not popular.

While other tools can affect the money supply, open market operations have two advantages over them: precision and secrecy. This is why open market operations remain the Fed's primary means of changing the money supply.

The Fed's ability to conduct its policies in secret—and its independent status in general—is controversial. Some argue that secrecy and independence are needed so that the Fed can do what is best for the country—keeping the price level stable—without undue pressure from Congress or the president. Others argue that there is something fundamentally undemocratic about an independent Federal Reserve, whose governors are not elected and who can, to some extent, ignore the popular will. In recent years because the Fed has been so successful in guiding the economy, the controversy has largely subsided.

USING THE THEORY

BANK FAILURES AND BANKING PANICS

A bank failure occurs when a bank is unable to meet the requests of its depositors to withdraw their funds. Typically, the failure occurs when depositors begin to worry about the bank's financial health. They may believe that their bank has made unsound loans that will not be repaid, so that it does not have enough assets to cover its demand deposit liabilities. In that case, everyone will want to be first in line to withdraw cash, since banks meet requests for withdrawals on a first-come, first-served basis. Those who wait may not be able to get any cash at all. This can lead to a **run on the bank,** with everyone trying to withdraw funds simultaneously.

RUN ON THE BANK An attempt by many of a bank's depositors to withdraw their funds.

Ironically, a bank can fail even if it is in good financial health, with more than enough assets to cover its liabilities, just because people think the bank is in trouble. Why should a false rumor be a problem for the bank? Because many of its assets are illiquid, such as long-term loans. These cannot be sold easily or quickly enough to meet the unusual demands for withdrawal during a run on the bank.

For example, look back at Table 1, which shows a healthy bank with more assets than liabilities. But notice that the bank has only $2 million in vault cash. Under normal circumstances, that would be more than enough to cover a day of heavy withdrawals. But suppose that depositors hear a rumor that the bank has made many bad loans, and they want to withdraw $40 million. The bank would soon exhaust its $2 million in cash. It could then ask the Federal Reserve for more cash, using the $8 million in its reserve account, and the Fed would likely respond quickly, perhaps even delivering the cash the same day. The bank could also sell its $25 million in government bonds and obtain more cash within a few days. But all together, this will give the bank only $35 million with which to honor requests for withdrawals. What then? Unless the bank is lucky enough to have many of its long-term loans coming due that week, it will be unable to meet its depositors' requests for cash. A false rumor can cause a bank to fail.

A **banking panic** occurs when many banks fail simultaneously. In the past, a typical panic would begin with some unexpected event, such as the failure of a large bank. During recessions, for example, many businesses go bankrupt, so fewer bank loans are repaid. A bank that had an unusual number of "bad loans" would be in trouble, and if the public found out about this, there might be a run on that bank. The bank would fail, and many depositors would find that they had lost their deposits.

BANKING PANIC A situation in which depositors attempt to withdraw funds from many banks simultaneously.

But that would not be the end of the story. Hearing that their neighbors lost their deposits might lead others to question the health of their own banks. Just to be sure, they might withdraw their own funds, preferring to ride out the storm and keep their cash at home. As we've seen, even healthy banks can fail under the pressure of a bank run. They, too, would have to close their doors, stoking the rumor mill even more, and so on.

Banking panics can cause serious problems for the nation. Besides the hardship suffered by people who lose their accounts when their bank fails, there is another problem: The withdrawal of cash—even when banks do not fail—decreases the banking system's reserves. As we've seen, the withdrawal of reserves leads—through the demand deposit multiplier—to a larger decrease in the money supply. In the next chapter, you will learn that a decrease in the money supply can cause a recession. In a banking panic, the money supply can decrease suddenly and severely, causing a serious recession.

There were five major banking panics in the United States from 1863 to 1907. Indeed, it was the banking panic of 1907 that convinced Congress to establish the Federal Reserve System. From the beginning, one of the Fed's primary functions was to act as a lender of last resort, providing banks with enough cash to meet their obligations to depositors.

But the creation of the Fed did not, in itself, solve the problem. Figure 4 shows the number of bank failures each year since 1920. As you can see, banking panics continued to plague the financial system even after the Fed was created. The Fed did not always act forcefully enough or quickly enough to prevent the panic from spreading.

The Great Depression is a good example of this problem. In late 1929 and 1930, many banks began to fail because of bad loans. Then, from October 1930 until March 1933, more than one-third of all banks failed as frantic depositors stormed bank after bank, demanding to withdraw their funds—even from banks that were in reasonable financial health. Many economists believe that the banking panic of 1930–1933 turned what would have been just a serious recession into the Great Depression. Officials of the Federal Reserve System, not quite grasping the seriousness of the problem, stood by and let it happen.[5]

As you can see in Figure 4, banking panics were largely eliminated after 1933. Indeed, except for the moderate increase in failures during the late 1980s and early 1990s, the system has been almost failure free. Why the dramatic improvement?

Largely for two reasons. First, the Federal Reserve learned an important lesson from the Great Depression, and it now stands ready to inject reserves into the sys-

5 Milton Friedman and Anna Jacobson Schwartz, *A Monetary History of the United States, 1867–1960* (Princeton University Press, 1963), especially p. 358.

FIGURE 4

BANK FAILURES IN THE UNITED STATES, 1920–

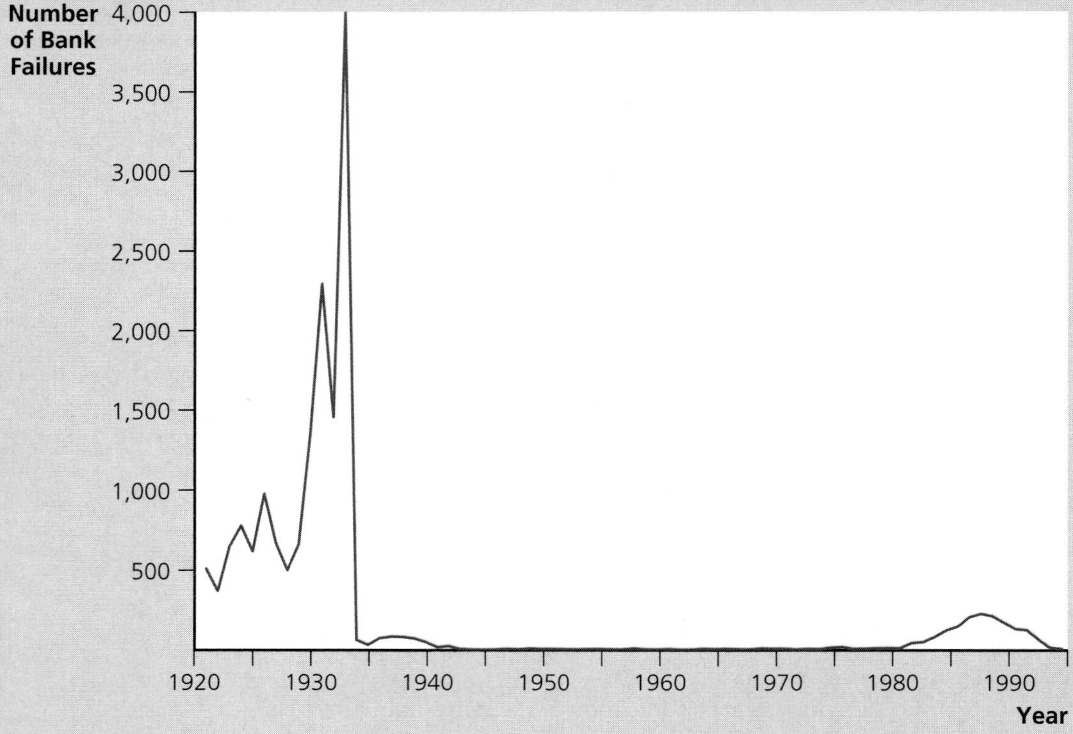

Bank failures continued after the Fed was created in 1913. During the Great Depression, a large number of banks failed. The Fed learned a hard lesson: It needed to inject reserves into the banking system whenever a crisis threatened. The creation of the Federal Deposit Insurance Corporation in 1933 also strengthened faith in the stability of the banking system. Few banks have failed since that time.

tem more quickly in a crisis. Moreover, in 1933 Congress created the Federal Deposit Insurance Corporation (FDIC) to reimburse those who lose their deposits. If your bank is insured by the FDIC (today, accounts are covered in 99 percent of all banks) and cannot honor its obligations for any reason—bad loans, poor management, or even theft—the FDIC will reimburse you up to the first $100,000 you lose. (If you have more than $100,000 in a bank account, you are not insured for the amount over $100,000.)

The FDIC has had a major impact on the psychology of the banking public. Imagine that you hear your bank is about to go under. As long as you have less than $100,000 in your account, you will not care. Why? Because even if the rumor turns out to be true, you will be reimbursed in full. The resulting calmness on your part, and on the part of other depositors, will prevent a run on the bank. This makes it very unlikely that bank failures will spread throughout the system.

FDIC protection for bank accounts has not been costless. Banks must pay insurance premiums to the FDIC, and they pass this cost on to their depositors and borrowers by charging higher interest rates on loans and higher fees for their services. And there is a more serious cost. If you are thoroughly protected in the event of a bank failure, your bank's managers have little incentive to develop a reputation for prudence in lending funds, since you will be happy to deposit your money there anyway. Without government regulations, banks could act irresponsibly, taking great risks with your money, and you would remain indifferent. Many more banks would fail, the FDIC would have to pay off more depositors, and banks—and their customers—would bear the burden of higher FDIC premiums. This is the logic behind the Fed's continuing regulation of bank lending. Someone must watch over the banks to keep the failure rate low, and if the public has no incentive to pay attention, the Fed must do so. Most economists believe that if we want the freedom from banking panics provided by the FDIC, we must also accept the strict regulation and close monitoring of banks provided by the Fed.

Look again at Figure 4 and notice the temporary rise in bank failures of the late 1980s and the early 1990s. Most of these failures occurred in state-chartered banks, which are less closely regulated by the Fed, and are often insured by state agencies instead of the FDIC. When a few banks failed because highly speculative loans turned sour, insurance funds in several states were drained. Citizens in those states began to fear that insufficient funds were left to insure their own deposits, and the psychology of banking panics took over. To many observers, the experience of the late 1980s and early 1990s was a reminder of the need for a sound insurance system and close monitoring of the banking system.

SUMMARY

In the United States, the standard measure of money—M1—includes currency, checking account balances, and travelers' checks. Each of these assets is liquid and widely acceptable as a means of payment. Other, broader measures go beyond M1 to include funds in savings accounts and time deposits.

The amount of money in the economy is controlled by the Federal Reserve, operating through the banking system. Banks and other financial intermediaries are profit-seeking firms that collect loanable funds from households and businesses, then repackage them to make loans to other households, businesses, and governmental agencies,

The Federal Reserve injects money into the economy by altering banks' balance sheets. In a balance sheet, assets always equal liabilities plus net worth. One important kind of asset is *reserves*—funds that banks are required to hold in proportion to their demand deposit liabilities. When the Fed wants to increase the money supply, it buys bonds in the open market and pays for them with a check. This is called an *open market purchase.* When the Fed's check is deposited in a bank, the bank's balance sheet changes. On the asset side, reserves increase; on the liabilities side, demand deposits (a form of money) also increase. The bank can lend some of the reserves, and the money loaned will end up in some other banks where it supports creation of still more demand deposits. Eventually, demand deposits, and the M1 money supply, increase by some multiple of the original injection of reserves by the Fed. The *demand deposit multiplier*—the inverse of the required reserve ratio—gives us that multiple.

The Fed can decrease the money supply by selling government bonds—an open market sale—causing demand deposits to shrink by a multiple of the initial reduction in reserves. The Fed can also change the money supply by changing either the required reserve ratio or the discount rate it charges when it lends reserves to banks.

KEY TERMS

liquidity
cash in the hand of the public
demand deposits
M1
M2
financial intermediary
balance sheet
bond
loan
reserves
required reserves
required reserve ratio
net worth
central bank
Federal Open Market Committee
discount rate
open market operations
excess reserves
demand deposit multiplier
run on the bank
banking panic

REVIEW QUESTIONS

1. Describe the main characteristics of money. What purpose does money serve in present-day economies?

2. Which of the following is considered part of the U.S. money supply?
   a. A $10 bill you carry in your wallet
   b. A $100 travelers' check you bought but did not use
   c. A $100 bill in a bank teller's till
   d. The $325.43 balance in your checking account
   e. A share of General Motors stock worth $40

3. Given the following data, calculate the value of the M1 money supply (the data are in billions of dollars):

Bank reserves	50
Cash in the hands of the public	400
Demand deposits	400
Noninstitutional MMMF balances	880
Other checkable deposits	250
Savings-type account balances	1,300
Small time deposits	950
Travelers' checks	10

4. What is a depository institution? Give an example of each of the four types of depository institutions.

5. What are reserves? What determines the amount of reserves that a bank holds? Explain the difference between required reserves and excess reserves.

6. What are the main functions of the Federal Reserve System?

7. Explain how the Federal Reserve can use open market operations to change the level of bank reserves. How does a change in reserves affect the money supply? (Give answers for both an increase and a decrease in the money supply.)

8. Suppose that the money supply is $1 trillion. Decision makers at the Federal Reserve decide that they wish to reduce the money supply by $100 billion, or by 10 percent. If the required reserve ratio is 0.05, what does the Fed need to do to carry out the planned reduction?

9. How does a "run on a bank" differ from a "banking panic"? What are their implications for the economy? What steps have been taken to reduce the likelihood of bank runs and bank panics?

PROBLEMS AND EXERCISES

1. Suppose the required reserve ratio is 0.2. If an extra $20 billion in reserves is injected into the banking system through an open market purchase of bonds, by how much can demand deposits increase? Would your answer be different if the required reserve ratio were 0.1?

2. Suppose bank reserves are $100 billion, the required reserve ratio is 0.2, and excess reserves are zero. Now suppose that the required reserve ratio is lowered to 0.1 and that banks once again become fully "loaned up" with no excess reserves. What is the new level of demand deposits?

3. For each of the following situations, determine whether the money supply will increase, decrease, or stay the same.
   a. Depositors become concerned about the safety of depository institutions.
   b. The Fed lowers the required reserve ratio.
   c. The economy enters a recession and banks have a hard time finding credit-worthy borrowers.
   d. The Fed sells $100 million of bonds to First National Bank of Ames, Iowa.

4. Suppose that the Fed decides to increase the money supply. It purchases a government bond worth $1,000 from a private citizen. He deposits the check in his account at First National Bank, as in the chapter example. But now, suppose that the required reserve ratio is 0.2, rather than 0.1 as in the chapter.
   a. Trace the effect of this change through three banks—First National, Second Federal, and Third State. Show the changes to each bank's balance sheet as a result of the Fed's action.
   b. By how much does the money supply change in each of these first three rounds?
   c. What will be the ultimate change in demand deposits in the entire banking system?

CHALLENGE QUESTION

1. Sometimes banks wish to hold reserves in excess of the legal minimum. Suppose the Fed makes an open market purchase of $100,000 in government bonds. The required reserve ratio is 0.1, but each bank decides to hold additional reserves equal to 5 percent of its deposits.
   a. Trace the effect of the open market purchase of bonds through the first three banks in the money expansion process. Show the changes to each bank's balance sheet.
   b. Derive the demand deposit multiplier in this case. Is it larger or smaller than when banks hold no excess reserves?
   c. What is the ultimate change in demand deposits in the entire banking system?

WWW

Visit the Federal Reserve Bank of New York (http://www.ny.frb.org/).

a. Review "FedPoint 13: The New York Fed: Who We Are and What We Do" (http://www.ny.frb.org/pihome/fedpoint/fed13.html). Briefly summarize the key operations of the New York Fed.
b. Review "Open Market Operations" (http://www.ny.frb.org/pihome/fedpoint/fed32.html). How do Reserve Bank officials and staff conduct open market operations?
c. Review "The Federal Reserve System: Purposes and Functions" (http://www.bog.frb.fed.us/pf/pf.htm). Note that this publication is an Adobe Portable Document Format (PDF) file, viewable in *Adobe Acrobat*. You may download Acrobat Reader for free (http://www.adobe.com/prodindex/acrobat/readstep.html). Describe the typical day in the conduct of open market operations.

CHAPTER

12

THE MONEY MARKET AND THE INTEREST RATE

CHAPTER OUTLINE

Which of the following two newspaper headlines might you see in your daily paper?

1. "Motorists Fear Department of Energy Will Raise Gasoline Prices."
2. "Wall Street Expects Fed to Lower Interest Rates."

You probably know the answer—the first headline is entirely unrealistic. The Department of Energy, the government agency that makes energy policy, has no authority to set prices in any market. The Federal Reserve, by contrast, has full authority to determine the interest rate—the price of borrowing money. And it exercises this authority every day. This is why headlines such as the second one appear in our newspapers so often.

In this chapter, you will learn how the Fed, through its control of the money supply, also controls the interest rate. We'll continue our focus on the short run, postponing any discussion about longer time horizons until the next chapter.

THE DEMAND FOR MONEY

Re-read the title of this section. Does it appear strange to you? Don't people always want as much money as possible? Isn't their demand for money infinite?

You already learned the answer to this apparent paradox several chapters ago, when you studied the classical model. There, as here, the "demand for money" does not mean how much money people would *like* to have in the best of all possible worlds. Rather, it means *how much money people would like to hold, given the constraints that they face.* Let's first consider the demand for money by an individual, and then turn our attention to the demand for money in the entire economy.

An Individual's Demand for Money

You've been reminded several times, but since it's a very common mistake, another reminder won't hurt. Money and wealth are *stock* variables, not flow variables. They refer to amounts held *at a particular moment in time.* Do not confuse them with flow variables such as *income* or *saving.* Your income is what you earn *over a period of time.* Your saving is the part of your disposable income that you do not spend *over a period of time.*

DANGEROUS CURVES

Money is one of the ways that each of us, as individuals, can hold our *wealth*. Unfortunately, at any given moment, the total amount of wealth we have is a given; we can't just snap our fingers and have more of it. Therefore, if we want to hold more wealth in the form of money, we must hold less wealth in other forms—savings accounts, money market funds, time deposits, stocks, bonds, and so on. Indeed, individuals exchange one kind of wealth for another millions of times a day, in banks, stock markets, and bond markets. If you sell shares in the stock market, for example, you give up wealth in the form of corporate stock and acquire money. The buyer of your stock gives up money and acquires the stock.

These two facts—that wealth is given, and that you must give up one kind of wealth in order to acquire more of another—determine an individual's **wealth constraint.** Whenever we speak about the demand for money, the wealth constraint is always in the background, as in the following statement:

WEALTH CONSTRAINT At any point in time, wealth is fixed.

An individual's demand for money *is the amount of wealth that the individual chooses to hold as money, rather than as other assets.*

Why do people want to hold some of their wealth in the form of money? The most important reason is that money is a *means of payment;* you can buy things with it. Other forms of wealth, by contrast, cannot be used for purchases. (Imagine trying to pay for your groceries with stocks or bonds.) However, the other forms of wealth provide a financial return to their owners. For example, bonds, savings deposits, and time deposits pay interest, while stocks pay dividends. Money, by contrast, pays either very little interest (some types of checking accounts) or none at all (cash and most checking accounts). Thus,

when you hold money, you bear an opportunity cost—the interest you could have earned.

OPPORTUNITY COST

Each of us must continually decide how to divide our total wealth between money and other assets. The upside to money is that it can be used as a means of payment. The more of our wealth we hold as money, the easier it is to buy things at a moment's notice, and the less often we will have to pay the costs (in time, trouble, and commissions to brokers) to change our other assets into money. The downside to money is that it pays little or no interest.

To keep our analysis as simple as possible, we'll use bonds as our representative nonmoney asset. We'll also assume money pays *no* interest at all. In our discussion, therefore, people will choose between two assets that are mirror images of each other. Specifically,

individuals choose how to divide wealth between two assets: (1) money, *which can be used as a means of payment but earns no interest; and (2)* bonds, *which earn interest, but cannot be used as a means of payment.*

This choice involves a clear tradeoff: The more wealth we hold as money, the less often we will have to go through the inconvenience of changing our bonds into money . . . but the less interest we will earn on our wealth.

What determines how much money an individual will decide to hold? While tastes vary from person to person, three key variables have rather predictable impacts on most of us.

- *The price level.* The greater the number of dollars you spend in a typical week or month, the more money you will want to have on hand to make your purchases. A rise in the price level, which raises the dollar cost of your purchases, should therefore increase the amount of money you want to hold.
- *Real income.* Suppose the price level remains unchanged, but your income increases. Your purchasing power or *real* income will increase, and so will the number of dollars you spend in a typical week or month. Once again, since you are spending more dollars, you will choose to hold more of your wealth in the form of money.
- *The interest rate.* Interest payments are what you give up when you hold money—the *opportunity cost* of money. The greater the interest rate, the greater the opportunity cost of holding money. Thus, a rise in the interest rate *decreases* your quantity of money demanded.

The effect of the interest rate on the quantity of money demanded will play a key role in our analysis. But before we go any further, you may be wondering whether it is realistic to think that changes in the interest rate—which are usually rather small—affect an individual's demand for money. Here, as in many aspects of economic life, you may not find yourself consciously thinking about the interest rate in deciding how to adjust your money-holding habits. Just as you don't rethink all your habits about using lights and computers every time the price of electricity changes, you may respond to interest rates more casually. But when we add up everybody's behavior, we find a noticeable and stable tendency for people to hold less money when it is more expensive to hold money—that is, when the interest rate is higher.

THE DEMAND FOR MONEY BY BUSINESSES. Our discussion of money demand has focused on the typical individual. But some money (not a lot in comparison to what individuals hold) is held by businesses. Stores keep some currency in their cash registers, and firms generally keep funds in business checking accounts. Businesses face the same types of constraints as individuals: They have only so much wealth, and they must decide how much of it to hold as money rather than other assets. The quantity of money demanded by businesses follows the same principles we have developed for individuals: They want to hold more money when real income or the price level is higher. And less money when the opportunity cost (the interest rate) is higher.

THE ECONOMY-WIDE DEMAND FOR MONEY

When we use the term *demand for money* without the word "individual," we mean the total demand for money by all wealth holders in the economy—businesses and individuals. And just as each person and each firm in the economy has only so much wealth, so, too, there is a given amount of wealth in the economy as a whole at any given time. In our analysis, this total wealth must be held in one of two forms: money or bonds.

THE DEMAND FOR MONEY

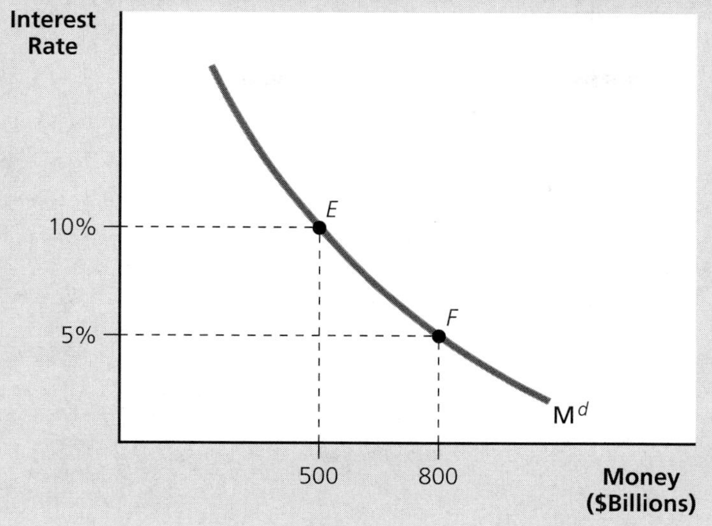

FIGURE 1

The downward-sloping money demand curve shows that, for given real GDP and a given price level, the amount of money demanded by households and firms is inversely related to the interest rate. At an interest rate of 10 percent, $500 billion of money is demanded; at the lower interest rate of 5 percent, $800 billion is demanded.

The (economy-wide) demand for money is the amount of total wealth in the economy that all households and businesses, together, choose to hold as money rather than as bonds.

The demand for money in the economy depends on the same three variables that we discussed for individuals. In particular, (1) a rise in the price level will increase the demand for money; (2) a rise in real income GDP will increase the demand for money; and (3) a rise in the interest rate will *decrease* the demand for money.

THE MONEY DEMAND CURVE. Figure 1 shows a **money demand curve,** which tells us *the total quantity of money demanded in the economy at each interest rate.* Notice that the curve is downward sloping. As long as the other influences on money demand don't change, a drop in the interest rate—which lowers the opportunity cost of holding money—will increase the quantity of money demanded.

MONEY DEMAND CURVE A curve indicating how much money will be willingly held at each interest rate.

Point *E,* for example, shows that when the interest rate is 10 percent, the quantity of money demanded is $500 billion. If the interest rate falls to 5 percent, we move to point *F,* where the quantity demanded is $800 billion. As we move along the money demand curve, the interest rate changes, but other determinants of money demand (such as the price level and real income) are assumed to remain unchanged.

SHIFTS IN THE MONEY DEMAND CURVE. What happens when something *other* than the interest rate changes the quantity of money demanded? Then the curve shifts. For example, suppose that real income increases. Then, at each interest rate, individuals and businesses will want to hold *more* of their wealth in the form of money. The entire money demand curve will shift rightward. This is illustrated in Figure 2, where the money demand curve shifts from the solid line to the dashed line. At an interest rate of 10 percent, the quantity of money demanded rises from $500 billion to $700 billion; if the interest rate were 5 percent, it would rise from $800 billion to $1,000 billion.

FIGURE 2

A SHIFT IN THE DEMAND FOR MONEY

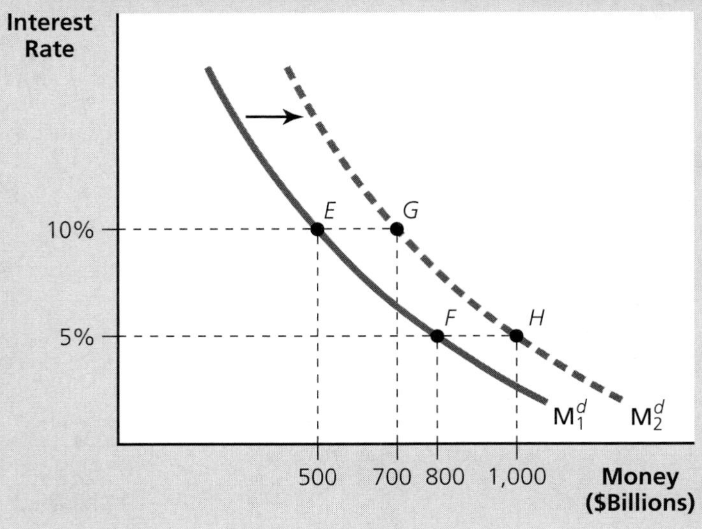

An increase in real GDP or in the price level will shift the money demand curve to the right. At each interest rate, more money will be demanded.

A change in the interest rate moves us along the money demand curve. A change in money demand caused by something other *than the interest rate (such as real income or the price level) will cause the curve to shift.*

Table 1 summarizes how the key variables we've discussed so far affect the demand for money.

THE SUPPLY OF MONEY

Just as we did for money demand, we would like to draw a curve showing the quantity of money *supplied* at each interest rate. In the previous chapter, you learned how the Fed controls the money supply: It uses open market operations to inject or withdraw reserves from the banking system and then relies on the demand deposit multiplier to do the rest. Since the Fed decides what the money supply will be, we treat it as a fixed amount. That is, the interest rate can rise or fall, but the money supply will remain constant unless and until the Fed decides to change it.

TABLE 1

EFFECTS OF KEY CHANGES ON THE MONEY DEMAND CURVE

	Interest Rate		Price Level or Income	
	Increases	**Decreases**	**Increases**	**Decreases**
Effect on Money Demand Curve	Movement leftward along curve	Movement rightward along curve	Entire curve shifts rightward	Entire curve shifts leftward

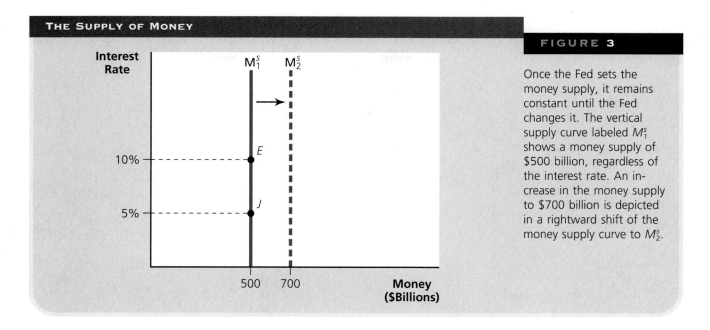

THE SUPPLY OF MONEY

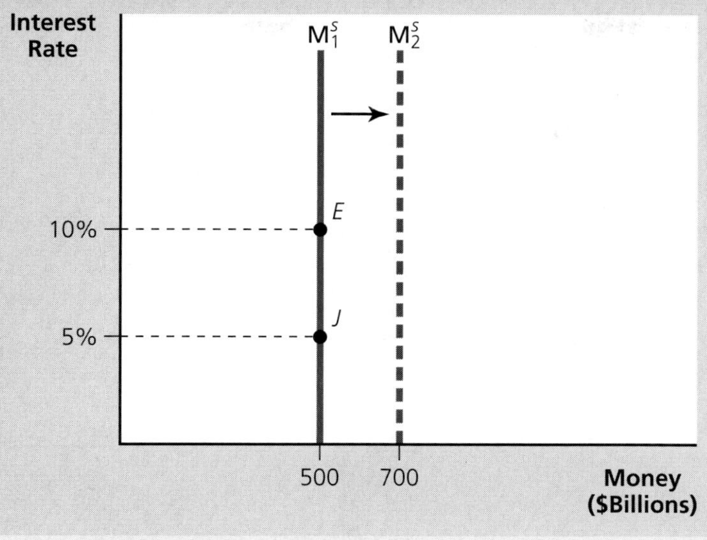

FIGURE 3

Once the Fed sets the money supply, it remains constant until the Fed changes it. The vertical supply curve labeled M_1^s shows a money supply of $500 billion, regardless of the interest rate. An increase in the money supply to $700 billion is depicted in a rightward shift of the money supply curve to M_2^s.

Look at the solid vertical line in Figure 3. This is the economy's **money supply curve,** which shows the total money supply at each interest rate. The line is vertical because once the Fed sets the money supply, it remains constant until the Fed changes it. In the figure, the Fed has chosen to set the money supply at $500 billion. A rise in the interest rate from, say, 5 percent to 10 percent would move us from point *J* to point *E* along the solid money supply curve, leaving the money supply unchanged.

MONEY SUPPLY CURVE A line showing the total quantity of money in the economy at each interest rate.

Now suppose the Fed, for whatever reason, were to *change* the money supply. Then there would be a *new* vertical line, showing a different quantity of money supplied at each interest rate. Recall from the previous chapter that the Fed raises the money supply by purchasing bonds in an open market operation. For example, if the demand deposit multiplier is 10, and the Fed purchases government bonds worth $20 billion, the money supply increases by 10 × $20 billion = $200 billion. In this case, the money supply curve shifts rightward, to the dashed line in the figure.

Open market purchases of bonds inject reserves into the banking system, and shift the money supply curve rightward by a multiple of the reserve injection. Open market sales have the opposite effect: They withdraw reserves from the system and shift the money supply curve leftward by a multiple of the reserve withdrawal.

EQUILIBRIUM IN THE MONEY MARKET

Now we are ready to combine what you've learned about money demand and money supply to find the interest rate in the economy. But before we do, a question may have occurred to you. Haven't we already discussed how the interest rate is deter-

FIGURE 4

MONEY MARKET EQUILIBRIUM

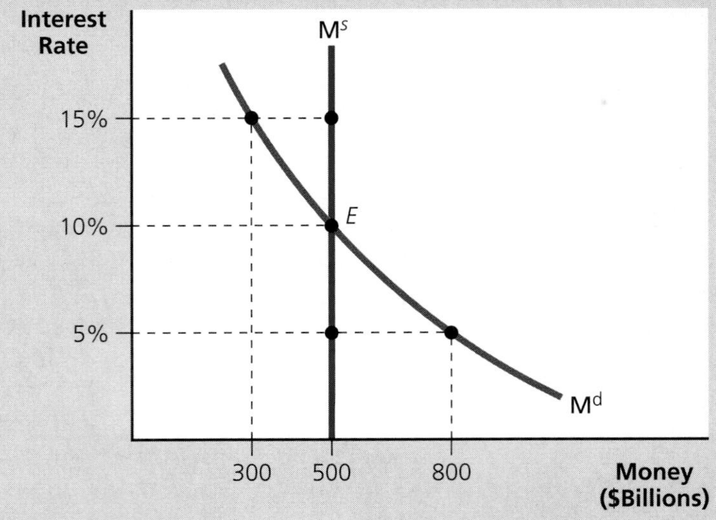

Money market equilibrium occurs when households and firms are content to hold the amount of money they are actually holding. At point *E*—at an interest rate of 10 percent—the quantity of money demanded equals the quantity supplied, and the market is in equilibrium. At a higher interest rate, such as 15 percent, there would be an excess supply of money, and the interest rate would fall. At a lower interest rate, such as 5 percent, there would be an excess demand for money, and the interest rate would rise.

mined? Indeed, we have. The classical model tells us that the interest rate is determined by equilibrium in the *financial market*—where a flow of loanable funds is offered by lenders to borrowers. But remember: The classical model tells us how the economy operates in the *long run.* We can rely on its mechanisms to work only over long periods of time. Here, we are interested in how the interest rate is determined in the *short run,* so we must change our perspective. Toward the end of the chapter, we'll come back to the classical model and explain why its theory of the interest rate does not apply in the short run.

In the short run—our focus here—we look for the *equilibrium* interest rate in the money market: the interest rate at which the quantity of money demanded and the quantity of money supplied are equal. Figure 4 combines the money supply and demand curves. Equilibrium occurs at point *E,* where the two curves intersect. At this point, the quantity of money demanded and the quantity supplied are both equal to $500 billion, and the equilibrium interest rate is 10 percent.

It is important to understand what equilibrium in the money market actually means. First, remember that the money supply curve tells us the quantity of money, determined by the Fed, that *actually exists* in the economy. Every dollar of this money—either in cash or in checking account balances—is held by *someone.* Thus, the money supply curve, in addition to telling us the quantity of money supplied by the Fed, also tells us the quantity of money that people are actually holding at any given moment. The money demand curve, on the other hand, tells us how much money people *want* to hold at each interest rate. Thus, when the quantity of money supplied and the quantity demanded are equal, all of the money in the economy is being *willingly held.* That is, people are *satisfied* holding the money that they are *actually* holding.

MARKETS AND EQUILIBRIUM

Equilibrium in the money market occurs when the quantity of money people are actually *holding (quantity supplied) is equal to the quantity of money they* want *to hold (quantity demanded).*

Can we have faith that the interest rate will reach its equilibrium value in the money market, such as 10 percent in our figure? Indeed we can. In the next section, we explore the forces that drive the money market toward its equilibrium.

HOW THE MONEY MARKET REACHES EQUILIBRIUM

To understand how the money market reaches its equilibrium, suppose that the interest rate, for some reason, were *not* at its equilibrium value of 10 percent. For example, suppose the interest rate were 15 percent. As Figure 4 shows, at this interest rate the quantity of money demanded would be $300 billion, while the quantity supplied would be $500 billion. Or, put another way, people would *actually* be holding $500 billion of their wealth as money, but they would *want* to hold only $300 billion as money. There would be an **excess supply of money** (the quantity of money supplied would exceed the quantity demanded) equal to $500 billion − $300 billion = $200 billion.

EXCESS SUPPLY OF MONEY The amount of money supplied exceeds the amount demanded at a particular interest rate.

Now comes an important point. Remember that in our analysis, money and bonds are the only two assets available. If people want to hold *less* money than they are currently holding, then, by definition, they must want to hold *more* in bonds than they are currently holding—an **excess demand for bonds.**

EXCESS DEMAND FOR BONDS The amount of bonds demanded exceeds the amount supplied at a particular interest rate.

When there is an excess supply of money in the economy, there is also an excess demand for bonds.

To understand this more clearly, imagine that instead of the money market, which can seem rather abstract, we were discussing something more concrete: the arrangement of books in a bookcase. Suppose that you have a certain number of books, and you have only two shelves on which to hold all of them—top and bottom. One day, you look at the shelves and decide that, the way you've arranged things, the top shelf has *too many* books. Then, by definition, you must also feel that the bottom shelf has *too few* books. That is, an excess supply of books on the top shelf (it has more books than you want there) is the same as an excess demand for books on the bottom shelf (it has fewer books than you want there).

A similar conclusion applies to the money market. People allocate a given amount of wealth between two different assets: money and bonds. Too much in one asset implies too little in the other.

So far, we've established that if the interest rate were 15 percent, which is higher than its equilibrium value, there would be an excess supply of money, and an excess demand for bonds. What would happen? The public would try to convert the undesired money into bonds. That is, people would try to *buy* bonds. Just as there is a market for money, there is also a market for bonds. And as the public begins to demand more bonds, making them scarcer, *the price of bonds will rise.* We can illustrate the steps in our analysis so far as follows:

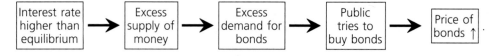

[Interest rate higher than equilibrium] → [Excess supply of money] → [Excess demand for bonds] → [Public tries to buy bonds] → [Price of bonds ↑].

We conclude that, when the interest rate is higher than its equilibrium value, the price of bonds will rise. Why is this important? In order to take our story further, we must first take a detour for a few paragraphs.

AN IMPORTANT DETOUR: BOND PRICES AND INTEREST RATES. A bond, in the simplest terms, is a promise to pay back borrowed funds at a certain date or dates in the future. There are many types of bonds. Some promise to make payments each month or each year for a certain period and then pay back a large sum at the end. Others promise to make just one payment—perhaps one, five, ten, or more years from the date the bond is issued. When a large corporation or the government wants to borrow money, it issues a new bond and sells it in the marketplace; the amount borrowed is equal to the price of the bond.

Let's consider a very simple example: a bond that promises to pay to its holder $1,000 in exactly one year. Suppose that you purchase this bond from the issuer—a firm or government agency—for $800. Then you are lending $800 to the issuer, and you will be paid back $1,000 in one year. What interest rate are you earning on your loan? Let's see: You will be getting back $200 more than you lent, so that is your *interest payment*. The interest *rate* is the interest payment divided by the amount of the loan, or $200/$800 = 0.25 or 25 percent.

Now, what if instead of $800, you paid a price of $900 for this very same bond. The bond still promises to pay $1,000 in one year, so your interest payment would now be $100, and your interest rate would be $100/$900 = 0.11 or 11 percent—a considerably lower interest rate. As you can see, the interest rate that you will earn on your bond depends entirely on the *price* of the bond. *The higher the price, the lower the interest rate.*

This general principle applies to virtually all types of bonds, not just the simple one-time-payment bond we've considered here. Bonds promise to pay various sums to their holders at different dates in the future. Therefore, the more you pay for any bond, the lower your overall rate of return, or interest rate, will be. Thus:

When the price of bonds rises, the interest rate falls; when the price of bonds falls, the interest rate rises.[1]

The relationship between bond prices and interest rates helps explain why the government, the press, and the public are so concerned about the *bond market*, where bonds issued in previous periods are bought and sold. This market is sometimes called the *secondary* market for bonds, to distinguish it from the *primary* market where newly issued bonds are bought and sold. When you hear that "the bond market rallied" on a particular day of trading, it means that prices rose in the secondary bond market. This is good news for bond holders. But it is also good news for any person or business that wants to borrow money. When prices rise in the secondary market, they immediately rise in the primary market as well, since newly issued bonds and previously issued bonds are perfect substitutes for each other. Therefore, a bond market rally not only means lower interest rates in the secondary market, it also means lower interest rates in the primary market, where

1 In our macroeconomic model of the economy, we refer to *the* interest rate. In the real world, there are many types of interest rates—a different one for each type of bond, and still other rates on savings accounts, time deposits, car loans, mortgages, and more. However, all of these interest rates move up and down together, even though some may lag behind a few days, weeks, or months. Thus, when bond prices rise, interest rates *generally* will fall, and vice versa.

firms borrow money by issuing new bonds. Sooner or later, it will also lead to a drop in the interest rate on mortgages, car loans, credit card balances, and even many student loans. This is good news for borrowers. But it is bad news for anyone wishing to lend money by buying bonds, for now they will earn less interest.

Now that you understand the relationship between bond prices and interest rates, let's return to our analysis of the money market.

DANGEROUS CURVES

We've shown that when the money market is not in equilibrium, the public *tries* to buy or sell bonds. The word "tries" is important. On any given day, the total number of bonds—like the money stock—is some fixed amount. (We ignore the relatively small number of newly issued bonds added to the market each day.) Therefore, it is impossible for the public as a whole to acquire more bonds, or to get rid of them. A single individual may be able to acquire bonds or money by exchanging with another individual. But the total amount of bonds and money held by the public will remain unchanged.

How, then, does the money market achieve equilibrium? When many people simultaneously try to sell bonds, they cause the price of bonds to fall. The price of bonds stops falling only when the public, as a whole, is happy holding the same bonds they were holding originally. When many people simultaneously try to acquire bonds, they cause the price of bonds to rise until the public is, once again, satisfied holding what it started with. *Individuals* may buy and sell bonds, but the public, as a whole, can only *try* to.

BACK TO THE MONEY MARKET. Look back at Figure 4, and let's recap what you've learned so far. If the interest rate were 15 percent, there would be an excess supply of money, and therefore an excess demand for bonds. The public would try to buy bonds, and the price of bonds would rise. Now we can complete the story. As you've just learned, a rise in the price of bonds means a *decrease* in the interest rate. The complete sequence of events is:

[Interest rate higher than equilibrium] → [Excess supply of money and excess demand for bonds] → [Public tries to buy bonds] → [Price of bonds ↑] → [Interest rate ↓].

Thus, if the interest is 15 percent in our figure, it will begin to fall. Therefore, 15 percent is *not* the equilibrium interest rate.

How far will the interest rate fall? As long as there continues to be an excess supply of money, and an excess demand for bonds, the public will still be trying to acquire bonds and the interest rate will continue to fall. But notice what happens in the figure as the interest rate falls: The quantity of money demanded *rises*. Finally, when the interest rate reaches 10 percent, the excess supply of money, and therefore the excess demand for bonds, is eliminated. At this point, there is no reason for the interest rate to fall further. Ten percent is, indeed, our equilibrium interest rate.

We can also do the same analysis from the other direction. Suppose the interest rate were *lower* than 10 percent in the figure? Then, as you can see in Figure 4, there would be an *excess demand for money,* and an *excess supply of bonds.* In this case, the following would happen:

[Interest rate lower than equilibrium] → [Excess demand for money and excess supply of bonds] → [Public tries to sell bonds] → [Price of bonds ↓] → [Interest rate ↑].

The interest rate would continue to rise until it reached its equilibrium value: 10 percent.

Name:
Federal Reserve System, Board of Governors
Description:
Overseer of the Federal Reserve System, the central bank of the United States
Resources:
The Federal Reserve Board publishes detailed information about the conduct of U.S. monetary policy; the *Summary of Commentary on Current Economic Conditions,* commonly known as the "Beige Book," minutes from the Federal Open Market Committee (FOMC); and publications, press releases, land reports.
Address:
http://www.bog.frb.fed.us/

WHAT HAPPENS WHEN THINGS CHANGE?

Now that we have seen how the interest rate is *determined* in the money market, we turn our attention to *changes* in the interest rate. We'll focus on two questions: (1) What *causes* the equilibrium interest rate to change? and (2) What are the *consequences* of a change in the interest rate? As you are about to see, the Fed can change the interest rate as a matter of policy, or the interest rate can change on its own, as a by-product of other events in the economy. We'll begin with the Fed.

How the Fed Changes the Interest Rate

Changes in the interest rate from day to day, or week to week, are often caused by the Fed. Later in this chapter, you'll learn *why* the Fed often wants to manipulate the interest rate. For now, we'll focus on *how* the Fed does this.

Suppose the Fed wants to *lower* the interest rate. Fed officials cannot just *declare* that the interest rate should be lower. To change the interest rate, the Fed must change the *equilibrium* interest rate in the money market, and it does this by changing the money supply.

Look at Figure 5. Initially, with a money supply of $500 billion, the money market is in equilibrium at point *E,* with an interest rate of 10 percent. To lower the interest rate, the Fed *increases* the money supply through open market purchases of bonds. In the figure, the Fed raises the money supply to $800 billion, shifting the money supply curve rightward to the dashed line. (This is a much greater shift than the Fed would engineer in practice, but it makes the graph easier to read.) At the old interest rate of 10 percent, there would be an excess supply of money and an excess demand for bonds. This will drive the interest rate down until it reaches its new equilibrium value of 5 percent, at point *F.* The process works like this:

Fed conducts open market purchases → Money supply ↑ → Excess supply of money and excess demand for bonds → Public tries to buy bonds → Price of bonds ↑ → Interest rate ↓.

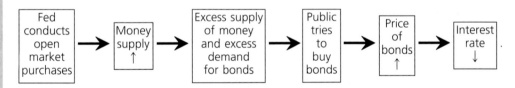

The Fed can *raise* the interest rate as well, through open market *sales* of bonds. In this case, the money supply curve in Figure 5 would shift leftward (not shown), setting off the following sequence of events:

Fed conducts open market sales → Money supply ↓ → Excess demand for money and excess supply of bonds → Public tries to sell bonds → Price of bonds ↓ → Interest rate ↑.

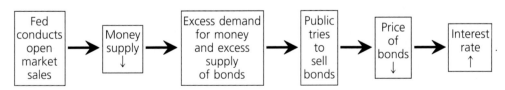

If the Fed increases the money supply by buying government bonds, the interest rate falls. If the Fed decreases the money supply by selling government bonds, the interest rate rises. By controlling the money supply through purchases and sales of bonds, the Fed can also control the interest rate.

An Increase in the Money Supply

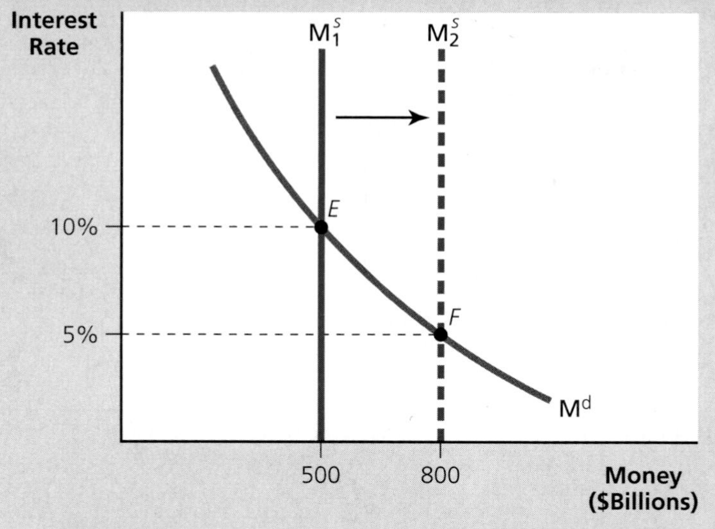

FIGURE 5

If the Fed wishes to lower the interest rate, it can do so by increasing the money supply. At point *E,* the money market is in equilibrium at an interest rate of 10 percent. To lower the rate, the Fed could increase the money supply to $800 billion. At the original interest rate, there would be an excess supply of money (and an excess demand for bonds). Bond prices would rise, and the interest rate would fall until a new equilibrium is established at point *F* with an interest rate of 5 percent.

The Fed in Action

When the Fed tries to achieve a macroeconomic goal by controlling or manipulating the money supply, it is conducting *monetary policy.* During periods of economic calm, such as 1993 through 1997, the Fed's monetary policy tends to be stable, and the interest rate remains at about the same level from year to year. Occasionally, however, the Fed sees the need to act dramatically—to adjust the money stock aggressively and engineer large changes in interest rates. Such an episode occurred in the period from 1988 to 1990. In 1988, the Fed believed that the economy was becoming overheated and that it needed to be slowed down by a rise in the interest rate (you'll learn why a higher interest rate slows the economy in the next section).

Figure 6 shows what happened. Starting in July 1988, the Fed began to conduct open market sales of bonds, withdrawing reserves from the banking system. As you can see in panel (a) of the figure, from mid-1988 to mid-1989, banking system reserves fell by about $2 billion. This, in turn, shrank demand deposits and similar checking account balances by about $20 billion—ten times the withdrawal of reserves. (The previous chapter explained why the decrease in checking-type accounts is greater than the decrease in reserves.)

Because checking account balances are part of the money supply, the Fed's action shifted the money supply curve leftward. This, in turn, caused the interest rate to rise. Panel (c) of the figure shows changes in the *federal funds rate*—a key interest rate in the economy. The **federal funds rate** is the interest rate that banks with excess reserves charge for lending reserves to other banks. The federal funds rate varies closely with other interest rates in the economy, so it gives us a good idea of how interest rates in general were changing during this period. As you can see, the federal funds rate rose sharply, from less than 8 percent to almost 10 percent over the period.

FEDERAL FUNDS RATE The interest rate charged for loans of reserves among banks.

FIGURE 6

THE FED IN ACTION

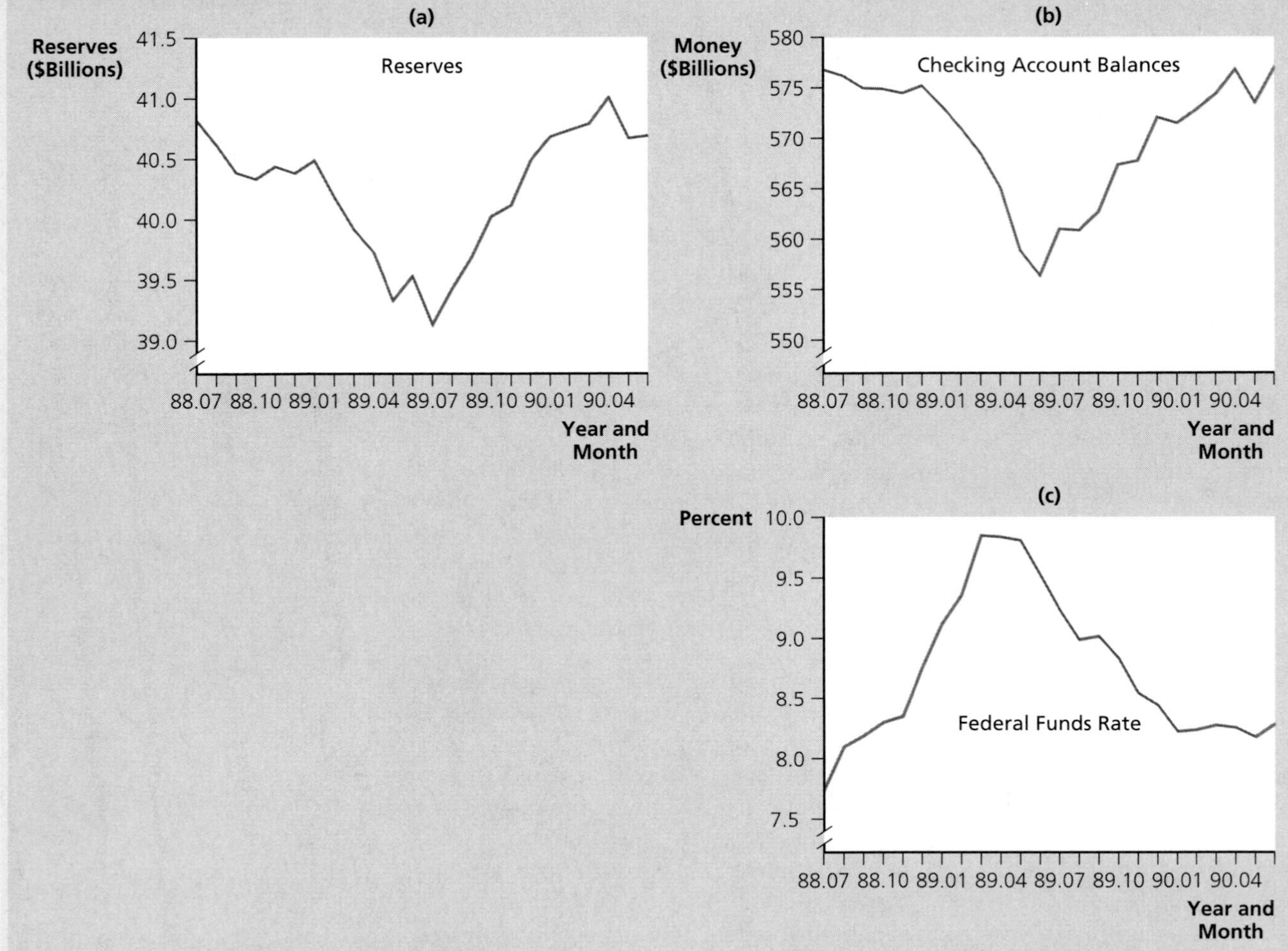

In July 1988, the Fed began to sell bonds and withdraw reserves from the banking system. As a result, checking account balances fell and the federal funds rate increased. In July 1989, the Fed reversed course and injected reserves. Checking balances rose and the federal funds rate fell.

Starting in July 1989, the Fed reversed course. It began to *purchase* government bonds, thereby injecting reserves into the banking system. This caused checking account balances to rise, and shifted the money supply curve rightward. As a result, the interest rate fell back to a little over 8 percent.

The contraction and expansion of the money supply from 1988 to 1990 raises some important questions. Why would the Fed feel the need to raise interest rates in the first place? And why would it reverse course? We'll be answering questions like these in the next two chapters. But we can begin to understand the Fed's motives by learning how interest rate changes affect the economy, which is the subject of the next section.

How Do Interest Rate Changes Affect the Economy?

Suppose the Fed increases the money supply through open market purchases of bonds. The interest rate falls, for the reasons discussed earlier in this chapter, and strongly confirmed by the data shown in Figure 6. But what then? How is the macroeconomy affected? The answer is: *A drop in the interest rate will boost several different types of spending in the economy.*

How the Interest Rate Affects Spending. First, a lower interest rate stimulates business spending on plant and equipment. This idea came up a few chapters ago in the classical model, but we will go back over it here.

Remember that the interest rate is one of the key costs of any investment project. If a firm must borrow funds, it will have to pay for them at the going rate of interest—for example, by selling a bond at the going price. If the firm uses its *own* funds, so it doesn't have to borrow, the interest rate *still* represents a cost: Each dollar spent on plant and equipment *could* have been lent to someone else at the going interest rate. Thus, the interest rate is the *opportunity cost* of the firm's own funds when they are spent on plant and equipment.

A firm deciding whether to spend on plant and equipment compares the benefits of the project—the increase in future income—with the costs of the project. With a lower interest rate, the costs of funding investment projects are lower, so more projects will get the go-ahead. Other variables affect investment spending as well. But for given values of these other variables, a drop in the interest rate will cause an increase in spending on plant and equipment.

Interest rate changes also affect another kind of investment spending: spending on new houses and apartments that are built by developers or individuals. Most people borrow to buy houses or condominiums, and most developers borrow to build apartment buildings. The loan agreement for housing is called a *mortgage,* and mortgage interest rates move closely with other interest rates. Thus, when the Fed lowers the interest rate, families find it more affordable to buy homes, and landlords find it more profitable to build new apartments. Total investment in new housing increases.

Finally, in addition to investment spending, the interest rate affects consumption spending on "big ticket" items such as new cars, furniture, and dishwashers. Economists call these *consumer durables* because they usually last several years. People often borrow to buy consumer durables, and the interest rate they are charged tends to rise and fall with other interest rates in the economy. Spending on new cars, the most expensive durable that most of us buy, is especially sensitive to interest rate changes. When the interest rate falls, consumption spending rises at *any* level of disposable income. It causes a *shift* in the consumption function, not a movement along it. Therefore, we consider this impact on consumption to be a rise in autonomous consumption spending, called *a* in our discussion of the consumption function.

We can summarize the impact of monetary policy as follows:

When the Fed increases the money supply, the interest rate falls, and spending on three categories of goods increases: plant and equipment, new housing, and consumer durables (especially automobiles). When the Fed decreases the money supply, the interest rate rises, and these categories of spending fall.

FIGURE 7

MONETARY POLICY AND THE ECONOMY

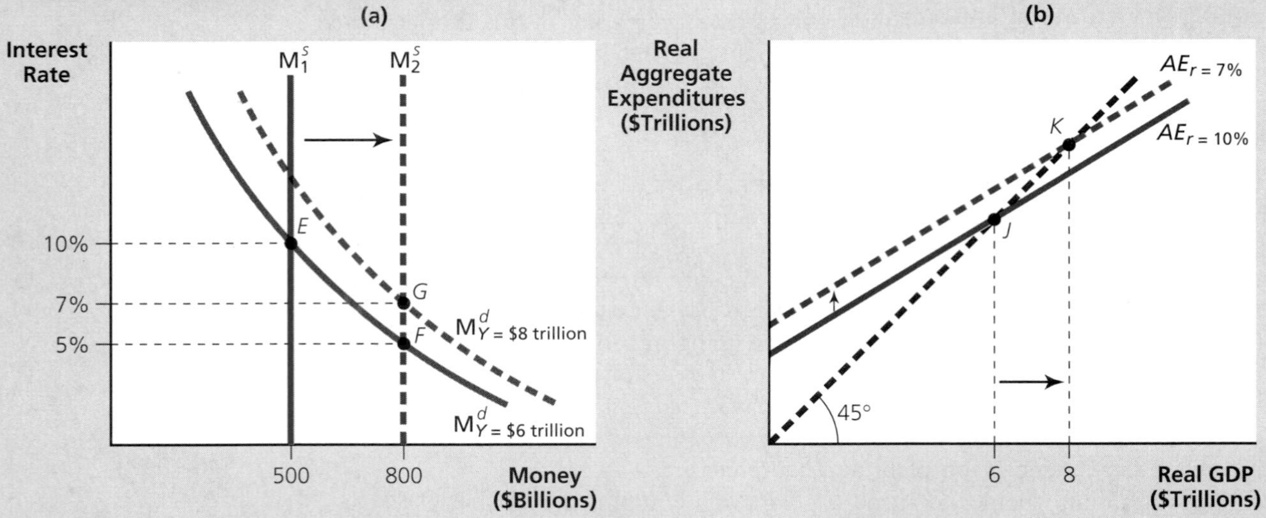

Monetary policy involves an interaction between the interest rate and equilibrium real GDP. Initially, the Fed has set the money supply at $500 billion, so the interest rate is 10 percent (point *E*). Given that interest rate, aggregate expenditure is $AE_{r=10\%}$ in panel (b), and real GDP is $6 trillion (point *J*).

If the Fed increases the money supply to $800 billion, money market equilibrium moves to point *F* in panel (a). The interest rate falls, stimulating interest-sensitive spending and driving aggregate expenditures upward in panel (b). Through the multiplier process, real GDP increases. As it does, the money demand curve shifts rightward in panel (a). In the new equilibrium, real GDP is $8 trillion and the interest rate is 7 percent.

MONETARY POLICY AND THE ECONOMY. Now we can finally see how monetary policy affects the economy overall. The only remaining step is one you learned two chapters ago: how a change in spending affects output and employment. This is what the short-run Keynesian model was all about.

In Figure 7, we revisit the short-run Keynesian model, but we now include the money market in our analysis. In panel (a), the Fed has initially set the money supply at $500 billion. Equilibrium is at point *E,* with an interest rate (*r*) of 10 percent. Panel (b) shows the familiar short-run Keynesian diagram, with equilibrium at point *J,* and equilibrium GDP equal to $6 trillion.

But notice the new labels in the figure. The aggregate expenditure line has the label "r = 10%," and the money demand curve has the label "Y = $6 trillion." These are necessary because of the *interdependence* between the interest rate and equilibrium GDP. Recall that the money demand curve will shift if there is a change in real income. Therefore, our money demand curve is drawn for a particular level of real income—the level determined in panel (b), or $6 trillion. Similarly, as you are about to see, a change in the interest rate will cause the aggregate expenditure line to shift. Therefore, our aggregate expenditure line is drawn for a particular interest rate—the one determined in the money market, or 10 percent. As you can see, the equilibrium in each panel depends on the equilibrium in the other panel.

Now we suppose that the Fed increases the money supply to $800 billion. (Again, this is an unrealistically large change in the money supply, but it makes it easier to see the change in the figure.) In panel (a), the money market equilibrium moves from

> **DANGEROUS CURVES**
>
> When thinking about the effects of monetary policy, try not to confuse movements *along* the aggregate expenditure line with *shifts* of the line itself. We move along the line only when a change in *income* causes spending to change. We shift the line when something *other* than a change in income causes spending to change.
>
> When the Fed changes the interest rate, both types of changes occur, but it's important to keep the order straight. *First,* the drop in the interest rate (something other than income) causes interest-sensitive spending to change, *shifting* the aggregate expenditure line. *Then,* increases in income in each round of the multiplier cause further increases in spending, moving us *along* the new aggregate expenditure line.

point E to point F, and the interest rate begins to drop. (It would drop all the way down to 5 percent, except that the money demand curve will shift as well before we are finished.) The drop in the interest rate causes spending on plant and equipment, new housing, and consumer durables (especially automobiles) to rise. That is, both investment spending (I) and autonomous consumption spending (a) will rise. In panel (b), the rise in spending causes the aggregate expenditure line to shift upward, setting off the multiplier effect and increasing equilibrium GDP. The rise in income causes the money demand curve to shift rightward, since the demand for money is greater when income is higher.

The new equilibrium will be at point G in the money market and point K in the aggregate expenditure diagram. The interest rate ends up at 7 percent, so the aggregate expenditure line is labeled "$r = 7\%$." Equilibrium GDP has risen to \$8 trillion, so the new money demand curve is labeled "$Y = \$8$ trillion." In the end, we see that the Fed, by increasing the money supply and lowering the interest rate, has increased the level of output.

We've covered a lot of ground to reach our conclusion, so let's review the highlights of how monetary policy works. This is what happens when the Fed conducts open market purchases of bonds:

[Open market purchases] → [Money supply ↑] → [Interest rate ↓] → [a and I ↑] —Multiplier effect→ [Real GDP ↑].

Open market *sales* by the Fed have exactly the opposite effects. In this case, the money supply curve in Figure 7 would shift leftward (not shown), driving the interest rate up. The rise in the interest rate would cause a decrease in interest-sensitive spending (a and I), shifting the aggregate expenditure line downward. Equilibrium GDP would fall by a multiple of the initial decrease in spending.

[Open market sales] → [Money supply ↓] → [Interest rate ↑] → [a and I ↓] —Multiplier effect→ [Real GDP ↓].

Fiscal Policy (and Other Spending Changes) Revisited

Two chapters ago, we discussed how fiscal policy affects the economy in the short run. For example, an increase in government spending causes output to rise, and in successive rounds of the multiplier, spending and output rise still more. Now that we've added the money market to our analysis, it's time to revisit fiscal policy. As you'll see, its effects are now a bit more complicated.

Figure 8 shows the money market and the familiar short-run Keynesian diagram. Initially, we have equilibrium in both panels. In panel (a), the money mar-

FIGURE 8

FISCAL POLICY AND THE MONEY MARKET

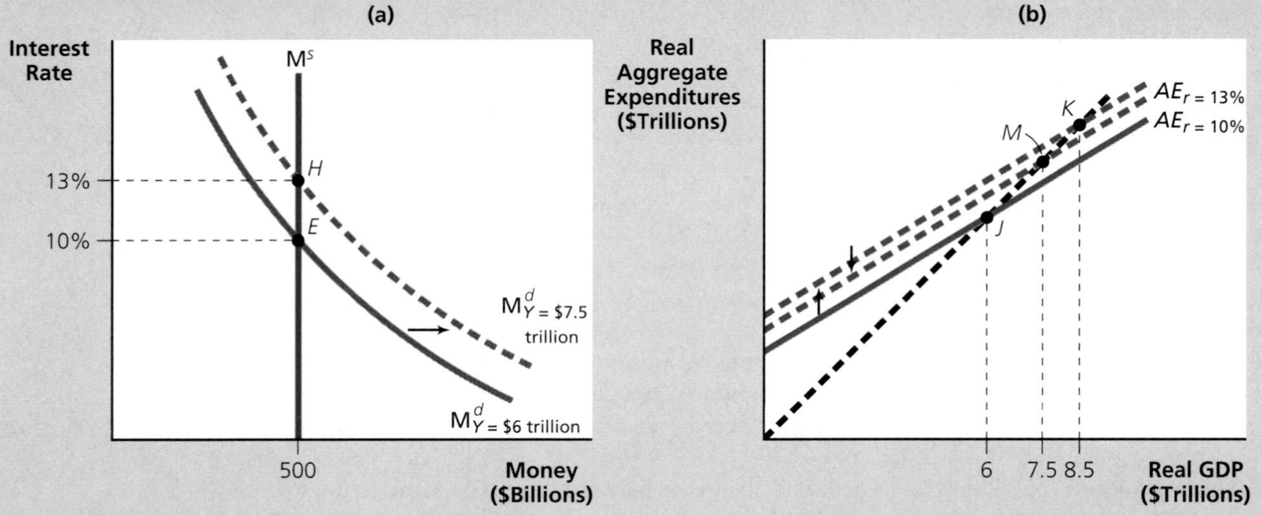

The economy is initially in equilibrium with an interest rate of 10 percent in panel (a) and real GDP of \$6 trillion in panel (b). An increase in government purchases shifts the aggregate expenditure line upward, triggering the multiplier process. If the interest rate did not change, equilibrium would be reestablished at point *K* in panel (b) with real GDP of \$8.5 trillion. But the increase in GDP stimulates money demand in panel (a), driving the interest rate upward to 13 percent at point *H*. That reduces interest-sensitive spending, lowering aggregate expenditure to $AE_{r=13\%}$ in panel (b) so that the real GDP at the new equilibrium is \$7.5 trillion (point *M*).

ket equilibrium is point *E*, with the interest rate at 10 percent. In panel (b), the solid aggregate expenditure line, labeled "$r = 10\%$," is consistent with the interest rate we've found in the money market. As you can see, with this aggregate expenditure line, the equilibrium is at point *J*, with real GDP equal to \$6 trillion, just as we assumed when we drew the money demand curve in panel (a).

AN INCREASE IN GOVERNMENT PURCHASES. Now let's see what happens when the government changes its fiscal policy, say, by increasing government purchases by \$1 trillion. Panel (b) shows the initial effect: The aggregate expenditure line shifts upward, by \$1 trillion, to the topmost dashed line. This new aggregate expenditure line is drawn for the same interest rate as the original line: $r = 10\%$. The shift illustrates what *would* happen if there were no change in the interest rate, as in our analysis of fiscal policy two chapters ago.

As you've learned, the increase in government purchases will set off the multiplier process, increasing GDP and income in each round. *If this were the end of the story,* the result would be a rise in real GDP equal to $[1/(1 - MPC)] \times \Delta G$. In our example, with an MPC of 0.6, the multiplier would be $1/(1 - 0.6) = 2.5$. The new equilibrium would be at point *K*, with GDP equal to \$8.5 trillion—a rise of \$2.5 trillion.

But point *K* is *not* the end of our story—not when we include effects in the money market. As income increases, the money demand curve in panel (a) will shift rightward, raising the interest rate. As a result, autonomous consumption (*a*) and investment spending (*I*) will decrease and shift the aggregate expenditure line downward. That is, *an increase in government purchases, which by itself shifts the aggregate expenditure line upward, also sets in motion forces that shift it downward.*

We can outline these forces as follows:

$G\uparrow$ $\xrightarrow[\text{effect}]{\text{Multiplier}}$ GDP $\uparrow$ $\rightarrow$ Increase in money demand $\rightarrow$ $r\uparrow$ $\rightarrow$ a and $I\downarrow$ $\xrightarrow[\text{effect}]{\text{Multiplier}}$ *GDP* $\downarrow$.

Thus, at the same time as the increase in government purchases has a *positive* multiplier effect on GDP, the decrease in a and I have *negative* multiplier effects. Which effect dominates? The positive multiplier effect. Why? Because the only force pulling GDP down—a higher interest rate—*depends upon* a rise in GDP. (It is the rise in GDP that shifts the money demand curve and drives up the interest rate.) If the negative effect on GDP were stronger, GDP would actually decrease in the end, so the interest rate would be lower, not higher, and there would be no force pulling GDP down at all.

Thus, we know that an increase in government purchases causes GDP to rise. But the rise is smaller than the simple multiplier formula suggests. That's because the simple multiplier ignores the effect of a rise in the interest rate on GDP.

In the short run, an increase in government purchases causes real GDP to rise, but not by as much as it would have risen if the interest rate had not increased.

Let's sum up the characteristics of the new equilibrium after an increase in government purchases:

- The aggregate expenditure line is higher, but by less than ΔG.
- Real GDP and real income are higher, but the rise is less than $[1/(1 - MPC)] \times \Delta G$.
- The money demand curve has shifted rightward, because real income is higher.
- The interest rate is higher, because the money demand curve has shifted rightward.
- Autonomous consumption and investment spending are lower, because the interest rate is higher.

Figure 8 indicates one possible result that is consistent with all of these requirements: In the figure, the new equilibrium GDP is $7.5 trillion (point M) and the new equilibrium interest rate is 13 percent (point H). Notice that real GDP has risen, but by only $1.5 trillion—not the $2.5 trillion suggested by the simple multiplier formula. Moreover, the two panels of the diagram are consistent with each other. The aggregate expenditure line (labeled $r = 13\%$) corresponds to the equilibrium interest rate in the money market. The money demand curve, (labeled "$Y =$ $7.5 trillion") corresponds to the equilibrium GDP in the aggregate expenditure diagram.

Crowding Out Once Again. Our analysis illustrates an interesting byproduct of fiscal policy. Comparing our initial equilibrium (points E and J) to the final equilibrium (points H and M), we see that government spending increases, but—because of the rise in the interest rate—*investment spending has decreased.*

What about consumption spending? It is influenced by two opposing forces. The rise in the interest rate causes *some* types of consumption spending (e.g., on automobiles) to decrease, but the rise in *income* makes other types of consumption spending *increase.* Thus, an increase in government purchases may increase or decrease consumption spending, depending on which effect is stronger.

Summing up:

POLICY TRADEOFFS

> *When effects in the money market are included in the short-run Keynesian model, an increase in government spending raises the interest rate and* crowds out *private investment spending. It* may *also crowd out consumption spending.*

This should sound familiar. In the classical, long-run model, an increase in government purchases also causes crowding out. But there is one important difference between crowding out in the classical model and the effects we are outlining here. In the classical model, there is *complete crowding out:* Investment spending and consumption spending fall by the same amount that government purchases rise. As a result, total spending does not change at all, and neither does GDP. This is why, in the long run, we expect fiscal policy to have no effect on equilibrium GDP.

In the short run, however, our conclusion is somewhat different. While we expect *some* crowding out from an increase in government purchases, *it is not complete.* Investment spending falls, and consumption spending *may* fall, but together, they do not drop by as much as the rise in government purchases. In the short run, real GDP rises.

A DECREASE IN GOVERNMENT PURCHASES. A decrease in government purchases would have precisely the opposite effects as an increase in government purchases. In this case, real GDP and income would decrease, shifting the money demand curve *leftward.* The interest rate would fall, causing a and I to rise:

$G\downarrow$ → (Multiplier effect) → GDP $\downarrow$ → Decrease in money demand → $r\downarrow$ → a and $I\uparrow$ → (Multiplier effect) → $GDP\uparrow$.

To test your understanding, try drawing a diagram similar to Figure 8, but for a *decrease* in government purchases. If you do this correctly, your new equilibrium should have the following characteristics:

- The aggregate expenditure line is lower, but not by the full ΔG.
- Real GDP and real income are lower, but the drop is less than $[1/(1 - MPC)] \times \Delta G$.
- The money demand curve has shifted leftward, because real income is lower.
- The interest rate is lower, because the money demand curve has shifted leftward.
- Autonomous consumption and investment spending are higher, because the interest rate is lower.

Notice that the decrease in government purchases—by lowering the interest rate—causes investment spending to *increase,* and may or may not cause consumption spending to increase.

OTHER SPENDING CHANGES. So far, we've focused on the impact on the economy of a change in government purchases. But our analysis extends to *any* shock that shifts the aggregate expenditure line. Positive shocks would shift the aggregate expenditure line upward, just as in Figure 8. More specifically:

Increases in government purchases, investment, and autonomous consumption, as well as decreases in taxes, all shift the aggregate expenditure line upward. Real GDP rises, but so does the interest rate. The rise in equilibrium GDP is smaller than would occur if the interest rate remained constant.

For example, a \$1 trillion increase in investment spending shifts the aggregate expenditure line upward by \$1 trillion, as in Figure 8. If there were no rise in the interest rate, real GDP would rise according to the simple multiplier of $1/(1 - MPC) = 2.5$, or by a full \$2.5 trillion. But once again, the rise in GDP does drive up the interest rate in the money market, which works to decrease investment and interest-sensitive consumption. Once again, GDP will rise, but not by as much as the simple multiplier suggests.

Negative shocks shift the aggregate expenditure line *downward.* More specifically:

Decreases in government purchases, investment, and autonomous consumption, as well as increases in taxes, all shift the aggregate expenditure line downward. Real GDP falls, but so does the interest rate. The decline in equilibrium GDP is smaller than would occur if the interest rate remained constant.

What About the Fed? In our analysis of spending shocks, we've made an implicit but important assumption. Look back at Figure 8. Notice that, from beginning to end, the money supply curve never shifts. This implies that the Fed just stands by, not interfering at all with the changes we've been describing. More specifically, we've been assuming that *the Fed does not change the money supply in response to shifts in the aggregate expenditure line.*

While this assumption has helped us focus on the impact of spending shocks, it is not very realistic. In the Using the Theory section at the end of this chapter, we'll consider how the Fed is likely to respond to spending shocks, and how its response changes their impact on the economy.

Shifts in the Money Demand Curve

So far, we've considered changes in the interest rate engineered by the Fed, or caused by a spending shock that shifts the aggregate expenditure line upward or downward. Here, we discuss one additional source of interest rate changes: a *shift in the money demand curve.* Note that you've already seen what happens when the money demand curve shifts as a by-product of a spending shock (Figure 8). Here, we explore what happens when the *initial shock* to the economy is a shift in the money demand curve.

What could cause the money demand curve to shift besides a spending shock? There are several possibilities. Tastes for holding money can change. For example, if the public began to fear that criminals would steal their credit card numbers and began to prefer making payments by cash or check, the demand for money curve would shift rightward. New technology (such as electronic money cards) can lead to new substitutes for money, shifting the money demand curve leftward. Finally, *expectations about the future interest rate* can dramatically affect the demand for money in the present. This is the case we'll explore in detail.

Expectations and Money Demand. Why should expectations about the future interest rate affect money demand *today*? Because bond prices and interest rates are negatively related. If you expect the interest rate to rise in the future, then you also expect the price of bonds to fall in the future.

To see this more clearly, imagine (pleasantly) that you hold a bond promising to pay you $100,000 in exactly one year and that the interest rate is currently 10 percent. The going price for your bond will be $90,900. Why? At that price, a buyer would earn $100,000 – $90,900 = $9,100 in interest. Since the bond cost $90,900, the buyer's rate of return would be $9,100/$90,900 = 0.10 or 10 percent—the going rate of interest. If you tried to charge more than $90,900 for the bond, its rate of return would be less than 10 percent, so no one would buy it—they could always earn 10 percent by buying another bond that pays the going rate of interest.

Now suppose that you *expect* the interest rate to rise to 15 percent in the near future, say, next week. (This is an unrealistically large change in the interest rate in so short a time, but it makes the point dramatically.) Then next week, the going price for your bond would be only about $87,000. At that price, a buyer would earn $100,000 – $87,000 = $13,000 in interest, so the buyer's rate of return would be $13,000/$87,000 = 0.15 or 15 percent. Thus, if you believe that the interest rate is about to rise from 10 to 15 percent, you also believe the price of your bond is about to fall from $90,900 to $87,000—a drop of almost $4,000.

What would you do?

Logically, you would want to sell your bond *now,* before the price drops. If you still want to hold this type of bond later, you can always buy it back next week at the lower price, and gain from the transaction. Thus, if you expect the interest rate to rise in the future, you will want to exchange your bonds for money *today.* Your demand for money will increase.

Of course, if *you* expect the interest rate to drop, and your expectation is reasonable, others will probably feel the same way. They, too, will want to trade in their bonds for money. Thus, if the expectation is widespread, there will be an increase in the demand for money economy-wide.

A general expectation that interest rates will rise (bond prices will fall) in the future will cause the money demand curve to shift rightward in the present.

Notice that when people expect the interest rate to rise, we *shift* the money demand curve, rather than move along it. People will want to hold more money at any *current* interest rate.

Figure 9 shows what will happen in the money market when people expect the interest rate to rise. Initially, with the money supply equal to $500 billion, the equilibrium is at point *E* and the interest rate is 10 percent. But the expected rise in the interest rate shifts the money demand curve rightward. After the shift, there is an excess demand for money and an excess supply of bonds at the original interest rate of 10 percent. As the public attempts to sell bonds, the price of bonds will fall, which means the interest rate will rise.

How far will the interest rate rise? That depends. Imagine a simple case where *everyone* in the economy expected the interest rate to rise to 15 percent next week. Then *no one* would want to hold bonds at any *current* interest rate less than 15 percent. For example, if the interest rate rose to 14 percent, people would still expect it to rise further, so they would still want to sell their bonds. Therefore, to return the money market to equilibrium, the interest rate would rise to exactly the level that people expected. This is the case we've illustrated in Figure 9, where the money demand curve shifts rightward by just enough to raise the interest rate to 15 percent. More generally:

INTEREST RATE EXPECTATIONS

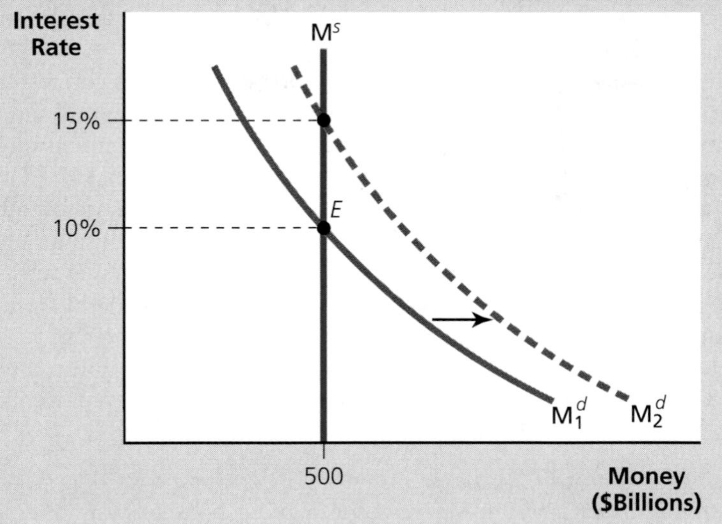

FIGURE 9

If households and firms expect the interest rate to rise in the future, their demand for money will increase today. Starting from equilibrium at point *E*, an expected increase in the interest rate from 10 percent to 15 percent will increase money demand to M_2^d. The result is a self-fulfilling prophecy: The interest rate increases to 15 percent *today*.

When the public as a whole expects the interest rate to rise in the future, they will drive up the interest rate in the present.

When information comes along that makes people believe that interest rates will rise and bond prices fall in the near future, the result is an immediate rise in the interest rate and a fall in bond prices. This principle operates even if the information is false and there is ultimately no reason for the interest rate to rise. Thus, a general expectation that interest rates will rise can be a *self-fulfilling prophecy:* Because people believe it, it actually happens. Their expectation alone is enough to drive up the interest rate.

This immediate response to information about the future—and the possibility of a self-fulfilling prophecy—works in the opposite direction as well:

When the public expects the interest rate to drop in the future, they will drive down the interest rate in the present.

In this case, the public expects bond prices to rise, so they try to shift their wealth from money to bonds. In Figure 9, the money demand curve would shift leftward (not shown). The price of bonds would rise, and the interest rate would fall, just as was originally expected.

EXPECTATIONS AND THE FED. Changes in interest rates due to changes in expectations can have important consequences. First, fortunes can be won and lost depending on how people bet on the future. For example, suppose you believe the interest rate is about to drop, so you buy bonds, thinking their price is about to rise. But suppose the interest rate actually *rises* instead. Then your bonds will immediately drop in price and be worth less than what you paid for them. In fact, it is not unusual for major bondholders—such as pension funds or money market mutual funds—to gain or lose millions of dollars in a single day based on a good or a bad bet.

Another consequence is one we discussed earlier in this chapter: Changes in the interest rate affect aggregate expenditure, and therefore output. Fortunately, the Fed can counteract these changes with open market purchases or sales of bonds, as needed, and we'll discuss this a bit later.

Still, the public's ever-changing expectations about future interest rates make the Fed's job more difficult. Expectations can change interest rates, and changes in interest rates can affect individual fortunes as well as the economy as a whole. This observation helps explain some seemingly mysterious Fed behavior. Public policy statements made by the Fed's chair (currently Alan Greenspan) or by other Fed officials are remarkably tentative, and sometimes downright confusing. You can read them again and again and still have no idea what the Fed intends to do about interest rates in the future. For example, on July 9, 1993, the Federal Reserve's Open Market Committee (FOMC) released a summary of the minutes of its May 1993 meeting. Here is the part of the statement explaining the Fed's future intentions regarding the money supply and interest rates. See if you can tell what the Fed planned to do.

In the view of a majority of the members . . . developments over recent months were sufficiently worrisome to warrant positioning policy for a move toward restraint should signs of continuing inflation continue to multiply. . . . Slightly greater reserve restraint would or slightly lesser reserve restraint might be acceptable.[2]

This is the kind of writing that causes English teachers heartache. But from the Fed's point of view, the obfuscation is understandable. If the officials of the FOMC had given stronger hints about their thinking, the money and bond markets might have gone into overdrive, as people rushed to buy or sell bonds in order to profit (or avoid loss) from the Fed's action. On rare occasions, Fed officials—by speaking more clearly—have given unintentional hints and then had to quickly undo the damage with further statements or open market operations.

Even the policy statement quoted above caused a minor flurry of bond selling and a rise in the interest rate. Why? Look at the last sentence in the Fed's statement. On the day the statement was issued, many bondholders thought the word "would" was stronger than the word "might." They therefore thought the Fed was hinting that it would probably withdraw reserves from the banking system, which would decrease the money supply, raise the interest rate, and cause bond prices to drop.

ARE THERE TWO THEORIES OF THE INTEREST RATE?

At the beginning of this chapter, you were reminded that you had already learned a different theory of how the interest rate is determined in the economy. In the classical model, the interest rate was determined in the *market for loanable funds.* In this chapter, you learned that the interest rate is determined in the *money market,* where people make decisions about holding their wealth as money and bonds. Which theory is correct?

The answer is: Both are correct. The classical model, you remember, tells us what happens in the economy in the *long run.* Therefore, when we ask what changes

2 *New York Times,* July 10, 1993.

the interest rate over long periods of time—many years or even a decade—we should think about the market for loanable funds. But over shorter time periods—days, weeks, or months—we should think about the money market.

Why can't we use the classical loanable funds market to determine the interest rate in the short run? Because, as you've seen, the economy behaves differently in the short run than it does in the long run. For example, in the classical model, output is automatically at full employment. But in the short run, output changes as the economy goes through booms and recessions. These changes in output affect the loanable funds market in ways that the classical model does not consider. For example, look back at Figure 8 in the chapter on the classical model. Recession, which decreases household income, also decreases household saving at any given interest rate: With less income, households will spend less *and* save less. The supply of loanable funds curve would shift leftward in the diagram, and the interest rate would rise. The classical model ignores this possibility.

The classical model also ignores an important idea discussed in this chapter: that the public continuously chooses how to divide its wealth between money and bonds. In the short run, the public's preferences over money and bonds can change, and this, in turn, can change the interest rate. This idea does not appear in the classical model.

Of course, in the long run, the classical model gives us an accurate picture of how the economy—and the interest rate—behaves. Recessions and booms don't last forever, so the economy returns to full employment. Thus, we don't have to worry about shifts in the supply of loanable funds curve in the long run. Also, changes in preferences for holding money and bonds are rather short lived. We can ignore these changes when we take a long-run view.

Our view of the interest rate depends on the time period we are considering. In the long run, the interest rate is determined in the market for loanable funds, where household saving is lent to businesses and the government. In the short run, the interest rate is determined in the money market, where wealth holders adjust their wealth between money and bonds.

SHORT-RUN VERSUS LONG-RUN OUTCOMES

ACTIVE VERSUS PASSIVE POLICY

USING THE THEORY

Throughout this chapter, we've assumed that the Fed's response to changes in spending, or to shifts in the money demand curve, is a **passive monetary policy**—that is, it conducts neither open market purchases nor open market sales of bonds, and just keeps the money supply constant. While this was useful for understanding how different events can affect the economy, it is not a realistic description of Fed policy. Under most circumstances, the Fed wants a stable level of real GDP, rather than a stable money supply. Ideally, the Fed would like to keep the economy operating as close to its potential output as possible. If output falls below potential, the result is a costly recession; if output rises above potential, there is a danger of inflation, which we'll explore further in the next chapter.

In this section, we'll explore **active monetary policy**, in which the Fed responds to events in the economy by *changing* the money supply to achieve its goals—primarily a stable real GDP. As you'll see, the required change in the money supply depends on what type of change in the economy the Fed is responding to.

PASSIVE MONETARY POLICY Federal Reserve policy that holds the money supply constant in response to changes in economic conditions.

ACTIVE MONETARY POLICY Federal Reserve policy that adjusts the money supply in response to changes in economic conditions.

THE FED'S RESPONSE TO SPENDING SHOCKS

FIGURE 10

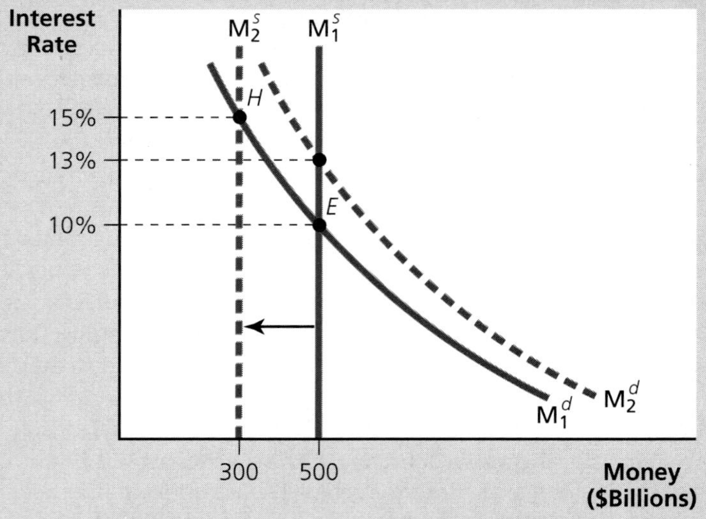

Starting from equilibrium at point *E*, a spending shock would increase real GDP. Under a passive monetary policy, the increase in GDP would shift the money demand curve outward, driving up the interest rate (to 13 percent) and crowding out interest-sensitive spending. The Fed can completely offset the spending shock by reducing the money supply and further increasing the interest rate (to point *H* along the original money demand curve).

THE FED'S RESPONSE TO SPENDING SHOCKS

As you've learned, shifts in the aggregate expenditure line—due to changes in autonomous consumption, investment, taxes, or government purchases—cause changes in real GDP. Even in this chapter, in which we've included effects in the money market that lead to crowding out and smaller changes in output, real GDP still responds to spending shocks. How can the Fed keep real GDP constant when there are spending shocks to the economy?

Figure 10 provides the answer. Initially, the money market is in equilibrium at point *E,* with a money supply of $500 billion and an interest rate of 10 percent. Now suppose a positive spending shock hits the economy, say, an increase in government purchases. Real income will rise, and this shifts the money demand curve rightward, to the dashed line in the figure. Under a *passive* monetary policy, the interest rate would rise (to 13 percent in the figure), and this would cause *some* decline of investment and interest-sensitive consumption. But as you've learned, the crowding out would be less than complete, so real GDP would still rise.

To prevent real GDP from increasing, the Fed will have to raise the interest rate even higher—enough to create *complete* crowding out, thereby counteracting the effect of the rise in government spending. The Fed can do this by *decreasing* the money supply in response to the positive spending shock. In the figure, an interest rate of 15 percent will do the trick, so that the Fed must decrease the money supply from $500 billion to $300 billion. (As in all of our examples, this is an unrealistically huge change in the money supply, but it makes the graph easier to read.) With the new, lower money supply, the equilibrium interest rate is the required 15 percent (point *H*).

Notice that the equilibrium in the money market, at point *H,* occurs along our *original* money demand curve, not the shifted dashed line. Why? Remember why the money demand curve shifted in the first place: because the spending shock caused *real income* to rise. But when the Fed brings real income back to its original level,

the money demand curve will shift back to its original position as well. This is why the Fed must decrease the money supply enough to raise the interest rate to 15 percent along the *original* money demand curve.

Now flip back to Figure 8, where we explored the impact of an increase in government purchases on the economy. There, we assumed that the Fed followed a passive monetary policy. Crowding out was less than complete, so the aggregate expenditure line shifted upward, and equilibrium GDP rose from \$6 trillion to \$7.5 trillion. But if the Fed actively decreases the money supply, to keep real GDP constant, the aggregate expenditure line would not shift at all, and equilibrium real GDP would remain at \$6 trillion.

What if there were a *negative* spending shock to the economy, say, a decrease in government purchases? Then the Fed—to keep real GDP constant—would follow the opposite policy. It would *increase* the money supply, thereby lowering the interest rate by just enough to prevent any downward shift in the aggregate expenditure line.

To stabilize real GDP, the Fed must change the money supply in response to a spending shock. Specifically, it must decrease the money supply in response to a positive spending shock and increase the money supply in response to a negative spending shock.

Notice that an active Fed policy to stabilize real GDP comes at a price: a greater change in the interest rate. In our example, in response to the fiscal stimulus, the Fed raises the interest rate all the way to 15 percent, higher than the passive policy interest rate of 13 percent.

In order to stabilize real GDP, the Fed must engineer greater fluctuations in the interest rate than would occur under a passive monetary policy.

Fluctuations in the interest rate are costly in some ways. They make it more difficult for households and business to plan, and they increase the risks to bondholders (remember that changes in interest rates translate into changes in bond prices). They can also cause problems for the interest-sensitive sectors of the economy, especially housing construction and automobiles. Nevertheless, fluctuations in real GDP are costly too, and the Fed—especially in recent decades—has concluded that it is a good idea to adjust the interest rate aggressively when necessary to stabilize real GDP.

THE FED'S RESPONSE TO CHANGES IN MONEY DEMAND

As you've seen several times in this chapter, shifts in the money demand curve are a natural consequence of spending shocks that change income in the economy. But the money demand curve can also shift on its own. For example, earlier in the chapter, you saw that changes in the expected future interest rate can shift the money demand curve, even when there is no other change in the economy. Changes in tastes for holding money and other assets, or changes in technology, can also shift the money demand curve. For example, the increasing use of substitutes for money—such as credit cards or, in the future, electronic money cards—can decrease the demand for money. When the initial shock to the economy comes from a shift in the money demand curve, the Fed must respond in a different way than we've just discussed.

FIGURE 11

THE FED'S RESPONSE TO CHANGES IN MONEY DEMAND

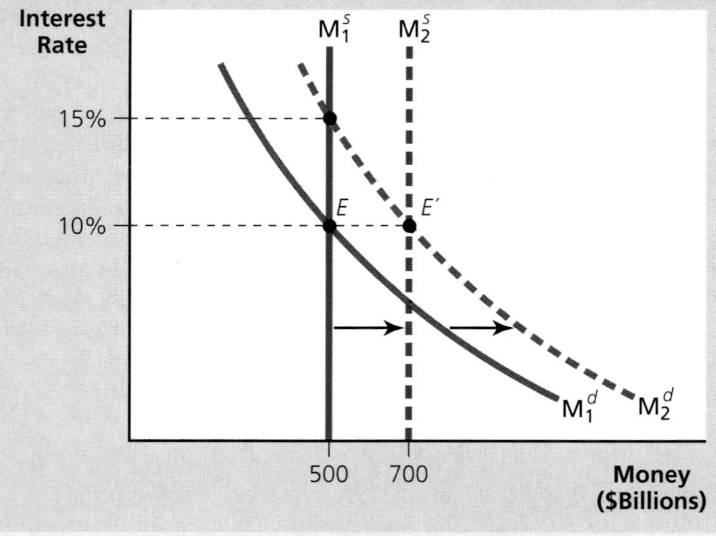

A spontaneous increase in money demand would disturb the equilibrium at point *E.* In the absence of a Fed response, the interest rate would increase to 15 percent. The Fed can offset this increase in the interest rate by raising the money supply (from $500 billion to $700 billion). At *E′*, the interest rate is the same as it was originally.

Figure 11 illustrates this case. Initially, the money supply is $500 billion and the money market is in equilibrium at point *E,* with an interest rate of 10 percent. Now, suppose that people *expect* the interest rate to rise (and bond prices to fall), so they want to shift out of bonds and into money. The money demand curve will shift rightward. If the Fed does nothing, the interest rate will rise—to 15 percent in the figure.

But if the Fed's goal is to stabilize real GDP, it cannot sit by while these events occur. For if the Fed does nothing, the rise in the interest rate will *decrease* investment and interest-sensitive consumption spending, shifting the aggregate expenditure line downward. Real GDP will decrease. What can the Fed do to keep real GDP constant? In this case, the Fed must *neutralize* the change in the interest rate by increasing the money supply. In the figure, a money supply of $700 billion will do the trick. With the equilibrium interest rate back at 10 percent, there is no cause for a shift in the aggregate expenditure line, and no change in equilibrium GDP.

To stabilize real GDP when money demand changes on its own (not in response to a spending shock), the Fed must change the money supply. Specifically, it must increase the money supply in response to an increase in money demand, and decrease the money supply in response to a decrease in money demand.

Notice an interesting (and pleasant) by-product of this policy. In order to stabilize real GDP, the Fed must also stabilize the interest rate. This gives it an easy guideline to follow when disturbances to the economy arise from changes in money demand:

To prevent changes in money demand from affecting real GDP, the Fed should keep the interest rate constant.

In normal times, when there are no significant spending shocks to the economy, the Fed can concentrate its efforts on neutralizing shifts in the money demand curve. For example, this has been the Fed's main activity during the period from 1994 through 1997. In practice, keeping the interest rate constant during such periods is straightforward. When the interest rate rises, the Fed knows the money demand curve has shifted to the right. When the interest rate falls, it knows the money demand curve has shifted leftward.

The Fed does not even need to know the precise amount of the shift in the money demand curve in order to stabilize the interest rate. It can operate successfully with educated guesses. A mistake that it makes one day can be fixed the next day, because the mistake will show up in the interest rate. Since the Fed conducts open market operations each day, it is able to use continuous feedback to keep the interest rate relatively constant. While small changes occur between one day and the next, the changes largely disappear when the interest rate is averaged over several weeks.

In this chapter, you've only just begun to learn about the Fed's policy goals and the practice of monetary policy. We will come back to this important topic soon, in a chapter devoted to monetary policy. But before we do, we need to take a closer look at a major concern of the Fed: inflation. In the next chapter, we extend our analysis of the short run to explore changes in the price level.

SUMMARY

The interest rate is a key macroeconomic variable. This chapter explores how the supply and demand for money interact to determine the interest rate in the short run, and how the Federal Reserve can adjust the money supply to hit and maintain an interest rate target.

An individual's demand for money indicates the fraction of wealth that person wishes to hold in the form of money, for different interest rates. Money is useful as a means of payment, but holding money means sacrificing the interest that could be earned by holding bonds instead. The higher the interest rate, the larger the fraction of their wealth people will hold in the form of bonds, and the smaller the fraction they will hold as money.

The demand for money is sensitive to the interest rate, but also depends upon the price level, real income, and expectations. An increase in the price level, higher real income, or an increase in the expected future interest rate can each shift the money demand curve to the right.

The money supply is under the control of the Fed and is independent of the interest rate. Equilibrium in the money market occurs at the intersection of the downward-sloping money demand curve and the vertical money supply curve. The interest rate will adjust so that the quantity of money demanded by households and firms just equals the quantity of money supplied by the Fed and the banking system.

Conditions in the money market mirror conditions in the bond market. If the interest rate is above equilibrium in the money market, there will be an excess supply of money there. People *want to* hold less money than they actually *do* hold, which means that they wish to hold more bonds than they do hold. An excess supply of money means an excess demand for bonds. As people try to obtain more bonds, the price of bonds rises, and the interest rate falls. Thus an excess supply of money will cause the interest rate to fall. Similarly, an excess demand for money will cause the interest rate to rise.

The Fed can increase the money supply through an open market purchase of bonds, and decrease it through an open market sale. An increase in the money stock creates an excess supply of money. Very quickly, the interest rate will fall so that the public is willing to hold the now-higher money supply. A decrease in the money stock will drive up the interest rate.

Changes in the interest rate affect interest-sensitive forms of spending—firms' spending on plant and equipment, new housing constructions, and households' purchases of "big ticket" consumer durables. By lowering the interest rate, the Fed can stimulate aggregate expenditures and increase GDP through the multiplier process.

Fiscal policy, and other spending shocks, have a smaller effect on output when we include interest-rate changes in our model. The Fed can neutralize the impact of spending shocks on GDP by using active, rather than passive, monetary policy.

KEY TERMS

wealth constraint
money demand curve
money supply curve
excess supply of money
excess demand for bonds
federal funds rate
passive monetary policy
active monetary policy

REVIEW QUESTIONS

1. Why do individuals choose to hold some of their wealth in the form of money? Besides individual tastes, what factors help determine how much money an individual holds?

2. Why is the money demand curve downward sloping? Which of the following result in a shift of the money demand curve and which result in a movement along the curve? If there is a shift, in what direction?
   a. The Fed lowers interest rates.
   b. The Fed raises interest rates.
   c. The price level falls.
   d. The price level rises.
   e. Income increases.
   f. Income decreases.

3. Why is the economy's money supply curve vertical? What causes the money supply curve to shift?

4. What sequence of events brings the money market to equilibrium if there is an excess supply of money? An excess demand for money?

5. The text mentions that starting in July 1989 the Fed began purchasing government bonds, and as a result, the interest rate fell to a little over 8 percent. Explain how the Fed's purchase of bonds led to a lower interest rate.

6. Describe how an increase in the interest rate affects spending on the following:
   a. plant and equipment
   b. new housing
   c. consumer durables

7. Does a change in expectations about the interest rate result in a shift in the money demand curve or a movement along it? Explain what happens in the money market when people expect the interest rate to fall.

8. Why do we have both a short-run and a long-run theory of the interest rate? Briefly, what determines the interest rate in the short run? In the long run?

9. In the face of increased government spending, what could the Fed do to maintain a stable level of real GDP? In the case of a decrease in government spending, how can the Fed maintain a stable level of real GDP?

PROBLEMS AND EXERCISES

1. Assume the demand deposit multiplier is 10. By how much will the money supply change and in what direction will the money supply curve shift if:
   a. the Fed purchases bonds worth $10 billion?
   b. the Fed sells bonds worth $5 billion?

2. A bond promises to pay $500 one year from now. For the following prices, find the corresponding interest payments and interest rates that the bond offers.

Price	*Amt. Paid in One Year*	*Interest Payment*	*Interest Rate*
$375	$500	______	______
$425	$500	______	______
$450	$500	______	______
$500	$500	______	______

As the price of the bond rises, what happens to the bond's interest rate?

3. "A general expectation that the interest rate will fall can be a self-fulfilling prophecy." Explain what this means.

4. Suppose that, in an attempt to prevent the economy from overheating, the Fed raises the interest rate. Illustrate graphically, using a diagram similar to Figure 7 in the chapter, the effect on the money supply, interest rate, and GDP.

5. The government is interested in raising GDP, so it cuts taxes. Use a diagram similar to Figure 8 in the chapter to illustrate the effects of a cut in taxes. Comparing the old and the new equilibrium, what has happened to GDP and the interest rate?

6. Assume that the Fed's goal is to stabilize GDP. How would it respond to the following changes in money demand? How will the interest rate and GDP be affected in each case? How would the effects be different if the Fed were using a passive rather than an active policy? Illustrate each case with a diagram.
   a. People believe the interest rate will fall in the near future, so money demand falls.
   b. Many credible financial advisors recommend buying bonds, and consequently the demand for bonds increases.
   c. Tired of credit card debt, the general public begins to use credit cards less frequently and money more frequently.

CHALLENGE QUESTION

Is fiscal policy more or less effective in changing GDP when autonomous consumption and investment spending are very sensitive to changes in the interest rate? What about monetary policy?

Visit the Federal Reserve Board of Governors site (http://www.bog.frb.fed.us/).

a. Review the minutes from the most recent meeting of the Federal Open Market Committee. Relate the concepts discussed in the minutes to the text discussion of monetary policy. In your opinion, what do the minutes indicate about possible action by the FMOC?
b. Look within "Statistics: Releases and Historical Data" for historical data on selected interest rates. Review the annual discount rate for the New York Fed (http://www.bog.frb.fed.us/releases/H15/data/a/dwb.txt). From this data, what do you suppose were the economic conditions and the Fed's monetary strategy for the following time periods: 1978–1985 and 1992–1994?

C H A P T E R

13

AGGREGATE DEMAND AND AGGREGATE SUPPLY

CHAPTER OUTLINE

From 1929 to 1933, in the early phase of the Great Depression, U.S. output fell by 30 percent, and the unemployment rate rose from 3.2 percent to about 25 percent. But something else of interest happened as well: The price level fell dramatically. A basket of goods that cost $100 in 1929 cost only about $76 in 1933.

In 1990, the U.S. economy experienced a sharp recession. Although not nearly as serious as the Great Depression, its effects were painful and wide ranging. As plants closed, millions of workers lost their jobs, and the unemployment rate rose from 5.3 percent to 7.5 percent. At the same time, prices rose more rapidly than in previous years.

In both of these periods, output fell. But the price level behaved differently in each case. What are we to make of these apparently contradictory experiences? Did the fundamental rules governing the macroeconomy change between the 1930s and the 1990s? Actually, no. In this chapter, you'll learn that as output falls, the price level can either decrease (as in the Great Depression) or increase (as in 1990). The same holds for an *increase* in output. As you'll see, by adding changes in the price level to our model, we can improve our understanding of economic fluctuations—and explain more fully how the economy returns to normal after a boom or recession.

We'll begin the chapter by exploring the relationship between the price level and output. This is a two-way relationship, as you can see in Figure 1. On the one hand, changes in the price level causes changes in real GDP. This causal relationship is illustrated by the *aggregate demand curve,* which we will discuss shortly. On the other hand, changes in real GDP cause changes in the price level. This relationship is summarized by the *aggregate supply curve,* to which we will turn later.

Once we've developed the aggregate demand and supply curves, we'll be able to use them to understand the role of the price level, both in the short run—a period of a year or so following a change in the economy—and over longer time horizons as well.

THE TWO-WAY RELATIONSHIP BETWEEN OUTPUT AND THE PRICE LEVEL

FIGURE 1

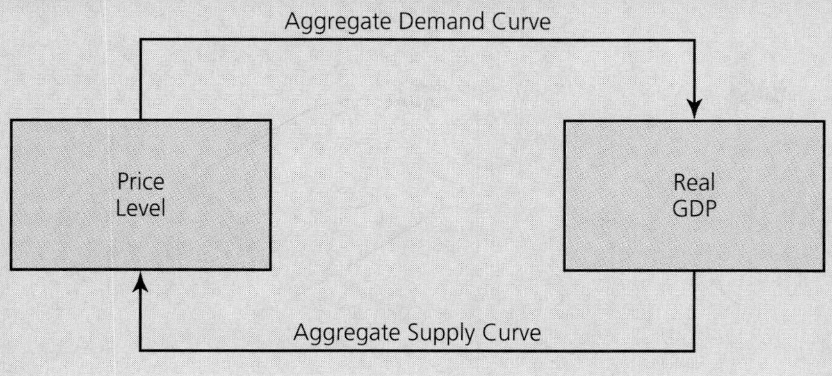

THE AGGREGATE DEMAND CURVE

In this section, we'll focus on how changes in the price level affect equilibrium real GDP. We'll postpone till later the question of *why* the price level might change.

Let's suppose that, initially, the price level (measured by the GDP Price Index) is 100. In Figure 2, we show our familiar money market and aggregate expenditure diagram. For now, focus on the solid lines in the two top panels, (a) and (b). In panel (a), the money market is in equilibrium at point *A*, with an interest rate of 10 percent. Notice that the money demand curve is now marked "$P = 100$, $Y = \$6$ trillion." This is because changes in either the price level (P) or income (Y) shift the money demand curve, so we always draw the curve for particular values of P and Y.

In panel (b), equilibrium GDP is at point *E*, with output equal to $6 trillion. The aggregate expenditure line is marked "$r = 10\%$," which is the equilibrium interest rate found in the money market.

Now let's imagine a rather substantial rise in the price level—from 100 to 140. What will happen in the economy? The initial impact is in the money market. With higher prices, people's dollar spending will rise at any given level of the interest rate and real GDP. The money demand curve will start to shift rightward, and the interest rate will rise. Next, in panel (b), the higher interest rate decreases interest-sensitive spending—business investment, new housing, and consumer durables. The aggregate expenditure line shifts downward, and equilibrium real GDP decreases. All of these changes continue until we reach a new, consistent equilibrium in both panels. Compared with our initial position, this new equilibrium will have the following characteristics:

- The money demand curve will have shifted rightward.
- The interest rate will be higher.
- The aggregate expenditure line will have shifted downward.
- Equilibrium GDP will be lower.

Remember that all of these changes are caused by a rise in the price level.

The dashed lines in the figure show one possible new, short-run equilibrium consistent with these requirements. In panel (a), the money demand curve has shifted to the dashed line, marked "$P = 140$, $Y = \$5$ trillion." The interest rate has risen

FIGURE 2

DERIVING THE AGGREGATE DEMAND CURVE

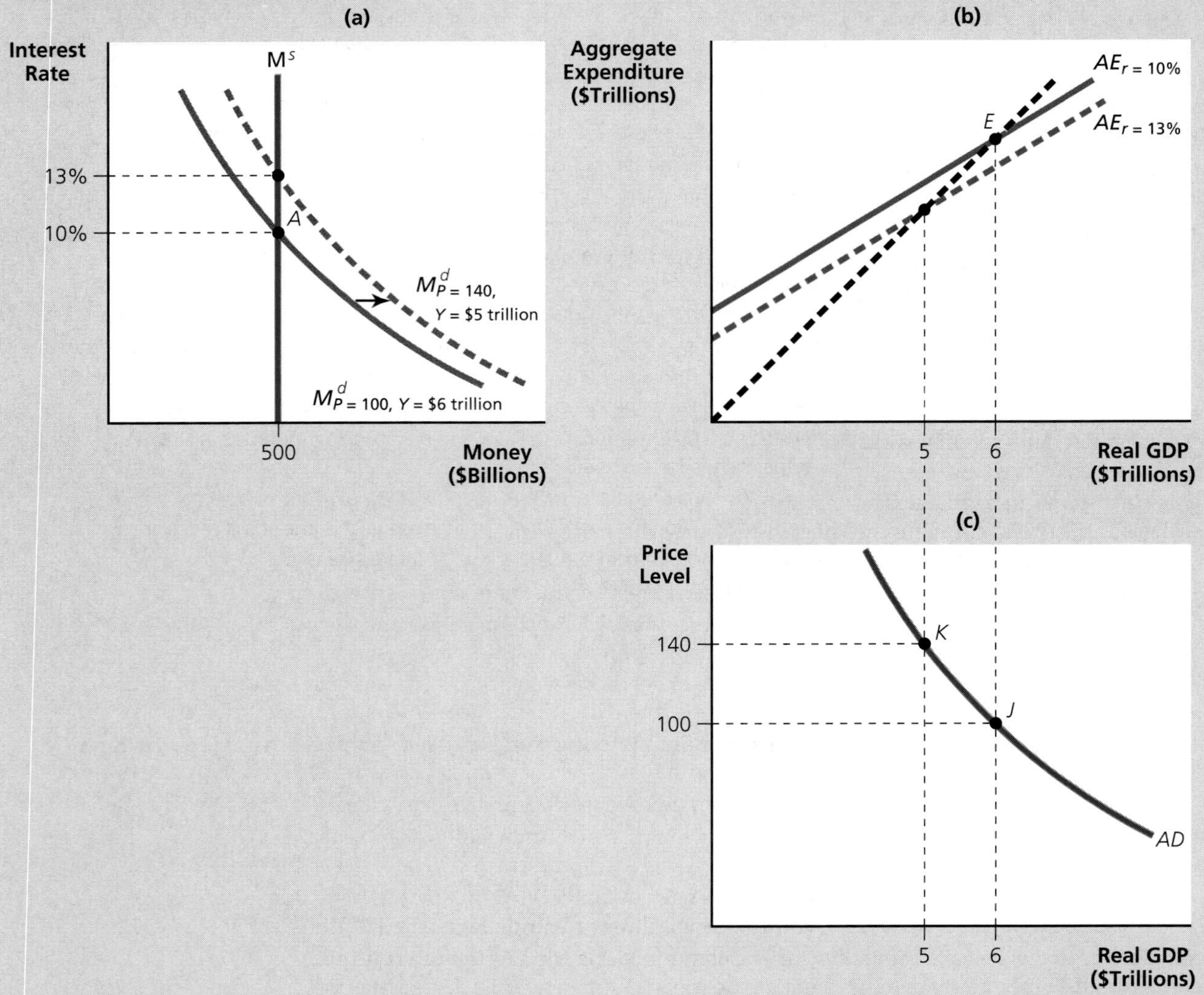

With a price level of 100 and real GDP of $6 trillion, the money market is in equilibrium at point *A* in panel (a), and aggregate expenditure equals real GDP at point *E* in panel (b). That price–output combination determines point *J* in panel (c). A higher price level—140—increases money demand, raises the interest rate, reduces interest-sensitive spending, and lowers aggregate expenditure. Through the multiplier process, equilibrium real GDP falls to $5 trillion. The new price–output combination determines point *K* in panel (c). Connecting points like *J* and *K* yields the downward-sloping aggregate demand (*AD*) curve.

to 13 percent. The aggregate expenditure line has shifted downward, to the one marked "$r = 13\%$." Finally, equilibrium output has fallen to $5 trillion.

Now recall the initial event that caused real GDP to fall: a rise in the price level. We've thus established an important principle:

A rise in the price level causes a decrease in equilibrium GDP.

In panel (c), we introduce a new curve that summarizes the negative relationship between the price level and equilibrium GDP more directly. In this panel, the price level is measured along the vertical axis, while real GDP is on the horizontal. Point *J* represents our initial equilibrium, with *P* = 100 and equilibrium GDP = $6 trillion. Point *K* represents the new equilibrium, with *P* = 140 and equilibrium GDP = $5 trillion. If we continued to change the price level to other values—raising it further to 150, lowering it to 85, and so on—we would find that each different price level results in a different equilibrium GDP. This is illustrated by the downward-sloping curve in the figure, which we call the *aggregate demand curve.*

DANGEROUS CURVES

Watch out for two common mistakes about the aggregate demand curve. The first is thinking that it is simply a "total demand" or "total spending" curve for the economy, telling us the total quantity of output that purchasers want to buy at each price level. This is an oversimplification. Rather, the *AD* curve tells us the *equilibrium real GDP* at each price level. Remember that equilibrium GDP is the level of output at which total spending *equals* total output. Thus, total spending is only part of the story behind the *AD* curve; the other part is the requirement that total spending and total output be equal.

A second, related mistake is thinking that the *AD* curve is obtained by adding up demand curves for every product in the economy. This, too, is wrong; *microeconomic* demand curves for individual products rely on an entirely different mechanism than the one we've described for the *AD* curve. In the market for maple syrup, for example, a rise in price causes quantity demanded to decrease mostly because people switch to other goods that are now relatively cheaper. But along the *AD* curve, a rise in the price level generally causes the prices of all goods to increase *together.* In this case, there are no relatively cheaper goods to switch to!

The *AD* curve works in an entirely different way from microeconomic demand curves. Along the *AD* curve, an increase in the price level raises the interest rate, which decreases spending on interest-sensitive goods, causing a drop in equilibrium GDP.

*The **aggregate demand** (AD) **curve** tells us the equilibrium real GDP at any price level.*

AGGREGATE DEMAND (*AD*) CURVE A curve indicating equilibrium GDP at each price level.

UNDERSTANDING THE *AD* CURVE

The *AD* curve is unlike any other curve you've encountered in this text. In all other cases, our curves have represented simple behavioral relationships. For example, the demand curve for maple syrup shows us how a change in price affects the behavior of buyers in a market. Similarly, the aggregate expenditure line shows how a change in income affects total spending in the economy.

But the *AD* curve represents more than just a behavioral relationship between two variables: Each point on the curve represents a short-run *equilibrium* in the economy. For example, point *J* in Figure 2 tells us that when the price level is 100, *equilibrium* GDP is $6 trillion. Thus, point *J* doesn't just tell us that total spending is $6 trillion; rather, it tells us that, when *P* = 100, the level of output at which *total spending and total output are equal* is $6 trillion.

As you can see, a better name for the *AD* curve would be the "equilibrium output at each price level" curve—not a very catchy name. The *AD* curve gets its name because it *resembles* the demand curve for an individual product. It's a downward-sloping curve, with the price level (instead of the price of a single good) on the vertical axis and total output (instead of the quantity of a single good demanded) on the horizontal axis. But there the similarity ends. The *AD* curve is not a demand curve at all, in spite of its name.

MOVEMENTS ALONG THE *AD* CURVE

As you will see later in this chapter, a variety of events can cause the price level to change, and move us *along* the *AD* curve. It's important to understand what happens in the economy as we make such a move.

Look again at the *AD* curve in panel (c) of Figure 2. Suppose the price level rises, and we move from point *J* to point *K* along this curve. Then the following sequence of events occurs: The rise in the price level increases the demand for money, raises the interest rate, decreases autonomous consumption (*a*) and investment spending (*I*), and works through the multiplier to decrease equilibrium GDP. The process can be summarized as follows:

$P\uparrow$ → Increase in money demand → $r\uparrow$ → a and $I\downarrow$ —Multiplier effect→ Equilibrium GDP $\downarrow$

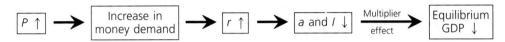

The opposite sequence of events will occur if the price level falls, moving us rightward along the *AD* curve:

$P\downarrow$ → Decrease in money demand → $r\downarrow$ → a and $I\uparrow$ —Multiplier effect→ Equilibrium GDP $\uparrow$

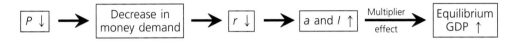

SHIFTS OF THE *AD* CURVE

When we move along the *AD* curve in Figure 2, we assume that the price level changes, but that other influences on equilibrium GDP are held constant. When any of these other influences on GDP changes, the *AD* curve will shift. The distinction between movements along the *AD* curve and shifts of the curve itself is very important. Always keep the following rule in mind:

> *When a change in the price level causes equilibrium GDP to change, we move along the AD curve. Whenever anything* other *than the price level causes equilibrium GDP to change, the AD curve itself shifts.*

What are these other influences on GDP? They are the very same changes you learned about in previous chapters. Specifically, equilibrium GDP will change whenever there is a change in any of the following:

- government spending
- taxes
- autonomous consumption spending
- investment spending
- the money supply
- the money demand curve

Let's consider some examples and see how each causes the *AD* curve to shift.

SPENDING SHOCKS. Spending shocks initially affect the economy by shifting the aggregate expenditure line. Here, we'll see how these spending shocks—which you've encountered several times in this book already—shift the *AD* curve.

In Figure 3, we assume that the economy begins at a price level of 100. In the money market (not shown), the equilibrium interest rate is 10 percent, and equilibrium output—given by point *E* in the upper panel—is $6 trillion. The lower panel shows the same equilibrium as represented by point *J* on AD_1.

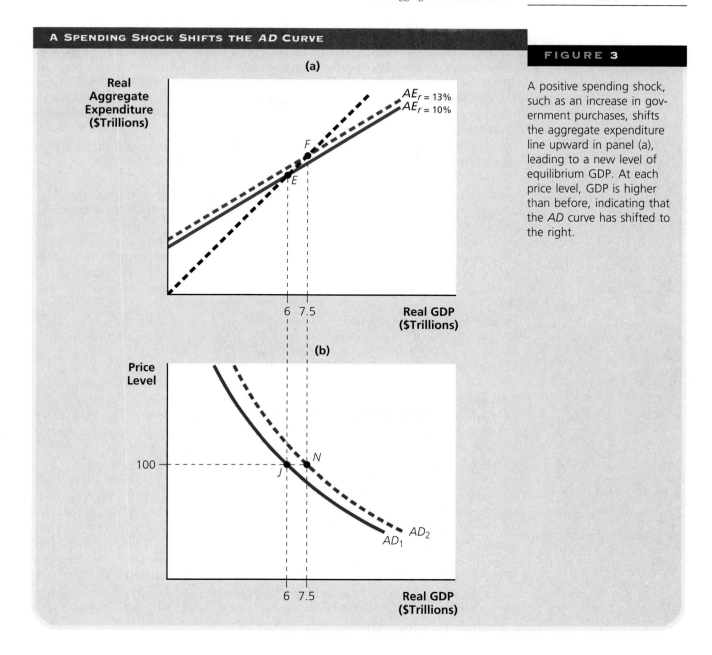

A SPENDING SHOCK SHIFTS THE *AD* CURVE

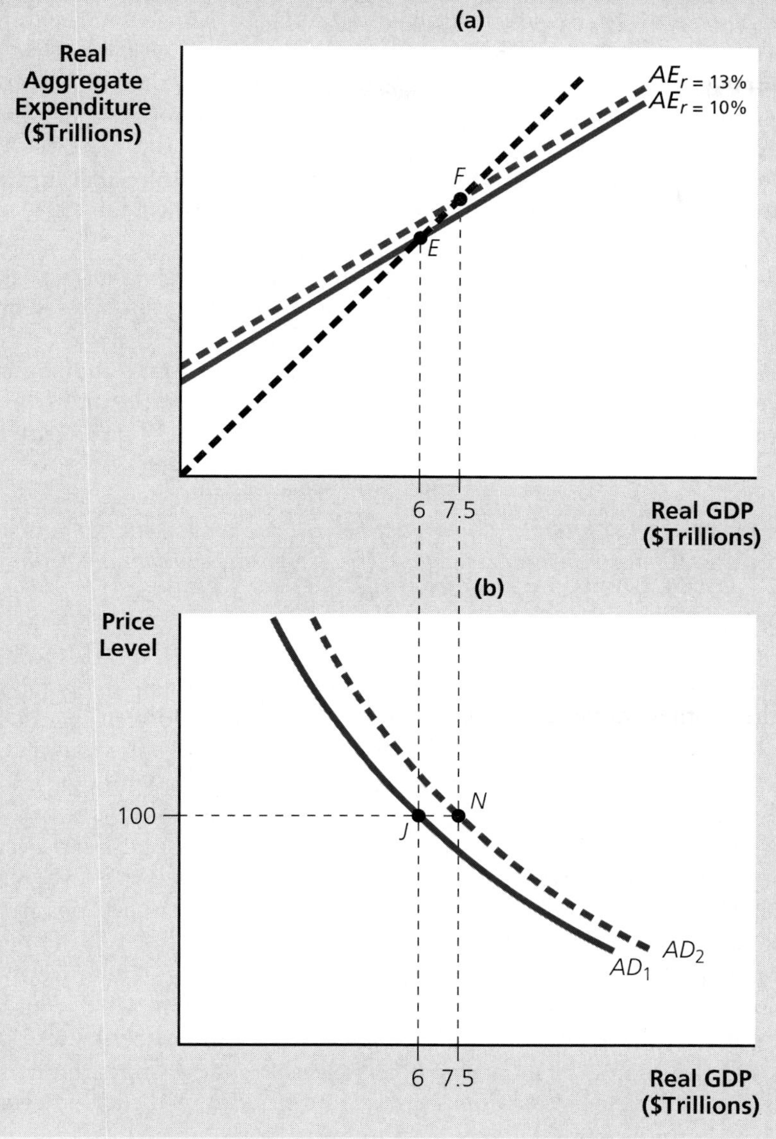

FIGURE 3

A positive spending shock, such as an increase in government purchases, shifts the aggregate expenditure line upward in panel (a), leading to a new level of equilibrium GDP. At each price level, GDP is higher than before, indicating that the *AD* curve has shifted to the right.

Now let's repeat an experiment from the previous chapter: We'll increase government purchases by $1 trillion and ask what happens if the price level remains at 100. If you flip back to Figure 8 in the previous chapter, you'll see that this rise in government purchases caused the *AE* line to shift upward, but it also caused the equilibrium interest rate to rise to 13 percent, causing the *AE* line to shift back downward a bit. The result was that equilibrium GDP rose to $7.5 trillion. This new equilibrium is also shown in the upper panel of Figure 3. The aggregate expenditure line shifts upward to the dashed line, and the equilibrium moves to point *F*. With the price level remaining at 100, equilibrium GDP increases.

Now look at the lower panel of Figure 3. There, the new equilibrium is represented by point *N* (P = 100, real GDP = $7.5 trillion). This point lies to the right of our original curve AD_1. Point *N*, therefore, must lie on a *new AD* curve—a curve that tells us equilibrium GDP at any price level *after the increase in government spending*. The new *AD* curve is the dashed line, AD_2, which goes through point *N*. What about the other points on AD_2? They tell us that, if we had started at any *other* price level, an increase in government spending would have increased equilibrium GDP at that price level, too. We conclude that *an increase in government purchases shifts the entire AD curve rightward.*

Other spending shocks that shift the aggregate expenditure line upward shift the *AD* curve rightward just as in Figure 3. More specifically,

> *the AD curve shifts rightward when government purchases, investment spending, or autonomous consumption spending increases, or when taxes decrease.*

Our analysis also applies in the other direction. For example, at any given price level, a *decrease* in government spending shifts the aggregate expenditure line *downward*, decreasing equilibrium GDP. This in turn shifts the *AD* curve leftward. More generally,

> *the AD curve shifts leftward when government purchases, investment spending, or autonomous consumption spending decreases, or when taxes increase.*

CHANGES IN THE MONEY MARKET. Changes that originate in the money market will also shift the aggregate demand curve. To see why, look at Figure 4, which illustrates the effect of an increase in the money supply. Initially, the price level is equal to 100, and the Fed has set the money stock at $500 billion. Our initial equilibrium is represented by points *A*, *E*, and *J* in the figure.

Now suppose the Fed conducts an open market purchase of bonds, increasing the money supply from $500 billion to $800 billion, but the price level remains at 100. Then the money supply curve shifts rightward, from M_1^s to M_2^s, and the interest rate falls. (It *would* fall all the way to 5 percent, except that the money demand curve will shift before we are finished.) As the interest rate drops, the aggregate expenditure line shifts upward, increasing equilibrium GDP. This, in turn, causes a rightward shift in the money demand curve, raising the interest rate back up a bit. Panels (a) and (b) show one possible result: a new, short-run equilibrium at points *B* and *F*. The equilibrium interest rate has dropped to 7 percent, and—importantly—equilibrium GDP has risen to $8 trillion.

Throughout our analysis, we've assumed that the price level remains constant at $P = 100$. At this price level, the increase in the money supply raises equilibrium GDP to $8 trillion. Therefore, in the lower panel, the economy moves to point *L*. The *AD* curve has *shifted* from AD_1 to AD_2.

A decrease in the money supply would have the oppo-

DANGEROUS CURVES

Be very careful when thinking about the effects of a change in autonomous consumption (*a*) or investment spending (*I*), or a shift in the money demand curve. If you look back at Figure 2, you'll see that these changes occur automatically as we move *along* the *AD* curve. So how can we distinguish when such changes cause the *AD* curve to shift?

Actually, there is a very simple rule: If *a* or *I* or the money demand curve changes *because a change in the price level has changed the interest rate,* we move along a given *AD* curve. If *a* or *I* or the money demand curve change *for any other reason*—a reason we *cannot* trace back to a change in the price level—the *AD* curve shifts.

A CHANGE IN THE MONEY SUPPLY SHIFTS THE *AD* CURVE

FIGURE 4

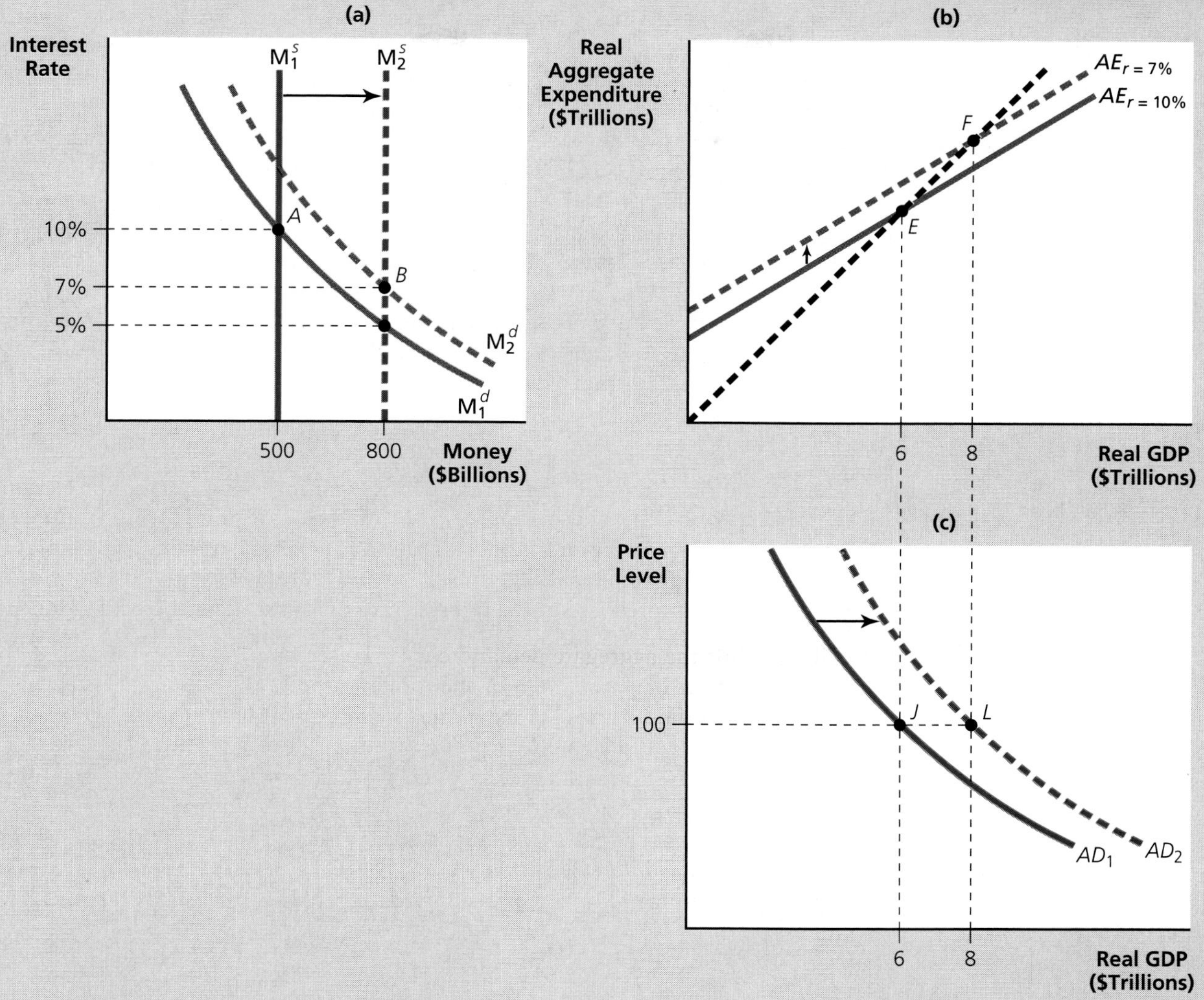

With a money supply of $500 billion, the money market is in equilibrium at point *A;* the interest rate is 10 percent. In panel (b), real GDP of $6 trillion is determined at point *E.* Given a price level of 100, the economy is at point *J* on AD_1 in panel (c). An increase in the money supply to $800 billion will lower the interest rate and raise aggregate expenditures. In the new equilibrium at point *F* in panel (b), real GDP is higher, at $8 trillion. Panel (c) shows that the *AD* curve has shifted right—there is a higher level of GDP associated with each price level.

site effect in Figure 4: The money supply curve would shift leftward. As a result, the interest rate would rise, the aggregate expenditure line would shift downward, and *equilibrium GDP at any price level would fall.* We conclude that

an increase in the money supply shifts the AD curve rightward. A decrease in the money supply shifts the AD curve leftward.

TABLE 1

EFFECTS OF KEY CHANGES ON THE AGGREGATE DEMAND CURVE

	Price Level		Government Purchases, Autonomous Consumption, or Investment Spending		Taxes		Money Supply		Money Demand	
	Increases	Decreases	Increases	Decreases	Increase	Decrease	Increases	Decreases	Increases	Decreases
Effect on *AD* Curve	Movement upward along curve	Movement downward along curve	Shifts right-ward	Shifts left-ward	Shifts left-ward	Shifts right-ward	Shifts right-ward	Shifts left-ward	Shifts left-ward	Shifts right-ward

Changes in the money demand curve can also shift the *AD* curve. For example, if the public *expects* the interest rate to rise (the price of bonds to fall), they will want to sell bonds and acquire money. To test your understanding, put down the book and—with a three-panel diagram similar to Figure 4—see if you can trace out the effects of an expected rise in the interest rate. If you do this correctly, your new equilibrium will show the following: The money demand curve has shifted rightward, the interest rate is higher, the aggregate expenditure line has shifted downward, and the *AD* curve has shifted leftward.

Changes in money demand cause the AD curve to shift. If the money demand curve shifts rightward, the AD curve shifts leftward. If the money demand curve shifts leftward, the AD curve shifts rightward.

SHIFTS VS. MOVEMENTS ALONG THE *AD* CURVE: A SUMMARY. Table 1 summarizes how different events in the economy cause a movement along, or a shift in, the *AD* curve. You can use the table as an exercise; drawing diagrams similar to Figures 3 and 4 to illustrate each case.

Notice that the table tells us how a variety of events affect the *AD* curve, but *not* how they affect *real* GDP. The reason is that, even if we know which *AD* curve the economy is on, we could be at *any point* along that curve, depending on the price level.

But how is the price level determined? Our first step in answering that question is to understand the other side of the relationship between GDP and the price level.

THE AGGREGATE SUPPLY CURVE

Look back at Figure 1, which illustrates the *two-way* relationship between the price level and output. On the one hand, changes in the price level affect output. This is the relationship—summarized by the *AD* curve—that we explored in the previous section. On the other hand, changes in output affect the price level. This relationship—summarized by the *aggregate supply curve*—is the focus of this section.

The effect of changes in output on the price level is complex, involving a variety of forces. Current research is helping economists get a clearer picture of this relationship. Here, we will present a simple model of the aggregate supply curve that focuses on the link between prices and costs. Toward the end of the chapter, we'll discuss some additional ideas about the aggregate supply curve.

PRICES AND COSTS IN THE SHORT RUN

The price *level* in the economy results from the pricing behavior of millions of individual business firms. In any given year, some of these firms will raise their prices, and some will lower them. For example, during the 1990s, personal computers and long-distance telephone calls came down in price, while college tuition and the prices of movies rose. These types of price changes are subjects for *micro*economic analysis, because they involve individual markets.

But often, all firms in the economy are affected by the same *macro*economic event, causing prices to rise or fall throughout the economy. This change in the price *level* is what interests us in macroeconomics.

To understand how macroeconomic events affect the price level, we begin with a very simple assumption:

A firm sets the price of its products as a markup over cost per unit.

For example, if it costs Burger King \$2.00, on average, to produce a Whopper (cost per unit is \$2.00), and Burger King's percentage markup is 10 percent, then it will charge \$2.00 + (0.10 × \$2.00) = \$2.20 per Whopper.[1]

The percentage markup in any particular industry will depend on the degree of competition there. If there are many firms competing for customers in a market, all producing very similar products, then we can expect the markup to be relatively small. Thus, we expect a relatively low markup on fast-food burgers or personal computers. In industries where there is less competition—such as daily newspapers or jet aircraft—we would expect higher percentage markups.

In macroeconomics, we are not concerned with how the markup differs in different industries, but rather with the *average percentage markup* in the economy:

The average percentage markup in the economy is determined by competitive conditions in the economy. The competitive structure of the economy changes very slowly, so the average percentage markup should be somewhat stable from year to year.

But a stable markup does not necessarily mean a stable price level, because unit costs can change. For example, if Burger King's markup remains at 10 percent, but the unit cost of a Whopper rises from \$2.00 to \$3.00, then the price of a Whopper will rise to \$3.00 + (0.1 × \$3.00) = \$3.30. Extending this example to all firms in the economy, we can say:

1 In microeconomics, you learn more sophisticated theories of how firms' prices are determined. But our simple markup model captures a central conclusion of those theories: that an increase in costs will result in higher prices.

In the short run, the price level rises when there is an economy-wide increase in unit costs, and the price level falls when there is an economy-wide decrease in unit costs.

Our primary concern in this chapter is the impact of *output* on unit costs and, therefore, on the price level. Why should a change in output affect unit costs and the price level? We'll focus on three key reasons. As total output in the economy increases:

- *Greater amounts of inputs may be needed to produce a unit of output.* As output increases, firms hire new, untrained workers who may be less productive than existing workers. Firms also begin using capital and land that are less well-suited to their industry. As a result, greater amounts of labor, capital, land, and raw materials are needed to produce each unit of output. Even if the prices of these inputs remain the same, unit costs will rise. For example, imagine that Intel increases its output of computer chips. Then it will have to be less picky about the workers it employs, hiring some who are less well-suited to chip production than those already working there. Thus, more labor hours will be needed to produce each chip. Intel may also have to begin using older, less efficient production facilities, which require more silicon and other raw materials per chip. Even if the prices of all of these inputs remain unchanged, unit costs will rise.
- *The prices of non-labor inputs rises.* This is especially true of inputs like land and natural resources, which may be available only in limited quantities in the short run. An increase in the output of final goods raises the demand for these inputs, causing their prices to rise. Firms that produce final goods experience an increase in unit costs, and raise their own prices accordingly.
- *The nominal wage rate rises.* Greater output means higher employment, leaving fewer unemployed workers looking for jobs. As firms compete to hire increasingly scarce workers, they must offer higher nominal wage rates to attract them. Higher nominal wages increase unit costs, and therefore result in a higher price level. Notice that we use the nominal wage, rather than the real wage we've emphasized elsewhere in this book. That's because we are interested in explaining how firms' prices are determined. Since price is a nominal variable, it will be marked up over *nominal* costs.

A decrease in output affects unit costs through the same three forces, but with the opposite result. As output falls, firms can be more selective in hiring the best, most efficient workers and in choosing other inputs, decreasing input requirements per unit of output. Decreases in demand for land and natural resources will cause their prices to drop. And as unemployment rises, wages will fall as workers compete for jobs. All of these contribute to a drop in unit costs, and a decrease in the price level.

All three of our reasons are important in explaining why a change in output affects the price level. However, they operate within different time frames. When total output increases, new, less productive workers will be hired rather quickly. Similarly, the prices of certain key inputs—such as lumber, land, oil, and wheat—may rise within a few weeks or months.

But our third explanation—changes in the nominal wage rate—is a different story. While wages in some lines of work might respond very rapidly, we can expect wages in many industries to change very little or not at all for a year or more after a change in output.

For a year or so after a change in output, changes in the average nominal wage are less important than other forces that change unit costs.

Here are some of the more important reasons why wages in many industries respond so slowly to changes in output:

- Many firms have union contracts that specify wages for up to three years. While wage increases are often built into these contracts, a rise in output will not affect the wage increase. When output rises or falls, these firms continue to abide by the contract.
- Wages in many large corporations are set by slow-moving bureaucracies.
- Wage changes in either direction can be costly to firms. Higher wages must be widely publicized in order to raise the number of job applicants at the firm. Lower wages can reduce the morale of workers—and their productivity. Thus, many firms are reluctant to change wages until they are reasonably sure that any change in demand for their output will be long lasting.
- Firms may benefit from developing reputations for paying stable wages. A firm that raises wages when output is high and labor is scarce may have to lower wages when output is low and labor is plentiful. Such a firm would develop a reputation for paying unstable wages, and have difficulty attracting new workers.

In this section, we focus exclusively on the short run—a time horizon of a year or so after a change in output. Since the average wage rate changes very little over the short run, we'll make the following simplifying assumption: *The nominal wage rate is fixed in the short run.* More specifically,

we assume that changes in output have no effect on the nominal wage rate in the short run.[2]

Keep in mind, though, that our assumption of a constant wage holds only in the *short run.* As you will see later, wage changes play a very important role in the economy's adjustment over the long run.

Since we assume a constant nominal wage in the short run, a change in output will affect unit costs through the other two factors we mentioned earlier. Specifically, in the short run, a rise in real GDP raises firms' unit costs because (1) the prices of non-labor inputs rise; and (2) input requirements per unit of output rise. With a constant percentage markup, the rise in unit costs translates into a rise in the price level. Thus,

in the short run, a rise in real GDP, by causing unit costs to increase, will also cause a rise in the price level.

In the other direction, a *drop* in real GDP lowers unit costs because (1) the prices of non-labor inputs fall; and (2) input requirements per unit of output fall. With a constant percentage markup, the drop in unit costs translates into a fall in the price level.

2 This simplifying assumption is not entirely realistic. In some industries, wages will respond to changes in output, at least somewhat, even in the short run. However, assuming that the nominal wage remains constant in the short run makes our model much simpler, without affecting any of our essential conclusions.

THE AGGREGATE SUPPLY CURVE

FIGURE 5

Beginning at point *A*, an increase in output will raise unit costs. For given percentage markups, firms will raise the prices they charge. An increase in output from \$6 trillion to \$8 trillion might raise the price level from 100 to 140 at point *B*. A decrease in output would lower unit costs and lead firms to lower their prices. The price level might fall to 80 at point *C*. Connecting points such as *A*, *B*, and *C* traces out the economy's *AS* curve.

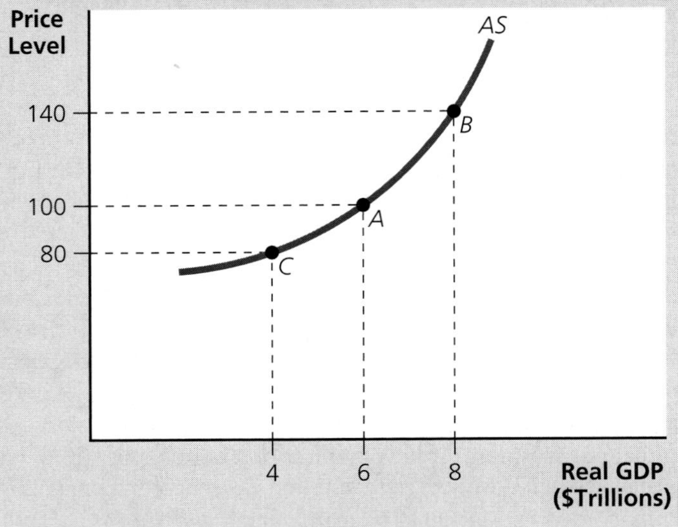

In the short run, a fall in real GDP, by causing unit costs to decrease, will also cause a decrease in the price level.

DERIVING THE AGGREGATE SUPPLY CURVE

Figure 5 summarizes our discussion about the effect of output on the price level in the short run. Suppose the economy begins at point *A*, with output at \$6 trillion and the price level at 100. Now suppose that output rises to \$8 trillion. What will happen in the short run? Even though wages are assumed to remain constant, the price level will rise because of the other forces we've discussed. In the figure, the price level rises to 140, indicated by point *B*. If, instead, output *fell* to \$4 trillion, the price level would fall—to 80 in the figure, indicated by point *C*.

As you can see, each time we change the level of output, there will be a new price level in the short run, giving us another point on the figure. If we connect all of these points with a line, we obtain the economy's *aggregate supply curve:*

AGGREGATE SUPPLY (*AS*) CURVE A curve indicating the price level consistent with firms' unit costs and markups for any level of output over the short run.

*The **aggregate supply curve** (or **AS curve**) tells us the price level consistent with firms' unit costs and their percentage markup at any level of output* over the short run.

An entirely accurate name for the *AS* curve would be the "short-run-price-level-at-each-output-level" curve, but that is not a very catchy name. The AS curve gets its name because it *resembles* a microeconomic market supply curve. Like the supply curve for maple syrup we discussed in Chapter 3, the AS curve is upward sloping, and it has a price variable (the price level) on the vertical axis, and a quantity variable (total output) on the horizontal axis. But there, the similarity ends.

Movements Along the *AS* Curve

When a change in output causes the price level to change, we *move along* the economy's *AS* curve. But what happens in the economy as we make such a move?

Look again at the *AS* curve in Figure 5. Suppose we move from point *A* to point *B* along this curve in the short run. The increase in output raises the prices of raw materials and other (non-labor) inputs and also raises input requirements per unit of output at many firms. Both of these changes increase costs per unit. As long as the markup remains somewhat stable, the rise in unit costs will lead firms to raise their prices, and the price level will increase. Thus, as we move upward along the *AS* curve, we can represent what happens as follows:

DANGEROUS CURVES

A very common mistake about the *AS* curve is thinking that it is obtained by summing up the supply curves for all the different products in the economy. There are two reasons why this is wrong.

First, the direction of causation between price and output is reversed for the *AS* curve. For example, when we draw the supply curve for maple syrup, we view changes in the price of maple syrup as causing a change in quantity supplied. But along the *AS* curve, a change in output causes a change in the price level.

Second, the basic assumption behind the *AS* curve is very different from that behind a single market supply curve. When we draw the supply curve for an individual product, we assume that all other prices in the economy, including the prices of inputs used in producing the good, remain fixed. This is a sensible thing to do, because an increase in production for a single good is unlikely to have much effect on input prices in the economy as a whole.

But when we draw the *AS* curve, we imagine an increase in *real GDP,* in which *all* firms are increasing their output. In this case, it is unrealistic to assume that input prices remain fixed since the demand for inputs *in general* will be rising. Indeed, the rise in input prices is one of the important reasons for the *AS* curve's upward slope.

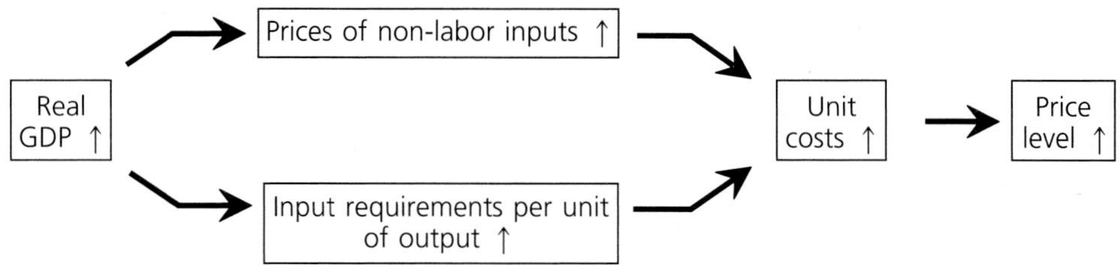

The opposite sequence of events occurs when real GDP falls, moving us downward along the *AS* curve:

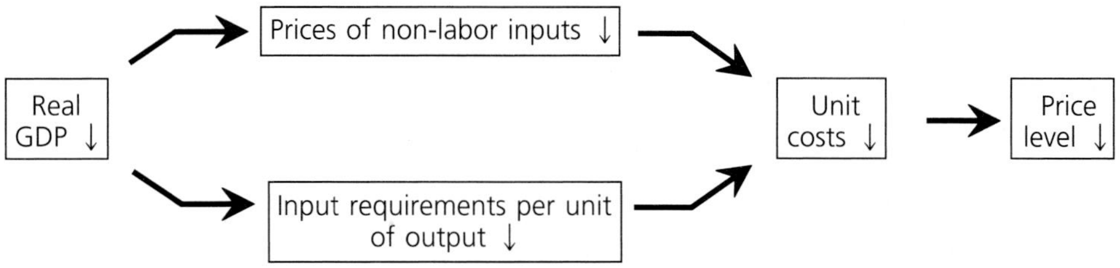

Shifts of the *AS* Curve

When we drew the *AS* curve in Figure 5, we assumed that a number of important variables remained unchanged. In particular, we assumed that the only changes in unit costs were those caused by a change in output. But in the real world, unit costs—and the price level—sometimes change for reasons *other* than a change in

FIGURE 6

SHIFTS IN THE AGGREGATE SUPPLY CURVE

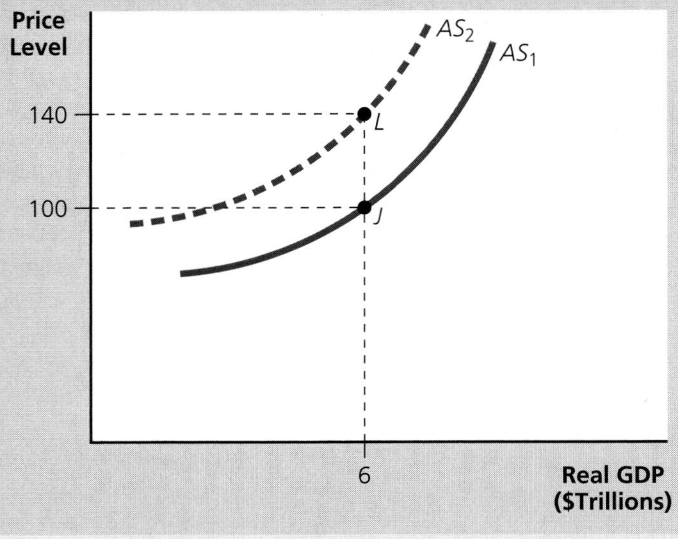

Any factor that changes firms' unit prices will shift the *AS* curve. An increase in world oil prices would shift the *AS* curve upward; the price level would be higher at each level of real GDP. An improvement in weather would shift the curve downward; the price level would be lower at each level of real GDP.

output. When this occurs, unit costs—and the price level—will change at *any* level of output, so the *AS* curve will shift.

In general, we distinguish between a movement along the *AS* curve, and a shift of the curve itself, as follows:

> *When a change in real GDP* causes *the price level to change, we* move along *the AS curve. When anything* other *than a change in real GDP causes the price level to change, the AS curve itself* shifts.

Figure 6 illustrates the logic of a shift in the *AS* curve. Suppose the economy's initial *AS* curve is AS_1. Now suppose that some economic event *other* than a change in output—for the moment, we'll leave the event unnamed—causes firms to raise their prices. Then the price level will be higher at *any* level of output we might imagine, so the *AS* curve must shift *upward*—for example, to AS_2 in the figure. At an output level of $6 trillion, the price level would rise from 100 to 140. At any other output level, the price level would also rise.

In practice, we can distinguish two different types of events that cause the *AS* curve to shift.

SHORT-RUN CHANGES IN UNIT COSTS. You've seen that as we move along the *AS* curve, unit costs are changing *because* output is changing. But unit costs can change for other reasons, too.

- *Changes in world oil prices.* Oil is traded on a world market, where prices can fluctuate even when output in the United States does not. Indeed, over the last few decades, changes in world oil prices have caused major shifts in the *AS* curve. An oil embargo by Arab oil-producing nations in 1973–74, the Iranian revolution in 1978–79, and Iraq's invasion of Kuwait in 1990 all caused large

EFFECTS OF KEY CHANGES ON THE AGGREGATE SUPPLY CURVE

TABLE 2

	Short-Run Changes in Unit Costs Caused by Changes in Output		**Short-Run Changes in Unit Costs *Not* Caused by Changes in Output**		**Adjustment over the Long Run**	
	Unit Costs Increase	**Unit Costs Decrease**	**Unit Costs Increase**	**Unit Costs Decrease**	**Wage Rate Increases**	**Wage Rate Decreases**
Effect on *AS* Curve	Movement upward along curve	Movement downward along curve	Shifts upward	Shifts downward	Shifts upward	Shifts downward

jumps in the price of oil. Each time, unit costs rose, and at any output level, firms charged higher prices than before. As in Figure 6, the *AS* curve shifted upward. Conversely, in 1991, the price of oil decreased dramatically. This caused unit costs to decrease at many firms, shifting the *AS* curve downward.

- *Changes in the weather.* Good crop-growing weather increases farmers' yields for any given amounts of land, labor, capital, and other inputs used. This decreases farms' unit costs, and the price of agricultural goods falls. Since many of these goods are final goods (such as fresh fruit and vegetables), the price drop will contribute directly to a drop in the price level, and a downward shift of the *AS* curve. Additionally, agricultural products are important inputs in the production of many other goods. (For example, corn is an input in beef production.) Good weather thus leads to a drop in input prices for many other firms in the economy, causing their unit costs—and their prices—to decrease. For these reasons, we can expect good weather to shift the *AS* curve downward. Bad weather, which decreases crop yields, increases unit costs at any level of output, and shifts the *AS* curve upward.

CHANGES IN UNIT COSTS DURING ADJUSTMENT TO THE LONG RUN. We've assumed that, in the short run, the nominal wage remains unchanged as output changes. But as we extend our time horizon beyond the first year after a change in output, our assumption of a constant wage becomes increasingly unrealistic. As you will see a bit later, when output rises beyond its full-employment level, we can expect nominal wage rates to rise as part of the long-run adjustment process in the economy. Similarly, if output falls below potential, wage rates will eventually fall, shifting the *AS* curve, since we assume that the wage is constant when we draw the curve.

SHIFTS VS. MOVEMENTS ALONG THE *AS* CURVE: A SUMMARY. Table 2 summarizes how different events in the economy cause a movement along, or a shift in, the *AS* curve.

The *AS* curve tells only half of the economy's story: It shows us the price level *if* we know the level of output. The *AD* curve tells the other half of the story: It

FIGURE 7

SHORT-RUN MACROECONOMIC EQUILIBRIUM

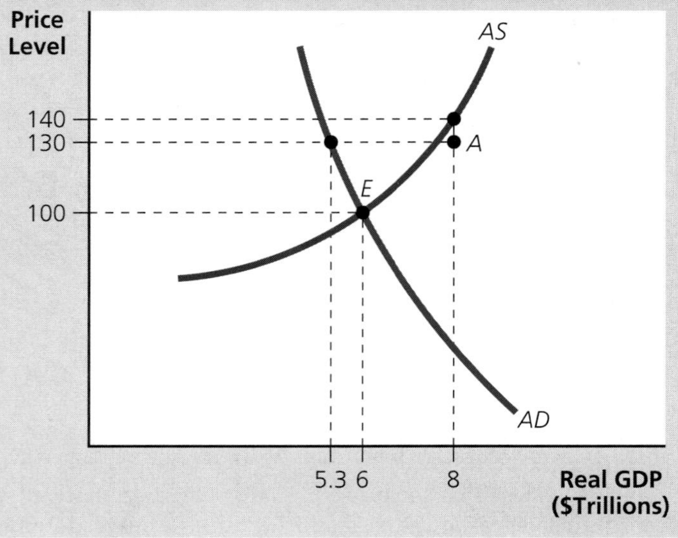

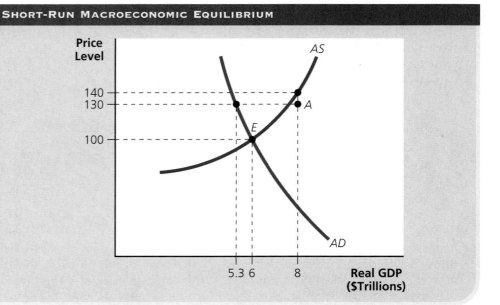

Short-run equilibrium occurs where the *AD* and *AS* curves intersect. At point *E,* the price level of 100 is consistent with an output of $6 trillion along the *AD* curve. The output level of $6 trillion is consistent with a price level of 100 along the *AS* curve. At any other combination of price level and output, such as point *A,* at least one condition for equilibrium will not be satisfied.

shows us the level of output *if* we know the economy's price level. In the next section, we finally put the two halves of the story together, allowing us to determine both the price level and output.

AD AND *AS* TOGETHER: SHORT-RUN EQUILIBRIUM

SHORT-RUN MACROECONOMIC EQUILIBRIUM A combination of price level and GDP consistent with both the *AD* and *AS* curves.

Where will the economy settle in the short run? That is, where is our **short-run macroeconomic equilibrium**? Figure 7 shows how to answer that question, using both the *AS* curve and the *AD* curve. If you suspect that the equilibrium is at point *E,* the intersection of these two curves, you are correct. At that point, the price level is 100, and output is $6 trillion. But it's worth thinking about *why* point *E*—and only point *E*—is our short-run equilibrium.

First, we know that the economy must be at some point on the *AD* curve. Otherwise, real GDP would not be at its equilibrium value. For example, consider point *A,* which lies to the right of the *AD* curve. At this point, the price level is 130, and output is $8 trillion. But the *AD* curve tells us that with a price level of 130, *equilibrium* output is $5.3 trillion. Thus, at point *A,* real GDP would be greater than its equilibrium value. As you learned several chapters ago, this situation cannot persist for long, since inventories would pile up, and firms would be forced to cut back on their production. Thus, point *A* cannot be our short-run equilibrium.

Second, short-run equilibrium requires that the economy be operating on its *AS* curve. Otherwise, firms would not be charging the prices dictated by their unit costs and the average percentage markup in the economy. For example, point *A* lies *below* the *AS* curve. But the *AS* curve tells us that when output is $8 trillion, based on the average percentage markup and unit costs, the price level should be 140, not 130, as at point *A.* That is, prices are *too low* for equilibrium. This situation will not last long either.

We could make a similar argument for other points that are off the *AS* and *AD* curves, always coming to the same conclusion: Unless the economy is on *both* the *AS* and the *AD* curve, the price level and the level of output will change. Only when the economy is at point *E*—on *both* curves—will we have reached a sustainable level of real GDP and the price level.

WHAT HAPPENS WHEN THINGS CHANGE?

Now that we know how the short-run equilibrium is determined, and armed with our knowledge of the *AD* and *AS* curves, we are ready to put the model through its paces. In this section, we'll explore how different types of events cause the short-run equilibrium to change.

Our short-run equilibrium will change when either the *AD* curve, the *AS* curve, or both *shift*. Since the consequences for the economy are very different for shifts in the *AD* curve as opposed to shifts in the *AS* curve, economists have developed a shorthand language to distinguish between them:

An event that causes the AD curve to shift is called a ***demand shock****. An event that causes the AS curve to shift is called a* ***supply shock****.*

DEMAND SHOCK Any event that causes the *AD* curve to shift.

SUPPLY SHOCK Any event that causes the *AS* curve to shift.

In much of this section, we'll explore the effects of demand shocks, both in the short run and during the adjustment process to the long run. Then, we'll take up the issue of supply shocks.

DEMAND SHOCKS IN THE SHORT RUN

Table 1, which lists the reasons for a shift in the *AD* curve, also serves as a list of demand shocks to the economy. Let's consider some examples.

AN INCREASE IN GOVERNMENT PURCHASES. You've learned that an increase in government purchases shifts the *AD* curve rightward. Now we can see how it affects the economy in the short run. Figure 8 shows the initial equilibrium at point *E,* with the price level equal to 100 and output at $6 trillion. Now, suppose that government purchases rise by $1 trillion. Table 1 tells us that the *AD* curve will shift rightward. What will happen to equilibrium GDP?

In our example in the previous chapter, a $1 trillion rise in government purchases increased output to $7.5 trillion, and also raised the interest rate in the money market to 13 percent. (Flip back to Figure 8 in that chapter to refresh your memory.) But nowhere in our previous analysis did we consider any change in the price level. Thus, the rise in GDP to $7.5 trillion in the previous chapter makes sense *only if the price level does not change.* In Figure 8 in the current chapter, this *would* be a movement rightward, from point *E* to point *F*. However, *point* F *does not describe the economy's short-run equilibrium.* Why not? Because it ignores two facts that you've learned about in this chapter: The rise in output will change the price level, and the change in the price level will, in turn, affect equilibrium GDP.

To see this more clearly, let's first suppose that the price level did *not* rise when output increased, so that the economy actually *did* arrive at point *F* after the *AD* shift. Would we stay there? Absolutely not. Point *F* lies below the *AS* curve, telling us that when GDP is $7.5 trillion, the price level consistent with firms' unit costs and average markup is 130, not 100. Firms would soon raise prices, and this would cause a movement upward along AD_2. The price level would keep rising, and out-

FIGURE 8

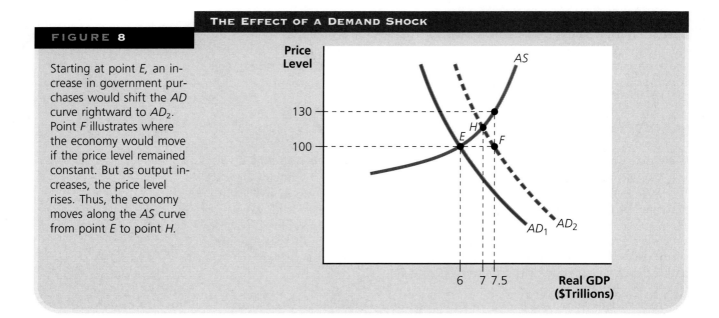

THE EFFECT OF A DEMAND SHOCK

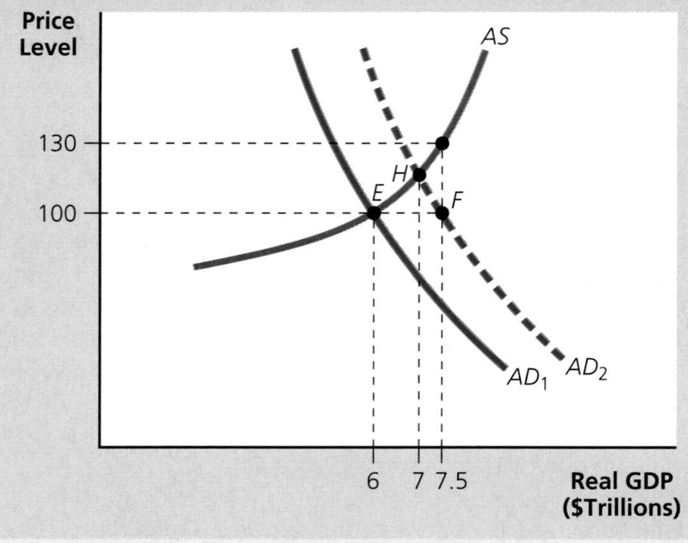

Starting at point *E*, an increase in government purchases would shift the *AD* curve rightward to AD_2. Point *F* illustrates where the economy would move if the price level remained constant. But as output increases, the price level rises. Thus, the economy moves along the *AS* curve from point *E* to point *H*.

put would keep falling, until we reached point *H*. At that point—with output at $7 trillion—we would be on both the *AS* and *AD* curves, so there would be no reason for a further rise in the price level and no reason for a further fall in output.

However, the process we've just described is not entirely realistic. It assumes that when government purchases rise, *first* output increases (the move to point *F*), and *then* the price level rises (the move to point *H*). In reality, output and the price level tend to rise *together*. Thus, the economy would likely *slide along* the *AS* curve from point *E* to point *H*. As we move along the *AS* curve, output rises, increasing unit costs and the price level. At the same time, the rise in the price level *reduces equilibrium GDP—the level of output toward which the economy is heading on the* AD *curve*—from point *F* to point *H*.

We can summarize the impact of a rise in government purchases this way:

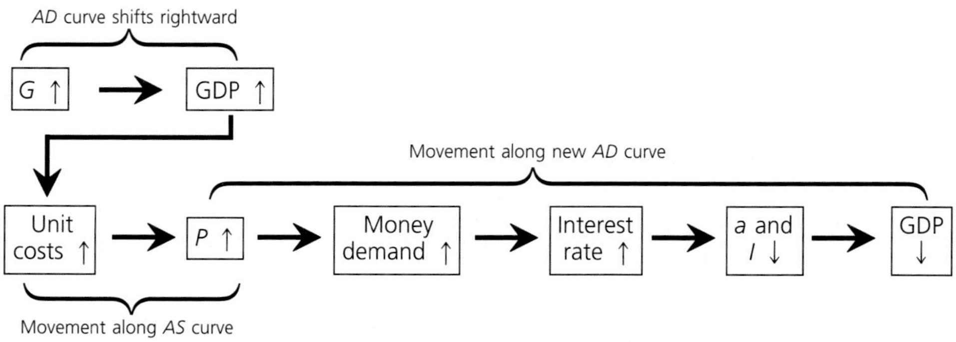

Net Effect: GDP ↑, but by less than if *P* did not increase.

Let's step back a minute and get some perspective about this example of fiscal policy. This is the third time in this text that we've considered fiscal policy in the short run. Each time, the discussion became more realistic, and we've seen that the effect of fiscal policy becomes weaker. In our first analysis, we ignored any increase in the interest rate, and found that a rise in government purchases increased equilibrium GDP according to the simple multiplier formula $1/(1 - MPC)$. In our second analysis, in the chapter before this one, you learned that a rise in government purchases increases the interest rate, crowding out some interest-sensitive spending, thus making the rise in GDP smaller than it would otherwise be. The multiplier, therefore, was smaller than $1/(1 - MPC)$. Now you've learned that the rise in government purchases *also* increases the price level. This leads to a *further* rise in the interest rate, crowding out still *more* interest-sensitive spending, and making the rise in GDP smaller still. The size of the multiplier has been reduced yet again. (In our example, a $1 trillion increase in government purchases increases equilibrium GDP by $1 trillion, so the multiplier would be 1.0.) However, as you can see in Figure 8, a rise in government purchases—even when we include the rise in the price level—still raises GDP in the short run.

We can summarize the impact of price-level changes this way:

> *When government purchases increase, the horizontal shift of the AD curve measures how much real GDP* would *increase* if the price level remained constant. *But because the price level rises, real GDP rises by* less *than the horizontal shift in the AD curve.*

Now let's switch gears into reverse: How would we illustrate the effects of a *decrease* in government purchases? In this case, the *AD* curve would shift *leftward,* causing the following to happen:

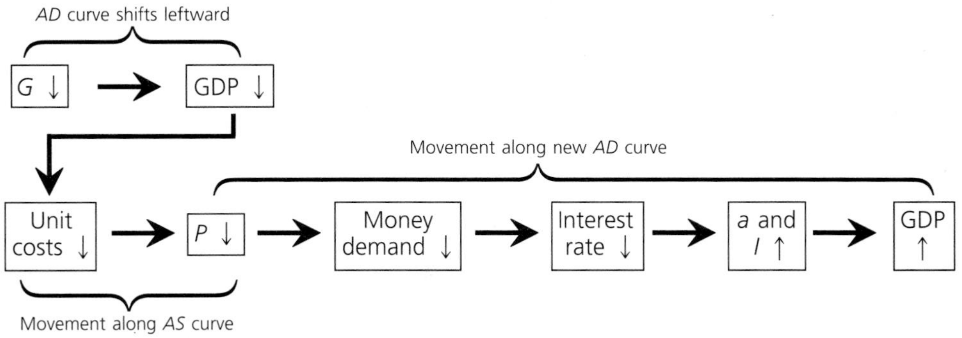

Net Effect: GDP ↓, but by less than if *P* did not decrease.

As you can see, the same sequence of events occurs in the same order, but each variable moves in the opposite direction. A decrease in government purchases decreases equilibrium GDP, but the multiplier effect is smaller because the price level falls.

An Increase in the Money Supply. Although monetary policy stimulates the economy through a different channel than fiscal policy, once we arrive at the *AD* and *AS* diagram, the two look very much alike. For example, an increase in the money supply, which reduces the interest rate, will stimulate interest-sensitive consumption and investment spending. Real GDP then increases, and the *AD* curve shifts rightward, just as in Figure 8. Once output begins to rise, we have the same sequence of events as in fiscal policy: The price level rises, so the increase in GDP will be smaller. We can represent the situation as follows:

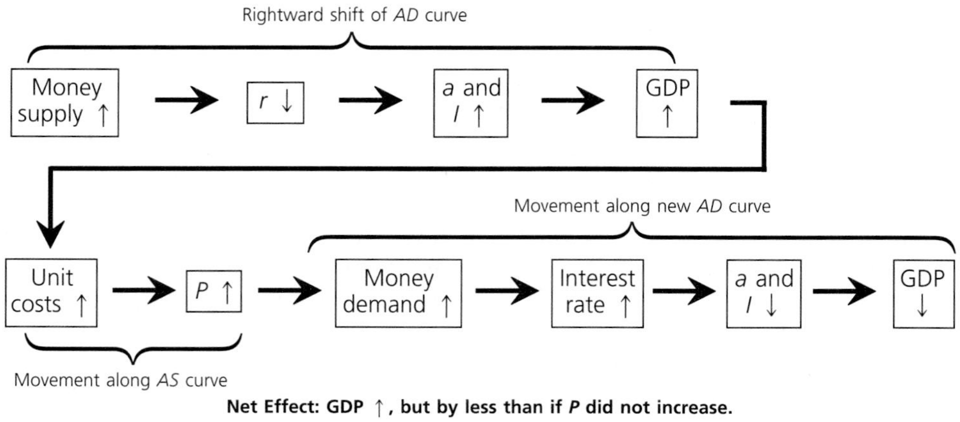

OTHER DEMAND SHOCKS. You may want to go through the demand shocks in Table 1 on your own and explain the sequence of events in each case that causes output and the price level to change. This will help you verify the following general conclusion about demand shocks:

> *A positive demand shock—one that shifts the AD curve rightward—increases both real GDP and the price level in the short run. A negative demand shock—one that shifts the AD curve leftward—decreases both real GDP and the price level in the short run.*

AN EXAMPLE: THE GREAT DEPRESSION. As mentioned at the beginning of the chapter, the U.S. economy collapsed far more seriously during 1929 through 1933—the onset of the Great Depression—than it did at any other time in the country's history. Because the price level fell during the contraction, we know that the contraction was caused by an adverse demand shock. An adverse supply shock would have caused the price level to *rise* as GDP fell.

What do we know about the demand shocks that caused the depression? This question has been debated by economists almost continuously in the 70 years since the contraction began. The candidates are numerous, and it appears that a combination of bad developments was responsible. The 1920s were a period of optimism—with high levels of investment by businesses and spending by families on houses and cars. The stock market soared. In the fall of 1929, the bubble of optimism burst. The stock market crashed, and investment and consumption spending plummeted. Similar events occurred in other countries, and the demand for products exported by the United States fell. The Fed—then only 16 years old—reacted by cutting the money supply sharply, which added an adverse monetary shock to all of the cutbacks in spending. Each of these events contributed to a leftward shift of the *AD* curve, causing both output and the price level to fall.

DEMAND SHOCKS: ADJUSTING TO THE LONG RUN

In Figure 8, point *H* shows the new equilibrium after a positive demand shock *in the short run*—a year or so after the shock. But point *H* is not necessarily where the economy will end up in the long run. For example, suppose full-employment

THE LONG-RUN ADJUSTMENT PROCESS

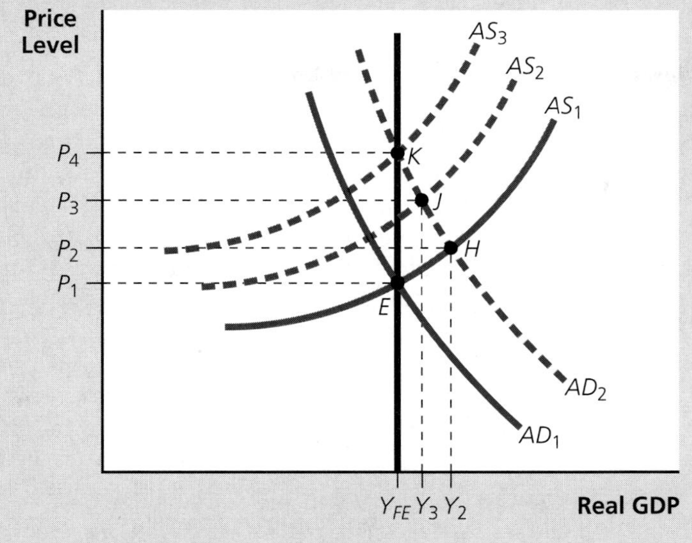

FIGURE 9

Beginning at point E, a positive demand shock would shift the aggregate demand curve to AD_2, raising both output and the price level. At point H, output is above the full-employment level, Y_{FE}. Firms will compete to hire scarce workers, thereby driving up the wage rate. The higher wage rate will shift the AS curve to AS_2 and then to AS_3. Only when the economy returns to full-employment output at point K will there be no further shifts in AS.

output is \$6 trillion, and point H—representing an output of \$7 trillion—is above full-employment output. Then—with employment unusually high and unemployment unusually low—business firms will have to compete to hire scarce workers, driving up the wage rate. It might take a year or more for the wage rate to rise significantly—recall our earlier list of reasons that wages adjust only slowly. But when we extend our horizon to several years or more, we must recognize that if output is beyond its potential, the wage rate will rise. Since the *AS* curve is drawn for a *given wage,* a rise in the wage rate will *shift* the curve upward, changing our equilibrium.

Alternatively, we could imagine a situation in which short-run equilibrium GDP was *below* its potential. In this case, with abnormally high unemployment, workers would compete to get scarce jobs, and eventually the wage rate would fall. Then the *AS* curve would shift downward, once again changing our equilibrium GDP.

SHORT-RUN VERSUS LONG-RUN OUTCOMES

In the short run, we treat the wage rate as given. But in the long run, the wage rate can change. When output is above full employment, the wage rate will rise, shifting the AS curve upward. When output is below full employment, the wage rate will fall, shifting the AS curve downward.

Now we are ready to explore what happens over the long run in the aftermath of a demand shock. Figure 9 shows an economy in equilibrium at point E. We assume that the initial equilibrium is at full-employment output (Y_{FE}), since—as you are about to see—this is where the economy always ends up after the long-run adjustment process is complete. To make our results as general as possible, we'll use symbols, rather than numbers, to represent output and price levels.

Now suppose the *AD* curve shifts rightward, say, due an increase in government purchases. In the short run, the equilibrium moves to point H, with a higher price level (P_2) and a higher level of output (Y_2). Point H tells us where the economy will be about a year after the increase in government purchases, before the wage rate has a chance to adjust. (Remember, along any given AS curve, the wage rate is assumed to be constant.)

But now let's extend our analysis beyond a year. Notice that Y_2 is greater than Y_{FE}. The wage will begin to rise, raising unit costs at any given output level and causing firms to raise prices. In the figure, the AS curve would begin shifting upward. The new aggregate supply curve, AS_2, shows where the economy might be two years after the shock, after the long-run adjustment process has begun. With this AS curve, the economy would be at point J, with output at Y_3. The rise in the price level has moved us along the new aggregate demand curve, AD_2.

Now, is point J our final, long-run equilibrium? No, it cannot be. At Y_3, output is *still* greater than Y_{FE}, so the wage rate will continue to rise, and the AS curve will continue to shift upward. At point J, the long-run adjustment process is not yet complete. When will the process end? Only when the wage rate stops rising—that is, only when output has returned to Y_{FE}. This occurs when the AS curve has shifted all the way to AS_3, moving the economy to point K—our new, long-run equilibrium.

SELF-CORRECTING MECHANISM The adjustment process through which price and wage changes return the economy to full-employment output in the long run.

As you can see, the increase in government purchases has no effect on equilibrium GDP in the long run: The economy returns to full employment, which is just where it started. This is why the long-run adjustment process is often called the economy's **self-correcting mechanism.** And this mechanism applies to any demand shock, not just an increase in government purchases:

SHORT-RUN VERSUS LONG-RUN OUTCOMES

If a demand shock pulls the economy away from full employment, changes in the wage rate and the price level will eventually cause the economy to correct itself and return to full-employment output.

For a positive demand shock that shifts the AD curve rightward, the self-correcting mechanism works like this:

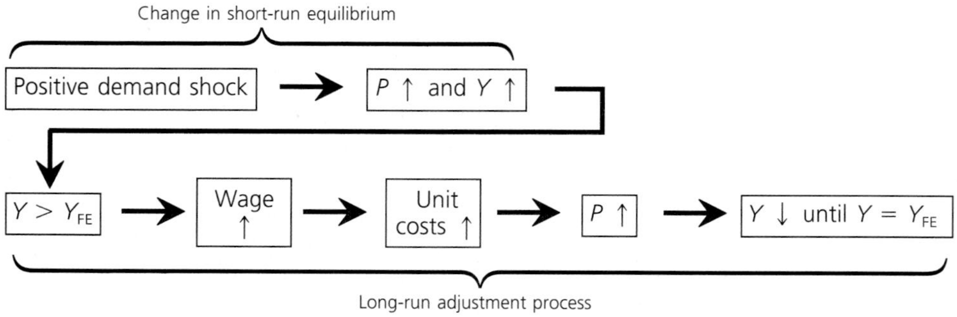

Figure 10 illustrates the case of a negative demand shock, in which the AD curve shifts leftward. In this case, the short-run equilibrium GDP is *below* Y_{FE}. Over the long run, unusually high unemployment drives the wage rate down, shifting the AS curve down as well. The price level decreases, causing equilibrium GDP to rise along the AD_2 curve. The process comes to a halt only when output returns to Y_{FE}. Thus, in the long run, the economy moves from point E to point M, and the negative demand shock causes no change in equilibrium GDP. The complete sequence of events after a negative demand shock looks like this:

LONG-RUN ADJUSTMENT AFTER A NEGATIVE DEMAND SHOCK

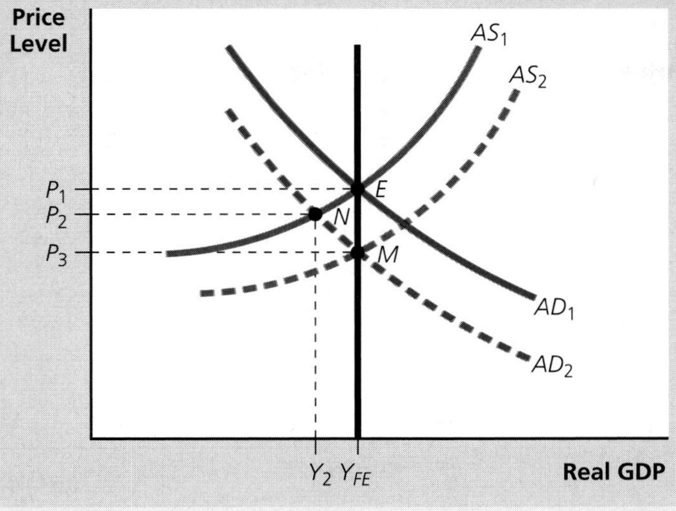

FIGURE 10

Starting from point *E*, a negative demand shock shifts the *AD* curve to AD_2, lowering GDP and the price level. At point *N*, output is below the full-employment level. With unemployed labor available, wages will fall, enabling firms to lower their prices. The *AS* curve shifts downward until full employment is regained at point *M*, with a lower price level.

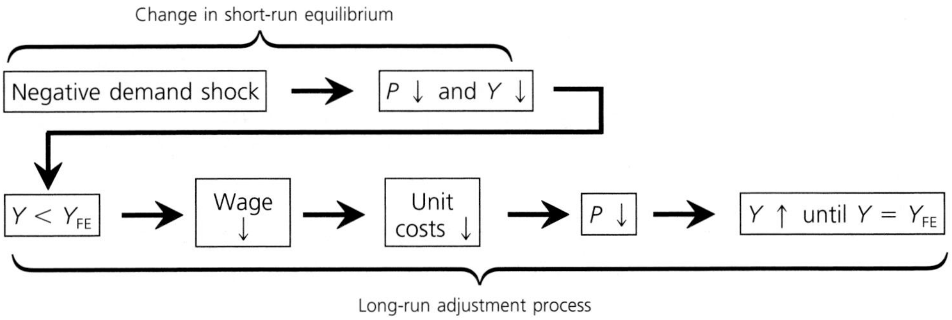

Pulling all of our observations together, we can summarize the economy's self-correcting mechanism as follows:

> *Whenever a demand shock pulls the economy away from full employment, the self-correcting mechanism will eventually bring it back. When output exceeds its full-employment level, wages will eventually rise, causing a rise in the price level and a drop in GDP until full employment is restored. When output is less than its full-employment level, wages will eventually fall, causing a drop in the price level and a rise in GDP until full employment is restored.*

THE LONG-RUN AGGREGATE SUPPLY CURVE

The self-correcting mechanism provides an important link between the economy's long-run and short-run behavior. It helps us understand why booms and recessions don't last forever. Often, however, we are primarily interested in the long-run effects of a demand shock. In these cases, we may want to skip over the self-correcting mechanism and go straight to its end result. A new version of the *AS* curve helps us do this.

FIGURE 11

THE LONG-RUN AGGREGATE SUPPLY CURVE

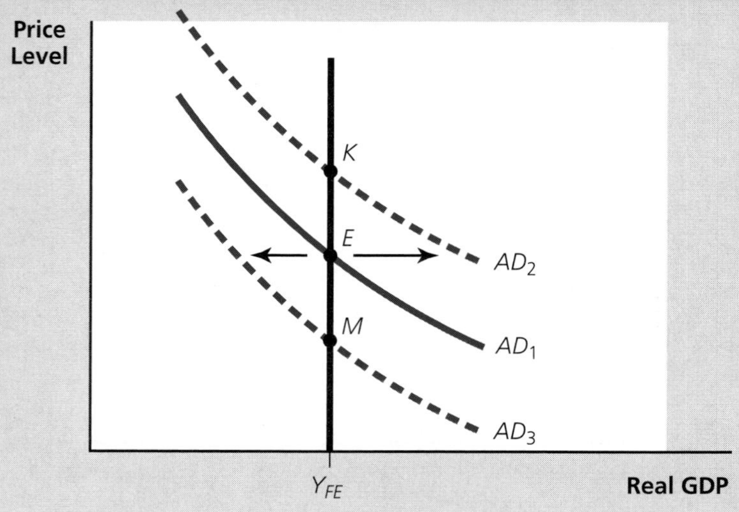

In the long run, GDP will be at its full-employment level regardless of the position of the *AD* curve. A positive demand shock would shift *AD* rightward to AD_2, moving the economy from point *E* to point *K* with a higher price level. A negative shock would shift *AD* to AD_3, leading to a lower price level at point *M*. The long-run *AS* curve is vertical at full-employment output.

Look again at Figure 9, which illustrates the impact of a positive demand shock. The economy begins at full employment at point *E*, then moves to point *H* in the short run (before the wage rate rises), and then goes to point *K* in the long run (after the rise in wages). If we skip over the short-run equilibrium, we find that the positive demand shock has moved the economy from *E* to *K*, which is vertically above *E*. That is, in the long run, the price level rises, but output remains unchanged.

LONG-RUN AGGREGATE SUPPLY CURVE A vertical line indicating all possible output and price-level combinations at which the economy could end up in the long run.

Now look at Figure 11, which shows another way of illustrating this long-run result. In the figure, the vertical line is the economy's **long-run aggregate supply curve.** It summarizes all possible output and price-level combinations at which the economy could end up in the long run. It is vertical because, in the long run, GDP will be the same—full-employment output—*regardless* of the position of the *AD* curve. The price level, however, will depend on the position of the *AD* curve. In the figure, a positive demand shock would shift the *AD* curve rightward, moving the economy from *E* to *K*: a higher price level, but the same level of output. A negative demand shock would shift the *AD* curve leftward, moving the economy from *E* to *M*: a lower price level with the same level of output.[3]

Figure 11 tells us something very important about the economy: In the long run, after the self-correcting mechanism has done its job, *the economy behaves very much as the classical model predicts.* In particular, the classical model tells us that neither fiscal policy nor monetary policy can change equilibrium GDP in the long run. The figure brings us to the same conclusion: While fiscal and monetary policy shift the *AD* curve, this only moves the economy up or down along a vertical long-run *AS* curve, leaving output unchanged.

Figure 11 also illustrates another classical conclusion. In the classical model, an increase in government purchases causes *complete crowding out*—the rise in gov-

3 Of course, full-employment output can increase from year to year, as you learned in the chapter on economic growth. When the economy is growing, the long-run *AS* curve will shift rightward. In that case, the level of output at which the economy will eventually settle increases from year to year.

THE EFFECT OF SUPPLY SHOCKS

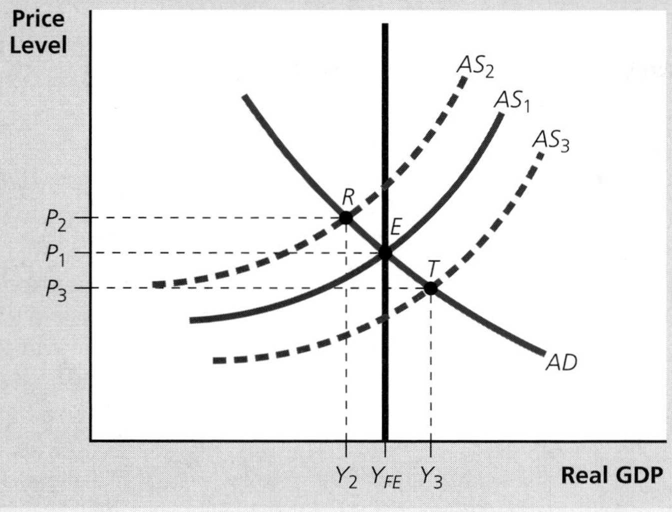

FIGURE 12

An adverse supply shock would shift the *AS* curve upward from AS_1 to AS_2. In the short-run equilibrium at point *R*, the price level is higher and output is below Y_{FE}. Eventually, wages will fall, causing unit costs to fall, and the *AS* curve will shift back to its original position. A positive supply shock would have just the opposite effect.

ernment purchases is precisely matched by a drop in consumption and investment spending, leaving total output and total spending unchanged. In Figure 11, the same result holds. How do we know? The figure tells us that, in the long run, the rise in government purchases causes no change in GDP. But if GDP is the same, and government purchases are higher, then the other components of GDP—consumption and investment—must decrease by the amount that government purchases increased.

The self-correcting mechanism shows us that, in the long run, the economy will eventually behave as the classical model predicts.

SHORT-RUN VERSUS LONG-RUN OUTCOMES

But notice the word *eventually* in the previous statement. It can take several years before the economy returns to full employment after a demand shock. This is why governments around the world are reluctant to rely on the self-correcting mechanism alone to keep the economy on track. Instead, they often use fiscal and monetary policy in an attempt to return the economy to full employment more quickly. We'll explore fiscal and monetary policy in more detail in the next two chapters.

SUPPLY SHOCKS

In recent decades, supply shocks have been important sources of economic fluctuations. The most dramatic supply shocks have resulted from sudden changes in world oil prices. As you are about to see, supply shocks affect the economy differently from demand shocks.

SHORT-RUN EFFECTS OF SUPPLY SHOCKS. Figure 12 shows an example of a supply shock: an increase in world oil prices that shifts the aggregate supply curve upward, from AS_1 to AS_2. As rising oil prices increase unit costs, firms will begin raising prices, and the price level will increase. The rise in the price level decreases equilibrium GDP along the *AD* curve. In the short run, the price level will continue to rise, and the economy will continue to slide leftward along its *AD* curve, until we reach the AS_2 curve at point *R*. At this point, the price level is consistent with firms' unit costs and average markup (we are on the *AS* curve), and total output is equal to total spending (we are on the *AD* curve). As you can see, the short-run impact of higher oil prices is a rise in the price level and a fall in output. We call this a *negative* supply shock, because of the negative effect on output.

In the short run, a negative *supply shock shifts the AS curve upward, decreasing output and increasing the price level.*

Notice the sharp contrast between the effects of negative supply shocks and negative demand shocks in the short run. After a negative demand shock (see, for example, Figure 10), both output and the price level fall. After a negative supply shock, however, output falls, but the price level rises. Economists and journalists have coined the term **stagflation** to describe a *stag*nating economy experiencing in*flation*.

STAGFLATION The combination of falling output and rising prices.

A negative supply shock causes stagflation *in the short run.*

Stagflation caused by increases in oil prices is not just a theoretical possibility. Three of our recessions in the last quarter century—in 1973–74, 1978–79, and 1990–91—followed increases in world oil prices. And each of these three recession also saw jumps in the price level.

Positive supply shocks increase output by shifting the *AS* curve downward, as in the shift from AS_1 to AS_3 in Figure 12. As you can see in the figure,

a positive supply shock shifts the AS curve downward, increasing output and decreasing the price level.

Unusually good weather or a drop in oil prices are examples of positive supply shocks. In addition, a positive supply shock can sometimes be caused by government policy. A few chapters ago, we discussed how the government could use tax incentives and other policies to increase the rate of economic growth. These policies work by shifting the *AS* curve downward, thus increasing output while tending to decrease the price level.

Another type of policy tries to deal directly with negative supply shocks. For example, after the oil price shocks of the 1970s, the federal government decided to accumulate a strategic reserve of oil in huge underground storage areas. The idea was to release oil from the reserve if another oil price shock hit, in order to stabilize the price. The reserve was used in this way in 1990, but not enough to make much difference in the world oil price.

LONG-RUN EFFECTS OF SUPPLY SHOCKS. What about the effects of supply shocks in the long run? In some cases, we need not concern ourselves with this question, because some supply shocks are temporary. For example, except in unusual cases, periods of rising oil prices are followed by periods of falling oil prices. Similarly, supply shocks caused by unusually good or bad weather, or by natural disasters, are always short lived. A temporary supply shock causes only a temporary shift in the *AS* curve; over the long run, the curve simply returns to its initial position, and the economy returns to full employment. In Figure 12, the *AS* curve would shift back from AS_2 to AS_1, and the economy would move from point *R* back to point *E*.

In other cases, however, a supply shock can last for an extended period. One example was the rise in oil prices during the 1970s, which persisted for several years. In cases like this, is there a self-correcting mechanism that brings the economy back to full employment after a long-lasting supply shock? Indeed, there is, and it is the same mechanism that brings the economy back to full employment after a demand shock.

Look again at Figure 12. At point *R*, output is below full-employment output. In the long run, as workers compete for scarce jobs, the wage rate will decline. This will cause the *AS* curve to shift *downward*. The wage will continue to fall until the economy returns to full employment; that is, until we are back at point *E*.

In the long run, the economy self-corrects after a supply shock, just as it does after a demand shock. When output differs from its full-employment level, the wage rate changes, and the AS curve shifts until full employment is restored.

SHORT-RUN VERSUS LONG-RUN OUTCOMES

SOME IMPORTANT PROVISOS ABOUT THE *AS* CURVE

The upward-sloping aggregate supply curve we've presented in this chapter gives a realistic picture of how the economy actually behaves after a demand shock. In the short run, positive demand shocks that increase output also raise the price level. Negative demand shocks that decrease output generally put downward pressure on prices.

However, the story we have told about what happens as we move along the *AS* curve is somewhat incomplete.

First, we made the assumption that prices are completely flexible—that they can change freely over short periods of time. In fact, however, some prices take time to adjust, just as wages take time to adjust. Firms print catalogs containing prices that are good for, say, six months. The regulatory commission in your state generally sets the prices of electricity, gas, water, and basic telephone service in advance for a year or more.

Second, we assumed that wages are completely *inflexible* in the short run. But in *some* industries, wages respond quickly. For example, in the construction industry, contractors hire workers for projects lasting a few months. When they can't find the workers they want, they immediately offer higher wages—they don't wait for a year.

Third, there is more to the process of recovering from a shock than the adjustment of prices and wages. As we discussed a few chapters ago, during a recession, many workers lose their jobs at the same time—there is a burst of job destruction. It takes time for those workers to become re-established in new jobs. As time passes, and job losers become job finders, the economy tends to recover. This process, in addition to the changes in wages and prices we've discussed, is part of the long-run adjustment process and helps to bring the economy back to full employment after a shock.

USING THE THEORY

THE RECESSION AND RECOVERY OF 1990–92

The aggregate demand and aggregate supply curves are not just graphs and concepts; they are tools that help us understand important economic events. In this section, we'll look at how we can use these tools to understand our most recent recession.

Our story begins in mid-1990, when Iraq invaded Kuwait, a major oil producer. During this conflict, Kuwait's oil was taken off the world market, and so was Iraq's. The reduction in oil supplies resulted in an immediate and substantial increase in the price of oil, a key input to many industries. Panel (a) of Figure 13 shows that the price of oil rose from $14 to $27 per barrel in 1990.

Figure 14 shows our *AS–AD* analysis of the shock. Initially, the economy is on both AD_1 and AS_1, with equilibrium at point *E*, and output at its full-employment level. Then, the oil price shock shifts the *AS* curve upward, to AS_2.

FIGURE 13

THE PRICE OF OIL, REAL GDP, AND THE PRICE LEVEL, 1990–92

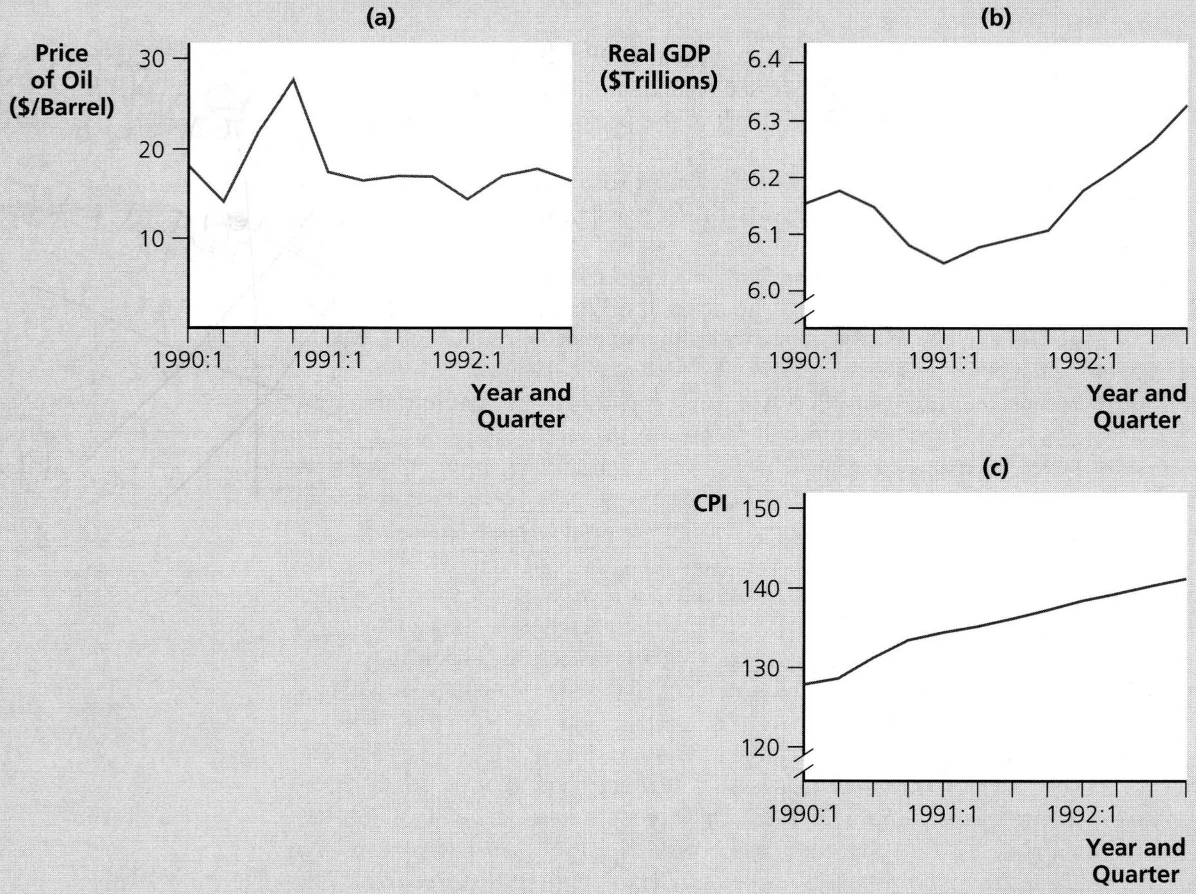

In mid-1990, Kuwaiti and Iraqi oil was taken off the world market, resulting in a substantial increase in the world price of oil, as shown in panel (a). U.S. GDP fell, and the consumer price index rose. When oil prices fell in 1991, GDP recovered.

AN *AD–AS* ANALYSIS OF THE OIL PRICE SHOCK

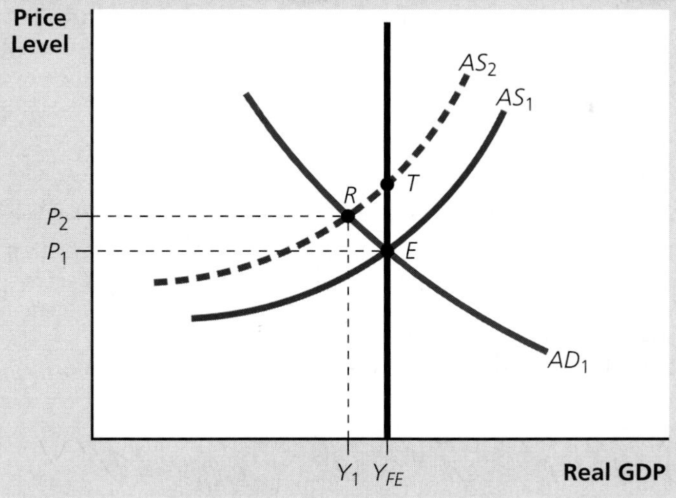

FIGURE 14

Beginning at point *E,* the increase in the world price of oil shifted the *AS* curve from AS_1 to AS_2. Output fell and the price level rose. When oil prices fell in 1991, the *AS* curve shifted back to AS_1. Because the Fed simultaneously increased the money supply, the *AD* curve shifted rightward. By 1992, output was back to Y_{FE}, but with a higher price level at point *T.*

As the short-run equilibrium moves to point *R,* real GDP falls and the price level rises. Going back to Figure 13, we see that this is indeed what happened. Panel (b) shows that real GDP did fall in the period after the shock, from $6.175 trillion in mid-1990 to about $6 trillion in early 1991. In panel (c), you can see that the Consumer Price Index rose especially rapidly during this period. Late 1990 through early 1991 was clearly a period of stagflation.

Now let's return to our *AS–AD* analysis in Figure 14. At point *R,* output is below its full-employment level. If the price of oil had remained high, our theory tells us, the self-correcting mechanism would have begun to work: Falling wages would have decreased unit costs, shifting the *AS* curve back down to AS_1. However, the self-correcting mechanism wasn't needed in this case: As you can see in Figure 13, the oil price shock was temporary. Oil prices fell back down in early 1991, shifting the *AS* curve back to AS_1. In panel (b) of Figure 13, you can see that real GDP began to recover in early 1991, and continued moving back to its full-employment level in the succeeding years.

But something looks fishy here. In our *AS–AD* analysis, the price level should rise when the negative supply shock hits and then gradually *fall* back to its original level when the shock proves temporary. But panel (c) of Figure 13 shows that this prediction was not borne out by the experience of 1990–92. Instead, while the price level rose more rapidly in the year after the shock, it *continued to rise* in the next two years as the economy self-corrected. Have we missed something?

Yes, we have. In our analysis of demand and supply shocks in this chapter, we've been focusing on only one change at a time. And here, too, we've been looking at the events of 1990–92 by considering *only* the shift in the *AS* curve. In particular, as the *AS* curve shifts upward and then downward, we've assumed that the *AD* curve stays put.

But that is not what happened in the early 1990s. Instead, in the period after the shock, the Fed increased the money supply, shifting the *AD* curve rightward. Thus, instead of moving from point *R* back to *E,* the economy moved from *R* to

T. (You can draw in the new *AD* curve to help you see the move.) Output rose, but the price level rose as well.

Why did the Fed increase the money supply, rather than hold it constant and let the economy adjust back to point *E*? This is a question about monetary policy and the Fed's motives in conducting it—a subject we will consider in detail in the next chapter.

SUMMARY

The model of aggregate supply and demand explains how the price level and output are determined in the short run—a period of a year or so following a change in the economy—and how the economy adjusts over longer time periods as well.

The aggregate demand (*AD*) curve shows how changes in the price level affect equilibrium real GDP. A change in the price level shifts the money demand curve and alters the interest rate in the money market. The change in the interest rate, in turn, affects interest-sensitive forms of spending, shifts the aggregate expenditure curve, triggers the multiplier process, and leads to a new level of equilibrium real GDP. A lower price level means a higher equilibrium real GDP, and a higher price level means lower GDP. The downward-sloping *AD* curve is drawn for given values of government spending, taxes, autonomous consumption spending, investment spending, the money supply, and the public's preferences for holding money and bonds. Changes in any of those factors will cause the *AD* curve to shift.

The aggregate supply (*AS*) curve summarizes the way changes in output affect the price level. To draw the *AS* curve, we assume that firms set the price of individual products as a markup over their costs per unit, and that the economy's average markup is determined by competitive conditions. We also assume that the nominal wage rate is fixed in the short run. As we move upward along the *AS* curve, a rise in real GDP, by raising unit costs, causes the price level to increase. When anything other than a change in real GDP causes the price level to change, the entire *AS* curve shifts.

AD and *AS* together determine real GDP and the price level. The economy must be on the *AD* curve or real GDP would not be at its equilibrium level. It must be on the *AS* curve or firms would not be charging prices dictated by their unit costs and markups. Both conditions are satisfied at the intersection of the two curves.

The *AD*/*AS* equilibrium can be disturbed by a demand shock. An increase in government purchases, for example, shifts the *AD* curve rightward. As a result, the price level rises, and so does real GDP. In the long run, if GDP is above potential, wages will rise. This causes unit costs to rise and shifts the *AS* curve upward. Eventually, GDP will return to potential and the only long-run result of the demand shock is a higher price level. This implies that the economy's long-run aggregate supply curve is vertical at potential output.

The short-run *AD*/*AS* equilibrium can also be disturbed by a supply shock, such as an increase in world oil prices. With unit costs higher at each level of output, the *AS* curve shifts upward, decreasing real GDP and increasing the price level. Eventually, the shock will be self-correcting: With output below potential, the wage rate will fall, unit costs will decrease, and the *AS* curve will shift back downward until full employment is restored.

KEY TERMS

aggregate demand (*AD*) curve
aggregate supply (*AS*) curve
short-run macroeconomic equilibrium
demand shock
supply shock
self-correcting mechanism
long-run aggregate supply curve
stagflation

REVIEW QUESTIONS

1. What causal relationship does the aggregate demand curve describe? Why is the *AD* curve downward sloping? What does each point on the *AD* curve represent?
2. "Only changes in spending shift the aggregate demand curve." True or false? Explain.
3. List three reasons why a change in output affects unit costs and subsequently the price level.
4. What causal relationship does the aggregate supply curve describe? Why is the *AS* curve upward sloping?

5. Why does equilibrium occur only where the *AD* and *AS* curves intersect?

6. What is meant by the economy's *self-correcting mechanism* after a demand shock?

7. What is the long-run aggregate supply curve? Why is it vertical?

8. Does the vertical shape of the long-run aggregate supply curve support the predictions of the classical model with regard to the effectiveness of policy and crowding out? Explain.

9. How does an economy recover from a negative supply shock?

PROBLEMS AND EXERCISES

1. Illustrate graphically how an increase in the use of credit cards affects the interest rate, real aggregate expenditure, and the aggregate demand curve. (Assume that the price level does not change.)

2. Using a graph, describe how an increase in taxes affects the interest rate, real aggregate expenditure, and the aggregate demand curve. (Assume that the price level does not change.) What other spending changes would result in these same effects?

3. Suppose firms become pessimistic about the future and consequently investment spending falls. Describe the short-run effects on GDP and the price level. If the price level were constant, how would your answer change?

4. Explain, using graphs, the short-run effect of a decrease in the money supply on GDP and the price level. What is the effect in the long run? Assume the economy begins at full employment.

5. A new government policy successfully lowers unit costs to firms. What are the short-run and the long-run effects of such a policy? (Assume full-employment output does not change.)

CHALLENGE QUESTIONS

1. Suppose that wages were slow to adjust downward but rapidly adjust upward. What would the *AS* curve look like? How would this affect the economy's adjustment to spending shocks (compared to the analysis given in the chapter)?

2. Because of increases in the capital stock, technological change, and population growth, full-employment output grows every year. Using this fact, illustrate the long-run effects of a positive spending shock. (*Hint:* What happens to the long-run *AS* curve over time?)

Visit the National Bureau of Economic Research (NBER) (http://www.nber.org/) and look within "Online Data." Using "Macro Data," review the "NBER Official Business Cycle Dates." Answer the following questions:

a. How many business cycles have there been since 1854?
b. Has the average duration of the expansion phase been increasing, decreasing, or constant?
c. Has the average duration of the contraction phase been increasing, decreasing, or constant?
d. How does NBER define a recession?

CHAPTER

14

INFLATION AND MONETARY POLICY

In the late 1970s, the annual inflation rate in the United States reached 13 percent. Polls showed that the public considered inflation the most serious economic problem facing the country. Since the mid-1980s, however, the annual inflation rate has never exceeded 6 percent, and the problem has receded as a matter of public concern. Keeping the inflation rate low has been one of the solid victories of national economic policy.

How did the Fed achieve this victory? Why was it less successful in earlier periods? Are there costs, as well as benefits, to a lower inflation rate? And how should the Fed respond to economic disturbances as it faces the future?

In this chapter, we'll be addressing these and other questions as we take a closer look at the Fed's conduct of monetary policy. Our earlier discussions of monetary policy were somewhat limited, because we lacked the tools—aggregate demand and aggregate supply—to explain changes in the price level. In this chapter, we'll explore monetary policy more fully, making extensive use of the *AD* and *AS* curves.

THE OBJECTIVES OF MONETARY POLICY

The Fed's objectives have changed over the years. When the Fed was first established in 1913, its chief responsibility was to ensure the stability of the banking system. By acting as a "lender of last resort"—injecting reserves into the banking system in times of crisis—the Fed was to alleviate financial panics.

By the 1950s, the stability of the banking system had become a minor concern, largely because the United States had not had a banking panic since the 1930s. (Deposit insurance programs started during that period effectively eliminated panics.) Accordingly, the Fed's objective in the 1950s and 1960s changed to keeping the interest rate low and stable. In the 1970s, the Fed's objectives shifted one more time: As stated in the Federal Reserve Banking Act of 1978, which is still in force, the Fed is now responsible for achieving a low, stable rate of inflation, and full employment of the labor force. Let's consider each of these goals in turn.

Low, Stable Inflation

Why is a low rate of inflation important? Several chapters ago, we reviewed the social costs of inflation. When the inflation rate is high, society uses up resources coping with it—resources that could have been used to produce goods and services. Among these resources are the labor needed to update prices at stores and factories, as well as the additional time spent by households and businesses to manage their wealth and protect it from a loss of purchasing power.

In addition to keeping the inflation rate low, the Fed tries to keep it *stable* from year to year. For example, the Fed would prefer a steady yearly inflation rate of 3 percent to an inflation rate of 5 percent half the time, and 1 percent the other half, even though the average inflation rate would be 3 percent in both cases. The reason is that unstable inflation is difficult to predict accurately; it will often turn out higher or lower than people expected. As you learned several chapters ago, an inflation rate higher than expected redistributes real income from lenders to borrowers, while an inflation rate lower than expected has the opposite effects. Thus, unstable inflation adds to the risk of lending and borrowing, and interferes with long-run financial planning.

The Fed, as a public agency, chooses its policies with the costs of inflation in mind. And the Fed has another concern: Inflation is very unpopular with the public. Surveys show that most people associate high rates of inflation with a general breakdown of government and the economy.[1] A Fed chairman who delivers low rates of inflation is seen as popular and competent, while one who tolerates high inflation goes down in history as a failure.

Full Employment

"Full employment" means that unemployment is at normal levels. But what, exactly, is a "normal" amount of employment?

Recall that there are different types of unemployment. Some of the unemployed in any given month will find jobs after only a short time of searching. This *frictional* unemployment is part of the normal working of the labor market, and is not a serious social problem. Other job seekers will spend many months or years out of work because they lack the skills that employers require, or because they lack information about available jobs. While this *structural* unemployment is a serious social problem, it is best solved with microeconomic policies, such as job-training programs or improved information flows.

Cyclical unemployment, by contrast, is a *macro*economic problem. It occurs during a recession, in which millions of workers lose their jobs and remain unemployed as they seek new ones. This is why macroeconomists use the term "full employment" to mean *the absence of cyclical employment.* When the economy achieves full employment according to this definition, macroeconomic policy has done all that it can do.

The Fed is concerned about cyclical unemployment for two reasons. First is its *opportunity cost*: the output that the unemployed could have produced if they were

1 Robert J. Shiller, "Public Resistance to Inflation: A Puzzle," *Brookings Papers on Economic Activity,* 1997.

working. Part of this opportunity cost is paid by the unemployed themselves, in the form of lost earnings, and part is paid by people who remain employed, but pay higher taxes to provide unemployment benefits to job losers. By maintaining full employment, the Fed can help society avoid this cost.

Second, cyclical unemployment represents a social failure. In a recession, people who have the right skills and who could be working actually *lose* their jobs. Excess unemployment lingers for several years after a recession strikes. Thus, cyclical unemployment caused by a recession is a partial breakdown of the system. The economy is not doing what it should do: provide a job for anyone who wants to work and who has the needed skills.

But why should the Fed try to eliminate only *cyclical* unemployment? Why not go further—pushing output beyond its full-employment level? After all, at higher levels of output, business firms would be more willing to hire *any* available workers. The frictionally unemployed would find jobs more easily, and some of the structurally unemployed would be hired as well. If unemployment is a bad thing, shouldn't the Fed aim for the lowest possible unemployment rate possible?

The answer is no. If the unemployment rate falls too low, GDP rises beyond its potential, full-employment level. As you learned in the last chapter, this causes the economy's self-correcting mechanism to kick in: The *AS* curve shifts upward, increasing the price level. Thus, unemployment that is too low compromises the Fed's other chief goal by creating inflation. And, as you will see later in the chapter, the Fed could not keep the economy operating beyond full employment for more than a short time anyway. In the long run, its attempts to push the economy too hard would only create more inflation and would not succeed in lowering unemployment.

The unemployment rate at which GDP is at its full-employment level—that is, with no cyclical unemployment—is called the **natural rate of unemployment.**

NATURAL RATE OF UNEMPLOYMENT The unemployment rate when there is no cyclical unemployment.

> *When the unemployment rate is* below *the natural rate, GDP is greater than potential output. The economy's self-correcting mechanism will then create inflation. When the unemployment rate is* above *the natural rate, GDP is below potential output. The self-correcting mechanism will then put downward pressure on the price level.*

The word "natural" must be interpreted with care. The natural unemployment rate is not etched in stone, nor is it the outcome of purely natural forces than can't be influenced by public policy. But it is determined by rather slow-moving forces in the economy: how frequently workers lose their jobs, how efficiently the unemployed can search for jobs and firms can search for new workers, and how well the skills of the unemployed match the skills needed by employers. The natural rate can also be influenced by government policies that provide incentives or disincentives for workers to find jobs quickly, or for employers to hire them. The natural rate can change when any of these underlying conditions change. Indeed, economists generally believe that over the past decade, the natural rate has decreased in the United States—from 6 or 6.5 percent in the mid-1980s to about 5.5 percent today. Meanwhile, in many European countries, the natural rate of unemployment has increased in recent years—exceeding 10 percent in France and close to 20 percent in Spain. The causes of these changes in the natural rate, as well as the *extent* of the changes, are hotly debated by economists. But there is general agreement about the direction: down in the United States, up in Europe.

Why use the term "natural" for such a changeable feature of the economy? The term makes sense only from the perspective of *macro*economic policy: Simply put, there isn't much that macroeconomic policy can do about the natural rate. Stimulating the economy with fiscal or monetary policy may bring the *actual* unemployment rate down for a time, but it will not change the natural rate itself. And pushing unemployment below the natural rate would cause inflation. Thus, the natural rate of unemployment can be seen as a kind of goalpost for the Fed. The location of the goalpost may change over the years, but during any given year, it tells us where the Fed is aiming.

THE FED'S PERFORMANCE

How well has the Fed achieved its goals? Panel (a) of Figure 1 shows the annual inflation rate since 1950, as measured by the Consumer Price Index. You can see that monetary policy permitted extended periods of high inflation in the 1970s and early 1980s. You can also see, as noted at the beginning of the chapter, that the Fed has achieved great success in controlling inflation since then. Indeed, in the 12 years from 1984 to 1996, the annual inflation rate exceeded 4.6 percent only once—in 1990, during the supply shock caused by higher oil prices. Note also that the rate of inflation fell to practically zero during 1986, when oil prices declined. Except for these two brief episodes, inflation was held steady at around 3 percent.

Panel (b) shows the monthly rate of unemployment since 1950. Over the last decade or so, the Fed's performance on unemployment has been somewhat mixed. From 1984 to 1996, the unemployment rate was 7 percent or greater—significantly above its natural rate—during 41 months. The most recent period of high unemployment was during the recession of the early 1990s, when the unemployment rate stayed above 7.5 percent for half a year. But notice the remarkable improvement in unemployment from mid-1992 and after. Through 1997, the Fed kept the unemployment rate hovering very close to 5 percent, *without* heating up inflation.

As you can see, the Fed has had a good—and improving—record in recent years. The inflation rate has been kept low and relatively stable, and—especially in the last few years—unemployment has been near most estimates of the natural rate. How has the Fed done it? Are there any general conclusions we can reach about how a central bank should operate to achieve the twin goals of full employment and a stable, low inflation rate? Indeed there are, as you'll see in the next section.

FEDERAL RESERVE POLICY: THEORY AND PRACTICE

Two chapters ago, we discussed the difference between *active* and *passive* monetary policy. With a passive policy, the Fed does not change the money supply in response to events in the macroeconomy. Under an active policy, the Fed responds to events in the economy with changes in the money supply, in order to improve the economy's performance over time.

In recent years, the Fed has been following an active monetary policy—carefully gauging its actions according to conditions in the economy.

FIGURE 1

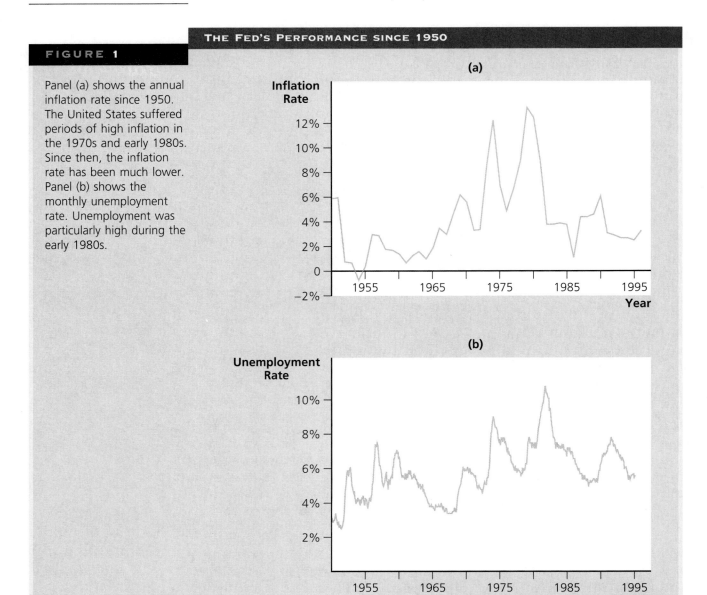

THE FED'S PERFORMANCE SINCE 1950

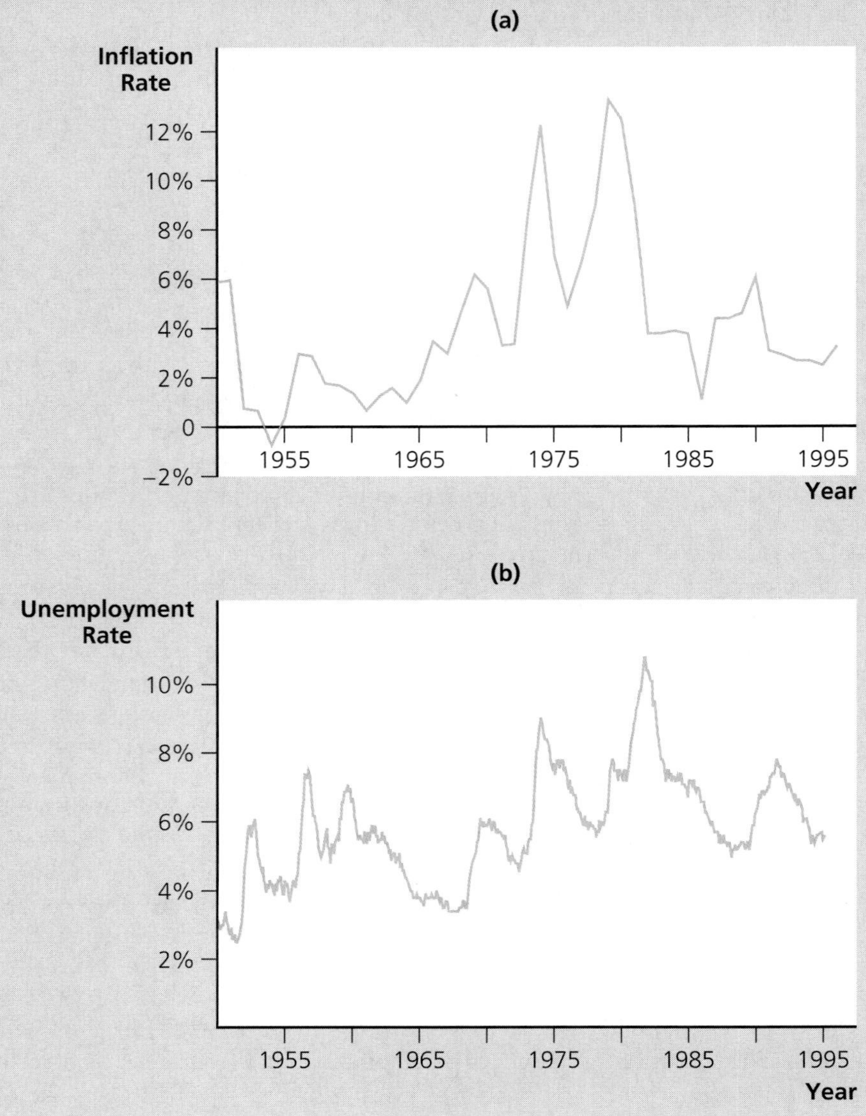

Panel (a) shows the annual inflation rate since 1950. The United States suffered periods of high inflation in the 1970s and early 1980s. Since then, the inflation rate has been much lower. Panel (b) shows the monthly unemployment rate. Unemployment was particularly high during the early 1980s.

In this section, we'll explore how the Fed has responded to different types of shocks, and why it has responded as it has. In some cases, the proper response is easy to determine, because the same action that maintains full employment also helps maintain low inflation. But in other cases, the Fed must trade off one goal for another: Responses that maintain full employment will worsen inflation, and responses that alleviate inflation will create more unemployment.

We'll make a temporary simplifying assumption in this section: that the Fed's goal for the inflation rate is *zero*. In reality, the Fed's goal is *low,* but not zero, inflation. A bit later, we'll discuss why the Fed prefers a low inflation rate to a zero rate, and how this modifies our analysis.

RESPONDING TO SHIFTS IN MONEY DEMAND

FIGURE 2

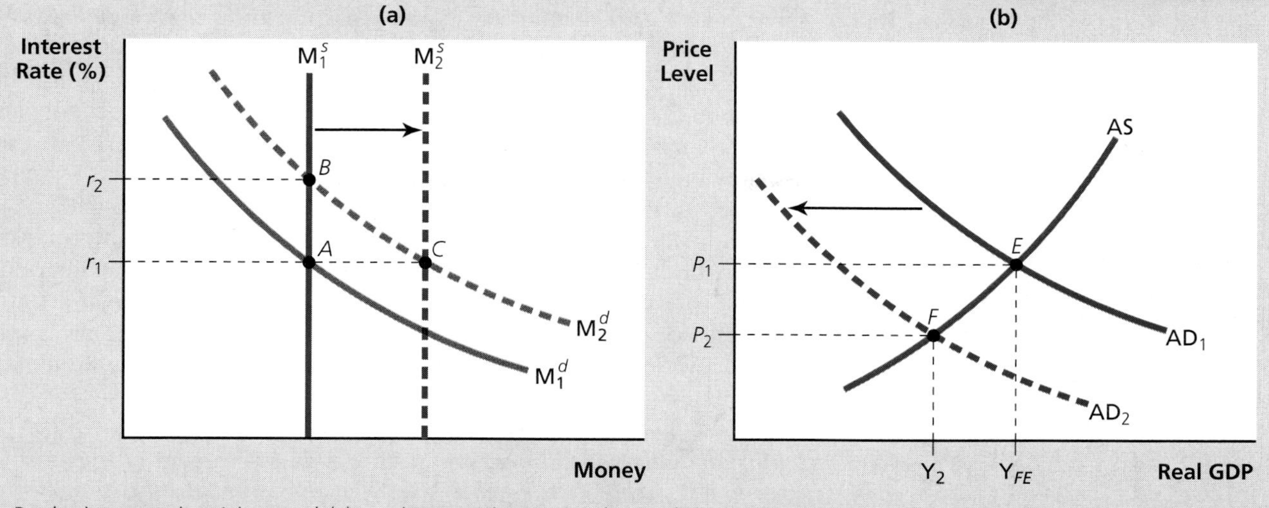

Beginning at point *A* in panel (a), an increase in money demand drives the interest rate up to r_2 (point *B*). Under a passive monetary policy, this would cause interest-sensitive spending to decrease. In panel (b), the aggregate demand curve would shift to AD_2, decreasing GDP from Y_{FE} (at point *E*) to Y_2 (at point *F*)—a recession. To maintain full employment, the Fed could increase the money supply to M_2^s, preventing any change in the interest rate and any shift in *AD*.

RESPONDING TO SHIFTS IN THE MONEY DEMAND CURVE

Potential disturbances to the economy sometimes arise from a shift in the money demand curve. For example, two chapters ago, you learned about the effects of expectations on money demands. If people expect the interest rate to rise (the price of bonds to fall) in the near future, they will want to hold less wealth in the form of bonds and more in money, so the money demand curve will shift rightward. Larger and longer-lasting shifts in the money demand curve may occur for reasons that are not well understood, although leading suspects are the development of new types of financial assets and new methods of making payments.

How should the Fed respond to shifts in the money demand curve? We considered this question two chapters ago, but let's review what we found. Figure 2 shows the effect of a rightward shift of the money demand curve. Look first at panel (a). Initially, the money market is in equilibrium at point *A*, with the interest rate equal to r_1. When the money demand curve shifts rightward, to M_2^d, the equilibrium moves to point *B*, with the higher interest rate r_2. Under a passive monetary policy—leaving the money supply unchanged—the rise in the interest rate would cause interest-sensitive spending to fall. This, in turn, would decrease equilibrium GDP at any given price level.

Panel (b) shows another way to view the effect of the change in money demand: the AD curve shifts leftward, from AD_1 to AD_2. With a passive monetary policy, the economy would slide down the *AS* curve from point *E* to point *F*. Since the economy began at full-employment output (Y_{FE}), the passive monetary policy would result in a recession. Unemployment would rise above the natural rate, and the price level would decrease.

If the Fed wants to maintain full employment with zero inflation—an unchanged price level—then a passive monetary policy is clearly the wrong response. Is there a better policy?

Indeed there is—an *active* monetary policy. By increasing the money stock—shifting the money supply curve from M_1^s to M_2^s—the Fed moves the money market to a new equilibrium at point *C*, *preventing any rise in the interest rate.* If the Fed acts quickly enough, there will be no decrease in interest-sensitive spending and no shift in the *AD* curve. In panel (b), the economy remains at point *E*, and the Fed maintains full employment with zero inflation.

As you can see, shifts in the money demand curve present the Fed with a no-lose situation: By adjusting the money supply to prevent changes in the interest rate, the Fed can achieve both price stability and full employment. During most periods, when the economy is not affected by any shocks other than money demand shifts, the constant interest rate policy will keep the economy on an even keel. This is why, in its day-to-day operations, the Fed sets and maintains an **interest rate target** and then adjusts the money supply to achieve that target:

INTEREST RATE TARGET The interest rate the Federal Reserve aims to achieve by adjusting the money supply.

> *To deal with money demand shocks, the Fed sets an interest rate target and changes the money supply as needed to maintain the target. In this way, the Fed can achieve its goals of price stability and full employment simultaneously.*

HOW THE FED KEEPS THE INTEREST RATE ON TARGET. A quick review of the day-to-day mechanics of Fed policy making shows how it sets and maintains its interest rate target in practice. Fed officials meet each morning to determine that day's monetary policy, based on information gathered the previous afternoon and earlier that morning. A key piece of information is what actually happened to the interest rate since the morning before. A rise in the interest rate means that the money demand curve has shifted rightward; a drop in the interest rate means the curve has shifted leftward.

Using this and other information about the banking system and the economy, the Fed decides what to do. At 11:30 A.M., if the interest rate is above target, the Fed buys government bonds. This increases the money supply and brings the interest rate back down to its target level, as in Figure 2. If, instead, the interest rate is below target, the Fed sells government bonds, decreasing the money supply and raising the interest rate back up to its target level.

THE FED'S RESPONSE TO SPENDING SHOCKS

The Fed has a somewhat more difficult job responding to spending shocks than to shifts in money demand. Figure 3 illustrates why. In panel (a) the money market is initially in equilibrium at point *A*, and in panel (b) the economy's short-run equilibrium is at point *E*, with output at full employment. Now suppose that there is a positive spending shock. The shock might originate with the government—an increase in government spending or a decrease in taxes—or in the private sector—an increase in investment or autonomous consumption. Whatever the source, the impact in Figure 3 is the same: the *AD* curve will shift rightward, from AD_1 to AD_2. Now let's consider three possible responses by the Fed.

First, the Fed could follow a *passive* monetary policy, leaving the money supply unchanged. In this case, the economy would slide upward along the *AS* curve, moving to point *F*. Both output and the price level would rise.

RESPONDING TO SPENDING SHOCKS

FIGURE 3

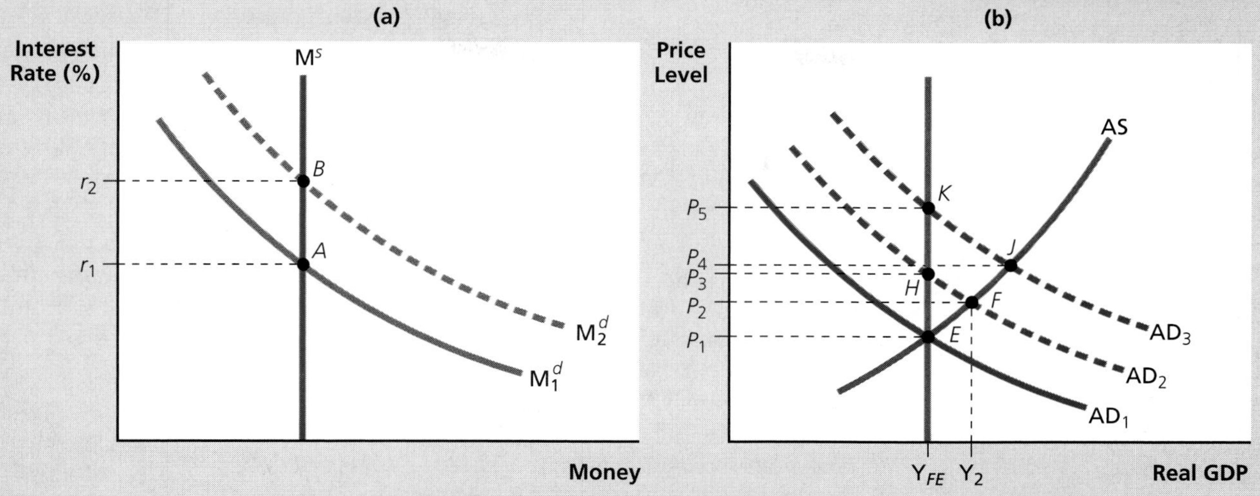

A positive spending shock would shift *AD* rightward to AD_2 in panel (b), causing both the price level and output to rise. Under a passive monetary policy, that rise in income would cause the money demand curve to shift to M_2^d in panel (a), driving the interest rate upward from r_1 to r_2.

An active policy of maintaining the interest rate at r_1 would make matters worse. To maintain the interest rate target, the Fed would have to increase the money supply, causing an additional rightward shift of the *AD* curve to AD_3 and pushing the economy even further above full employment. The price level would increase to P_4 in the short run and P_5 in the long run.

As you can see, the Fed would not want to respond to a spending shock with a passive monetary policy. Output would rise, bringing the unemployment rate below the natural rate. The price level would rise as well—to P_2. In the long run, the price level would rise further—to P_3—as the self-correcting mechanism returned the economy to full employment at point *H*.

Would the active policy described earlier—maintaining an interest rate target—be an improvement? Actually, no—it would be even worse. To maintain the interest rate at r_1, the Fed would have to increase the money supply (not shown). But with no rise in the interest rate to crowd out some consumption and investment spending, the spending shock would shift the *AD* curve rightward even further—say, to AD_3. The new short-run equilibrium would then be at point *J*. As you can see, maintaining the interest rate target would push the economy even further beyond its potential output, and increase the price level even more—both in the short run (to P_4) and in the long run (P_5).

How, then, should the Fed respond to the spending shock? To maintain full employment and a stable price level, the Fed must shift the *AD* curve back to AD_1. And it can, indeed, do so, as illustrated in Figure 4. Once again, the figure shows a spending shock that shifts the *AD* curve rightward to AD_2, increasing both output and the price level. In the money market, the higher prices and higher incomes shift the money demand curve rightward, raising the interest rate to r_2. But the rise to r_2 is not enough to choke off the increase in spending; it causes *some* crowding out of consumption and investment, but not *complete* crowding out. In order to shift the *AD* curve back to AD_1, the Fed must raise the interest rate enough to cause

FIGURE 4

THE BEST RESPONSE TO A SPENDING SHOCK

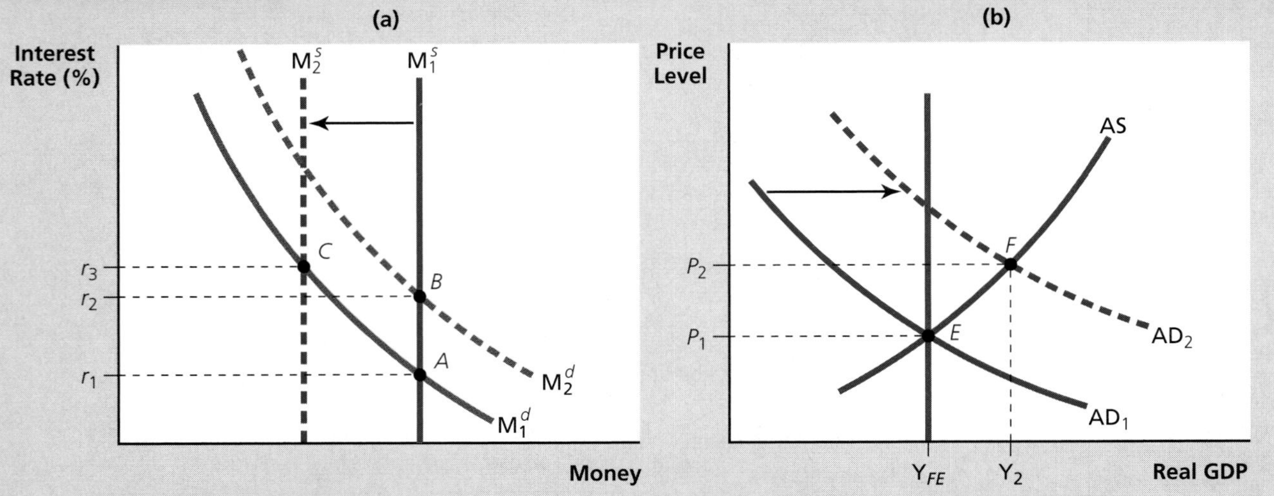

A spending shock that shifts the *AD* curve to AD_2 threatens to raise output beyond its full-employment level, and increase the price level as well. The Fed can neutralize that shift by decreasing the money supply to M_2^s. The resulting rise in the interest rate (to r_3) would reduce interest-sensitive spending and return the *AD* curve to AD_1.

complete crowding out. That is, it must raise the interest rate by just enough so that consumption and investment spending decline by an amount equal to the initial spending shock. In the figure, we assume that an interest rate of r_3 will do the trick (point *C*). The Fed must decrease the money supply to M_2^s. If the Fed acts quickly enough, it can prevent the spending shock from shifting the *AD* curve at all:[2]

To maintain full employment and price stability after a spending shock, the Fed must change *its interest rate target. A positive spending shock requires an increase in the target; a negative spending shock requires a decrease in the target.*

In recent years, the Fed has changed its interest rate target as frequently as needed to keep the economy on track—sometimes the target changes every few weeks, and sometimes it remains unchanged for most of a year. If the Fed observes that the economy is overheating—and that the unemployment rate has fallen below its natural rate—it will raise its target. In this way, it responds to forces that shift the *AD* curve rightward by creating an opposing force—a higher interest rate—to shift it leftward again. When the Fed observes that the economy is sluggish—and the unemployment rate has risen above its natural rate—the Fed will lower its target. This tends to neutralize leftward shifts of the *AD* curve.

As you can see, spending shocks present the Fed with another no-lose situation: The same policy that helps to keep unemployment at its natural rate also helps to maintain a stable price level. However, spending shocks present a challenge to the Fed that it doesn't face during other, less eventful periods. To change the interest

2 Notice that the new money market equilibrium is along the original money demand curve M_1^d, since the policy will return both the price level and income to their original values.

rate target by just the right amount, the Fed needs accurate information about how the economy operates. We'll return to this and other problems in conducting monetary policy in the "Using the Theory" section of this chapter.

THE INTEREST RATE TARGET AND THE FINANCIAL MARKETS. The members of the Open Market Committee think very hard before they vote to change the interest rate target. In addition to its effects on the level of output and the price level, changes in the interest rate target can create turmoil in the stock and bond markets.

Why? Recall that the interest rate and the price of bonds are negatively related. Thus, when the Fed moves the interest rate to a higher target level, the price of bonds drops. Because the public holds trillions of dollars in government and corporate bonds, even a small rise in the interest rate—say, a quarter of a percentage point—causes the value of the public's bond holdings to drop by billions of dollars.

The stock market is affected in a similar way. People hold stocks because they pay dividends—which come from firms' profits—and because stock prices are usually expected to rise as the economy grows and firms become more profitable. But stocks must remain competitive with bonds, or else no one would hold them. The lower the price of a stock, the more attractive it is to a potential buyer.

When the Fed raises the interest rate, the rate of return on bonds increases, so bonds become more attractive. As a result, stock prices must fall, so that stocks, too, will become more attractive. And that is typically what happens. Unless other changes are affecting the stock market, a rise in the interest rate causes people to try to sell their stocks in order to acquire the suddenly-more-attractive bonds. This causes stock prices to fall, until stocks are once again as attractive as bonds. Thus, a rise in the interest rate causes stock prices, as well as bond prices, to fall:

The stock and bond markets move in the opposite direction of the Fed's interest rate target: When the Fed raises its target, stock and bond prices fall; when it lowers its target, stock and bond prices rise.

The destabilizing effect on stock and bond markets is one reason the Fed prefers not to change its interest rate target very often. Frequent changes in the target would make financial markets less stable, and the public more hesitant to supply funds to business firms by buying stocks and bonds.

Importantly, financial markets are also affected by *expected* changes in the interest rate target—whether or not they occur. If you expect the Fed to raise its target, you also expect stock and bond prices to fall. Therefore, you would want to dump these assets *now,* before their price drops. Similarly, an expectation of a drop in the interest rate target would make you want to buy stocks and bonds now, before their prices rise. Thus, *changes in expectations* about the Fed's future actions can be as destabilizing as the actions themselves.

This is why the financial press speculates constantly about the likelihood of changes in the interest rate target. Most of the time, the news is of the dog that didn't bark—the Open Market Committee meets and decides to keep the target unchanged. Interest rates and stock prices often jump around in the days leading up to meetings of the Open Market Committee.

These observations can help us understand a phenomenon that—at first glance—appears mystifying: Stock and bond prices often fall when good news about the economy is released, and rise when bad news is released. For example, if the Bureau of Labor Statistics announces that jobs are plentiful and the unemployment rate

FIGURE 5

RESPONDING TO SUPPLY SHOCKS

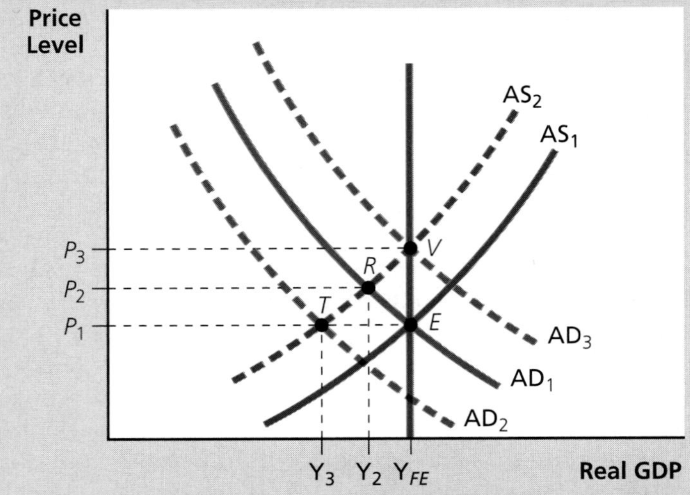

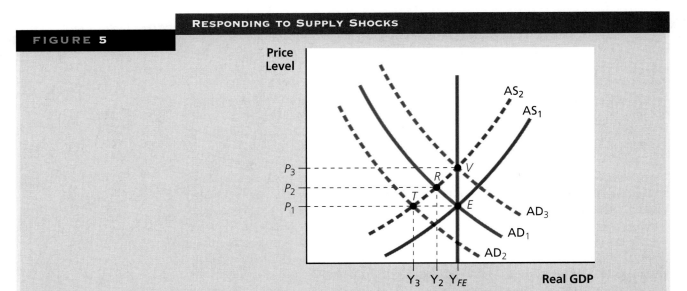

Starting at point *E*, a negative supply shock shifts the *AS* curve upward to AS_2. Under a passive monetary policy, a new short-run equilibrium would be established at point *R*, with a higher price level (P_2) and a lower level of output (Y_2). The Fed could prevent inflation by decreasing the money supply and shifting *AD* to AD_2, but output would fall to Y_3. At the other extreme, it could increase the money supply and shift the *AD* curve to AD_3. This would keep output at the full-employment level, but at the cost of a higher price level, P_3.

has dropped, or the Department of Commerce announces that real GDP has grown rapidly in the previous quarter, the stock and bond markets may plummet. Why? Because owners of stocks and bonds know that the Open Market Committee might interpret the good news as evidence that the economy is overheating. They expect the Committee to raise its interest rate target, so they try to sell their stocks and bonds before the committee even meets. Similarly, bad news about the economy often creates expectations of a drop in the interest rate target, causing stock and bond prices to rise.

RESPONDING TO SUPPLY SHOCKS

So far in this chapter, you've seen that demand shocks, in general, present the Fed with easy policy choices. By sticking to its interest rate target, it can neutralize any demand shocks that arise from shifts in money demand. And by changing its interest rate target from time to time, it can deal with demand shocks caused by changes in spending. In each of these cases, the very policy that maintains a stable price level also helps to maintain full employment.

But negative *supply* shocks present the Fed with a true dilemma: If the Fed tries to preserve price stability, it will worsen unemployment; if it tries to maintain high employment, it will worsen inflation.

SHORT-RUN RESPONSE TO SUPPLY SHOCKS. Figure 5 illustrates the Fed's dilemma in the short run. Initially, the economy is at point *E* (full employment). Then, a supply shock—say, a rise in world oil prices—shifts the *AS* curve up to AS_2. Under a passive monetary policy, the Fed would not change the money stock, keeping the *AD* curve at AD_1. The short-run equilibrium would then move from point *E* to point *R*, and the economy would experience stagflation—both inflation and a recession—with output falling to Y_2 and the price level rising to P_2.

HAWK AND DOVE POLICIES

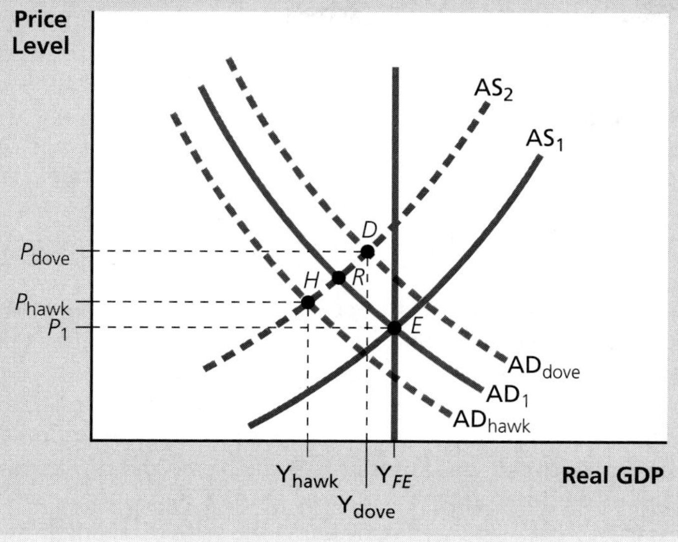

FIGURE 6

Starting at point *E*, an adverse supply shock shifts the *AS* curve to AS_2. Under a dove policy, the Fed would shift the *AD* curve to AD_{dove}. The equilibrium moves to point *D* instead of *R*, moderating the drop in output, but at the cost of a higher price level. Under a hawk policy, the Fed would shift *AD* to AD_{hawk}. The equilibrium moves to point *H*—a larger fall in output and a smaller rise in the price level.

But the Fed can instead respond with an active monetary policy, changing the money stock in order to alter the short-run equilibrium. Which policy should it choose? The answer will depend on whether it is mostly concerned about rising prices or rising unemployment. Let's start by imagining two extreme positions.

First, the Fed could prevent inflation entirely by decreasing the money stock, shifting the *AD* curve leftward to AD_2. This would move the short-run equilibrium to point *T*. Notice, though, that while the price level remains at P_1, output decreases to Y_3—even lower than under the passive policy.

At the other extreme, the Fed could prevent any fall in output. To accomplish this, the Fed would *increase* the money stock and shift the *AD* curve rightward, to AD_3. The equilibrium would then move to point *V*, keeping output at its full-employment level. But this policy causes more inflation, raising the price level all the way to P_3.

In practice, the Fed is unlikely to choose either of these two extremes to deal with a supply shock, preferring instead some intermediate policy. But the extreme positions help illustrate the Fed's dilemma:

POLICY TRADEOFFS

A negative supply shock presents the Fed with a short-run trade-off: It can limit the recession, but only at the cost of more inflation; and it can limit inflation, but only at the cost of a deeper recession.

The choice between the two policies is a hard one. After supply shocks, there are often debates within the Fed—and in the public arena—about how best to respond. Inflation *hawks* lean in the direction of price stability, and are willing to tolerate more unemployment in order to achieve it. Inflation *doves* lean in the direction of a milder recession, and are more willing to tolerate the cost of higher inflation.

Figure 6 shows how we can illustrate the hawk and dove positions. Once again, a negative supply shock shifts the *AS* curve from AS_1 to AS_2. The hawk position would shift the *AD* curve leftward, to AD_{hawk}, moving the short-run equilibrium from point *E* to point *H*. The hawk policy is less extreme than the no-inflation policy depicted in Figure 5, but it still leans somewhat against inflation. The price level rises to P_{hawk}, and output falls to Y_{hawk}.

The dove position, by contrast, leans toward maintaining high employment. Under a dove policy, the *AD* curve shifts rightward, to AD_{dove}. Output still falls—to Y_{dove}—but by less than under the hawk policy. However, the price level rises by more than under the hawk policy.

POLICY TRADEOFFS

In response to a supply shock, inflation hawks lean more toward controlling inflation, at the cost of greater unemployment. Inflation doves lean more toward limiting unemployment, at the cost of higher inflation.

LONG-RUN RESPONSE TO SUPPLY SHOCKS. So far, we've been considering the Fed's response to a supply shock in the short run. What about the long run? We know that if the supply shock is long-lasting, the self-correcting mechanism will kick in after a year or so. With unemployment above the natural rate, wages will fall, and the *AS* curve will shift back down to its original position. The economy will eventually return to full employment. Do the hawk and dove policies give any different results in the long run?

Not necessarily. Look again at Figure 6. As the self-correcting process shifts the *AS* curve back toward AS_1, monetary policy can be used to shift the *AD* curve back to AD_1. If the Fed responded in the short run with a hawk policy, then over the long run, it would shift the *AD* curve rightward as the *AS* curve shifted downward. Under the dove policy, the Fed would have to shift the *AD* curve leftward as the *AS* curve shifted downward, to prevent the economy from overshooting full employment. In either case, we can end up back at point *E*. The difference between hawk and dove policies is largely in what happens in the interim, before the self-correcting process is complete. Under the hawk policy, the unemployment rate remains higher than under the dove policy, until the economy has self-corrected. But under the dove policy, the temporary rise in the price level is greater than under the hawk policy.

CHOOSING BETWEEN HAWK AND DOVE POLICIES. When a supply shock hits, should the Fed use a hawk policy, should it employ a dove policy, or should it keep the *AD* curve unchanged? That depends. Over time, as the economy is hit by supply shocks, the hawk policy maintains more stability in the price level, but less stability in output and employment. The dove policy gives the opposite result: more stability in output and less stability in the price level. The Fed should choose the hawk policy if it cares more about price stability, and the dove policy if it cares more about the stability of output and employment. Or it can pick an intermediate policy—one that balances price and employment stability more evenly.

The proper choice depends on how the Fed weights the harm caused by unemployment against the harm caused by inflation. And since the Fed is a public institution, its views should reflect the assessment of society as a whole. This is why supply shocks present such a challenge to the Fed: The public itself is divided among hawks and doves. Both inflation and unemployment cause harm, but of very different kinds. Inflation imposes a more general cost on society—the resources used up to cope with it. If the inflation is unexpected, it will also redistribute income between borrowers and lenders. The costs of unemployment are borne largely by the unemployed themselves—who suffer the harm of job loss—but partly by taxpayers, who provide funds for unemployment insurance. Balancing the gains and losses from hawk and dove policies is no easy task.

In recent years, some officials at the Fed have argued that having two objectives—stable prices *and* full employment—is unrealistic when there are supply shocks. The current chair of the Board of Governors, Alan Greenspan, has asked Congress to change the Fed's mandate to one of controlling inflation, period. But it would be difficult for the Fed to ignore the costs of higher unemployment, even if it was legally permitted to do so. Regardless of any future change in the Fed's mandate, the debate between hawks and doves is destined to continue.

EXPECTATIONS AND ONGOING INFLATION

So far in this chapter, we've assumed that the Fed strives to maintain *zero* inflation, and that the price level remains constant when the economy reaches its long-run, full-employment equilibrium. But as we discussed earlier, this is not entirely realistic. Look again at panel (a) of Figure 1. There you can see that the U.S. economy has been characterized by *ongoing inflation.* Even in the mid 1990s—with unemployment at its natural rate—the annual inflation rate has remained close to 3 percent. That means that, even though the economy is at full employment, prices are *continually rising.*

Why should the price level continue to rise when unemployment is at its natural rate? And how does ongoing inflation change our analysis of the effects of monetary policy, or the guidelines that the Fed should follow? We'll consider these questions next.

HOW ONGOING INFLATION ARISES

The best way to begin our analysis of ongoing inflation is to explore how it arises in an economy. We can do this by revisiting the 1960s, when the inflation rate rose steadily, and ongoing inflation first became a public concern.

What was special about the economy in the 1960s? First, it was a period of exuberance and optimism, for both businesses and households. Business spending on plant and equipment rose, and household spending on new homes and automobiles rose as well. At the same time, government spending rose—both military spending for the war in Vietnam and social spending on programs to help alleviate poverty. These increases in spending all contributed to a rightward shift of the *AD* curve—a positive demand shock. The unemployment rate fell below the natural rate—hovering around 3 percent in the late 1960s. And, as expected, the economy's self-correcting mechanism kicked in: Higher wages shifted the *AS* curve upward, causing the price level to rise.

As you've learned in this chapter, the Fed could have neutralized the positive demand shocks by raising its interest rate target. Alternatively, the Fed could have done nothing, allowing the self-correcting mechanism to bring the economy back to full employment with a higher—but stable—price level. But in the late 1960s, the Fed made a different choice: It maintained its low interest rate target. This required the Fed to increase the money supply, thus adding its *own* positive demand shock to the spending shocks already hitting the economy.

Why did the Fed act in this way? No one knows for sure, but one likely reason is that, in the 1960s, the Fed saw its job differently than it does today. The Fed's goal was to keep the interest rate stable and low, both to maintain high investment spending and to avoid instability in the financial markets. This is what it had been doing for years, with good effect: Americans had prospered in the previous decade, the 1950s, and financial markets were, indeed, stable.

FED POLICY IN THE 1960S

FIGURE 7

During the 1960s, a rightward shift of *AD* to AD_2 increased both output and the price level (point *B*). As the economy began to self-correct, the Fed shifted *AD* to AD_3, holding output above the full-employment level at point *C*. This was done several times, and the price level rose year after year—to P_2, P_3, and P_4. When the public began to expect continuing inflation, the *AS* curve shifted to AS_4 (point *E*). This brought the economy back to full employment.

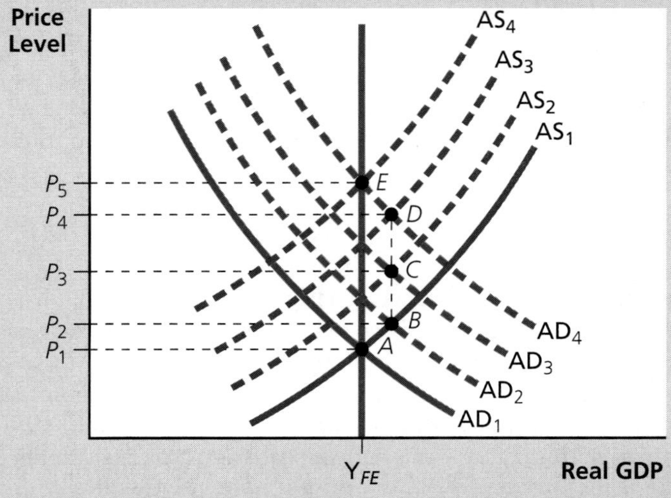

But while this policy worked well in the 1950s, it did not serve the economy well during and after the demand shocks of the 1960s. Figure 7 illustrates what happened. The initial increases in consumption, investment, and government spending—along with the Fed's increase in the money stock—shifted the *AD* curve from AD_1 to AD_2, moving the equilibrium from point *A* to point *B*. As the economy began to self-correct, and the *AS* curve shifted upward from AS_1 to AS_2, the Fed shifted the *AD* curve further rightward, to AD_3, creating a new equilibrium at point *C*. Notice that, by increasing the money supply, the Fed allowed the economy to continue operating beyond its potential, causing the price level to rise further.

And this was done more than once. Each time the economy began to self-correct, with the *AS* curve shifting upward, the Fed would respond by increasing the money supply, shifting the *AD* curve to match it. In Figure 7, the equilibrium continued to move—from *B* to *C* and *C* to *D*. Year after year, the price level rose.

Now comes a crucial part of the story: As the price level continued to rise, the public began to *expect* it to rise at a similar rate in the future.

When inflation continues for some time, the public develops expectations that the inflation rate in the future will be similar to the inflation rates of the recent past.

Why are expectations of inflation so important? Because when managers and workers expect inflation, it gets built into their decision-making process. Union contracts that set wages for the next three years will include automatic increases to compensate for the anticipated loss of purchasing power caused by future inflation. Non-union wages will tend to rise each year as well, to match the wages in the unionized sector. And contracts for future delivery of inputs—like lumber, cement, and unfinished goods—will incorporate the higher prices everyone expects by the date of delivery.

LONG-RUN EQUILIBRIUM WITH BUILT-IN INFLATION

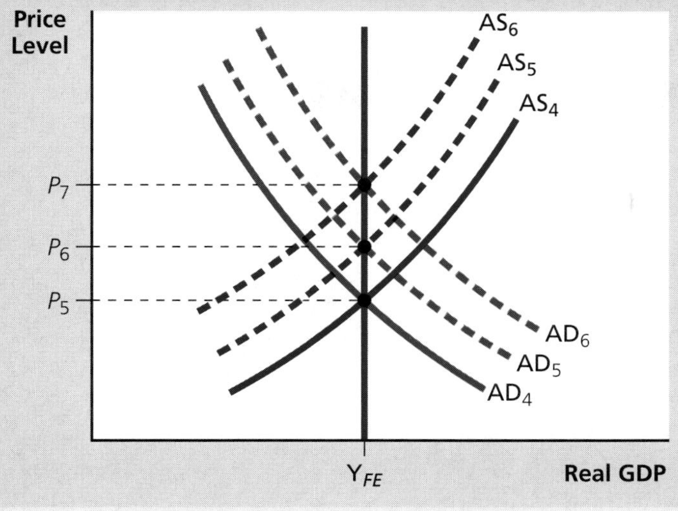

FIGURE 8

Each year, the aggregate supply curve shifts upward by the built-in rate of inflation. To keep the economy at full employment, the Fed shifts the *AD* curve rightward each year, by continually increasing the money supply.

A continuing, stable rate of inflation gets built into the economy. The built-in rate is usually the rate that has existed for the past few years.

Look again at Figure 7. There, the *AS* curve shifts up each year—from AS_1 to AS_2 to AS_3 and so on—because of the self-correcting mechanism: Unemployment is below the natural rate, so labor is scarce and the wage rate is rising. This increases unit costs and shifts the *AS* curve upward. But once the public begins to expect continuing inflation, there is *another* reason for the *AS* curve to shift up as well: Wages and input prices are rising because everyone *expects* inflation. Thus, as soon as the public expects inflation, the *AS* curve will shift up even further during the year, finally causing the economy to self-correct back to full employment. In the figure, this occurs when the *AS* curve shifts upward from AS_3 to AS_4—a larger shift than previously—bringing us to point *E*. But at *E*, even though the economy has returned to full employment, the public expects inflation to continue. Therefore, the *AS* curve continues to shift up, year after year.

Figure 8 shows the economy's new long-run equilibrium. With output at full employment, the self-correcting mechanism has done its job. Unemployment is at its natural rate, so the self-correction mechanism is no longer contributing to any rise in wages or unit costs. But something else *is* causing unit costs to increase: inflationary expectations. Based on recent experience, the public still expects the price level to rise as it has been rising in the past, so wages and input prices will continue to increase, *even though output remains unchanged at full employment*. Thus,

in an economy with built-in inflation, the AS *curve will shift up each year, even when output is at full employment and unemployment is at its natural rate. The upward shift of the* AS *curve will equal the built-in rate of inflation.*

For example, if the public expects inflation of 3 percent per year, then contracts will call for wages and input prices to rise by 3 percent per year. This means that unit costs will increase by 3 percent. Firms—marking up prices over unit costs—

FIGURE 9

THE FED'S RESPONSE TO ONGOING INFLATION

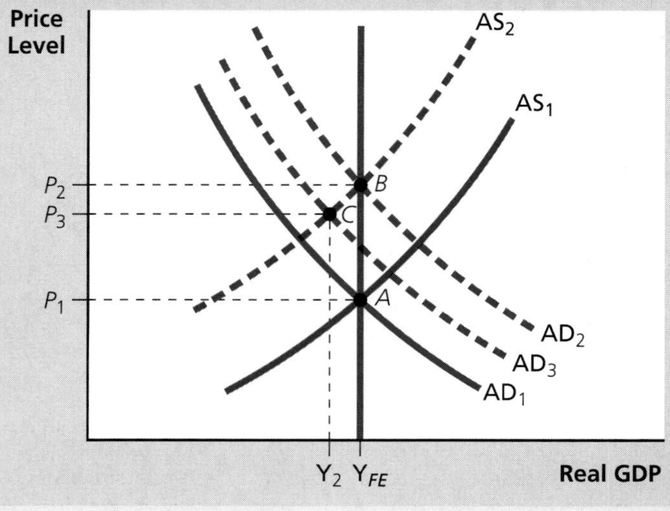

In an economy experiencing ongoing inflation, the *AS* curve will shift upward at the built-in rate of inflation (to AS_2). The Fed can maintain full employment by shifting *AD* to AD_2, bringing the economy to point *B*. But it may decide to reduce inflation by shifting the curve only to AD_3 (point *C*). This slows inflation, but at the cost of a recession.

will raise their prices by 3 percent as well, and the *AS* curve will shift upward by 3 percent each year.

Notice that, in Figure 8, the economy is in equilibrium, but the nature of this equilibrium is different from that of the others we've discussed. Instead of an unchanging price level, there is an *unchanging rate of inflation.* Output remains constant, but each year the price level rises at the constant, built-in rate of inflation.

THE FED'S ROLE IN ONGOING INFLATION. Explaining why the *AS* curve shifts up is only half the story of the long-run equilibrium in Figure 8. We must also explain why the *AD* curve continues to shift rightward. The simple answer is: The *AD* curve shifts rightward because the Fed continues to increase the money supply. But *why* does the Fed shift the *AD* curve rightward, when it knows that doing so only prolongs inflation? One reason is that reducing inflation is *costly* to the economy.

Figure 9, which shows one year in an economy with built-in inflation, illustrates this cost. During the year, the *AS* curve will shift up from AS_1 to AS_2—a percentage shift equal to the built-in rate of inflation. This will happen *no matter what the Fed does,* because the shift is based on wage and price decisions that, in turn, are based on past experiences of inflation. There is nothing the Fed can do today to affect what has happened in the past, so this year, it must accept the upward shift to AS_2 as a given.

If the Fed continues to act this year as it has in past years, it will shift the *AD* curve to AD_2, maintaining full employment while moving the economy from point *A* to point *B*. But now suppose the Fed decides to reduce inflation by shifting the *AD* curve by *less* than it has in the past—say, to AD_3. Then, since the *AS* curve still shifts up to AS_2, the equilibrium will move to point *C*. The Fed achieves its goal of bringing down inflation this year: The price level will rise from P_1 to P_3, instead of from P_1 to P_2. But the reduction in inflation is not without cost: When the economy moves to point *C*, we will be in a recession.

POLICY TRADEOFFS

In the short run, the Fed can bring down the rate of inflation by reducing the rightward shift of the AD curve, but only at the cost of creating a recession.

If the Fed continues to hold tight, limiting the shift of the *AD* curve year after year and maintaining a lower inflation rate, what will happen in the long run? The public will begin to *expect* lower inflation. This will cause the *AS* curve to shift up at a slower rate. The Fed can then position the *AD* curve to return the economy to full employment, and continue shifting the *AD* curve by the amount needed to maintain full employment. But since the *AS* curve is then shifting upward more slowly, the built-in inflation rate will be lower.

In the long run, if the Fed lowers the rate of inflation and holds it at the lower rate, expectations of inflation will adjust downward. At that point, the Fed can move the economy back to full employment with a lower inflation rate.

As you can see, to eliminate built-in inflation from the economy, the Fed must engineer a recession by slowing down the rightward shifts of the *AD* curve.

The idea that the Fed would purposely create a recession to reduce inflation is not just a theoretical possibility; the Fed has actually done this more than once. By far the most important episode occurred during the early 1980s. As Figure 1 shows, inflation reached the extraordinary level of 13.3 percent in 1979. Soon after, with the support of the newly elected president, the Fed embarked on an aggressive campaign to bring inflation down. The interest rate was set at sky-high levels, a recession began in July of 1981, and unemployment peaked, as shown in Figure 1, at 10.8 percent at the end of 1982. With tremendous slack in the economy, inflation fell rapidly, to below 4 percent in 1982. The Fed deliberately created a serious recession, but it took care of high inflation.

Creating a recession is not a decision that the Fed takes lightly. Recessions are costly to the economy and painful to those who lose their jobs. The desire to avoid a recession is one reason that the Fed tolerates ongoing inflation and continues to play its role by shifting the *AD* curve rightward. We'll discuss other reasons for the Fed's tolerance of ongoing inflation a bit later.

ONGOING INFLATION AND MONETARY POLICY

How does ongoing inflation change our analysis of monetary policy? For one thing, it means that the Fed must cope with an upward-shifting *AS* curve, even when there are no supply shocks. As long as the public continues to expect inflation, the *AS* curve will automatically shift up each year.

As a consequence, we must recognize a subtle, but important, change in the Fed's objectives: While the Fed still desires full employment, its other goal—price stability—becomes a *low and stable inflation rate.*

Figure 10 shows how this new goal changes our analysis of spending shocks. At the beginning of the year, the economy is at point *E*, on AD_1 and AS_1. During the year, because of built-in inflation, the *AS* curve will shift up to AS_2, *no matter what the Fed does this year.* Normally, the Fed would increase the money supply by enough to shift the *AD* curve to AD_2, maintaining output at full employment.

But a positive spending shock will also move the *AD* curve rightward, which will make prices rise even more during the year. This might raise inflationary expectations and lead to a higher built-in rate of inflation. What can the Fed do?

FIGURE 10

SPENDING SHOCKS DURING AN ONGOING INFLATION

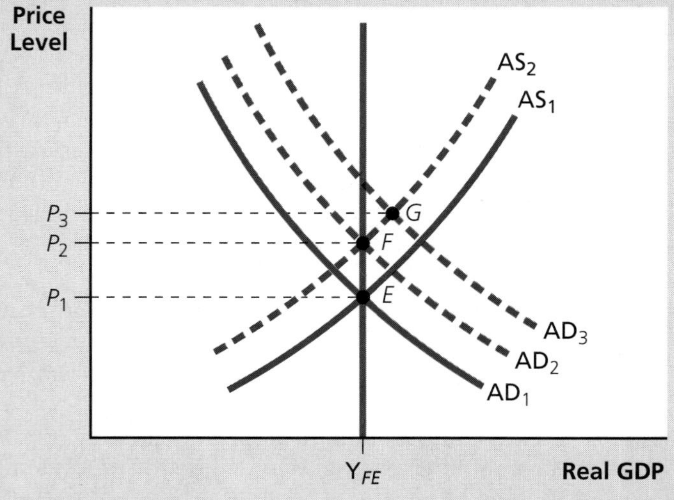

Beginning at point *E*, built-in inflation would cause the *AS* curve to shift to AS_2. The Fed ordinarily would maintain full employment by shifting *AD* to AD_2. A positive spending shock would mean a further shift—to AD_3. At that point, the Fed could choose a passive policy, increasing the money supply at the same rate as in the past. This would allow the price level to rise to P_3. Or it could slow the rate of increase in the money supply to bring the *AD* curve to AD_2. In that case, the price level would rise only to P_2.

First, it could follow a passive monetary policy—ignoring the demand shock. But with ongoing inflation, a passive monetary policy no longer means holding the money stock constant:

When there is built-in inflation, a passive monetary policy means that the Fed increases the money supply at the same rate as in the past, thereby shifting the AD *curve rightward at the same rate as in the past.*

When we add the impact of the spending shock to a passive monetary policy, the *AD* curve shifts rightward beyond AD_2—say, to AD_3. The *inflation rate rises.*

But the Fed can also choose (and in the recent past, has chosen) an active policy to neutralize the effect of a spending shock. How? In much the same way we discussed earlier in the chapter: by raising its interest rate target. To do this, the Fed will increase the money supply by less than it has in the recent past. The combined effect of the demand shock, and the Fed's less-than-normal increase in the money supply, will shift the *AD* curve to AD_2. By raising its interest rate target, the Fed can maintain full employment and a stable rate of inflation:

To neutralize a positive spending shock when there is built-in inflation, the Fed should follow the same policy described earlier: raise the interest rate target. This policy can maintain full employment, while keeping the rate of inflation equal to the built-in rate.

What about a supply shock? Here, too, our earlier analysis still applies. Figure 11 shows an economy in long-run equilibrium with built-in inflation. During the year, the *AS* and *AD* curves would ordinarily shift up to AS_2 and AD_2, moving the equilibrium from *E* to *F*. But a supply shock—say, a rise in world oil prices—causes

SUPPLY SHOCKS DURING AN ONGOING INFLATION

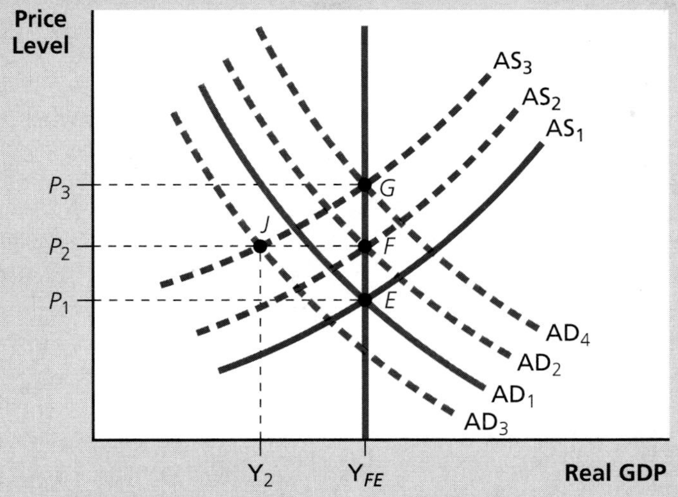

FIGURE 11

Beginning at point *E*, built-in inflation would cause the *AS* curve to shift to AS_2. The Fed could maintain full employment by shifting the *AD* curve to AD_2. But a supply shock would cause a further shift of *AS* to AS_3. The Fed could respond by moving to AD_3 (point *J*), which would maintain stable inflation but worsen the recession. Or it could prevent the recession by moving to AD_4 (point *G*), but at the cost of an even higher inflation rate.

the *AS* curve to shift up by *more* during the year—to AS_3. The supply shock causes a recession combined with a *rising inflation rate.* As before, the Fed must make some unpleasant choices. To prevent any rise in the inflation rate, it could move the *AD* curve to AD_3, but that would worsen the recession. To prevent the recession, the Fed could move the *AD* curve to AD_4, but this would result in an even higher inflation rate. More generally,

with built-in inflation, a negative supply shock causes a recession combined with a rise in the inflation rate. A hawk policy will lean toward reducing the inflation rate, at the cost of deepening the recession. A dove policy will lean toward a milder recession, increasing the inflation rate.

POLICY TRADEOFFS

THE PHILLIPS CURVE

As you've seen, once inflation is built into the economy, the long-run equilibrium is an *inflationary* equilibrium. In order for the Fed to *decrease* the rate of inflation, it will have to begin shifting the *AD* curve by less than it has in the recent past. This will bring down inflation, but it will also cause unemployment to rise above the natural rate for a time, until the public expects a new, lower rate of inflation.

Economists often illustrate this process with the aid of a *Phillips curve,* named after the late British economist A.W. Phillips, who did early research on the relationship between inflation and unemployment:

*The **Phillips curve** illustrates the Fed's choices between inflation and unemployment in the short run, for a given built-in inflation rate.*

PHILLIPS CURVE A curve indicating the Fed's choice between the inflation and unemployment in the short run.

The solid line in Figure 12 shows a Phillips curve for the U.S. economy. The inflation rate is measured on the vertical axis, the unemployment rate on the horizontal. Point *E* is the long-run equilibrium in this economy when the built-in in-

FIGURE 12

THE PHILLIPS CURVE

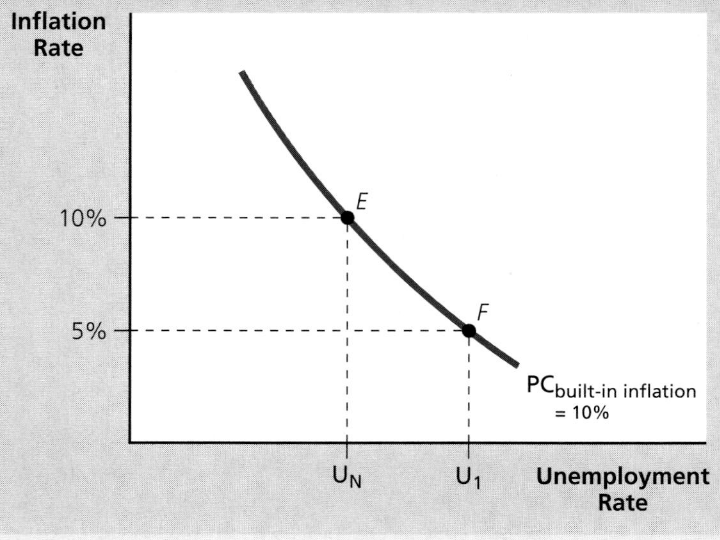

The Phillips curve illustrates the Fed's choices between inflation and unemployment in the short run, with a given built-in inflation rate. Point *E* represents the long-run equilibrium, with the economy at the natural rate of unemployment, U_N, and inflation at the built-in rate of 10 percent. If the Fed wishes to decrease the inflation rate to 5 percent, it must accept a higher unemployment rate—U_1 at point *F*.

flation rate is 10 percent. At point *E*, unemployment is at its natural rate—U_N—and inflation remains constant from year to year at the built-in rate of 10 percent.

Notice that the Phillips curve is downward-sloping. Why? Because it tells the same story we told earlier—with *AD* and *AS* curves—about the Fed's options in the short run. If the Fed wants to decrease the rate of inflation from 10 percent to 5 percent, it must slow the rightward shifts of the *AD* curve. This would cause a movement *along* the Phillips curve from point *E* to point *F*. As you can see, at point *F*, the economy is in a recession—unemployment is higher than the natural rate.

POLICY TRADEOFFS

In the short run, the Fed can move along *the Phillips curve by adjusting the rate at which the* AD *curve shifts rightward. When the Fed moves the economy downward and rightward along the Phillips curve, the unemployment rate increases, and the inflation rate decreases.*

Now suppose the Fed keeps the economy at point *F*. In the long run, the public—observing a 5-percent inflation rate—will come to expect 5-percent inflation in the future. Thus, in the long run, 5 percent will become the economy's built-in rate of inflation. Figure 13 shows the effect on the Phillips curve: It shifts downward, to the lower dashed line. At any unemployment rate, the inflation rate will be lower, now that the public expects inflation of only 5 percent, rather than 10 percent.

In the long run, a decrease in the actual inflation rate leads to a lower built-in *inflation rate, and the Phillips curve shifts downward.*

Once the Fed has reduced the built-in inflation rate, it can begin shifting the *AD* curve rightward by just enough to return the economy to full employment. This will move the economy upward and leftward along the new, lower Phillips curve. The long-run equilibrium will be at point *G*, with unemployment at its natural rate,

THE SHIFTING PHILLIPS CURVE

FIGURE 13

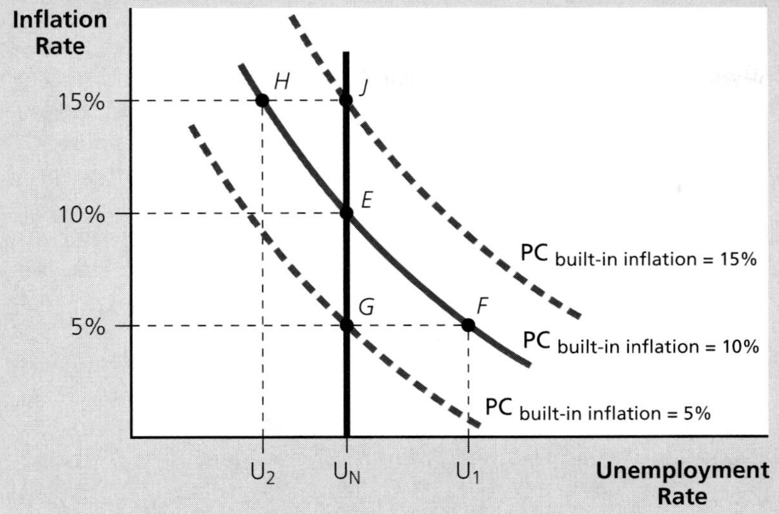

Initially, the economy is at point *E,* with inflation equal to the built-in rate of 10 percent. If the Fed moves the economy to point *F* and keeps it there, the public will eventually come to expect 5 percent inflation in the future. At that point, the built-in inflation rate will fall and the curve will shift down to $PC_{\text{built-in inflation} = 5\%}$. The economy will move to point *G* in the long run, with unemployment at the natural rate and an actual inflation rate equal to the built-in rate of 5 percent.

Starting again at point *E,* a demand shock that was not neutralized by the Fed would move the economy to point *H;* the inflation rate would rise to 15 percent, and the unemployment rate would fall to U_2. If the Fed then held the economy at point *H,* the built-in inflation rate would rise to 15 percent, and the Phillips curve would shift up to $PC_{\text{built-in inflation} = 15\%}$. Eventually, the economy would move to point *J.* The vertical line connecting points *E, G,* and *J* is the long-run Phillips curve.

and the inflation rate remaining constant at 5 percent. *In the long run, the actual inflation rate will be equal to the expected inflation rate: 5 percent.*

The distinction between the short run and the long run is important when thinking about the Phillips curve:

> *In the short run, the Fed can move the economy* along *the Phillips curve. But this will cause the Phillips curve to* shift *in the long run, after inflationary expectations adjust to the change in actual inflation.*

SHORT-RUN VERSUS LONG-RUN OUTCOMES

RIDING UP THE PHILLIPS CURVE. The process we've described—moving down the Phillips curve and causing it to shift downward—also works in reverse: Moving *up* the Phillips curve will cause it to shift *upward.* Figure 13 also illustrates this case. Once again, the economy begins at point *E,* with a built-in inflation rate of 10 percent and unemployment at its natural rate. Now look back at Figure 8, and imagine that the *AD* curve there began shifting rightward more rapidly. This could happen, for example, if a demand shock hit the economy and the Fed chose not to neutralize it (as occurred during the 1960s). In the short run, the economy would move *along* the Phillips curve from point *E* to point *H* in Figure 13. The inflation rate would rise to 15 percent, and the unemployment rate would fall below its natural rate—in the short run.

But suppose the Fed keeps the economy at point *H* for some time—continuing to shift the *AD* curve rightward at a faster rate than before. Then, in the long run, the public will begin to expect 15-percent inflation, and that will become the new built-in rate of inflation. The Phillips curve will then shift upward. At this point, if the Fed returns the economy to full employment, we end up at point *J*. The economy will be back in long-run equilibrium—but with a higher built-in inflation rate.

THE LONG-RUN PHILLIPS CURVE. Figure 13 demonstrates something important about the unemployment-inflation relationship in the short run and the long run:

SHORT-RUN VERSUS LONG-RUN OUTCOMES

In the short run, there is a tradeoff between inflation and unemployment: The Fed can choose lower unemployment at the cost of higher inflation, or lower inflation at the cost of higher unemployment. But in the long run, since unemployment always returns to its natural rate, there is no such tradeoff.

Now let's reconsider what we've learned about the Fed's options in the long run. Figure 13 shows us that, when the Fed slows the rightward shifts of the *AD* curve, unemployment returns to the natural rate, but the inflation rate is lower. The figure also shows us that, when the Fed allows the *AD* curve to shift rightward more rapidly than in the past, unemployment returns once again to the natural rate, but the inflation rate is higher. As you can see,

in the long run, monetary policy can change the rate of inflation, but not the rate of unemployment.

LONG-RUN PHILLIPS CURVE A vertical line indicating that in the long run, unemployment must equal the natural rate, regardless of the rate of inflation.

Now look at the vertical line in Figure 13. It tells us how monetary policy affects the economy in the long run, without the distractions of the short-run story. The vertical line is the economy's **long-run Phillips curve,** which tells us the combinations of unemployment and inflation that the Fed can choose in the long run. No matter what the Fed does, unemployment will always return to the natural rate, U_N, in the long run. However, the Fed can use monetary policy to select any rate of inflation it wants:

The long-run Phillips curve is a vertical line at the natural rate of unemployment. The Fed can select any point along this line in the long run, by using monetary policy to speed or slow the rate at which the AD *curve shifts rightward.*

WHY THE FED ALLOWS ONGOING INFLATION

Since the Fed can choose any rate of inflation it wants, and since inflation is costly to society, we might think that the Fed would aim for an inflation rate of zero. But a look back at panel (a) of Figure 1 shows that this is not what the Fed has chosen to do. In recent years, with unemployment very close to its natural rate, the Fed has maintained annual inflation at around 3 percent. Why doesn't the Fed eliminate inflation from the economy entirely?

One reason is a widespread belief that the Consumer Price Index (CPI) and other measures of inflation actually *overstate* the true rate of inflation in the economy. For example, many economists believe that the CPI overstates the true inflation rate by 1 to 2 percent per year. If the Fed forced the *measured* rate of inflation down to zero, the result would be a true rate of inflation that was negative—prices would actually *fall* each year. But negative rates of inflation can be as costly to society as positive rates: People are as likely to make errors in financial planning when the price level is falling at 2 percent per year as they are when the price level is rising at the same rate. And if the price level drops by more or less than expected, real income will be shifted between borrowers and lenders.

Some economists have offered another explanation for the Fed's behavior: low, stable inflation makes the labor market work more smoothly. The argument goes as follows: While no one wants a cut in their *real* wage rate, people seem to react differently, depending on *how* the real wage is decreased. For example, suppose there is an excess supply of manufacturing workers, and a wage cut of 3 percent is needed to bring that labor market back to equilibrium. Workers would strongly resist a 3-percent cut in the nominal wage. But they would more easily tolerate a freeze in the nominal wage while the price level rises by 3 percent, even though in both scenarios, the real wage falls by 3 percent. If this argument is correct, then a low or modest inflation rate would help wages adjust in different markets. In some labor markets, real wages can be raised by increasing nominal wages faster than prices. In other labor markets, real wages can be cut by increasing nominal wages more slowly than prices, or not at all.

But the strongest reason for the Fed's tolerance of low inflation is one we've already discussed: Once inflation is built into the economy, it is costly to reduce it. For example, to reduce the built-in inflation rate from its current 3 or 4 percent, the Fed would have to engineer a recession. Even if the Fed believed that the economy would be better off with lower inflation, it would not necessarily choose to pursue this goal. In fact, as a result of the Fed's success in controlling inflation for the past several years, popular concern about inflation has practically disappeared. Since a further reduction in inflation is not valued highly by the public, it is not politically worthwhile to pay the costs of achieving it.

WWW POLICY DEBATE

What should the Fed's inflation policy be? Learn more in the Policy Debates portion of the ECONOMICS web site.
Address:
http://hall-lieb.swcollege.com

The Fed has tolerated measured inflation at 3 to 4 percent per year because it knows that the true rate of inflation is lower, because low rates of inflation may help labor markets adjust more easily, and because there is not much payoff to lowering inflation further.

POLICY TRADEOFFS

CONDUCTING MONETARY POLICY IN THE REAL WORLD

USING THE THEORY

So far in this chapter, we've described some clear-cut guidelines the Fed *can* and *does* follow in conducting monetary policy. We've seen that the proper policy for dealing with day-to-day changes in money demand is to set and maintain an interest rate target. The proper response to a spending shock is a change in the interest rate target. Dealing with a supply shock is more problematic, since it requires the Fed to balance its goal of low, stable inflation with its goal of full employment. But even here, once the Fed decides on the proper balance, its policy choice is straightforward: Shift the *AD* curve to achieve the desired combination of inflation and unemployment in the short run, and then bring the economy back to full employment in the long run.

In most of our discussion, we've assumed that the Fed has all of the information it needs to determine where the economy *is* operating, where it *should* be operating, and what change in monetary policy will get it there. Unfortunately, the real world is not that simple: The information available to the Federal Open Market Committee is far from perfect. As a result, the Fed's selection and execution of policy are sometimes more complicated than we've suggested so far. In this section, we'll consider some of the problems of monetary policy, and how the Fed has adapted to them.

Information about the Money Demand Curve

The easiest job facing the Fed is responding to shifts in the money demand curve. As you saw in Figure 2, the Fed can stop money demand shocks from affecting output or the price level by adjusting the money stock to keep the interest rate unchanged. If the money demand curve shifts to M_2^d, the interest rate rises, so the Fed knows it must increase the money supply to keep the interest rate at r_1. The Fed maintains the interest rate by moving *along* the new money demand curve.

But Figure 2 also reveals a potential problem: The Fed cannot know by how much to increase the money stock unless it knows the *slope* of the new money demand curve. For example, if the money demand curve has become flatter, the Fed will have to increase the money supply beyond M_2^s in order to maintain its interest rate target.

How does the Fed deal with this problem? In two ways. First, the Fed's research staff tries to estimate the changes in the position and slope of the money demand curve from available data. While the techniques are not perfect, they enable the Fed to make reasonable guesses about the required change in the money supply on any given day.

Second, the Fed uses the trial-and-error procedure that we discussed earlier. For example, suppose the interest rate rises and Fed officials underestimate the required change in the money supply. Then the interest rate will remain above its target rate, and the Fed can try again the next day, increasing the money supply further. In recent years, using a combination of research on the one hand and trial and error on the other, the Fed has been quite successful in reaching and maintaining its interest rate target.

Information about the Sensitivity of Spending to the Interest Rate

The proper response to spending shocks presents the Fed with a more significant problem. Look back at Figure 3, in which a positive spending shock shifts the *AD* curve rightward to AD_2. The Fed will want to neutralize the shock by shifting the *AD* curve back to AD_1. To do so, it will raise its interest rate target. But by how much? That depends on the sensitivity of consumption and investment spending to the interest rate. If spending is *very* sensitive to interest rate changes, only a small rise in the target is needed; if spending is less sensitive, the Fed will need to raise its target rate by more.

Once again, the Fed has adapted to this problem with both research and trial-and-error methods. The research in this case focuses on how households and businesses change their spending plans when the interest rate rises and falls. This enables the Fed to make reasonable guesses about the required change in the interest rate target.

Trial and error helps the Fed get even closer. In Figure 3, maintaining an interest rate target of r_2 neutralizes the effect of the spending shock. But suppose the Fed makes an error, and selects a target *lower* than r_2. Then the *AD* curve will shift rightward somewhat, and the economy will begin to overheat. As output rises beyond full employment, the price level (or the inflation rate) will rise. The Fed then observes the changes in output and prices, and adjusts its interest rate target again.

There is one major drawback to this procedure, however: It may take many months for the Fed's error to show up. GDP is measured only once each quarter. The Consumer Price Index is released each month, but prices may be slow to adjust to the increase in output. Thus, in contrast to the case of money-demand shifts—where the Fed can correct its errors within days—spending shocks often require the Fed to "wing it" for many months.

Uncertain and Changing Time Lags

We've just seen that it can take many months before the Fed observes how a change in its interest rate target is affecting output and the price level. More importantly, the Fed does not know precisely *how* many months it will take. This presents a serious challenge for monetary policy. Suppose Fed officials believe that the economy is beginning to overheat, and they raise the interest rate target. The new, higher target might not reduce spending for some time. Business firms will finish building the new plants and new homes that they've already started, even at higher interest rates. Investment spending will finally come down only at the point when canceled investment projects *would* have entered the pipeline, many months later. By the time the higher interest rate target has its maximum effect, the economy may be returning to full employment on its own, or it may be hit by a negative demand shock. In this case, the Fed—by raising its interest rate target—will be reining in the economy at just the wrong time, causing a recession.

Economists often use an analogy to describe this problem. Imagine that you are trying to drive a car with a very special problem: When you step on the gas, the car will go forward . . . but not until five minutes later. Similarly, when you step on the brake, the car will slow, but also with a five-minute lag. It would be very difficult to maintain an even speed with this car: You'd step on the gas, and when nothing happened, you'd be tempted to step on it harder. By the time the car begins to move, you will have given too much gas and find yourself speeding down the road. So you try to slow down, but once again, hitting the brakes makes nothing happen. So you brake harder, and when the car finally responds, you come to a dead halt.

The Fed can make—and, in the past, has made—a similar mistake. When it tries to cool off an overheated economy, it may find that nothing is happening. Is it just a long time lag, or has the Fed not hit the brakes hard enough? If it hits the brakes harder, it runs the risk of braking the economy too much; if it doesn't, it runs the risk of continuing to allow the economy to overheat. Even worse, the time lag before monetary policy affects prices and output can change over the years: Just when the Fed may think it has mastered the rules of the game, the rules change.

The Natural Rate of Unemployment

Finally, we come to the most controversial information problem facing the Fed: uncertainty over the natural rate of unemployment. While there is wide agreement that the natural rate rose in the 1970s and has fallen since the late 1980s, economists remain uncertain about its value during any given period. Many economists believe that today the natural rate is around 5.5 percent, but no one is really sure.

Why is this a problem? It's very much like the two mountain climbers who become lost. One of them pulls out a map. "Do you see that big mountain over there," he says, pointing off into the distance. "Yes," says the other. "Well," says the first, "according to the map, we're standing on top of it." In order to achieve its twin goals of full employment and a stable, low rate of inflation, the Fed tries to maintain the unemployment rate as close to the natural rate as possible. If its estimate of the natural rate is wrong, it may believe it has succeeded when, in fact, it has not.

For example, suppose the Fed believes the natural rate of unemployment is 5.5 percent, but the rate is really 5 percent. Then—at least for a time—the Fed will be steering the economy toward an unemployment rate that is unnecessarily high, and an output level that is unnecessarily low. We've already discussed the costs of cyclical unemployment; and an overestimate of the natural rate makes society bear these costs needlessly. On the other hand, if the Fed believes the natural rate is 5 percent when it is really 5.5 percent, it will overheat the economy. This will raise the inflation rate—and a costly recession may be needed later in order to reduce it.

Trial and error can help the Fed determine the true natural rate. If the Fed raises unemployment above the true natural rate, the inflation rate will drop. If unemployment falls below the true natural rate, the inflation rate will rise. But—as we discussed earlier—trial and error works best when there is continual and rapid feedback. It can take some time for changes in the inflation rate to reveal the problem—six months, a year, or even longer. In the meantime, the Fed will believe it has been successful, even while causing avoidable unemployment, or planting the seeds for a future rise in the inflation rate.

Estimating the natural rate of unemployment is made even more difficult because the economy is constantly buffeted by shocks of one kind or another. If the Fed observes that the inflation rate is rising, does that mean that unemployment is below the natural rate? Or is the higher inflation being caused by a negative supply shock? Or by the Fed's response to an earlier, negative demand shock? This information is difficult to sort out, although the Fed has become increasingly sophisticated in its efforts to do so.

As you can see, conducting monetary policy is not easy. The Fed has hundreds of economists carrying out research and gathering data to improve its information about the status of the economy and its understanding of how the economy works. And the effort seems to have paid off, especially over the last decade. But years from now, this period may be seen as the golden age of successful monetary policy. After all, the 1950s also seemed to be a period of good policy, but then the 1960s and especially the 1970s turned into disasters for monetary policy. Because we don't know what kinds of shocks will hit the economy in the future (oil price shocks came out of the blue in the 1970s) or how the Fed will respond to them, we cannot say that monetary policy will necessarily continue to work well in the future.

SUMMARY

As the nation's central bank, the Federal Reserve bears primary responsibility for maintaining a low, stable rate of inflation and for maintaining full employment of the labor force as the economy is buffeted by a variety of shocks. The money demand curve, for example, may shift, causing a change in the interest rate, a shift in the *AD* curve, and a change in output and employment. The Fed can neutralize such money demand shocks by setting an interest rate target. To maintain the target, it increases the money supply whenever money demand increases, and decreases the money supply when money demand decreases. This policy enables the Fed to stabilize both inflation and unemployment.

Spending shocks—spontaneous shifts in aggregate expenditures—can also shift the *AD* curve, causing output to deviate from its full-employment level. The Fed can neutralize spending shocks by adjusting its interest rate target—changing the money supply to shift the *AD* curve back to its original position.

The Fed's most difficult problem is responding to supply shocks. A negative supply shock—an upward shift of the *AS* curve—presents the Fed with a dilemma. In the short run, it must choose a point along that new *AS* curve. If it wishes to maintain price stability, it must shift the *AD* curve to the left and accept higher unemployment. If the Fed wishes to maintain full employment, it must shift the *AD* curve to the right and accept a higher rate of inflation. A "hawk" policy puts greater emphasis on price stability, while a "dove" policy emphasizes lower unemployment.

If Fed policy leads to ongoing inflation, then business and households come to expect the prevailing inflation rate to continue. As a result, the *AS* curve continues to shift at that built-in expected inflation rate. To maintain full employment, the Fed must shift the *AD* curve rightward, creating an inflation rate equal to the expected rate.

If the Fed wishes to change the built-in inflation rate, it must first change the expected inflation rate. For example, to lower the expected inflation rate, the Fed will slow down the rightward shifts of the *AD* curve. The actual inflation rate will fall, and expectations will eventually adjust downward. While they do so, however, the economy will experience a recession.

The Fed's short-run choices between inflation and unemployment can be illustrated with the Phillips curve. In the short run, the Fed can move the economy along the downward-sloping Phillips curve by adjusting the rate at which the *AD* curve shifts. If the Fed moves the economy to a new point on the Phillips curve and holds it there, the built-in inflation rate will eventually adjust and the Phillips curve will shift. In the long run, the economy will return to the natural rate of unemployment with a different inflation rate. This is why we draw the long-run Phillips curve as a vertical line at the natural rate of unemployment.

KEY TERMS

natural rate of unemployment

interest rate target

Phillips curve

long-run Phillips curve

REVIEW QUESTIONS

1. Why is one of the Fed's chief objectives a low, stable rate of inflation? Why is its other objective low unemployment?

2. List and describe the different categories of unemployment. What type of unemployment do macroeconomists address?

3. "The Fed should aim for the lowest possible unemployment rate." True or false? Explain.

4. What effect does a change in the Fed's interest rate target have on financial markets? How do changes in expectations regarding the Fed's position on the interest rate target affect financial markets?

5. "The Fed should respond to any shift in the *AD* curve by maintaining its interest rate target." True or false? Explain.

6. Explain the tradeoff that the Fed faces with regard to negative supply shocks. What do "hawks" and "doves" have to do with this tradeoff?

7. Why do expectations of inflation have a significant impact on the economy? What is the impact?

8. What is the meaning of passive monetary policy when there is ongoing inflation?

9. What relationship does the Phillips curve illustrate? How does the Fed control movements along the Phillips curve? Why is the long-run Phillips curve vertical?

10. List and explain three reasons why the Fed tolerates some ongoing inflation.

PROBLEMS AND EXERCISES

1. For each of the following, compare the Fed's reaction under its 1960s' objectives with the Fed's reaction since the Federal Reserve Banking Act of 1978:
   a. a money demand shock
   b. a spending shock

   Why did the objectives of the Fed change?

2. Suppose that by law the central bank must do everything possible to keep the inflation rate equal to zero. How would it deal with (a) a money demand shock, (b) a spending shock, and (c) an aggregate supply shock? What would the costs and benefits of such a law be?

3. Suppose that in an economy experiencing ongoing inflation, the government raises taxes. Describe the effects on the economy if the Fed practices a passive monetary policy. Alternatively, how could the Fed neutralize the spending shock?

4. Suppose the economy has been experiencing a low inflation rate. A new chair of the Federal Reserve is named, and she is known to be highly sympathetic to dove policies. Explain the possible effects on the Phillips curve.

5. Using a graph, illustrate why the Fed, if it practices interest rate targeting, is concerned about the slope of the money demand curve. What are the implications of incorrectly estimating the slope?

6. Suppose that initially the price level is at P_1 and GDP is at Y_1, with no built-in inflation. The Fed reacts to a negative spending shock by shifting the aggregate demand curve. The next time the Fed receives data on GDP and the price level, it finds that prices are above P_1 and GDP is above Y_1. Give two possible explanations for this finding.

CHALLENGE QUESTION

Suppose the economy is experiencing ongoing inflation. The Fed wants to reduce expected inflation, so it *announces* that in the future it will tolerate less inflation. How does the Fed's credibility affect the success of the reduction? How can the Fed build its credibility? Are there costs to building credibility? If so, what are they?

CHAPTER

15

FISCAL POLICY: TAXES, SPENDING, AND THE BUDGET DEFICIT

Every few years, a best-selling new book predicts economic disaster for the United States and the world. In most of these books, the U.S. federal government plays a central role. Arguments and statistics are offered to show that the U.S. federal budget is out of control: Government spending is growing by leaps and bounds, while tax revenue is not keeping up. As a result, the national debt is skyrocketing. Who is at fault? In the disaster books, the blame falls on politicians who curry favor with voters and avoid tough decisions; on the public, which is too shortsighted to see disaster looming on the horizon; and usually one or two other, inexorable, forces that are driving the world toward an economic apocalypse.

Do these predictions of disaster have merit? In this chapter, we'll take another, closer look at the government's role in the macroeconomy. You'll learn how to interpret trends in the government's budget, and how to identify the causes and effects of those trends. As you'll see, the disaster books—and some ideas widely held by the public—are based on myths and misunderstandings.

CHAPTER OUTLINE

THINKING ABOUT SPENDING, TAXES, AND THE DEFICIT

Let's start with some simple numbers. In 1959, the federal government's total spending—for goods and services, transfer payments, and interest on its debt—was \$89 billion. By 1996, the total had grown to \$1,700 billion, an increase of 1,900 percent. Government spending is out of control—right?

Or consider the national debt—the total amount that the government owes to the public from past borrowing. In 1959, the national debt was \$235 billion; by the end of 1996, it had grown to $3,850 billion.[1] This amounts to about $14,500 for every man, woman, and child in the United States—a sum that would be very painful for each of us, individually, to repay. Can the economy survive such a crushing burden?

Actually, these figures are highly misleading. The first problem is that they are *nominal* values. Between 1959 and 1996, the price level—as measured by the Consumer Price Index—increased by more than a factor of five. Thus, even if the government continued to spend the same amount or owe the same amount in *purchasing power,* the nominal figures would have more than quintupled over the period. If we translate these nominal values into *real values,* we find much smaller increases: From 1959 to 1996, *real* government spending and the *real* national debt each roughly tripled (compared to the nominal values, which increased more than fifteen-fold). Thus,

THE IMPORTANCE OF REAL VALUES

when examining budget-related figures over time, it is grossly misleading to use nominal figures, since the price level rises over time.

But even if we use real values to make our comparisons, we are still making a serious mistake. From 1959 to 1996, the U.S. population grew, the labor force grew, and the average worker became more productive. As a result, real GDP and real income tripled during this period. Why is that important? Because *spending and debt make sense only when viewed in relation to income.*

We automatically recognize this principle when we think about an individual household or business. Suppose you are told that a household is spending $50,000 each year on goods and services, and has a total debt—a combination of mortgage debt, car loans, student loans, and credit card balances—of $200,000. Is this household acting responsibly? Or is its spending and borrowing out of control? That depends. If the income of the household is $40,000 per year and is expected to remain roughly constant, there is serious trouble. This household would be spending more than it is earning, and its debt would grow each year until it could not handle the monthly interest payments.

But what if the household's income is $800,000 per year? Then our conclusion would change dramatically: We'd wonder, why does this household spend so *little*? And if it owed $200,000, we would not think it irresponsible at all. After all, the household could pay the interest on its debt—or even many times that interest—with a small fraction of its income.

What is true for an individual household is also true for the nation. Spending and debt are important only as *relative* concepts. As a country's total income grows, it will want more of the things that government can provide—education, high environmental standards, police protection, programs to help the needy, and more. Therefore, we expect government spending to rise as a nation becomes richer. Moreover, as its income grows, a country can *handle* higher interest payments on its

1 There are many ways to measure the national debt. Some measures include amounts that the U.S. Treasury owes to other government agencies. But this part of the debt, since it is owed by one branch of government to another, could be canceled out at the stroke of a pen. Other measures include unfunded liabilities of U.S. government for Social Security, Medicare, and other benefits in future years. While unfunded liabilities are a concern for policymakers, they are not yet actual government debt. In this chapter, the national debt is defined as U.S. government bonds currently held outside of U.S. government agencies.

debt. Government spending and the total national debt, considered in isolation, tell us nothing about how responsibly or irresponsibly the government is behaving.

Budget-related figures such as government spending or the national debt have meaning only when considered relative to a nation's total income. This is why we should always look at these figures as percentages of GDP.

When we take this last step in adjusting our figures, we discover that both government spending and the national debt were, indeed, higher in 1996 than in 1959. Government spending as a fraction of GDP grew from 17 percent to 22 percent, and the national debt grew from 46 percent of GDP to 50 percent. But while this growth is significant, it is nowhere near as great as that suggested by the unadjusted figures often cited in the press or the latest paperback book.

In the rest of this chapter, as we explore recent trends in fiscal behavior and their effects on the economy, we'll do so with these lessons in mind: All variables will be viewed as percentages of GDP.[2]

GOVERNMENT SPENDING, TAXES, AND THE BUDGET DEFICIT: SOME BACKGROUND

Our ultimate goal in this chapter is to understand how fiscal changes have affected, and continue to affect, the macroeconomy. But before we do this, some background will help. What has happened to the *composition* of government spending in recent decades? How does the U.S. tax system work, and what has happened to the government's tax revenues? Why has the national debt risen more rapidly in some periods than in others? This section provides answers to these and other questions about the government's finances. Although state and local spending also play an important role in the macroeconomy, most of the significant macroeconomic changes in recent decades have involved the *federal* government. This is why we'll focus on spending, taxing, and borrowing at the federal level.

GOVERNMENT SPENDING

The federal government's *spending*—the total amount spent or disbursed by the federal government in all of its activities—can be divided into three categories:

- *government purchases*—the total value of the goods and services that the government buys.
- *transfer payments*—income supplements the government provides to people, such as social security benefits, unemployment compensation, and welfare payments.
- *interest on the national debt*—the interest payments the government must make to those who hold government bonds.

2 It makes no difference whether we use nominal or real figures when dividing by GDP, as long as we're consistent. For example, we get the same fraction whether we divide nominal government spending by nominal GDP, or real government spending by real GDP.

FIGURE 1

FEDERAL GOVERNMENT PURCHASES AS A PERCENTAGE OF GDP

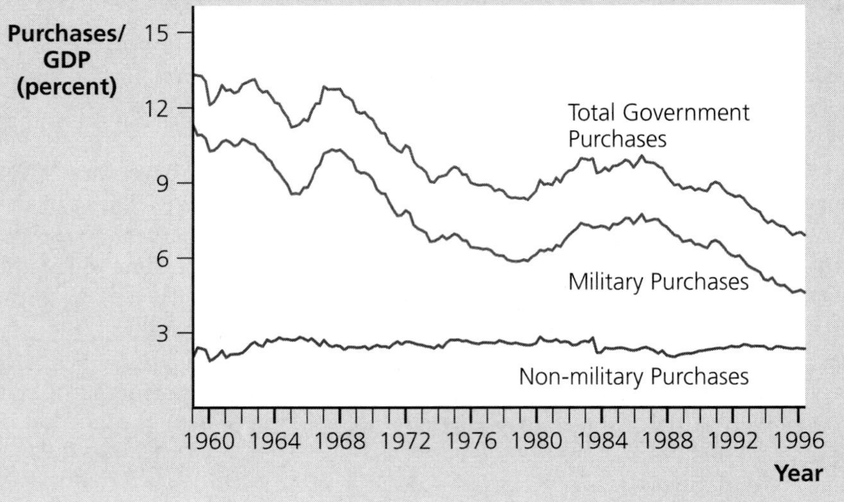

The federal government's purchases have declined dramatically (relative to GDP) over the past 40 years. Non-military purchases have always been a stable, small percentage of GDP. Military purchases have declined, except for temporary buildups during the Vietnam War in the late 1960s and during the Reagan administration in the early 1980s.

GOVERNMENT PURCHASES. Until the 1980s, government purchases of goods and services were the largest component of government spending. To understand how these purchases have changed over time, it's essential to divide them into two categories: military and non-military. Figure 1 shows total federal purchases, as well as federal military and non-military purchases, from 1960 to 1996.

One fact stands out from the figure: The federal government uses up only a tiny fraction of our national resources for non-military purposes. These non-military purchases include the salaries paid to all government workers outside the Defense Department (for example, federal judges, legislators, and the people who run federal agencies), as well as purchases of buildings, equipment, and supplies. Added together, all the different kinds of non-military government purchases account for a stable, low 2.5 percent of GDP.

This strongly contradicts a commonly held notion: that government spending is growing by leaps and bounds because of bloated federal bureaucracies. If government spending has become a growing concern, we must look somewhere besides non-military purchases for the reason.

Viewed as a percentage of GDP, non-military government purchases have remained very low and stable. They have not contributed to growth in total government spending.

What about military purchases? Here, we come to an even stronger conclusion:

Viewed as a percentage of GDP, military purchases have declined dramatically *over the past several decades. Like non-military purchases, they have not contributed to any growth in government spending.*

The decline in military purchases is shown by the middle line in Figure 1. They were around 11 percent of GDP in 1959 and fell almost continuously, to a level of

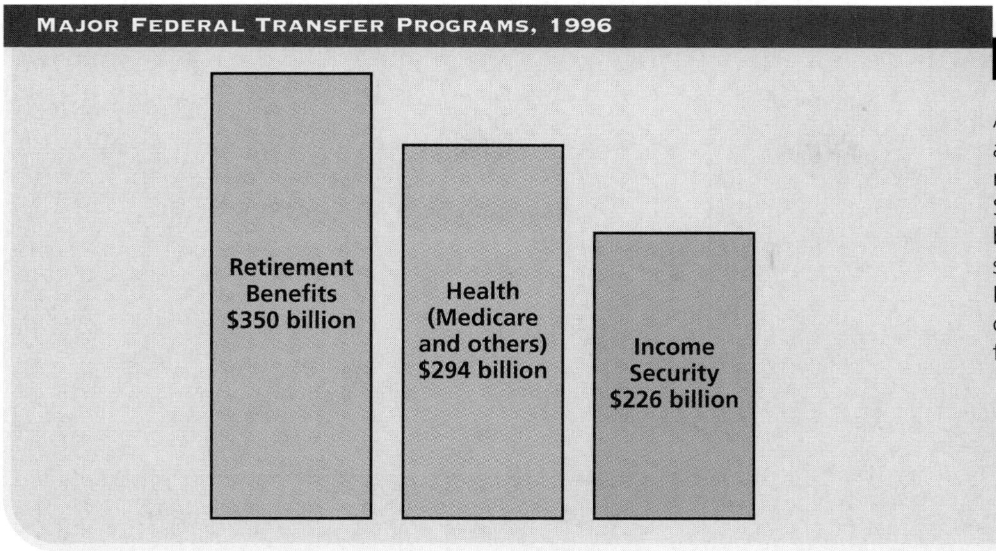

FIGURE 2

Approximately equal amounts of transfer payments were made for Social Security retirement benefits, health programs such as Medicare and Medicaid, and income security programs such as food stamps and welfare.

4 percent recently. Two buildups interrupted the decline, one associated with the Vietnam War in the late 1960s and the other during the Reagan administration in the 1980s. But both of these buildups were temporary.

The decline of military spending freed up resources amounting to 7 percent of GDP over the span shown in Figure 1. There are debates about whether U.S. defense spending can be cut even more, but given the current U.S. role in global politics, it is unlikely that any future cuts would be substantial. The implications are tremendously important for thinking about the recent past and the future of the federal government's role in the economy:

The decline in military spending in relation to GDP since the 1950s has made huge amounts of resources available for other purposes. Because military spending is now only 4 percent of GDP and probably cannot drop much further, there cannot be any similar flow of resources in coming decades.

The resources freed up by military spending eased many otherwise tough decisions about resource allocation in the economy. In particular, they made it easy for the federal government to provide huge increases in resources to some parts of the population, through transfers.

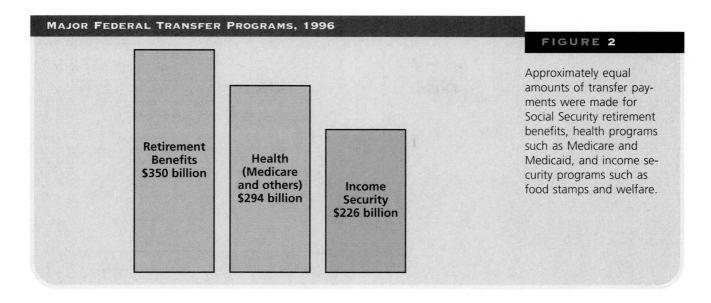

SOCIAL SECURITY AND OTHER TRANSFERS. Transfer programs provide cash and in-kind benefits to people whom the federal government designates as needing help. Figure 2 shows the three major categories of transfers. As you can see, they are roughly equal in size.

The largest category is retirement benefits—the payments made by the social security system to retired people. Although the benefits are loosely related to past contributions to the social security system, workers whose earnings are low receive benefits that are worth far more than their contributions. And after age 72, even someone with no history of contributions receives the minimum benefit.

FIGURE 3

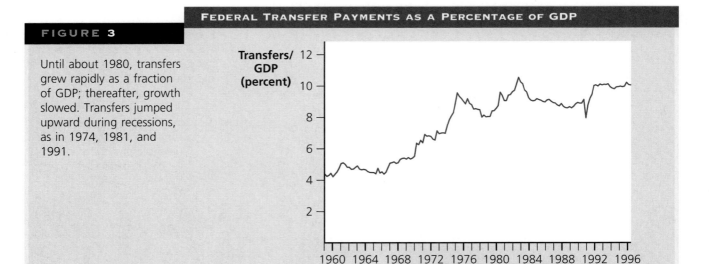

Until about 1980, transfers grew rapidly as a fraction of GDP; thereafter, growth slowed. Transfers jumped upward during recessions, as in 1974, 1981, and 1991.

FEDERAL TRANSFER PAYMENTS AS A PERCENTAGE OF GDP

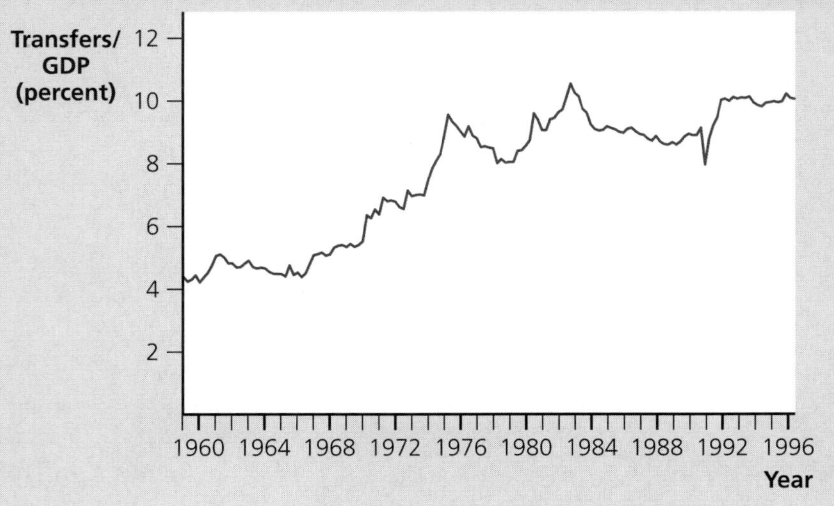

The second largest category of transfers occurs in health programs. The social security system provides health-related benefits to everyone aged 62 and over through Medicare. This is a health insurance plan in which people can go to any doctor they choose, as often as they want, and Medicare will pay 80 percent of the bills. Reform of Medicare to reduce its rapidly growing cost has been proposed, but little progress has been made so far. In addition to funding Medicare, the federal government helps finance state-operated health plans for the poor, through a program called Medicaid. The costs of these programs have been rising rapidly as well.

The third and smallest of the three categories of transfers is *income security*—programs to help poor families. Within this category, the largest component is the food stamp program, which gives coupons or special credit cards—good only for buying food—to qualified families. Welfare payments—known as Aid to Families with Dependent Children—are also in this category, but are much smaller than outlays on food stamps.

Do transfer payments account for any of the growth in government spending? Indeed, they do. All three categories of transfer programs have grown rapidly in recent decades, and Figure 3 shows that total transfer payments as a percentage of GDP have risen as well. In fact,

transfers are the fastest growing part of federal government spending and are currently equal to about 10 percent of GDP.

Growth in transfers in relation to GDP was most rapid in the 1970s during the Nixon administration. During this period, government-financed retirement benefits became much more generous, food stamps were introduced, and Medicare expanded. Since then, transfers have remained high, but they have not grown in relation to GDP.

Notice that transfers are sensitive to the ups and downs of the economy. Transfers as a fraction of GDP rise during recessions, as in 1974, 1981, and 1991.

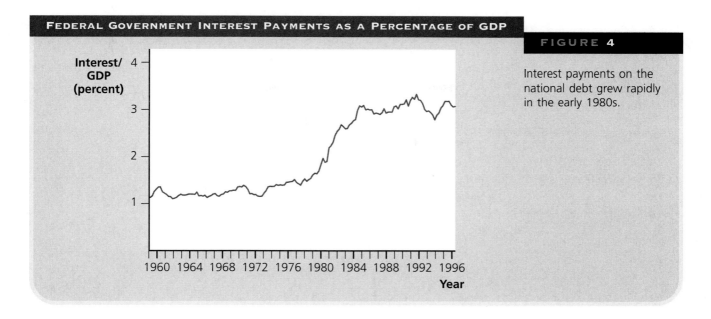

FEDERAL GOVERNMENT INTEREST PAYMENTS AS A PERCENTAGE OF GDP

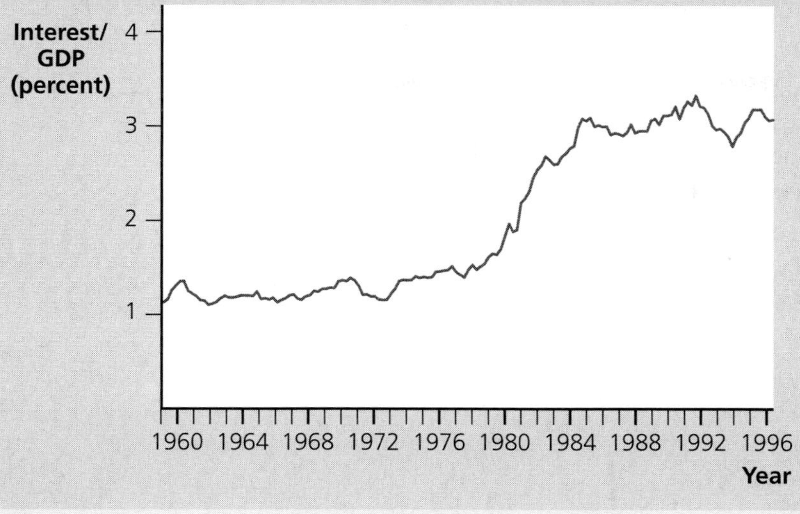

FIGURE 4

Interest payments on the national debt grew rapidly in the early 1980s.

This is for two reasons: First, the number of needy recipients rises in a recession, so transfer payments—the numerator of the fraction—increase; second, GDP—the denominator—falls in a recession. We will come back to the importance of these movements in transfers toward the end of the chapter.

INTEREST ON THE NATIONAL DEBT. Figure 4 shows the behavior of the third and smallest category of government spending: interest on the national debt. As you can see, interest as a percentage of GDP grew rapidly in the early 1980s, when the debt was growing and interest rates were rising. We'll discuss the reasons for the rise in debt a bit later.

TOTAL GOVERNMENT SPENDING. Figure 5 shows total spending in relation to GDP over the past several decades. There are two important things to notice in the figure. The first is the *fluctuations* in government spending over the period. There was a sharp increase in spending in each recession due to the jump in transfers that we saw in Figure 3. The recession of 1981–82 is a striking example. Also visible is the increase in military spending for the Vietnam War in the late 1960s.

The second thing to notice is the *upward trend* of federal spending as a percentage of GDP:

Over the past several decades, federal government spending as a percentage of GDP has risen steadily. The main causes have been increases in transfer payments and increases in interest on the national debt.

The rise in government spending has been an important long-run trend. But in order to understand its impact on the macroeconomy, we must look at the other side of the budget: tax revenue.

FIGURE 5

TOTAL FEDERAL SPENDING AS A PERCENTAGE OF GDP

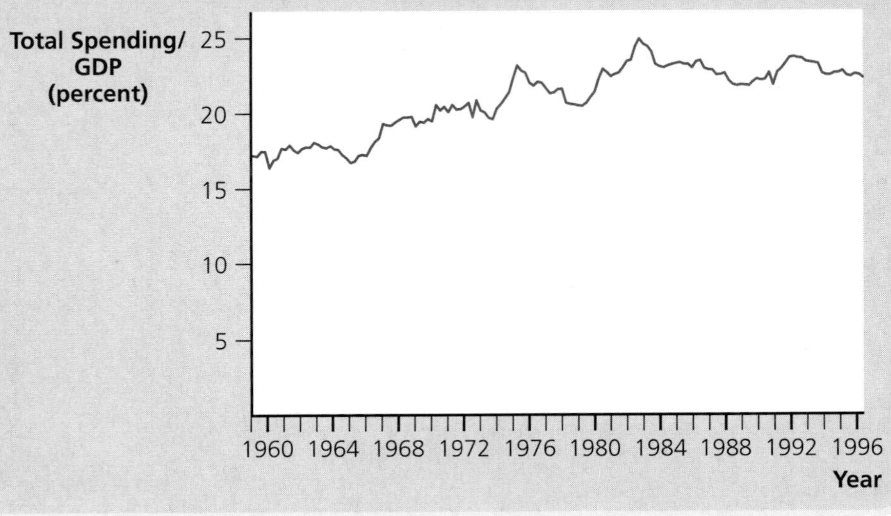

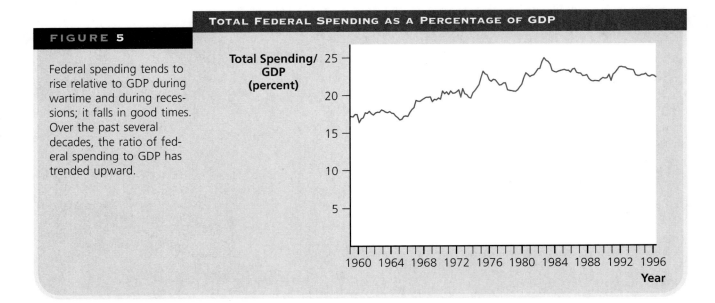

Federal spending tends to rise relative to GDP during wartime and during recessions; it falls in good times. Over the past several decades, the ratio of federal spending to GDP has trended upward.

FEDERAL TAX REVENUES

The federal government obtains most of its revenue from two sources: the personal income tax and the social security tax. Table 1 breaks down the revenue from these and the other less important sources.

THE PERSONAL INCOME TAX. The personal income tax is the most important source of revenue for the federal government and also the most conspicuous and painful. Almost every adult has to file Form 1040 or one of its shorter cousins. One of the signs of success as an American is seeing your federal tax return swell to the size of a magazine. Proposals to reduce both the amount of taxes people pay and the complexity of the tax forms are immensely popular.

PROGRESSIVE TAX A tax whose rate increases as income increases.

The personal income tax is designed to be **progressive**—to tax those at the higher end of the income scale at higher rates than those at the lower end of the scale, and to excuse the poorest families from paying any tax at all. Table 2 shows how the

TABLE 1

SOURCES OF FEDERAL REVENUE, 1996

Source	Revenue (billions of dollars)
Personal income taxes	656
Corporate income taxes	172
Social security taxes	509
Excise taxes	54
Other sources	62
Total	1,453

Source: *Economic Report of the President, 1997,* Table B-79.

THE PERSONAL INCOME TAX FOR A MARRIED COUPLE WITH TWO CHILDREN

TABLE 2

Income	Tax	Average Tax Rate	Marginal Tax Rate
$ 10,000	$ 0	0%	0%
20,000	465	3	15
30,000	1,965	7	15
50,000	4,965	10	15
75,000	11,055	15	28
150,000	33,141	22	31
250,000	68,411	27	36
400,000	126,708	32	40

Calculated from the 1996 Form 1040 tax table with the standard deduction of $6,700 and four exemptions.

income tax works, in theory, by computing the amount of tax a family of four should pay if it takes the standard deduction.[3] The table also shows the **average tax rate**—the fraction of total income a family pays in taxes—and the **marginal tax rate**—the tax rate paid on *each additional dollar* of income.

AVERAGE TAX RATE The fraction of a given income paid in taxes.

MARGINAL TAX RATE The fraction of an additional dollar of income paid in taxes.

We can see from Table 2 that the income tax is designed to be quite progressive. A family in the middle of the income distribution, earning $50,000 per year, should pay 10 percent of its income in taxes, while a family at the top should pay 32 percent of its income in taxes. The table also shows that marginal tax rates on families with the highest income are in the range of 28 to 40 percent.

But the tax system shown in the table does not reflect the ways that people can avoid tax. Many people have deductions far above the standard deduction. Some people earn income that they never report to the government, thereby evading taxes entirely. And people can shelter income in their employer's retirement plan or in a plan of their own. Studies have shown that higher income households avoid more taxes than poorer families and that the tax system—while still progressive—is much less progressive than suggested by Table 2.

In addition to making the tax system less progressive, tax avoidance reduces the total tax revenues of the federal government. If we use Table 2—along with the incomes people actually earn—to estimate tax revenue, we'd predict that the government would collect between 15 and 20 percent of total personal income. But in reality, the income tax revenues amount to only about 10 percent of total personal income.

THE SOCIAL SECURITY TAX. The social security tax applies to wage and salary income only. It was put in place in 1936, to finance the social security system created in that year. Generally, the benefits paid to retired workers are about equal to the revenue from the social security tax. Whereas the personal income tax is a nightmare of complex forms and rules, the social security tax is remarkably simple. The

3 The federal government allows households to deduct certain expenses (like medical care or the costs of moving to a new job) from their income before calculating the tax that they owe. Alternatively, they may deduct a standard amount from their income, regardless of their spending patterns.

FIGURE 6

FEDERAL GOVERNMENT REVENUE AS A PERCENTAGE OF GDP

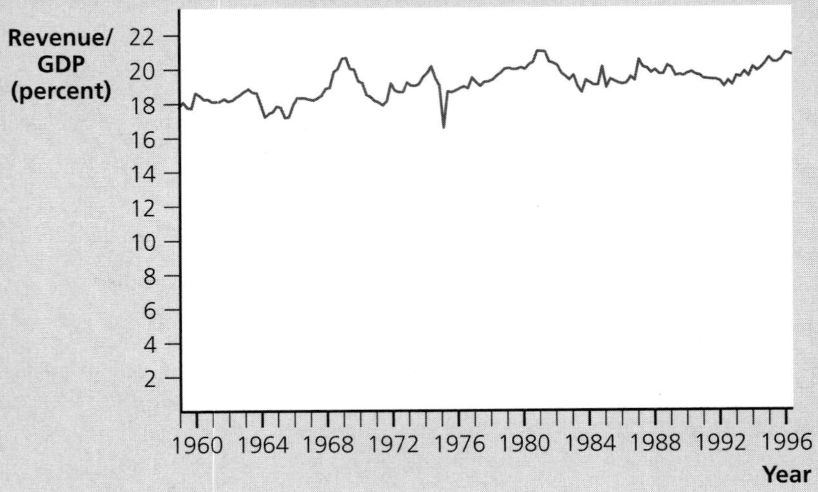

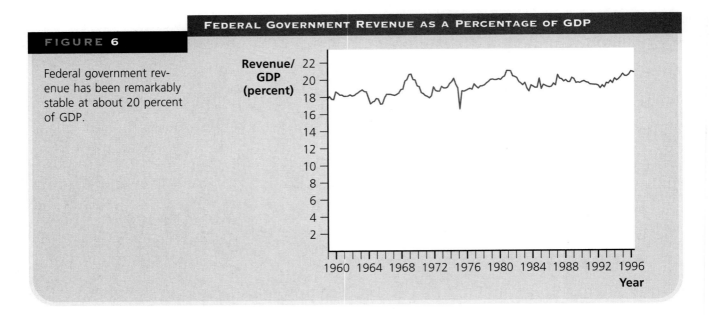

Federal government revenue has been remarkably stable at about 20 percent of GDP.

current tax rate is a flat 15.3 percent, except for one complication: The tax is applied only on earnings below about $70,000 per year.[4]

The social security tax is actually the largest tax paid by many Americans, especially those with lower incomes. These families pay little or no income tax, but pay the social security tax on all of their wage earnings. For example, a family with $30,000 of earnings in Table 2 would pay $1,965 in federal income tax, but social security taxes on those earnings would be $4,590.

OTHER FEDERAL TAXES. Table 1 shows that the federal government also collects a little less than $300 billion from other taxes. The most important of these is the *corporate profits tax,* which raises $172 billion by taxing the profits earned by corporations at a rate of 35 percent.

The corporate profits tax is widely criticized by economists because of two important problems. First, it only applies to corporations. Thus, a business owner can avoid it completely by setting up a sole proprietorship or partnership instead of a corporation. As a result, the tax causes many businesses to forgo the benefits of being corporations because of the extra tax they would have to pay.

Second, the corporation tax results in *double taxation* on the portion of corporate profits that corporations pay to their owners. This portion of profits is taxed once when the corporation is taxed and again when the profits are included as part of personal income. The corporation tax is thus a prime target for tax reform. Almost all reform proposals put forward by economists involve integrating the taxation of corporations into the tax system in a way that avoids these two distortions.

4 If you look at your own paycheck, it may seem that the social security tax is only 7.65 percent instead of the 15.3 percent we've just mentioned. The reason is that your employer pays half the tax and you pay the other half. But the amount paid on your earnings is the sum, 15.3 percent.

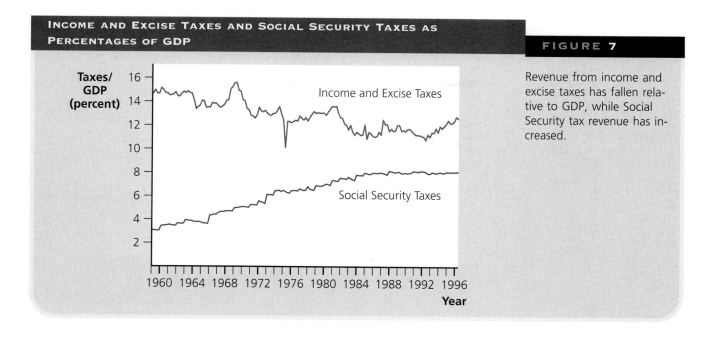

INCOME AND EXCISE TAXES AND SOCIAL SECURITY TAXES AS PERCENTAGES OF GDP

FIGURE 7

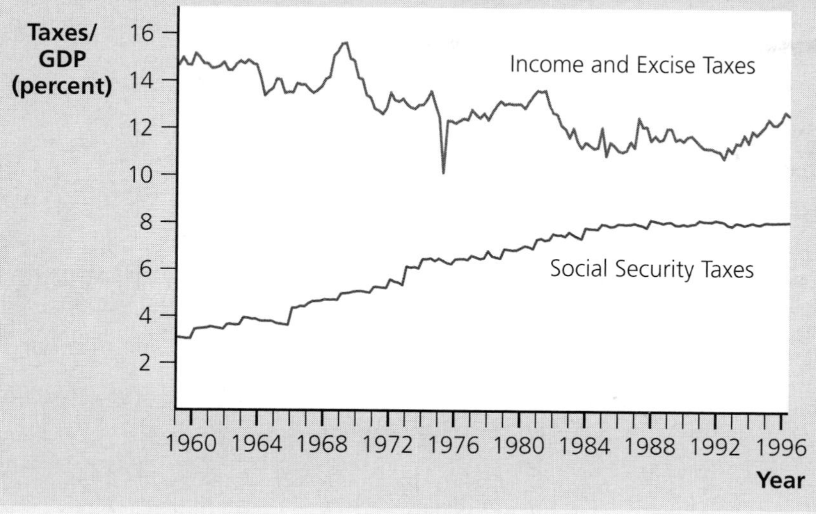

Revenue from income and excise taxes has fallen relative to GDP, while Social Security tax revenue has increased.

The federal government also taxes the consumption of certain products, such as gasoline, alcohol, tobacco, and air travel. These are called *excise taxes.* Excise taxes raise additional revenue for the government, but they are usually put in place for other, nonrevenue reasons as well. The excise tax on gasoline is seen, in part, as a fee on drivers for the use of federal highways. The taxes on alcohol and tobacco are intended to discourage consumption of these harmful products.

TRENDS IN FEDERAL TAX REVENUE. Figure 6 shows total federal government revenue, as a percentage of GDP, from all of the taxes we've discussed. Over the 38 years shown in the figure, revenue has been remarkably stable, at around 20 percent. Although, as we will see shortly, there have been important changes in the ways that the government collects and spends its revenue, the share of the nation's resources that flows to the government through taxes has been held—as if by some unwritten law—at around 20 percent.

Federal revenue is close to constant at around 20 percent of GDP.

While total federal revenue has remained a stable fraction of GDP, its *composition* has changed dramatically. Figure 7 divides total federal revenue between social security taxes, on the one hand, and all other taxes, on the other. Notice the steady upward trend in social security tax revenue. Other sources of revenue—led by the personal income tax—have declined just enough over the same period to keep total federal revenue at its stable level of 20 percent of GDP.

Why have social security taxes grown in importance? First, a little background. The social security system operates on a pay-as-you-go principle—it taxes people who are working now in order to pay benefits to those who worked earlier and are now retired. But it also pays more benefits to those who have worked longer.

FIGURE 8

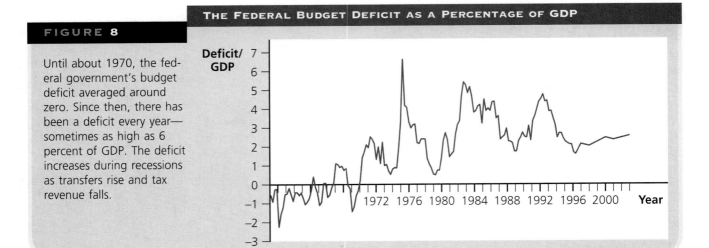

THE FEDERAL BUDGET DEFICIT AS A PERCENTAGE OF GDP

Until about 1970, the federal government's budget deficit averaged around zero. Since then, there has been a deficit every year—sometimes as high as 6 percent of GDP. The deficit increases during recessions as transfers rise and tax revenue falls.

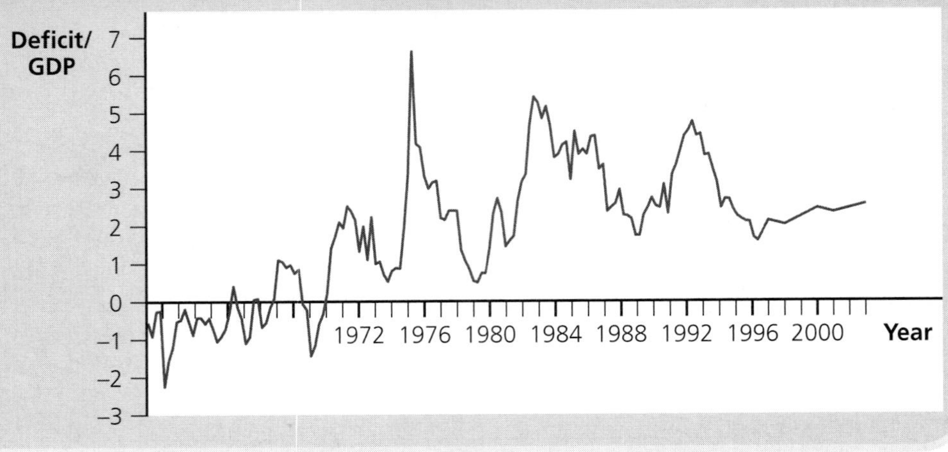

Over the years, the system has benefited from a number of favorable circumstances. In its early decades, most retirees who received benefits had started working before the system began, so their benefits were small in relation to the earnings of those at work. More recently, there have been two favorable demographic factors: first, a relatively small number of retirees due to very low birth rates during the 1930s; and second, a large number of people born in the 1950s who were reaching their peak earning—and taxpaying—years.

Now, these favorable factors have weakened, so benefits are growing in relation to earnings. This is one reason the government has raised social security tax rates. But there are two additional reasons: (1) The tax rate has been increased above the pay-as-you-go level in order to build up a reserve for retiring baby boomers in the coming decades; and (2) improved health is allowing people to spend a larger fraction of their lives in retirement, so each year of work has to pay for more retirement.

THE FEDERAL DEFICIT AND THE NATIONAL DEBT

People often confuse the federal *deficit* with the national *debt*. The two totals are related, but they are not the same. As you learned earlier in this text, the federal deficit is a *flow* variable—the amount by which federal government spending exceeds tax revenue *over a given period*, usually a year. The national debt, by contrast, is a *stock* variable—the total amount that the federal government owes *at a given point in time*. Each year that the government runs a deficit, it must borrow funds to finance it, adding to the national debt. For example, in 1996, the federal government ran a deficit of $125 billion. During that year, the national debt grew by about the same amount—from $3,712 to $3,846 billion. (The increase in debt is not precisely the same as the increase in the deficit, because of accounting details.)

THE DEFICIT. Figure 8 shows the history of the deficit in recent decades. This line in the figure is actually just the difference between the federal spending line in

Figure 5 and the federal revenue line in Figure 6. The deficit graph looks much choppier because the scale of the diagram is different here. As you can see, there was a dramatic change in the behavior of the deficit around 1970. Until that year, the deficit had small ups and downs, but averaged around zero. In many years, the budget was almost balanced, and surpluses were as common as deficits. But from 1970 on, the federal budget has been in deficit every year.

Notice the large rise in the deficit that occurred in the early 1980s. This was the combined result of a severe recession, which caused transfers to rise as shown in Figure 3, the buildup in military spending shown in Figure 1, and a large cut in income taxes during President Reagan's first term in office. Since 1983, the deficit has generally declined, although it jumped up again in the recession of 1991. With a strong economy, higher tax rates, and declining military spending, the deficit fell below 2 percent of GDP by 1996. Figure 8 also incorporates a projection of the deficit made in January 1997 by the Congressional Budget Office (CBO), an organization with a reputation for honest analysis of controversial economic matters.[5] The projection shows a continuation of the deficit at a little below 2 percent of GDP.

How should we reform the current tax system? Learn more about this issue in the Policy Debates portion of the ECONOMICS web site.

Address:
http://hall-lieb.swcollege.com

THE NATIONAL DEBT. When the federal government runs a deficit, it finances that deficit by issuing new government bonds and selling them to the public. When the government runs a surplus, it uses the additional funds to buy back some of the government bonds it issued in the past. We can measure the national debt as the total value of government bonds held by the public. Thus,

> *deficits—which add to the public's holdings of government bonds—add to the national debt. Surpluses—which decrease the public's bond holdings—subtract from the national debt.*

Since the cumulative total of the government's deficits has been greater than its surpluses, the national debt has grown in recent decades. It has also grown relative to GDP, as shown in Figure 9.

The rise in the national debt also explains another trend we discussed earlier: the rise in *interest payments* the government must make to those who hold government bonds. The greater the national debt, the greater will be the government's yearly interest payments on the debt. As you saw in Figure 4, total interest payments rose rapidly during the 1980s—the same period in which the national debt zoomed upward.

Figure 9 also shows the CBO's projection for the national debt until the year 2002. It looks as if the national debt will decline in the coming years. Wait a minute! you may say. How can the debt fall when the deficit is projected to remain positive, at about 2 percent of GDP? Doesn't it take a budget surplus for the government to pay back some of its debt? Yes, it does. But remember that in Figure 9, we view the national debt, as we view all variables in this chapter, as a *percentage of GDP*. The figure does not say that the debt itself will decline. Rather, it says that the *ratio of debt to GDP* will decline. With rising GDP, the debt can grow,

5 Congressional Budget Office, *The Economic and Budget Outlook: Fiscal Years 1998–2007*, January 1997.

FIGURE 9

FEDERAL DEBT AS A PERCENTAGE OF GDP

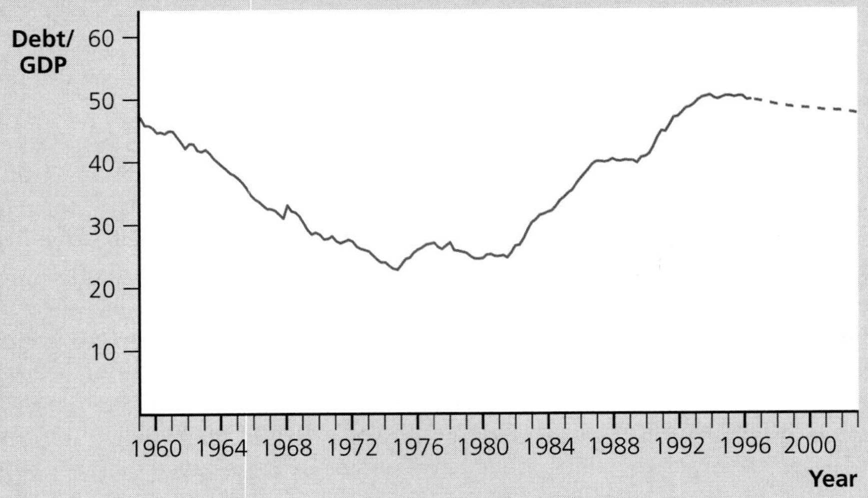

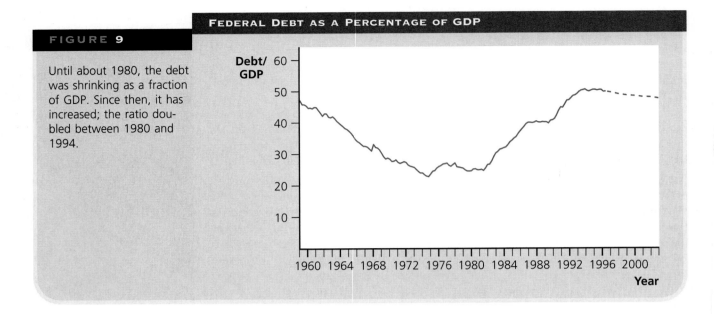

Until about 1980, the debt was shrinking as a fraction of GDP. Since then, it has increased; the ratio doubled between 1980 and 1994.

but the ratio will still fall as long as the debt grows more slowly than GDP. That's exactly what the CBO says will happen:

Although the federal debt is expected to grow, the ratio of the debt to GDP is expected to decline, because the debt is expected to grow at a slower rate than GDP.

SPENDING, TAXES, AND THE NATIONAL DEBT: A GENERAL CONCLUSION. This section has outlined some important changes in the federal government's budget over the past several decades. As you've seen, government purchases have decreased relative to GDP, because of a decrease in defense purchases. At the same time, total federal spending has increased, because transfer payments and interest on the national debt rose by more than military spending fell.

But these changes are not all independent of one another. For example, the rise in interest payments resulted from the growth in the national debt. And the national debt grew because of continuing deficits which, in turn, resulted from changes in government spending. Thus, we can trace the continuing deficits, the high levels of debt relative to GDP, and high interest payments relative to GDP all back to the same source: increased government spending relative to GDP, caused by the rise in transfer payments relative to GDP.

Continuing deficits and high levels of debt relative to GDP have been the result of fundamental choices the federal government has made in the past 30 years. In broad summary, the government has increased transfer payments without increasing taxes to pay for them.

Now that we've outlined the recent history of federal government spending, taxes, and debt, we can turn our attention to how fiscal changes affect the economy. But before we do, we need to dispel a common myth about the relationship between fiscal and monetary policy.

A MYTH ABOUT FINANCING THE BUDGET DEFICIT

MYTHS

"Governments Finance Their Budget Deficits by Printing Money"

A commonly-held myth about the deficit is that it is financed by printing up new money. At best, this is a gross oversimplification, and it is often flat wrong.

Let's take the United States as an example. When the U.S. government runs a deficit, the Treasury Department must *borrow* the funds by issuing new government bonds and selling them to the public. The Treasury is not legally entitled to create money; only the Federal Reserve can do that. In the following figure, deficit financing is illustrated by the arrows between the Treasury and the U.S. public. Note that while the public pays for its bonds with money, this does *not* increase the money supply; it is only a transfer of money from the public to the Treasury.

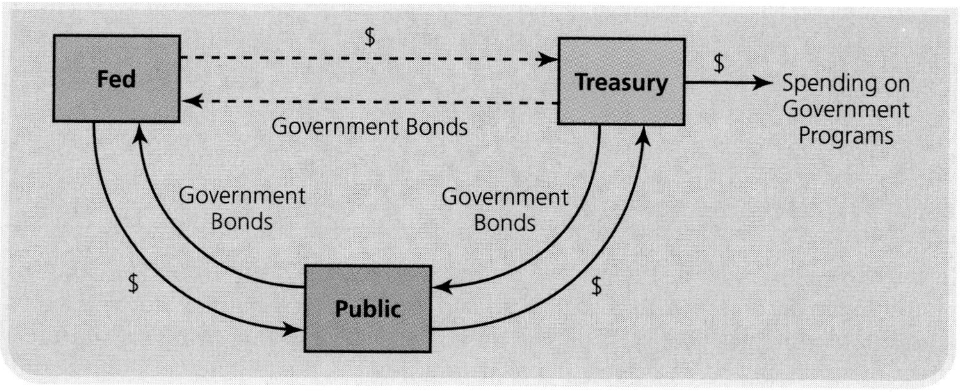

Now consider what happens when the Fed increases the money supply through open market purchases. The Fed buys government bonds from the public—the same bonds that the Treasury has issued to finance the government's past deficits. This is illustrated by the arrows between the Fed and the public. Notice that here, the Fed pays with reserves, which leads—through the demand deposit multiplier—to an increase in the money supply.

Now, if the government is running a deficit (as it usually is) at the same time as the Fed is increasing the money supply (as it usually is), something interesting happens: The Treasury's bonds end up going to the Fed. The public, in this case, plays the role of "middleman"—buying bonds from the Treasury and selling them to the Fed. At the same time, the Fed's newly created money goes to the Treasury, which spends it on government programs.

The dashed arrows between the Fed and the Treasury show these movements of money and bonds. If we look only at these dashed arrows, it *appears* that the Treasury has issued bonds and given them to the Fed, and the Fed has created money that it has passed along to the Treasury. That is, it appears that the deficit has been financed by money creation. This is how the public often understands the process of deficit financing. But the dashed arrows ignore an important fact: The decision to run a deficit and the decision to increase the money supply are made by two separate agencies: the Treasury and the Fed. The Fed does not *have* to increase the money supply just because the government is running a deficit, and it often chooses not to.

Our analysis of deficit financing in the U.S. applies to most other countries as well. For example, in England, Germany, and Japan, the central bank has some independence from the rest of the government. Running a deficit and increasing the money supply are seen as *separate decisions,* so it is incorrect to say that the deficit is financed by money creation.

However, there have been recent cases, in other countries, in which the central bank was subservient to the rest of the government. In these cases, the central bank's financing of the government's deficit was standard policy. Economists call this sort of arrangement **monetizing the deficit**—increasing the money supply so that the government can run a deficit. But automatic monetization of deficits is rare today. Many countries that previously relied on monetization to finance deficits—such as Argentina, Brazil, and Russia—have recently introduced reforms that prevent their central banks from bailing out their governments in that way.

In the United States, the Fed views increases in government spending and tax cuts as positive demand shocks and has typically responded by *decreasing* the money supply (or, at least, decreasing its rate of growth) in response to higher deficits. That is, the Fed has *not* behaved as shown in the figure. Therefore, it is wrong to say that the U.S. budget deficit is financed—even indirectly—by money creation.

THE EFFECTS OF FISCAL CHANGES IN THE SHORT RUN

In the short run, there is a two-way relationship between the government's budget and the macroeconomy. On the one hand, changes in the economy affect the government's spending and taxes; on the other hand, changes in spending and taxes affect the economy. Let's begin by considering how economic fluctuations—booms and recessions—affect the government's budget.

HOW BOOMS AND RECESSIONS AFFECT SPENDING, TAXES, AND THE BUDGET DEFICIT

Economic fluctuations affect both transfer payments and tax revenues. In a recession, in which many people lose their jobs, the federal government contributes larger amounts to state-run unemployment insurance systems and pays more in transfers to the poor, since more families qualify for these types of assistance. Thus, a recession causes transfer payments to rise. Recessions also cause a drop in tax revenue, because household income and corporate profits—two important sources of tax revenue—decrease during recessions.

In a recession, because transfers rise and tax revenue falls, the federal budget deficit rises.

A boom has the opposite effects on the federal deficit: With lower unemployment and higher levels of output and income, federal transfers decrease and tax revenues increase. Thus, *in a boom, because transfers decrease and tax revenue rises, the budget deficit falls.*

Because the business cycle has systematic effects on spending and revenue, economists find it useful to divide the deficit into two components. The **cyclical deficit** is the part that can be attributed to the current state of the economy. It turns positive (a cyclical deficit) during recessions, and negative (a cyclical surplus) during booms. When the economy is operating just at full employment, the cyclical deficit is, by definition, zero.

CYCLICAL DEFICIT The part of the federal budget deficit that varies with the business cycle.

The **structural deficit** is the part of the deficit that is not caused by economic fluctuations. As the economy recovers from a recession, for example, the cyclical deficit goes away, but any structural deficit in the budget will remain.

STRUCTURAL DEFICIT The part of the federal budget deficit that is independent of the business cycle.

Changes in the cyclical deficit are not a cause for concern, because, on average, these changes tend to cancel each other out as recessions are followed by booms. Thus, the cyclical deficit should not contribute to a long-run rise in the national debt.

Moreover, changes in the cyclical deficit are actually a good thing for the economy: They help to make economic fluctuations milder than they would otherwise be. Recall that spending shocks have a multiplier effect on output. The larger the multiplier, the greater will be the fluctuations in output caused by any given spending shock. Changes in the cyclical deficit make the multiplier smaller, and thus act as an *automatic stabilizer*. How?

Let's use unemployment insurance as an example. In normal times, with unemployment at around 5.5 percent, federal transfers for unemployment insurance are modest. But when a negative spending shock hits the economy, and output and income begin to fall, the unemployment rate rises. Federal transfers for unemployment insurance rise *automatically*. Without assistance from the government, many of the newly unemployed would have to cut back their consumption spending substantially. But unemployment insurance cushions the blow for many such families, allowing them to make smaller cutbacks in consumption. As a result, the total decline in consumption is smaller, and GDP declines by less. Unemployment insurance thus reduces the multiplier.

Other transfer programs have a similar stabilizing effect on output. More people receive food stamps and welfare during recessions. Consequently, their consumption falls by less than it would if they did not have this help. And the tax system contributes to economic stability in a similar way. Income tax payments, for example, fall in a recession. With the government siphoning off a smaller amount of income from the household sector, the drop in consumption is smaller than it would be if tax revenues remained constant.

The same principle applies when a positive spending shock hits the economy. Transfer payments automatically decline, as the unemployed find jobs and fewer families qualify for government assistance. And tax revenues automatically rise, since income rises. As a result, the spending shock causes a smaller rise in GDP than would otherwise occur.

Many features of the federal tax and transfer systems act as automatic stabilizers. As the economy goes into a recession, these features help to reduce the decline in consumption spending, and they also cause the cyclical deficit to rise. As the economy goes into a boom, these features help to reduce the rise in consumption spending, and they also cause the cyclical deficit to fall.

COUNTERCYCLICAL FISCAL POLICY?

In the previous section, you learned that changes in government spending and taxes that occur automatically in booms and recessions help to stabilize the economy. This immediately raises a question: Can the government *purposely* change its spending or tax policy to make the economy even more stable? For example, suppose the *AD* curve shifts leftward, and the economy enters a recession. Perhaps the government could increase its purchases of goods and services, or cut income tax rates, thereby shifting the *AD* curve rightward again. If a government changes its spending or taxes specifically to counteract a boom or recession, it is engaging in **countercyclical fiscal policy.**

COUNTERCYCLICAL FISCAL POLICY Changes in taxes or government spending designed to counteract a boom or recession.

In the 1960s and early 1970s, many economists and government officials believed that countercyclical fiscal policy could be an effective tool to counteract the business cycle. Today, however, very few economists hold this position. Instead, they would put the Fed in charge of stabilizing the economy and reserve fiscal policy for addressing long-run issues of resource allocation. Indeed, the last clear use of countercyclical fiscal policy occurred in 1975, when the government gave tax rebates in the depths of a serious recession in order to stimulate consumption. (In Figure 7, you can see the especially large downward spike in tax revenue relative to GDP in that year.)

Why do economists recommend against using countercyclical fiscal policy, and why does Washington follow their advice? There are several reasons.

TIMING PROBLEMS. It takes many months or even longer for a fiscal change to be enacted. Consider, for example, a decision to change taxes in the United States. A tax bill originates in the House of Representatives and then goes to the Senate, where it is usually modified. Then a conference committee irons out the differences between the House and Senate versions, and the tax bill goes back to each chamber for a vote. Even if all goes smoothly, this process can take many months.

But in most cases, it will *not* go smoothly: The inevitable political conflicts will cause further delays. First, there is the thorny question of distributing the cost of a tax hike, or the benefits of a tax cut, among different income groups within the country. Each party may argue for changes in the tax bill in order to please its constituents. And some senators and representatives will see the bill as an opportunity to improve the tax system in more fundamental ways, causing further political debate.

All of these problems create the danger that the tax change will take effect long after it is needed. And changes in transfer payments or government purchases would suffer from similar delays. As a result, a fiscal stimulus might take effect after the economy has recovered from a recession and is headed for a boom; or a fiscal contraction might take effect just as the economy is entering a recession. Fiscal changes would then be a *de*stabilizing force in the economy—stepping on the gas when we should be hitting the brakes, and vice versa.

The Fed, by contrast, can increase or decrease the money supply *on the very day it decides that the change is necessary.* While there are time lags in the *effectiveness* of monetary policy (see the previous chapter), the ability to execute the policy in short order gives monetary policy an important advantage over fiscal policy for stabilizing the economy.

IRREVERSIBILITY. A second reason for favoring monetary rather than fiscal policy to stabilize the economy is the difficulty of reversing changes in government spending or taxes. Spending programs that create new government departments or expand existing ones tend to become permanent, or at least difficult to terminate. Many temporary tax changes become permanent as well—the public is never happy to see a tax cut reversed, and the government is often reluctant to reverse a tax hike that has provided additional revenue for government programs.

Reversing monetary policy, while not always painless, is easier to do. For one thing, the Fed makes its decisions secretly—neither government officials nor the public knows for sure what course the Fed has set until six weeks after the Federal Open Market Committee meets. Thus, the Fed is somewhat insulated from the political process in making its decisions. While there are limits to the Fed's independence (Congress could change the Fed's charter, or even eliminate the Fed entirely if it became too unhappy with its performance), these limits do not affect the Fed's ability to act quickly when it sees the need.

The Fed's Reaction. Even if the government attempted to stabilize the economy with fiscal policy, it could not do so very effectively, because—to put it simply—the Fed will not allow it. The Fed views a change in fiscal policy just as it views other spending shocks: as a shift in the *AD* curve that needs to be neutralized. For example, suppose the Fed believes that the *AD* curve is shifting leftward and the economy is entering a recession. Then the Fed will increase the money supply to shift the *AD* curve rightward by the amount it thinks necessary, long before any fiscal change takes effect. The fiscal change, when it is finally enacted, will simply be counteracted with an offsetting change in the money supply. As long as the Fed is free to set its own course, and as long as it continues to see its goal as stabilizing the economy at the natural rate of unemployment and low inflation, there is simply no opportunity—and no need—for countercyclical fiscal policy.

THE EFFECTS OF FISCAL CHANGES IN THE LONG RUN

Because the Fed acts to neutralize them, fiscal changes have little short-run effect on the macroeconomy. But fiscal changes do have important long-run effects. To analyze them, we'll use the model best suited for long-run analysis: the classical model.

We've already considered some of the long-run effects of fiscal policy in this book. In the chapter titled "The Classical, Long-run Model," we discussed the long-run impact of changes in government purchases. In the chapter titled "Economic Growth and Rising Living Standards," we discussed how government tax and transfer policies can affect the incentives of workers and firms, in turn affecting the economy's long-run growth rate.

Here, we once again explore the effect of fiscal changes in the long run. But rather than revisit the topic in a general way, we'll analyze one specific fiscal change—we'll ask, "What are the long-run effects of a policy of increasing transfers without increasing taxes?"

Our analysis centers on the classical model's *loanable funds market,* illustrated in Figure 10, where household saving (the supply of loanable funds) is made available for borrowing by businesses and the government (the demand for loanable funds). The supply of funds curve slopes upward because households will save more (supply more funds) at higher interest rates. The demand for funds curve slopes downward because business firms spend less on plant and equipment, and therefore borrow less, at higher interest rates. Initially, the market is in equilibrium at

FIGURE 10

THE IMPACT OF DEFICIT-FINANCED TRANSFER PROGRAMS

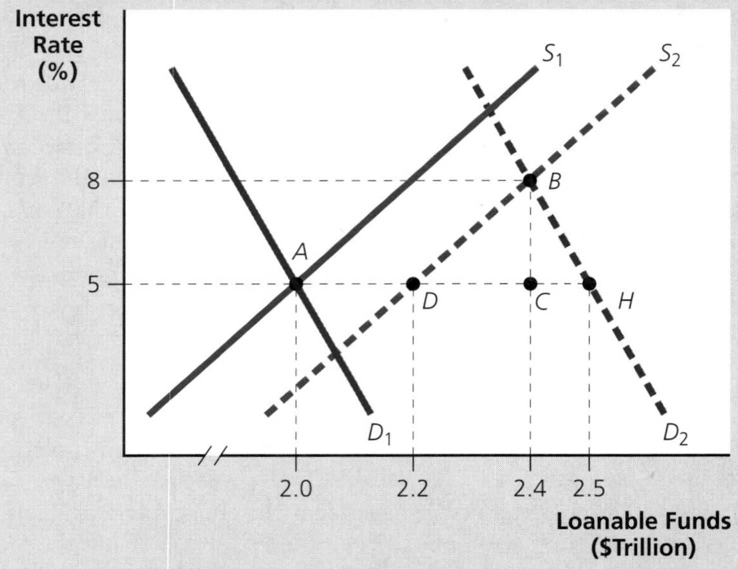

The financial market is originally in equilibrium at point *A* with an interest rate of 5 percent. A $500 billion government transfer program causes the household sector to increase its saving. The supply of funds curve shifts rightward to S_2. With no change in tax revenues, the government's budget deficit increases by $500 billion, shifting the demand for funds curve to D_2. The resulting excess demand for funds (*DH*) drives the interest rate up to 8 percent. Private investment falls by *CH,* but the higher interest rate causes saving to increase—by the distance *DC*—for a total increase in saving of *AC*. In the end, consumption rises by $100 billion, $100 billion of investment is crowded out, and total spending remains unchanged.

point *A*, with an interest rate of 5 percent, and $2 trillion in loanable funds supplied and demanded.

Now let's see what happens when the government launches a program of $500 billion in transfers. To keep things simple, we'll assume that there are no changes in tax revenue or government purchases. As you are about to see, the rise in transfer payments has an impact on *both* the supply and demand for loanable funds.

Let's first consider the impact on the supply of loanable funds curve. When more unemployment insurance, social security, or welfare payments are paid to households, they will *not* spend the entire amount. Instead, they will save some part of the additional funds, thereby increasing the supply of funds. Thus, the increase in transfers causes a rightward shift in the supply of funds curve—the household sector will supply more at any interest rate. In the figure, we assume that households spend 60 percent of their transfers ($300 billion) and save the remaining 40 percent ($200 billion). The supply of funds curve shifts rightward by $200 billion. (In reality, households are likely to spend 90 percent or more of their transfers, so the shift will be much smaller; but our assumption makes the diagram easier to read.)

Now let's turn to the demand curve for loanable funds. With no change in tax revenues, the $500 billion increase in transfer payments will increase the government's budget deficit by the full $500 billion. The government will have to borrow the additional funds to finance the larger deficit. As a result, the demand curve for funds shifts to the right by the full $500 billion.

After these shifts occur, the equilibrium in the loanable funds market will change. To see why, note that—at the original interest rate of 5 percent—there is an excess demand for funds equal to the distance *DH*—$2.5 trillion of funds are demanded (point *H*), while only $2.2 trillion are supplied (point *D*). The excess demand for funds drives the interest rate up to 8 percent. Investment falls as a result, moving us along the new demand for funds curve from point *H* to point *B*. As you can see, *the rise in transfers raises the interest rate, and reduces investment spending*—in our example, by the amount *CH*, or $100 billion.

At the same time, the rise in the interest rate will cause saving to increase, moving us along the new supply of funds curve, from point *D* to point *B*. Importantly, this is the second time saving has increased after the rise in transfers: First, saving increased by $200 billion at the original interest rate of 5 percent; and now, it increases *by another* $200 billion because of the rise in the interest rate. The total increase in saving is $200 billion + $200 billion = $400 billion.

Now let's examine how the increase in transfers affects the three categories of spending: *C*, *I*, and *G*. By assumption, there has been no change in government purchases (*G*). Second, investment (*I*) fell by $100 billion because the transfer program raised interest rates. Third, consumption (*C*) spending rose by $100 billion. How do we know? Because households received an additional $500 billion in transfers from the government. Since they are saving $400 billion of this, they must be spending the remainder. Thus, the final effect of the rise in transfers is: consumption spending increases by $100 billion, and investment spending falls by $100 billion. Total spending remains unchanged.

While the numbers are specific to our example, we have reached an important general conclusion:

> *Increases in transfer payments that are not funded by additional tax revenue shift the nation's resources from investment goods to consumption goods. That is, the increase in transfer payments causes consumption spending to* crowd out *investment spending.*

Why does the increase in transfers crowd out investment spending? With no change in taxes, the government must borrow the funds to pay for the increased transfers. By borrowing, it takes funds away from some other sector—in this case, the business sector—that would otherwise have borrowed them and used them for investment. True, households make more funds available to businesses by saving more, but they don't increase their saving by as much as the government increases its borrowing. This is why businesses, in the end, must borrow and invest less.

Recall from the chapter "Economic Growth and Rising Living Standards" that investment in new plant and equipment is one of the sources of growth of the economy. Deficit financing of transfers results in lower growth because it reduces capital formation. Many economists have suggested that the growth of spending without comparable growth of tax revenue has been responsible for low rates of capital formation and growth in the U.S. economy at some times in recent decades. Although transfers have benefited those who have received them, and have helped millions of people maintain acceptable living standards, the cost has been a lower rate of economic growth.

DANGEROUS CURVES

This section has shown that rising transfer payments have come at the cost of lower investment spending and therefore reduce the rate of economic growth. This does not mean that government spending for *other* purposes necessarily slows growth. In particular, some government purchases support the legal, financial, and physical infrastructure of the economy and *contribute* to economic growth. Even if these purchases crowd out private investment spending, their net effect on growth could be favorable anyway.

But remember that rising transfers relative to GDP have been financed only *in part* by deficit spending. Military spending has also decreased relative to GDP, and this has made room in the budget for much of the increase in transfer payments. This shift from military spending to transfer payments—which doesn't add to the deficit—does *not* cause the kinds of adverse effects on investment and growth that we've outlined here.

Nevertheless, the rise in transfer payments still imposes an opportunity cost on society. If transfer payments had *not* increased, the decrease in military spending *would have* led to a decrease in total government spending. This would have meant a smaller deficit, lower interest rates, and greater investment spending. The increase in transfer payments required society to forgo these gains from a shrinking military budget. Thus,

OPPORTUNITY COST

> *whether rising transfers are financed by deficits or by reduced military spending, the opportunity cost of transfers is the same: lower investment and slower economic growth.*

Our discussion so far has focused on economic flows, as described by the loanable funds market diagram. Over the years, rising transfers have contributed to continuing deficits. (There are other reasons for the deficit as well, which we've discussed earlier in the chapter, but transfers have been an important part of the story.) As you've seen, these deficits have caused a decrease in consumption and investment spending.

But we can also view the impact of deficits in terms of a stock variable: the national debt. Over the years, continuing deficits have accumulated into high levels of debt.

> *Over the last several decades, continuing deficits have led to a steady rise in the national debt.*

We'll have more to say about the problem of a rising national debt in the "Using the Theory" section of the chapter.

A CONTRARY VIEW: RICARDIAN EQUIVALENCE

Some economists—most notably, Robert Barro of Harvard University—find the preceding analysis incomplete in an important way. When increased government spending is financed by government borrowing, a far-sighted taxpayer may figure out that taxes will need to be raised in the future to deal with the debt. And how should this insightful taxpayer respond? By saving more today in preparation for future higher taxes. In this view, the choice between financing government outlays by taxes or by borrowing is only a question of timing—borrowing is a way of postponing, but not eliminating, taxes. This idea was first proposed by the 19th-century British economist David Ricardo, so it is called *Ricardian equivalence*. Deficit financing and taxation are equivalent because they differ only by when taxpayers actually make their tax payments.

The Ricardian equivalence critique of the analysis presented in Figure 10 is straightforward: The figure *understates* the increase in saving resulting from the transfer program. Not only do the recipients of transfers increase their saving, as shown in the figure, but taxpayers who do not enjoy the transfers also increase saving, in order to pay higher taxes in the future. According to this view, we should redraw Figure 10 so that the rightward shift in the supply of funds curve is just as large as the rightward shift in the demand for funds curve. In that case, the interest rate would not rise, and investment would not fall. The transfers would simply increase the consumption spending of those who receive them, and decrease consumption by taxpayers who will save more to pay higher taxes in the future. There would be no crowding out of investment spending.

The dispute between economists who believe in crowding out and those who believe in Ricardian equivalence is unresolved. The latter group cannot point to any increase in private saving in the United States after the policy of deficit-financed transfers went into effect—in fact, saving has generally declined. But the Ricardians' notion that households look to the future is compelling. The truth may lie somewhere between the hypothesis of substantial crowding out, as in Figure 10, and the Ricardian equivalence case of zero crowding out.

ARE WE HEADED FOR A DEBT DISASTER?

USING THE THEORY

On a billboard in Manhattan, a giant digital display tracks the U.S. national debt and how it is changing each minute. Through 1996, the clock showed debt growing by about $240,000 per minute; the last four digits on the display changed so rapidly that they appeared as a blur. And on December 31, 1996, for a split second, the national debt reached $3,846,000,000,000.[6]

How can we ever hope to repay all of this debt? Are we headed for a debt disaster? While many economists are *concerned* about budget deficits and growing debt—because of their effects on resource allocation and growth that we discussed in the previous section—there is widespread agreement that we are *not* headed for a disaster.

Why?

First, it's important to realize that the national debt *never has to be paid back*. That may sound surprising. How can the government keep borrowing funds without every paying them back? Surely, no business could behave that way. Right?

Actually, wrong. Many successful businesses *do* behave this way and continue to prosper. For example, the debt of many major corporations—like AT&T and General Motors—continues to grow, year after year. While they continue to pay interest on their debt, they have no plans to pay back the amount originally bor-

6 The national debt clock showed a greater figure at that moment, because it included the part of the debt owed to U.S. government agencies.

rowed in the foreseeable future. As these companies' bonds become due, they simply *roll them over*—they issue new bonds to pay back the old ones.

Why don't these firms pay back their debt? Because they believe they have a better use for their funds: investing in new capital equipment and research and development to expand their businesses. This will lead to higher future profits. And as long as their profits continue to grow, they can continue to increase their debt.

Of course, this does not mean that *any* size debt would be prudent. Recall the important principle we discussed earlier in the chapter: *Debt and interest payments have meaning only in relation to income.* If a firm's income is growing by 5 percent each year, but its interest payments are growing by 10 percent per year, it would eventually find itself in trouble. Each year, its interest payments would take a larger and larger fraction of its income, and at some point interest payments would exceed total income. And even *before* this occurred, the firm would find itself in trouble. Lenders, anticipating the firm's eventual inability to pay interest, would cut the firm off. At that point, the firm would reach its *credit limit*—the maximum amount it can borrow based on lenders' willingness to lend. Since it could no longer roll over its existing debt with further borrowing, it would have to pay back any bonds coming due, until its debt was comfortably below its credit limit.

All of these observations apply to the federal government as well. As long as the nation's total income is rising, the government can safely take on more debt. More specifically, if the nation's income is growing at least as fast as total interest payments, the debt can continue to grow indefinitely, without putting the government in danger.

The federal government *could* pay back the national debt—by running budget surpluses for many years—but few people believe this would be a good thing for the economy. The government, in deciding not to pay back its debt, is acting just like corporations, which behave in similar fashion: It believes it has better uses for its revenue than debt repayment.

But how fast can the government continue to accumulate debt? Or, equivalently, how large can the federal deficit be without making the national debt a greater and greater burden for our citizens to bear?

Let's see. As long as total national income grows at least as fast as interest payments on the debt, the ratio of interest payments to income will not grow. In that case, we could continue to pay interest without increasing the average tax rate on U.S. citizens. For example, suppose that the nominal GDP is \$10 trillion and the national debt is \$5 trillion. Suppose, too, that interest payments average out to 10 percent of the national debt, or \$500 billion. Then the ratio of interest payments to nominal GDP would be \$500 billion/\$10 trillion = 0.05. Now suppose that, over some period of time, both nominal GDP and the national debt double, to \$20 trillion and \$10 trillion, respectively. Then interest payments will double as well, to \$1 trillion. But the ratio of interest payments to nominal GDP will remain constant, at \$1 trillion/\$20 trillion = 0.05.

More generally,

> *as long as the debt grows by the same percentage as nominal GDP, the ratios of debt to GDP and interest payments to GDP will remain constant. In this case, the government can continue to pay interest on its rising debt without increasing the average tax rate in the economy.*

This establishes an important *minimal guideline for responsible government*: The debt should grow no faster than nominal GDP. Currently, nominal GDP is growing at about 6 percent per year—2.5-percent growth in real GDP, plus a 3.5-percent increase in the price level. So the debt can grow 6 percent per year without any rise in the average tax rate.

But what size yearly *deficit* would keep the *debt* growing at 6 percent? That is easy to calculate. The debt is about half as large as GDP, so when the debt grows by 6 percent, it grows by 3 percent of GDP. Now, remember that the deficit is equal to the increase in the debt. Therefore,

the deficit can be as large as 3 percent of GDP without causing an increase in the ratio of debt or interest to GDP, and without requiring any increase in the average tax rate.

If the deficit exceeds 3 percent of GDP, then the ratios of debt to GDP, and interest payments to GDP, will rise. In that case, higher and higher tax rates would be needed to pay the growing interest on the debt. But as long as the deficit is 3 percent of GDP or less, the debt can grow indefinitely without danger.

But what if the ratio of debt to GDP—today, around 0.50—is *already* too high? Could the United States be dangerously close to its credit limit—the amount of debt that would make lenders worry about the government's ability to continue paying interest? If so, we would be flirting with disaster—a tiny increase in the ratio could lead to a cutoff of further lending and require the budget to be balanced immediately. It might also cause a financial panic, as everyone tried to dump their U.S. government bonds, causing their prices to fall and household wealth to plummet. This is a common scenario in the disaster books discussed at the beginning of the chapter. Are we facing this danger?

Not really. There is, indeed, some credit limit for the U.S. government, but we are probably far from it at the current time. At the conclusion of World War II, the ratio of federal debt to GDP was 1.08. At that time, there was little concern that the government would not honor its debt obligations, and in fact, the debt–GDP ratio was brought down dramatically: Thirty years after the end of the war, in 1975, the debt was down to about 23 percent of GDP. From this experience, we might guess that ratio of debt to GDP could exceed 1.0 before the federal government would reach its credit limit. In 1996, the national debt was about 50 percent of GDP—far from this credit limit.

In early 1997, the Congressional Budget Office projected deficits of around 2 percent of GDP for the next several years. This will keep the government on an even keel for the indefinite future. But the deficit cannot rise much above that figure. We've seen that if the deficit stayed above 3 percent of GDP, the debt–GDP ratio would begin to rise again. And this would create a vicious cycle: A higher debt–GDP ratio would lead to a higher interest–GDP ratio. To pay the higher interest, the government would probably run higher deficits relative to GDP, raising the debt–GDP ratio still more. Unless something was done to raise revenue or cut spending, the situation would gradually get out of control—the debt–GDP ratio would rise faster and faster. Within a decade or two, the government would reach its credit limit. Thus, a critical factor for the stability of the government is that it keep its deficit within the range where the debt–GDP ratio remains stable—3 percent of GDP or less. So far, the U.S. government has stayed safely within that range.

SUMMARY

The U.S. federal government finances its spending through a combination of taxes and borrowing. Whenever government spending exceeds tax revenue, the government runs a budget deficit. It finances that deficit by selling bonds, thereby adding to the national debt.

Federal government spending consists of government purchases, transfer payments, and interest on the national debt. Nonmilitary government purchases have traditionally accounted for about 2.5 percent of real GDP. Military purchases vary according to global politics; in recent years, they have declined dramatically relative to GDP. Transfer programs—such as Social Security, Medicare, and welfare—are the fastest growing part of government spending. They currently equal about 10 percent of GDP.

On the revenue side, the government relies on personal and corporate income taxes, Social Security taxes, and some smaller excise taxes and user fees. For several decades, federal revenue has been almost constant at 20 percent of GDP.

In every year since 1970, federal spending has exceeded federal revenues so that the government has run a budget deficit. Particularly large deficits occurred in the early 1980s; since then the deficit has generally declined relative to GDP. As a result of the excess of spending over revenue, the national debt—the cumulative total of budget deficits minus surpluses—has continued to grow. The ratio of debt to GDP, however, has declined.

In the short run, there is a two-way relationship between government spending and taxes on the one hand, and the level of output on the other. First, changes in output affect government spending and taxes. In recessions, for example, government tax revenues fall and transfer payments rise. In this way, the tax and transfer system acts as an automatic stabilizer, helping to smooth out fluctuations.

Second, changes in government spending and taxes affect output. In principle, the government could use countercyclical fiscal policy—changing taxes and spending in order to offset booms and recessions. However, because of practical problems, countercyclical fiscal policy is seldom used.

In the long run, fiscal changes do have important effects. Increases in transfer payments that are not funded by additional tax revenue raise the interest rate and crowd out investment spending. Over long periods of time, this causes the capital stock to be smaller than it would otherwise be, and slows the rate of economic growth.

KEY TERMS

progressive tax
average tax rate
marginal tax rate
cyclical deficit
structural deficit
countercyclical fiscal policy

REVIEW QUESTIONS

1. Why is it misleading to compare the national debt in 1959 of $235 billion with the national debt in 1996 of $3,850 billion?
2. List the categories of federal government spending. What is the largest component? What is the fastest growing part?
3. What is a progressive income tax? How do people avoid paying income taxes?
4. List the main sources of federal revenue. How and why has the composition changed recently?
5. Explain the difference between the federal deficit and the national debt.
6. What does "monetizing the deficit" mean? What is the Fed's policy regarding monetizing the deficit?

7. Define the cyclical deficit and the structural deficit. Why are changes in the cyclical deficit not a major long-run concern?

8. What is countercyclical fiscal policy? Is it an effective tool? Explain.

9. "An increase in transfers slows economic growth." True or false? Explain.

10. What is Ricardian equivalence?

11. While the national debt is an important concern, most economists don't believe we're headed for imminent disaster. Explain.

PROBLEMS AND EXERCISES

1. Use the following statistics, in billions of units, to calculate the real national debt and the debt relative to GDP, in 1968 and 1998 for this particular country. Which figures would you use to compare the national debt in the two years?

National Debt in 1968:	1.2
National Debt in 1998:	13.84
Nominal GDP in 1968:	101.7
Nominal GDP in 1998:	552.2
CPI in 1968:	35.2
CPI in 1998:	113.3

2. Suppose there is a country with 30 households divided into three categories (A, B, and C), with 10 households of each type. If a household earns 20,000 units (the country's currency) or more in a year it must pay 15 percent in tax to the government. If the household earns below 20,000 units, it doesn't pay any tax. When the economy is operating at full employment, household income is 250,000 units for type A households, 50,000 units for type B households, and 20,000 units for type C households per year.
   a. If the economy is operating at full employment, how much revenue does the government collect in taxes for the year?
   b. Suppose a recession hits and household income falls for each type of household. Type A households now earn 150,000 units, type B households earn 30,000 units, and type C households earn 10,000 units for the year. How much does the government collect in tax revenue for the year? Assume the government spends all of the revenue it *would* collect if the economy were operating at full employment. What is the effect of the recession on the government budget deficit?
   c. Suppose instead that a boom hit and household incomes rose to 400,000 units, 75,000 units, and 30,000 units respectively for the year. How much tax would the government collect for the year? What is the effect on the government deficit (assume again that the government spends exactly the amount of revenue it collects when household income is at the values in part [a])?

   What is the relationship between shocks to the economy and the budget deficit? How does this relate to the cyclical deficit as an automatic stabilizer?

3. Assume that the government is not running a deficit initially. The government cuts taxes by $150 billion, but it doesn't change government spending. How does this affect the loanable funds market according to (a) a critic of Ricardian equivalence, and (b) a supporter of Ricardian equivalence?

4. Why do many economists view an independent central bank as a stabilizing force in the economy?

5. According to the minimal guideline for responsible government outlined in the text, are either of the following two countries having a national debt crisis?

Country A
(figures are in billions of $)

	Debt	*GDP*
1997	1	100
1998	2	110
1999	3	150

Country B
(figures are in billions of $)

	Debt	*GDP*
1997	1236	1400
1998	1346	1550
1999	1406	1707

CHALLENGE QUESTION

Suppose the government finances a tax cut today by borrowing. According to Ricardian equivalence, people realize that the tax cut will require greater taxes in the future, so their current saving increases by the amount of the tax cut. What if, however, people believe that the government won't increase taxes during their lifetimes, but will instead impose higher taxes on future generations. Does Ricardian equivalence still hold? Why or why not?

WWW

Can you balance the Federal budget? Visit the "National Budget Simulation," a project developed by UC–Berkeley's Center for Community Economic Research (http://garnet.berkeley.edu:3333/budget/budget.html).

a. Tabulate the changes you make in the budget. Are you successful in balancing the budget? How much of a deficit or surplus are you left with? What does this exercise suggest about the process of creating a balanced budget?
b. Examine again the budget cuts or increases you made. What challenges would such changes pose for a politician facing reelection?
c. This budget simulator allows you only to change spending and tax expenditures over a one-year period. What problems does this pose to finding a realistic economic solution for balancing the budget?

CHAPTER

16

COMPARATIVE ADVANTAGE AND THE GAINS FROM TRADE

CHAPTER OUTLINE

Consumers love bargains. And the rest of the world offers U.S. consumers bargains galore—cars from Japan, computer memory chips from Korea, shoes from China, tomatoes from Mexico, lumber from Canada, and sugar from the Caribbean. Should we let these bargain goods into the country? Consumers certainly benefit when we do let them in. But don't cheap foreign goods threaten the jobs of American workers and the profits of American producers? How do we balance the interests of specific workers and producers on the one hand with the interests of consumers in general? These questions are important not just in the United States, but in every country of the world.

Over the post-World War II period, there has been a worldwide movement toward a policy of *free trade*—the unhindered movement of goods and services across national boundaries. A new international body, the World Trade Organization (WTO), has been created as a forum for negotiations to remove restrictions on trade all over the world.

Thanks to the WTO and earlier efforts, import taxes, import limitations, and all kinds of crafty regulations designed to keep out imports are gradually falling away. In addition to lower trade barriers, a new mechanism for settling trade disputes has been put in place. And some 30 other countries, including China and Russia, seem eager to join the free-trade group.

But while many barriers have come down, others are being put up. Asian governments have been dragging their feet on allowing U.S. firms to sell financial services there. The United States has moved to protect its maritime industry from foreign shipping companies and has renewed its long-standing quota on sugar imports. Europeans have restricted the sale of American satellite communications services. Poor countries have imposed tariffs on computers, semiconductors, and software exported by rich countries. Rich countries have announced their intention to maintain, at least through the year 2005, existing quotas on textiles and clothing sold by poor countries.

Looking at the contradictory mix of trade policies that exist in the world, we are left to wonder: Is free international trade a good thing that makes us better off, or is it bad for us and something that should be kept in check? In this chapter, you'll learn some of the tools economists use to analyze the issues surrounding international trade.

THE LOGIC OF FREE TRADE

Many of us like the idea of being self-reliant. Some would even prefer to live by themselves in a remote region of Alaska or the backcountry of Montana. But consider the defects of self-sufficiency: If you lived all by yourself, you would be poor. You could not *export* or sell to others any part of your own production, nor could you *import* or buy from others anything they have produced. You would be limited to consuming the goods and services that you produced. Undoubtedly, the food, clothing, and housing you would manage to produce by yourself would be small in quantity and poor in quality—nothing like the items you currently enjoy. And there would be many things you could not get at all—electricity, television, cars, airplane trips, or the penicillin that could save your life.

The defects of the self-sufficient state explains why most people choose *not* to be self-sufficient, but rather to specialize and trade with each other. In Chapter 2, you learned the *basic principle of specialization and exchange:*

SPECIALIZATION AND EXCHANGE

Specialization and exchange enable us to enjoy greater production and higher living standards than would otherwise be possible. As a result, all economies have been characterized by high degrees of specialization and exchange.

This principle applies not just to individuals, but also to *groups* of individuals, such as those living within the boundaries that define cities, counties, states, or nations. That is, just as we benefit when *individuals* specialize and exchange with each other, so, too, we can benefit when groups of individuals specialize in producing different goods and services, and exchange them with other groups.

Imagine what would happen if the residents of your state insisted on self-sufficiency and refused to import anything from "foreign states" or to export anything to them. Such an arrangement would be preferable to individual self-sufficiency—specialization and trade within the state would raise the quantities and qualities of goods available—but it would surely continue to involve many sacrifices. Lacking the necessary inputs for their production, for instance, your state might have to do without bananas, cotton, or tires. And the goods that *were* made in your state would likely be produced inefficiently. For example, while residents of Vermont *could* drill for oil, and Texans *could* produce maple syrup, they could do so only at great cost of resources.

Thus, it would make no sense to insist on the economic self-sufficiency of each of the 50 states. And the founders of the United States knew this. They placed prohibitions against tariffs, quotas, and other barriers to interstate commerce right in the U.S. Constitution. The people of Vermont and Texas are vastly better off under free trade among the states than they would be if each state were self-sufficient.

What is true for states is also true for entire nations. The members of the WTO have carried the argument to its ultimate conclusion: National specialization and exchange can expand world output through free *international* trade. Such trade involves the movement of goods and services across national boundaries. Goods and services produced domestically, but sold abroad, are called **exports;** those produced abroad, but consumed domestically, are called **imports.** The long-term goal of the WTO is to remove all barriers to exports and imports in order to encourage among nations the specialization and trade that has been so successful within nations.

EXPORTS Goods and services produced domestically, but sold abroad.

IMPORTS Goods and services produced abroad, but consumed domestically.

THE THEORY OF COMPARATIVE ADVANTAGE

Economists who first considered the benefits of international trade focused on a country's *absolute advantage*. A country has an **absolute advantage** in a good when it can produce it using fewer resources than another country. As the early economists saw it, the citizens of every nation could improve their economic welfare by specializing in the production of goods in which they had an absolute advantage and exporting them to other countries. In turn, they would import goods from countries that had an absolute advantage in those goods.

ABSOLUTE ADVANTAGE The ability to produce a good using fewer resources than another country.

Way back in 1817, however, the British economist David Ricardo disagreed. Absolute advantage, he argued, was not a necessary ingredient for mutually beneficial international trade. The key was *comparative advantage:*

COMPARATIVE ADVANTAGE The ability to produce a good at a lower opportunity cost than elsewhere.

> *A nation has a* ***comparative advantage*** *in producing a good if it can produce it with a lower opportunity cost than some other country.*

OPPORTUNITY COST

We measure the opportunity cost of producing a good not by the resources used to produce it, but rather by the *other goods* whose production must be sacrificed.

Ricardo argued that a potential trading partner could be absolutely inferior in the production of every single good—requiring more resources per unit of each good than any other country—and still have a comparative advantage in some good. The comparative advantage would arise because the country was *less* inferior at producing some goods than others. Likewise, a country that had an absolute advantage in producing everything could—contrary to common opinion—still benefit from trade. It, too, would have a comparative advantage only in some—but not all—goods.

> *Mutually beneficial trade between any two countries is possible whenever one country is relatively better at producing a good than the other country is. Being relatively better means having the ability to produce a good at a lower opportunity cost—that is, at a lower sacrifice of other goods foregone.*

OPPORTUNITY COST

OPPORTUNITY COST AND COMPARATIVE ADVANTAGE

To illustrate Ricardo's insight, let's consider a hypothetical world of two countries, Germany and the United States. Both are producing only two goods, cameras and computers. Could they better themselves by trading with one another? Ricardo would have us look at opportunity costs; to find them, let's consider what it costs to produce these goods in each country. To keep our example simple, we'll assume that the costs per unit—for both cameras and computers—remain the same no matter how many units are produced.

Look at Table 1. Naturally, German firms keep books in deutsche marks (DM) and American firms in dollars, so our cost data are expressed accordingly.

We can use the data in the table to calculate the opportunity cost of producing more of each good in each country.

TABLE 1

COSTS OF PRODUCTION

	Per camera	Per computer
Germany	DM125	DM2,500
United States	\$100	\$1,000

First, suppose Germany were to produce one additional computer. Then it would have to divert DM2,500 of resources from the camera industry. This, in turn, would require Germany to produce fewer cameras. How many fewer? Since each camera uses up DM125 in resources, using DM2500 for one computer would require producing DM2,500/DM125 = 20 fewer cameras.

In the United States, producing an additional computer requires diverting \$1,000 of resources from camera making, losing \$1,000/\$100, or 10 cameras. Thus, the U.S. opportunity cost is smaller (10 < 20), and *the United States has a comparative advantage in making computers.*

We can do the same calculation for cameras, determining the opportunity cost in terms of *computers forgone.* Our computations are summarized in Table 2. The numbers allow us to see which country has the lower opportunity cost in which good. Thus, Germany has the comparative advantage in cameras, and the United States has it in computers.

Now we can use our conclusions about comparative advantage to show how both countries can gain from trade. The explanation comes in two steps. First, we show that if Germany could be persuaded to produce more cameras and the United States more computers, the world's total production of goods will increase. Second, we show how each country can come out ahead by trading with the other.

SPECIALIZATION AND WORLD PRODUCTION

According to Table 2, if Germany produced, say, 20 more cameras, it would have to sacrifice the production of one computer as resources were shifted between the two industries. If the United States, simultaneously, produced one extra computer, it would have to sacrifice 10 cameras—again because fully employed resources would have to be moved. But note: As a result of even this small change, the world output of cameras would increase by 10, while computer production would be unchanged—despite the fact that no more resources were used than before. Table 3 summarizes the changes.

The extra cameras in this example represent the gain from specializing according to comparative advantage—a gain, as the next section will show, that the two trading partners will share. It is also the kind of gain that, multiplied a million times, lies behind the substantial benefits countries enjoy from free trade.

TABLE 2

OPPORTUNITY COSTS

	Per camera	Per computer
Germany	1/20 computer	20 cameras
United States	1/10 computer	10 cameras

A Small Change in Production — TABLE 3

	Camera production	Computer production
Germany	+20	−1
United States	−10	+1
World	+10	0

The particular example given here is not the only one that can be derived from our table of opportunity costs. For example, if Germany produced 10 more cameras and, therefore, cut back by half a computer, the world output of cameras would be unchanged, while computer production would rise. Other examples illustrate simultaneous increases in the world output of both goods. As an exercise, try to create such an example on your own.

In all cases, however, the key insight remains the same:

If countries specialize according to comparative advantage, a more efficient use of given resources occurs. As a result, the world output of at least one good rises, without decreasing that of any other good.

Specialization and Exchange

Gains from International Trade

Now we proceed to the second step in Ricardo's case, showing that both sides can gain from trade. In our example so far, each country would have more of one good but *less* of another. However, with the net increase in *world* output, international trade flows could be arranged so that no country would have less of anything, while each country would get a piece of the gain in total output. Many different arrangements are possible; here is one that would apportion the world output gain equally:

Germany exports (and the U.S. imports) 15 cameras.
Germany imports (and the U.S. exports) 1 computer.

Table 4 summarizes the end result. The *gains from trade* (5 extra cameras for both Germany and the United States) add up precisely to the gain in world output noted earlier. This is no coincidence: With only two countries in our example, when world output rises by 10 cameras, one country or the other must end up with the additional cameras.

The Gains from Specialization and Trade — TABLE 4

	Production	Loss from exports (−) or gain from imports (+)	Net gain
Germany			
Cameras	+20	−15	+5
Computers	−1	+1	none
United States			
Cameras	−10	+15	+5
Computers	+1	−1	none

TABLE 5

LABOR INPUTS NEEDED

	Per camera	Per computer
Germany	12.5 hours	250 hours
United States	10 hours	100 hours

It is worth reiterating that the mutually beneficial changes summarized in Table 4 are based on *comparative* advantage, not *absolute* advantage. A quick recasting of Table 1 can make the point. We will simplify our example further and suppose that the only resource countries use in production is labor. Further, we'll suppose arbitrarily that an hour of labor costs DM10 in Germany and $10 in the U.S. Then the DM125 it costs to make a camera in Germany would mean that 12.5 hours of labor are needed to make a camera there, since 12.5 hours × DM10 per hour = DM125. Thus, in Table 5, we enter 12.5 hours for the labor needed per camera in Germany.

Making similar calculations, we find that it takes 250 hours to make a computer in Germany; and in the United States, it takes 10 hours to make a camera and 100 hours to make a computer.

Now it's easy to see that the United States has an absolute advantage—using less input per unit of output than Germany—in the production of *both* goods. Would specialization and mutually beneficial trade still be possible? Very much so. The opportunity cost data in Table 2 would be unchanged, and so would be all the conclusions we derived from that table. Thus,

SPECIALIZATION AND EXCHANGE

as long as opportunity costs differ, specialization and trade can be beneficial to all involved. This remains true regardless of whether the parties involved are nations, states, counties, or individuals. It remains true even if one party holds an all-round absolute advantage or disadvantage.

THE TERMS OF TRADE

TERMS OF TRADE The ratio at which a country can trade domestically produced products for foreign-produced products.

In our ongoing example, Germany exports 15 cameras in exchange for 1 computer. This exchange ratio (15 cameras for 1 computer) is known as the **terms of trade.** Our particular choice of 15 to 1 for the terms of trade happened to apportion the gain in world output equally between the two countries. (See Table 4.) With different terms of trade, however, the benefit would have been distributed unequally. We won't consider here precisely *how* the terms of trade are determined (it is a matter of supply and demand), but we can establish the limits within which they must fall.

Look again at Table 2. Germany would never give up *more* than 20 cameras to import 1 computer. Why not? Because it could always get 1 computer for 20 cameras *domestically,* by shifting resources into computer production.

Similarly, the United States would never export a computer for *fewer than* 10 cameras, since it can substitute 1 computer for 10 cameras domestically (again, by switching resources between the industries). Therefore, the equilibrium terms of trade must lie between 20 and 10 cameras for 1 computer. Outside of that range, one of the two countries would refuse to trade. Note that in our example, we assume terms of trade of 15 cameras for 1 computer—well within the acceptable range.

COMPARATIVE ADVANTAGE: A GRAPHICAL ILLUSTRATION

The theory of comparative advantage can be illustrated graphically with two countries' production possibilities frontiers (PPFs). Recall from Chapter 2 that a PPF shows the different combinations of two goods that a country can produce. Figure 1 shows two PPFs—line *AG* for Germany and line *HR* for the United States. The PPFs differ because the two countries have different quantities and qualities of resources and, possibly, technical knowledge.

But notice that the PPFs are straight lines. This reflects an assumption, made for simplicity, that the opportunity cost of one good in terms of the other does not

COMPARATIVE ADVANTAGE AND THE GAINS FROM TRADE

FIGURE 1

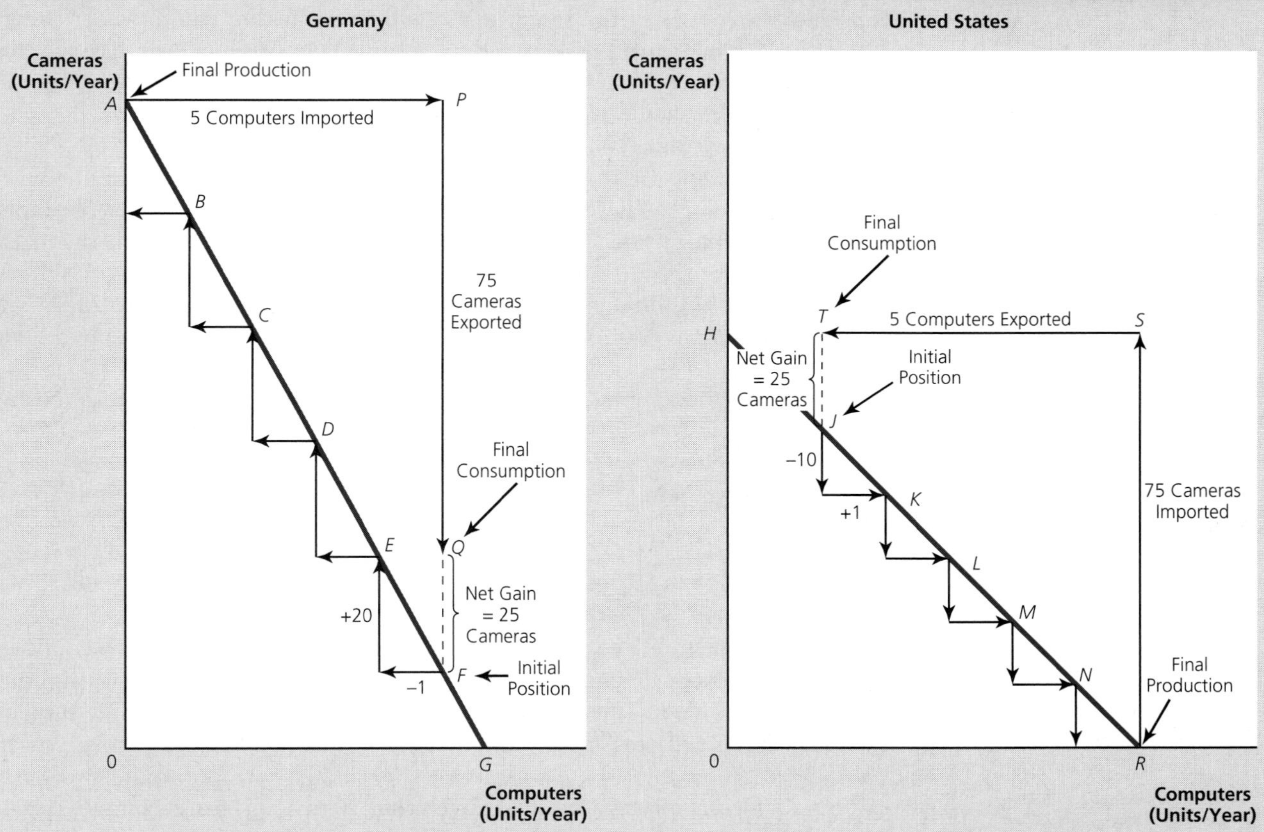

The two production possibility curves show the combinations of cameras and computers that can be produced in Germany and in the United States. Before trade, Germany is at point *F* and the United States is at *J.* When trade opens up, Germany begins moving up its PPF, freeing up resources capable of producing 20 cameras for each computer it sacrifices. The United States moves down its PPF, producing fewer cameras and using freed-up resources to produce more computers.

If the two countries trade cameras for computers at a rate such as 25:1, both can benefit. The United States ends up specializing in computers, exports five computers to Germany in exchange for 75 cameras, and ends up consuming at *T,* a point above its PPF. Germany specializes in cameras, exports 75 of them to the United States, imports five computers, and consumes at point *Q,* above its PPF. Both nations gain from trade.

vary as the volume of production changes. Thus, regardless of the totals of cameras and computers produced by either country, we assume that Germany can always switch 20 cameras for 1 computer in the process of production, and the United States can switch 10 cameras for 1 computer. These numbers equal the absolute values of the two slopes and reflect the opportunity costs found in Table 2.

Complete Specialization

In our example, the assumption of constant opportunity costs has an important implication: To maximize world production and the ultimate gain from international trade, each country must specialize completely, rather than partially, in producing the good in which it has a comparative advantage. Let's see why.

Suppose that Germany is initially at point *F*, and the United States starts at *J*. Now let's have each country shift resources toward the good in which it has a comparative advantage. We'll start by having Germany cut computer production by 1 unit and use the freed-up resources to produce 20 more cameras, moving to point *E*. (Follow the arrows.) At the same time, we'll have the United States cut camera production by 10 units and use the freed-up resources to produce 1 additional computer, moving from *J* to *K*. (Again, note the arrows.) As a result of this first step toward specialization, world output of cameras increases by 10, with no change in world output of computers—just as we saw earlier, in Table 3.

But after this step, the opportunity costs in the two countries continue to diverge exactly as before. Therefore, the same logic that suggested to us the moves from *F* to *E* in Germany and from *J* to *K* in the United States suggests further, identical steps: Germany should continue to move from *E* to *D*, and then to *C*, *B*, and *A*. The United States should continue to move from *K* to *L* and then to *M*, *N*, and *R*. In the end, Germany would produce nothing but cameras and the United States nothing but computers—*complete* specialization in each country.

In our graphical example, the ultimate changes in output would be as follows:

Germany (moving from *F* to *A*):	+100 cameras	−5 computers
United States (moving from *J* to *R*):	−50 cameras	+5 computers
World:	+50 cameras	No change

Consumption beyond the Frontier

So far, we've used Figure 1 to illustrate changes in *production* in the two countries. But we can also use the diagram to illustrate changes in *consumption*—the amount of each good available to consumers in each country. Assuming the same terms of trade as earlier (25 cameras for 1 computer), let's imagine that Germany exports, and the United States imports, 75 cameras in exchange for 5 computers. As a result, Germany's *consumption* would move from *A* to *P* (5 more computers) and then to *Q* (75 fewer cameras). Comparing Germany's initial consumption (point *F*) with its final consumption (point *Q*), we see that Germany enjoys 25 more cameras and the same number of computers as a result of specializing and trading.

Now we'll imagine that the U.S. exports the 5 computers that Germany imports and imports the 75 cameras that Germany exports. This would move the United States from *R* to *S* (75 more cameras) and on to *T* (5 fewer computers). Comparing the United States' initial consumption at point *J* with its final consumption at point *T*, we see that it, too, gains 25 cameras, with no sacrifice of computers, as a result of specialization and trade. Notice that each country consumes a combination of goods (at *Q* and *T*, respectively) that lies beyond its own PPF:

PRICES IN GERMANY AND THE UNITED STATES WITH AN EXCHANGE RATE OF DM2 FOR $1

TABLE 6

	Per camera	Per computer
Germany	**DM125** ($62.50)	**DM2,500** ($1,250)
United States	**$100** (DM200)	**$1,000** (DM2,000)

If opportunity costs differ and countries specialize according to their comparative advantage, they can consume combinations of goods that lie outside their production possibilities frontiers. Both countries are better off as a result.

SPECIALIZATION AND EXCHANGE

TURNING POTENTIAL GAINS INTO ACTUAL GAINS

So far in this chapter, we have discussed the *potential* advantages of specialization and trade among nations, but one major question remains: How is that potential realized? Who or what causes a country to shift resources from some industries into others and then to trade in the world market?

Do foreign trade ministers at WTO meetings decide who should produce and trade each product? Does some group of omniscient and benevolent people in Washington and other world capitals make all the necessary arrangements? Not at all. Within the framework of the WTO, government officials are supposed to create the environment for free trade, but they do not decide who has a comparative advantage in what, or what should be produced in this or that country. In today's market economies around the world, it is individual consumers and firms who decide to buy things—at home or abroad—and who, by their joint actions, determine where things are produced and what things are traded. The promise of Ricardo's theory is achieved through markets.

With competitive markets for all goods (cameras, computers, and such) and competitive markets for all currencies (German marks, dollars, and such), people only have to do what comes naturally: buy products at the lowest price. Without their knowing it, they are promoting Ricardo's dream!

Let's see how this works. In the absence of trade, the prices of goods within a country will generally reflect their opportunity costs. That is, if producing one more computer in the United States requires the sacrifice of 10 cameras, then the price of a computer will be about 10 times the price of a camera.[1]

Let's imagine the situation before trade between two countries begins. We'll suppose that prices in each country are precisely equal to the costs of production in each country, as given earlier in Table 2. These prices are shown again in Table 6, in bold type. For the moment, ignore the prices in parentheses.

1 If you've studied microeconomics, you might remember that prices will more closely reflect opportunity costs the more closely markets satisfy the conditions of pure competition.

Now suppose we allow trade to open up between the two countries. Consider the decision of a U.S. consumer, who can choose to purchase cameras and computers in either country. To buy goods from German producers, Americans must pay in deutsche marks. In order to obtain that currency, Americans must go to the *foreign exchange market* and trade their dollars for deutsche marks at the going *exchange rate*. Here, to illustrate how countries are pushed to produce according to their comparative advantage, we'll just assume that the exchange rate is 2 deutsche marks for 1 dollar.

Now, at this exchange rate, an American can purchase a German camera priced at DM125 by exchanging $62.50 for DM125 and then buying the camera. Thus, to the American, the *dollar price of German cameras* is $62.50, which appears in parentheses below the price in deutsche marks. Similarly, the dollar price of a DM2,500 German computer is $1,250—also in parentheses. Looking at the table, you can see that, to an American, German cameras at $62.50 are cheaper than U.S. cameras at $100, so *Americans will prefer to buy cameras from Germany*. But when it comes to computers, we reach the opposite conclusion: a U.S. computer at $1,000 is cheaper than a German computer at $1,250, so *Americans will prefer to buy computers in the United States.*

Now take the viewpoint of a German consumer who can buy U.S. or German goods. To buy U.S. goods, German consumers will need dollars, which they can obtain at the going exchange rate: DM2 for $1. The bottom row of the table shows the prices in deutsche marks of the U.S. goods, in parentheses. German cameras at DM125 are cheaper than U.S. cameras at DM200, while U.S. computers at DM2,000 are cheaper than German computers at DM2,500. Thus, *a German, just like an American, will prefer to buy computers from the United States and cameras from Germany.*

Now suppose that trade in cameras and computers had previously been prohibited, but is now opened up. Everyone would buy cameras in Germany and computers in the United States, and the process of specialization according to comparative advantage would begin. German camera makers would expand their production, while German computer makers would wither on the vine. Unemployed computer workers in Germany would find jobs in the camera industry. And analogous changes would occur in the United States. These changes in production patterns would continue until Germany specialized in camera production and the U.S. specialized in computer production—that is, until each country produced according to its comparative advantage.

Our example illustrates a general conclusion:

When consumers are free to buy at the lowest prices, they will naturally buy a good from the country that has a comparative advantage in producing it. A country's industries respond by producing more of that good and less of other goods. In this way, countries naturally tend to specialize in those goods in which they have a comparative advantage.[2]

2 Something may be bothering you about the way we reached this conclusion: We merely *asserted* that the exchange rate was DM2 for $1. What if we had chosen another exchange rate? With a little work, you can verify that at any exchange rate between DM1.25 for $1 and DM2.5 for $1, our conclusion will still hold: Countries will automatically produce according to their comparative advantage. Further, you can verify that if the exchange rate went *beyond* those bounds, the residents of both countries would want to buy both goods from just one country. This would increase the demand for deutsche marks and force the exchange rate back between DM1.25 for $1 and DM2.5 for $1.

Some Important Provisos

The real world is much more complicated than our simplified graphical and numerical examples might suggest. Despite divergent opportunity costs, sometimes it does *not* make sense for two countries to trade with each other, or it might make sense to trade, but *not* completely specialize as in Figure 1. Following are some real-world considerations that can lead to reduced trade or incomplete specialization.

Costs of Trading. If there are high transportation costs or high costs of making deals across national boundaries, trade may be reduced and even become prohibitively expensive. High transportation costs are especially important for perishable goods, such as ice cream, which must be shipped frozen, and most personal services, such as haircuts, eye exams, and restaurant meals. None of these are typically traded internationally. (Imagine the travel cost for an American barber who would like to sell a haircut to a resident of Germany.) Such high costs associated with trading help explain why nations continue to produce some goods in which they do not have a comparative advantage and why there is less than complete specialization in the world.

Sizes of Countries. Our earlier example featured two large economies capable of fully satisfying each other's demands. But sometimes a very large country, such as the United States, trades with a very small one, such as the Pacific island nation of Tonga. Even if their PPFs were straight lines, as in Figure 1, and the smaller country specialized completely, its output would be insufficient to fully meet the demand of the larger one. The larger country would continue to produce both goods and would specialize only in the sense of producing *more* of its comparative-advantage good rather than *nothing but* that good. The smaller country would specialize completely. This helps to explain why the United States continues to produce bananas, even though we do so at much higher opportunity cost than many small Latin American nations.

Increasing Opportunity Cost. In our example, we have assumed that opportunity cost remains constant as production changes, giving us the straight-line PPFs in Figure 1. But more typically, opportunity cost rises as production increases and falls as production falls. (Why? You may want to review the law of increasing opportunity cost in Chapter 2.) In that case, each step on the road to specialization would change the opportunity cost and thus change the slope of the production function. PPFs will then be *curved,* just as they were in Chapter 2, and trading partners will move along them only to a limited degree—to the point at which opportunity costs have become equalized. In the end, while trading will occur, there will not be complete specialization. Instead, each country will produce both goods, just as Germany and the United States each produce cameras *and* computers in the real world.

Government Barriers to Trade. Governments can enact barriers to trading. In some cases, these barriers increase trading costs; in other cases, they make trade impossible. We'll consider government-imposed barriers a bit later in the chapter.

Name:
U.S. Department of Commerce, International Trade Administration (ITA)
Description:
International trade policy developer for the federal government
Resources:
The International Trade Administration gathers statistics and information on international trade and aims to assist U.S. businesses with imports and exports.
Address:
http://www.ita.doc.gov/

THE SOURCES OF COMPARATIVE ADVANTAGE

We've just seen how nations can benefit from specialization and trade when they have comparative advantages. But what determines comparative advantage in the first place? In many cases, the answer is differences in natural resources. The top part of Table 7 contains some examples. Saudi Arabia has a comparative advantage in the production of oil because it has oil fields with billions of barrels of oil that can be extracted at low cost. Canada is a major exporter of timber because its climate and geography make its land more suitable for growing trees than other crops. Canada is a good example of comparative advantage without absolute advantage—it grows a lot of timber not because it can do so using fewer resources than other countries, but because its land is even more poorly suited to grow other crops.

The bottom part of Table 7 shows examples of international specialization in which comparative advantage arises from some cause *other* than natural resources. Japan has a huge comparative advantage in making automobiles—over 40 percent of the world's automobiles are made there. And that number would be even larger, except for laws that ban the import of Japanese cars into Europe. Yet none of the natural resources needed to make cars are available in Japan; the iron ore, coal, and oil that provide the basic ingredients for cars are all imported.

Countries often specialize in products based on their own particular endowments of natural resources. But natural resources are not the only basis for comparative advantage.

Explaining the origins of the specialties in the bottom part of Table 7 is not easy. For example, if you think you know why Japan completely dominates the world market for VCRs and other consumer electronics—say, some unique capacity to develop technical expertise—be sure you have an explanation for why Japan is a distant second in computer printers. The company that dominates the market for printers—Hewlett-Packard—is a U.S. firm. Moreover, the ability to mass-produce high-quality products is not unique to Japan, as Switzerland showed long ago in developing its international specialty in watches.

In even the most remote corner of the world, the cars, cameras, and VCRs will be Japanese, the movies and music American, the clothing from Hong Kong, and the bankers from Britain. Although we can't explain the reasons behind these countries' comparative advantages, we *can* explain why a country retains its comparative advantage once it gets started. Japan today enjoys a huge comparative advantage in cars and consumer electronics in large part because it has accumulated a capital stock—both physical capital and human capital—very well suited to producing those goods. The physical capital stock includes the many manufacturing plants and design facilities that the Japanese have built over the years. But Japan's human capital is no less important. Japanese managers know how to anticipate the features that tomorrow's buyers of cars and electronic products will want around the world. And Japanese workers have developed skills adapted for producing these products. The stocks of physical and human capital in Japan sustain its comparative advantage in much the way as stocks of natural resources lead to comparative advantages in other countries. More likely than not, Japan will continue to have a comparative advantage in cars and electronics, just as Saudi Arabia will continue to have a comparative advantage in producing oil.

EXAMPLES OF NATIONAL SPECIALTIES IN INTERNATIONAL TRADE

TABLE 7

Country	Specialty resulting from natural resources or climate
Saudi Arabia	Oil
Canada	Timber
United States	Grain
Spain	Olive oil
Mexico	Tomatoes
Jamaica	Aluminum ore
Italy	Wine
Israel	Citrus fruit
	Specialties not based on natural resources
Japan	Cars, consumer electronics
United States	Software, movies, music
Switzerland	Watches
Korea	Steel, ships
Hong Kong	Textiles
Great Britain	Financial services

Countries often develop strong comparative advantages in the goods they have produced in the past, regardless of why they began producing those goods in the first place.

WHY SOME PEOPLE OBJECT TO FREE TRADE

Given the clear benefits that nations can derive by specializing and trading, why would anyone *ever* object to free international trade? Why do the same governments that join the WTO turn around and create roadblocks to unhindered trade? The answer is not too difficult to find: Despite the benefit to the nation as a whole, some groups within the country, in the short run, are likely to lose from free trade, even while others gain a great deal more. Opening up trade is a potential Pareto improvement—a change in which the gains to the gainers are greater than the losses to the losers. But opening up trade is rarely a *simple* Pareto improvement, in which no one loses. Instead of finding a way to compensate the losers—to make them better off as well—we often allow them to block free-trade policies. The simple model of supply and demand helps illustrate this story.

In our earlier example, after trade opens up, the U.S. exports computers and Germany imports them. Figure 2 illustrates the impact on the computer market in the two countries. To keep things simple, we'll let the vertical axis represent the *dollar* price of computers in both countries, even though computers in Germany are actually sold for deutsche marks. (To obtain the dollar prices of computers in Germany, we would translate from deutsche marks, using the exchange rate between the two currencies.)

FIGURE 2

THE IMPACT OF TRADE

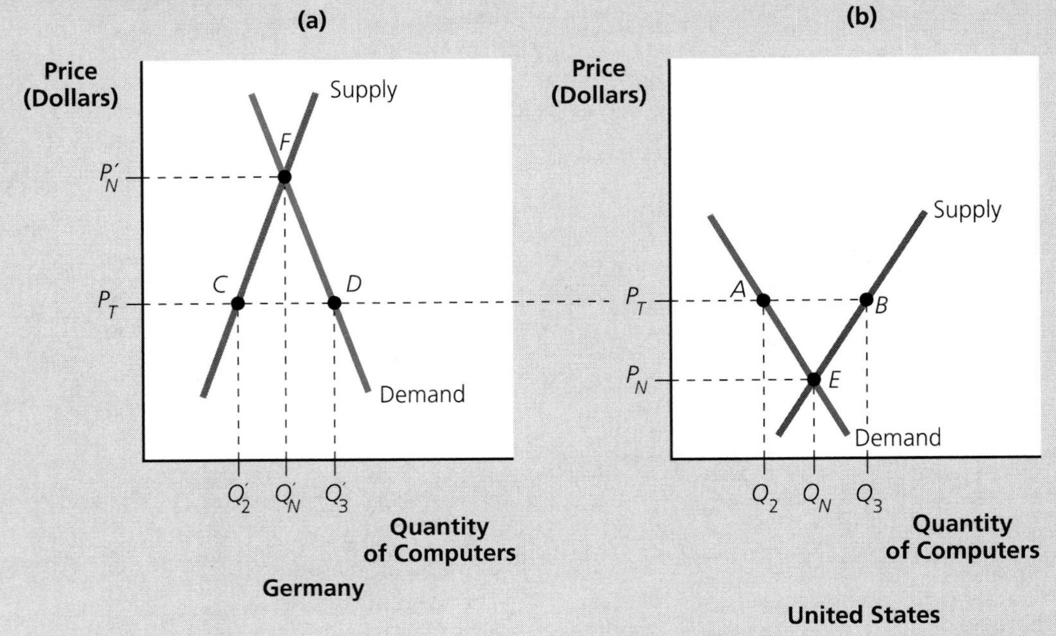

Before trade, the U.S. computer market is in equilibrium at point *E*, and the German market is in equilibrium at *F*. When trade begins, Germans buy the cheaper U.S. computers, driving up their price. In response, U.S. computer manufacturers increase output, and U.S. consumers decrease their purchases. At world equilibrium price P_T, Americans buy Q_2 computers, Germans buy $Q_3 - Q_2$ American computers, and the total quantity of American computers produced and sold is Q_3. Distance *CD*, which shows German imports of computers, equals distance *AB*, which shows U.S. exports.

As a result of trade, U.S. computer producers sell more units at a higher price, but U.S. consumers pay more for computers. In Germany, computer producers are worse off, but computer buyers benefit from the lower price there.

Before trade opens up, the U.S. computer market is in equilibrium at point *E*, with price equal to P_N (for "no trade") and quantity equal to Q_N. The German computer market is in equilibrium at point *F*, with price P'_N and quantity Q'_N. Notice that before trade opens up, the price is lower in the United States—the country with a comparative advantage in computers.

Now, when trade opens up, Germans will begin to buy U.S. computers, driving the price of U.S. computers upward. As the price in the United States rises from P_N to P_T (for "trade"), U.S. producers increase their output of computers, moving from *E* to *B* along the supply curve, and U.S. consumers decrease their purchases of computers, moving from *E* to *A* along the demand curve. This seems to create an "excess supply" of computers in the United States, equal to *AB*, but it is not *really* an excess supply, because *AB* is precisely the number of computers that are exported to Germany.

Now let's consider the effects in Germany. There, consumers are switching from German computers to the U.S. ones. With less demand for German computers, their price will fall. With free trade, Germans must be able to buy U.S. computers at the same price as Americans (ignoring transportation costs), so the price of German computers must fall to P_T. As it does, German producers will decrease their output, from F to C along the supply curve, and German consumers will increase their purchases, from F to D along the demand curve. This seems to create a shortage of computers in Germany, equal to CD, but it is not a shortage, because CD will equal the number of computers imported from the United States.

Now let's see how different groups are affected by the opening up of trade.

The Impact of Trade in the Exporting Country

When trade opens up in computers, the United States is the exporting country. How are different groups affected there?

- *U.S. computer producers and workers are better off.* Before international trade, producers sold Q_N units at price P_N, but with trade, they sell the higher quantity Q_3 at the higher price P_T. The industry's workers are equally delighted because they undoubtedly share in the bonanza as the number of workers demanded rises along with the level of production. Both management and labor in the U.S. computer industry are likely to favor free trade.
- *U.S. computer buyers are worse off.* Why? Before trade, they bought Q_N units at price P_N, and now they must pay the higher price P_T and consume the smaller quantity Q_2. Consumers are likely to lobby the government to restrict free trade:

When the opening of trade results in increased exports of a good, the producers of the good are made better off and will support increased trade. Consumers of the good will be made worse off and will oppose increased trade.

The story told here is anything but hypothetical. A dramatic example is provided by American agriculture, which not so long ago exported a huge percentage of various crops to the Soviet Union. Growers of wheat, rye, and corn did everything they could to promote this trade. All kinds of people in grain-growing areas, ranging from car dealers to sellers of fertilizer, were equally behind the Russian trade deal; they benefited indirectly. American consumers, however, complained bitterly. Bread, cereals, and flour were more expensive. So were eggs and chicken, because chickens were fed with more expensive grain.

The Impact of Trade in the Importing Country

Now let's consider the impact of free trade in computers on Germany, the importing country. Once again, it is easy to figure out who is happy and who is unhappy with the new arrangement.

- *German computer producers and workers are worse off.* They used to sell quantity Q'_N at price P'_N, but now they are furious because they sell the lower quantity Q'_2 at the lower price P_T. The industry's workers suffer, too, because the number of workers demanded falls with the level of production. Both management and labor are likely to oppose free trade.
- *German computer buyers are better off.* They used to buy quantity Q'_N at price P'_N, but now they pay the lower price, P_T and consume the larger quantity, Q'_3. German consumers will favor free trade:

When the opening of trade results in increased imports of a product, the domestic producers of the product are made worse off and will oppose the increased trade. Consumers are better off and will favor the increased trade.

TABLE 8

ATTITUDES TOWARD FREE TRADE

	In export sectors that enjoy comparative advantage	In import sectors that suffer from comparative disadvantage
Pro Trade	Owners of firms, workers	Consumers
Anti Trade	Consumers	Owners of firms, workers

This story, too, is anything but hypothetical. A vivid example was provided recently by the American clothing industry. A Ukrainian clothing maker produced stylish, high-quality women's coats and sold them in the United States. With the coats priced between $89 and $139, over a million of them were sold. When American coat makers complained bitterly about the new competitor, the U.S. government stepped in. A tight import limitation killed off half of the Ukrainian imports in 1995. On top of that, the United States imposed a 21.5-percent tax on the offending coats. The interests of U.S. coat makers prevailed over the interests of U.S. coat consumers.

ATTITUDES TOWARD FREE TRADE: A SUMMARY

In our examples, we've been discussing the impact of free trade in computers. We could tell the same story about free trade in cameras. In this case, Germany has the role of exporter, and the U.S. is the importer. But our conclusions about the impacts on different groups in exporting and importing countries would remain the same. And so would our conclusions about who favors, and who opposes, free trade. Table 8 summarizes the stance toward trade we can expect from these different groups.

HOW FREE TRADE IS RESTRICTED

So far in this chapter, you've learned that specialization and trade according to comparative advantage can dramatically improve the well-being of entire nations. This is why governments generally favor free trade. Yet international trade can, in the short run, hurt particular groups of people. These groups often induce governments to restrict free trade.

When governments decide to accommodate the opponents of free trade, they are apt to use one of two devices to restrict trade: tariffs or quotas.

TARIFFS

TARIFF A tax on imports.

A **tariff** is a tax on imported goods. It can be a fixed dollar amount per physical unit, or it can be a percentage of the good's value. In either case, the effect in the tariff-imposing country is similar: Domestic producers and their workers are helped, domestic consumers are hurt, and the nation as a whole is hurt, since the Ricardian gains from trade are reduced.

Figure 3 illustrates the effects of a German tariff on U.S. computers. Initially, before the tariff is imposed, the price of computers in both countries is P_T, and the

THE EFFECTS OF A TARIFF ON COMPUTERS

FIGURE 3

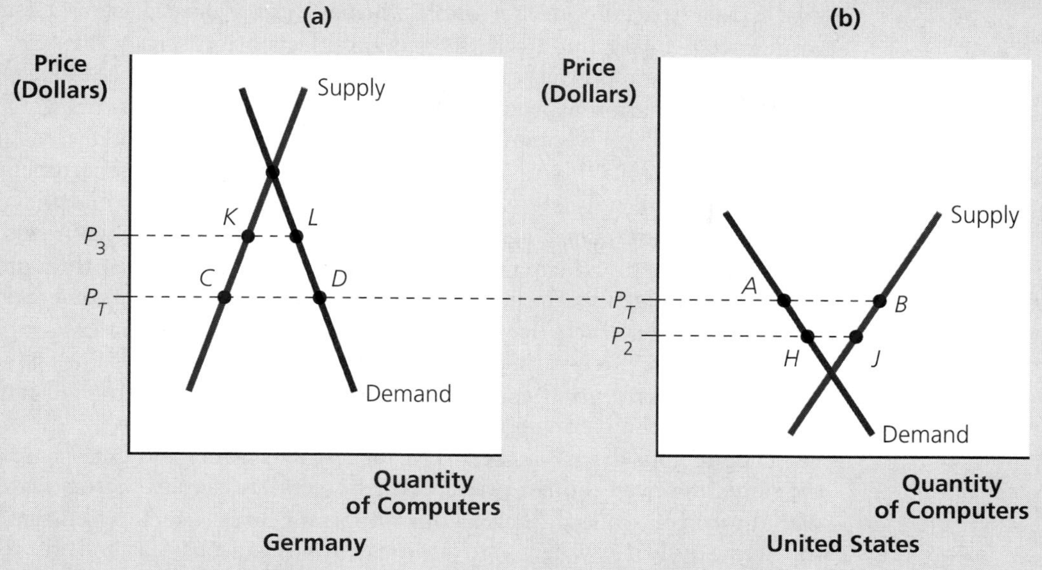

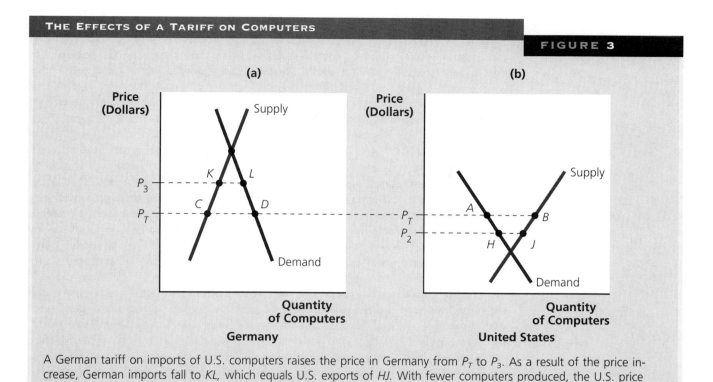

A German tariff on imports of U.S. computers raises the price in Germany from P_T to P_3. As a result of the price increase, German imports fall to *KL*, which equals U.S. exports of *HJ*. With fewer computers produced, the U.S. price falls to P_2.

United States exports *AB* computers, while Germany imports the same number (represented by the distance *CD* in the German market). Now, suppose Germany imposes a tariff on U.S. computers that raises the price there to P_3. In Germany, the rise in price will increase the quantity of computers supplied and decrease the quantity demanded. German imports are accordingly cut back to *KL*. In the United States, exports must shrink to the new level of German imports, so the new U.S. export level is *HJ*. With fewer computers exported, the price in the U.S. market will fall to P_2.

As you can see, German consumers are worse off—they pay a higher price for fewer computers. German producers, on the other hand, are much better off: They sell more computers at a higher price. In the United States, the impact is the opposite: The price of computers falls, so U.S. producers lose and U.S. consumers gain.

But we also know this: Since the volume of trade has decreased, the gains from trade according to comparative advantage have been reduced as well. Both countries, as a whole, are worse off as a result of the tariff:

Tariffs reduce the volume of trade and raise the domestic prices of imported goods. In the country that imposes the tariff, producers gain and consumers lose. But the world as a whole loses, because tariffs decrease the volume of trade and therefore decrease the gains from trade.

MARKETS AND EQUILIBRIUM

QUOTAS

QUOTA A limit on the physical volume of imports.

A **quota** is a government decree that limits the imports of a good to a specified maximum physical quantity, such as 500,000 Ukrainian coats per year. Because the goal is to restrict imports, a quota is usually set below the level of imports that would occur under free trade. Its general effects are precisely the same as those of a tariff: Domestic producers and their workers are helped, domestic consumers are hurt, and the nation as a whole loses part of Ricardo's net benefit.

Figure 3, which we used to illustrate tariffs, can also be used to analyze the impact of a quota. In this case, we suppose that the German government simply decrees that it will only allow *KL* computers into the country and that it is able to enforce this quota. Once again, the market price in Germany will rise to P_3. (Why? Because at any price lower than P_3, total imports of *KL* plus the domestic quantity supplied, given by the supply curve, would be smaller than quantity demanded. This would cause the price to rise.) And once again, the decrease in German imports translates into a shrinkage in U.S. exports—down to *HJ*. Both countries' computer markets end up in exactly the same place as if Germany had imposed a tariff that raised the German price to P_3.

The previous discussion seems to suggest that tariffs and quotas are pretty much the same. But even though prices in the two countries may end up at the same level with a tariff or a quota, there is one important difference between these two trade-restricting policies. When a government imposes a tariff, it collects some revenue every time a good is imported. (See if you can determine the amount of tariff revenue in Figure 3.) This revenue can be used to fund government programs or reduce other taxes, to the benefit of the country as a whole. When a government imposes a quota, however, it gains no revenue at all.[3]

Quotas have effects similar to tariffs—they reduce the quantity of imports and raise domestic prices. While both measures help domestic producers, they reduce the benefits of trade to the nation as a whole. However, a tariff has one saving grace: increased government revenue.

Economists, who generally oppose measures such as quotas and tariffs to restrict trade, argue that, if one of these devices must be used, tariffs are the better choice. While both policies reduce the gains that countries can enjoy from specializing and trading with each other, the tariff provides some compensation in the form of additional government revenue.

PROTECTIONISM

PROTECTIONISM The belief that a nation's industries should be protected from foreign competition.

This chapter has outlined the *gains* that arise from international trade, but it has also outlined some of the *pain* trade can cause to different groups within a country. While the country as a whole benefits, some citizens in both the exporting and importing countries are harmed. The groups who suffer from trade with other nations have developed a number of arguments against free trade. Together, these arguments form a position known as **protectionism**—the belief that a nation's industries should be *protected* from free trade with other nations. Some protectionist arguments are rather sophisticated and require careful consideration. We'll consider some of these a bit later. But antitrade groups have also promulgated a number of myths to support their protectionist beliefs. Let's consider some of these myths.

3 In theory, a government could auction off the right to import, and in this way collect just as much revenue under a quota as it could under a tariff. However, this does not happen in the United States.

MYTHS ABOUT FREE TRADE

"A HIGH-WAGE COUNTRY CANNOT AFFORD FREE TRADE WITH A LOW-WAGE COUNTRY. THE HIGH-WAGE COUNTRY WILL EITHER BE UNDERSOLD IN EVERYTHING AND LOSE ALL OF ITS INDUSTRIES, OR ELSE ITS WORKERS WILL HAVE TO ACCEPT EQUALLY LOW WAGES AND EQUALLY LOW LIVING STANDARDS."

It's true that some countries have much higher wages than others. Here are 1995 figures for average hourly wages, including benefits such as holiday pay and health insurance: Germany $31.88; Japan $23.66; United States $17.20; Mexico $1.51; Russia $0.60; China and India $0.25. As you can see, the wealthier, more developed countries have wages far higher than poorer, less developed countries. This leads to the fear that the poorer countries will be able to charge lower prices for their goods, putting American workers out of jobs unless they, too, agree to work for low wages. But this argument is incorrect, for two reasons. First, workers in different countries are not equally productive. American workers, for example, are more highly skilled than their counterparts in China and work with more sophisticated machinery than they do. If an American could produce 80 times as much output as a Chinese worker in an hour, then even though wages in the United States are about 70 times greater, cost *per unit* produced would still be lower in the United States.

But even if cost per unit *were* lower in China, there is another, more basic argument against the fear of a general job loss or falling wages in the United States: comparative advantage. Let's take an extreme case. Suppose that labor productivity were the same in the United States and China, so that China—with lower wages—could produce *everything* more cheaply than the United States could. Both would still gain if China specialized in products in which its cost advantage was relatively large and the United States specialized in goods in which China's cost advantage was relatively small. That is, even though China would have an absolute advantage in everything, the United States would still have a comparative advantage in some things. The mutual gains from trade arise not from absolute advantage, but from comparative advantage.

"A LOW-PRODUCTIVITY COUNTRY CANNOT AFFORD FREE TRADE WITH A HIGH-PRODUCTIVITY COUNTRY. THE FORMER WILL BE CLOBBERED BY THE LATTER AND LOSE ALL OF ITS INDUSTRIES."

This argument is the flip side of the first myth. Here, it is the poorer, less developed country that is supposedly harmed by trade with a richer country. But this myth, like the first myth, confuses absolute advantage with comparative advantage. Suppose the high-productivity country (say, the United States) could produce *every* good at lower cost per unit than the low-productivity country (say, China). Once again, the low-productivity country would *still* have a comparative advantage in *some* goods. It could then gain, just as do Germany and the United States, by producing those goods and trading with the high-productivity country.

To make the point even clearer, let's bring it closer to home. Suppose there is a small, poor town in the United States where workers are relatively uneducated and work with little capital equipment, so their productivity is very low. Would the residents of this town be better off sealing their borders and not trading with the rest of the United States, which has higher productivity? Before you answer, think what this would mean: The residents of the poor town would have to produce everything on their own—grow their own food, make their own cars and television sets, and even make their own movies and television programs. Clearly, they would be worse off in isolation. And what is true *within* a country is also true *between* different countries: Closing off trade will make a nation, as a whole, worse off, regardless of its level of wages or productivity; trading with other nations makes it better off.

"In Recent Times, America's Unskilled Workers Have Suffered Because of Ever-Expanding Trade Between the United States and Other Countries."

True enough, unskilled workers have been losing ground since around 1980, for *some* reason. College graduates have enjoyed growing purchasing power from their earnings, while those with only a grade school education have lost about 25 percent of their 1980 purchasing power. Rising trade with low-wage countries has been blamed for this adverse trend.

Our discussion earlier in this chapter tells us where to look for effects that come through trade. If the opening of trade has harmed low-skilled workers in the United States, it has done so by lowering the prices of products that employ large numbers of those workers in this country. For example, if the United States has been flooded recently with cheap clothes, then we should see a decline in U.S. clothing prices and reductions in earnings among clothing workers. A recent study taking this approach found almost no change in the relative prices of products in this country that employ large numbers of unskilled workers. Studies that take the different approach of asking whether categories of imports that have grown rapidly also account for large amounts of unskilled employment have found only modest effects. In general, economists who have looked at the relation between changes in trade patterns and the depressed earnings of unskilled American workers have concluded that foreign trade is a small contributor.[3]

SOPHISTICATED ARGUMENTS FOR PROTECTION

While most of the protectionist arguments we read in the media are based on a misunderstanding of comparative advantage, some more recent arguments for protecting domestic industries are based on a more sophisticated understanding of how markets work. These arguments have become collectively known as *strategic trade policy*. According to its proponents, a nation can benefit in some circumstances by assisting certain "strategic" industries that can provide benefits to society as a whole, but that may not thrive in an environment of free trade.

Strategic trade policy is most effective in situations where a market is dominated by a few large firms.[4] With few firms, the forces of competition—which ordinarily reduce profits in an industry to very low levels—will not operate. Therefore, each firm in the industry may earn high profits. These profits benefit not only the owners of the firm, but also the nation more generally, since the government will be able

3 The studies include Robert Z. Lawrence and Matthew J. Slaughter, "Trade and U.S. Wages: Giant Sucking Sound or Small Hiccup?" *Brookings Papers on Economic Activity: Microeconomics,* 2:1993, pp. 161–210, and Jeffrey D. Sachs and Howard J. Shatz, "Trade and Jobs in U.S. Manufacturing," *Brookings Papers on Economic Activity,* 1:1994, pp. 1–84.

4 Why are there only a few firms in the market? If you've studied *microeconomics,* you've already learned some of the reasons. These include economies of scale, legal barriers like patent protection, and strategic behavior on the part of existing firms to keep out competitors.

to capture some of the profit with the corporate profits tax. When a government helps an industry compete internationally, it increases the likelihood that high profits—and the resulting general benefits—will be shifted from a foreign country to its own country. Thus, interfering with free trade—through quotas, tariffs, or even a direct subsidy to domestic firms—might actually benefit the country as a whole.

An argument related to strategic trade policy is the *infant industry argument*. This argument begins with a simple observation: In order to enjoy the full benefits of trade, markets must allocate resources toward those goods in which a nation has a comparative advantage. This includes not only markets for goods and markets for resources such as labor and land, but also *financial markets,* where firms obtain funds for new products. But in some countries—especially developing countries—financial markets do not work very well. Poor legal systems or incomplete information about firms and products may prevent a new industry from obtaining financing, even though the country would have a comparative advantage in that industry once it was formed. In this case, government assistance to the "infant industry" may be warranted until the industry can "stand on its own feet."

Strategic trade policy and support for infant industries are controversial. Opponents of these ideas stress three problems:

1. Once the principle of government assistance to an industry is accepted, special-interest groups will lobby to get the assistance, whether it benefits the general public or not.
2. When one country provides assistance to an industry, other nations may respond in kind. If they respond with tariffs and quotas of their own, the result is a shrinking volume of world trade and falling living standards. If subsidies are used to support a strategic industry, and another country responds with its own subsidies, then both governments lose revenue, and neither gains the sought-after profits.
3. Strategic trade policy assumes that the government has the information to determine which industries, infant or otherwise, are truly strategic and which are not.

This last point—insufficient information—is the one that opponents of free trade policy cite most often. They point to the European firm Airbus as an example of a costly government mistake. During the 1970s, Airbus received $1.5 billion from European governments to help it produce the A300 aircraft, in competition with Boeing's 767 aircraft. In the end, in spite of the subsidy, Airbus suffered a loss, Boeing continued to produce the 767, and European governments had spent a lot of money with very little return.

Still, the arguments related to strategic trade policy suggest that government protection or assistance *may* be warranted in some circumstances, even if putting this support into practice proves difficult. Moreover, the arguments help to remind us of the conditions under which free trade is most beneficial to a nation:

Production is most likely to reflect the principle of comparative advantage when firms can obtain funds for investment projects and when they can freely enter industries that are profitable. Thus, free trade, without government intervention, works best when markets are working well.

MARKETS AND EQUILIBRIUM

This may explain, in part, why the United States, where markets function relatively well, has for decades been among the strongest supporters of the free-trade ideal.

Does the U.S. economy benefit from foreign trade? Learn more about the arguments in the Policy Debates section of the ECONOMICS web site.
Address:
http://hall-lieb.swcollege.com

TRADE RESTRICTIONS IN THE UNITED STATES

USING THE THEORY

No country has completely free trade with the rest of the world; every government limits trade in one way or another. And in spite of its strong protrade stance, the United States has restricted imports in many cases. Among the trade restrictions currently imposed by the U.S. government are the following:

- Foreign airlines may not carry domestic passengers from one point to another inside the United States.
- Canadian lumber can enter the United States only in limited quantities.
- Imports of fibers and textiles are tightly limited.
- Importers of many products have to pay tariffs.
- The amount of sugar that can be imported is tightly limited and is far less than would occur with free trade.

In addition, the government often takes temporary steps to limit certain kinds of imports or to raise their prices. For example, the United States has required Japan to limit exports of automobiles during certain periods, and the government required Asian manufacturers of computer memory chips to double the U.S. prices of their products for a time. Again, these practices, though restrictive, are not nearly as severe as those of many other governments: Japanese carmakers sell millions of cars in the United States, but almost none in Europe, where there is a flat ban on imports of their cars.

As we learned earlier in the chapter (see Table 8), opening up trade to a foreign country with a comparative advantage in a product is against the interest of domestic makers of that product. But, though protection is good for the makers of the protected product, it is bad for consumers. As a result, there is a tug-of-war between consumer interests and producer interests. Generally, in the United States, consumers have won the tug-of-war. Because so many imports are allowed into the country free of tariffs, the average U.S. tariff rate for all imports (which once approached 50 percent) was down to 3 percent by the mid-1990s. Thus, U.S. consumers enjoy the benefits of importing many of the products listed in Table 5—olive oil from Spain, tomatoes from Mexico, and cars and VCRs from Japan. Consumers also benefit from products made from imported oil, aluminum, timber, and steel.

On the other side of the ledger, U.S. consumers suffer, and U.S. producers gain, from some persistent quotas, such as the sugar import quota. As you saw in Figure 3, a quota on imports raises the price to domestic residents. It is no surprise that the price of sugar in the United States is about ten times higher than the world market price. But quotas—like the U.S. sugar quota—create further problems of their own. First, because a quota raises the domestic price above prices elsewhere in the world, importers have an incentive to buy the good on the international market, violating the quota. The U.S. sugar quota, for example, has to be enforced by the "sugar police"—customs inspectors who prevent the importation of the extra sugar that would eliminate the price differential and reduce the price of sugar in the United States to the free-trade price, like P_T in Figure 3. In this way, valuable resources—such as the labor of the sugar police—are used up to enforce the quota.

The second problem with a quota is how to decide who gets to import the restricted good. Importers have a lot to gain, since they can buy at the lower world price and sell at the artificially high domestic price. One logical approach would be to auction tickets that entitled the holder to import a given amount of the restricted good. Then the government would collect the difference between the U.S.

and world price as revenue, making the quota similar to a tariff in its total impact. That approach is never used in practice. Instead, the right to import is typically *given* away by the government, as in the case of sugar.

The impact of quotas in general can be understood by looking closely at the harm caused by the U.S. sugar quota:

1. It denies U.S. consumers the benefits of free trade—the ability to buy sugar cheaply from countries that have comparative advantages in sugar production.
2. It lowers the incomes of sugar producers in the generally poor countries in tropical regions that have comparative advantages in sugar production.
3. The gap between the U.S. and world market price creates an incentive for illegal and wasteful activities, such as smuggling sugar, bribing the sugar police, or importing candy and refining it back into sugar. (Some people are actually in jail for defying the sugar import quota.)
4. The government's power to grant sugar-importing rights causes people to waste resources lobbying for those rights, and it may cause corruption of the government officials in charge.
5. The government does not collect revenue that it could.

Who benefits from the sugar quota? A look back at Table 8 provides the answer: U.S. sugar producers and foreign sugar consumers. But as the principle of comparative advantage shows, the world as a whole is the loser.

SUMMARY

International specialization and trade enable people throughout the world to enjoy greater production and higher living standards than would otherwise be possible. The benefits of unrestrained international trade can be traced back to the idea of comparative advantage. Mutually beneficial trade is possible whenever one country can produce a good at a lower opportunity cost than its trading partner can. Whenever opportunity costs differ, countries can specialize according to their comparative advantage, trade with each other, and end up consuming more.

Despite the net benefits to each nation as a whole, some groups within each country lose while others gain. When trade leads to increased exports, domestic consumers will be made worse off. When imports increase as a result of trade, domestic producers suffer. The losers often encourage government to block or reduce trade through the use of tariffs—taxes on imported goods—and quotas—limits on the volume of imports.

A variety of arguments have been proposed in support of protectionism. Some are clearly invalid and fail to recognize that employment patterns and wage differentials reflect productivity differences between nations. More sophisticated arguments include strategic trade policy—the notion that governments should assist certain strategic industries—and the idea of protecting "infant" industries when financial markets are imperfect.

KEY TERMS

exports
imports
absolute advantage
comparative advantage
terms of trade
tariff
quota
protectionism

REVIEW QUESTIONS

1. Describe the theory of comparative advantage.
2. What is the difference between absolute advantage and comparative advantage?
3. What are the terms of trade and why are they important?
4. What are the sources of comparative advantage?

5. What is a tariff? What are its main economic effects? How does a quota differ from a tariff?

6. What arguments have been made in support of protectionism? Which of them may be valid, and under what circumstances?

7. List the ways in which a quota on imported coffee would harm the nation that imposes it.

PROBLEMS AND EXERCISES

Questions 1 through 3 refer to the following situation: Suppose two countries—Andorra and Monaco—have equal amounts (100 units) of labor, which is the only resource used to produce two goods, watches and music boxes. Three alternative sets of production possibilities frontiers for the two goods are shown in Figures A, B, and C on page 469. Answer the following questions:

1. In each of the three situations, determine which country (if either) has an absolute advantage in which good. Do this by determining how much labor it takes to produce each good in each country.

2. In each of the three situations, determine which country (if either) has a comparative advantage in which good. Do this by determining the opportunity cost of producing each good in each country.

3. Assume that the terms of trade are 1:1 on the world market, and that initially each country produces at the midpoint of its production possibilities frontier. For the pair of PPFs shown in Figure A, give an example in which trade based upon specialization and comparative advantage yields gains to at least one of the countries while leaving the other country no worse off.

4. The following table gives information about the supply and demand for beef in Paraguay and Uruguay. (You may wish to draw the supply and demand curves for each country to help you visualize what is happening.)

Paraguay			*Uruguay*		
Price	*Quantity Supplied*	*Quantity Demanded*	*Price*	*Quantity Supplied*	*Quantity Demanded*
0	0	1200	0	0	1800
5	200	1000	5	0	1600
10	400	800	10	0	1400
15	600	600	15	0	1200
20	800	400	20	200	1000
25	1000	200	25	400	800
30	1200	0	30	600	600
35	1400	0	35	800	400
40	1600	0	40	1000	200
45	1800	0	45	1200	0

a. In the absence of trade, what is the equilibrium price and quantity in Paraguay? In Uruguay?
b. If the two countries begin to trade, what will happen to the price of beef? How many sides of beef will be purchased in Paraguay and how many in Uruguay at that price?
c. How many sides of beef will be produced in Paraguay and how many in Uruguay? Why is there a difference between quantity purchased and quantity produced in each country?
d. Who benefits and who loses from the opening of trade between these two countries?

5. Use the data on supply and demand given in question 4 to answer the following questions:
a. Suppose that Uruguay imposed a tariff that raised the price of beef imported from Paraguay to $25 per side. What would happen to beef consumption in Uruguay? To beef production there? How much beef would be imported from Paraguay?

(A)

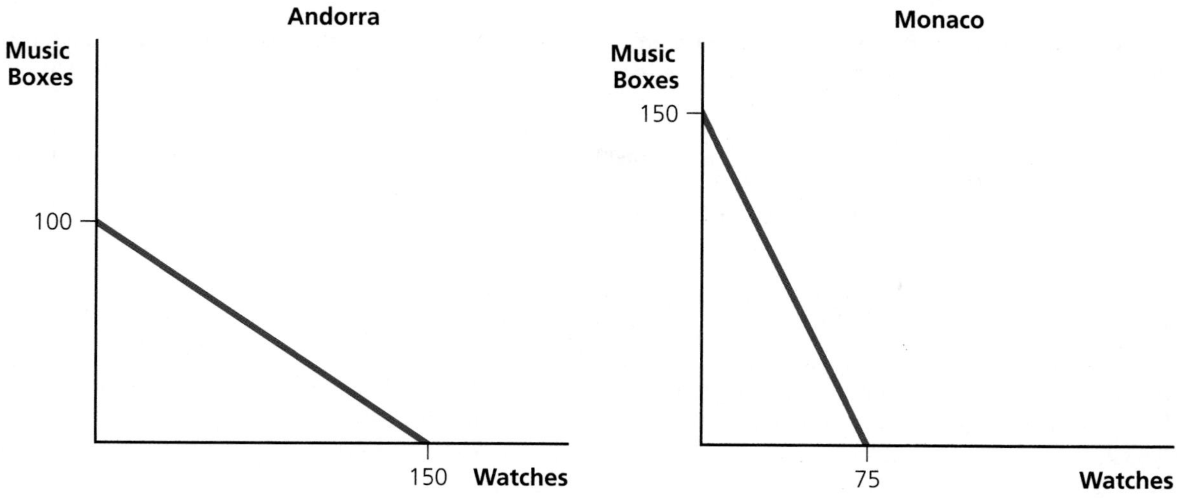
Andorra
Music Boxes
100
150
Watches
Monaco
Music Boxes
150
75
Watches

(B)

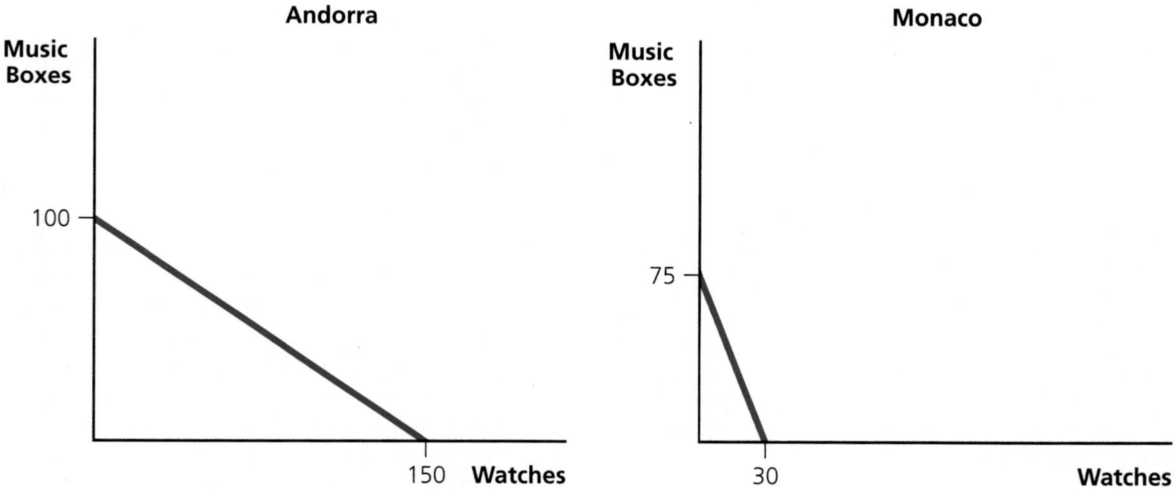
Andorra
Music Boxes
100
150
Watches
Monaco
Music Boxes
75
30
Watches

(C)

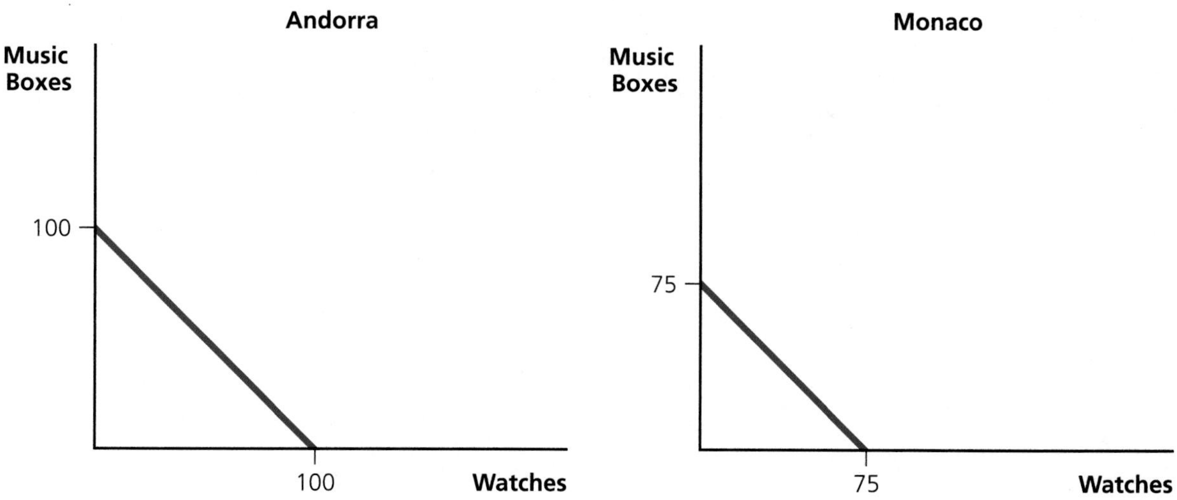
Andorra
Music Boxes
100
100
Watches
Monaco
Music Boxes
75
75
Watches

b. How would the tariff affect Paraguay? What would happen to the price of beef there after Uruguay imposed its tariff? How would domestic production and consumption be affected?
c. Suppose, instead, that Uruguay imposed a quota on import of beef from Paraguay—only 200 sides of beef can be imported each year. What would happen to the price of beef in Uruguay? What would happen to beef consumption in Uruguay? To beef production there?
d. How would the quota affect Paraguay? What would happen to the price of beef there after Uruguay imposed its quota? How would domestic production and consumption be affected?

CHALLENGE QUESTION

Suppose that the Marshall Islands does not trade with the outside world. It has a competitive domestic market for VCRs. The market supply and demand curves are reflected in this table:

Price ($/VCR)	*Quantity Demanded*	*Quantity Supplied*
500	0	500
400	100	400
300	200	300
200	300	200
100	400	100
0	500	0

a. Plot the supply and demand curves and determine the domestic equilibrium price and quantity.
b. Suddenly, the islanders discover the virtues of free exchange and begin trading with the outside world. The Marshall Islands is a very small country, and so its trading has no effect on the price established in the world market. It can import as many VCRs as it wishes at the world price of $100 per VCR. In this situation, how many VCRs will be purchased in the Marshall Islands? How many will be produced there? How many will be imported?
c. After protests from domestic producers, the government decides to impose a tariff of $100 per imported VCR. Now how many VCRs will be purchased in the Marshall Islands? How many will be produced there? How many will be imported?
d. What is the government's revenue from the tariff described in part (c)?

Visit the U.S. Department of Commerce, International Trade Administration (ITA).
a. Examine the industry and market information for computers and software (http://www.ita.doc.gov/industry/computers/). Given this information, does domestic and international regulation favor or hinder free trade? Why or why not?
b. Visit the Office of Trade and Economic Analysis (OTEA), a division of the ITA, and examine the *U.S. Global Trade Outlook 1995–2000* report (http://www.ita.doc.gov/industry/otea/gto/global.html/). In the view of the OTEA, will foreign trade improve or worsen as we approach the year 2000? What reasons does the OTEA give for this prediction?
c. Recall your answer in (a). What economic and trade forecast does the *U.S. Global Trade Outlook 1995–2000* report make for the computer and software industry? What reasons are given for this forecast?

CHAPTER

17

EXCHANGE RATES AND OPEN-ECONOMY MACROECONOMICS

CHAPTER OUTLINE

If you've ever traveled to a foreign country, you were a direct participant in the **foreign exchange market**—a market in which one country's currency is traded for that of another. For example, if you traveled to Mexico, you might have stopped near the border to exchange some dollars for Mexican pesos, so that you could buy things in Mexico. By exchanging currencies, you were a trader in a particular foreign exchange market—the market for exchanging dollars and pesos.

Even if you have never traveled abroad, you've been involved, at least indirectly, in all kinds of foreign exchange dealings. For example, suppose you buy a bottle of Bertolli extra-virgin olive oil in the United States, where you pay with dollars. Except for shipping and retailing services, the resources used to produce that bottle of olive oil were Italian. An Italian farmer grew the olives; Italian truckers transported them to the Bertolli factory in Italy; and Italian workers, machinery, and raw materials were used to bottle the oil. The Italian resource owners—those who provided labor, land, and capital—want to be paid in Italian lire, regardless of who buys the final product. After all, they live in Italy, so they need lire to buy things there. But you, as an American, want to pay for your bottle of olive oil with dollars.

Let's think about this for a moment. You pay for olive oil in dollars, but the Italian resource owners are paid in lire. How is this possible?

The answer: *Someone,* here or abroad, uses the foreign exchange market to exchange dollars for lire. Most likely, your supermarket pays some of the dollars you spend to a U.S. distributor of Italian olive oil, who, in turn, sends a check in dollars, to the Bertolli company in Italy. Bertolli, in turn, turns the check over to an Italian bank, which exchanges them for lire. In this case, the actual changing of dollars into lire takes place in an Italian bank.

Alternatively, the U.S. distributor might itself exchange dollars for lire at a bank in the United States and then pay Bertolli directly with lire. Regardless of the pre-

FOREIGN EXCHANGE MARKET The market in which one country's currency is traded for another country's.

cise procedure, somehow, somewhere in the world, dollars are exchanged for lire. Otherwise, you could not purchase Italian olive oil with dollars.

In this chapter, we'll look at the markets in which Americans exchange dollars for other currencies. We'll also expand our macroeconomic analysis to include trading with other nations. As you'll see, what happens in the foreign exchange market affects the economy, and changes in the economy affect the foreign exchange market. We will need to revisit fiscal and monetary policy in this chapter, since they have additional effects when we incorporate international trade. Finally, in the "Using the Theory" section, you'll see how the tools of the chapter can help us understand the origins of the ongoing U.S. trade deficit.

FOREIGN EXCHANGE MARKETS AND EXCHANGE RATES

Every day, all over the world, more than a hundred different national currencies are exchanged for one another in banks, hotels, stores, and kiosks in airports and train stations. Traders exchange dollars for Mexican pesos, Japanese yen, French francs, Indian rupees, Chinese yuan, and so on. In addition, traders exchange each of these foreign currencies for one another: pesos for francs, yen for yuan, francs for yen. . . . There are literally thousands of combinations. How can we hope to make sense of these markets, and come up with some general conclusions about how they operate and how they affect us?

Our basic approach is to regard the exchange of each pair of currencies as a separate market. That is, there is one market in which dollars are exchanged for French francs, another in which Angolan kwanzas trade for German marks, and so on. The physical locations where the trading takes place don't matter: Whether you exchange your dollars for francs in France, in the United States, or even in Ecuador, you are a trader in the same dollar–franc market.

EXCHANGE RATE The amount of one country's currency that is traded for one unit of another country's currency.

In any foreign exchange market, the rate at which one currency is traded for another is called the **exchange rate** between those two currencies. For example, if you happened to trade dollars for British pounds on June 25, 1997, each British pound would have cost you about $1.66. On that day, the exchange rate was $1.66 per pound.

DOLLARS PER POUND OR POUNDS PER DOLLAR?

Table 1 lists exchange rates between the dollar and various foreign currencies on a particular day in 1997. But notice that there are two different exchange rates listed for each currency. That's because we can think of any exchange rate in two ways: as so many units of foreign currency per dollar, or so many dollars per unit of foreign currency. For example, the table shows the exchange rate between the British pound and the dollar as 0.6011 pounds per dollar, or 1.6636 dollars per pound. We can always obtain one form of the exchange rate from the other by taking its reciprocal: $1/0.6011 = 1.6636$, and $1/1.6636 = 0.6011$.

In this chapter, we'll always define the exchange rate as "dollars per unit of foreign currency," as in the last column of the table. That way, from the American point of view, the exchange rate is just another price. In other words, the same way you pay a certain number of dollars for a gallon of gasoline (the price of gas), so, too, you pay a certain number of dollars for a British pound (the price of pounds).

The exchange rate is the price of foreign currency in dollars.

FOREIGN EXCHANGE RATES, JUNE 25, 1997

TABLE 1

Country	Name of Currency	Symbol	Units of Foreign Currency per Dollar	Dollars per Unit of Foreign Currency
Brazil	real	R	1.0764	$0.9290
China	yuan	Y	8.3214	0.1202
France	franc	F	5.8145	0.1720
Germany	mark	DM	1.7235	0.5802
Great Britain	pound	£	0.6011	1.6636
India	rupee	R	35.810	0.0279
Italy	lira	L	1,682.00	0.000595
Japan	yen	¥	113.80	0.008787
Mexico	peso	P	7.9420	0.125913
Russia	ruble	R	5,761.00	0.000174

Table 1 raises some important questions: Why, in early 1997, did a pound cost $1.66? Why not $1? Or $5? Why did one Japanese yen cost a little less than a penny? And a Russian ruble about one-fiftieth of a penny?

The answer to these questions certainly affects Americans who travel abroad. Suppose you are staying in a hotel in London that costs 100 pounds per night. If the price of the pound is $1, the hotel room will cost you $100, but if the price is $5, the room will cost you $500. And exchange rates affect Americans who stay at home, too: They influence the prices of many goods we buy in the United States, they help determine which of our industries will expand and which will contract, and they affect the wages and salaries that we earn from our jobs.

How are all these exchange rates determined? In most cases, they are determined by the familiar forces of supply and demand. As in other markets, each foreign exchange market reaches an equilibrium at which the quantity of foreign exchange demanded is equal to the quantity supplied.

In the next several sections, we'll build a model of supply and demand for a representative foreign exchange market: the one in which U.S. dollars are exchanged for British pounds. Taking the American point of view, we'll call this simply "the market for pounds." The other currency being traded—the dollar—will always be implicit.

THE DEMAND FOR BRITISH POUNDS

To analyze the demand for pounds, we start with a very basic question: *Who* is demanding them? The simple answer is, anyone who has dollars and wants to exchange them for pounds.

In the real world, this includes many different parties, residing in many different countries. But the most important buyers of pounds in the pound–dollar market will be American households and businesses. When Americans want to buy things from Britain, they will need to acquire pounds. And to buy them, they will offer what they already have: U.S. dollars. Over any given period, then, we expect Americans to do most of the buying in the market for pounds. To keep our analy-

FIGURE 1 THE DEMAND FOR BRITISH POUNDS

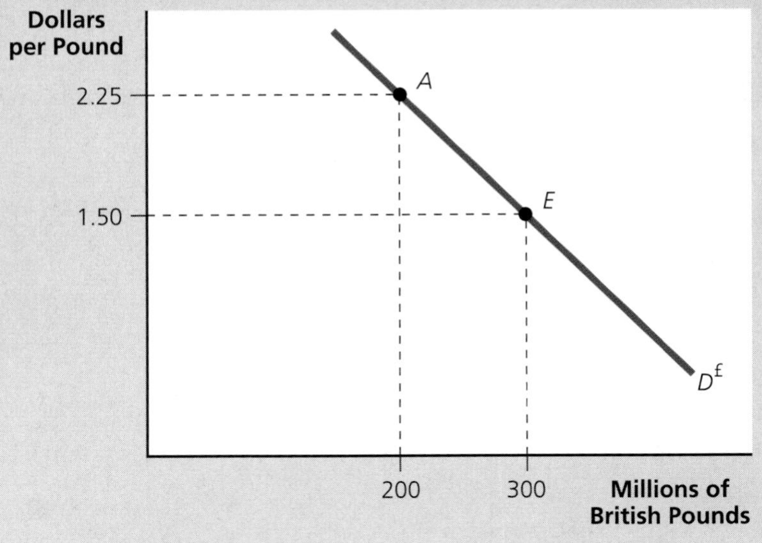

Americans demand British pounds in order to buy British goods and services and British assets. At lower exchange rates, British goods and services become less expensive to American buyers (in dollar terms). Thus, Americans buy more of those items and demand more British pounds to carry out their transactions. The demand for pounds curve slopes downward.

sis simple, we'll focus on just these American buyers. We'll also—for now—ignore any demand for pounds by the U.S. government.

In our model of the market for pounds, we assume that American households and businesses are the only buyers.

Why do Americans want to buy pounds? There are two reasons:

- *To buy goods and services from British firms.* Americans buy sweaters knit in Edinburgh, airline tickets sold by Virgin Airways, and insurance services offered by Lloyd's. American tourists also stay in British hotels, use British taxis, and eat at British restaurants. To buy goods and services from British firms, Americans need to acquire pounds in order to pay for them.
- *To buy British assets.* Americans buy British stocks, British corporate or government bonds, and British real estate. In each case, the British seller will want to be paid in pounds, so the American buyer will have to acquire them.

THE DEMAND FOR POUNDS CURVE

DEMAND CURVE FOR FOREIGN CURRENCY A curve indicating the quantity of a specific foreign currency that Americans will want to buy, during a given period, at each different exchange rate.

Figure 1 shows an example of a **demand curve for foreign currency**, in this case, the demand curve for pounds. The curve tells us *the quantity of pounds Americans will want to buy in any given period, at each different exchange rate.* Notice that the curve slopes downward: The lower the exchange rate, the greater is the quantity of pounds demanded. For example, at an exchange rate of $2.25 per pound, Americans would want to purchase £200 million (point *A*). If the exchange rate fell to $1.50 per pound, Americans would want to buy £300 million (point *E*).

Why does a lower exchange rate—a lower price for the pound—make Americans want to buy more of them? Because at a lower price for the pound, British goods and services are less expensive to American buyers. Remember that Americans think

SHIFTS IN THE DEMAND FOR POUNDS CURVE

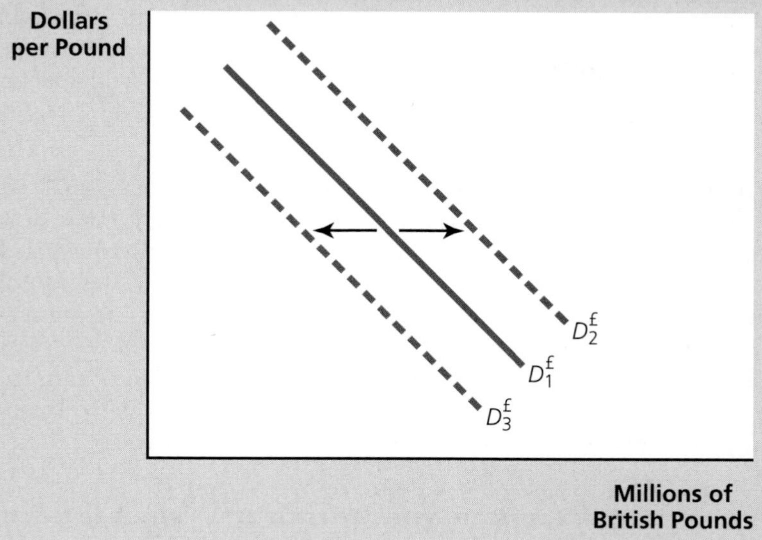

FIGURE 2

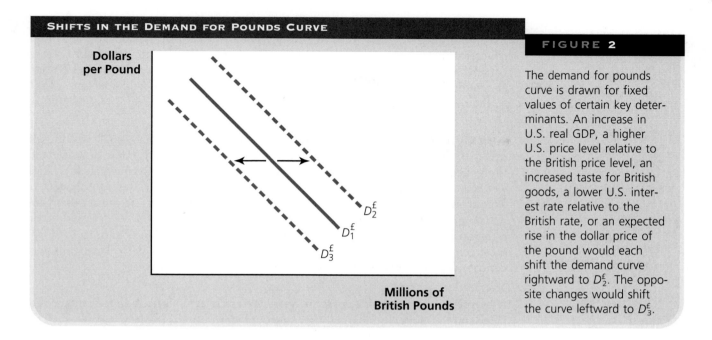

The demand for pounds curve is drawn for fixed values of certain key determinants. An increase in U.S. real GDP, a higher U.S. price level relative to the British price level, an increased taste for British goods, a lower U.S. interest rate relative to the British rate, or an expected rise in the dollar price of the pound would each shift the demand curve rightward to $D_2^£$. The opposite changes would shift the curve leftward to $D_3^£$.

of prices in dollar terms. A British compact disc that costs £10 will cost an American $22.50 at an exchange rate of $2.25 per pound, but only $15 if the exchange rate is $1.50 per pound. Thus, the lower the price of the pound, the more British goods Americans will buy, and the more pounds they will need to make their purchases.

Thus, as we move rightward *along* the demand for pounds curve, as in the move from point *A* to point *E:*

Price of pounds ↓	→	British goods cheaper to Americans	→	Americans buy more British goods	→	Quantity of pounds demanded ↑

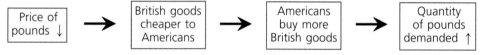

A rise in the exchange rate would have exactly the opposite effects: British goods would become more expensive to Americans, they would buy fewer of them, and they would demand fewer pounds.

SHIFTS IN THE DEMAND FOR POUNDS CURVE

In Figure 1, you saw that a change in the exchange rate moves us *along* the demand for pounds curve. But other variables besides the exchange rate influence the demand for pounds. If any of these other variables changes, the entire curve will shift. As we consider each of these variables, keep in mind that we are assuming that only one of them changes at a time; we suppose the rest to remain constant.

U.S. REAL GDP. Suppose real GDP and real income in the United States rise—say, because of a recovery from a recession. Then, Americans will buy more of everything, including goods and services from Britain. Thus, at any given exchange rate, Americans will demand more pounds. This is illustrated, in Figure 2, as a rightward shift of the demand curve from $D_1^£$ to $D_2^£$. A fall in U.S. real GDP will have the opposite effect, shifting the demand curve from $D_1^£$ to $D_3^£$.

RELATIVE PRICES IN THE UNITED STATES. Suppose that the U.S. price level rises by 8 percent, while that in Britain rises by 5 percent. Then, although both countries' prices have risen, U.S. prices have risen *relative* to British prices. As Americans shift from buying their own goods toward the relatively cheaper British goods, their demand for pounds rises (with the exchange rate held constant). That is, the demand for pounds curve would shift rightward.

AMERICANS' TASTES FOR BRITISH GOODS. All else being equal, would you prefer to drive a General Motors Aurora or a Jaguar? Do you prefer British-made films, like *Sense and Sensibility* and *Hamlet,* or America's offerings, such as *The Terminator* or *Lost World*? These are matters of taste, and tastes can change. If Americans come to develop a taste for British cars, films, tea, or music, their demand for these goods will increase, and the demand for pounds curve will shift rightward. In the opposite direction, the "mad cow disease" in Britain in 1996 almost completely eliminated the demand for British beef products by Americans and contributed to a leftward shift in the demand for pounds curve.

RELATIVE INTEREST RATE IN THE UNITED STATES. A few chapters ago (Monetary Policy), you learned that rates of return on all financial assets—such as stocks and bonds—tend to rise and fall together. Thus, a rise in a country's interest rate generally means a rise in rates of return on all of its assets. When a country's interest rate is high relative to that of another country, the first country's assets, *in general,* will have higher rates of return.

Now, suppose you're an American trying to decide whether to hold some of your wealth in British financial assets or American financial assets. You will look very carefully at the rate of return you expect to earn in each country. All else being equal, a lower U.S. interest rate, relative to the British rate, will make British assets more attractive to you. Accordingly, as you and other Americans demand more British assets, you will need more pounds to buy them. The demand for pounds curve will shift rightward.

EXPECTED CHANGES IN THE EXCHANGE RATE. Once again, imagine you are an American deciding whether to buy American or British bonds. Suppose British bonds pay 10 percent interest per year, while U.S. bonds pay 5 percent. All else equal, you would prefer the British bond, since it pays the higher rate of return. You would then exchange dollars for pounds at the going exchange rate and buy the bond.

But what if the price of the pound falls before the British bond becomes due? Then, when you cash in your British bond for pounds, and convert the pounds back into dollars, you'll be *selling your pounds at a lower price* than you bought them for. While you'd benefit from the higher interest rate on the British bond, you'd lose on the foreign currency transaction—buying pounds when their price is high, and selling them when their price is low. If the foreign currency loss is great enough, you would be better off with U.S. bonds, even though they pay a lower interest rate.

As you can see, it is not just relative interest rates that matter to wealth holders; it is also *expected changes in the exchange rate. The expectation that the price of the pound will fall* will make British assets less appealing to Americans, since they will expect a foreign currency loss, and *the demand for pounds curve will shift leftward.*

Effects of Key Changes on the Demand for Pounds Curve

TABLE 2

Exchange Rate (price of the pound):		U.S. GDP: American Tastes for British Goods: or Relative Prices in the United States:		Relative Interest Rates in the United States:		Expectation That the Price of the Pound Will:	
Increases	**Decreases**	**Increase**	**Decrease**	**Increase**	**Decrease**	**Rise**	**Fall**
Movement leftward along curve	Movement rightward along curve	Shifts rightward	Shifts leftward	Shifts leftward	Shifts rightward	Shifts rightward	Shifts leftward

The opposite holds as well. If Americans *expect the price of the pound to rise,* they will expect a foreign currency *gain* from buying British assets. This will cause the *demand for pounds curve to shift rightward.*

The Demand for Pounds Curve: A Summary

Table 2 summarizes our discussion of movements along, and shifts of, the demand for pounds curve.

THE SUPPLY OF BRITISH POUNDS

The demand for pounds is one side of the market in which dollars and pounds are exchanged. Now we turn our attention to the other side: the supply of pounds. And we'll begin with our basic question: *Who* is supplying pounds in this market?

In the real world, pounds are supplied from many sources. Anyone who has pounds, and wants to exchange them for dollars can come to the market and supply pounds. But the most important sellers of pounds are British households and businesses—who naturally have pounds and who want to make purchases from Americans with payment in dollars. To keep our analysis simple, will focus on just these British sellers, and we'll ignore—for now—any pounds supplied by the British government:

> *In our model of the market for pounds, we assume that British households and firms are the only sellers.*

The British supply pounds in the dollar–pound market for only one reason: because they want dollars. Thus, to ask why the British supply pounds is to ask why they want dollars. We can identify two separate reasons:

- *To buy goods and services from American firms.* The British buy airline tickets on United, computers made by IBM and Apple, and the rights to show films made in Hollywood. British tourists stay in American hotels and eat at American restaurants. The British demand dollars—and supply pounds—for all of these purchases.

FIGURE 3

THE SUPPLY OF BRITISH POUNDS

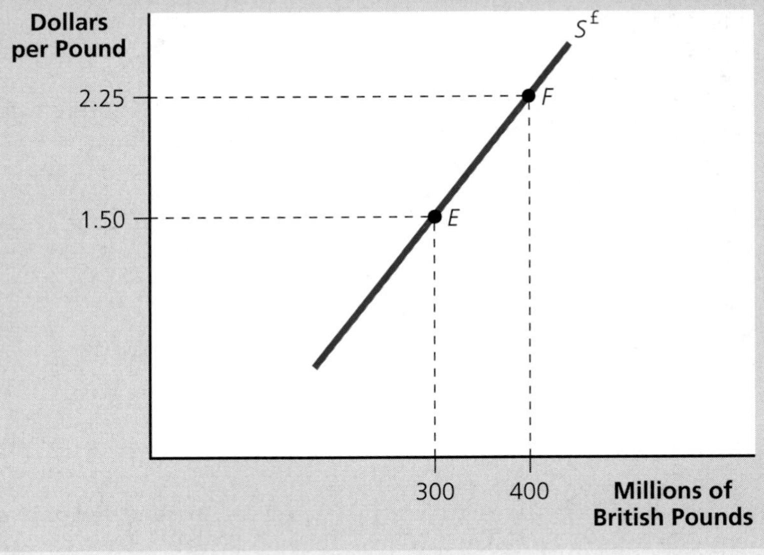

The British supply pounds in order to buy U.S. goods and services and U.S. assets. At higher exchange rates, U.S. goods and services become less expensive (in pounds) to British buyers. Thus, Britons buy more of those items and supply more British pounds to carry out their transactions. The supply of pounds curve slopes upward.

- *To buy American assets.* The British buy American stocks, American corporate or government bonds, and American real estate. In each case, the American seller will want to be paid in dollars, and the British buyer will acquire dollars by offering pounds.

THE SUPPLY OF POUNDS CURVE

SUPPLY CURVE FOR FOREIGN CURRENCY A curve indicating the quantity of a specific foreign currency that will be supplied, during a given period, at each different exchange rate.

Figure 3 shows an example of a **supply curve for foreign currency**—here, British pounds. The curve tells us *the quantity of pounds the British will want to sell in any given period, at each different exchange rate.* Notice that the curve slopes upward: The higher the exchange rate, the greater is the quantity of pounds supplied. For example, at an exchange rate of $1.50 per pound, the British would want to supply £300 million (point *E*). If the exchange rate rose to $2.25 per pound, they would supply £400 million (point *F*).

Why does a higher exchange rate—a higher price for the pound—make the British want to sell more of them? Because with a higher price for the pound, the British will get more dollars for each pound traded. This makes U.S. goods and services less expensive to British buyers, who will want to buy more of them. Of course, the more U.S. goods they buy, the more dollars they will need. Thus, the more pounds they will supply to obtain dollars.[1]

To summarize, as we move rightward *along* the supply of pounds curve, such as the move from point *E* to point *F:*

1 Actually, it is not a logical necessity for the supply of pounds curve to slope upward. Why not? When the price of the pound rises, it is true that the British will buy more U.S. goods and need more dollars to buy them. However, each dollar they buy costs *fewer pounds.* It might be that—even though the British obtain more dollars—they actually supply fewer pounds to get them at the higher exchange rate. In this case, the supply of pounds curve would slope downward. Economists believe, however, that a downward-sloping supply curve for foreign currency—while theoretically possible—is very rare.

SHIFTS IN THE SUPPLY OF POUNDS CURVE

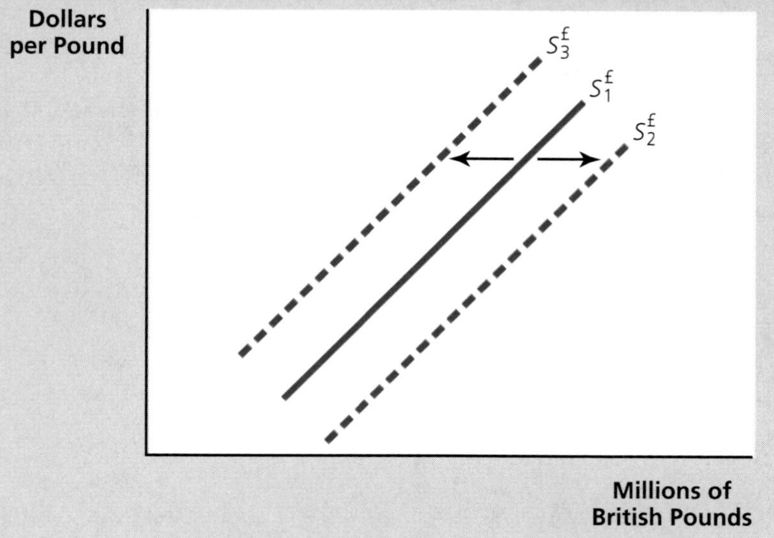

FIGURE 4

The supply of pounds curve is drawn for fixed values of certain key determinants. Higher real GDP in Britain, a lower U.S. price level relative to the British price level, a shift in British tastes toward American goods, a higher U.S. interest rate relative to the British rate, or an expected fall in the dollar price of the pound would each shift the supply curve rightward to $S_2^£$. The opposite changes would shift the curve leftward to $S_3^£$.

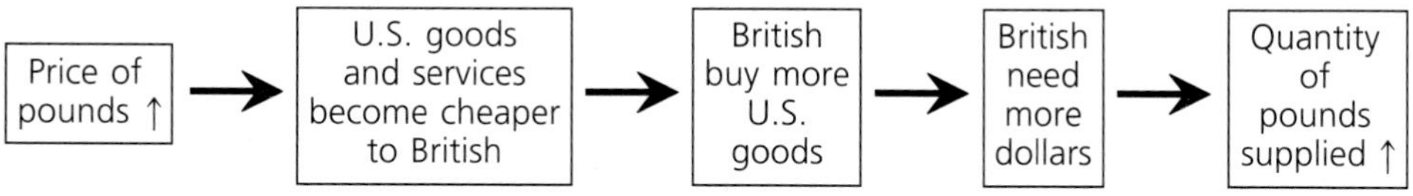

A fall in the price of the pound would have exactly the opposite effects: U.S. goods would become more expensive to the British, they would buy less of them and need fewer dollars, so they would supply fewer pounds.

SHIFTS IN THE SUPPLY OF POUNDS CURVE

When the exchange rate changes, we *move along* the supply curve for pounds. But other variables can affect the supply of pounds besides the exchange rate. When any of these variables changes, the supply of pounds curve will shift. In this section, we'll discuss the most important variables that can shift the supply curve.

REAL GDP IN BRITAIN. When real GDP and real income rise in Britain, British residents will buy more goods and services, including those produced in the United States. Since they will need more dollars to buy U.S. goods, they will supply more pounds. This is illustrated, in Figure 4, as a rightward shift of the supply curve, from $S_1^£$ to $S_2^£$. Similarly, if GDP falls in Britain, the supply curve will shift leftward, from $S_1^£$ to $S_3^£$.

RELATIVE PRICES IN THE UNITED STATES. Earlier, you learned that a rise in the relative price level in the U.S. makes British goods more attractive to Americans. But it also makes *American* goods *less* attractive to the British. Since the British will want to buy fewer U.S. goods, they will want fewer dollars and will supply fewer pounds. Thus, a rise in the U.S. price level relative to that in Britain shifts the supply of pounds curve leftward. A *fall* in relative prices in the U.S. will have the opposite effect, shifting the supply of pounds curve rightward.

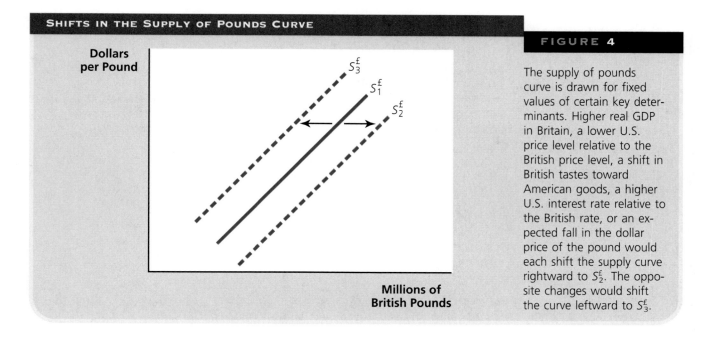

TABLE 3

EFFECTS OF KEY CHANGES ON THE SUPPLY OF POUNDS CURVE

Exchange Rate (price of the pound):		British GDP: British Tastes for U.S. Goods: or Relative Interest Rates in the United States:		Relative Prices in the United States:		Expectation that the Price of the Pound Will:	
Increases	**Decreases**	**Increase**	**Decrease**	**Increase**	**Decrease**	**Rise**	**Fall**
Movement rightward along curve	Movement leftward along curve	Shifts rightward	Shifts leftward	Shifts leftward	Shifts rightward	Shifts leftward	Shifts rightward

BRITISH TASTES FOR U.S. GOODS. Recall our earlier discussion about the effect of American tastes on the demand for pounds. The same reasoning applies to the effect of British tastes on the *supply* of pounds. The British could begin to crave things American—or recoil from them. A shift in British tastes toward American goods will shift the supply of pounds curve rightward. A shift in tastes *away* from American goods will shift the curve leftward.

RELATIVE INTEREST RATE IN THE UNITED STATES. You've already learned that a rise in the relative U.S. interest rate makes U.S. assets more attractive to Americans. It has exactly the same effect on the British. As British residents seek to buy more U.S. assets, they will need more dollars and will supply more pounds. The supply of pounds curve will then shift rightward. Similarly, a *decrease* in the U.S. interest rate relative to that of Britain will shift the supply of pounds curve leftward.

EXPECTED CHANGE IN THE EXCHANGE RATE. In deciding whether to hold their wealth in their own assets or the assets of a foreign country, the British have the same concerns as Americans. They will look, in part, at relative rates of return; but they will *also* look ahead to possible gains or losses on foreign currency transactions. If the British *expect the price of the pound to fall,* then—by holding U.S. assets—they can anticipate a foreign currency gain—selling pounds at a relatively high price and buying them back again when their price is relatively low. This will make U.S. assets more attractive, and the British will buy more of them. *The supply of pounds curve will shift rightward.*

An *expected rise in the price of the pound,* by contrast, will make British assets more attractive, since buying U.S. assets would entail a foreign currency loss. The British demand for U.S. assets will decline, and *the supply of pounds curve will shift leftward.*

THE SUPPLY OF POUNDS CURVE: A SUMMARY

Table 3 summarizes our discussion of movements along, and shifts of, the supply of pounds curve.

THE EQUILIBRIUM EXCHANGE RATE

Now we will make an important—and in most cases, realistic—assumption: that the exchange rate between the dollar and the pound *floats*. A **floating exchange rate** is one that is freely determined by the forces of supply and demand, without government intervention to change it or keep it from changing. Indeed, many of the world's leading currencies, including the Japanese yen, the British pound, the French franc, the German mark, and the Italian lira, do float freely against the dollar most of the time.

FLOATING EXCHANGE RATE An exchange rate that is freely determined by the forces of supply and demand.

In some cases, however, governments do not allow the exchange rate to float freely, but instead manipulate its value by intervening in the market, or even *fix* it at a particular value. We'll discuss government manipulation of the exchange rate a bit later. In this section, we assume that both the British and U.S. governments leave the dollar–pound market alone.

When the exchange rate floats, the market for foreign exchange works just like the market for maple syrup or any other market in which many buyers and sellers trade the same thing. In equilibrium, the price will settle at the level where quantity supplied and quantity demanded are equal. Here, buyers and sellers are trading British pounds, and the price is the exchange rate—the *price of the pound.*

Look at Figure 5. The equilibrium in the market for pounds occurs at point *E,* where the supply and demand curves intersect. The equilibrium price is $1.50 per pound. Now, imagine that the exchange rate were higher, say, $2.25 per pound. Then there would be an *excess supply* of pounds, given by the distance *AF.* Frustrated sellers would have to lower the price in order to sell their pounds, and the price of the pound would fall. As the price fell, the quantity of pounds demanded would rise, and we'd move rightward along the demand curve from point *A.* At the same time, the quantity of pounds supplied would fall, and we'd move leftward along the supply curve from point *F.* These movements would continue until the excess supply was eliminated at point *E,* our equilibrium point.

As you can verify, a similar process would occur if the price of the pound were *lower* than the equilibrium price of $1.50. In that case, there would be an *excess demand* for pounds, driving the exchange rate back up to $1.50.

When the exchange rate floats—that is, when the government does not intervene in the foreign currency market—the equilibrium exchange rate is determined by the intersection of the demand curve and the supply curve.

MARKETS AND EQUILIBRIUM

WHAT ABOUT THE MARKET FOR DOLLARS?

Something may be bothering you about our analysis of the market for pounds. We have considered the demand and supply of pounds, but what about the other side of this market: the demand and supply of dollars? After all, when Americans demand pounds, they are supplying dollars; and when the British supply pounds, they are demanding dollars. To determine the equilibrium exchange rate, don't we have to worry about the quantity of dollars supplied and demanded, as well as the quantity of pounds?

Actually, we don't have to worry about trading in dollars at all, and here is why: If the quantity of *pounds* demanded and supplied are equal at some exchange rate, then the quantity of *dollars* demanded and supplied are automatically equal at that same exchange rate. How do we know?

FIGURE 5

THE EQUILIBRIUM EXCHANGE RATE

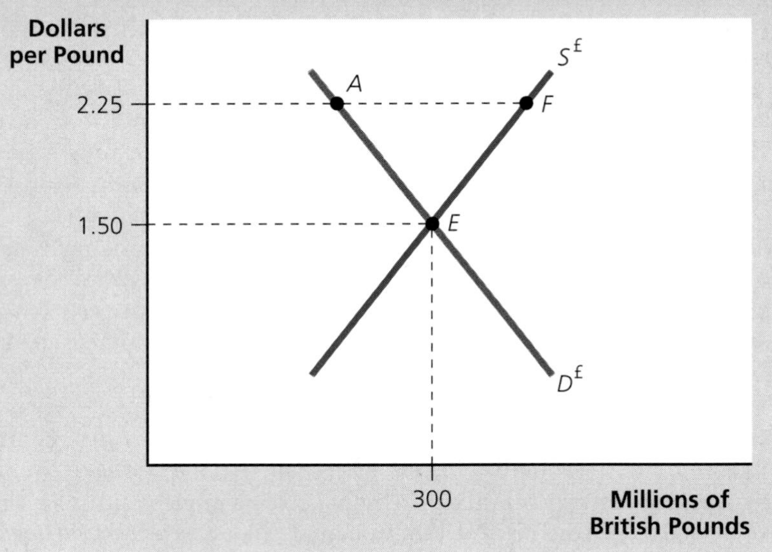

Equilibrium in the market for pounds occurs at point *E,* where the supply and demand curves cross. The equilibrium price is $1.50 per pound. At a higher price, such as $2.25, an excess supply of pounds (equal to *AF*) would put downward pressure on the exchange rate. The rate would continue to fall until the excess supply was eliminated at point *E.*

Look at Figure 5 again. At the equilibrium exchange rate of $1.50, point *E* tells us that Americans want to buy £300 million per year. How many dollars will they offer to sell to get these pounds? The answer is, 300 million × $1.50 = $450 million. That is, when Americans demand 300 million pounds at a price of $1.50 per pound, it follows that they supply $450 million. Likewise, since the British are supplying £300 million at $1.50 per pound, they must be demanding 300 million × $1.50 = $450 million—the same quantity of dollars that the Americans are supplying.

This result should not surprise us. In the dollar–pound market, a decision to buy pounds is a decision to sell dollars, and a decision to sell pounds is a decision to buy dollars. Thus, once we have found the exchange rate at which the quantity of pounds demanded and supplied are equal, we have also found the exchange rate at which the quantity of dollars demanded and supplied are equal. This leaves us free to concentrate on either pounds or dollars, as we choose. And in this chapter, we've chosen to focus on pounds.

WHAT MAKES EXCHANGE RATES CHANGE?

What would cause the price of the pound to rise or fall? The simple answer to this question is, the forces of supply and demand. More specifically, the price of the pound will change whenever there is a shift in the demand for pounds curve, or in the supply curve, or in both curves together. Have another look at Tables 2 and 3. They summarize the major factors that can shift the demand and supply curves for pounds and therefore change the equilibrium price of the pound.

Let's illustrate with a simple example. In Figure 6, the initial equilibrium in the market for pounds is at point *E,* with an exchange rate of $1.50 per pound. Now suppose that Americans develop an increased taste for British goods. As you've learned (see Table 2), this change in tastes will shift the demand for pounds curve

CHANGES IN THE EXCHANGE RATE

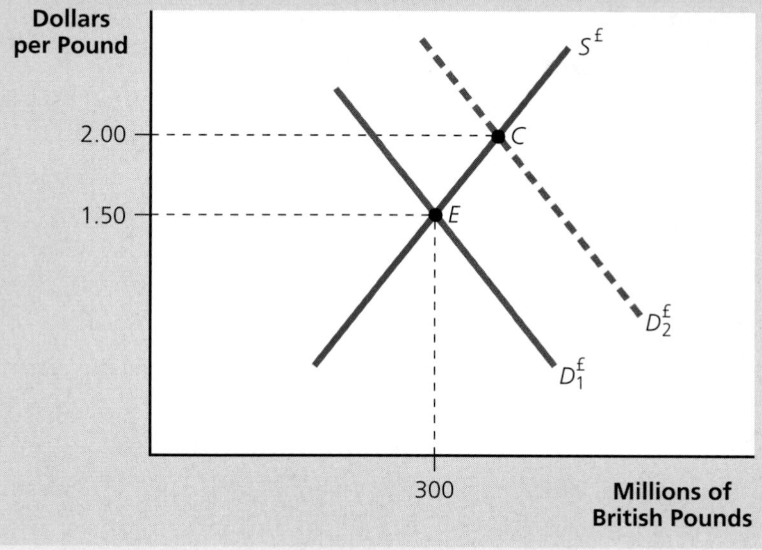

FIGURE 6

The market for pounds is initially in equilibrium at point *E*, with an exchange rate of $1.50 per pound. An increased American taste for British goods would shift the demand curve rightward to $D_2^£$. At the original exchange rate, the excess demand for pounds would put upward pressure on the exchange rate, which would rise to $2 per pound at point *C*.

rightward, from $D_1^£$ to $D_2^£$ in the figure. At the old exchange rate of $1.50, there would be an excess demand for pounds, which would drive the price of the pound higher. The new equilibrium—where the quantity of pounds supplied and demanded are equal—occurs at point *C*, and the new equilibrium exchange rate is $2.00 per pound.

To recap, the increase in American tastes for British goods causes the price of the pound to rise from $1.50 to $2.00. When the price of any foreign currency rises because of a shift in the demand curve, the supply curve, or both, we call it an **appreciation** of the currency. In our example, the pound appreciates against the dollar. Notice, though, that while the price of the pound in dollars has risen, *the price of the dollar in pounds* has *fallen*. That is, at point *E*, it takes 0.66 pounds to buy one dollar, while at point *C*, it takes 0.5 pounds to buy one dollar. Because of the appreciation of the pound, there has been a **depreciation** of the dollar—a fall in its price.[2]

APPRECIATION An increase in the price of a currency in a floating-rate system.

DEPRECIATION A decrease in the price of a currency in a floating-rate system.

When a floating exchange rates changes, one country's currency will appreciate (rise in price) and the other country's currency will depreciate (fall in price).

We can also explore other types of changes in tastes with a diagram like Figure 6. For example, if *British* tastes changed, say, toward U.S. goods, then the *supply* of pounds curve would shift rightward. In that case, the pound would depreciate, and the dollar would appreciate.

We could continue in this way, changing each of the variables in Tables 2 and 3 one by one, as we did with tastes, and determining how the dollar-pound ex-

2 You may have heard two other terms used to describe changes in the exchange rate: "devaluation" and "revaluation." These terms are used only when a government has *fixed* its exchange rate at a particular value, and then raises or lowers that value. When exchange rates *float*, however, the correct terms are "depreciation" and "appreciation."

FIGURE 7

THE EXCHANGE RATE IN THE POUND–DOLLAR MARKET

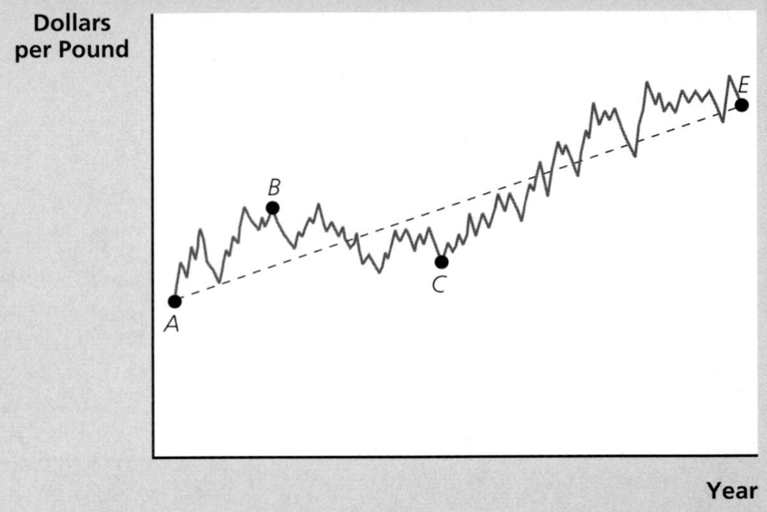

These hypothetical data show typical patterns of exchange rate fluctuations. Over the course of a few minutes, days, or weeks, the exchange rate can experience sharp up-and-down spikes. Over several months or a year or two, the exchange rate may rise or fall, as in the appreciation of the pound from points *A* to *B* and the depreciation from *B* to *C*. Over the long run, there may be a general upward or downward trend, like the appreciation of the pound illustrated by the dashed line connecting points *A* and *E*.

change rate would be affected. However, we'll organize our discussion of exchange rate changes in a slightly different way.

HOW EXCHANGE RATES CHANGE OVER TIME

When we examine the actual behavior of exchange rates over time, we find three different kinds of movements. For example, look at Figure 7, which shows the exchange rate in the pound–dollar market. The figure is based on hypothetical data, designed to make these three kinds of movement stand out more clearly than they usually do in practice.

Notice first the sharp up-and-down spikes. These fluctuations in exchange rates occur over the course of a few weeks, a few days, or even a few minutes—periods of time that we call the *very short run*.

Second, we see a gradual rise and fall of the exchange rate over the course of several months or a year or two. An example is the appreciation of the pound from point *A* to *B* and the depreciation of the pound from point *B* to *C*. These are *short-run* movements in the exchange rate.

Finally, notice that while the price of the pound fluctuates in the very short run and the short run, we can also discern a general *long-run* trend: The pound seems to be appreciating in the figure. This long-run trend is illustrated by the dashed line connecting points *A* and *E*.

In this section, we'll explore the causes of movements in the exchange rate over all three periods: the very short run, the short run, and the long run.

THE VERY SHORT RUN: "HOT MONEY." Sometimes, at a moment's notice, billions of dollars are moved from the assets of one country into the assets of another country. Who or what is behind these movements of "hot money"?

Banks and other large financial institutions—and a few very rich individuals—have hundreds of billions of dollars available to move from one type of investment to another. If they perceive even a tiny advantage in moving funds to a different country's assets—say, because its interest rate is slightly higher—they will do so. Often, decisions to move tens of billions of dollars are made in split seconds, by traders watching computer screens showing the latest data on exchange rates and interest rates around the world. The term *hot money* comes from the speed needed to keep up with rapid changes in the markets. Because hot money investors move such large volumes of funds, they have immediate effects on exchange rates.

Let's consider an example of a shift of hot money from one country to another and see how and why it changes the exchange rate. Suppose that the relative interest rate in the U.S. rises suddenly and significantly. Then, as you've learned, U.S. assets will suddenly be more attractive to residents of both the U.S. and England, including managers of hot-money accounts in both countries. As these managers shift their funds from British to U.S. assets, they will be dumping billions of pounds on the foreign exchange market in order to acquire dollars to buy U.S. assets. This will cause a significant rightward shift of the supply of pounds curve.

In addition to affecting managers of hot-money accounts, the higher relative interest rate in the U.S. will affect ordinary investors. British investors will prefer to buy American assets, contributing further to the rightward shift in the supply of pounds curve. And American investors will want to buy fewer British assets than they were buying before, causing some decrease in the *demand* for pounds. Thus, in addition to the very large rightward shift in the supply of pounds, there will be a more moderate leftward shift in the demand for pounds.

Both of these shifts are illustrated in Figure 8: The supply of pounds curve shifts from $S_1^{£}$ to $S_2^{£}$, and the demand for pounds curve shifts from $D_1^{£}$ to $D_2^{£}$. The result is easy to see: The equilibrium in the market for pounds moves from point E to point G, and the price of the pound *falls* from \$1.50 to \$1.00. The pound depreciates and the dollar appreciates.

Figure 8 also illustrates what would happen if American and British residents suddenly *expected* the pound to depreciate against the dollar. Managers of hot-money accounts, as well as ordinary British investors, would anticipate foreign currency gains from holding U.S. assets, shifting the supply of pounds curve rightward. At the same time, U.S. investors—anticipating foreign currency losses from holding British assets—would shy away from them. This would cause the demand for pounds curve to shift leftward. As you can see in Figure 8, the expectation that the pound will depreciate actually *causes* the pound to depreciate—a self-fulfilling prophecy.

Sudden changes in relative interest rates, as well as sudden expectations of an appreciation or depreciation of a nation's currency, occur frequently in foreign exchange markets. They can cause massive shifts of hot money from the assets of one country to those of another in very short periods of time. For this reason,

> *relative interest rates and expectations of future exchange rates are the dominant forces moving exchange rates in the very short run.*

THE SHORT RUN: BUSINESS CYCLES. As mentioned earlier, Figure 7 shows movements in the exchange rate that take place over a somewhat longer period of time—many months or a few years. These are *short-run* changes in exchange rates and can be attributed mostly to economic fluctuations taking place in one or more countries.

FIGURE 8

HOT MONEY IN THE VERY SHORT RUN

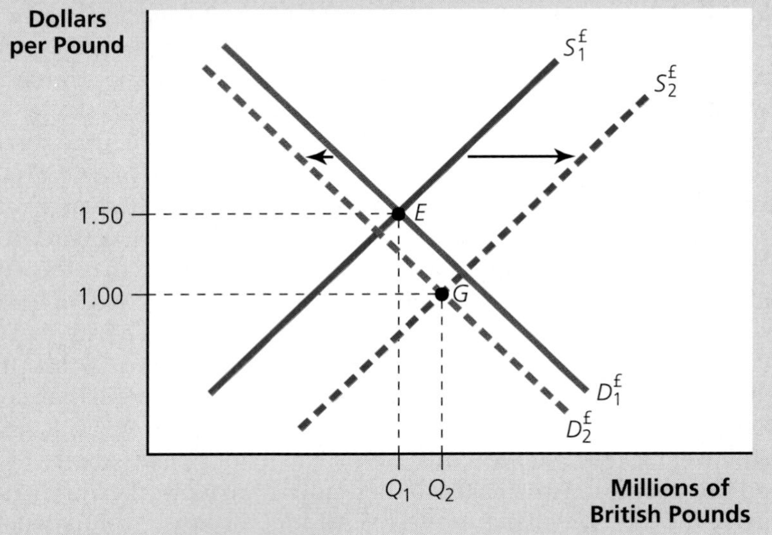

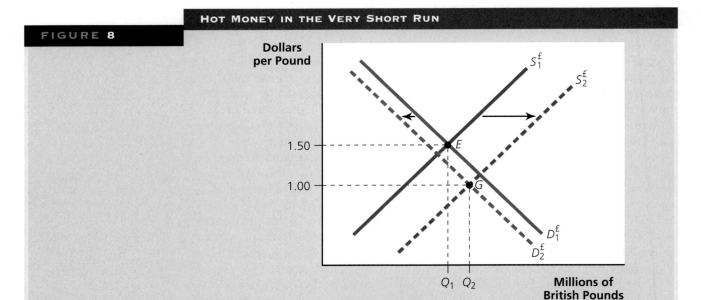

The market for pounds is initially in equilibrium at point *E*, with an exchange rate of $1.50 per pound. A rise in the U.S. interest rate relative to the British rate will make U.S. assets more attractive to both Americans and Britons. Hot-money managers in both countries will shift funds from British to U.S. assets, causing a significant rightward shift of the supply of pounds curve. American investors will want to buy fewer British assets, causing a decrease in the demand for pounds. The net effect is a lower exchange rate—$1.00 per pound at point *G*.

Suppose, for example, that both Britain and the United States are in a recession, and the U.S. economy begins to recover while the British slump continues. As real GDP rises in the U.S., so will Americans' demand for foreign goods and services, including those from Britain. The demand for pounds curve will shift rightward, and—as shown in panel (a) of Figure 9—the pound will appreciate.

A year or so later, when Britain recovers from *its* recession, its real GDP will rise. British residents will begin to buy more U.S. goods and services, and supply more pounds so they can acquire more dollars. The supply of pounds curve will shift rightward, and—as shown in panel (b)—the pound will depreciate. Thus,

in the short run, movements in exchange rates are caused largely by economic fluctuations. All else equal, a country whose GDP rises relatively rapidly will experience a depreciation *of its currency. A country whose GDP falls more rapidly will experience an* appreciation *of its currency.*

This observation contradicts a commonly held myth: that a strong (appreciating) currency is a sign of economic health, and a weak (depreciating) currency denotes a sick economy. The truth may easily be the opposite. Over the course of several quarters or a few years, the dollar could be strong because the U.S. economy is *weak*—suffering a serious recession—and Americans are not spending much on domestic *or* foreign goods. In this case, it's the weak American demand for foreign goods that decreases the demand for foreign currency, and causes the dollar to appreciate. Similarly, a strong U.S. economy—in which Americans are earning and spending at high levels—would increase the U.S. demand for foreign currency and—all else equal—cause the dollar to depreciate.

Exchange Rates in the Short Run

Figure 9

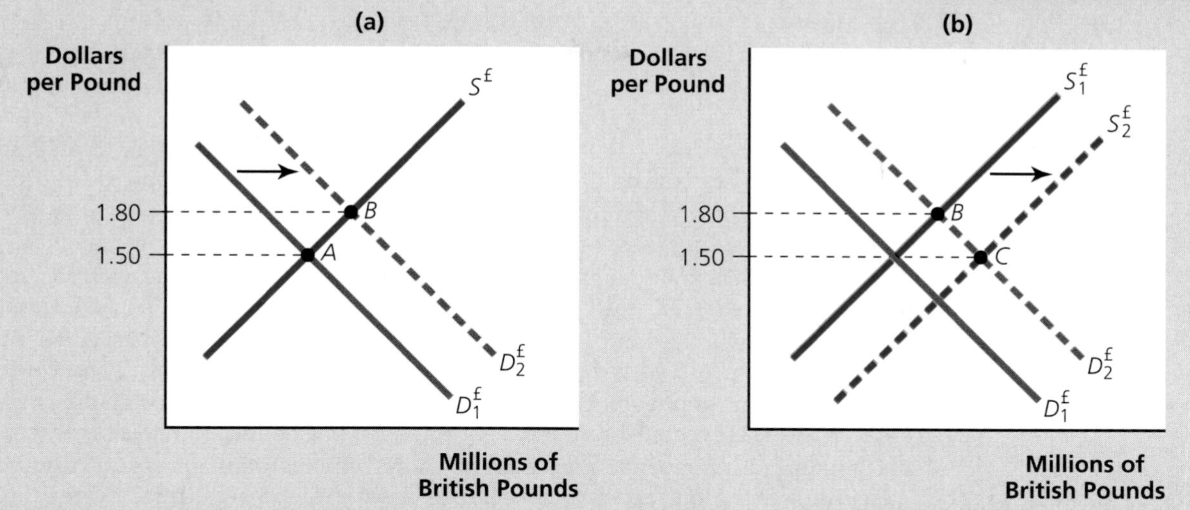

Panel (a) shows a situation in which the U.S. recovers from a recession first. U.S. demand for foreign goods and services increases, shifting the demand for pounds curve to the right. The result is an appreciation of the pound. Panel (b) shows Britain's subsequent recovery from its recession. As Britons begin to buy more U.S. goods and services, the supply of pounds curve shifts rightward, causing the pound to depreciate.

Although we've highlighted the impact of changes in real GDP on exchange rates, other variables can change over the business cycle as well, including interest rates and price levels in the two countries. For example, a recession can be caused by a monetary contraction that raises the relative interest rate in a country. Or a monetary stimulus in the midst of a recession could result in a relatively low interest rate. These changes, too, will influence exchange rates over the business cycle.

The Long Run: Purchasing Power Parity. In mid-1992, you could buy about 100 Russian rubles with one dollar. In mid-1997, that same dollar would get you almost 6,000 rubles. What caused the ruble to depreciate by so much against the dollar during those five years?

This is a question about exchange rates over many years—the long run. Movements of hot money—which explain sudden, temporary movements of exchange rates—cannot explain this kind of long-run trend. Nor can business cycles, which are, by nature, temporary. What, then, causes exchange rates to change over the long run?

In general, long-run trends in exchange rates are determined by *relative price levels* in two countries. We can be even more specific:

> *According to the* ***purchasing power parity (PPP) theory****, an exchange rate between two countries will adjust in the long run until the average price of goods is roughly the same in both countries.*

Purchasing-power parity (PPP) theory The idea that the exchange rate will adjust in the long run so that the average price of goods in two countries will be roughly the same.

To see why the PPP theory makes sense, imagine a basket of goods that costs \$750 in the United States and £500 in Britain. If these prices do not change, then, according to the PPP theory, the exchange rate will adjust to \$750/£500 = \$1.5 dollars per pound. Why? Because at this exchange rate, \$750 can be exchanged for £500, so the price of the basket is the same to residents of either country—\$750 for Americans, and £500 for the British.

Now, suppose the exchange rate was *below* its PPP rate of \$1.50 per pound—say, \$1 per pound. Then a trader could take \$500 to the bank, exchange it for £500, buy the basket of goods in Great Britain, and sell it in the United States for \$750. She would earn a profit of \$250 on each basket of goods traded. In the process, however, traders would be increasing the demand for pounds and raising the exchange rate. When the price of the pound reached \$1.50, purchasing power parity would hold, and special trading opportunities would be gone.

On the other hand, suppose the exchange rate was *higher* than the PPP rate—say, \$5 per pound. In this case, a trader could take £150 to the bank, exchange it for \$750, buy the basket of goods in the United States, and sell it in Great Britain for £500. The profit would be £350 per basket traded. In the process, however, the rising supply of pounds in the foreign exchange market would lower the exchange rate. When the exchange rate fell back to \$1.50 per pound, purchasing power parity would hold, and there would be no more opportunities for special trading. As you can see, trading activity will tend to drive the exchange rate toward the PPP value.[3]

The PPP theory has an important implication:

In the long run, the currency of a country with a higher inflation rate will depreciate against the currency of a country whose inflation rate is lower.

Why? Because in the country with the higher inflation rate, the relative price level will be rising. As that country's basket of goods becomes relatively more expensive, only a depreciation of its currency can restore purchasing power parity. And traders—taking advantage of opportunities like those just described—would cause the currency to depreciate.

PURCHASING POWER PARITY: SOME IMPORTANT CAVEATS. While purchasing power parity is a good general guideline for predicting long-run trends in exchange rates, it does not work perfectly. For a variety of reasons, exchange rates can deviate from their PPP values for many years.

First, some goods—by their very nature—are difficult to trade. Suppose a haircut costs £5 in London and \$30 in New York, and the exchange rate is \$1.50 per pound. Then British haircuts are cheaper for residents of both countries. Could traders take advantage of this? Not really. They cannot take \$30 to the bank in exchange for £20, buy four haircuts in London, ship them to New York, and sell them for a total of \$120 there. Haircuts and most other personal services are generally nontradable.

Second, high transportation costs can reduce trading possibilities even for goods that *can* be traded. Our earlier numerical example would have quite a different ending if moving the basket of goods between Great Britain and the United States involved \$500 of freight and insurance costs.

3 The adjustment process could be more complicated than described here. It may involve, for instance, changes in the domestic prices of the two baskets of goods as the demand for them, or the supply of them, was affected by international trade. But in the end, purchasing power parity would come to prevail.

Third, artificial barriers to trade, such as the tariff and import quotas described in the previous chapter, can hamper traders' ability to move exchange rates toward purchasing power parity.

Still, the purchasing power parity theory is useful in many circumstances. Under floating exchange rates, a country whose relative price level is growing rapidly will almost always find that the price of its currency is falling rapidly. If not, all of its goods would soon be priced out of the world market. Indeed, we often observe that countries with very high inflation rates have currencies depreciating against the dollar by roughly the amount needed to preserve purchasing power parity. For example, we've already mentioned the sharp depreciation of the Russian ruble from 1992 to 1997. During those five years, the number of rubles that exchanged for a dollar rose from around 100 to about 5,700. Over the same period, average yearly inflation rate was about 200 percent in Russia, but only about 3 percent in the United States. As a result, the relative price level in Russia skyrocketed, leading to a dramatic depreciation of the ruble against the dollar. Other countries with unusually high inflation rates have also experienced rapid currency depreciations. For example, from mid-1996 to mid-1997, Turkey's price level almost doubled, while the dollar price of its currency was cut in half.

Managed Float

As you've seen, when exchange rates float, they can rise and fall for a variety of reasons. But a government may not be content to let the forces of supply and demand change its exchange rate. If the exchange rate rises too high, the country's goods will become much more expensive to foreigners, causing harm to its export-oriented industries. If the exchange rate falls too low, goods purchased from other countries will rise in price. Since many imported goods are used as inputs by U.S. firms (such as oil from the Middle East and Mexico, or computer screens from Japan), a drop in the exchange rate will cause a general rise in prices in the United States. Finally, if the exchange rate is too volatile, it can make trading arrangements riskier or require traders to acquire special insurance against foreign currency losses, which costs them money, time, and trouble. For all of these reasons, governments have sometimes intervened in foreign exchange markets involving their currency.

For example, look back at Figure 8. Suppose the British government does not want the price of the pound to fall to $1 as hot money is shifted out of British assets. Then it could begin trading in the dollar–pound market itself—buying British pounds with dollars, thereby shifting the demand for pounds curve rightward. If it buys just the right amount of pounds, it can prevent the pound from depreciating at all. Alternatively, the U.S. government might not be happy with the appreciation of the dollar in Figure 9. In that case, the Federal Reserve can enter the market and buy British pounds with dollars, once again shifting the demand for pounds curve rightward.

The central banks of European countries often influence exchange rates in the fashion just noted. So does the Federal Reserve. When a government buys or sells its own currency or that of a trading partner for the purpose of influencing floating exchange rates, the intervention is called a "managed float" or a "dirty float."

Under a managed float, a country's central bank buys its own currency to prevent a depreciation, and sells its own currency to prevent an appreciation.

Managed floats are used most often in the very short run, to prevent large, sudden changes in exchange rates such as the one depicted in Figure 9. Often, central

FIGURE 10

BILATERAL ARBITRAGE

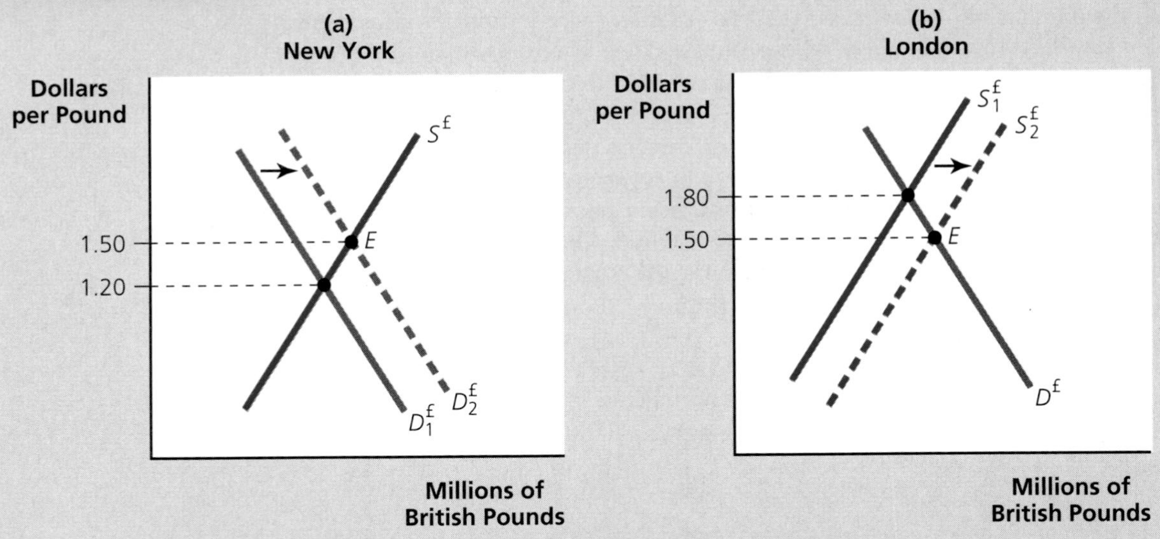

Initially, the price of the pound is $1.20 in New York—panel (a)—and $1.80 in London—panel (b). Traders take advantage of this exchange rate differential by buying pounds in New York and simultaneously selling them in London. As they do so, the demand curve shifts rightward in New York, and the supply curve shifts rightward in London. Arbitrage continues until the exchange rate attains the same value—$1.50 per pound—in both locations.

banks cooperate with each other to offset what would otherwise be a change in an exchange rate. For example, they might all sell deutsche marks and buy pounds in order to prevent the pound from depreciating relative to the German currency. Where the fundamental forces behind the appreciation or depreciation are strong, however, a managed float only delays the change in the exchange rate.

INTERDEPENDENT MARKETS: THE ROLE OF ARBITRAGE

The market for pounds—like any other foreign exchange market—is not a centralized market in a single location. Rather, pounds and dollars are exchanged at tens of thousands of locations—at banks, hotels, airports, and train stations in hundreds of cities and towns around the world. How do we know that the equilibrium exchange rate, such as the one we found back in Figure 5, will be the exchange rate in *all* of these locations? Couldn't it be that in New York pounds sell for $1.50 each, while in London they sell for $1.60, and in Paris, for $1.35?

Actually, no. An exchange rate between two currencies will be the same in every location, except for tiny differences that will exist for only a few seconds. Why? Because of the process of **arbitrage**—the simultaneous buying and selling of a foreign currency in order to profit from any difference in exchange rates.

ARBITRAGE Simultaneous buying and selling of a foreign currency in order to profit from a difference in exchange rates.

BILATERAL ARBITRAGE Arbitrage involving one pair of currencies.

Figure 10 can help us visualize how **bilateral arbitrage**—in which only one pair of currencies is traded—drives an exchange rate to the same, equilibrium value around the world. Suppose that in New York (panel (a)) the equilibrium price of the pound was $1.20, while in London (panel (b)) the price was $1.80. Then astute traders could make fortunes in minutes. American and British traders could buy pounds in New York for $1.20 each, while simultaneously selling them in London for $1.80 each. On each pound traded, they would make a profit of 60 cents. This may not sound like much, but in the foreign exchange market, a professional trader can easily buy and sell millions of dollars worth of currency in a matter of seconds, with a few keystrokes on a computer. In our example, someone buying $10 million worth of pounds in New York and selling them in London would make a nice profit of $6 million—not bad for the few seconds it took to make the trade.

But before you decide to quit college and become a foreign exchange trader, you should know that differences in exchange rates as large as the one in Figure 10 never actually occur. Why not? Because traders—in their pursuit of profits—immediately take advantage of even the tiniest differences in exchange rates, and their efforts wipe out those differences entirely.

Let's go back to Figure 10 and see how bilateral arbitrage eliminates potential profits. As traders buy pounds in New York, the demand curve there shifts rightward, from $D_1^{\pounds}$ to $D_2^{\pounds}$, thereby increasing the price of the pound in New York. As traders sell pounds in London, the supply curve there shifts rightward, from $S_1^{\pounds}$ to $S_2^{\pounds}$, thereby decreasing the price of pounds in London. The process continues until the exchange rate reaches the same value of $1.50 in both markets and there are no more profit opportunities for traders.

Bilateral arbitrage ensures that the exchange rate between any two currencies is the same everywhere in the world.[4]

MARKETS AND EQUILIBRIUM

TRIANGULAR ARBITRAGE. Another form of arbitrage—called **triangular arbitrage**—involves trades among *three* (or more) countries' currencies. Triangular arbitrage ensures that the number of dollars that exchange for one pound is the same whether you make the trade *directly*—in the dollar–pound market—or *indirectly,* by buying and selling a third currency.

TRIANGULAR ARBITRAGE Arbitrage involving trades among three (or more) currencies.

To see how triangular arbitrage works, suppose that the exchange rates among the dollar, pound, and French franc are as shown in the left-hand column of Table 4: The price of a pound in dollars is $1.80, the price of a franc in dollars is $0.10, and the price of a pound in francs is 10 FF.

With these exchange rates, the *direct* price of the pound to Americans is $1.80. But the *indirect* price is $1.00. Why? Because an American, starting with $1.00, could purchase 10 francs in the dollar–franc market and then use those 10 francs to purchase 1 pound in the franc–pound market.

This difference between the direct and indirect prices for the pound would allow traders to make huge profits. They could acquire pounds *indirectly* for $1.00 each and then sell them *directly* for $1.80 each, for a huge profit of 80 cents per pound sold.

However, such large potential profits from triangular arbitrage would never arise in practice. Even the tiniest potential profits are eliminated, almost immediately, by the arbitrage process itself. In our example, when traders buy francs with

4 Exchange rates will sometimes *appear* different in different locations because a commission for the broker is often built into the rate. These commissions can differ by location, depending on the cost structure and degree of competition among brokers. For example, if you buy pounds in a small-town bank, which faces little competition and may have higher costs, you may pay more for them than if you bought them in a big-city bank. But this is only because the small-town bank is charging a higher commission.

TABLE 4

BEFORE AND AFTER TRIANGULAR ARBITRAGE

	Exchange Rate Before Arbitrage	Exchange Rate After Arbitrage
Price of pound in dollar–pound market	\$1.80	\$1.50
Price of franc in dollar–franc market	\$0.10	\$0.125
Price of pound in pound–franc market	10 FF	12 FF

dollars, they *drive up the price of the franc in the dollar–franc market.* When they buy pounds with francs, they *drive up the price of the pound in the pound–franc market.* Finally, when they buy dollars with pounds, they *drive down the price of the pound in the dollar–pound market.*

Each of these movements decreases the potential profits from arbitrage, and the process ends when no opportunity for such profits remains. The last column in Table 4 shows where the exchange rates might end up after the arbitrage process is completed. With these exchange rates, the direct price of the pound is \$1.50. And this is also what it would cost to buy a pound *indirectly:* \$1.50 gets you 12 FF, and 12 FF gets you one pound. There are no more opportunities for arbitrage, because arbitrage has eliminated them.

MARKETS AND EQUILIBRIUM

Triangular arbitrage ensures that the price of a foreign currency is the same whether it is purchased directly—in a single foreign exchange market—or indirectly, by buying and selling a third currency.[5]

MACROECONOMICS IN AN OPEN ECONOMY

CLOSED ECONOMY An economy that does not trade with the rest of the world.

OPEN ECONOMY An economy in which trade with other nations plays a significant role.

So far in this book, we've built our macroeconomic models for a **closed economy**—an economy that does not trade with other nations. This was for good reason: It's easier to learn the fundamental forces guiding the economy when you start with a simple model that does not include international trade. But even in the U.S. economy—where most of what we buy is produced domestically—trading with other nations is important. Every year, about 10 percent of the goods and services bought by U.S. households, businesses, and government agencies are produced abroad, and a slightly lower percentage of U.S. output is sold abroad. In this section, we'll explore how output and employment are determined in an **open economy**—an economy in which trade with other nations plays a significant role.

AGGREGATE EXPENDITURE IN AN OPEN ECONOMY

In previous chapters, you've learned that a basic requirement for macroeconomic equilibrium is that aggregate expenditure and total output be equal. Unless business firms sell just the level of output they produce, they will change their level of production in future periods. In our closed-economy model, we divided aggregate

5 Because brokerage commissions are sometimes built into the price of foreign currency, small differences between the direct and indirect price may remain, even after arbitrage has eliminated all possibilities of profit. This is because two commissions are paid when a person buys indirectly, but only one commission is paid when buying directly.

expenditure into three components: consumption spending by U.S. households (C), investment spending by U.S. business firms (I), and purchases by U.S. government agencies (G). Thus,

$$\text{Aggregate expenditure in a closed economy} = C + I + G$$

With international trade, however, we will need to adjust our expression for aggregate expenditure. First, some American goods and services are sold to *foreign* consumers, businesses, and governments. These are *exports* from the U.S. point of view. Since aggregate expenditure should include *all* spending on U.S. output, we must *add total exports* purchased by foreigners.

But we have one additional correction to make. A portion of the products bought by U.S. consumers, firms, and government agencies were produced abroad. From the U.S. point of view, these are *imports*—spending on foreign, rather than U.S., output. We must *subtract total imports* in our definition of aggregate expenditure.

When we make these adjustments, we find that aggregate expenditure in an open economy is

$$C + I + G + \text{Exports} - \text{Imports}$$
$$= C + I + G + NX$$

where NX stands for net exports, or exports − imports.

In an open economy, some production is sold to foreigners as exports, and some domestic spending is for imports rather than domestic production. Thus,

$$\text{Aggregate expenditure in an open economy} = C + I + G + NX$$

If exports are larger than imports, NX is positive, so international trade *increases* aggregate expenditure. If imports exceed exports, NX is negative, so trade *decreases* aggregate expenditure.

In Figure 11, the solid line shows aggregate expenditure for a closed economy, the dashed line aggregate expenditure for an open economy. Notice two differences between the lines. First, as we just discussed, in an open economy the aggregate-expenditure line includes net exports. In the figure, we assume that net exports are positive, so international trade shifts the line upward. Second, the open-economy line is *flatter* than the closed economy line. Why? Because as U.S. GDP rises, Americans will buy more of *everything*—including imports. Thus, as we move rightward along the aggregate expenditure line, imports rise. Exports, by contrast, are not directly affected by our own GDP—they depend on the incomes of foreigners.

Will the European Monetary Union succeed? Learn more about this issue in the Policy Debates portion of the ECONOMICS web site.
Address: http://hall-lieb.swcollege.com

DANGEROUS CURVES

Watch out for two common mistakes involving the terms *exports* and *imports*. The first is applying these terms too broadly, by including *everything* that is traded among nations. In fact, exports and imports refer to trade in *goods and services* only. They do *not* include trading in assets, as when a British citizen buys a U.S. bond.

The second mistake is applying the terms too narrowly—by including only *goods* that are actually shipped from one country to another. In fact, a large percentage of exports and imports involves goods and services that never cross an international border. For example, when an American stays in a hotel room in London and buys a serving of bread pudding there, she is *importing* hotel services and prepared food to the United States, even though she consumes them in Britain. As far as the American economy is concerned, it makes no difference whether the goods travel to Americans or Americans travel to the goods.

FIGURE 11

EQUILIBRIUM REAL GDP IN CLOSED AND OPEN ECONOMIES

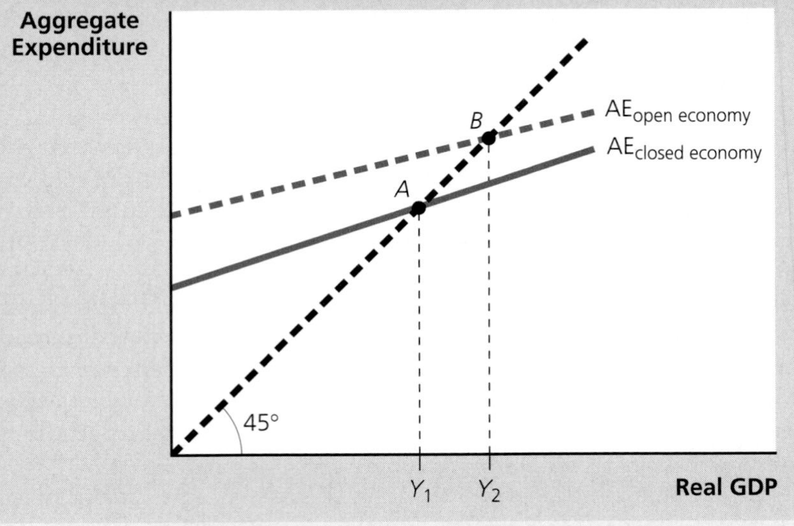

The aggregate expenditure line for the *closed* economy crosses the 45° line at point *A* to determine a real GDP of Y_1. In an otherwise similar *open* economy, the aggregate expenditure line is higher (if net exports are positive) and flatter (because imports rise as real GDP rises). The open-economy aggregate expenditure line crosses the 45° line at point *B* to determine an equilibrium GDP of Y_2.

An increase in a nation's GDP raises its imports, but leaves its exports unaffected. Hence, increases in GDP decrease *net exports.*

The automatic shrinkage of net exports as GDP rises is illustrated by the shrinking distance between the solid and dashed lines in the figure. The result is a flatter aggregate expenditure line for an open economy.

Figure 11 also illustrates a feature of the open economy that we mentioned earlier in the book: Imports are one of the economy's *automatic stabilizers.* As income rises in a boom, some of the increased spending is on *foreign* products. This may stimulate further production in *foreign* countries, but does not affect U.S. firms. Thus, a positive spending shock raises output by less than it otherwise would. Similarly, as income falls in a recession, some of the decrease in household spending affects foreign, rather than domestic, firms. As a result, a negative spending shock causes a smaller decline in output than would otherwise occur.

Imports—which depend on domestic income—act as an automatic stabilizer for an economy, reducing the size of the multiplier. As a result, spending shocks cause smaller changes in GDP in an open economy than in a closed economy.

EQUILIBRIUM OUTPUT IN AN OPEN ECONOMY

Once we draw the aggregate expenditure line for an open economy, we can find equilibrium real GDP just as we did earlier in a closed economy. We simply find the level of output at which the aggregate expenditure line—now including net exports—crosses the 45-degree line. In Figure 12, using the solid aggregate expenditure line, we find that equilibrium is at point *E,* with output equal to Y_1. At any other level of GDP, total *spending* on U.S. output would be larger than or smaller than output, and U.S. firms would change their production levels in future periods.

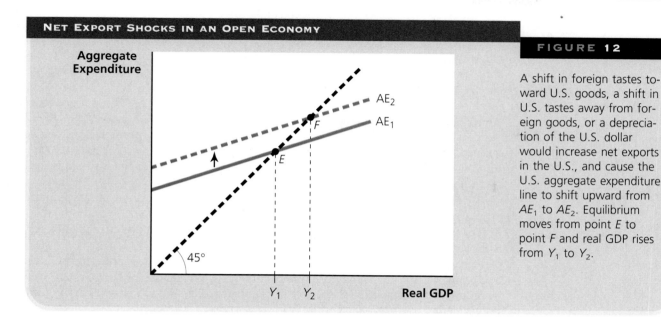

NET EXPORT SHOCKS IN AN OPEN ECONOMY

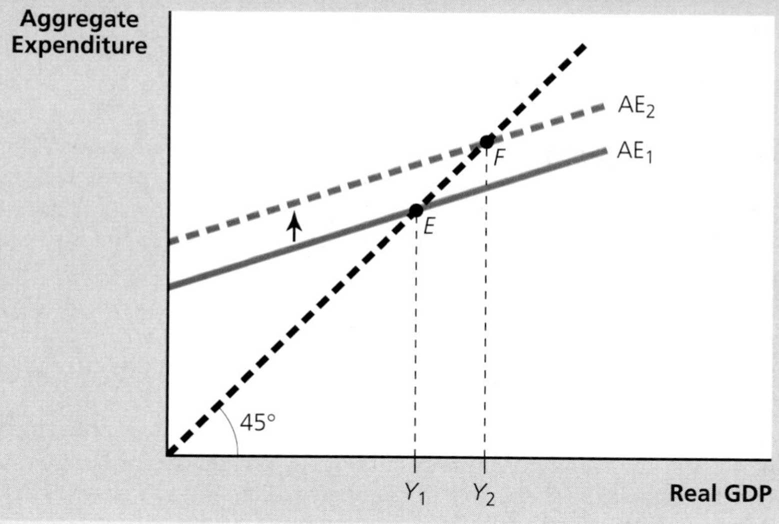

FIGURE 12

A shift in foreign tastes toward U.S. goods, a shift in U.S. tastes away from foreign goods, or a depreciation of the U.S. dollar would increase net exports in the U.S., and cause the U.S. aggregate expenditure line to shift upward from AE_1 to AE_2. Equilibrium moves from point E to point F and real GDP rises from Y_1 to Y_2.

SPENDING SHOCKS IN AN OPEN ECONOMY

Spending shocks—which change aggregate expenditure at each level of output—change equilibrium GDP in an open economy just as they do in a closed economy. But in addition to the spending shocks we've discussed elsewhere in the book, an open economy has a new type of spending shock: a change in net exports.

Suppose, for example, that foreign tastes change in favor of U.S. goods. This will increase net exports at each level of output, shifting the aggregate expenditure line in Figure 12 upward, to the dashed line. The equilibrium moves to point F, and real GDP rises to Y_2. The same would occur if U.S. tastes shifted away from foreign goods toward American goods. In this case, imports would decrease at every level of income. Once again, net exports would rise, and the aggregate expenditure line would shift upward.

A change in the exchange rate can also cause a net-export shock, leading to a shift like that in Figure 12. If the dollar depreciates against the foreign currencies of its major trading partners, U.S. goods would become cheaper to foreigners, and net exports would rise.

A rise in net exports—due to a change in tastes toward U.S. goods or a depreciation of the dollar—will shift the aggregate expenditure line upward, increasing equilibrium GDP. A fall in net exports—due to a change in tastes away from U.S. goods or an appreciation of the dollar—will shift the aggregate expenditure line downward, decreasing equilibrium GDP.

The impact of net-export shocks on equilibrium GDP—and the fact that they can arise from changes in the exchange rate—helps us understand one reason why governments are often concerned about their exchange rates: An unstable exchange rate can result in repeated shocks to the economy. At worst, this can cause fluctuations in GDP; at best, it makes the central bank's job more difficult as it tries to keep the economy on an even keel.

EXCHANGE RATES AND ECONOMIC POLICY

Monetary and fiscal policies, which we've explored in several earlier chapters, can change GDP in an open economy as well as a closed one. But in an open economy, these policies have additional effects because *they also cause changes in the exchange rate.*

ENHANCED EFFECTIVENESS OF MONETARY POLICY. Suppose the United States is in a recession, and the Fed decides to increase equilibrium GDP. As you've learned, the Fed—by increasing the money supply—brings down the interest rate. Interest-sensitive spending rises, and the aggregate expenditure line shifts upward. In an open economy, however, this is not the only effect on aggregate expenditure.

By lowering the U.S. interest rate, the Fed makes foreign financial assets more attractive to Americans, which raises their demand for foreign currency. In the market for pounds, for example, this will shift the demand for pounds curve rightward, as in Figure 6. At the same time, U.S. financial assets become less attractive to foreigners, which decreases the supply of foreign exchange (in the market for pounds, a leftward shift in the supply of pounds curve). As long as the exchange rate floats, the combined effect of these changes in supply and demand is a *depreciation of the dollar* against the currencies of its trading partners.

This depreciation will have further effects on the economy. With dollars now cheaper to foreigners, American goods and services are cheaper to them as well. Foreigners will thus buy more U.S. goods, raising U.S. exports. At the same time, the depreciation of the dollar makes foreign goods and services more expensive to Americans, decreasing U.S. imports.

Both the increase in exports and the decrease in imports contribute to a rise in net exports, *NX*. This in turn causes an upward shift in the aggregate expenditure line, like the shift illustrated in Figure 12. Thus, as you can see, the expansionary monetary policy causes the aggregate expenditure line to rise in two ways: first, by increasing interest-sensitive spending, and second, by increasing net exports. As a result, equilibrium GDP rises by more than it would in a closed economy. Expansionary monetary policy—with floating exchange rates—is more effective in raising equilibrium GDP in an open economy.

We can outline the channels through which monetary policy works as follows. The top line shows the familiar effect on interest-sensitive spending, while the bottom line shows the *additional* effect on net exports:

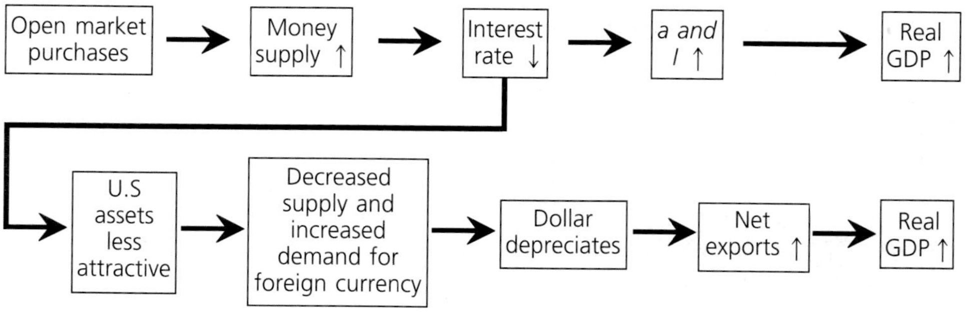

Net Effect: GDP ↑ by more than in a closed economy.

The analysis of contractionary monetary policy is the same, but in reverse. A decrease in the money supply will not only decrease interest-sensitive spending, it will also cause the dollar to appreciate and net exports to drop. Thus, it will cause equilibrium GDP to fall by more than in a closed economy.

The channel of monetary influence through exchange rates and the volume of trade is an important part of the full story of monetary policy in the United States. In countries where exports are relatively large fractions of GDP—such as those of Europe—the trade channel is the main way that monetary policy has its effects.

Monetary policy has a stronger effect in an open economy than in a closed economy because changes in the interest rate affect net exports as well as investment.

REDUCED EFFECT OF FISCAL CHANGES. While monetary policy is more effective when we add the impact on net exports, fiscal policy becomes *less* effective. This is because fiscal policy causes net exports to change in a way that *counteracts* the fiscal policy itself.

Consider an increase in government purchases, which—as you've learned earlier—increases aggregate expenditure. You've also learned that a rise in government purchases has an important by-product: It raises the interest rate in the money market, causing some crowding out of interest-sensitive spending.

But in an open economy, the higher U.S. interest rate has further effects. First, it makes U.S. financial assets more attractive to foreigners, shifting their supply of foreign currency rightward. Second, it makes foreign financial assets less attractive to Americans, shifting U.S. demand for foreign currency leftward. These two shifts cause an *appreciation* of the dollar.

Now, with a higher price for the dollar, American goods are more expensive to foreigners, and U.S. exports fall. Also, foreign goods are cheaper to Americans, so U.S. imports of goods and services rise. American net exports, therefore, decline. Thus, the increase in government purchases—which *increases* aggregate expenditure—also causes net exports to fall—which tends to *decrease* aggregate expenditure. The final rise in aggregate expenditure will be smaller, and so will the final rise in equilibrium GDP.

We can outline the full effects of fiscal policy on GDP as follows:

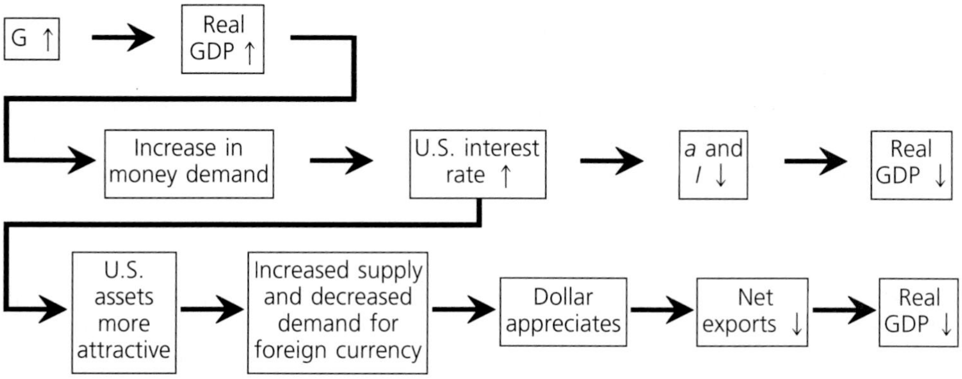

Net Effect: GDP ↑, but by less than in a closed economy.

Notice that, in an open economy, an increase in government purchases not only crowds out interest-sensitive spending (autonomous consumption and investment), but also crowds out net exports. Although it still causes an increase in equilibrium GDP—since the crowding-out effects occur only *as a result* of the rise in GDP—GDP will increase by much less in an open economy than in a closed economy.

A contractionary fiscal change—say, a decrease in government purchases—has exactly the opposite effects: It will cause the U.S. interest rate to fall, the dollar to depreciate, and net exports to rise.

Fiscal policy has a weaker effect on real GDP in an open economy than in a closed economy. By changing the exchange rate, it causes net exports to change in the opposite direction to real GDP.

USING THE THEORY

UNDERSTANDING THE U.S. TRADE DEFICIT

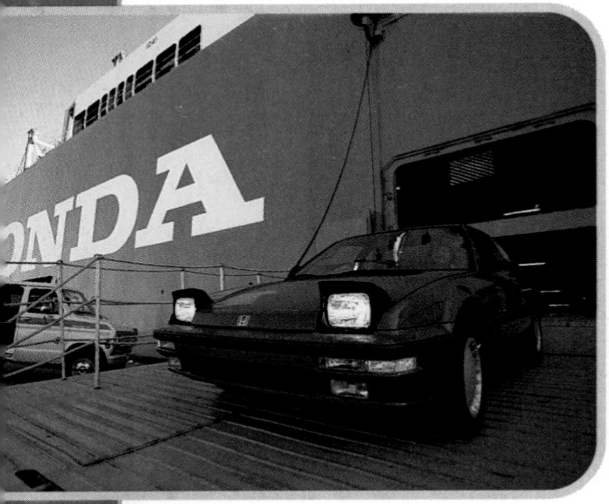

The U.S. trade deficit is often in the news. What, exactly, is it? It is the extent to which a country's imports exceed its exports:

$$\textbf{Trade deficit} = \text{imports} - \text{exports}$$

On the other hand, when exports exceed imports, a nation has a trade surplus:

$$\textbf{Trade surplus} = \text{exports} - \text{imports}$$

As you can see, the trade surplus is nothing more than positive net exports (NX). When net exports are negative, we have a trade deficit.

The United States has had continuing, large trade deficits with the rest of the world since the early 1980s. In 1996, for example, the trade deficit totaled \$99.5 billion. Simply put, Americans bought almost \$100 billion more goods and services from other countries than their residents bought from the United States.

TRADE DEFICIT The excess of a nation's imports over its exports during a given period.

TRADE SURPLUS The excess of a nation's exports over its imports during a given period.

Why does the U.S. have a trade deficit with the rest of the world? A variety of explanations have been offered in the media, including the relatively low quality of U.S. goods (compared to, say, Japan), poor U.S. marketing savvy in selling to foreigners, and a greater degree of protectionism in foreign markets. But economists believe that there is a much more important reason. In this section, we'll use what you've learned about floating exchange rates to show how the U.S. trade deficit arose and why it continues. Our analysis will be simpler if we analyze the U.S. trade deficit with just one country—say, Japan—but our results generalize to the trade deficit with other countries as well.

Before we analyze the causes of the trade deficit, we need to do a little math. Let's begin by breaking down the total quantity of yen demanded by Americans ($D^{¥}$) into two components: the yen demanded to purchase Japanese goods and services (U.S. imports from Japan) and the yen demanded to buy Japanese assets:

$$D^{¥} = \text{U.S. imports} + \text{U.S. purchases of Japanese assets}$$

Similarly, we can divide the total quantity of yen supplied by the Japanese ($S^{¥}$) into two components: the yen exchanged for dollars to purchase American goods

(U.S. exports to Japan), and the yen exchanged for dollars to purchase American assets like stocks, bonds or real estate:

$$S^{¥} = \text{U.S. exports} + \text{Japanese purchases of U.S. assets}$$

As long as the yen floats against the dollar without government intervention—which is true during most periods—we know that the exchange rate will adjust until the quantity of yen supplied and demanded are equal, or $D^{¥} = S^{¥}$. Substituting the foregoing breakdowns into this equation, we have

$$\text{U.S. imports} + \text{U.S. purchases of Japanese assets} = \text{U.S. exports} + \text{Japanese purchases of U.S. assets}$$

Now let's rearrange this equation—subtracting U.S. exports from both sides, and subtracting American purchases of Japanese assets from both sides, to get

$$\text{U.S. imports} - \text{U.S. exports} = \text{Japanese purchases of U.S. assets} - \text{U.S. purchases of Japanese assets}$$

The term on the left should look familiar: It is the U.S. trade deficit. But what is the expression on the right? It tells us the extent to which the Japanese are buying more of our assets than we are buying of theirs. It is often called the **net capital inflow** into the United States, because when the Japanese buy U.S. assets, funds flow into the U.S. financial market, where U.S. firms and the U.S. government can borrow them. Thus, the equation we've derived—which must hold true when exchange rates float—can also be expressed as

NET CAPITAL INFLOW An inflow of funds equal to a nation's trade deficit.

$$\text{U.S. trade deficit} = \text{U.S. net capital inflow}$$

Why have we bothered to derive this equation? Because it tells us two very important things about the U.S. trade deficit. First, it tells us how the trade deficit is *financed*. Think about it: If the U.S. is running a trade deficit with Japan, it means that the Japanese are providing more goods and services to Americans—more automobiles, VCRs, memory chips, and other goods—than Americans are providing to them. The Japanese are not doing this out of kindness. They must be getting *something* in return for the extra goods we are getting, and the equation tells us just what that is: U.S. assets. This is one reason why the trade deficit concerns U.S. policy makers: It results in a transfer of wealth from Americans to foreign residents.

The second important insight provided by the equation is that a trade deficit can arise *because* of a net capital inflow. That is, if forces in the global economy make the right side of the equation positive, then the left side must be positive as well, and we will have a trade deficit. Indeed, economists believe this is just what has happened to the United States: that the U.S. trade deficit has been caused by a massive capital inflow that arose in the early 1980s, as illustrated in Figure 13. That capital inflow was unprecedented in size and duration, and it reversed a longstanding pattern of ownership between the United States and other countries. For decades, American holdings of foreign assets far exceeded foreign holdings of U.S. assets. But the capital inflows of the 1980s changed that: By 1988, foreigners held \$533 billion more in U.S. assets than Americans held in foreign assets.

FIGURE 13

NET CAPITAL FLOWS INTO THE UNITED STATES AS A PERCENT OF GDP

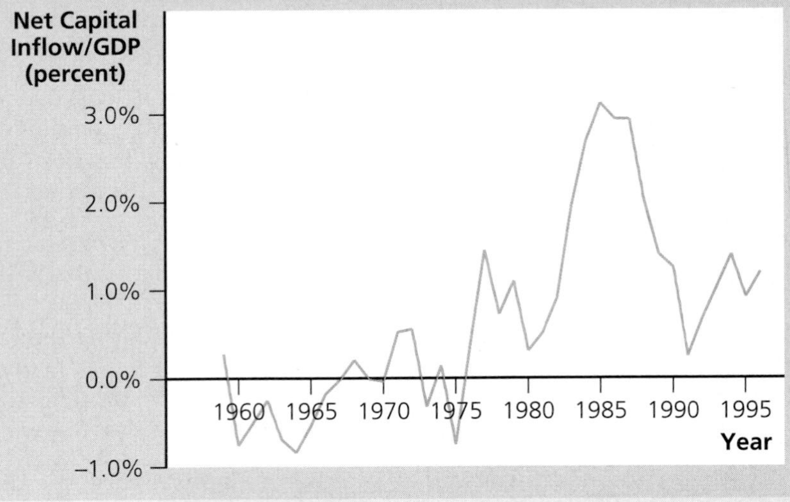

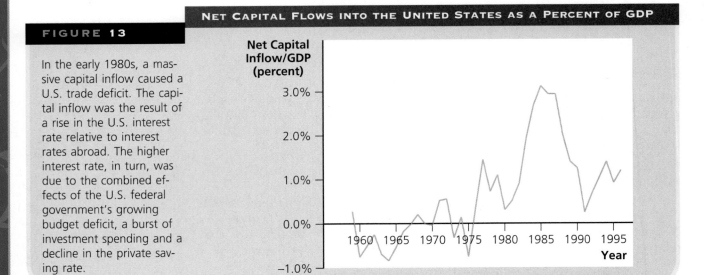

In the early 1980s, a massive capital inflow caused a U.S. trade deficit. The capital inflow was the result of a rise in the U.S. interest rate relative to interest rates abroad. The higher interest rate, in turn, was due to the combined effects of the U.S. federal government's growing budget deficit, a burst of investment spending and a decline in the private saving rate.

But how does a capital inflow *cause* a trade deficit? When foreigners start buying more of our assets than we are buying of theirs, the dollar will appreciate above the value it would have if there were no net capital inflow. This causes U.S. goods to appear more expensive to foreigners, and foreign goods to appear cheaper to Americans. Thus,

an increase in the net capital inflow contributes to an appreciation of the domestic currency. As a result, exports—which become more expensive for foreigners—decline. Imports—which appear cheaper to Americans—increase. The result is a rise in the trade deficit (or a fall in the trade surplus).

How can we explain this huge capital inflow of the 1980s? An important part of the story is *a rise in U.S. interest rates relative to interest rates abroad,* which made U.S. assets more attractive to foreigners, and foreign assets less attractive to Americans. We can discern three separate causes of this phenomenon, which occurred sequentially.

One cause was the federal government's budget deficit. Because of tax cuts phased in since 1981, and also the recession of 1981–82, the deficit mushroomed from 1981 to 1983. The rise in the budget deficit increased U.S. interest rates relative to rates abroad, making U.S. assets more appealing to foreigners. After reaching a maximum of over 4 percent of GDP, the budget deficit gradually declined.

But by then, another economic event occurred: a rise in investment spending relative to GDP in the United States. Investment had fallen to low levels during the recession of 1981–82, but it rose rapidly in 1984–85. The rise in investment spending increased the demand for loanable funds and contributed to the rise in the U.S. interest rate relative to interest rates abroad.

From 1985 onward, investment spending gradually declined. But then a third cause sustained the rise in the U.S. interest rate relative to interest rates abroad: a fall in private saving relative to GDP. Private saving had been stable until about 1985, and then it fell gradually for the second half of the decade. The decrease in saving translated into a decrease in the supply of loanable funds, raising the interest rate and attracting foreign funds into the loanable funds market.[6]

Remember that, under floating exchange rates, the capital inflow equals the trade deficit. Thus, the story of the U.S. capital inflow of the 1980s is also the story of the U.S. trade deficit:

We can trace the rise in the trade deficit during the 1980s to three important sources: a rising budget deficit in 1981–83, followed by a burst of investment spending in 1984–85, followed by a drop in the private saving rate from 1985 until the end of the decade. Each of these contributed to a higher relative U.S. interest rate, sustaining a large capital inflow.

As Figure 13 shows, the trade deficit almost disappeared during the recession of 1991 and then rose to about 1 percent of GDP. Although this is far below its level of the 1980s, the trade deficit persists. Why?

As you now know, another way to phrase this question is, Why does the United States continue to attract funds from foreign countries (the capital inflow)? For three reasons: First, there is a continuing, though much smaller, budget deficit. Second, investment spending became strong again by the mid-1990s as growth in the United States outpaced that in many other large industrialized countries. And third, private saving, while higher than in the 1980s, remains low in comparison to other countries.

6 In this section, we've used the loanable funds model—a classical idea—to explain the rise in the U.S. interest rate because it reflects a trend taking place over many years. But we can also understand why the interest rate rose in a Keynesian framework. Each of our three causes—a rising budget deficit, rising investment spending, and falling saving (rising consumption) were positive spending shocks to the economy. As you've learned previously, these spending shocks increase money demand and drive up the interest rate. And the Fed often responded by raising the interest rate further in order to prevent the economy from overheating.

SUMMARY

When residents of two countries trade with one another, one party ordinarily makes use of the foreign exchange market to trade one national currency for another. In this market, suppliers of a currency interact with demanders to determine an exchange rate—the price of one currency in terms of another.

In the market for U.S. dollars and British pounds, for example, demanders are mostly Americans who wish to obtain pounds in order to buy goods and services from British firms, or to buy British assets. A higher dollar price for the pound will lead Americans to demand fewer pounds—the demand curve is downward sloping. Changes in U.S. real GDP, the U.S. price level relative to the British price level, Americans' tastes for British goods, interest rates in the U.S. relative to Britain, or expectations regarding the exchange rate, can each cause the demand curve to shift.

Suppliers of pounds are mostly British residents who wish to buy American goods, services, or assets. A higher dollar price for the pound will lead Britons to supply more pounds—the supply curve slopes upward. The supply curve will shift in response to changes in British real GDP, prices in Britain relative to the United States, British tastes for U.S. goods, the British interest rate relative to the U.S. rate, and expectations regarding the exchange rate.

The equilibrium exchange rate is determined where the supply and demand curves cross. If the equilibrium is disturbed by, say, a rightward shift of the demand curve, then the currency being demanded will appreciate—the exchange rate will rise. (The other country's currency will depreciate.) In a similar way, a rightward shift of the supply curve will cause the currency being supplied to depreciate.

In practice, each country's currency is traded in a variety of markets around the world. Currency traders, in a search for profits, engage in arbitrage whenever the exchange rate differs between two markets. This activity—buying low and selling high—serves to eliminate any exchange rate differentials. A more complex form of arbitrage ensures that the direct and indirect prices of one currency in terms of another will be the same.

International trade can be an important determinant of a country's level of GDP. An increase in net exports will shift the *AE* line upward, increasing equilibrium GDP. A decrease in net exports will have the opposite effect.

Monetary policy is more effective in an open economy than in a closed economy. In addition to its impact on interest-sensitive spending, monetary policy also changes the exchange rate and net exports, adding to changes in output. Fiscal policy, by contrast, is less effective in an open economy. In this case, the changes in the exchange rate and net exports work to counteract the impact of fiscal policy on GDP.

KEY TERMS

foreign exchange market
exchange rate
demand curve for foreign currency
supply curve for foreign currency
floating exchange rate
appreciation
depreciation
purchasing power parity (PPP) theory
arbitrage
bilateral arbitrage
triangular arbitrage
closed economy
open economy
trade deficit
trade surplus
net capital inflow

REVIEW QUESTIONS

1. Why do Americans demand foreign currency? Why is the demand curve for foreign currency downward sloping? What shifts the demand curve for foreign currency to the right? What shifts it to the left?

2. Why do foreigners supply foreign currency? Why does the supply of foreign currency curve slope upward? What shifts the supply curve for foreign currency to the right? What shifts it to the left?

3. Explain how the expected appreciation of a foreign currency can become a self-fulfilling prophecy.

4. What moves exchange rates in the very short run? In the short run?

5. "A weak currency is a sign of a sick economy." True or false? Explain.

6. What is purchasing power parity? Why might exchange rates deviate from purchasing power parity?

7. What is a managed float and why would a government use it?

8. What is the difference between bilateral arbitrage and triangular arbitrage? What would be different about foreign exchange market equilibria if neither type of arbitrage took place?

9. What changes would occur in a country's aggregate expenditure line if the country were formerly a closed economy and suddenly became open?

10. How do imports act as an automatic stabilizer?

11. How does the appreciation of the dollar affect real GDP?

12. According to economists, what caused the trade deficit in the 1980s? Why does the trade deficit persist?

PROBLEMS AND EXERCISES

1. Do the following events cause the dollar to appreciate against the French franc or to depreciate?
   a. Health experts discover that red wine, especially French red wine, lowers cholesterol.
   b. France's GDP falls rapidly.
   c. The U.S. experiences a higher inflation rate.
   d. The U.S. runs a large budget deficit.

2. Let the demand for English pounds and the supply of English pounds be described by the following equations:

$$\text{Demand for pounds} = 10 - 2e$$
$$\text{Supply of pounds} = 4 + 3e,$$

   where the quantities are in millions of pounds and e is dollars per pound.
   a. Find the equilibrium exchange rate.
   b. Suppose the U.S. government intervenes in the foreign currency market and uses U.S. dollars to buy 2 million pounds. What happens to the exchange rate? Why might the U.S. government do this?

3. Suppose the following are the exchange rates among the U.S. dollar, French franc, and deutsche mark.

dollars per franc = 0.2
dollars per deutsche mark = 0.5
deutsche marks per franc = 0.3

Is there an opportunity for triangular arbitrage? If so, how would it work?

4. Suppose the U.S. and Mexico are sole trading partners with each other. The Fed, afraid that the economy is about to overheat, decreases the U.S. money supply.
   a. Will the dollar appreciate or depreciate against the Mexican peso? Illustrate with a diagram of the dollar–peso foreign exchange market.
   b. What will happen to equilibrium GDP in the U.S.? Illustrate with an open-economy aggregate expenditure diagram.
   c. How would your analyses in (a) and (b) change if, at the same time that the Fed was increasing the interest rate, the Mexican central bank increased the Mexican interest rate by an equivalent amount?

5. Suppose that the U.S. government raises taxes. Illustrate the effects on the open-economy aggregate expenditure line. How would your analysis change if the supply of foreign currency were completely insensitive to changes in the U.S. interest rate?

CHALLENGE QUESTION

1. It is often stated that the U.S. trade deficit with Japan results from Japanese trade barriers against U.S. goods.
   a. Suppose that Japan and the U.S. trade goods but not assets. Show—with a diagram of the dollar–yen market—that a trade deficit is impossible. (*Hint:* With no trading in assets, the demand for yen is equal to U.S. imports measured in yen, and the supply of yen is equal to U.S. exports measured in yen.)
   b. In the diagram, illustrate the impact of a reduction in Japanese trade barriers. Would the dollar appreciate or depreciate against the yen? What would be the impact on U.S. net exports?
   c. Now suppose that the United States and Japan also trade assets, but that the Japanese buy more U.S. assets than we buy of theirs. Could the elimination of Japanese trade barriers wipe out the U.S. trade deficit with Japan? Why, or why not? (*Hint:* What is the relationship between the U.S. trade deficit and U.S. net capital inflow?)

MATHEMATICAL APPENDIX

TABLES AND GRAPHS

A brief glance at this text will tell you that graphs are important in economics. Graphs provide a convenient way to display data. Take the example of Len & Harry's, an up-and-coming manufacturer of high-end ice cream products, located in Texas. Suppose that you've just been hired to head Len & Harry's advertising department, and you want to learn as much as you can about how advertising can help the company's sales. One of the simplest things you can do as you begin to analyze the data that have been collected is to organize the information in the form of a table.

Table A1 records the company's total advertising outlay per month in the left-hand column, and the company's ice cream sales during that same month are shown in the right-hand column. Notice that the data are organized so that advertising outlay increases as we move down the first column. Often, just looking at such a table can reveal useful patterns. In this case, it seems that higher advertising outlays are associated with higher monthly sales. This suggests that there may be some *causal relationship* between advertising and sales.

To explore this relationship further, we might decide to plot the data and draw a graph. First, we need to choose units for our two variables. We'll measure both advertising and sales in thousands of dollars. Different values of one variable are then measured along the horizontal axis, increasing as we move rightward from the origin. The corresponding values of the other variable are measured along the vertical axis, increasing as we move upward, away from the origin.

Using the data in the table, let X stand for advertising outlay per month, and let Y stand for sales per month. Notice that each row of the table gives us a pair of numbers: The first is always the value of the variable we are calling X, and the second is the value of the variable we are calling Y. We often write such pairs in the form (X,Y). For example, we would write the first three rows of the table as (2,46), (3,49) and (6,58), respectively.

To plot the pair (X,Y) on a graph, begin at the origin, where the axes cross, count rightward X units along the horizontal axis, then count upward Y units parallel to the vertical axis, and then mark the spot. Thus, to plot the pair (2,46), we go rightward 2 units along the horizontal axis and then upward 46 units along the vertical axis, arriving at the point marked A in Figure A1. To plot the next pair, (3,49), we go rightward from the origin 3 units and then upward 49 units, arriving at the point marked B. Carrying on in just this way, we can plot all remaining pairs in Table A1 as the points C, D, E, and F.

If we connect points A through F, we see that they all lie along the same straight line. Now we are getting somewhere. The relationship we've discovered appears from the graph to be very regular, indeed.

Study the graph closely. You will notice that each time advertising increases (moves rightward) by \$1,000, Y moves upward by \$3,000. For example, when advertising rises from \$2,000 to \$3,000, sales rise from \$46,000 to \$49,000. By checking between any other two points on the graph, you will see that every time X increases horizontally by one unit (here, a unit is \$1,000), Y increases vertically by three units (here, by \$3,000). Thus, we conclude that that the *rate of change* in Y is three units of Y for every one-unit increase in X.

TABLE A1

ADVERTISING AND SALES AT LEN & HARRY'S

Advertising ($1,000s per month)	Sales ($1,000s per month)
2	46
3	49
6	58
7	61
11	73
12	76

FIGURE A1

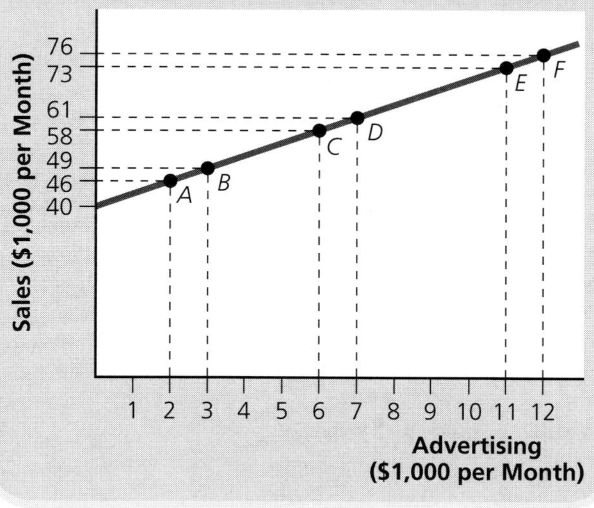

The *slope* of a graph tells us the rate at which the Y-variable changes for every one-unit change in the X-variable. The slope of a straight line between any two points (X_1,Y_1) and (X_2,Y_2) is defined as the change in Y—the vertical "rise"—divided by the change in X—the horizontal "run." This is why the slope is often described as "rise over run." Supposing we start at (X_1,Y_1) and end at (X_2,Y_2); then the change in the X-variable is $(X_2 - X_1)$. The corresponding change in the Y-variable is $(Y_2 - Y_1)$. We therefore compute the slope as follows:

$$\text{Slope of the line from } (X_1,Y_1) \text{ to } (X_2,Y_2) = \frac{\text{Rise along vertical axis}}{\text{Run along horizontal axis}} = \frac{Y_2 - Y_1}{X_2 - X_1}$$

We sometimes use the capital Greek letter, Δ ("delta"), to denote a change in a variable. Here we would write $\Delta X = X_2 - X_1$ to denote the change in X, and $\Delta Y = Y_2 - Y_1$ to denote the corresponding change in Y. We then could write that same formula for the slope more compactly as

$$\text{Slope of the line from } (X_1,Y_1) \text{ to } (X_2,Y_2) = \frac{\Delta Y}{\Delta X}.$$

NONLINEAR GRAPHS

Although many of the relationships we encounter in economics have straight-line graphs, many do not. Still, graphs can help us understand the underlying relationships, and the concept of slope remains very useful.

As an example, look at the data in Table A2, which records the price of a share of Len and Harry's stock at different points in time since the stock first appeared on the market. To understand how the price of this stock has behaved over time, we might again start by plotting a graph of the data in the table. It seems natural to measure time—in "weeks since launch"—on the X-axis and stock price—in "dollars per share" —on the Y-axis. As you can see in Figure A2, Len and Harry's has had a rocky ride since it came on the market. In its first 10 weeks, each additional week of time was associated with an increase in the stock's price, so the slope of the underlying relationship was positive during that time. Over the next 10 weeks, the story changed: Each additional week saw a decrease in the stock's price from the previous week, so the slope of the relationship was negative then. Between weeks 20 and 30, things leveled off: As those weeks passed by, there was no change in the stock's price, so the slope of the graph was zero during that time. However, between weeks 30 and 40 things picked up, and once again the slope turned positive, with each additional week accompanied by an increase in the price of the stock.

From this example, we can see the following:

- *The slope is positive whenever an increase in* X *is associated with an increase in* Y.
- *The slope is negative whenever an increase in* X *is associated with a decrease in* Y.
- *The slope is equal to zero whenever an increase in* X *is associated with no change in* Y.

TABLE A2

PRICE OF LEN & HARRY'S STOCK SINCE LAUNCH

Weeks Since Launch	Stock Price
3	$20
10	50
18	35
20	20
25	20
30	20
40	75

FIGURE A2

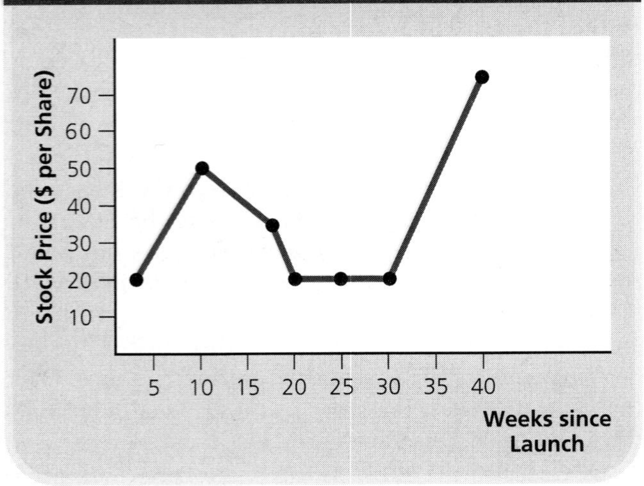

LINEAR EQUATIONS

What if the boss were to stop you in the hallway and ask how much sales the firm could expect if it spent \$5,000 on advertising next month? What if it spent \$8,000? How about \$9,000? Wouldn't it be nice to be able to answer questions like this without having to pull out tables and graphs to do it? As it turns out, any time the relationship you are studying has a straight-line graph, it is easy to figure out the equation for the entire relationship. You then can use the equation to answer any such question that might be put to you.

All straight lines have the same general form. If Y stands for the variable on the vertical axis and X for the variable on the horizontal axis, every straight line has an equation of the form

$$Y = a + bX,$$

where a stands for some number and b for another number. The number a is called the vertical *intercept,* because it marks the point where the graph of this equation hits (intercepts) the vertical axis; this occurs when X takes the value zero. (If you plug $X = 0$ into the equation, you will see that, indeed, $Y = a$.) The number b is the slope of the line, telling us how much Y will change every time X changes by one unit. To confirm this, note that as X increases from 0 to 1, Y goes from a to $a + b$. The number b is therefore the change in Y corresponding to a one-unit change in X—exactly what the slope of the graph should tell us.

More generally, if X changes from some value X_1 to some other value X_2, Y will change from

$$Y_1 = a + bX_1$$

to

$$Y_2 = a + bX_2.$$

If we subtract Y_1 from Y_2 to compute how much Y has changed (ΔY), we find that

$$\begin{aligned} \Delta Y = Y_2 - Y_1 &= (a + bX_2) - (a + bX_1) \\ &= a + bX_2 - a - bX_1 \\ &= b(X_2 - X_1) \\ &= b\Delta X. \end{aligned}$$

Dividing both sides by ΔX, we get

$$\frac{\Delta Y}{\Delta X} = b,$$

confirming that b really does measure the slope.

If b is a positive number, a one-unit increase in X causes Y to increase by b units, so the graph of our line would slope upward, as illustrated by the red line in panel (a) of Figure A3. If b is a negative number, then a one-unit increase in X will cause Y to *decrease* by b units, so the graph would slope downward, as the blue line does in panel (a). Of course, b could equal zero. If it does, a one-unit increase in X causes no change in Y, so the graph of the line is flat, like the black line in panel (a).

The value of a has no effect on the slope of the graph. Instead, different values of a determine the graph's position. When a is a positive number, the graph will intercept the vertical Y-axis above the origin, as the red line does in panel (b) of Figure A3. When a is negative, however, the graph will intercept the Y-axis *below* the origin, like the blue line in panel (b). When a is zero, the graph intercepts the Y-axis right at the origin, as the black line does in panel (b).

Let's see if we can figure out the equation for the relationship depicted in Figure A1. There, X denotes advertising and Y denotes sales. It is easy to see that when advertising expenditure is zero, sales are \$40,000. Therefore, our equation will have a *vertical* intercept of $a = 40$. Earlier, we calculated the slope of this graph to be 3. Therefore, the equation will have $b = 3$. Putting these two observations together, we find that the equation for the line in Figure A1 is

$$Y = 40 + 3X.$$

FIGURE A3

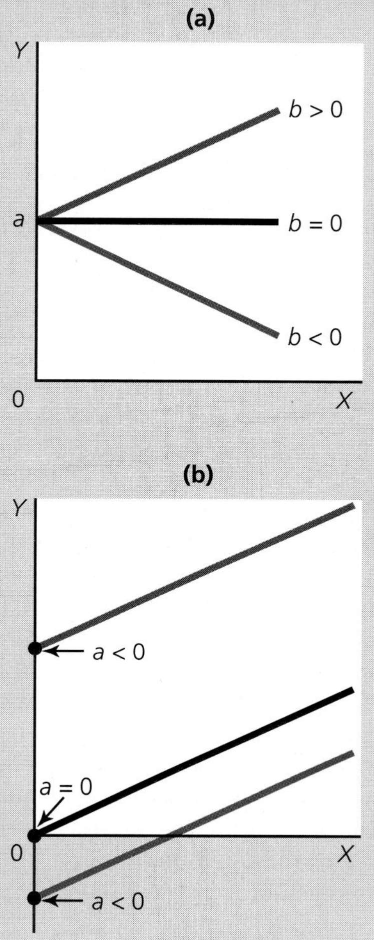

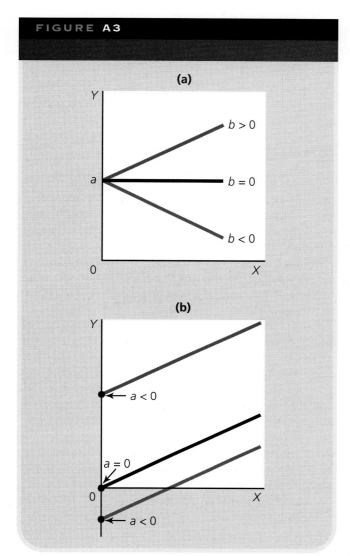

Now if the boss asks you how much in sales to expect from a particular expenditure on advertising, you'd be able to come right back with an answer: You'd simply multiply the amount spent on advertising by 3, add $40,000, and that would be your sales. To confirm this, plug in for X in this equation any amount of advertising from the left-hand column of Table A1. You'll see that you get the corresponding amount of sales in the right-hand column.

HOW LINES AND CURVES SHIFT

So far, we've focused on relationships where some variable Y depends on a single other variable, X. But in many of our theories, we recognize that some variable of interest to us is actually affected by more than just one other variable. When Y is affected by both X and some third variable, changes in that third variable will usually cause a *shift* in the graph of the relationship between X and Y. This is because whenever we draw the graph between X and Y, we are holding fixed every other variable that might possibly affect Y.

A graph between two variables X *and* Y *is only a picture of their relationship when all other variables affecting* Y *are constant. Changes in any one or more of those other variables will shift the graph of* X *and* Y.

Think back to the relationship between advertising and sales. Earlier, we supposed sales depend only on advertising. But suppose we make an important discovery: Ice cream sales are *also* affected by how hot the weather is! What's more, all of the data in Table A1 on which we previously based our analysis turns out to have been from the month of June, when the average temperature in Texas is always 80 degrees. What's going to happen in July, when the temperature rises to its usual sweltering 100 degrees?

In Figure A4 we've redrawn the graph from Figure A1, this time labeling the line "June." Often, a good way to determine how a graph will shift is to perform a simple experiment like this: Put your pencil tip anywhere on the graph labeled June, let's say at point C. Now ask the following question: If I hold advertising constant at $6,000, do I expect to sell more or less ice cream as temperature rises in July? If you expect to sell

FIGURE A4

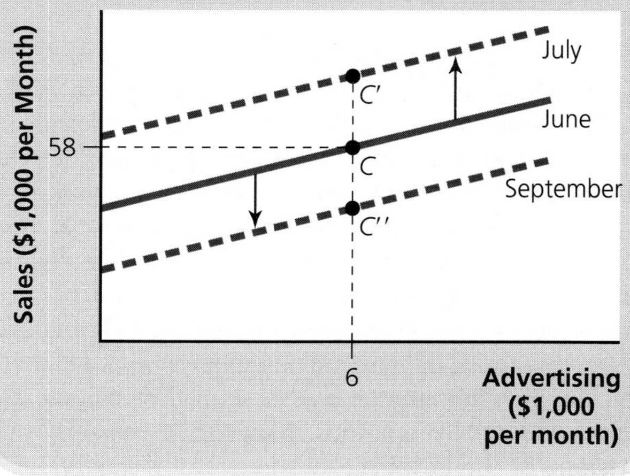

FIGURE A5

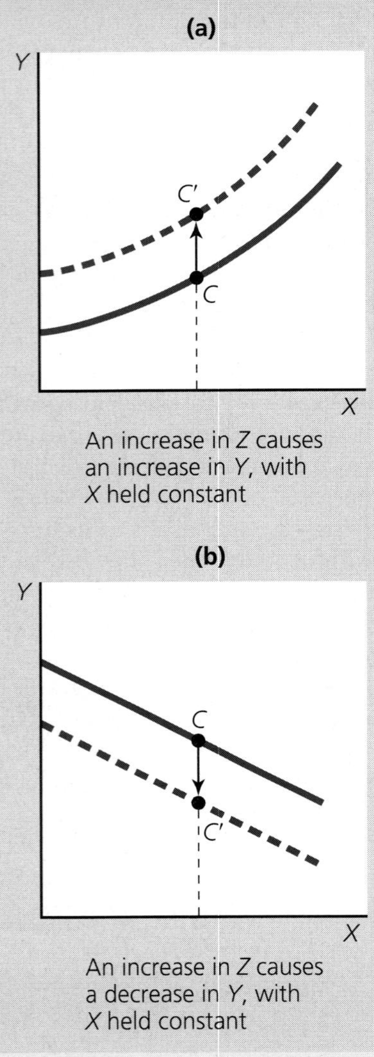
(a)
Y
C′
C
X
An increase in Z causes an increase in Y, with X held constant
(b)
Y
C
C′
X
An increase in Z causes a decrease in Y, with X held constant

more, then the amount of sales corresponding to \$6,000 of advertising will be *above* point C, at a point such as C′. From this, we can tell that the graph will shift upward as temperature rises. In September, however, when temperature falls, the amount of sales corresponding to \$6,000 in advertising would be less than it is at point C. It would be shown by a point such as C″. In that case, the graph would shift downward.

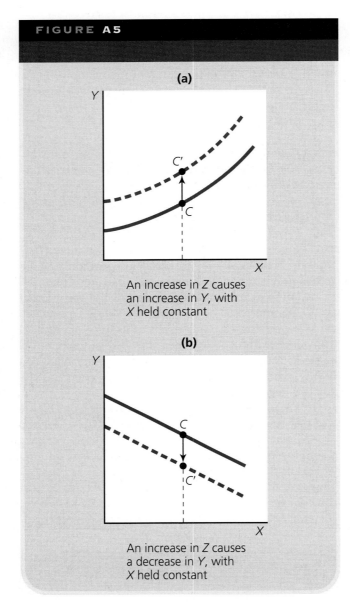

The same procedure works well whether the original graph slopes upward or downward, and whether it is a straight line or a curved one. Figure A5 sketches two examples. In panel (a), an increase in some third variable, *Z*, increases the value of *Y* for each value of *X*, so the graph of the relationship between *X* and *Y* shifts upward as *Z* increases. We often phrase it this way: "An increase in *Z* causes an increase in *Y*, *with X held constant*." In panel (b), an increase in *Z decreases* the value of *Y*, with *X* held constant, so the graph of the relationship between *X* and *Y* shifts *downward* as *Z* increases.

SOLVING EQUATIONS

When we first derived the equation for the relationship between advertising and sales, we wanted to know what level of sales to expect from different amounts of advertising. But what if we're asked a slightly different question? Suppose, this time, you are told that the sales committee has set an ambitious goal of \$64,000 for next month's sales. The treasurer needs to know how much to budget for advertising, and you have to come up with the answer.

Since we know how advertising and sales are related, we ought to be able to answer this question. One way is just to look at the graph in Figure A1. There, we could first locate sales of \$64,000 on the vertical axis. Then, if we read over to the line and then down, we find the amount of advertising that would be necessary to generate that level of sales. Yet even with that carefully drawn diagram, it is not always easy to see just exactly how much advertising would be required. If we need to be precise, we'd better use the equation for the graph, instead.

According to the equation, sales (*Y*) and advertising (*X*) are related as follows:

$$Y = 40 + 3X.$$

In the problem before us, we know the value for sales, and we need to solve for the corresponding amount of advertising. Substituting the sales target of \$64,000 for *Y*, we need to find that value of *X* for which

$$64 = 40 + 3X.$$

Here, *X* is the unknown value for which we want to solve.

Whenever we solve one equation for one unknown, say, *X*, we need to *isolate* *X* on one side of the equals sign and everything else on the other side of the equals sign. We do this by performing identical operations on both sides of the equals sign. Here, we can first subtract 40 from both sides, getting

$$24 = 3X.$$

We can then divide both sides by 3 and get

$$8 = X.$$

This is our answer; if we want to achieve sales of \$64,000, we'll need to spend \$8,000 on advertising.

By looking back over what we just did, we can come up with a useful formula that will help to solve similar equations. Starting with an equation of the form

$$Y = a + bX,$$

we first subtracted a from both sides to get

$$Y - a = bX.$$

We then divided both sides by b to get our answer:

$$\frac{Y - a}{b} = X.$$

This is a formula you can use to solve for X whenever X and Y are linearly related and whenever b is not equal to zero. Of course, not all relationships are linear, so this formula will not work in every situation. But no matter what the underlying relationship, the idea remains the same:

> *To solve for* X *in any equation, rearrange the equation, following the rules of algebra, so that* X *appears on one side of the equals sign and everything else in the equation appears on the other side.*

PERCENTAGE CHANGES

It is often convenient to express changes in percentage terms, rather than absolute terms. While we are all quite used to thinking in percentages, a quick review of how to calculate them may be helpful. If some variable X starts at one value and ends at another, the percentage change in X, denoted, $\%\Delta X$, is computed as follows:

$$\%\Delta X = \frac{\text{ending value of } X - \text{starting value of } X}{\text{starting value of } X} \times 100$$

Look at this formula for a moment. It says that, to calculate the *percentage* change in X, first compute the *change* in X by subtracting the ending value from the starting value, and then divide by the "base," or starting value, of X. The resulting fraction is then multiplied by 100. The formula shows us that:

- *Whenever a variable decreases, the percentage change in its value will be negative.*
- *Whenever a variable increases, the percentage change in its value will be positive.*

Sometimes, we are interested in computing the percentage change in a product or a ratio. There are some useful rules of thumb that can simplify those computations. Specifically, we have:

Product Rule: If $A = B \times C$, then $\%\Delta A = \%\Delta B + \%\Delta C$.

Quotient Rule: If $A = B/C$, then $\%\Delta A = \%\Delta B - \%\Delta C$.

The first rule says that when A is the product of B and C, to find the percentage change in A, we simply *add* the percentage change in B to the percentage change in C. The second rule says that when A is the quotient, B/C, to find the percentage change in A, simply *subtract* the percentage change in C from the percentage change in B.

Strictly speaking, these rules are *approximations.* They are most accurate when the percentage changes in B and C are extremely small. Yet, as long as those percentage changes remain "relatively small," the rules will provide "reasonably good" approximations. A few examples will help to convince you.

Suppose B rises from 100 to 103, while C rises from 20 to 21. To keep things straight, we've recorded the relevant data in Table A3. The first two rows of the table record the beginning and ending values of B and C, and the percentage change in each variable. The last

TABLE A3

RULES OF THUMB FOR PERCENTAGE CHANGES

Variable	Beginning value	Ending value	Calculated percentage change
B	100	103	+3
C	20	21	+5
$B \times C$	2,000	2,163	+8.15
B/π	5	4.905	−1.90

two rows show the beginning and ending values for the product $B \times C$ and the quotient B/C, respectively, and the percentage change in each of these, calculated exactly.

Now look at what we have. Moving across the third row, we see that $B \times C$ rises from 2,000 to 2,163, a percentage increase of 8.15% when computed exactly. Notice that this is very close to what we would get if, instead, we just applied our product rule, adding the 3% change in B to the 5% change in C to get an estimate of 8% for the change in the product $B \times C$. Thus, our approximation is very close. Similarly, moving across the fourth row, we find that the quotient B/C declines from 5 to 4.905, a percentage decrease of exactly 1.9%. Had we applied our quotient rule instead, we would have taken the 3% increase in B and subtracted the 5% increase in C to get 3% − 5% = −2%—again, very close to the exact result of −1.9%.

A SPECIAL SUM

In economics, we sometimes need to evaluate the sum of an infinite number of terms. A common example is the sum of a *geometric series,* in which some number or expression is raised to higher and higher powers. If H is the number we are raising to higher powers, then we can write the sum (S) of the geometric series as

$$S = 1 + H + H^2 + H^3 + H^4 + \ldots .$$

In all of the geometric series you will encounter in this book, H will be a fraction between 0 and 1. For example, when H is the fraction $\frac{1}{2}$, the sum of the geometric series is

$$\begin{aligned} S &= 1 + \tfrac{1}{2} + (\tfrac{1}{2})^2 + (\tfrac{1}{2})^3 + (\tfrac{1}{2})^4 + \ldots \\ &= 1 + 1/2 + 1/4 + 1/8 + 1/16 + \ldots . \end{aligned}$$

Notice that each time we add a term, it is smaller than the term before. Eventually, as we continue to add terms, they will become so small that we can safely ignore them. That is, the sum *converges* (becomes closer and closer to) some finite number, which we are calling S.

It turns out that, as long as H is a fraction between 0 and 1, we can use a very simple formula to calculate S. To get this formula, we'll start with the equation for S itself:

$$S = 1 + H + H^2 + H^3 + H^4 + \ldots .$$

Next, we multiply both sides of the previous equation by H, to get

$$\begin{aligned} H \times S &= H(1 + H + H^2 + H^3 + H^4 + \ldots) \\ &= H + H^2 + H^3 + H^4 + H^5 + \ldots . \end{aligned}$$

Now we subtract this expression from the original expression, yielding

$$\begin{aligned} S &= 1 + H + H^2 + H^3 + H^4 + \ldots \\ -(H \times S) &= \quad\; - H - H^2 - H^3 - H^4 - \ldots \end{aligned}$$

You can see that all the terms cancel out except for "1" from the first equation. Therefore, we end up with

$$S - HS = S(1 - H) = 1.$$

Finally, we divide both sides by $(1 - H)$ to get the formula for S, the sum of the geometric series that we've been seeking:

$$S = 1/(1 - H)$$

When H is a fraction between 0 and 1, our formula gives us a very simple way to compute a rather complicated-looking sum:

> *When H is a positive fraction less than 1, the sum of the infinite geometric series*
>
> $$S = 1 + H + H^2 + H^3 + H^4 + \ldots .$$
>
> *resolves to the simple expression*
>
> $$S = 1/(1 - H)$$

When we use this formula in the text, H will sometimes be an expression involving other variables. For example, suppose $H = (1 - a)$, so that our geometric series is

$$S = 1 + (1 - a) + (1 - a)^2 + (1 - a)^3 + (1 - a)^4 + \ldots .$$

Then, as long as $(1 - a)$ is a fraction between 0 and 1, we can still use our formula. The sum of the infinite geometric series will be $1/(1 - H) = 1/[1 - (1 - a)] = 1/a$.

GLOSSARY

A

absolute advantage The ability to produce a good or service using fewer resources than other producers use.

active monetary policy Federal Reserve policy that adjusts the money supply in response to changes in economic conditions.

aggregate demand (*AD*) curve A curve indicating equilibrium GDP at each price level.

aggregate expenditure (*AE*) The sum of spending by households, business firms, and the government on final goods and services.

aggregate production function The relationship showing how much total output can be produced with different quantities of labor, and with land, capital, and technology held constant.

aggregation The process of combining different things into a single category.

alternate goods Other goods that a firm could produce using some of the same types of inputs as the good in question.

appreciation An increase in the price of a currency in a floating-rate system.

arbitrage Simultaneous buying and selling of a foreign currency in order to profit from a difference in exchange rates.

autonomous consumption spending The part of consumption spending that is independent of income; also, the vertical intercept of the consumption function.

average standard of living Total output (real GDP) per person.

average tax rate The fraction of a given income paid in taxes.

B

balance sheet A financial statement showing assets, liabilities, and net worth at a point in time.

banking panic A situation in which depositors attempt to withdraw funds from many banks simultaneously.

basic principles of economics A small set of basic ideas that are used repeatedly in analyzing economic problems. They form the foundation of economic theory.

bilateral arbitrage Arbitrage involving one pair of currencies.

black market An illegal market in which goods are sold at prices above the legal ceiling.

bond An IOU issued by a corporation or government agency when it borrows funds.

boom A period of time during which real GDP exceeds full-employment, potential GDP.

budget deficit The difference between government purchases and net taxes.

business cycles Fluctuations in real GDP around its long-term growth trend.

C

capital Long-lasting tools used in producing goods and services.

capital gains tax A tax on profits earned when a financial asset is sold at more than its acquisition price.

capitalism An economic system in which most resources are owned privately.

capitalized value The present value of the future income stream generated by an asset.

capital per worker The total capital stock divided by total employment.

capital stock The total value of all goods that will provide useful services in future years.

cash in the hand of the public Currency and coins held outside of banks.

central bank A nation's principal monetary authority.

change in demand A shift of a demand curve in response to a change in some variable other than price.

change in quantity demanded A movement along a demand curve in response to a change in price.

change in quantity supplied A movement along a supply curve in response to a change in price.

change in supply A shift of a supply curve in response to a change in some variable other than price.

circular flow A diagram that shows how goods, resources, and dollar payments flow between households and firms.

classical dichotomy The classical idea that real variables are independent of the quantity of money in the economy.

classical model A macroeconomic model that explains the long-run behavior of the economy, assuming that all markets clear.

closed economy An economy that does not trade with the rest of the world.

command system An economic system in which resources are allocated according to explicit instructions from a central authority.

communism An economic system in which most resources are owned in common.

comparative advantage The ability to produce a good or service at a lower opportunity cost than other producers.
complement A good that is used *together with* some other good.
complete crowding out A dollar-for-dollar decline in one sector's spending caused by an increase in some other sector's spending.
Consumer Price Index An index of the cost, through time, of a fixed market basket of goods purchased by a typical household in some base period.
consumption The part of GDP purchased by households as final users.
consumption function A positively-sloped relationship between real consumption spending and real disposable income.
consumption–income line A line showing aggregate consumption spending at each level of real income or GDP.
consumption tax A tax on the part of their income that households spend.
corporate profits tax A tax on the profits earned by corporations.
countercyclical fiscal policy Changes in taxes or government spending designed to counteract a boom or recession.
critical assumption Any assumption that affects the conclusions of a model in an important way.
crowding out A decline in one sector's spending caused by an increase in some other sector's spending.
cyclical deficit The part of the federal budget deficit that varies with the business cycle.
cyclical unemployment Joblessness arising from changes in production over the business cycle.

D

deflation A period during which the price level is falling.
demand curve The graphical depiction of a demand schedule; a line showing the quantity of a good or service demanded at various prices, with all other variables held constant.
demand curve for foreign currency A curve indicating the quantity of a foreign currency that Americans will want to buy, during a given period, at each different exchange rate.
demand deposit multiplier The number by which a change in reserves is multiplied to determine the resulting change in demand deposits.
demand deposits Checking accounts that do not pay interest.
demand-management policies Government policies designed to change the level of spending in the economy.
demand schedule A list showing the quantities of a good that consumers would choose to purchase at different prices, with all other variables held constant.
demand shock Any event that causes the *AD* curve to shift.
depreciation A decrease in the price of a currency in a floating-rate system.
depression An unusually severe recession.
discount rate The interest rate the Fed charges on loans to banks.
discouraged workers Individuals who would like a job, but have given up searching for one.
disequilibrium A situation in which a market does not clear—quantity supplied is not equal to quantity demanded.
disposable income The part of household income that remains after paying taxes.
diversifiable risk Risk that can be reduced through diversification.

E

economics The study of choice under conditions of scarcity.
economic system A system of resource allocation and resource ownership.
equilibrium A state of rest; a situation that, once achieved, will not change unless some external factor, previously held constant, changes.
equilibrium income (equilibrium GDP) The level of real income at which aggregate spending equals aggregate income.
excess demand At a given price, the excess of quantity demanded over quantity supplied.
excess demand for bonds The amount of bonds demanded exceeds the amount supplied at a particular interest rate.
excess reserves Reserves in excess of required reserves.
excess supply At a given price, the excess of quantity supplied over quantity demanded.
excess supply of money The amount of money supplied exceeds the amount demanded at a particular interest rate.
exchange The act of trading with others to obtain what we desire.
exchange rate The amount of one country's currency that trades for one unit of another country's currency.
expansion A period of increasing real GDP.
expenditure approach Measuring GDP by adding the value of goods and services purchased by each type of final user.
expenditure multiplier The amount by which equilibrium real GDP changes as a result of a one-dollar change in autonomous consumption, investment, or government purchases.
exports Goods and services produced domestically, but sold abroad.

F

factor payments Payments to the owners of resources that are used in production.
factor payments approach Measuring GDP by summing the factor payments made by all firms in the economy.
federal funds rate The interest rate charged for loans of reserves among banks.
Federal Open Market Committee A committee of Federal Reserve officials that establishes U.S. monetary policy.
Federal Reserve System The central bank and national monetary authority of the United States.
fiat money Anything that serves as a means of payment by government declaration

final good A good sold to its final user.
financial intermediary A business firm that specializes in brokering between savers and borrowers.
fiscal policy A change in government purchases or net taxes designed to change total spending and total output.
floating exchange rate An exchange rate that is freely determined by the forces of supply and demand.
foreign exchange market The market in which one country's currency is traded for another country's.
frictional unemployment Joblessness experienced by people who are between jobs or who are just entering or reentering the labor market.
full employment A situation in which there is no cyclical unemployment.
full-employment output level The level of real GDP produced when the labor market clears.

G

GDP price index An index of the price level for all of the final goods and services included in GDP.
government demand for funds curve Indicates the amount of government borrowing at various interest rates.
government purchases Spending by federal, state, and local governments on goods and services.
gross domestic product (GDP) The total value of all final goods and services produced for the marketplace during a given year, within the nation's borders.

H

household saving The portion of after-tax income that households do not spend on consumption goods.
human capital The skills and training of the labor force.

I

imperfectly competitive market A market in which a single buyer or seller has the power to influence the price.
imports Goods and services produced abroad, but consumed domestically.
income The amount that a person or firm earns over a particular period.
index A series of numbers used to track a variable's rise or fall over time.
indexation Adjusting the value of some payment in proportion to a price index.
inferior good A good that people demand less of as their income rises.
inflation rate The percent change in the price level from one period to the next.
injections Spending from sources other than households.
interest rate target The interest rate the Fed aims to achieve by adjusting the money supply.
intermediate goods Goods used up in producing final goods.
investment demand curve Indicates the level of investment spending at various interest rates.
investment tax credit A reduction in taxes for firms that invest in certain favored types of capital.
involuntary part-time workers Individuals who would like a full-time job, but who are working only part time.

J

job creation Increases in employment at expanding firms.
job destruction Decreases in employment at contracting firms.

L

labor The time human beings spend producing goods and services.
labor demand curve Indicates how many workers firms will want to hire at various wage rates.
labor force Those people who have a job or who are looking for one.
labor productivity Total output, real GDP, per worker.
labor supply curve Curve indicating the number of people who want jobs in a labor market at each wage rate.
land The physical space on which production occurs, together with the natural resources found beneath it.
law of demand As the price of a good increases, the quantity demanded decreases.
law of increasing opportunity cost The more of something that is produced, the greater is the opportunity cost of producing one more unit.
law of supply As the price of a good increases, the quantity supplied increases.
leakages Income earned, but not spent, by households during a given year.
liquidity The property of being easily converted into cash.
loan An IOU issued by a household or noncorporate business when it borrows funds.
loanable funds market The market in which financial capital is traded.
long-run aggregate supply curve A vertical line indicating all possible output and price level combinations at which the economy could end up in the long run.
long-run Phillips curve A vertical line indicating that, in the long run, unemployment must equal the natural rate, regardless of the rate of inflation.

M

M1 A standard measure of the money supply, including cash in the hand of the public, checking account deposits, and travelers' checks.
M2 M1 plus savings account balances, noninstitutional money market mutual fund balances, and small time deposits.
macroeconomics The study of the economy as a whole.
marginal product of labor The additional output produced when one more worker is hired.
marginal propensity to consume The amount by which consumption spending changes when disposable income changes by one dollar.
marginal rate of substitution of good *y* for good *x* ($MRS_{y,x}$) The decrease in the quantity of good *y* needed to keep the consumer indifferent following a one-unit increase in good *x;* the slope of an indifference curve at a given point.

marginal tax rate The fraction of an additional dollar of income paid in taxes.

market A group of buyers and sellers with the potential to trade.

market clearing Adjustment of prices until quantities supplied and demanded are equal.

market economy An economic system in which resources are allocated through individual decision making.

market system An economic system involving resource allocation by the market and private resource ownership.

means of payment Anything acceptable as payment for goods and services.

microeconomics The study of the behavior of individual households, firms, and governments, the choices they make, and their interaction in specific markets and industries.

minimum wage A price floor imposed in a labor market.

model An abstract, simplified representation of reality.

monetary policy Manipulation of the money supply to achieve some macroeconomic goal.

monetizing the deficit Increasing the money supply to finance the government's budget deficit.

money demand curve A curve indicating how much money will be willingly held at each interest rate.

money supply curve A line showing the total quantity of money in the economy at each interest rate.

N

national debt The total amount of government debt outstanding as a result of financing earlier budget deficits.

natural rate of unemployment The unemployment rate when there is no cyclical unemployment.

net capital inflow An inflow of funds equal to a nation's trade deficit.

net exports (*NX*) Total exports minus total imports.

net investment spending Total investment spending minus depreciation.

net taxes Government tax revenues minus transfer payments.

net worth The difference between assets and liabilities.

nominal variable A variable measured without adjustment for the dollar's changing value.

nominal wage A wage measured in current dollars.

nonmarket production Goods and services that are produced, but not sold in a market.

normal good A good that people demand more of as their income rises.

normative economics The study of what *should be;* it is used to make value judgments, identify problems, and prescribe solutions.

O

open economy An economy in which trade with other nations plays a significant role.

open market operations Purchases or sales of bonds by the Federal Reserve system.

opportunity cost The value of the best alternative sacrificed when taking an action.

P

passive monetary policy Federal Reserve policy that holds the money supply constant in response to changes in economic conditions.

patent protection A government grant of exclusive rights to use or sell a new technology.

peak The point at which real GDP reaches its highest level during an expansion.

Phillips curve A curve indicating the Fed's choice between inflation and unemployment in the short run.

positive economics The study of what *is,* of how the economy works.

potential output The level of output the economy could produce if operating at full employment.

price The amount of money that must be paid to a seller to obtain a good or service.

price ceiling A governmentally imposed price that may not legally be exceeded.

price floor A governmentally imposed minimum price below which a good or service may not be sold.

price level The average level of dollar prices in the economy.

principle of markets and equilibrium To understand how the economy behaves, economists divide the world into separate markets and then examine the equilibrium in each of those markets.

principle of opportunity cost All economic decisions taken by individuals or society are costly. The correct way to measure the cost of a choice is its opportunity cost—that which is given up to make the choice.

principle of specialization and exchange Specialization and exchange enable us to enjoy greater production and higher living standards than would otherwise be possible. As a result, all economies are characterized by high degrees of specialization and exchange.

private investment spending The sum of business plant and equipment purchases, new home construction, and inventory changes.

production possibilities frontier (PPF) A curve showing all combinations of two goods that can be produced with the resources and technology currently available.

progressive tax A tax whose rate increases as income increases.

protectionism The belief that a nation's industries should be protected from foreign competition.

purchasing power parity (PPP) theory The idea that the exchange rate will adjust in the long run so that the average price of goods in two countries will be roughly the same.

purely competitive labor market A market with many indistinguishable sellers of labor, and many buyers, and that involves no barriers to entry or exit.

purely competitive market A market in which no buyer or seller has the power to influence the price.

Q

quantity demanded The total amount of a good that all buyers in a market would choose to purchase at a given price.

quantity supplied The total amount of a good or service that all producers in a market would choose to produce and sell at a given price.

quantity theory of money The idea that the long-run price level depends on the supply of money.

quota A limit on the physical volume of imports.

R

real interest rate The percentage by which the *purchasing power* returned to a lender exceeds the purchasing power loaned.

real variable A variable adjusted for changes in the dollar's value.

real wage A wage measured in terms of purchasing power.

recession A period during which real GDP declines to an abnormally low level.

recovery The period after a recession during which output and employment return to their full-employment levels.

rent controls A government-imposed maximum on rents that may be charged for apartments or homes.

required reserve ratio The minimum fraction of checking account balances that banks must hold as reserves.

required reserves The minimum amount of reserves a bank must hold, depending upon the amount of its deposit liabilities.

reserves Vault cash plus balances held at the Fed.

resource allocation A method of determining which goods and services will be produced, how they will be produced, and who will get them.

resource markets Markets in which households sell resources—land, labor, and natural resources—to firms.

resources The land, labor, and capital that are used to produce goods and services.

run on the bank An attempt by many of a bank's depositors to withdraw their funds.

S

Say's law The idea that total spending will be sufficient to purchase the total output produced.

scarcity A situation in which the amount of something available is insufficient to satisfy everyone's desire for it.

seasonal unemployment Joblessness related to changes in weather, tourist patterns, or other seasonal factors.

self-correcting mechanism The adjustment process through which price and wage changes return the economy to full-employment output in the long run.

shock A change in spending that ultimately affects the entire economy.

short run A time horizon during which at least one of the firm's inputs cannot be varied.

short-run aggregate supply (*AS*) curve A curve indicating the price level consistent with firms' unit costs and markups for any level of output over the short run.

short-run Keynesian model A macroeconomic model that explains how changes in spending can affect real GDP in the short run.

short-run macroeconomic equilibrium A combination of price level and GDP consistent with both the *AD* and *AS* curves.

simplifying assumption Any assumption that makes a model simpler without affecting any of its important conclusions.

socialism An economic system in which most resources are owned by the state.

specialization A method of production in which each person concentrates on a limited number of activities.

stagflation The combination of falling output and rising prices.

stock options Rights to purchase shares of a stock at a prespecified price.

structural deficit The part of the federal budget deficit that is independent of the business cycle.

structural unemployment Joblessness arising from mismatches between workers' skills and employers' requirements or between workers' locations and employers' locations.

substitute A good that can be used in place of some other good and that fulfills more or less the same purpose.

substitution effect As the price of a good decreases, the consumer substitutes that good in place of other goods whose prices have not changed.

supply curve A graphical depiction of a supply schedule; a line showing the quantity of a good or service supplied at various prices, with all other variables held constant.

supply curve for foreign currency A curve indicating the quantity of a foreign currency that will be supplied, during a given period, at each different exchange rate.

supply of funds curve Indicates the level of household saving at various interest rates.

supply schedule A list showing the quantities of a good or service that firms would choose to produce and sell at different prices, with all other variables held constant.

supply shock Any event that causes the *AS* curve to shift.

systematic risk Risk that cannot be reduced through diversification.

T

tariff A tax on imports.

technical efficiency A situation in which the maximum possible output is being produced from a given collection of inputs.

technological change The invention or discovery of new inputs, new outputs, or new production methods.

terms of trade The ratio at which a country can trade domestically produced products for foreign-produced products.

total demand for funds curve Indicates the total amount of borrowing at various interest rates.

trade deficit The excess of a nation's imports over its exports during a given period.

trade surplus The excess of a nation's exports over its imports during a given period.

triangular arbitrage Arbitrage involving trades among three currencies.

trough The point at which real GDP reaches its lowest level during a recession.

U

unemployment rate The fraction of the labor force that is without a job.

unit of value A common unit for measuring how much something is worth.

V

value added The revenue a firm receives minus the cost of the intermediate goods it buys.

value-added approach Measuring GDP by summing the value added by all firms in the economy.

W

wealth The total value of everything a person or firm owns, at a point in time, minus the total value of everything owed.

wealth constraint At any point in time, wealth is fixed.

INDEX

Note: Italicized letters *f* and *t* following page numbers indicate figures and tables, respectively.

D

T

U

V

W

PHOTO CREDITS

Page	7	© 1996, PhotoDisc, Inc.
	39	© Ian Shaw/Tony Stone Images
	51	© Robert E. Daemmrich/Tony Stone Images
	68	© Keith Wood/Tony Stone Images
	82	© J. Nourok/PhotoEdit
	112	© David Hanover/Tony Stone Images
	121	© David Young-Wolff/Tony Stone Images
	131	© Dan Bosler/Tony Stone Images
	161	© Jim Pickerell/Tony Stone Images
	187	© Janet Gill/Tony Stone Images
	194	© Hugh Sitton/Tony Stone Images
	211	© Cyberimage/Tony Stone Images
	227	© David Young-Wolff/PhotoEdit
	251	© Robert Van Der Hilst/Tony Stone Images
	269	© Jeff Greenberg/Unicorn Stock Photos
	280	© UPI/Corbis-Bettmann
	296	© Paul Conklin/PhotoEdit
	311	© Reuters/Corbis-Bettmann
	345	© Christopher Allibon/Impact Visuals
	371	© Susan Van Etten/PhotoEdit
	372	© Martin Rogers/Tony Stone Images
	389	© Robert E. Daemmrich/Tony Stone Images
	415	© Ron Sherman/Tony Stone Images
	425	© Jeff Greenberg
	426	© Gary Braasch/Tony Stone Images
	453	© Thierry Chesnot/Sipa Press
	458	© Alan Levenson/Tony Stone Images